The Life of
JOHN J. KEANE

Keane in 1878, at the time of his consecration as Bishop of Richmond (courtesy of Miss Mary V. Merrick).

The Life of
JOHN J. KEANE
Educator and Archbishop
1839-1918

Patrick Henry Ahern, M.A., Ph.D.

THE BRUCE PUBLISHING COMPANY
Milwaukee

NIHIL OBSTAT:

JOHN TRACY ELLIS
Censor Deputatus

IMPRIMATUR:

✠ JOHN GREGORY MURRAY
Archbishop of St. Paul

June 24, 1954

Library of Congress Catalog Card Number: 54–12980

MADE IN THE UNITED STATES OF AMERICA

Preface

THE history of the Catholic Church in the United States for the last quarter of the nineteenth century and the early years of the twentieth cannot be fully known without a close acquaintance with three of the most famous prelates of the period, namely: James Cardinal Gibbons, Archbishop John Ireland, and Archbishop John Joseph Keane. Each member of this triumvirate of intimate friends was a strenuous actor in the scenes of that day. Each was cast in a role which called for searching scrutiny by national and international critics.

In this volume John J. Keane's part in the exciting drama is revealed. As the fifth Bishop of Richmond (1878–1888), first rector of the Catholic University of America (1878–1896), a titular archbishop with residence in Rome (1896–1898), and second Archbishop of Dubuque (1900–1911), he was not always the most important figure on the ecclesiastical stage. Nonetheless, the applause of a discerning audience was frequently for him alone, owing to his engaging personality, his unfeigned selflessness, and the industrious and conscientious exercise of his unusual talents. At other times Keane found himself portrayed in the villain's part in the numerous controversies of the day.

By utilizing his oratorical talents and organizational ability to promote the temperance cause and to create effective societies among the Catholics in the city of Washington, Keane won the admiration of his ecclesiastical superiors, who appointed him to the See of Richmond in 1878 — just twelve years after his ordination. While he administered the Virginia bishopric, his apostolic zeal was evident in his tireless evangelizing among the Negroes and the white Protestants and in his promotion of Catholic education in the face of many obstacles. The Third Plenary Council of Baltimore held in 1884 provided the opportunity for a majority of the prelates in the United States to gain a personal knowledge of Keane's exceptional talents. When their representatives chose him in 1887 as the first rector of the Catholic University of America, therefore, they regarded the selection with favor. Overcoming the handicap of a lack of formal training in university administration by an enthusiastic and selfless devotion to his work, Keane succeeded more than any other single person in building, staffing, and endowing the institution. During the nine years in which he served as rector of the University, Bishop Keane also figured prominently in the German question, the school controversy, and the Parliament of Religions at Chicago in 1893. To his part in these burning public issues, as well as to a clash of personalities, must be attributed the succession of dissensions in the institution over which he presided and which disturbed his administration. For what was considered to be the welfare of the University, but with little regard for the position in which it would place Keane in the eyes of the world, Pope Leo XIII removed him from the rectorship and invited him to take up residence in Rome. During his two years' stay in the Eternal City, Keane's engaging personality and evident spirituality won for him the friendship of many prominent ecclesiastics. At the same time his critics ruthlessly pursued him, and by means that were not always fair sought to destroy his reputation completely in the great controversy known as Americanism. Exhausted from the battle to vindicate his honor in Rome, Archbishop Keane returned to the United States and within a short time received an appointment to the See of Dubuque, where he labored for eleven years until failing health forced him to resign the charge. For seven years he lived on at Dubuque in quiet retirement and prepared for the welcome call of the Master whom he had always served to the best of his ability.

Although Keane preserved very little of his personal correspondence, the source material for this volume was abundant and rich, owing to the large number of his own letters and letters pertaining to him in the principal archival deposits in the United States. Moreover, the newspapers in the United States and in Europe devoted considerable space to him because of his prominent position in the Church, and principally because of his part in the major controversies of the day. Without this valuable source the story of his life could not have been told so completely and so honestly.

During his research on the life of Archbishop Keane, the author was rendered generous help which he gratefully acknowledges and without which the present volume could not have been written. In the first place, his thanks are especially due to the Reverend John Tracy Ellis, professor of American church history in the Catholic University of

America, for indicating the possibilities of the subject, for the loan of copies of numerous documents, for the critical reading of the manuscript, and for his continual encouragement.

For permission to use diocesan or institutional archives and for courtesies extended during the period of research the writer is indebted to the late Most Reverend Michael J. Curley and to his successor as Archbishop of Baltimore, the Most Reverend Francis P. Keough, and to the Reverend Paul L. Love, archivist of the Archdiocese of Baltimore; to the Most Reverend Peter L. Ireton, Bishop of Richmond, and to his former and present chancellors, the Very Reverends Robert O. Hichman and Justin D. McClunn; to the Most Reverend Henry P. Rohlman, Archbishop of Dubuque, and to his former chancellor, the Right Reverend Dorance V. Foley; to the Most Reverend Patrick O'Boyle, Archbishop of Washington; to the Right Reverend John M. A. Fearns, rector of St. Joseph's Seminary, Yonkers, New York, and to the Reverend Jeremiah J. Brennan, archivist of the Archdiocese of New York; to the Reverend Thomas T. McAvoy, C.S.C., archivist of the University of Notre Dame; to the Very Reverend James A. Laubacher, S.S., rector of St. Mary's Seminary, Roland Park, and to the Reverend William J. O'Shea, S.S., professor of church history at Roland Park; to the Reverend Joseph I. Malloy, C.S.P., former archivist of the Paulist Fathers, and to the Reverend Joseph McSorley, C.S.P., of the Church of St. Paul the Apostle, New York City; to the Right Reverend Matthew A. Howard of St. Charles Seminary, Columbus, Ohio; and to the Right Reverend Charles J. Plauché, chancellor of the Archdiocese of New Orleans.

To the staffs of the Mullen Library of the Catholic University of America, the Library of Congress, the Public Library, Dubuque, Iowa, and to the Reverend Fidelis J. Kaufmann, former librarian of Loras College, Dubuque, Iowa, grateful thanks are likewise due for valuable help during the search through newspaper files.

For other papers and manuscripts, or for information leading thereto, a debt of gratitude is owed to the Right Reverend James H. Moynihan, pastor of the Church of the Incarnation, Minneapolis, the Reverend Colman J. Barry, O.S.B., of St. John's University, Collegeville, Minnesota, the Reverend Peter E. Hogan, S.S.J., of Epiphany Apostolic College, Newburg, New York, the late Right Reverend William H. Russell of the Catholic University of America, the Reverend Vincent F. Holden, C.S.P., archivist of the Paulist Fathers, the Reverend

Thomas B. Finn of the Diocese of Covington, and the Right Reverend Isidore Semper of Loras College, Dubuque, Iowa.

Grateful acknowledgments are also owing to Professor John T. Farrell of the Catholic University of America and to the Reverend Henry J. Browne, archivist of the same institution, for reading the manuscript, for suggestions by which it has been improved, and for the use and loan of important documents. Finally to the Most Reverend John Gregory Murray, Archbishop of St. Paul, who allowed him to pursue graduate studies, and to his mother, Mrs. Rose Ahern, who made graduate studies financially possible, the writer will always be grateful. In its original form this work was submitted as a doctoral dissertation at the Catholic University of America.

PATRICK HENRY AHERN

The St. Paul Seminary
St. Paul, Minnesota
May 27, 1954

Contents

Key to Abbreviations

AAB — Archives of the Archdiocese of Baltimore.

AAD — Archives of the Archdiocese of Dubuque.

AANO — Archives of the Archdiocese of New Orleans.

AANY — Archives of the Archdiocese of New York.

AASP — Archives of the Archdiocese of Saint Paul.

ACUA — Archives of the Catholic University of America.

ADC — Archives of the Diocese of Covington.

ADR — Archives of the Diocese of Richmond.

AJF — Archives of the Josephite Fathers.

APF — Archives of the Paulist Fathers.

ASMS — Archives of St. Mary's Seminary, Baltimore.

AUND — Archives of the University of Notre Dame.

LCLD — Loras College Library, Dubuque.

MMBT — Minutes of the Meetings of the Board of Trustees.

The Life of
JOHN J. KEANE

CHAPTER I

Path to the Altar

WESTWARD, across the narrowest part of Ireland, the Erne River flows three miles from Lough Erne to the Atlantic Ocean. Before these waters empty into the southeast side of Donegal Bay, they fall about 140 feet over a succession of rapids, the highest of which is fifteen feet. Below this picturesque spot the town of Ballyshannon is situated. It is the southernmost town of County Donegal, the northernmost county in the northwestern corner of Ireland. During Ireland's early history this town was known as Athseanaigh. It was then the principal seat of the O'Connells, who were the rulers of that area for centuries. Unfortunately, nothing was done during its long history to develop its possibilities. If a canal, which had been begun and then abandoned for lack of funds, had afforded a means of cheap communication with Lake Erne, a large area of the interior would have been opened to its wonderful port. Also, if the potential water power of the natural falls had been harnessed, industry would have flourished. Nevertheless, in the 1840's Ballyshannon was a prosperous town. With the exception of Coleraine and Ballina, it enjoyed the most extensive salmon fishing in Ireland. Besides exporting that item to England, the town boasted of a large distillery, where 100,000 gallons of whisky were produced annually, and of copper, lead, and zinc mines, recently discovered in the immediate neighborhood. Furthermore, the excellently protected harbor assured the town of a certain number of commercial activities according to the limited needs of the surrounding area.[1]

[1] Thomas Campbell Foster, *Letters on the Condition of the People of Ireland* (London, 1846), pp. 67–79; Anthony Marmion, *The Ancient and Modern History of the Maritime Ports of Ireland* (3rd ed.; London, 1858), pp. 422–424.

Hugh Keane and his wife, Fannie Connolly, chose this spot for their home after their marriage in the third decade of the nineteenth century. Although Mr. Keane did not directly depend upon the commercial and business prosperity of the town, nevertheless, as a tailor, the fortunes of those engaged in commerce and business affected his purse. Providence, fortunately, took care that the purse was amply filled adequately to supply the needs of his wife and of the three boys and two girls born to them.[2]

John Joseph, the oldest of the three boys, was born on September 12, 1839. Shortly thereafter, according to custom, he was taken to the nearest church in the parish of Killbarn, for baptism.[3] Like his sisters, who died in their infancy, and like his brothers, Terrence and Thomas, John suffered from delicate health during these early years and indeed until he had reached early manhood.[4] Yet, it seems that his uncertain health did not retard the boy mentally, since he claimed to have been sent to school when he was three years old. It may have been that customs differed from those of our day, or that he was a precocious child. The latter possibility seems more likely as the following story from his own lips in later life would indicate:

> I remember well the first day I went to school, how the servant boy took me to the mall, and how, just as we passed out of the mall into the main street there came a tremendous hailstorm, and we had to take refuge in Chiswisk's bakery near the corner. When the hailstorm was over I was taken on to school that day to Mistress Molly. I was at school with dear old Mistress Molly until I was seven years old. . . . I remember the dear old lady used to think me a good sort of boy, and take me aside to read for her the lives of the saints. It is singular, but I remember clearly to this day — I was then six years of age — how I read for her the story of St. Cassian. . . .[5]

When Hugh Keane had married and settled in Ballyshannon he had intended to grow old there with his family. Circumstances, however, forced a change in his plans. Terrifying hunger stalked parts of Ireland in the spring and summer of 1842, but it did not come close enough to Hugh to startle him into apprehensiveness. In 1846

[2] LCLD, clippings. An account of Keane's life which he gave in 1901 on the occasion of a visit to Ireland. Some sources indicate that there was only one girl in the Keane family, John T. Reily, *Collections in the Life and Times of J. Card. Gibbons* (McSherrytown, Pa., 1893–), II, 648.

[3] ASMS, Daybook. Register in St. Mary's Seminary, Vol. I, 116.

[4] Reily, *op. cit.*, II, 648.

[5] LCLD, clippings.

a more terrible famine, attended by widespread disease and death, affected many parts of Ireland.[6] Although Keane's family was not suffering undue hardship at the time, he resolved to leave Ireland one day after he had passed by the soup house which had been established in Ballyshannon and saw there people whom he had known in better circumstances waiting in line for food to sustain their lives. He said to his wife that day, "Fannie, we are going to leave, I cannot stand it any longer." Shortly afterward he went to Londonderry and booked passage for North America.[7]

Naturally, the sea was not a mystery to those who had watched it for years alternately caress and beat Erin's shores. Perhaps they had often been hypnotized by its ceaseless motion, and under the spell they may have been transported westward to a fabulous land known as America. But now, this was different. To the children, the prospect of crossing to unknown shores may have brought the thrill of anticipated adventure. To the parents, however, preparations for leaving their people and land could have brought only sorrow and anxiety.

With Ireland's shores gradually hidden in the haze, Hugh Keane and his family turned their gaze westward to await the appearance of unfamiliar shores. The vessel was bound for St. John, New Brunswick. Many British colonists had settled in that maritime province of Canada in the years 1830 to 1850, or at least they took passage there on British vessels at special rates and then made their way to other parts of Canada or to the United States. A settlement of loyalists on the St. John's River had formed the nucleus of what became the Province of New Brunswick in 1784.[8] In 1846, when the Keanes approached its shores it was a huntsman's paradise,[9] but it still presented a forbidding aspect to the unseasoned colonist. The Keane family may have watched as their vessel passed Nova Scotia on the right and then entered the Bay of Fundy. Soon they were approaching

[6] For the condition of the Irish just before the famine, cf. William Forbes Adams, *Ireland and the Irish Emigration to the New World from 1815 to the Famine* (New Haven, 1932); also Marcus Lee Hansen, *The Atlantic Migration, 1607–1860* (Cambridge, 1940), for the conditions in Ireland that fostered emigration prior to and during the famine. Also cf. Justin McCarthy, *A History of Our Own Times* (New York, 1880), I, 278–283; Bernard O'Reilly, *John McHale, Archbishop of Tuam* (New York, 1890), I, 597.

[7] LCLD, clippings.

[8] Justin Winsor (ed.), *Narrative and Critical History of America* (Boston and New York, 1889), VIII, 136–137.

[9] R. G. A. Levinge, *Echoes from the Backwoods* (London, 1846). According to this description New Brunswick was, indeed, a huntsman's paradise.

St. John, part way up the northwest side of the bay. As they drew near they found that it was a well-protected town on the left bank of a large river where it rushed over rapids to become one with the sea. They probably thought to themselves that November day in 1846[10] that it did look a little bit like good old Ballyshannon.

In the town the family had a choice of two good hotels and of several smaller ones for temporary living accommodations, if they had not made previous arrangements to occupy one of the older frame houses or the new brick structures that made up the town. Once they were settled, they could become acquainted with their countrymen who were the most numerous among the 30,000 inhabitants. An English traveler remarked of the city in 1843: "The number of Irish names on the signboards of the groceries and whisky-shops show that the Irish habits have been imported also."[11] Since there were so many Irish there, it was inevitable that the Catholic congregation would be the most numerous, and their two churches, among the fourteen in the city, were among the largest and best. The chief occupations in St. John were shipbuilding, fishing, and exporting of lumber. The educational facilities consisted of two public schools, one for the higher branches of knowledge, called the Grammar School, and the other for the elementary subjects, called the Madras Central School, in which the Lancaster method of teaching was employed.[12] Very probably John Keane attended the latter school during his year and a half at St. John, New Brunswick.

It is impossible to determine the manner in which Mr. Keane reached his decision to leave New Brunswick. Possibly before leaving Ireland he had determined to make St. John only a temporary home. It also is possible that upon his arrival he realized that opportunities for one in his trade were limited. At any rate, it seems evident that shortly after arriving in St. John, he set out alone for Baltimore, Maryland, in the hope of finding economic security.[13] Baltimore

[10] ASMS, Daybook. Register in St. Mary's Seminary, Vol. I, 116. According to this register the Keane family arrived in New Brunswick in November, 1847. John Keane claimed to have been brought to America when he was seven years old (ADR, Bishops' Diary, p. 73). Hence, the family must have left Ireland sometime between September 12, 1846, and before September 12, 1847. For additional evidence to indicate that the Keanes came to North America in 1846, cf. n. 13.

[11] James S. Buckingham, *Canada, Nova Scotia, New Brunswick, and the Other British Provinces in North America* (London, [1843]), p. 410.

[12] *Ibid.*, pp. 399–411.

[13] *Matchett's Baltimore Directory of 1847* (Baltimore, 1847), p. 132. This lists a Hugh Kane [*sic*], tailor, residing at 122 E. Fayette Street. There was no Hugh Kane,

must have pleased his discriminating eye, for in December, 1848,[14] the rest of the family joined him at 122 East Fayette Street, now a part of Old Town. It was here that John J. Keane grew to manhood.[15]

As the middle of the nineteenth century neared, Baltimore was a prosperous city with 165,000 inhabitants striving hard to surpass New York. It had started late as the youngest city on the Atlantic seaboard, having been founded in 1730 and incorporated in 1797. In 1752, it had only twenty-five houses and very few ships in its harbor.[16] The excellent harbor so far inland on the Patapsco River gave Baltimore marked advantages for rapid growth and satisfying prosperity. The extensive and fertile countryside made it the natural focus of trade. Those with capital, who were not blind to its possibilities, made it a center for manufactures of various kinds, chief among which was that "peculiar business,"[17] the manufacture of shot. Also as the middle of the nineteenth century approached, Baltimore might have been called a Catholic city in so far as any American city could be so designated. There had been many changes for the Catholics since Father Ashton came from Carroll Manor to say the first Mass for the Acadians (1756) in the first brick house and the

---

Keene, Keane, or Kain mentioned in the directory for the previous year. Later directories have various spellings for the name until they are consistent in giving the correct spelling. No matter what spelling they used, the address was always the same, namely, 122 E. Fayette Street. This indicates that Hugh Keane was in Baltimore in 1847, prior to the arrival of the family from New Brunswick.

[14] ASMS, Daybook. Register in St. Mary's Seminary, Vol. I, 116.

[15] The Keane family (entered as Keene, Hugh, tailor) lived at 122 East Fayette Street in 1851 (*Matchett's Baltimore Directory for 1851* [Baltimore, 1851], p. 146). By 1856 the family had moved to 124 East Fayette Street (*Wood's Baltimore Directory for 1856–57* [Baltimore, 1856], p. 140). From 1856 until 1873 the various Baltimore directories give 124 East Fayette as the address (*The Baltimore City Directory* [Baltimore, 1858], p. 184; *Wood's Baltimore City Directory* [Baltimore, 1860], p. 207; *ibid.*, [Baltimore, 1864], p. 212; *ibid.*, [Baltimore, 1867], p. 274; *ibid.*, [Baltimore, 1872], p. 322; *ibid.*, [Baltimore, 1873], p. 314). In 1874, after a second marriage, Mr. Keane moved to 27 North High Street and remained there until his death in 1877. His widow, John Keane's stepmother, lived there until 1895, according to *Wood's Baltimore City Directory* and the *R. L. Polk & Co's Baltimore City Directory,* which replaced the Wood's directory in 1887.

In 1886, the streets of Baltimore were officially renumbered, so that what had been 122, became 1228; 124 became 1230, 27 became 105 (*R. L. Polk & Co's Baltimore City Directory for 1887* [Baltimore, 1887], p. 45). All these residences were in the same area which today forms part of the widened East Fayette Street.

[16] J. S. Buckingham, *America, Historical, Statistic, and Descriptive* (London, [1840]), I, 396–397. Also cf. Reily, *op. cit.*, VI, 891.

[17] Henry Stockbridge, Sr., "Baltimore in 1846," *Maryland Historical Magazine,* VI (Mar., 1911), 25.

first two-story house in Baltimore which had been built by Edward Fottrell.[18] The tide of immigration had swelled Baltimore's Catholic population rapidly. The newcomers had worked hand in hand with the native sons of the Church to build the large cathedral which European travelers considered "plain enough externally, but very sumptuously adorned in the interior."[19] They also co-operated to provide adequate places of Catholic worship at convenient locations throughout the city.

Because of Baltimore's prosperity, Hugh Keane could look to the future with reasonable assurance. The heavily laden wagons that rumbled by his door as the straining oxen were urged on by the drivers; the changing breezes that crossed the harbor and wafted the odors of the world into his windows; and the shot tower that cast its shadow on his roof from its height of 234 feet,[20] all were tokens of a lively business center. Because of Baltimore's Catholicity, the Keane family could be assured of ample opportunities for the increase and renewal of the life of grace which were imperative for spiritual security and which were a deciding factor in the life of John.

The Church of St. Vincent de Paul on North Front Street, within a few blocks of the Keane residence, just up the street from the shot tower, was to play an important role in the lives of the Keanes practically from the moment of their arrival. The church was new then, having been built by John B. Gildea just seven years before they came. This venerable founder of the parish had died in 1845, and the new family was greeted by John B. Donelan (1846–1851).[21] From the hands of this pastor, young Keane received his first holy Communion during his first year in Baltimore.[22] In the same year and within the sanctuary of the same church, Archbishop Samuel Eccleston, S.S., conferred on him the sacrament of confirmation.[23]

St. Vincent de Paul School, conducted by the Christian Brothers, became equally familiar to young John. Mistress Molly in Ireland had only begun the work of teaching and John had hardly started the task of learning. So now he was presented to the Brothers and

[18] Reily, *op. cit.*, VI, 891.

[19] Alex. Mackay, *The Western World; or Travels in the United States in 1846–47* (4th ed.; London, 1850), I, 162.

[20] The tower is still standing.

[21] Reily, *op. cit.*, II, 614.

[22] ASMS, Daybook, Vol. I, 116.

[23] *Centenary Manual of St. Vincent de Paul, Baltimore, 1841–1941*. No publisher or pagination.

that introduction served as an entrée during the next four years while the elementary subjects were mastered.[24]

The sons of immigrants usually terminated their formal education after the elementary grades because they lacked either the necessary funds for further education, or the inclination to drink deeper of the fountains that ennoble man. For John Keane, the first normal deterrent was surmounted by his parents, and the second did not exist, for he was sent to Calvert Hall in Baltimore. This secondary school, conducted by the Christian Brothers, stood on ground once occupied by a simple brick church called St. Peter's. It was there that John Carroll, the first Catholic bishop in the United States, was installed in 1790. This church served the area until 1840, when it was torn down to make way for Calvert Hall, the cornerstone of which was laid in 1842. The hall was originally intended to be a place for the meetings of Catholic societies, but when Brother Francis returned to Baltimore in 1845, after completing his studies in Montreal, the basement was given to him and his two associates from Canada for a school. The brothers lived in a house nearby until 1848, when they took possession of the entire building and established the academy which John Keane entered in 1852 for his secondary education.[25]

There are no extant records from which one could reconstruct the progress made by young John during his four years with the Christian Brothers at Calvert Hall. His later accomplishments, however, indicate that he derived great benefit from this period of scholastic endeavor. During his later life he manifested his affection for the men who had instructed him.[26] In 1856, when he was seventeen years old, he left their tutelage[27] and another phase of his life began.

In 1856 various avenues stretched before an ambitious young man of seventeen with a good secondary education. The many possible choices required him to pause and to make a difficult decision. His parents wanted him to continue his education "in the splendid college [George-

[24] Reily, *op. cit.*, II, 648. Brothers Ambrose, Urban, and Jeremy were his teachers at St. Vincent School. Cf. Keane's statement in the *Manhattan Quarterly* (July, 1906), cited by Brother Angelus Gabriel, F.S.C., *The Christian Brothers in the United States, 1848–1949* (New York, 1949), p. 293.

[25] Reily, *op. cit.*, II, 220. Cf. "Brothers of the Christian Schools," *United States Catholic Magazine,* IV, 660–664. A new Calvert Hall was dedicated on August 30, 1891. Keane preached the sermon on the occasion (Reily, *op. cit.*, II, 219).

[26] Brothers Aphraate, Basas, John Chrysostom, and John of Mary taught him at Calvert Hall (Gabriel, *op. cit.*, p. 293). He took French and German, among other things, and excelled in these studies. Cf. Cyrus J. Manning, "The Archbishop's Visit to Rome," *College Spokesman,* III (Nov., 1905), 19.

[27] Washington *Post,* Mar. 30, 1878.

town] kept by the Jesuit Fathers," but, as he related years later, "I was stubborn, for the first time in my life."[28] To impatient youth the time spent in learning Greek and Latin seemed a waste. Then, too, did not men talk incessantly about the possibilities for making money and becoming respected gentlemen like those successful businessmen who were driven in their fine carriages down East Fayette Street? For one with ambition and with sufficient education only one choice seemed possible, namely, business. So young John found employment, first with John Murphy & Company, a Catholic firm of booksellers, then, after a year, with John S. Barry & Company, a wholesale dry-goods commission house.[29]

Between the years 1856 and 1859, during which Keane tried his fortune in the business world, Baltimore was in a pitiful political condition. In 1852, the Know-Nothing Party, spawned in ignorance and nourished by hatred of foreigners and Catholics, first appeared in Baltimore. The strong-arm tactics of the adherents of the party, especially at election time, brought about increasingly bitter antagonism between them and the other parties seeking political preference. By election day in November, 1855, the smoldering hatred burst out of control and the Know-Nothings — then known as the American Party — won victories in Baltimore and in thirteen counties amid rioting and disorder.[30] Again in October, 1856, riots preceded and accompanied the city elections, when the American Party's candidate for mayor was fraudulently elected. Conditions were so critical during the national elections in November of that year that Governor Lignon proposed that the state militia be employed to preserve order.[31] After a few years of lawless rule, during which Catholics suffered from attacks, internal quarrels developed in the party, resulting in their loss of control of the Maryland state legislature in 1859. In 1860, even the city government in Baltimore slipped from their grasp.[32]

There was evidence of saner modern trends during these same years

[28] LCLD, clipping.

[29] Reily, *op. cit.,* II, 648. Thomas Fortune Ryan worked for Barry as an errand boy from 1868 to 1872. In 1873 he married Barry's daughter. Cf. Max Lerner, "Thomas Fortune Ryan," *Dictionary of American Biography,* XVI, 265–268. Keane may have become acquainted with Ryan at this time. In later years Keane considered him a friend (AASP, Keane to Ireland, Rome, June 4, 1897).

[30] Lawrence F. Schmeckebier, *History of the Know Nothing Party in Maryland* (Baltimore, 1899), pp. 13, 28–29.

[31] Clayton Colman Hall (ed.), *Baltimore, Its History and Its People* (New York, 1912), I, 155–160.

[32] Schmeckebier, *op. cit.,* pp. 33, 102, 112, 115.

which John Keane may have looked upon with a sense of pride and approval. In 1857, Baltimore was connected to Cincinnati and St. Louis by a railroad,[33] which opened a larger area to its market and to its manufactures and imports. In 1859, Baltimore's first streetcar, "with eight gray horses attached," began to transport passengers over a short route.[34]

It is impossible, of course, to judge the effect of political and economic trends upon the thinking of Keane during the three years that the business world claimed his time and energy. It is certain, however, that God's grace was working all the while to prepare him for his exalted vocation. The occasion seized by Providence for moving young John to consider a vocation other than that of business came on a Sunday morning when he was reading the *Catholic Mirror,* Baltimore's archdiocesan paper. The remarkable story is told best in the simple statement of the man himself. On that Sunday morning, he said, "I read about a good French woman whose son had been a priest, who was martyred in China, and every day she prayed to her martyred son, and it struck me at the moment, 'I will go and become a priest.' "[35] This was a momentous decision that required prayer and thought before it could be translated into action. First, he considered the reaction of his parents, who had lost their little girls in infancy, and who were now comforted only by himself, since Terrence had died and Thomas had drowned in 1853.[36] The love which he bore his parents prompted him to postpone the revelation of his decision to them. Meanwhile, he began to prepare himself for his new and sacred calling by studying Latin and the church history in leisure moments at the store. His fellow employees called him a "bookish sort of fellow" but he did not mind that. After some months of private study, he approached his parents and told them: "I have to go and be a priest." His father said: "Why didn't you go when we gave you the chance when your brother was alive?" John answered, "I didn't know it was the will of God." "Well," said the father, "we will not resist the will of God. Go and God bless you."[37]

The blessing of his parents released John from the anxiety under which he labored during the time that he was preparing in private

[33] Hall, *op. cit.,* I, 480.

[34] *Ibid.,* I, 542.

[35] LCLD, clippings. This may be taken as an indication of impulsiveness in the young man. In his later life there were further indications of this trait in his character.

[36] Reily, *op. cit.,* II, 648.

[37] LCLD, clippings.

for further education. Since Father Thomas Foley, the secretary to Archbishop Francis P. Kenrick, seems to have been John's confidant and spiritual adviser at this time, it is likely that he now heard from the lips of young Keane that he was free and ready to enter a minor seminary to begin his preparation for the priesthood. Father Foley, who was later Coadjutor Bishop of Chicago, may have perceived the signs of a true vocation before Keane realized it himself, and, perhaps, the spiritual adviser had subtly directed him in the ways that would lead to the seminary, for he now unhesitatingly arranged for John's entrance into St. Charles' College.[38] Consequently, as his twentieth birthday approached, John Keane turned from the business world without a backward glance.

When John Keane entered St. Charles' College on September 2, 1859,[39] he was the 300th student to have enrolled at the institution, and he was one of the 102 students who were then taking the various subjects in the six-year course of studies.[40] Father Oliver Lawrence Jenkins, S.S., the president, was also the founder of the college, since it was he who had accepted the land that had been donated by Charles Carroll in this sparsely settled district of Howard County, Maryland, not far from Baltimore, and it was he who had begun the modest school in 1848 with a few candidates for the priesthood.[41]

Since St. Charles' College was incorporated solely for the preparation of aspirants to the priesthood, the discipline was designed to prove the qualities of those who aspired to that vocation as well as to instill habits of life, such as the spirit of recollection and mortification, deemed essential for a happy and fruitful life in such a noble calling. Silence was required at all times except during recreation and on holidays. Living conditions were rather primitive, although not unlike

[38] Reily, *op. cit.*, III, Part III, 150. Cf. *Evening Star* (Washington), Aug. 26, 1878.

[39] *A Complete List of the Students Entered at Saint Charles' College, Ellicott City, Maryland, from the Opening October 31, 1848, until the Golden Jubilee, June 15, 1898.* No pagination.

[40] [George Ernest Viger, S.S.], *Golden Jubilee of St. Charles' College, near Ellicott City, Maryland, 1848–1898* (Baltimore, 1898), p. 31.

[41] *Ibid.*, p. 27. John T. Reily has this account of St. Charles' College: "St. Charles' College was founded in 1831 by Charles Carroll of Carrollton, who gave for the purpose two hundred and fifty-three acres of land contiguous to his patrimonial estate. He subsequently laid the corner-stone of the first building, and used his personal influence to obtain the charter of incorporation from the Legislature of Maryland. The College was not, however, opened until the year 1848" (*op. cit.*, III, Part III, 154–155). Old St. Charles' at Ellicott City, Maryland, was destroyed by fire on March 11, 1911; hence, student records for the period of Keane's stay are unavailable. A new institution bearing the same name was built at Catonsville, Maryland.

those that prevailed elsewhere. The students slept in a dormitory which was heated in the winter by a single stove in the middle of the large room. The more fortunate ones near the stove did not have to break the ice in their water pitchers when they washed on cold mornings. Of course, there were moments of relaxation when the students played such games as prisoner's base, handball, or football, or just went for a walk on the Frederick turnpike that leads to Ellicott City.[42]

Naturally, the classroom was one of the most important scenes of activity for those who entered St. Charles. It was here that the faculty became aware of the remarkable talents of their new student. He began immediately with the second year work, and within a year had completed the second and third years. Then he was allowed to pass by the fourth year and take during his second year (1860–1861) that which was usually assigned to the fifth year students. During his third and last year at St. Charles' he followed the sixth year curriculum.[43] To have finished six years work in three years speaks eloquently for the application of the young man, and his ability is evident from the fact that each year he received first prize in Latin, French, and German, and the same honors in fourth and second Greek, first German, algebra and geometry, bible history, profane history and church history, and in Christian doctrine.[44] Although it was not unusual for the students at St. Charles to finish the regular six-year course in less than that time, it was the exceptional student who was allowed to graduate after only three years' residence.[45]

When John was completing his second year at St. Charles, the Civil War burst upon the nation. Maryland, as one of the border states, experienced many trials that were spared her northern sisters. From Keane's later words and actions it seems safe to deduce that he was in sympathy with those who sought to preserve the Union. In Maryland, and in Baltimore especially, there were many who were strongly pro-South. One traveler wrote that when he arrived in Baltimore in 1861, just before the war started, "the whole feeling of the landed and respectable classes is with the South."[46] After the fighting had begun, troops proceeding south through Baltimore were set

[42] Allen Sinclair Will, *Life of Cardinal Gibbons* (New York, 1922), I, 24–32.
[43] *A Complete List of the Students Entered at Saint Charles' College.*
[44] *Catholic Mirror* (Baltimore), July 14, 1860; July 13, 1861; July 5, 1862.
[45] Will, *op. cit.*, I, 28. Gibbons completed the six-year course in two years. John J. Kain, Keane's classmate at St. Mary's Seminary, completed the course in five years.
[46] William Howard Russell, *My Diary North and South* (New York, 1863), p. 36.

upon by a group of citizens, thereby evidencing sympathy for the Confederacy. This attack on the troops brought about the establishment of martial law in Baltimore midway in 1861. During the summer "a number of Forts were constructed in and about Baltimore to overawe and control the city in case of an outbreak in favor of the Confederacy."[47] An English visitor to Baltimore in the fall of 1861 reported: "Terrible tales were told of threats uttered by one member of a family against another. Old ties of friendship were broken up. Society had so divided itself, and one side could hold no terms of courtesy with the other."[48]

Amid such disturbance John completed his course at St. Charles' College in July, 1862. True, the spacious grounds around the college partially shielded the students from the air of excitement that accompanied the war. Yet, it must have been difficult for the young man who was once bent on a business career to ignore entirely the people who were hurrying to make their fortune before it was too late— before the war was over. At any rate, in the fall of 1862, he began the final phase of his education for the priesthood.

At the time John Keane entered St. Mary's Seminary of the Society of St. Sulpice, in Baltimore, it had a long and enviable record of services to the Church in the United States. As a Baltimorean, John must have seen the institution, its faculty, and its seminarians on many occasions. He probably knew that it had been founded by Francis Charles Nagot, S.S., in 1791. As he came out Pennsylvania Avenue and turned into St. Mary's Court on September 19, 1862,[49] he must have recognized the old seminary building on his left and the St. Mary's College building on his right. Joseph Paul Dubreul, S.S., the rector of the seminary, may have welcomed him to the community and then assigned him to the former college building which was then used to house the students of philosophy.[50]

It is hardly possible the Dubreul and his faculty, Stanislas Ferté, Alphonse Flammant, Paulin François Dissez, Urbain Lequerré, Pierre

[47] Hall, *op. cit.,* I, 172–189.

[48] Anthony Trollope, *North America* (London, 1862), I, 464. Cf. William A. Russ, Jr., "Disfranchisement in Maryland, 1861–67," *Maryland Historical Magazine,* XXVIII (Dec., 1933), 309–328.

[49] ASMS, Daybook, Vol. I, 116.

[50] George Ernest Viger, S.S., *1791–1891 Memorial Volume of the Centenary of St. Mary's Seminary of St. Sulpice, Baltimore, Md.* (Baltimore, 1891), p. 37. For a description of the buildings and a list of the faculty, cf. Charles Herbermann, *The Sulpicians in the United States* (New York, 1916).

Paul Chapon, Sebastien Guilbaud — Sulpicians all,[51] were ignorant of Keane's record while he was studying under their confreres at St. Charles. If any of them had entertained any doubts as to his ability and application, they were to be convinced by the end of the first year. At that time the faculty of arts of St. Mary's University, which had been granted the power to confer degrees by Pius VII, held its first public disputation. On the afternoon of June 24, 1863, Francis Patrick Kenrick, Archbishop of Baltimore, Richard V. Whalen, Bishop of Wheeling, Michael O'Connor, Bishop of Pittsburgh, and about thirty clergymen, gathered in the seminary library with the faculty and student body for the event. Keane, one of the five candidates for the bachelor of arts degree,[52] defended his theses with such logic and in such fluent Latin that he was applauded when his examination was completed.[53] Because of his proficiency in Latin and because of his apparent grasp of the matter for examination, John Keane received his degree *summa cum laude*. As a reward he received, besides the diploma, a full set of Archbishop Kenrick's *Theologia Dogmatica*.[54] Such a premium was to be highly prized since it came from the hand of the greatest theologian in the American Church up to that time. Soon it was to be doubly prized for within a few weeks that hand also conferred the clerical tonsure on the young seminarian,[55] and then was stilled in death.

Each year the seminarians spent the summer months at St. Charles' College, where their Sulpician superiors came to know them more thoroughly.[56] During the month of September the young men returned to the seminary in Baltimore to continue their regular studies. Outside the normal routine of seminary life during the year 1863, there was no event of great importance to John Keane, except, perhaps, the transfer of Martin J. Spalding of Louisville to the See of Baltimore on May 3, 1864.[57]

51 *St. Mary's Seminary, Baltimore, List of the Superiors, Professors and Students Ordained, 1791–1916* (New York, 1917), no pagination.

52 Baltimore *Katholische Volkszeitung,* July 4, 1863. The five seminarians who received degrees on this occasion were Thomas Burke, Joseph O'Keefe, Michael Shea, John J. Kain, John J. Keane.

53 ASMS, Dubreul's Diary. In this diary the rector of the seminary wrote that he frowned on such a demonstration in favor of one of the students because it might reflect on the others.

54 *Ibid.*

55 Reily, *op. cit.,* III, Part III, 150.

56 ASMS, Dubreul's Diary.

57 Joseph B. Code, *Dictionary of the American Hierarchy* (New York, 1940), p. 331. Code gives April 3 as the date of transfer, while all the other sources agree on May 3.

The scholastic year which began in the fall of 1864 was to be more eventful in the life of young Keane. The Sulpicians made use of his ability in speaking and in reading by appointing him to conduct classes in reading along with his classmate John J. Kain.[58] Most of the Sulpician professors had been raised in France. Since the majority of them came to the United States late in life, few acquired facility and accuracy in expressing themselves in English. It was to their credit that they recognized this defect and sought to remedy it in this fashion. During the school year Keane was privileged to be present for the conferring of the pallium on Archbishop Spalding on March 26, 1865, and he was among the seminarians who took part in the funeral procession when a month later the remains of Lincoln passed through Baltimore.[59]

At the close of Keane's third year at St. Mary's the faculties of arts and of theology presented candidates for degrees for the third successive year. John was one of the four candidates for the baccalaureate in theology. After he had shown outstanding ability in refuting the objections to the dogma of the resurrection of the dead proposed by William Clarke, S.J., he was awarded his diploma *summa cum laude,* and once more he received a special prize. His friend and classmate, John Kain, the future Bishop of Wheeling and Archbishop of St. Louis, received the same degree *maxima cum laude.*[60]

John Keane had just celebrated his twenty-seventh birthday in the fall of 1865 when the seminarians returned to St. Mary's Seminary after their summer spent at St. Charles' College. This was to be his final year of preparation for the priesthood. Since he was one of the two seminarians from Baltimore in major orders he went frequently to the cathedral to take part in solemn ceremonies. His presence there was especially noticeable during Lent when he sang the Passion with others from the seminary and when he participated in the solemn ceremonies of Holy Week.[61]

It was the practice of the Sulpicians at St. Mary's, as in all their seminaries, to form an estimate of the qualities of the students in their charge. When the seminarians approached the end of their course a permanent record of these observations was made. The entry under John Joseph Keane's name shows that the faculty considered him

[58] ASMS, Dubreul's Diary.

[59] *Ibid.*

[60] *Catholic Mirror,* July 8, 1865. There were four candidates for the S.T.B. degree and two candidates for the A.B. degree on this occasion.

[61] ASMS, Dubreul's Diary.

the best student in his class, and, judging by the entries under other names during that period, one might conclude that they regarded him as one of the best students ever to have come under their direction. Out of a maximum of ten points that could be given to any student in their system of marking, Keane was allowed nine and one half points under talent and success. For general behavior and for piety and virtue he was given nine points. The Sulpician professors remarked that Keane had, as they put it, "a more than ordinary quickness of apprehension with a never failing felicity of expression, and an ever ready memory. His judgment, although sound, is occasionally carried by some precipitancy. A most generous heart, stronger in his affection than sensitive." For preaching, he was given the mark of nine and it was noted that "he was constantly the model and friend of all in the community."[62] The only other student in the class who approached this record was John J. Kain. The rest of the class, like the majority of those whose names appear in the record received marks ranging from six to two under the various headings.[63]

Finally, there came the dawn of that day for which Keane had prepared so diligently for more than seven years. Early in the morning of July 2, 1866, his father and mother joined the two hundred relatives and friends of fifteen young men who were to be ordained in the seminary chapel.[64] After Archbishop Spalding had completed the Church's ancient ceremony by which the priesthood is perpetuated, Father John Joseph Keane sought his parents so that he might extend his freshly anointed hands over them in priestly blessing.

Shortly after his ordination, Father Keane offered his first public Mass at St. Vincent de Paul's Church where he had received his first holy Communion and the sacrament of confirmation. The special happiness that follows ordination must have been intensified in his case since he had those whom he most dearly loved to share with him the blessings of his first days as a priest of God. Moreover, he surely did not forget those who shared his childhood joys as he ascended the holy mount to offer a requiem Mass for the deceased who had been instrumental in directing his path to the altar.

At the time of his ordination, Archbishop Spalding told the young priest to report to Father Jacob Ambrose Walter, pastor of St.

[62] ASMS, book containing an estimate of the character and talents of the students.
[63] *Ibid.*
[64] ASMS, Dubreul's Diary. Cf. *Catholic Mirror,* July 14, 1866. John J. Keane and Louis A. Morgan were the only students ordained on this occasion for the Archdiocese of Baltimore.

Patrick's Church in the city of Washington, after a short vacation in the mountains. Keane said later in life that his heart sank at the mere thought of being stationed in Washington, which, as he expressed it, "then had a reputation well calculated to terrify a young priest." Yet he asserted that he was happy over the appointment since he would be with Father Walter, whom he had seen for the first time during the previous year, and who in their very first meeting had inspired the young man with respect and confidence.[65] When Father Keane reported to his assignment in September,[66] therefore, he was psychologically prepared for harmonious relations with his superior. This happy state was furthered by the pastor when he greeted his new assistant with the words: "I asked for you, Keane, because I thought you were a man I could get along with." Then he added: "And now understand we are to be partners and brothers. This is not *my* house; it is *our* house, and your friends are as welcome here as mine." At that moment was forged the first link of a friendship never to be broken.[67] Together and in perfect harmony they lived and cared for the people of St. Patrick's Parish in Washington.

[65] Joseph M. Walter (ed.), *A Memorial Tribute to Rev. J. A. Walter, Late Pastor of St. Patrick's Church, Washington, D. C.* (Washington, 1895), pp. 70–71.

[66] St. Patrick's Church, Washington, D. C., Baptismal Register, Sept. 8, 1857, to Sept. 30, 1871. Keane's first recorded baptism at St. Patrick's was on September 5, 1866. His first recorded marriage was on September 14, 1866 (St. Patrick's Church, Washington, D. C., Marriage Register).

[67] Walter, *op. cit.*, p. 71.

CHAPTER II

Assistant at St. Patrick's in Washington

ST. PATRICK'S was one of the oldest churches in Washington. In 1794 when the seat of government was still in Philadelphia, although the decision had already been made to move it to Washington, Father Anthony Caffry, O.P.,[1] bought three lots from the commissioners of the District of Columbia "in square 376 bounded by Ninth and Tenth F and G streets Northwest."[2] A church was built on the F Street lots in 1796. During Father William Matthews' pastorate of fifty years (1804–1854), the original church was torn down and in its place a larger brick church was erected. By the purchase of nine more lots in square 376 in 1814 ample room was provided for the enlargements made on this structure.[3] The main entrance of the enlarged church faced Tenth Street near F, and the residence of the priests was toward G Street, connected to the church by a covered walk.[4] Across G Street, to the north of the square, was a small cemetery known as Graveyard Hill.[5] Another building was in

[1] Father Caffry's name had been spelled Caffrey and McCaffrey. Caffry seems to have been his own way of spelling it. Cf. [Milton E. Smith], *History of St. Patrick's Church, Washington, D. C.* (1933), p. 6.

[2] Much of the material in Smith, *op. cit.*, may be found in the *Catholic Red Book* (Baltimore, 1908). The *Catholic Mirror* of November 9, 1872, carried a summary of the history of the parish. David H. Fosselman, C.S.C., adds to our knowledge of this parish's history and corrects some of the errors in the older work in his sociological-historical study "The Parish in Urban Communities," *The Sociology of the Parish,* ed. by C. J. Nuesse and Thomas J. Harte, C.Ss.R. (Milwaukee, 1951), pp. 135–147.

[3] Fosselman, *op. cit.*, p. 137.

[4] Smith, *op. cit.*, p. 16.

[5] Such people as the Carrolls, Brents, Fenwicks, Dyers, Carberrys, Hobans, and Sweeneys, famous names in the early Catholic history of Washington, worshiped at St. Patrick's Church and were buried in Graveyard Hill (Reily, *op. cit.*, II, 762).

the initial stages of erection, on G Street between Ninth and Tenth, when Keane came to St. Patrick's in the summer of 1866. Father Walter had laid the cornerstone of Carroll Hall on June 29,[6] just three days before the new assistant was ordained. The pastor hoped that when the building was completed it would become the favorite meeting place for various church societies in the city of Washington and a veritable center of Catholic life in the nation's capital.[7] This was the St. Patrick's that Keane knew during his first years as assistant.

When Father Keane took up residence in the city of Washington in 1866, it was a separate municipality. The keener interest in the capital following the Civil War was responsible for the consideration of means for unifying the District of Columbia. The deliberations of Congress were crystallized into law in 1871, when the corporations of Washington and of Georgetown ceased to exist and the entire District of Columbia became a municipality with a so-called territorial government. This type of rule lasted for four years until evident corruption forced Congress to abolish it and provide for a temporary commission government. The commission government was made permanent in 1878,[8] just after Keane left Washington.

The national government in 1866 was in the hands of the "Black Republicans" who disgraced themselves by flagrant corruption and by their attempt to impeach President Andrew Johnson. The misery inflicted on the South by the enactments of these legislators has caused all unbiased historians to condemn them, while it would be difficult to convey the depth of contempt felt by the southern writers who lived through the years following the war. Indeed, those years after the Civil War were trying ones for the people of the nation, but they were interesting ones for those who had their residence in the District of Columbia. The young assistant at St. Patrick's was in a position to be fully aware of the happenings on the Hill, owing to the number of prominent people who were welcomed to the table and parlors of the rectory. Yet, so far as could be ascertained, Keane took no part in the politics of the city, nor did he become involved in the support of any national party. As a priest his one and only interest was work for the salvation of souls. As assistant at St. Patrick's Church in Washington he was afforded ample opportunity to do that work.

[6] *Catholic Mirror,* June 30, 1866.
[7] Walter, *op. cit.,* p. 73.
[8] William Tindall, *Standard History of the City of Washington* (Knoxville, 1914), Chaps. vii–ix.

Keane in 1866, at the time of his ordination.

Archbishop Keane at the time of his appointment to Dubuque, 1900.

Preaching came to be one of his chief duties and one for which he was admirably equipped. A person who heard one of his first sermons at the nine o'clock Mass on a Sunday morning remarked to his son as they were on their way home: "Il a un remarquable talent; il faudrait qu'il s'instruise."[9] Another who listened to him preach during those first days at St. Patrick's was brave enough to seek out the young priest and to advise him to take some lessons in elocution. If John Keane was prompted to reject the advice when it was first given, his manner changed when he was informed that his constructive critic was a famous opera singer who did not find fault with the material that was used, but who feared that to continue to use his voice as he was using it would cause him difficulty in later years. So, true to his nature, he sought out a teacher who could point out his mistakes in delivery and aid him in correcting his faults.[10]

Father Walter let it be clearly understood during Keane's first days in the parish that the routine parochial work would be equitably divided between them. In keeping with this plan, the pastor always had charge of the girls and Keane was given care of the boys in the preparation of the children for first Communion. That the boys were placed under the supervision and instruction of the younger priest was not owing merely to the whim of the pastor. It was his intention that Keane should direct the young men of the parish in their endeavors to form Catholic associations and it was in keeping with his plan that the young priest should preside over the parish temperance society.[11]

Keane did not need any urging to take more than ordinary interest in the Father Mathew Total Abstinence Society[12] since he himself had taken the pledge from Father Theobald Mathew when that remarkable priest was using his phenomenal persuasive power to curb the drink evil.[13] Hence, from the time of his election as president

[9] AAB, 118-Q Maria Longworth Storer to Gibbons, Saranac Lake, New York, September 18, 1918, in which she enclosed a copy of part of a letter from her son-in-law, the Marquis Pierre de Chambrun, under date of August 16, 1918. The quotation is from the enclosure. Another writes of him: "Even when very young we admired and appreciated his wonderful eloquence. Though we lived in St. Matthew's Parish, to please us my father always kept a pew in St. Patrick's" (Mary Merrick to the author, Chevy Chase, Maryland, July 9, 1951).

[10] Statement by the Very Reverend Louis B. Pastorelli, S.S.J., Jan. 22, 1949, personal interview.

[11] Walter, *op. cit.*, p. 79.

[12] It had been organized by Joseph O'Toole (1854–1860), the third pastor of St. Patrick's. Smith, *op. cit.*, p. 32.

[13] Reily, *op. cit.*, II, 649. Keane frequently stated that he had taken the pledge

of the parish society, when he first came to St. Patrick's, until he left Washington,[14] Father Keane devoted his energies to the promotion of the work of the organization. He became well known as a temperance lecturer in the city of Washington. In fact, he was called upon on numerous occasions to address audiences on the topic, and most especially when any special drive for members was being made by the various temperance organizations in the city.[15] In 1870 the Catholic total abstinence movement in the United States had reached the stage where some deemed it advisable to form state unions for greater effectiveness.[16] In 1871 Washington followed the lead of Connecticut by forming a Central Union of the Catholic Total Abstinence Societies.[17] As president of the society at St. Patrick's, Keane was instrumental in promoting and accomplishing the union.

More important to the temperance movement than the formation of state unions was the call for delegates to be sent to the first national convention of Catholic Total Abstinence Societies to be held in Baltimore on February 22 and February 23, 1872. Keane was sent to this convention as the *ex-officio* delegate of the temperance society at St. Patrick's.[18] As chairman of the Committee on Resolutions[19] at this first gathering of temperance men, he was instrumental in presenting

---

from Father Mathew (statement by Monsignor Valentine Casey, rector of St. Raphael's Cathedral, Dubuque, Iowa, Dec. 28, 1948, personal interview). He must have taken the pledge between 1849 and 1851 during the Irish priest's crusade in the United States.

[14] *Catholic Mirror,* July 19, 1873. On the occasion of a trip to Europe made by Keane this society presented him with the following resolution: "*Resolved,* that the thanks of the Society be presented to the Reverend President for his paternal, kind, and eminent services in promoting and maintaining the interests and efficiency of the Society during his presidency of the last seven years, with the prayers of the Society for a pleasant and prosperous voyage to the land of his fathers and a safe return to us" (*ibid.*).

[15] *Catholic Mirror,* January 6, 1872. He addressed the Catholic Total Abstinence Societies' meeting at St. Aloysius' Church on New Year's evening. On September 22, 1872, he was the principal speaker at the opening of the fall campaign of the Central Catholic Temperance Union in Carroll Hall. On this occasion he spoke for an hour and "several ladies and gentlemen took the pledge at the end" (*ibid.,* Sept. 28, 1872). In 1873 Keane lectured before the Georgetown Catholic Total Abstinence and Beneficial Society (*ibid.,* Dec. 6, 1873).

[16] Sister Francis Joseph McKeon, S.N.D., "The Formation of the Catholic Total Abstinence Union of America" (unpublished master's thesis, Dept. of History, The Catholic University of America, 1946), p. 33; Sister Joan Bland, S.N.D., *Hibernian Crusade, The Story of the Catholic Abstinence Union of America* (Washington, 1951), p. 49 ff.

[17] McKeon, *op. cit.,* p. 36.

[18] *Catholic Mirror,* Mar. 2, 1872.

[19] Bland, *op. cit.,* p. 64.

recommendations which came to be regarded as the platform of the Union. Among other things, the committee advocated the "formation of state unions, juvenile societies, lecture bureaus, club houses and reading rooms; all of which later became accomplished factors in the propagation of temperance."[20] During the convention Keane offered the resolution that the constitution and the bylaws of the Union be offered to the church authorities of the Archdiocese of Baltimore for their approval.[21] The delegates so resolved and ecclesiastical approbation was given.[22]

At the close of the convention the business of electing the first president occupied the delegates. That Father Keane was esteemed by those present is evident from the fact that he was nominated for the high office along with Father James McDevitt, and Messrs. James W. O'Brien and Francis McNerhany. When each of those who had been proposed for the post declined the nomination, the delegates, by unanimous request, had Keane cast the vote of the convention for James McDevitt, assistant at St. Matthew's Church in Washington, who had presided over the convention as the chairman appointed by the Committee on Organization.[23] For some years thereafter Keane attended the annual meetings of the national organization and submitted his report as the president of the subordinate union in the District of Columbia. Furthermore, at these national conventions Keane usually served on important committees, such as the Committee on Constitutional Amendments, and he gave brief addresses before the delegates at their request.[24] Thus, he gained the admiration of temperance workers throughout the nation, and he became almost as well known to them as he was to the members of the various units in Washington.[25]

[20] McKeon, *op. cit.*, pp. 57–58.

[21] *Catholic Mirror*, Mar. 2, 1872.

[22] *Ibid.*, Mar. 16, 1872.

[23] *The Constitution and the Proceedings of the Catholic Total Abstinence Union of America, issued from the First Annual Convention held at Baltimore, Maryland, February 22nd and 23rd, 1872* (Baltimore, 1872). According to this document the voting was distributed as follows: Keane had twenty-four, O'Brien got twenty-three, McDevitt polled nineteen, and McNerhany ended up with three.

[24] *Constitution and Proceedings of the Catholic Total Abstinence Union of America, issued from the Fourth Annual Convention held at Chicago, Ill., October 7th and 8th, 1874* (Philadelphia, 1874), pp. 24, 39, 48, 52–53. Keane did not attend the second convention in Cleveland. Cf. Bland, *op. cit.*, p. 76.

[25] At the Chicago convention of the national union a large minority supported Keane for president (Bland, *op. cit.*, p. 90). Shortly after Archbishop Spalding's death in 1872, Keane and McDevitt took an active part in the formation of the Spalding Temperance Guards in Washington (*Catholic Mirror*, Oct. 19, 1872). Dur-

Although Keane's efforts in behalf of temperance from the very beginning of his priestly career were extremely important owing to the fact that he maintained an active and effective interest in the work throughout the rest of his life, his introduction to the work on behalf of the poor in Washington was immeasurably more significant because of its probable effect on his character. Before him day after day was a model of charity in the person of St. Patrick's pastor. When Gibbons wrote on the spirit of poverty in his *Ambassador of Christ,* he singled out Father Walter as an example under that heading and he said of him:

> Whilst he was Rector of St. Patrick's Church, large sums of money fell into his hands; but none of it clung to them. It was distributed among the orphans, or secretly dispensed to the poor, and especially to genteel, but indigent applicants for office in the Departments, who daily called on him. Profuse in his hospitality to visiting clergy, his own private apartment was more destitute of ornaments and comforts than that of a seminarian.[26]

Father Walter was especially interested in promoting the aims of the Society of St. Vincent de Paul, a conference of which society had existed in St. Patrick's for many years and had been aggregated to the superior council of New York by the pastor in March, 1861.[27] Concerning his solicitude for this organization, Keane said in later years: "No matter how busy he was, or how ailing, he never missed the meeting of the parish conference . . . , and the meetings of the Particular Council of the same admirable society were his special delight."[28] Even though the pastor directed the work of the charitable members of the organization, Keane was not excluded from their meetings. Very often it was his voice that spurred them on in their work for the poor.[29]

From the bosom of the Society of St. Vincent de Paul there had

---

ing the next year Keane lectured for the benefit of the Guards in Odd Fellows' Hall on "England's Social Puzzle: How she got into it and how she may hope to get out of it" (*ibid.,* Mar. 1, 1873). Unfortunately, the journal did not give the text or a summary of the lecture. Usually the newspapers were content to publish only a few phrases from Keane's sermons and lectures during these years, or they merely noted that he had appeared before an audience.

[26] James Cardinal Gibbons, *The Ambassador of Christ* (Baltimore, 1896), pp. 122–123.

[27] Smith, *op. cit.,* p. 38.

[28] Walter, *op. cit.,* pp. 79–80.

[29] *Church News,* Oct. 17, 1896.

sprung an auxiliary association, the Young Catholics' Friend Society, which consisted of a group of apostolic Catholic men who raised funds to clothe poor children and to educate them in parochial schools. From his very first days in Washington, Keane was a true friend to this organization, lecturing for them,[30] being present at some of the quarterly meetings of the society[31] and attending their annual gathering.[32]

During the years that Keane was in Washington, the Young Catholics' Friend Society became the parent of an organization known as the Carroll Institute, which has proved valuable to the religious life of Washington. The institute was organized in 1873, to promote closer social relationships among those who professed the same faith, and to provide the means of mental culture through literary discussions and exercises. The idea originated with Major Edmond Mallet, the president of the parent society, who foresaw the proposed organization as an adjunct to the society of which he was president, from which talent could be drawn to contribute to the interest of the Young Catholics' Friend's meetings. The original association formed in September, 1873, was known as the Carroll Literary Association. Father Walter made the first floor of the house adjoining Carroll Hall available to the group, and Keane, as chairman of the library committee, had printed a circular asking for contributions of books and money so the allotted space would contain a good library. Because of the generous response to this appeal, it was soon announced that the New York daily papers, Catholic periodicals, and good books awaited the inspection of the members of the association. After the first public meeting of this association on December 22, 1873, to which both Fathers Walter and Keane contributed, it was made known that literary meetings would be held every Tuesday evening.[33]

When, on May 7, 1874, the members of the Association voted that a new constitution be adopted and that the name of the association be changed to Carroll Institute,[34] Keane was one of the five constituting the Board of Directors of the institute, the rest being laymen. When St. Patrick's assistant was called elsewhere in 1878 the institute had 1861 volumes and pamphlets, a free night school in which 102 pupils were taught, and it had won a place in the social life of

[30] *Catholic Mirror,* Nov. 23, 1872.
[31] *Ibid.,* Dec. 21, 1872.
[32] *Ibid.,* Sept. 7, 1872.
[33] Smith, *op. cit.,* pp. 49–50; *Catholic Mirror,* Dec. 27, 1873.
[34] Smith, *op. cit.,* p. 49.

Washington.[35] In later years, Keane was given the chief credit for the success of the organization. In 1896, on the occasion of a testimonial gathering to honor Keane, J. Havens Richards, S.J., president of Georgetown University, stated: "Carroll Institute is the work of Bishop Keane; it is the fruit of his religious influence over young men, intended to guard them from dangers by affording them healthy recreation and association, and the means of self-instruction."[36] On the twenty-fifth anniversary of the founding of the institute, a charter member testified: "He was our guiding star, and much of the society's success may properly be ascribed to his suggestions and advice."[37]

Keane gave further evidence of his interest in the welfare of young men when he joined with others in 1875 to bring about the formation of the Catholic Young Men's National Union.[38] The purpose of this group was a lofty one, namely:

> to band the Catholic young men of the country into a solid phalanx, not with any aggressive purpose, but that, by their fidelity to their religion and what it enjoins on them, their pure lives, the integrity of their business relations, and the faithful discharge of all their duties to God and man, they may by their example and influence stem the tide of dishonesty and sin.[39]

By lending the influence of his personality to this cause, John Keane contributed to its success. Furthermore, by pointedly mentioning the great amount of good accomplished by the organization and by warmly recommending it to all Catholic young men in the pastoral letter which he prepared for the fathers of the Third Plenary Council,[40] he helped the union to become by 1889 what John Gilmary Shea, the foremost Catholic Church historian at that time, called "the most influential after the German Verein."[41]

[35] *Catholic Mirror,* Jan. 12, 1878.

[36] *Church News,* Oct. 17, 1896.

[37] *Ibid.,* Sept. 19, 1898. Patrick J. Donahue, Bishop of Wheeling, another charter member of Carroll Institute, said of Keane in a letter to Edward J. Hannan: "In its struggling infancy he was ever the staunch friend of Carroll Institute" (letter to the president of the institute on September 6, 1898, quoted in *ibid.*).

[38] James J. Green, "The Organization of the Catholic Total Abstinence Union of America, 1866–1884," *Records of the American Catholic Historical Society of Philadelphia,* LXI (June, 1950), 89. Cf. W. L. Sullivan, "Catholic Young Men's National Union," *Catholic Encyclopedia,* X, 712.

[39] New York *Freeman's Journal,* July 15, 1876, quoted in Green, *op. cit.,* pp. 89–90.

[40] *The Memorial Volume: A History of the Third Plenary Council of Baltimore November 9–December 7, 1884* (Baltimore, 1885), Appendix, p. 29.

[41] John Gilmary Shea, "Catholic Congresses," in *Official Report of the Proceedings of the Catholic Congress, held at Baltimore, Md., November 11th and 12th, 1889*

While it is true to say that Keane concerned himself principally with organizations of young men, in accordance with the pastor's wise plan for the effective administration of the parish, the societies for women were not entirely neglected by him. The young ladies who were enrolled in the Sodality of the Blessed Virgin Mary were especially appreciative of the direction which St. Patrick's busy assistant gave them. One woman who had belonged to that sodality recalled how much his instructions to the sodalists had meant to her, when she wrote to him years later.[42] More tangible evidence of the gratitude of these young women for his contributions to their spiritual formation was given on the occasion of his leaving for Europe in 1873 when they "presented him with a well-filled purse."[43] Not to be outdone in generosity, Keane on his return preached a beautiful sermon in St. Aloysius' Church to a congregation of sodalists from every part of the city who had gathered to celebrate the thirteenth anniversary of the formation of that parish's Sodality of the Immaculate Conception of the Blessed Virgin Mary.[44]

By far the most notable project for women to which he lent his zeal and organizing ability was the formation of the Tabernacle Society. At the suggestion of a young lady, Miss Fannie Whelan, who had an interest in sewing for poor churches, and who devoted her life and her means to this work, he invited women of like mind to St. Joseph's Male Orphan Asylum (since 1928 it has been known as St. Joseph's Home and School) where the Washington Tabernacle Society was organized.[45] The members of such groups "pledge themselves to spend an hour each month before the Blessed Sacrament and to pay yearly dues into a fund for the benefit of poor churches. The contributions are used to purchase materials for vestments which are made by women members of the society and given to poor churches."[46] In 1877, Keane was successful in having the Washington society affiliated with the Arch-Association of the Perpetual Adoration and Work for Poor Churches in Rome.[47] In this charitable occupation

(Detroit, 1889), p. 22. The official title of the German society was the German Roman Catholic Central-Verein.

[42] ACUA, Margaret A. [Faherty] Custer to Keane, Washington, Jan. 18, 1890.

[43] *Catholic Mirror,* July 26, 873.

[44] *Ibid.,* Dec. 20, 1873.

[45] *Church News,* Oct. 18, 1897. Keane reviewed the history of the society when he spoke at their meeting at the Shoreham Hotel.

[46] Blanche M. Kelly, "Tabernacle Societies," *Catholic Encyclopedia,* XIV, 426.

[47] Smith, *op. cit.,* p. 53.

many prominent Washington women found a way to make a humble contribution to the service of the altar and to this work Keane was to contribute many hours of his time and substantial sums from his meager income.[48]

Despite the hours devoted to the numerous societies while he was assistant at St. Patrick's, Father Keane found time to give careful preparation to his sermons for such occasions as St. Patrick's Day, which was celebrated at that time with a great deal of ceremony. Not only did he preach at the Mass on the patronal feast in 1872, after the parading societies, led by the Fort McHenry band, had greeted a Baltimore contingent and then marched to St. Patrick's Church, but he also gave a lecture that evening at the Odd Fellows' Hall before the Knights of St. Patrick on "Ireland's Past, and Its Bearing on Her Future."[49] At St. Patrick's he also preached on such occasions as the opening of the Forty Hours' Devotion,[50] the solemn high Mass on Christmas Day,[51] the high Mass on Easter Sunday,[52] and at the funerals of distinguished parishioners.[53]

Among the many invitations to preach and lecture outside of the city of Washington which the young priest received,[54] one which probably gave him special pleasure came in 1869, when he was asked to preach in the cathedral of Baltimore on the occasion of the month's mind for Oliver Lawrence Jenkins, S.S., who had died on July 11, of that year. The curate of St. Patrick's had the highest esteem for all of his Sulpician professors, but he entertained a genuine affection for this priest who had directed St. Charles' College during its formative years.[55] Keane preached at the cathedral again in 1878, at the pontifical Mass of requiem celebrated for the repose of the soul of Pius IX, who had died on February 7.[56]

[48] In 1918 the headquarters of the society was in a building occupied by the Sisters of Perpetual Adoration and of Work for the Poor Churches. This building was a gift to the cause by Keane. "Archbishop Keane Obeys Summons," *Apostolate,* XIV (May and June, 1918, 4).

[49] *Catholic Mirror,* Mar. 23, 1872.

[50] *Ibid.,* May 25, 1872.

[51] *Ibid.,* Jan. 4, 1873.

[52] *Ibid.,* Apr. 19, 1873.

[53] *Ibid.,* Aug. 24, 1873.

[54] He conducted missions which entailed instructions after the morning Mass, an afternoon or an evening sermon, and confessions during the last three days of the mission (*ibid.,* Apr. 20, 1872). He delivered a lecture in Baltimore in 1873 (*ibid.,* Feb. 22, 1873).

[55] Viger, *Golden Jubilee of St. Charles' College,* p. 32.

[56] *Catholic Mirror,* Feb. 23, 1878.

Obviously, preaching and lecturing drained a good deal of the energy that John Keane brought to St. Patrick's. True, it was by this means that he came to be known to a majority of Washington's Catholics as well as to a good number of people of other faiths. But the strength spent in the pulpit and on the platform does not necessarily earn for the priest that childlike trust and deep affection that are reserved for those who are solicitous for the spiritual welfare and nourishment of the flock. That Keane did not neglect this aspect of parochial work while seemingly wholly occupied in the exercise of his vocal and mental talents is evident from the record of spiritual care found at St. Patrick's. From the time of his first baptism on September 5, 1866, nearly every page of the record book is filled with his flowing hand, indicating that the sacrament was conferred at the convenience of the people of the parish during the week and on Sunday. One thing that stands out in this record is the number of elderly Negro ladies whom Keane baptized.[57] After he had officiated at his first marriage at St. Patrick's on September 14, 1866, he witnessed the union of Noyes to Sweeney, Dyer to Magruder, and Hellen to Cowles by which the old names in Washington were perpetuated and, incidentally, through which some of the old fortunes were saved.[58] The Interment Register at St. Patrick's indicates that the number of deaths was a good deal smaller than the number of births, although from his first recorded burial on January 28, 1867, Keane witnessed many scenes of bereavement during those years.[59] His visits to the sick and the dying, his words of hope to despairing souls, the hungry he

[57] During 1869, the young priest baptized 70 persons, nine of whom were converts. In 1877, he had fifty-eight baptisms, fourteen of them after he had given private instructions to each one. Cf. St. Patrick's Church, Washington, D. C., Baptismal Register, Sept. 8, 1857, to Sept. 30, 1871, and Baptismal Register, Oct., 1871, to Jan., 1881.

[58] St. Patrick's Church, Washington, D. C., Marriage Registers. In 1868 he performed twenty-one marriages. Such a great number during a period of twelve months was due to the absence of the pastor who had gone to Europe in December, 1867, and returned in June, 1868, having recovered from an inflammation of the lungs. Cf. Walter, *op. cit.*, pp. 74–75. Archbishop Spalding learned that Keane's health was "not strong," so he sent him an assistant during Walter's absence. He warned the young priest to take care of his health and said: "I have other views in your regard, to be carried out in some months — this entre nous" (AAB, Letterbook — A-321 — Spalding to Keane, Baltimore, Feb. 15, 1868).

[59] St. Patrick's Church, Washington, D. C., Interment Register, Apr. 15, 1860, to Sept. 25, 1871. The *Catholic Mirror* furnished a record of the prominent people Keane consoled in their last moments, but no mention was made of many lonely vigils he spent at the side of the poor. For an example, cf. the *Catholic Mirror* for Mar. 30, 1872.

may have fed, the naked he may have clothed, are not, of course, a matter of record. Knowing his character, however, we can surmise that very few sought his help in vain.

Two years after Keane's ordination, almighty God called his mother to her reward.[60] She had spent twenty years in Baltimore without ever having an opportunity to return to the land of her birth, and during those years she saw God take all of her children, either to their home, or to His service.[61] In 1872, four years after his mother's death, and in the same year in which he became a citizen of the United States,[62] John Keane asked Archbishop James Roosevelt Bayley for permission to join the Missionary Society of St. Paul the Apostle, commonly known as the Paulist Fathers.[63] The young priest was drawn to the community by its founder and Superior General, Isaac Hecker, who visited St. Patrick's Church in Washington frequently at this time, and when he came, as one intimate friend of the assistant put it, "their conversations turned always upon the deeper interior life."[64] That Hecker was anxious for Keane's transfer is evident from a letter written in an effort to influence the archbishop's decision:

> It has come to the point which I had anticipated, F. Keane of Washington City, writes me that he has applied to you for leave to try his vocation with us.
>
> I have known him several years, and long before he expressed any inclination for our Community, I felt satisfied that he was called to a religious life.
>
> His vocation is so evident that no one who has discernment in such matters will hesitate about it, much less you who can sympathize with and appreciate such a call from the Holy Spirit. I am convinced that he will make a perfect religious, and be much more useful to the Church in that state.

[60] Reily, *op. cit.*, II, 648.

[61] His mother's sister Mary also lived in Baltimore. ADR, a bequest from Mary Connolly to her nephew, John Keane, in consideration for money expended for her care during two years at St. Agnes' Hospital. The document was written in Baltimore and bears the date, August 18, 1874.

[62] ADR, Certificate. Supreme Court of the District of Columbia, Feb. 5, 1872.

[63] For a short history of the community, cf. Walter Elliott, C.S.P., "Missionary Society of St. Paul the Apostle," *Catholic Encyclopedia,* X, 368–369.

[64] Denis O'Connell's funeral oration over the remains of John J. Keane, cited in Walter Elliott, C.S.P., "Personal Reminiscences of Archbishop Keane," *Catholic World,* CVII (Aug., 1918), 641. O'Connell also said on this occasion: "Father Hecker gave his young friend a copy of the Jesuit Father Lallemant's *Spiritual Doctrine,* then recently translated by Father Faber, which he read and assimilated perfectly."

In addition, I have a personal reason for your consent to his trying his vocation with us.

My strength for some time has not been what it was, and I am compelled to divide up my cases and duties among companions. To some extent I have already done so. But there is a place for which I find no one in the Community, that is the editing of the Catholic World. It is one of the mightiest of my responsibilities and most taxing of my cares. F. Keane has a good pen, a literary taste and turn of mind, and many other qualifications which make him suitable for such a position. He has written for the Catholic World. With little training and supervision he can relieve me in a great measure of this tax on my energies.[65]

Probably Hecker also saw certain traits in Keane's character which would undoubtedly appeal to him. There was a tendency in the young man to assimilate quickly and to accept as his own the ideas and especially the lofty ideals of those whom he admired. Furthermore, he could express the ideas that he had obtained from others in a form that increased their appeal, and he had the strength of character and the tenacity of will which enabled him to direct his life according to the lofty ideals that he had accepted, as well as the zeal needed to promote great causes and the optimism necessary to prevent discouragement if his efforts were not attended by notable success.[66]

In his reply to Father Hecker, the Archbishop of Baltimore said that he did not doubt that Keane "would make an excellent member of your congregation," but he could not conscientiously allow him to leave because, as he put it, "he makes also an excellent priest on the mission, . . . and we have much need of priests especially such as he is."[67] A member of the Community who was in a position to be

[65] AAB, 41-U-15a, Hecker to Bayley, New York, Oct. 22, 1872. It is impossible to determine how much Keane contributed to the *Catholic World* since the articles in that magazine were not signed in those days.

[66] In the opinion of the present writer, Fathers Hecker and Walter exercised the greatest influence on Keane during this period. To the inspiration of the former may be attributed the beginnings of Keane's great personal devotion to the Holy Spirit and his labors to promote that devotion. Moreover, to him we can trace some of Keane's ideas on temperance and on the role of the United States in the designs of Providence. To the latter's example of heroic charity we must undoubtedly attribute the impulse which resulted in the formation of a similar virtue in Keane. In later years, it appears that his thinking was influenced by Father Thomas Bouquillon, professor of Moral Theology in the Catholic University of America, Archbishop John Ireland and, above all others, Monsignor Denis O'Connell.

[67] APF, Bayley to Hecker, Baltimore, Nov. 6, 1872. Such statements as "at Archbishop Spalding's earnest solicitation, he consented to remain a secular priest" (Reily, *op. cit.*, II, 649), and "he thought of entering the community of Paulist

familiar with the case said in later years that Archbishop Bayley did not favor the change because he considered the young priest to be "destined for a bishopric."[68] The fact that the request was made reveals that Keane had no ambitions for ecclesiastical preferment, since the Paulists do not accept honors such as the episcopacy.

After he had been refused permission to join the Paulists, Keane decided to take a trip to Europe. Perhaps, this decision was influenced by the fact that his father was not in good health,[69] and his son considered an ocean voyage to Ireland would benefit him. They sailed from New York on July 19, 1873, on the *City of Montreal*. John left his father in Ireland and proceeded alone to the continent, visiting in France before he went to the center of Christendom.[70] In Rome he ascended the *Scala Regia* to the Pope's chamber for the first time, where he was granted an audience with Pius IX — "an occasion," as he said later, "that I never can forget."[71] After a month on the continent he rejoined his father, and both returned to the United States in the last week of October.[72]

Within six months after their return from Europe, Mr. Keane married again, choosing for his wife a young woman by the name of Mary Henry.[73] On September 10, 1877, three years after this second marriage, Keane's father, then seventy-two years old, died and was buried from St. Vincent's Church in Baltimore.[74] John Keane, as the executor of his father's will, transferred to his stepmother the entire estate, which consisted of the house at 27 North High Street and its furniture, some shares in St. Vincent's Building Society, and $145 and interest in the Savings Bank of Baltimore.[75] Hence by the fall of 1877, Father Keane had been deprived of his whole family and whatever earthly possessions they had accumulated.

Other events took place in 1877 that were to have a more lasting

---

Fathers, but was dissuaded by Archbishop Spalding" (William J. Kerby, "John Joseph Keane," *Dictionary of American Biography,* X, 267) are not true.

[68] Elliott, *Catholic World,* CVII (Aug., 1918), 641.

[69] Reily, *op. cit.,* II, 649.

[70] *Catholic Mirror,* July 19, 1873.

[71] Cyrus J. Manning, "The Archbishop's Visit to Rome," *College Spokesman,* III (Nov., 1905), 18.

[72] *Catholic Mirror,* July 19, 1873.

[73] St. Vincent de Paul's Church, Baltimore, Maryland, Marriage Register. They were married on May 28, 1874.

[74] Reilly, *op. cit.,* II, 718.

[75] ADR, Document, Baltimore, Oct. 26, 1877. This document would indicate that Keane's stepmother could not write, since her signature consisted of a witnessed (x). She died on November 25, 1895 (*Church News,* Nov. 30, 1895).

effect on the life of Father Walter's assistant. For a long time Archbishop Bayley had been planning to have James Gibbons, Bishop of Richmond, transferred to Baltimore as his coadjutor. It was also his idea to have John J. Kain, classmate of Keane's and then pastor of Harper's Ferry, succeed Gibbons in Richmond.[76] Before Bayley's moves could be executed, however, Kain was appointed the second Bishop of Wheeling to succeed Richard V. Whelan who had died on July 7, 1874.[77] So in 1877, when Gibbons' transfer to Baltimore was accomplished, just in time to take care of the archbishop before his death on October 3, 1877,[78] another was sought for the vacant See of Richmond and for the Vicariate of North Carolina. A few weeks after Gibbons had succeeded Bayley as the metropolitan of the Province of Baltimore, he called together the bishops of the province for the purpose of making nominations for Richmond. Bishops Lynch, Becker, Gross, and Kain were present and agreed on a *terna* (a list of names of candidates for episcopacy), consisting of Silas M. Chatard, rector of the North American College in Rome, John J. Keane, and Henry P. Northrop, a priest in Charleston,[79] who was destined to be Vicar-Apostolic of North Carolina and Bishop of Charleston. John Moore, Bishop of St. Augustine, concurred in the choice of his brother bishops by letter.[80] Following the meeting in Baltimore, Archbishop Gibbons recorded in his diary under December 7: "Wrote to Cardinal Franchi in relation to the Richmond appointment, strongly recommending Rev. Father Keane and expressing the fear that the removal of Mgr. Chatard at the present juncture from the rectorship of the American College would be injurious to the College." Gibbons also wrote that he considered Keane "a rare combination of head and heart."[81] The Archbishop of Baltimore had a sure knowledge of Keane's character by this time for they had been on intimate terms even while the young man was in the major seminary. Gibbons was at that time pastor of St. Bridget's parish, which Keane described in later years as the poorest in Baltimore.[82]

[76] AAB, 72-Q-14, Bayley to Gibbons, Madison, New Jersey, July 24, 1874.

[77] Kain was consecrated on May 23, 1875. Cf. Code, *op. cit.*, p. 171.

[78] Will, *op. cit.*, I, 174.

[79] *Ibid.*, pp. 178–179. The meeting was held on October 20.

[80] AAB, 73-F-12, Moore to Gibbons, St. Augustine, Oct. 16, 1877.

[81] Will, *op. cit.*, I, 178–179.

[82] Statement by Monsignor Valentine Casey, pastor of St. Raphael's Cathedral, Dubuque, Iowa, Dec. 28, 1948, personal interview. The parish was located in a section known as Canton, then located at the extreme eastern boundaries of the city. The people were poor and the pastor had only a few small rooms built against

There was no doubt in Gibbons' mind, therefore, that Keane was admirably equipped for the post.

The Archbishop of Baltimore was kept informed about the situation in Rome by his friend Denis J. O'Connell, a priest of the Diocese of Richmond, who was in the Eternal City to get Gibbons' pallium. Since we can assume that the Archbishop of Baltimore was anxious to have his friend appointed to the vacant see, the news he received from his Rome correspondent must have been disconcerting. O'Connell stated early in December that there was some talk of Chatard's appointment,[83] and by the last week of that month he wrote: "Cardinal Franchi said, as I am certain, that Mgr. Chatard will be named to Richmond. 'The Congregation will select him without doubt, and a desire of the Holy Father to retain him is the only possible disappointment I foresee.' "[84] The death of Pius IX on February 7 caused further delay in filling Richmond. The new pontiff, Leo XIII, soon confirmed the selection of Chatard for the See of Vincennes,[85] thus clearing the way for the appointment of Keane at the consistory held late in March. On April 13, 1878, Giovanni Simeoni, Cardinal Prefect of the Congregation of the Propaganda, notified Gibbons of Keane's appointment as Bishop of Richmond and Administrator of the Vicariate of North Carolina.[86]

While the appointment to Richmond was being considered in Rome, rumors linked Keane's name with the vacant see. One who was in a class of children at St. Patrick's at the time had this to say of those exciting days: "I can see him still, announcing to a class of half-grown boys, in which I was, that the rumors in regard to his appointment as Bishop were unfounded. He was blushing like a school girl when he was speaking: and a week later came the official announcement that he had been appointed Bishop of Richmond."[87] After it had become quite certain that Keane had been selected, he was the recipient of many manifestations of the affection in which he was held by the people in Washington. The Washington *Post* for

---

the wall of the church for living quarters. Cf. John Tracy Ellis, *The Life of James Cardinal Gibbons* (Milwaukee, 1952), I, 49.

[83] AAB, 73-J-10, O'Connell to Gibbons, Rome, Dec. 12, 1877.

[84] AAB, 73-K-4, O'Connell to Gibbons, Rome, Dec. 28, 1877.

[85] AAB, 73-P-10, Chatard to Gibbons, Rome, Mar. 19, 1878.

[86] AAB, 73-Q-10, Simeoni to Gibbons, Rome, Apr. 13, 1878 (Latin).

[87] AAB, 118-Q, Maria Longworth Storer to Gibbons, Saranac Lake, New York, September 8, 1918, in which she enclosed a copy of part of a letter from her son-in-law, the Marquis Pierre de Chambrun, under date of August 16, 1918. The quotation is from the enclosure.

March 30 remarked: "In his private life he is the courteous, kind-hearted, generous gentleman, with whom a forgetfulness of self and a suave consideration of others seems a part of his nature. The charitable side of his character was the unobtrusive, but the poor of Washington will miss him more than any other class."[88] The members of the Carroll Institute made the bishop-elect an honorary member of their group,[89] and the people and the papers generally had many heartwarming things to say about the curate who had won a lasting place in the hearts of the people whom he had served.

Just before he left St. Patrick's, the bishop-elect had another opportunity to manifest his high regard for the Sulpicians, and particularly for the man who had been an example of those priestly qualities which the Church seeks to form in all those who aspire to the altar. Joseph Paul Dubreul, rector of St. Mary's Seminary during Keane's seminary days, died on Holy Saturday, April 20, 1878. On the day of his burial, his former student preached an eloquent eulogy at the pontifical requiem Mass celebrated by Archbishop Gibbons for his former vicar-general.[90]

On June 3, Keane left St. Patrick's for St. Charles' College to make a retreat in preparation for his consecration. There was no formal ceremony of leave taking, nor did he preach at the last Mass the Sunday before, although a large congregation made up of people from throughout the city had come with the expectation of hearing the newly-appointed bishop deliver his farewell sermon.[91] Amid the scenes of his preparatory seminary days, he engaged in those studies that would prepare him for the correct performance of the pontifical liturgy and for the special duties of his new office.[92] This period between the first announcement of his appointment and his consecration lengthened way beyond his original plan, since the bulls of appointment miscarried after leaving Rome, and he could not be consecrated without having them in his possession. The documents announcing his appointment in the consistory of March 28 were dated March 31 and had been sent to Gibbons on April 13. When a reasonable time had elapsed to allow for unforeseen delays in communications as an explanation for not receiving them, an investigation was begun. The inquiry revealed that the letter containing the docu-

[88] Washington *Post,* Mar. 30, 1878.
[89] *Catholic Mirror,* June 8, 1878.
[90] Reily, *op. cit.,* II, 616–617.
[91] *Catholic Mirror,* June 8, 1878.
[92] ADR, Bishops' Diary.

ments had been addressed to "Giacomo Gibbons." The Baltimore post-office officials did not recognize the name as referring to the archbishop so they advertised an unclaimed letter addressed to "G. Gibbons." When it was not called for it was sent to the dead letter office in New York and only after Gibbons' inquiry about the letter was it recovered in Baltimore where it arrived on August 1.[93]

With the bulls at last in his possession, Keane could complete the arrangements for his consecration. Bishop John Kain suggested that the ceremony take place in St. Peter's Cathedral in Richmond, and in disclosing this proposal to Gibbons the Bishop of Wheeling told the archbishop: "Baltimore has more attractions — but Richmond more claims."[94] Kain's idea appealed to the bishop-elect who made arrangements for his consecration to take place there on August 25, 1878, less than a month before his thirty-ninth birthday.

Although Keane was now approaching middle age, he was, despite a receding hairline, still youthful in appearance. The contours of his face and slender frame suggested that he was slightly underweight for his age. His finely textured dark-brown hair he wore long over the ears and in the back after the fashion of the day; the thinning portion in the middle of the crown he combed to the left and back without a part. Seriousness was indicated by his deep-set eyes, Irish gray in color, which gave the impression of deep penetration as they gazed through small rimless glasses, and by his thin and tight-drawn lips. His finely shaped nose seemed to be large because his fair complexioned cheeks and chin, which neither jutted nor receded, were not filled out. Within a few years considerable additional weight matured his figure and erased the slight sharpness from his features. In spite of his youthful appearance, Keane carried himself with dignity, head and slightly sloping shoulders erect, as he set out in 1878, for his consecration in Richmond.[95]

[93] Will, *op. cit.*, I, 179. The vice-rector of the American College in Rome told Gibbons that the original documents had come back to Rome and that the duplicates had been held up when the originals were returned (AAB, 73-U-3, Louis E. Hostlot to Gibbons, Rome, July 17, 1878).

[94] AAB, 73-Q-12, Kain to Gibbons, Wheeling, West Virginia, Apr. 15, 1878.

[95] This description of Keane is based on a picture taken at the time of his consecration and on the answers made to a questionnaire by Miss Mary Merrick, who knew Keane when he was selected for Richmond, and Monsignor Isidore Semper, who knew the prelate in later years.

Chapter III

Richmond's Fifth Bishop

THE Bishop-elect of Richmond arrived in his see city on the afternoon of August 22, 1878. He immediately presented his bulls of appointment to Francis Janssens,[1] the administrator of the diocese, and then, as his first act of jurisdiction, appointed this Dutch-born priest as his vicar-general. Keane found that preparations had been made for the consecration to take place on August 25. Richmond had never before witnessed this solemn ceremony, and on the morning of the consecration, St. Peter's Cathedral overflowed with the crowd which included many from Baltimore and Washington. James Gibbons, Archbishop of Baltimore, who had but recently left this same cathedral for the older see, was the consecrator. Jacob Walter, pastor of St. Patrick's Church in Washington, under whom Keane had served and for whom he had great esteem, was the assistant priest. Alphonse Magnien, S.S., president of St. Mary's Seminary in Baltimore, and Thomas Griffin, chancellor of the Diocese of Springfield, were deacons of honor. The deacons of the Mass were Augustine Van de Vyver, who was destined to be Keane's successor as sixth Bishop of Richmond, and Denis J. O'Connell, whose interesting career was to end as seventh bishop of the See. For his chaplains, Keane had chosen two of his Sulpician professors, François P. Dissez and Jean-Baptiste Ménu. As one of the assistant consecrators, Keane had selected the man who had taken an interest in his vocation to the priesthood and who had paved the way for his entry into St. Charles College, namely, Thomas Foley, Coadjutor Bishop of Chicago, who died six months after this cere-

[1] Reily, *op. cit.,* II, 642–643.

mony. For the other assistant consecrator Keane invited John J. Kain, Bishop of Wheeling.

In his sermon, the preacher, Patrick N. Lynch, Bishop of Charleston, after naming Keane's predecessors in the See of Richmond and speaking of their labors, addressed himself to Richmond's new bishop. "Your predecessors have done much of the hard and heavy work," he said, "you may reap the fruit of their arduous labors. But you will find enough and more than enough still to do." Lynch concluded: "You will find in your office both consolation and sorrow, the mitre must ever be, to some degree at least, as a crown of thorns."[2]

The consecration ceremony was followed by a banquet which the priests of the Diocese of Richmond had provided for the bishop's friends. Besides those who had actively participated in the ceremonies, the guests included William H. Gross, Bishop of Savannah, John Moore, Bishop of St. Augustine, Honorable Frederick William Holliday, Governor of Virginia, about twenty priests from Virginia and North Carolina, about forty priests from other dioceses, and a number of distinguished friends of the bishop who had come from various parts of the country.[3]

Late in the afternoon on the day of the consecration, Gibbons officiated at pontifical vespers and Bishop Keane preached his inaugural sermon, which was outstanding for its simple beauty, its humble statement of his thoughts, and its clear manifestation of his convictions. After thanking the people of Richmond for the cordial welcome he had received, he told them:

> I recognize that this is indeed the turning point of my life, which, while it bestows on me spiritual privileges and graces, which I would never have dared to hope for, and for which I can never be sufficiently grateful to God, yet also forever puts out of my reach that which I have the most shrunk from. Nothing indeed could be more directly in opposition to all my desires than the position in which the Lord has seen fit to place me, and the responsibility which he has laid on me. The object of my most ardent desires and most earnest endeavors for

[2] *Catholic Mirror,* Aug. 31, 1878. Keane's episcopal robes were the gift of the parishioners of St. Patrick's Church in Washington. The chalice used during the Mass was given to Keane by the wife of the Minister from Peru. Accounts of the ceremony also appeared in the *Katholische Volkszeitung,* August 31, 1878, which reported that there were 600 people from Baltimore and 400 from Washington at the consecration. The *Evening Star* (Washington), August 26, 1878, described the ceremony and gave the names of the participants. Cf. Jesse W. Lonsway, *The Episcopal Lineage of the Hierarchy in the United States, 1790–1948* (New York, 1948), for Keane's lineage.

[3] ADR, Bishops' Diary, p. 79.

years past was a life of even greater hiddenness and retirement than that with which God blessed me during my twelve years in the priestly ministry. But in the voice of the Vicar of Christ, our Holy Father Pope Leo XIII, I recognize the command of the Divine Head of the Church Himself, who is my God and my Master, and I have no will but to submit. He gives graces to fulfill His commands, and I stop not to dwell on my weaknesses and shortcomings, which He knows better than I do, but trust all to His Providence. I place my poor nothingness in his hands, that He may do with me what He can for His glory and the good of your souls.

Turning from himself, the bishop next treated the Christian's duties to his God and his country. The latter subject gave him the opportunity to present his views on public school education, a subject which would engage his serious attention many times in the years to come.

Our country may think us unfriendly because we tell her of her mistakes — because we warn her that, by a system of Godless education, she is training generations that, for want of proper religious moulding and principles, will be as unfit to be good citizens as to be good Christians. Wedded to her views and plans, she may denounce us as enemies for our advice. . . . We must remind our country that our Church has not only the unfailing deposit of revealed truth, but also a practical wisdom, made up from her experience in all the ages and all the nations of modern times; that *her experience demonstrates* that Godless education trains unprincipled citizens, who are their country's scourge, and, finally, her ruin, — that the only way to make a prosperous and happy state is to mould the individual and the family in the mould of Christian principles and virtue, for such as are the individual and the family, such also must be the nation.

Keane ended his inaugural sermon by earnestly exhorting his listeners to petition for the grace that he would need to serve God and them "in spirit and in truth" — the motto he had chosen for his shield.[4]

After the guests had departed the Bishop of Richmond had time to survey the scene of his future labors. The first Mass had been offered in Richmond in 1791 by John Dubois, later Bishop of New York. During the ensuing years such men as T. C. Mongrand (1798),

[4] *Catholic Mirror,* Aug. 31, 1878. It was probably owing to the importance of the school agitation at this time that Keane expressed his views on public school education. Cf. Sister Mary Angela Carlin, O.S.U., "The Attitude of the Republican Party Toward Religious Schools, 1875–1880" (unpublished master's thesis, Dept. of Education, Catholic University of America, 1953).

Xavier Michel (1811), and John McElroy, S.J. (1813), had stopped in Richmond for short periods and performed their priestly functions in private homes. In 1820 the Archbishop of Baltimore was relieved of this portion of his jurisdiction when Richmond was erected as a see and Patrick Kelly named the first bishop. Upon his arrival from Ireland in 1821, Kelly made the church in Norfolk his cathedral. After a year had elapsed this bishop sought relief from his charge and returned to Ireland, when once more the Archbishop of Baltimore was responsible for the area embraced by the See of Richmond. Between 1822 and 1840, when the diocese was given its second bishop, the cornerstone of a cathedral had been laid in 1834 and completed in 1835; three Sisters of Charity had come to Richmond in 1834 and St. Joseph's Orphan Asylum had been built in 1840. With the transfer of Richard V. Whelan, the second bishop, to Wheeling in 1850, John McGill was appointed as his successor. During McGill's administration (1850–1872) the cornerstone of St. Mary's Church for the Germans was laid in 1851, the cathedral was enlarged the following year, and the first diocesan synod was held there four years later. In 1859 the cornerstone of St. Patrick's Church was laid and in 1866 the Convent of the Visitation opened at Mount Maria. Two years later the German Benedictine nuns came to the diocese. During the five years that James Gibbons administered the see (1872–1877), the cornerstone of the cathedral school was laid and the Little Sisters of the Poor were incorporated. Hence, when Keane took charge, he found in Richmond three churches: St. Peter's Cathedral, St. Patrick's, and St. Mary's, with a total of 5098 members, besides two orphan asylums, and one Catholic newspaper, the *Catholic Visitor*.[5] Outside the See city there were, in 1878, twenty-one churches and about the same number of missions, while in the twenty-six schools of the diocese there was a total attendance of 2250 children. To assist in the care of these scattered souls there were only twenty-four priests located strategically at the more heavily populated places.[6]

Following his consecration Bishop Keane adopted practices which would enable him to become thoroughly familiar with his priests and people. On the Sunday after his arrival he preached at the high Mass in the cathedral,[7] and then he visited the Sunday school, and

[5] [F. Joseph Magri], *The Catholic Church in the City and Diocese of Richmond* (Richmond, 1906), pp. 34–115. Cf. Reily, *op. cit.*, III, Part III, 144–145; ADR, Bishops' Diary, p. 79; Ellis, *op. cit.*, Chap. iv.

[6] *Catholic Standard* (Philadelphia), Oct. 27, 1877.

[7] Magri, *op. cit.*, p. 117.

attended meetings of the Conference of St. Vincent de Paul and of the temperance society of the cathedral. He recorded that all these organizations were flourishing. During the first few weeks he also found that the schools of the city were in good condition.[8]

Keane was anxious to begin his first visitation tour of the diocese and the vicariate so that he might report to Rome on the state of religion in his see. He wrote the pastors to inform them of his coming and on the morning of September 18 he set out.[9] During the next two and a half months he visited the missions of Virginia and North Carolina. While he did not go to every place where the priests ministered, he did visit nearly every church where a priest resided, and each mission where the resident pastors thought it worth while to visit at the time. During the visitation Keane confirmed 359, of whom seventy-four were converts.[10] Thus informed about the material and spiritual condition of his jurisdiction Keane returned and prepared the report for the Holy See.[11]

The diocesan financial statement at the end of the year 1878 gave Bishop Keane a picture of what was in store for him. There was "an annual deficit of over $1,500, arising from excess of expenditures on property over receipts therefrom, excess of seminary expenses over collection, and annuities to priests in poor missions." When he had arrived in Richmond, the last payment on some property had been received and used by the administrator to meet such expenses. Hence, the sole certain sources of revenue were the cathedraticum and some rents. Keane wrote "were it not for the $600 per year (or such portion of it as can be spared), which the Cathedral has been in the habit of paying the Bp. it would be impossible for him to make ends meet."[12] Because of these circumstances the bishop composed a strong

[8] ADR, Bishops' Diary, p. 80.

[9] *Ibid.*

[10] ADR, Visitation Record. This is a record book with notes on his observations during visitation tours. The Diary was a more complete record of diocesan affairs. On November 3, 1878, Keane visited Wilmington, North Carolina, at which time the Catholics of the city tendered him a reception. *Centennial Souvenir of St. Thomas the Apostle Catholic Church* (Wilmington, North Carolina, 1947), p. 7.

[11] ADR, Visitation Record.

[12] ADR, Bishops' Diary, p. 81. Keane told Gibbons that he could get only $20 or $30 a month from the cathedral as his salary (AAB, 74-F-6, Richmond, Dec. 23, 1878). In a letter to Gibbons a few years later in which he told the Cardinal about a request for Mass stipends from a Monsignor in Rome, Keane said: "As I have not had an intention for a very long time past and have none now, I venture to ask your Eminence whether you might not have some that you could send him" (AAB, 83-B-9, Richmond, July 2, 1887).

plea for funds to the Society of the Propagation of the Faith in France, which he sent to Gibbons with the request that he add his endorsement.[13] Shortly after the appeal was dispatched, the Bishop received a check from the Society for 1200 francs for North Carolina, but nothing for the Diocese of Richmond.[14] The non-pew holders of the cathedral were also tapped as a source of revenue when it was found that the unrented spaces would bring in as much as $1,206 annually, and the response to the appeal proved gratifying.[15]

Within four months, therefore, Bishop Keane had become familiar with the spiritual, material, and financial state of the diocese and vicariate. He then formulated plans to improve or correct the conditions which he had found. Some of his plans were slow to materialize because of circumstances, others bore fruit within a short time.

From his first days in Richmond, Keane was concerned about making better provisions for the spiritual welfare of the people in the Vicariate of North Carolina. The vicariate, embracing the whole state of North Carolina, had been established in 1868 with James Gibbons as its first vicar apostolic. When Gibbons was transferred to Richmond in 1872, he retained jurisdiction over North Carolina under the title of administrator. Rome had been asked to select a bishop for the vacant vicariate during Gibbons' administration, but the Congregation of the Propaganda had not acted. On the eve of Keane's consecration a meeting of the metropolitan and his suffragans resulted in their determination to write to Rome urging action and stating that, "if there be any objection to the list sent, another can be made out, on our being notified."[16] Upon receipt of this appeal Cardinal Simeoni informed Keane that it had been decided that the vicariate must remain under the Bishop of Richmond until a special report was forwarded, accompanied by new names of candidates for the succession.[17] When it was announced in the fall of 1879 that Mark S. Gross had been appointed to the vacant vicariate, Keane sent Gross a check for the vicariate's funds and announced that he would not carry out his proposed visitation.[18] Gross, however, declined the appointment and after the bulls had been in his possession for

[13] AAB, 74-G-1, Keane to Gibbons, Richmond, Jan. 1, 1879.

[14] ADR, Bishops' Diary, p. 83.

[15] *Ibid.*

[16] *Ibid.*, p. 80. For Gibbons' administration of the vicariate, cf. Ellis, *op. cit.*, Chap. iii.

[17] ADR, Bishops' Diary, p. 88.

[18] ADR, Gross to Keane, Wilmington, North Carolina, Sept. 16, 1879; *ibid.*, Dec. (n.d.), 1879.

several months he returned them to Rome. Lest the people be deprived of the opportunity to receive the sacrament of confirmation for an indefinite time, Keane immediately made arrangements with Gross to begin a confirmation tour that ultimately took him to sixteen locations in various parts of North Carolina.[19] While he was engaged in confirming in October, 1880, the bishop received the unwelcome news that Gross's resignation had been accepted and that he was to continue as administrator of North Carolina for the time being.[20]

Keane's preference for a less conspicuous position in the Church which he had revealed on the day of his consecration, was manifested once more when Gibbons summoned the bishops of the province to Baltimore for the purpose of nominating the candidates for the vicariate. The bishop's generous offer which would have entailed a real sacrifice was recorded in his own words:

> After mature and prayerful reflection, considering that it was hard to find a man both willing and able to do the peculiar work to be done in N. C. and to stand the hard life to be there expected; and that it would not be so in regard to the diocese of Richmond; and feeling confident, after having twice gone all over the Vicariate, that I could not only stand the life but love it; after consultations with my spiritual director; I proposed to the Bps. that I should, if the Holy See consented, be transferred to the Vicariate, and another be appointed to Richmond. After discussion it was agreed that my proposition should be submitted to the Holy See; and nominations were made, for replacing me, should Rome consent, or, should the consent not be given, for the Vicariate. My resolution has been dictated by no want of love for the Diocese, its priests, and the work in it, but through commiseration for the Vicariate, and the conviction that it would suit me exactly.[21]

But Rome did not accept Keane's offer. Instead, at the dawn of the year 1882, it relieved him of the vicariate by appointing Henry P. Northrop, a native of Charleston, South Carolina, for the uncoveted position.[22] The Bishop of Richmond turned over to Northrop all the papers and funds of the vicariate,[23] and rejoiced at the final solution of one of his problems.

[19] BCA, 76-E-3, Keane to Gibbons, Richmond, Sept. 21, [1880].

[20] ADR, Bishops' Diary, p. 106.

[21] *Ibid.*

[22] *Centennial Souvenir of St. Thomas the Apostle Catholic Church*, p. 4.

[23] ADR, Bishops' Diary, p. 116. Patrick N. Lynch, Bishop of Charleston, died a month after Northrop had assumed his duties in North Carolina. Within a year

Soon after he had assumed his duties as Bishop of Richmond, Keane undertook to solve another problem that challenged him. Nearly half the population of Richmond, approximately 36,000, were colored and of this large number only twenty-two were Catholics.[24] His predecessors had entertained the idea of establishing a separate church for the Negroes, but it had never materialized. Keane now decided to submit them to the test before putting an added strain on an overburdened treasury. It was with that in mind that on January 5, 1879, the bishop commenced a series of Sunday evening devotions for the colored which consisted of the singing of hymns, prayers, and an instructive sermon. Concerning the first Sunday's devotions, he entered in his diary: "The Church was *crowded* by them in every part. They behaved in the most respectful manner—seemed greatly pleased. . . . I intend to devote my own exertions to it whenever I am in Rd. May God grant fruit to our labors."[25] After these Sunday services had been conducted for a month, he commenced catechetical instructions on two evenings of the week, and soon there were sixteen in the class. Yet his efforts in behalf of the Negroes did not pass without criticism, for while he stated that the "interest in the church exercises continues unabated," he added that it was, "notwithstanding great opposition from white and black Prot. ministers."[26] But the bishop was not daunted and he informed Gibbons that the project was meeting with some success.[27] His interest bore fruit quickly when, on April 18 he received seven Negroes into the Church and at the same time baptized two of their children. Two days later he confirmed 171 persons in the cathedral, thirty-one of whom were converts, eleven being colored.[28]

Northrop was transferred to the city of his birth, retaining as well until 1888 the administratorship of the vicariate.

[24] *Ibid.*, p. 82.

[25] *Ibid.*

[26] *Ibid.*, p. 86.

[27] AAB, 74-I-5, Keane to Gibbons, Richmond, Feb. 5, 1879. The papers commented on the large crowd attending the exercises and said: "This is the first time that the Catholic bishops here have ever made any uniform or well directed efforts to convert the negroes to that faith. Some of the most prominent colored men here have united with the Catholic Church since the interest manifested in the race by the bishop" (LCLD, clippings).

[28] ADR, Bishops' Diary, p. 88. The catechism classes were discontinued during the summer months but the Sunday exercises were conducted throughout the year (*ibid.*, p. 91).

Five years later Keane sought the opinion of the American superior of Saint Joseph's Society for Foreign Missions about the possibility of these men devoting their energies to that work in his diocese. In a letter to Alfred Leeson, the American superior, he said:

> . . . Please also beg the dear Lord to enlighten you and me, as to what *can* be done and *ought* to be done, for our colored people here. Out of over 32,000 negroes in the city, we have not 50 Catholics! But I have been working hard among them for nearly five years, but made some impression and about 25 converts, in the face of bitter prejudice and desperate opposition, and have a school which last year had 50 scholars, and we hope for at least as many this year. The bulk of them are, of course, of Protestant parents and through them access might be had into their families. It is in the line of your vocation to undertake so entirely apostolic a work, in so difficult a field. An apostolic man, a saint in fact and one with abundance of *tact* to win his way into the hearts of these poor people, would be needed. . . . Please think and pray hard over all this.[29]

When Father Peter Benoit, the vicar-general of the Society, came to the United States in the fall of 1883, Keane asked him for a member of the society to give full time to the work among the colored in Richmond.[30] The canon informed him that a man would be sent provided a church and school would be placed at his disposal. Since Keane could not turn to the already overburdened diocesan treasury, he set to work immediately to raise the funds for this purpose since, as he said, "it is evidently a duty."[31] The president of the Society for the Propagation of the Faith responded to his letters and personal appeal by sending 10,000 francs in 1883 and 12,000 francs in 1884. Such large amounts were forwarded because, as the president expressed it, "of your need among so many thousand non-catholics and because of the negroes who are the object of your paternal solicitude."[32] To supplement these funds the bishop went on begging tours to New York and other cities where the generosity of the bishops and pastors

[29] AJF, Leeson Papers, Keane to Leeson, Richmond, Sept. 25, [1883]. Members of the Society came to the United States from England in 1871. Owing to the success enjoyed in missionary endeavors and the rapid increase in the society's membership, in 1892 it was made independent of the mother foundation. Cf. Michael Ott, "Saint Joseph's Society for Foreign Missions," and "Saint Joseph's Society for Coloured Missions," *Catholic Encyclopedia,* VIII, 521–522.

[30] AJF, Leeson Papers, Keane to Leeson, Richmond, Nov. 10, [1883].

[31] ADR, Bishops' Diary, p. 126.

[32] ADR, Verdiere to Keane, Paris, June 12, 1884 (French); *ibid.,* June 19, 1883 (French).

would allow it.[33] Moreover, he made appeals to members of the Virginia Mission Union, which he had established for the purpose of helping the poor missions in the diocese.[34] When notifying Keane that Father John R. Slattery, S.S.J., would arrive in Richmond to undertake the work among the Negroes, Canon Benoit expressed the opinion that the bishop, in his zeal for the cause, was taking upon himself a larger amount of the trouble and expense attending the commencement of such a mission than was necessary.[35] The united efforts of the bishop and the Mill Hill priest, however, ultimately insured the success of the project. In January, 1885, the first property was purchased, to which other parcels were added shortly thereafter. The work of constructing the church was well under way when the cornerstone was laid on Easter Sunday, an occasion that attracted, according to the bishop's estimate, about 10,000 people. In May work was begun on a school which was rushed to completion so that it would be ready for the fall term when a staff of Franciscan Sisters, who had come from St. Mary's Abbey in London, would take charge.[36]

On November 22, St. Joseph's Church for the colored was completed and the dedicatory services took place. It was a day of real joy for the handful of Richmond's Catholic Negroes who for years had dreamed of having their own parish. For Keane it was a triumph over the prejudice that had once prevented priests from bringing the sacraments to the servants of the whites. Fitting ceremonies marked the inauguration of St. Joseph's and proclaimed the beginning of a new era in the relations of the Catholic Church with the colored. Keane himself opened a mission on the evening of the dedication and preached every night during the week to what he characterized as a "fine audience."[37] Moreover, the bishop extended his apostolate for the colored beyond Richmond when he established schools for them at Petersburg and Norfolk.[38]

[33] ADR, Bishops' Diary, pp. 132–136, 140.

[34] AJF, Slattery Papers, Keane to Members of the Virginia Mission Union, Richmond, Oct. 21, 1886. Keane told the members that the funds collected that year would be given to Slattery for work among the Negroes. The union, he said, "has aided me to lay broad and firm the foundations of a great work for enlightenment and salvation of the colored race within the limits of my jurisdiction."

[35] ADR, Benoit to Keane (n.p.), Nov. 11, 1884.

[36] ADR, Bishops' Diary, pp. 133–134.

[37] *Ibid.*, p. 136. The land, church, school, and homes for priest and sisters cost about $24,000. The school and its furnishings were paid for by a generous benefactor from the North; some of the money came from the Propagation of the Faith; and Slattery collected about $7,000. Keane obtained the rest by begging.

[38] ADR, Bishops' Diary, pp. 141, 145.

Interested as the Bishop of Richmond was in the spiritual welfare of the colored among his flock, he was no less concerned with strengthening the faith of the white Catholics under his care, and with breaking down the prejudice of the Protestants, who so greatly outnumbered the Catholics in the state of Virginia. During the visitation and confirmation tours that took him to nearly all of the missions each year, the bishop attempted to accomplish both these objectives. He preached morning and evening in the churches he visited and often scheduled a lecture at a convenient place for some evening during the week. It made no difference to Keane where he spoke; at one time it would be in a Methodist Church;[39] at another, in a courthouse.[40] The comments in his diary show that the lectures and sermons were attended mostly by Protestants, who listened attentively to his exposition of Catholic doctrine. After he had followed such practices for a year, he wrote about one place: "The people tell me that a complete revolution in popular estimation of Catholicism has been wrought."[41]

On a few occasions Protestant ministers attempted to stir up bigotry by taking exception to something that Keane had said in his lectures. When this happened, the bishop demonstrated his charity and good sense by avoiding controversy or recrimination. When a minister at Petersburg denounced a lecture that he had given there on "The Church and Human Nature," the bishop told Gibbons that he was surprised that anything had been made of the talk, especially since, as he put it, "there was honestly nothing in the lecture calculated to wound, as numbers of Protestants in Washington, Richmond and Petersburg assured me." After he had promised Gibbons that he would continue to pursue a policy of peace, Keane added: "After all, I think the people must see the good spirit that animates us, and will only be roused to *think* — a most desirable result, where religious stagnation is so prevalent among non-Catholics."[42] On one occasion in Lynchburg when Keane refuted objections to the recently defined dogma of papal infallibility which had been presented by two Protestant ministers, a newspaper reported:

The announcement that the Right Rev. Bishop Keane would deliver

[39] *Ibid.*, p. 92.

[40] *Ibid.*, p. 85.

[41] *Ibid.*, p. 94. Keane visited the missions each year. Cf. ADR, Visitation Record. For the titles of some of the lectures and the places where they were given, cf. Washington *Post,* January 27, 1879; ADR, Bishops' Diary, pp. 83–85, 102.

[42] AAB, 74-I-5, Keane to Gibbons, Richmond, Feb. 5, 1879.

> a discourse on "Objections to Papal Infallibility" caused a vast audience to fill the Church of the Holy Cross on Sunday evening. Long before the hour of the lecture had arrived the spacious church was filled to overflowing, seats were improvised and nearly every foot of standing space was occupied and yet many went away unable to gain admittance. Many of the Catholics kindly surrendered their pews to their Protestant friends who had come to hear the Bishop. The audience was one of the finest that ever assembled in Lynchburg. . . . The Bishop spoke for more than two hours, and during all the time held the vast assemblage enchained by the charm of his manner, the power of his eloquence, and the wonderful fertility of his knowledge of ecclesiastical history. It is proper to say that the Bishop carefully avoided all harsh language and no word fell from his lips that would offend or irritate those opposed to him or that was unworthy of his exalted station. His discourse produced a profound impression on the audience.[43]

Reports of this kind on Keane's conciliatory attitude toward non-Catholics gradually circulated throughout the state and helped to placate prejudice. This would probably indicate the reason why the Protestants of Boydton in Mecklenburg County invited the bishop to come and preach to them, to which he responded with several doctrinal discourses in the courthouse, marking the first time that Catholicism had been preached in that county.[44]

Similar manifestations of friendly feeling for all the people in his diocese procured for Keane an invitation to open the House of Delegates of Virginia with prayer for a week during March, 1879. The Washington *Post* reported: "This is the first time in the history of Virginia that a minister of the Catholic faith ever officiated as a chaplain in either house of the state legislature."[45] Such indications of sympathetic understanding for those not of the Catholic faith would doubtless account likewise for the large number of converts reported among those confirmed during his first full year in Richmond,[46] and for the gratifying number of converts during the succeeding years.[47]

Nor did Bishop Keane ignore the written word as a means of

[43] LCLD, clipping. Pope Pius IX promulgated the new dogma on July 18, 1870, during the Vatican Council.

[44] ADR, Bishops' Diary, p. 102.

[45] Washington *Post,* Mar. 18, 1879.

[46] ADR, Bishops' Diary, p. 95. There were 143 converts among the 785 confirmed during the year 1879. According to Keane this represented "the largest number of confs. and the largest proportion of converts any year in the history of the diocese."

[47] In 1881, fifty-five converts were confirmed (ADR, Bishops' Diary, p. 113). In 1882, there were eighty-three converts confirmed (*ibid.,* pp. 118–120).

encouraging the members of his flock to greater spiritual endeavor. Each year at the beginning of Lent he issued a pastoral letter that treated a variety of subjects. Frequently he wrote about the dangers to salvation that followed from intemperance. He exhorted his people to avoid dangerous literature and amusements. He urged the faithful to discharge their duties as to Christian marriage and Christian education, and each year he begged them to strive for holiness of life.[48] One of his former professors at St. Mary's Seminary expressed his approval of Keane's first pastoral by commending him for what he called "the solidity of its doctrine, the clearness of the exposition, the practical wisdom of the points treated and the spirit of affectionate zeal which animates all the composition."[49] In the light of the opinion expressed in a recent study that Keane "may be considered as the major promoter of devotion to the Holy Ghost in the Catholic Church in the United States,"[50] his pastoral on that devotion issued on October 8, 1879, is especially significant, for it marked the beginning of his endeavors to implement his conviction that "the devotion to the Holy Ghost, together with the teaching concerning our spiritual life with which that devotion is inseparably connected, is unquestionably the best antidote for the materialistic and degrading tendencies of our times."[51] In the following year the bishop published a manual containing exercises and prayers to be used by the members of the Confraternity of the Servants of the Holy Ghost which he had instructed the pastors of the larger parishes of the diocese to establish.[52] Besides being a handy compilation of prayers to the Holy Ghost, the manual suggested the procedure to be followed by the confraternities at their monthly meetings until, as he expressed it,

[48] ADR, Keane's Pastoral Letters while he administered the See of Richmond.

[49] ADR, Dissez, S.S., to Keane, Baltimore, Mar. 11, 1879.

[50] Joseph Clifford Fenton, "Devotion to the Holy Ghost and Its American Advocates," *American Ecclesiastical Review,* CXXI (December, 1949), 492.

[51] ADR, Keane's Pastoral Letters. The pastoral is printed *in extenso* in Otto Zardetti, *Devotion to the Holy Ghost, I, Special Devotion to the Holy Ghost. A Manual for the Use of Seminarians, Priests, Religious and the Christian People* (Milwaukee, 1888). Of a letter which Keane had written as an introduction to Zardetti's work, Fenton stated: "Perhaps better than any other document of the time, this letter is indicative of the enlightened piety and zeal that animated Bishop Keane and the other great prelates who worked with him for the establishment of the University" (*op. cit.,* p. 495). A month after the pastoral had appeared, the bishop requested Henry Edward Cardinal Manning to be sure that the petition to the Holy See, asking approbation for the "Rosary of the Holy Ghost," include Keane's name (Manning Papers, Keane to Manning, Richmond, Dec. 18, 1879, copy through the kindness of Father Ellis).

[52] ADR, Bishops' Diary, p. 96.

"higher authority presents us with a form of organization and prayer more worthy of the great devotion which is so dear to all who are enlisted in it."[53]

It was natural, of course, that the people of Richmond should benefit most from Keane's apostolic work. Shortly after his arrival at the cathedral he established the St. Vincent de Paul Society on a firmer basis. When the pastors of St. Patrick's and St. Mary's Churches had reorganized the societies along the lines suggested by the bishop, the first general meeting of the conferences from the three parishes was held and the particular council was organized.[54] To aid the societies in meeting the expenses of their charitable works the bishop often gave lectures for their benefit, and though the Richmond societies profited most from these affairs, those in other towns also received their share.[55]

Richmond was also the scene of the bishop's strongest efforts for the cause of temperance. A few months after his consecration he responded to a request of the city's prominent citizens to assist in the endeavor to have the Sabbath properly observed, particularly by the suppression of the sale of intoxicating drink on that day. His speeches and letter to the Legislature on the subject were proclaimed valuable contributions to the partially successful campaign by the secular press, which spoke of the "great powers of his mind and tongue." In December of the following year, Keane called together the Catholic liquor dealers of the see city to try to induce them to abandon the business or, if that was impossible, to carry it on in a manner that would result in the least harm. At this meeting thirty men signified by their signature that they and their employees would not sell liquor to the intoxicated or those on the point of intoxication, nor open their places of business on the Lord's day.[56] Keane took advantage of the auspicious signs by following up this

[53] John Joseph Keane, *A Sodality Manual for the Use of the Servants of the Holy Ghost* (Baltimore, 1880), pp. ii–iii. The bishop told a Paulist friend: "I am amazed that the special adoration of the Holy Ghost is not more popular and widespread" (Elliott, "Personal Reminiscences of Archbishop Keane," *op. cit.*, p. 642). Leo XIII issued his Encyclical on Devotion to the Third Person of the Blessed Trinity and instituted the annual novena to the Holy Ghost in all Catholic parishes in 1897.

[54] ADR, Bishops' Diary, pp. 85–87.

[55] Washington *Post*, Jan. 27, 1879.

[56] *Daily Dispatch* (Richmond), Dec. 21, 1880; ADR, Bishops' Diary, p. 107. J. E. Rankin, president of Howard University, wrote to Keane in later years and said: "I learned to honor you, long ago, when you did fearless and faithful work on behalf of temperance in Richmond" (ACUA, Washington, Jan. 7, 1890).

gathering with meetings in the three parishes of the city.[57] The strength of the bishop's feelings on the subject of Catholics engaged in the liquor business are revealed in a letter to the president of the Catholic Total Abstinence Union of America written in 1884, four years after he had inaugurated his campaign in Richmond. He said: "May the Holy Ghost ever animate and direct the work of the Union, and may its efforts not relax till there remain in our country not a single Catholic drunkard, not a single Catholic liquor seller, to bring the blush of shame to the Church's cheek."[58] In another letter to the president of the Union, Keane stated: "I never lose an opportunity of saying a good word for the cause; and such, please God, shall be my principles and my course till the end of my career."[59] True to his word, he responded to appeals for temperance lectures in many parts of the diocese and a word about the advantage of total abstinence frequently found its way into the sermons preached during his visitation tours and into the pastorals sent to the people each year.

The people of Richmond were especially fortunate in having their bishop with them every year during the lenten season. Protestants as well as Catholics came to the Cathedral to hear his sermons on Sunday nights. During Lent of 1880 he preached a typical series on: "Christ the God Man," "Christ, the Mediator of Redemption," "Christ, the Mediator of Sanctification," "Christ, the Mediator of Religion," "Christ, the Head of the Church," and "Our Duties to Christ our Mediator."[60]

While the bishop was striving to promote the spiritual welfare of the laity throughout the diocese, he did not neglect his duty to the priests who labored under him. When they gathered at the Cathedral for the blessing of the oils on Holy Thursday the first year after he came to the see, he instituted the practice of detaining them for a meeting. The first year the meeting was a quasi-synod to revise the diocesan statutes. Keane had suggested the changes and additions

[57] ADR, Bishops' Diary, p. 107.

[58] Keane to James M. Cleary, Richmond, July 28, 1884, cited in the *Proceedings of the Fourteenth Annual Convention of the Catholic Total Abstinence Union of America, Chicago, August 6–7, 1884,* in bound volumes entitled *Miscellanea de temperantia* (Mullen Library, Catholic University of America), IV, 44.

[59] Keane to Hugh Roe O'Connell, Richmond, July 10, 1880, cited in the *Proceedings for the Tenth Annual Convention of the Catholic Total Abstinence Union of America, Scranton, August 4–5, 1880,* in bound volumes entitled *Miscellanea de temperantia* (Mullen Library, Catholic University of America), V, 32–33.

[60] ADR, Bishops' Diary, p. 99.

and left the clergy to deliberate under the presidency of the vicar-general, who called the bishop when they had finished and informed him that all his suggestions had been adopted.[61] At subsequent sessions of these Holy Thursday meetings the pastors discussed their problems with the bishop and considered legislation that he proposed to them. At the meeting in 1883, an association of priests was formed for the purpose of offering Masses for the deceased among their number, and it was then determined likewise to hold diocesan theological conferences each year.[62] Henceforth, at the Holy Thursday meeting Keane assigned material for consideration at the theological conferences which were held during June at Richmond and Harper's Ferry. The bishop hoped, as he said, that "great utility" would result for the conferences and meetings.[63] At the meeting on Holy Thursday in 1884, Keane insisted that the Forty Hours' Devotion become a regular practice in every mission with a resident pastor and a population of 100 or more souls. He also asked the pastors to change places "for a week once a year or so" so as to give the people an opportunity to go to confession to someone not ordinarily connected with the parish. Further, he insisted that canonical reasons be given before they could expect him to grant dispensations from matrimonial impediments, and he called the attention of his assembled clergy to the necessity of exercising special care for the records of the church and for the sacred vessels and materials used on the altar.[64]

During Bishop Keane's years as ordinary of the Diocese of Richmond the number of priests disappointingly enough remained stationary at around twenty-seven.[65] At times the losses suffered through sickness, old age, and death forced the bishop to borrow priests from other dioceses until the Richmond seminarians would be ordained.[66] In 1881, when he was very short of priests, he lost his vicar-general by elevation to the episcopacy. This move was not entirely unforeseen since William Henry Elder, after he had been transferred to Cincinnati as coadjutor in 1880, informed the Bishop of Richmond that he favored Francis Janssens for first place on the list of those nominated for

[61] *Ibid.*, pp. 87–88.

[62] *Ibid.*, p. 122.

[63] *Ibid.*, pp. 124–125. Alexandria was designated to replace Harper's Ferry as a meeting place in 1885 (*ibid.*, p. 134).

[64] *Ibid.*, p. 129.

[65] The statistical tables for the Diocese of Richmond in *Sadliers' Catholic Directory* (New York, 1879), pp. 364–365, and *Sadliers' Catholic Directory* (New York, 1884), pp. 423–424, furnished the factual material.

[66] ADR, Bishops' Diary, p. 109.

Natchez.[67] When certain news of the appointment reached Richmond, Keane wrote: "Natchez will have a model bishop, but this See loses its right arm."[68] Archbishop Gibbons acquiesced in the desire of Janssens and Keane to have the consecration in Richmond, where Keane thought, as he expressed it, that "he will feel infinitely more *at home*. . . . and so will most of those he may invite among his old friends."[69] The consecration of Janssens, which took place in St. Peter's Cathedral, was described as "the grandest ecclesiastical function ever seen in Richmond, and attracted the largest gathering known in the history of the Church in the State."[70] It was the second appearance of Gibbons as the consecrator of a bishop in Richmond's cathedral. Keane and Thomas A. Becker, Bishop of Wilmington, shared the honors with the metropolitan as co-consecrators, while Elder, the man whom Janssens replaced at Natchez, preached the sermon.[71] Upon the departure of Janssens, Bishop Keane appointed as his vicar-general Augustine Van de Vyver who was destined himself one day to be Bishop of Richmond.[72]

Fortunately for Keane, he experienced few disciplinary problems with his clergy. He attended retreats with them at St. Mary's Seminary in Baltimore along with the clergy of the archdiocese and then complied with their desire to have their own retreat by arranging for one at Georgetown College each year after 1885.[73] After their first retreat at Georgetown, Keane remarked: "All seemed greatly pleased, but it has cost me considerably."[74] Through the retreats, the annual visitations, and the Holy Thursday conferences he came to know each one of his priests intimately. His comments in the visitation book on the qualities of the individual priests, and on the parish sentiment which, on occasion, might seem to indicate the necessity of changing pastors, revealed his wish to utilize the ability of his men in a way that would promote their happiness as well as the good of religion.[75]

The visitations also gave the Bishop opportunity to study the material progress of the Church in Virginia. He noted the condition of the buildings and the evident repairs needed, and he indicated

[67] ADR, Elder to Keane, Natchez, Apr. 5, 1880.
[68] ADR, Bishops' Diary, p. 108.
[69] AAB, 75-T-5, Keane to Gibbons, Richmond, Mar. 30, [1881].
[70] John Gilmary Shea, *Our Faith. Its Defenders* (New York, 1894), p. 314.
[71] ADR, Bishops' Diary, p. 111.
[72] *Ibid.*
[73] *Ibid.*, pp. 135, 149.
[74] *Ibid.*, p. 135.
[75] ADR, Visitation Record, 1884–1886.

in various places the advisability of purchasing property adjoining that which the parish already possessed.[76] During his ten years as Bishop of Richmond he dedicated churches at Leesburg, Danville, Manasses Junction, Lynchburg, Jarrat's Station, Culpepper, Charlottesville, Low Moor, Roanoke, Amherst Court House, Front Royal, Elk Garden, Columbia, Gordonville, and Richmond.[77] In 1882, it became evident that repairs would have to be made on St. Peter's Cathedral. When this was proposed to the people, they protested that rather than spend money on repairing the old building they should tear it down and replace it. In their first enthusiasm, the parishioners decided that a new cathedral of granite, costing about $120,000, would be their goal, and with that in mind, a mass meeting was held on January 1, 1883, for the purpose of gathering subscriptions. But at a meeting a week later the bishop made it clear that the first plan was impractical, and ultimately a more modest edifice was decided upon. The laity were banded into a group called the Cathedral Building Association to gather sufficient money to justify the inception of the work.[78] When it became clear that it would be some time before a new cathedral could be built, the old edifice was painted inside and out, and the money that had been collected for the new cathedral was used to buy some property that might in the future be employed for that purpose in the west end of Richmond.[79]

Keane was particularly anxious to provide the young people with the means for a Christian education. Shortly after he had arrived in Richmond he approached the Christian Brothers, whom he had known well in Baltimore and Washington, with the hope that they would teach in the Cathedral school for boys. They were forced to refuse the offer, however, because the number of novices did not warrant their making any further commitments.[80] Through Archbishop Gibbons he then applied to the Xaverian Brothers, who promised to come in 1881. Meanwhile lay teachers were employed.[81] After the brothers had been in charge of the boys' school for a year, Keane recorded that they had given "special satisfaction especially in the sanctuary of the Cathedral."[82] The bishop also added to the con-

[76] ADR, Visitation Record.

[77] ADR, Bishops' Diary, *passim*.

[78] *Ibid.*, pp. 120–121.

[79] *Ibid.*, pp. 129–131. The new cathedral was not erected during Keane's administration.

[80] ADR, Brother Paulian to Keane, New York, May 4, 1879; *ibid.*, June 16, 1879.

[81] ADR, Bishops' Diary, p. 90.

[82] *Ibid.*, p. 118.

siderable number of schools operating in the diocese upon his arrival by directing that schools for white children be built at Harper's Ferry, Martinsburg, and Fortress Monroe and that schools for the colored be erected in Richmond, Petersburg, and Norfolk.[83]

Experience with the benefits derived from Carroll Institute in Washington prompted Keane in 1885 to experiment with a similar organization for the benefit of young men in Richmond. He bought the property of the McGill Lyceum, a Catholic society that had been in good measure dormant, and proceeded to hold meetings to organize what was called the McGill Catholic Union. In the bishop's estimation the union justified the additional expense that was incurred, because it served as a center of Catholic activity in the city of Richmond and counteracted the attraction of the Protestant Y.M.C.A.[84]

While Bishop Keane was in Richmond, therefore, he made it clear that he realized that all souls within his jurisdiction had a claim on his attention and care. Fortunately, his general health during these years made it possible for him to fulfill his manifold duties. By 1881, however, he began to experience a serious impairment of his sight. The oculist in Richmond gave an "alarming diagnosis" which induced him to consult specialists in New York. The New York doctors advised him to take a few months of complete rest in some bracing atmosphere. Keane followed their advice, and, after two months with the Paulists at Lake George, he returned to his duties in improved health, although his eyes were still weak,[85] so weak indeed, that he asked, and readily received,[86] the privilege of saying the one same votive office, in the event that improvement would allow him to read at all. During the period of his recuperation the Holy See had been considering the candidates who were nominated for the coadjutorship of Archbishop Joseph S. Alemany of San Francisco. Since Keane's name appeared first on the list[87] and since he had the support of some of the archbishops,[88] it was very likely, as he himself said, that the eyestrain saved him from what he called the "imminent danger of being made coadjutor of San Francisco."[89] Although his

[83] *Ibid., passim.*
[84] *Ibid.*, p. 138.
[85] *Ibid.*, p. 112.
[86] *Ibid.*, p. 116.
[87] AAB, Gibbons' Diary, Feb. 3, 1881.
[88] AAB, 76-B-2, Elder to Gibbons, Cincinnati, Aug. 8, 1881.
[89] ADR, Bishops' Diary, p. 112. For further information on the appointment of a coadjutor to Archbishop Alemany, cf. Ellis, *op. cit.*, pp. 190–192.

sight improved after care was exercised in its use, he was to experience mild recurrences of the disorder later in life.

John Keane seldom left his diocese during his first years as a bishop except to beg money for his missions. Naturally, as the young bishop of a see that was not very prominent, he was seldom called upon to use his oratorical talents at notable ecclesiastical functions. However, when St. Patrick's Cathedral in New York was dedicated in 1879, Cardinal McCloskey asked him to preach at the vesper service.[90] On the same occasion the prelates met in the cardinal's residence to work out some plan of relief for helping John B. Purcell, Archbishop of Cincinnati, out of the burden of crushing indebtedness which had befallen him with the bankruptcy of his brother. Keane was appointed one of a committee of three to draft an appeal to the Catholics of the United States. The bishop later related, "the task was thrown on me by Abp. Gibbons. After revision at hands of him and Bp. Spalding, it was put in the hands of the Card."[91] This was the first indication that Gibbons had recognized Keane's literary ability which the Baltimore prelate utilized for more important assignments later. During that year Keane also was invited to preach at St. Vincent de Paul's Church in Baltimore on the occasion of its consecration by Archbishop Gibbons.[92] The bishop, probably more than anyone else present that day, had reason for striving to speak eloquently of the parish patron, for within the shadow of that church he had played as a boy, within its walls he had received the sacraments, and on its altar he had offered the Holy Sacrifice for the first time.

Keane also made it a practice to attend and take an active part in the annual conventions of the Catholic Young Men's National Union.[93] Then, too, he tried to be present on November 4 for the annual celebration of the patronal feast of St. Charles College and he usually contributed something of value to the festivities. In 1884 he attended what was termed a *petite séance academique* in the

[90] Reily, *op. cit.*, II, 199; ADR, Bishops' Diary, p. 88.

[91] ADR, Bishops' Diary, p. 89. The letter was printed in the papers throughout the country over the signatures of Gibbons, Spalding, and Keane. New York *Herald*, May 29, 1879; *Morning Star and Catholic Messenger* (New Orleans), June 8, 1879.

[92] ASMS, Magnien's Diary, Mar. 25, 1879; ADR, Bishops' Diary, p. 86.

[93] ADR, Bishops' Diary, p. 102; AUND, McMaster Papers, John Bingham to James A. McMaster, Washington, Apr. 14, 1880; AUND, Edwards Papers, Thomas Scully to James F. Edwards, Chicago, Jan. 18, 1882. Keane presided over the Union for four years (Smith, *op. cit.*, p. 50). Cf. Peter Guilday, "John Gilmary Shea," *Historical Records and Studies*, XVII (July, 1926), 82.

evening and "spoke at length and in the most appropriate manner."[94] John B. Hogan, the gifted Sulpician who had delivered the sermon at the Mass in the morning, confided to his diary:

> My panegyric might and should have been much better, but it was well compensated for in the evening by Bishop Keane. Never have I heard a man speak for a full hour with such grace, tact and power. I consider such a discourse to be as good as a retreat for the boys.[95]

Bishop Keane took his first extended vacation in 1883 when he made his *ad limina* visit to Rome. With Father James F. Mackin, pastor of St. Joseph's Church in Baltimore, as traveling companion and secretary, he sailed from New York for London on the *Grecian Monarch* during the first week of April. From London they went to Paris, thence to Marseilles, where they took a steamer for the Holy Land on April 26.[96] They went first to Jerusalem, where Keane procured for his projected new cathedral a cornerstone which had been cut from the solid rock of Mount Olivet within the enclosure of the Garden of Gethsemane. In return for this favor, he promised the Franciscan Fathers, who were in charge of the spot, to take up a collection for them on the first Sunday of the next Lent.[97] After departing from the Holy City they went on horseback through Judea, Samaria, and Galilee, stopping at Nazareth, Mount Tabor, Cana, the Sea of Galilee, and finally, arriving at Mount Carmel. From there the bishop and his friend took a steamer back to Jaffa and were ready to leave the Holy Land on June 1. After a few days in Naples they continued to Rome, arriving on June 13, for a three-week stay.[98]

In Rome Keane handed to the officials of the Propaganda his report on the Diocese of Richmond. With this report, both Pope Leo XIII and Cardinal Simeoni were well pleased.[99] Beyond his diocesan concerns, however, Keane discussed questions of importance to the American Church with the Holy Father and some of the curia officials. One of these topics was the summons sent to the metropolitans of the

[94] ASMS, Magnien's Diary, Nov. 4, 1884.

[95] John B. Hogan's Diary, quoted in W. S[tephan] R[eilly], S.S., "St. Charles' Alumnus Writes Reminiscences," *Voice*, X (Feb., 1933), 9.

[96] Baltimore *Sun*, Apr. 2, 1883.

[97] ADR, Bishops' Diary, p. 123. A year later Keane received a letter from the Franciscans in the Holy Land asking him to interest himself in promoting pilgrimages to that area (ADR, Maria Alph[onse] Ratisbonne, O.F.M., to Keane, Jerusalem, Apr. 29, 1884 [French]).

[98] AAB, 77-H-8, Keane to Gibbons, Rome, June 25, 1883.

[99] ADR, Bishops' Diary, p. 123.

United States requesting that they come to the Eternal City to prepare the outline for a proposed plenary council in 1884. After these conferences, Keane wrote long and informative letters to Archbishop Gibbons to inform him of the thinking of the men he was soon to meet. In one letter he told the archbishop that he was convinced from his conversations with the officials in Rome that the summons had been issued in a spirit of friendliness and for the sole purpose of promoting harmonious relationships between the Holy See and the American hierarchy through better mutual understanding. He found also that the officials in Rome had misunderstood the request of the American bishops to be allowed to have a representative in Rome and, as he remarked, "it never will be understood" in the form in which it had originally been proposed.[100] In another letter he said:

> In my parting interviews with Mgr. Jacobini, Secr. of the Propaganda, with Card. Simeoni, and with the Holy Father, I found it necessary to speak very plainly and positively in regard to two impressions which I found existing in their minds.
>
> The first was a sort of suspicion or dread that there was not a perfect disposition of accord and union on the part of the American Hierarchy towards the Holy See. . . .
>
> The second point that I tried to impress on them was, that they had entirely misunderstood the request that the United States should have a representative in Rome, rather than Rome a representative in the U. S.

Keane believed that when the archbishops came to Rome these impressions could be entirely dispelled by the Americans by dealing with the Roman authorities in what he called "a frank, confiding, and even affectionate manner," and by clearly explaining their reasons for requesting a representative in Rome.[101]

After accomplishing their objectives in Rome, Keane and his companion set out for Florence, where they spent a quiet fourth of July, and then went on to Geneva en route to Lourdes.[102] At Lourdes Keane made a novena for his eyes, in compliance "with the wish of the people." The doctor consulted after the novena told him that the organic condition of his eyes was the same, although functionally they were somewhat better.[103] Paris was the next stopping place.

[100] AAB, 77-H-8, Keane to Gibbons, Rome, June 25, 1883.
[101] AAB, 77-I-1, Keane to Gibbons, Florence, July 4, 1883.
[102] *Ibid.*
[103] ADR, Bishops' Diary, p. 123.

Here he visited the treasurer of the Society for the Propagation of the Faith, and in Lyons he called on the president of that organization for the purpose of convincing them that they had made a mistake in discontinuing the appropriations for his diocese. So convincingly did Keane present his case that during the year 1883 the Diocese of Richmond received 10,000 francs, which were exchanged for the sum of $1,909.31.[104]

After visiting in Germany and Belgium, where the bishop added to his information about cathedrals which he had been gathering in other parts of Europe, Keane and his companion proceeded to London. Here the prelate sought out an architect who had been recommended by Cardinal Manning, and engaged him to make two sets of sketches of a new cathedral for Richmond, one embodying Keane's views, and one giving his own.[105] At length after an absence of nearly six months from the United States, Keane and Mackin returned to New York on September 19.[106]

During the years that John Keane was Bishop of Richmond the most important single event for the Church in the United States was the convening of the Third Plenary Council of Baltimore in 1884. Some Roman officials were bent upon selecting an Italian delegate to preside over the council but so strong was the opposition to the plan from Gibbons and the rest of the metropolitans assembled there for the preparatory conferences that the Holy Father appointed the Archbishop of Baltimore as apostolic delegate to preside over its sessions. From Bishop Keane the news of this elicited a heartfelt "Deo Gratias."[107] In a letter to Michael J. O'Farrell, Bishop of Trenton, late in March, Gibbons told him that he had been selected along with Archbishop Corrigan and Bishop Keane to prepare the pastoral letter

[104] *Ibid.*

[105] ADR, Bishops' Diary, pp. 123–124. During Keane's visit with Manning they discussed Manning's efforts to spread devotion to the Holy Ghost (Manning Papers, Keane to Manning, Richmond, Aug. 1, 1885, copy supplied by Father Ellis).

[106] ADR, Bishops' Diary, p. 124. Concerning the financial arrangements for the trip, Keane recorded: "Owing to the poverty of the Diocese I so managed that none of the expenses of my journey came from Diocesan funds, all having been obtained from friends outside the Diocese with the exception of about two hundred and fifty dollars presented me by the people of Richmond. My companion and secretary Father Mackin of Balto. paid all his own expenses" (*ibid.*).

[107] AAB, 77-M-4, Magnien to Gibbons, Baltimore, Dec. 28, 1883. Shortly after his ordination, Keane attended the Second Plenary Council in an official capacity as a chanter. Cf. *Concilii Plenarii Baltimorensis II* (Baltimore, 1894), p. xxii. For the appointment of the apostolic delegate to preside over the sessions, cf. Ellis, *op. cit.,* I, 217.

for the clergy and laity. Gibbons also asserted: "Rt. Rev. Dr. Keane you will find to be an able colaborer. He will relieve you, I think of the heaviest part of the work, and will submit to you what he will have written for your suggestions and emendating."[108] It was evident from the archbishop's remarks to O'Farrell that Keane was expected to furnish the framework of the pastoral to be gone over later by the other members of the committee. O'Farrell replied that he could not assist in preparing the text since he was to go to Rome in April.[109] Further, because of the fact that the *Acta et decreta* listed Corrigan, O'Farrell, and Keane as the deputation charged with the preparation of the letter,[110] one would seem warranted in concluding that the council's pastoral letter was primarily the work of Bishop Keane. If this was true, Keane deserved high praise, for it was a remarkable document. Consisting of thirty-one printed pages, liberally sprinkled with quotations from Sacred Scripture, the letter first summarized the more important events in the history of the universal and the American Church that had occurred since the "rude beginning of pioneer missionary toil" in the United States, and then it pointed to the means of spiritual advancement for the clergy and laity that had been considered during the council. After speaking about the solicitude of the bishops to provide for better education of aspirants to the priesthood, and to multiply parochial schools "till every Catholic child in the land shall have within its reach the means of education," the pastoral devoted a great deal of space to the importance of a thoroughly Christian home and to the means for accomplishing that end. The faithful were warned against profaning the Lord's day and against joining forbidden societies, and were urged to foster Catholic societies and home and foreign mission work. The strong plea for better Christian education, the warmth with which the Catholic temperance societies were recommended and the vehemence with which the selling of beer and liquors on Sundays was denounced, the special recommendation of the Catholic Young Men's National Union and of the Society of St. Vincent de Paul, and the particular plea for support of the Negro and Indian mission work, all point to Keane as the author of

[108] AAB, Gibbons' Copybook, p. 43, Gibbons to O'Farrell, Mar. 28, 1884.

[109] AAB, 77-R-2, O'Farrell to Gibbons, Trenton, Mar. 29, 1884.

[110] *Acta et decreta concilii plenarii Baltimorensis tertii* (Baltimore, 1884), p. vi. Hereafter referred to as *Acta et decreta*. In the twenty-eighth private congregation Keane asked to be excused when he was appointed to the committee to consider the "loca plurima" that had been noted for consideration in the pastoral letter (*ibid.*, p. xciv).

the pastoral, for we have already seen how close those activities were to his heart.[111] According to Denis O'Connell, the officials of the Holy See, when they examined the pastoral months later, were enthusiastic about it.[112]

Prior to the council the bishops of the Province of Baltimore were summoned by Archbishop Gibbons to examine and express their views on the first chapter of the outline entitled, "De clericorum educatione."[113] To Keane was also given the responsibility of preparing the portion of the plan of discussion that dealt with the rules which would govern the debates.[114]

By early November, 1884, the final arrangements were made, and by November 9, prelates from all over the nation had assembled in Baltimore for the solemn inauguration of the council. The record of the debates during the private sessions showed that Keane's voice was heard frequently, offering suggestions and placing objections.[115] When Gibbons appointed a special commission of bishops to consider the best means for promoting temperance, Keane was one of those appointed,[116] and it was this committee that was responsible for inserting into the outline the section entitled, "De societatibus ad temperantiam promovendum."[117] The Bishop of Richmond likewise tried to persuade the fathers of the council to prevent clerics from making alcoholic beverages, except wine for Mass. But here he was opposed principally by Rupert Seidenbush, O.S.B., vicar apostolic of Northern Minnesota, who voiced the majority opinion.[118]

During the conciliar debates Keane showed his particular concern for the welfare of the Negroes. The fathers favored his proposal that the committee designated to distribute the funds collected for the

[111] Peter Guilday (ed.), *The National Pastorals of the American Hierarchy (1792–1919)* (Washington, 1923), Chap. xii. Gibbons' part in the pastoral was demonstrated in a letter to Ireland, who had made some suggestions about its content. Baltimore's archbishop said: "I have requested the Prelates charged with preparing the Pastoral Letter to refer to the violation of the Sunday, and I think that Sunday violation and intemperance ought to receive special attention from them" (AAB, Gibbons' Letterbook, p. 112, Gibbons to Ireland, Aug. 21, 1884). No one would have been more interested in, and more eloquent on, these subjects than Keane.

[112] AAB, 79-F-9, O'Connell to Gibbons, Rome, Mar. 8, 1885.

[113] AAB, 77-S-8, Gibbons to his Suffragans, Baltimore, Apr. 3, 1884, copy.

[114] AAB, 78-Y-16. A rough draft in Keane's hand in Latin. With some changes in the Latin introduction, the rules were given in the *Acta et decreta*, pp. xi–xiii.

[115] *Acta et decreta*, pp. xxviii, xxxvi, xxxviii, lii, lvi, lx, lxvii, lxxiii, lxxiv, lxxxi, lxxxvi, lxxxix, xci.

[116] *Ibid.*, p. xxxix.

[117] *Ibid.*, p. xc.

[118] *Ibid.*, p. lxxxviii.

Negro and Indian missions should decide whether or not a college ought to be erected to educate those who had a vocation to serve these missions perpetually.[119] It was Keane's contention that the work among the Negroes should be energetically pursued as quickly as possible. However, he was not in favor of getting religious from Europe to convert the colored lest more harm than good result, since, as he said, he feared Protestants might make capital of this fact and through it "hold the Negro up to ridicule."[120]

The Bishop of Richmond was probably at his best when he ascended the pulpit of the Cathedral of the Assumption on the evening of November 25 to deliver a sermon on "Catholic Societies."[121] Many distinguished prelates mounted the pulpit during the weeks of the council, but few could grace it with more oratorical skill than Keane. Nor was there any more familiar with this particular subject since both as priest and bishop Keane had been active in establishing and promoting Catholic societies. His sermon reflected his conviction that societies were essential to the welfare of the people and that the activity of those enrolled in the organizations flowed from their being members of the Body of Christ, "the ever active and infinitely loving God." Although he mentioned and endorsed all of the associations instituted for promoting the spiritual and material welfare of the faithful, he singled out the Confraternity of the Servants of the Holy Ghost, the temperance societies, the Society of St. Vincent de Paul, and Catholic young men's associations as especially worthy of the zealous support of the Catholic laity.[122]

Following the pageantry of the final public session which concluded the council on December 7, Bishop Keane confided only one entry to his diary by way of observation on the council's work. He wrote: "We hope for assistance in work among negroes. Not much legislation that can affect small and poorly organized Dioceses."[123]

The Third Plenary Council proved to be an important event in Keane's career. The council itself did not change the course of his life; but it did furnish the occasion for him to display his talents and

[119] *Ibid.*, p. lxxv.

[120] Francis P. Cassidy, "Catholic Education in the Third Plenary Council of Baltimore, II," *Catholic Historical Review,* XXXIV (Jan., 1949), 422–423.

[121] *Acta et decreta,* p. xiv. Gibbons had asked Keane to preach in April (AAB, 77-Y-7, Keane to "Dear Doctor John" [Foley], Richmond, Apr. 29, [1884]).

[122] *Memorial Volume of the Third Plenary Council of Baltimore* (Baltimore, 1885), pp. 190–213.

[123] ADR, Bishops' Diary, p. 132.

winning traits of character before the assembled hierarchy of the United States. During the sessions the leaders of the Church became aware of the forcefulness of his ideas and the clarity of his expression in debate. Many must have known, too, of his principal authorship of the pastoral letter. At any rate, after the council of 1884, the Bishop of Richmond became more influential in ecclesiastical affairs and he was soon given a double role to play in the American Church.

CHAPTER IV

Additional Burdens

WITHIN the year after the Third Plenary Council of Baltimore Keane was invited to preach the sermon on the occasion of the consecration of Alphonsus J. Glorieux as second Vicar Apostolic of Idaho,[1] and to act as assistant consecrator with Northrop when Gibbons consecrated Jeremiah O'Sullivan for the See of Mobile.[2] He also preached at the pontifical Mass on the day that St. Patrick's Church in Washington was dedicated.[3] But more important to his future career than these manifestations of his growing reputation as a preacher was the fact that in May, 1885, Keane's name was added to the committee appointed by the Third Plenary Council to inaugurate the work of a Catholic university for the United States.[4] Then in November of the same year he was appointed by the committee as one of four bishops charged with raising funds among wealthy Catholics for the proposed university.[5] Hence he was identified with the real effort in behalf of a national university practically from the beginning, and thus, too, were the talents displayed during the council put to good use by his fellow bishops.

The Bishop of Richmond entered wholeheartedly into the work of collecting by beginning his efforts early in 1886 in New York. To his surprise, however, he found that the archbishop of that great financial

[1] AAB, Gibbons' Diary, Apr. 19, 1885. For Alphonsus J. Glorieux, cf. Shea, *Our Faith, Its Defenders*, p. 400.

[2] AAB, Gibbons' Diary, Sept. 20, 1885.

[3] Smith, *op. cit.*, pp. 46–47.

[4] ACUA, MMBT, Baltimore, May 7, 1885, pp. 8–9. For a complete account of the history of the Catholic University of America prior to its inauguration on November 13, 1889, cf. John Tracy Ellis, *The Formative Years of the Catholic University of America* (Washington, 1946).

[5] ACUA, MMBT, Baltimore, Nov. 11, 1885, p. 11.

center was not in sympathy with the project, principally because the institution had been located "in the South."[6] After Keane and Spalding reported to the university committee, which had incorporated as the Board of Trustees of the Catholic University of America, on the result of their collection efforts in New York, Brooklyn, Albany, Boston, and Philadelphia, it took a great deal of optimism to view the future of the project with any hope.[7] But optimists they were, for at the May, 1886, meeting of the board they proceeded with their plans and it was at this time that the Bishop of Richmond was selected to be rector of the institution. They were probably influenced in their choice by the pleasing and energetic manner in which he had entered upon the work of collecting. Because he was truly "broad-minded," as a philosopher, he had free access to the intellectual and, generally, to the ruling classes, from whom they hoped to obtain the means for establishing the University. Moreover, they undoubtedly agreed with contemporaries, who considered him to be genial and openhearted, affable and even affectionate, endowed with high ideals and broad sympathies. Besides, he was more learned than most of his contemporaries in the hierarchy, and, although he could not be called a man of extraordinary erudition, he made good use of his learning which he supplemented with natural powers of a high order.[8] The choice was a surprise to Keane, who had expected that John Lancaster Spalding, Bishop of Peoria, the only university-trained bishop in the United States, would be designated. When he was told that the post had been refused by Spalding, Keane then indicated that he was willing to assume the burden.[9] He later described his reaction to this development for his friend Monsignor O'Connell:

> Imagine my amazement when Archbishop Gibbons called me aside and told me that the Archbishops had unanimously decided that I was the only man who could ensure success, and that Bishop Spalding, whom they then consulted, was more emphatic than any of them in the decision! I pleaded that it was simply absurd for a man to under-

[6] ACUA, "Chronicles of the Catholic University of America from 1885," pp. 5–7. This document will hereafter be referred to as "Chronicles." It is a sixty-two page document written in a record book in Keane's hand. The pagination begins with three and ends with sixty-four. Cf. Ellis, *The Formative Years,* p. 170.

[7] ACUA, "Chronicles," p. 8. Cf. AAB, 80-G-2, Keane to Gibbons, New York, Feb. 11, 1886, for a partial account of the tour.

[8] "Pen-Pictures of the American Hierarchy" by Merwin-Marie Snell in the New York *Independent,* Apr. 27, 1893; ACUA, Keane Papers, William Barry to Walter Elliott, Wallingford, England, Aug. 28, 1890.

[9] ACUA, "Chronicles," pp. 8–9.

> take to organize and run a university who had never been in a university in his life. But all in vain. They insisted that by study and examinations I could gain all necessary acquaintance with plans and methods, that I would have the confidence of the Bishops and the people, and no one else would, that it was a more important work for me to devote my life to than the ruling of the Diocese of Richmond, that I would be in full sympathy with the Sulpicians in directing discipline, etc. Of course, there was only one thing for me to do, to say, as I could honestly, that to be one place or another, at one work or another was indifferent to me. . . . My decision seemed to rejoice them greatly, and I acknowledge it was a relief to myself, in view of possibilities like those of St. Louis. . . .

Bishop Keane added that his selection was not to be made public until it had first been laid before the Holy See in the fall when he and Bishop John Ireland of St. Paul would go to Rome to petition approval of the University. He warned his friend that in the meantime he should be on his guard to protect the work against what he termed "petty undermining" on the part of Archbishop Corrigan who, as he told O'Connell, had expressed his determination to establish a university in New York in charge of the Jesuits.[10]

Once having accepted the post of rector, in so far as the trustees were then capable of giving it to him, Keane had an added incentive for earnestly soliciting the funds which, when added to the original donation of $300,000 by Miss Mary Gwendoline Caldwell through Bishop John Lancaster Spalding of Peoria, would bring the University into being. He had cleverly prodded Gibbons before the meeting by saying: "It is rather galling that New York should be claiming to have done nearly all that has thus far been done for the cause. Does it not seem time for Baltimore to speak and act?"[11] Now he would have to use measures of a far more difficult character than dropping hints in letters to quicken the interest of the hierarchy if success was to be assured. Fortunately for the cause, Gibbons just at this time received an enhanced prestige in being named a cardinal.[12] The interest that this powerful friend manifested in the project would prove to be one of Keane's greatest aids in accomplishing the work that the hierarchy had placed upon his shoulders.

[10] ADR, Keane to O'Connell, Richmond, May 20, 1886.

[11] AAB, 80-S-8, Keane to Gibbons, Richmond, Apr. 13, [1886].

[12] ADR, Bishops' Diary, p. 144. Keane congratulated Gibbons when a premature rumor appeared in the press (AAB, 80-G-2, Keane to Gibbons, New York, Feb. 11, 1886), and again when it was an accomplished fact (AAB, 81-C-8, Keane to Gibbons, Richmond, June 8, [1886]).

The affectionate regard in which Cardinal Gibbons held Keane was demonstrated about this time by an act of real fraternal charity. Gossip, the exact nature of which is not known, but which the cardinal felt would work harm to religion and to the reputation of Keane, had reached the ears of the Archbishop of Baltimore and he determined to inform the bishop of it. To the letter that conveyed the unpleasant information, Keane replied:

> Permit me to thank you most sincerely for the very kind solicitude about me which prompted your letter. Rest assured that I fully appreciate both the prudence and the considerateness for my feelings which directed all your course in this matter. Let me again assure you that the personal considerations involved in it do not cost me the least anxiety or feeling of any sort, — beyond a feeling of thankfulness for being put upon my guard, — and that I will be exceedingly prudent in so using my information as to guard as far as possible against any injury being done to religion.

After expressing astonishment that an evil rumor had been circulated following his visits to a family who in years previous had been hosts to Archbishop Bayley and other prelates, he ended by saying: "However, it is useless to discuss that. Since in fact, evil has been made of it, it is well for me to know it, that being forewarned, I may be forearmed."[13] Gibbons surely did not overlook the sane attitude which Keane displayed in acknowledging the displeasing news, nor could he have been unmindful of the bishop's evident concern for the welfare of religion above all else. The occasion, therefore, probably served to increase Gibbons' esteem for his friend and suffragan while it enabled Keane to shield himself against further gossip.

In the fall of 1886, prior to the meeting of the Board of Trustees, the bishop began the study of university and seminary buildings by visiting Harvard and Laval Universities and the seminaries of Boston and Montreal. He told Gibbons after the trip: "My conferences with all the long-headed clerics and laics whom I could find, capable of giving advice on the University question, have considerably modified my views as to the best plan of organization."[14] A few months later he prepared a draft for Gibbons of the letters to Leo XIII and Cardinal Simeoni which would acquaint the Holy See with the progress of the work of foundation and request its approval of the institution and of the man chosen to be rector.[15]

[13] AAB, 81-B-4, Keane to Gibbons, Richmond, May 20, [1886].
[14] AAB, 81-R-9, Keane to Gibbons, Fortress Monroe, Virginia, Aug. 12, [1886].
[15] AAB, 82-B-9, Keane to Gibbons, Richmond, Oct. 12, [1886].

While Keane was engaged in this work, the Archbishop of Quebec revealed that Rome had condemned for the second time the Quebec branch of the labor organization known as the Knights of Labor on the grounds that it was a secret society.[16] After the American papers had printed the news there was considerable speculation about the future relations of the Knights with the Church in the United States. A reporter from a German paper in Baltimore approached the Bishop of Richmond for his judgment and received from him an optimistic opinion of the Knights of Labor in America.[17] This publicly identified Bishop Keane with those American prelates who were opposed to extending the condemnation of the Knights to this country. Hence, when the general assembly of the Knights gathered in Richmond from October 4 to 20, for the largest and most publicized meeting of labor held in the United States up to that time, Terence V. Powderly, the Grand Master Workman and a Catholic, visited Keane at least twice and discussed with him the relations of the Knights to the Catholic Church.[18] It is likely that at this time Keane gave Powderly the advice which led to his appearance on October 28 before some members of the committee appointed by the Third Plenary Council of Baltimore to investigate secret societies, at which time he left a favorable impression upon a majority of the prelates.[19] After one of Powderly's visits Keane told Gibbons:

> While there seems to be a rather general fear of some elements in their makeup, the impression, I think, is quite as general that we had better let such things correct themselves, as, in matters of mere pecuniary balance of interests, and in such a country as ours, is sure to take place.[20]

Bishop Keane stated his endorsement of the Knights more positively in a hastily composed five-page pencil-written document which, as he told Powderly, contained the "substance of an address to the Convention, should circumstances so form as to lead to my making one."[21] Had the address been delivered, he was prepared to tell the workers that he took pleasure in speaking to them both as an American citizen and as a Catholic bishop. He wrote:

[16] Henry J. Browne, *The Catholic Church and the Knights of Labor* (Washington, 1949), p. 182. This scholarly work contains a thorough treatment of the subject.

[17] *Ibid.*

[18] *Ibid.*, pp. 205–208.

[19] *Ibid.*, pp. 207–211, 213–215.

[20] AAB, 82-B-9, Keane to Gibbons, Richmond, Oct. 12, [1886].

[21] Browne, *op. cit.*, pp. 207–208.

. . . As an American citizen, I rejoice at every advance towards the perfect realization of that truest and noblest ideal of social organization and government; and therefore do I rejoice to behold you and the vast body of working men at your backs banded together, not for violence or injustice, but for the calm, orderly, dignified assertion and vindication of your God-given rights. The Catholic Church is the old Church of "the gospel preached to the poor." As a Catholic Bishop I welcome whatever really improves the poor man's condition, whatever lifts poverty out of squalor and degradation, places it beyond the power of oppression, and makes it worthy of the Divine Carpenter of Nazareth, who chose poverty for His Bride and deified labor in His sacred person; therefore do I hail this organization of the intelligence, the energy, and the conscientiousness of the sons of toil, which, if faithful to intelligence and conscience, cannot fail to win for them the respect as well as the justice that is their due. . . .

Keane would urge the Knights to live up to their motto: "Justice to all, injustice to none," for in so doing they would win the support of their fellow workers and the respect of their fellow Americans. "You must appeal to the law and the judiciary," he said, "for protection of your rights. . . . How powerful soever may be an instrument of offence or defense, cast it from you as soon as authority which we are all bound to respect, pronounces it an unlawful or dishonorable weapon." He concluded by expressing confidence in their patriotic unselfishness and in the victory that would follow from their faithful adherence to the spirit of their motto — a victory as he said "that will have on it the blessing of Church and of country, of God and of man."[22]

But Keane's favorable opinion of the Knights was not shared by all the members of the committee of archbishops which met at Baltimore on October 28 for the purpose of considering whether or not certain organizations fell under the Church's ban against secret societies. Since the unanimous agreement required for a complete settlement of any case brought before the committee could not be obtained concerning the Knights, the problem had to be forwarded to Rome.[23] As we shall see, it was there that the Bishop of Richmond did his most effective work for the Knights by helping to dissuade Roman authorities from condemning their organization in the United States.

The day before the archbishops met to consider secret societies, the Board of Trustees of the Catholic University of America, assembled

[22] *Ibid.*, pp. 363–364.
[23] *Ibid.*, pp. 213–220.

in Baltimore, signed the documents which Keane had prepared for Leo XIII and Simeoni and commissioned him to carry them to the Holy See. The bishop set out for Europe in October, 1886, in the company of John Ireland of St. Paul, who was to help Keane accomplish his mission while at the same time making his *ad limina* visit.[24] It was Keane's intention when he left for Europe to conclude his Roman mission with as much dispatch as possible and then visit some of the European universities to get further information about university organization and interview men suitable to fill the chairs of instruction in the university.[25] His intention was not to be realized, however, for many other matters of importance would claim his energy and force him to make an extended stay in the Eternal City.

In London the two bishops heard that there was an agent in Rome for a certain group of the German Catholics in the United States who was to present to the Holy See accusations of unfair treatment and persecution of the German minority at the hands of the Irish majority. To prevent the Holy See from acting precipitously, Ireland left for Rome immediately and arrived, as Keane expressed it, "just in time to delay action."[26] The Bishop of Richmond followed his friend at a more leisurely pace and upon his arrival they worked together to persuade the Roman officials of the falsity of the accusations against the Irish bishops contained in a memorial presented by the Reverend Peter M. Abbelen, spiritual director of the School Sisters of Notre Dame at Milwaukee, as the representative of the German element in the American Church. The bishops first presented to Simeoni a memorial that they had drawn up in answer to Abbelen's petition; then Keane composed and had printed a document entitled, *La question Allemande dans l'église des États-Unis,* which both signed early in 1887 and presented to the Holy See. It contained the replies of a number of American bishops to the accusations contained in the Abbelen memorial.[27] Shortly after this latter document had been pre-

[24] ACUA, "Chronicles," p. 11. Cf. ACUA, MMBT, Baltimore, Oct. 27, 1886, pp. 15–16.

[25] ACUA, MMBT, Baltimore, Oct. 27, 1886, p. 16.

[26] AAB, 82-G-4, Keane to Gibbons, Rome, Dec. 4, 1886. For a detailed treatment of this episode, cf. Colman J. Barry, O.S.B., *The Catholic Church and German Americans* (Milwaukee, 1953), pp. 62–69, and James H. Moynihan, *The Life of Archbishop John Ireland* (New York, 1953), pp. 55–60. While they were in England, Keane and Ireland visited Liverpool, where they addressed a large meeting on total abstinence at the invitation of Monsignor James Nugent, the famous English temperance leader. Cf. Bland, *op. cit.,* p. 136.

[27] Archives of the Archdiocese of Boston, Letter File, 1884–1908, *La question*

sented, Gibbons arrived in the Eternal City and exercised his influence to secure the rejection of the demands made in the Abbelen memorial which would have fomented discord in the American Church.[28] In a letter to Gibbons after the matter had been settled, Bishop Richard Gilmour of Cleveland said: "The church in America owes you and brave Bishops Ireland and Kean [*sic*] a debt of deep gratitude, assisted as we all were by the fortunate discovery of this vile attempt to snap legislation and the firm and prompt action taken by the American hierarchy." At the same time Gilmour prophesied correctly that their victory would not end the differences between some of the Germans and the majority of the American hierarchy.[29] In writing later of the incident Keane said:

> This defeat of the ultra-German Party in the U.S., and the fact that the names of Bishop Ireland & myself were united in all the documents presented by us, sufficed to earn for ourselves personally, and for the University which we represented, the hostility of that party & of all whom they could influence.[30]

Allemande dans l'église des États-Unis (Rome, 1887). Cf. Barry, *op. cit.*, Appendix III, and the *Freeman's Journal*, Dec. 24, 31, 1892; Jan. 7, 1893, for the documents presented by both sides.

[28] Cf. Barry, *op. cit.*, pp. 12–13. Keane wrongly stated that Gibbons' "influence sufficed to end the matter and secure the rejection of all the demands of the Memorial" (ACUA, "Chronicles," p. 16).

[29] AAB, 83-C-6, Gilmour to Gibbons, Cleveland, July 16, 1887. That the Irish bishops were watching German activity prior to this time was evident from a letter of the Bishop of St. Augustine to O'Connell: "This President of the German Cath. Union at their late meeting in Toledo made the prophecy that in fifteen years, the Germans would control the political parties in this country, and that they would remain German in language and manners in spite of the Anglo-American Bishops, who would have them become one with the American people. Evidently we did not misinterpret their sentiments and intentions" (ADR, Moore to O'Connell, St. Augustine, Sept. 31, 1886).

[30] ACUA, "Chronicles," p. 16. The hostility toward these two prelates did not die, rather it was fanned by a pamphlet that Abbelen had printed and distributed to the German priests of the country. Ireland described it as containing "both our documents, his own memorial, an introduction in which he states that he had the full approval of the Archbishop of Milwaukee, and that he was defeated by our representations. The translations of our documents are poorly made, and often incorrect. At the end he prints the answer of the congregation in a mutilated form; retaining the answers to the first three propositions, and leaving out the others which are unfavorable to him; giving the impression that on the whole, he gained his point. This document, and the many articles in the German press, misrepresent the whole case, and are doing a great deal of harm. It occurred to me that it would be well to publish on our own behalf a pamphlet containing correct versions of the several documents presented to Rome, calling attention to Abbelen's mutilation" (ACUA, Keane Papers, Ireland to Keane, St. Paul, Mar. 3, 1890).

Keane, it must be said, was never hostile to the great body of Catholics of German descent in the United States. Rather, he was conspicuous for his opposition to some of their leaders who sought special legislation which he considered to be "of the most ruinous character" because it would mean, as he said, "the introduction of Germanism and *nationalism* in general" which to his mind would be "disastrous to the unity of the Church in the United States."[31] In this opinion he was in agreement with the vast majority of the American hierarchy. However, because he had been actively engaged in the efforts to defeat their objectives, certain elements among the German-Americans began to carry on a campaign to discredit him before the Holy See. Inevitably, the University project with which he was identified was made to suffer.

While the two bishops were occupied with the German question, they also concerned themselves with promoting an unbiased consideration of the problem that arose as a result of the condemnation of the Knights of Labor in Canada. Logical procedure following upon the action in Canada would likely result in the condemnation of the same organization in the United States, and there were those who had a mind to be logical. Keane and Ireland submitted their own "respectful protest" against a hasty condemnation of the Knights in the United States pending the arrival of documents which would contain the studied opinions of the archbishops constituting the committee on secret societies after their meeting in Baltimore on October 28.[32]

[31] Manning Papers, Keane to Manning, Rome, Feb. 10, 1887, copy through the kindness of Father Ellis. Ten years later, Keane said that he was endeavoring to remove a "mistaken notion" in Europe and he urged Ireland to do the same in America. He argued along these lines: "*We* have no *German question.* We only hold to *true ideas* ag'st the clique of Germans who have attacked them, thro' revenge for their having been defeated in their ultra Germanism. That clique do not [*sic*] represent the German people of Europe or America. Multitudes of Germans are in no way committed to their ultra narrowness, but are, on the contrary, at least as far advanced as we in many lines of ideas. But even these are banded ag'st us, because of their mistaken notion that we are *hostile to the Germans as such,* which we of course are not. They must be undeceived. And my long conversation with the Baroness d'Eichthal convinces me that they are ready to be undeceived. The lines ought to be drawn between those who hold to true ideas and those who oppose them, — by no means between nationalities as such, a mediaeval and cursed notion" (AASP, Keane to Ireland, Rome, Jan. 11 [1897]).

[32] ACUA, "Chronicles," p. 16. In his notes on the subject, Soderini states that Keane feared that the prevailing attitude toward the Knights among Roman officials would result in condemnation of the organization in the United States. He consulted the Commissary of the Holy Office, Vincenzo Sallua, O.P., titular Archbishop of Calcedon, who remained inflexible, claiming that, according to private but trustworthy sources, there did exist a liaison between the Knights of Labor and the

They also saw the editors of the *Moniteur de Rome* about what was called a "poisonous article, making sweeping and ruinous assertions about the Irish in America, the Knights of Labor, and Powderly," and demanded its correction. As a result, the *Moniteur* published an editorial written by Keane in which it was explained that more reliable information from the United States made it clear that the Knights of Labor were not dangerous to the public peace since they were directed by Terence V. Powderly, who was an intelligent, conscientious, and conservative man.[33] After Gibbons had sent a résumé of the Baltimore meeting to the Propaganda, Keane handed in a copy of the Knights' constitution and its translation and thereafter acted as Gibbons' agent until he arrived in February, 1887.[34]

In a letter to the Archbishop of Baltimore informing him that he had put some material of his pertaining to the Knights of Labor, the German question, and the New Orleans succession into three Latin documents, and had presented them to the Propaganda, Keane continued in what was one of the most difficult and fearless letters that a subject bishop could write to his superior. He said:

> . . . I beg that you will permit me, dear and venerated friend, to go on and mention things which are exceedingly painful for me to pen, and which only high regard for yourself personally and for the exalted office which you hold, could induce me to write, for it is a hard task and often a risky one, to write painful truths to a friend, especially when he is a superior. Only *real* friendship can nerve one to the duty.
>
> I find to my intense regret, that an impression has taken shape in Rome to the effect that your Eminence is changeable in views, weak and vacillating in purpose, anxious to conciliate both parties on nearly

---

socialists and Freemasons. Keane and Ireland denied this. As a last resort they sought and obtained an audience with the Pope to discuss the matter, and he advised them to prepare, together with Gibbons, a memorandum on the subject and submit it to the Cardinals of the Congregations of Propaganda and of the Holy Office for study (an unpublished portion of Count Eduardo Soderini's manuscript on the pontificate of Leo XIII, entitled "Leone e gli Stati Uniti di America," and the Count's notes taken during research in archives that were opened to him as a personal favor, are in the Vatican Library. Father Thomas McAvoy, C.S.C., archivist of the University of Notre Dame, obtained permission to have a microfilm copy made of the manuscript and of the notes, which contain valuable material that was not incorporated in the manuscript. The present writer is indebted to Father McAvoy for permission to use a translation of the entire manuscript and of the notes, and to Monsignor James H. Moynihan, pastor of the Church of the Incarnation, Minneapolis, Minnesota, for translating some portions of a typescript of the most important sections of the manuscript which may be found in APF).

[33] AAB, 82-G-4, Keane to Gibbons, Rome, Dec. 4, 1886. Clipping enclosed.

[34] Browne, *op. cit.*, pp. 229–237.

every question; that it is hard to know, therefore, upon which side you stand concerning any important question. Hence I find a growing inclination to look elsewhere than to your Eminence for reliable information and judgment, — a tendency, not only here but among the Bishops of the United States, to look to New York rather than to Baltimore for the representative and leader of our Hierarchy.

The Bishop of Richmond then enumerated some of his acts which had caused unsureness in Rome about him. For example, he had given Abbelen a letter of introduction to Simeoni and then had written against Abbelen's mission. He had strongly recommended Placide L. Chapelle for the coadjutorship of New Orleans at the request of Archbishop Leray and then he had switched his support to Bishop Janssens of Natchez as the better man. He had sent Bishop Joseph Dwenger of Fort Wayne as a representative of the hierarchy to win approval in Rome for the decrees of the Third Plenary Council, and then, after denying that he had sent Dwenger, had had to acknowledge the fact. After mentioning these things to the Cardinal of Baltimore, Keane concluded:

. . . We have lately been pouring out our honest indignation at the charge that the signatures of the Prelates to the University petition could not be implicitly trusted as giving the real sentiment of the signers; but I cannot help recognizing with what crushing force they can say to us: "Why look, even your Cardinal puts his name to statements and recommendations which he will afterwards take back or modify; if even he can send us important documents, not because he believes them best for the interests of the Church, but in order to please this one or that one, what confidence can we repose in any of these signatures?" They do not always say this in honest words; but they say it quite as gallantly in meaning shrugs, and smiles, and insinuations. Even the Holy Father himself has thus intimated his apprehension that your Eminence was uncertain and vacillating in your views as to the University's location, etc.

I know well, dear and venerated friend, that whatever truth there may be in all this has its real source in your kindness of heart, your anxiety to be gracious and yielding to every one as far as you possibly can. But, as happened to the old man in the fable, by endeavoring to be over prudent and to please all, there is great danger that you eventually will please no one, — that both here and at home they will come to mistrust your consistency and strength of character, and to look elsewhere than to our beloved Cardinal for our exponent and our leader. It galls me to the heart to think that such injustice should be done to our Cardinal, to the leader whom Providence has given to us, — and it is this thought that has given me courage to write so plainly on so painful a subject. . . .[35]

The tone in which Keane conveyed the frank exposition of the impressions in Rome about the cardinal indicated only complete respect and continued affection for this friend, and Gibbons must have received the unpleasant information on that basis for there was no evident change in their relations. John Keane clearly showed that he was chiefly concerned for what he considered to be the best interests of the Catholic Church in the United States even though it could have meant the loss of a powerful friend.

The Bishop of Richmond continued his efforts on behalf of the Knights of Labor with undiminished zeal. During February, 1887, just prior to Gibbons' arrival in Rome, he enlisted the potent aid of Henry Edward Cardinal Manning. He requested him to beg the Holy Father "not to order or permit any overt decision of the American social questions at present, both because they have not ripened yet and taken shape, and because the action of the Holy See would hardly fail to be odious to the whole American public and to split up Catholic unity."[36] Gibbons later acknowledged that Manning's active support in this crisis had considerable bearing on the outcome.[37] Upon his arrival in the Eternal City the cardinal requested Keane and Ireland to prepare a memorial on the whole labor question and on the Knights of Labor in particular. Having signed this document on February 20, Gibbons presented it to Simeoni, and, as Keane said, "urged [it] with

[35] AAB, 82-J-4, Keane to Gibbons, Rome, Dec. 29, 1886. The New Orleans coadjutorship question, mentioned in this letter, was also used to harm Keane in Rome. Francis X Leray, Archbishop of New Orleans, told Chapelle that he had seen Simeoni and left with him a document asking for Chapelle as his coadjutor. He added: "Then I told the Card. S[imeoni] that J[anssens] of Natchez was much after the image and likeness of K[eane] of R[ichmond], less his shrewdness and gift of speaking. Then came in what K[eane] had done with McG[lynn] of New York; it was a good hit if I judge by the expression manifested by the Card." (AANO, Leray to Chapelle, Rome, July 1, 1887). Leray died on September 23, 1887, and Francis Janssens was transferred from Natchez to New Orleans on August 7, 1888. Chapelle was consecrated on November 1, 1891, as coadjutor to the Archbishop of Santa Fe and he became archbishop of that see in 1894. Finally, in 1897, he was transferred to New Orleans.

[36] Keane to Manning, Rome, Feb. 10, 1887, cited by Shane Leslie, *Henry Edward Manning, His Life and Labours* (London, 1921), p. 30. Father John Tracy Ellis obtained the Keane letters in the Manning Papers for the present writer. Leslie quotes them accurately.

[37] Gibbons to Manning, Rome, Mar. 14, 1887, cited in Leslie, *op. cit.*, pp. 361–362.

all his influence."[38] Contrary to Gibbons' desires the memorial reached the press. At first, he was apprehensive about the results, but soon telegrams, letters, and newspaper comments lauding the American cardinal for his stand on the labor question indicated that the American people were behind him and he gradually came to see that his fears were unfounded.[39] A recent student of the case maintained that this document "was undoubtedly the most important single factor in the settlement of the case."[40] In a letter to Manning at this time, Keane revealed the anxious moments which preceded the turn that indicated a satisfactory settlement of the case. He told the English cardinal:

> You will see how the utterances which have forever secured to your Eminence the noble title of "Friend of the People" have done our Cardinal good service in his defense of the rights of the working millions. He had an interview this morning on these subjects with the chief officials of the Holy Office, with most gratifying results. It was easy to see that in his words they felt the weight of the whole hierarchy, the whole clergy, and the whole people of America, and that his sentiments had already produced among them an evident change of front. A few weeks ago the drift was towards condemnation, regardless of the widespread disastrous consequences that would inevitably have ensued. To-day the keynote was that the convictions of the Bishops of America are the safest guide to the Holy Office in its action on American affairs, and that they will let well enough alone. . . .[41]

With a view to prevent any attempt to reopen the question, which had been practically settled by the time the cardinal left for home,[42] Keane followed a practical course which he outlined for Gibbons later. He reported:

> I have handed in to both the Propaganda and the Holy Office a French translation of all the letters of endorsement received in regard to your labor document,—also a large compilation of newspaper extracts, thoroughly annotated in French, to be sent by Mgr. Jacobini to Cardinal Monaco. After consulting with Dr. O'Connell, I also handed

[38] ACUA, "Chronicles," p. 16; Browne, *op. cit.*, pp. 238–239. The text of the memorial, entitled "The Question of the 'Knights of Labor,'" is found in Browne, *op. cit.*, Appendix III. It was pointed out in the memorial that, because Doctor Edward McGlynn was "regarded as the friend of the people," the consequences of his condemnation were deplorable for the peace of the Church.

[39] Keane to Manning, Rome, Mar. 14, 1887, cited by Leslie, *op. cit.*, p. 361.

[40] Browne, *op. cit.*, p. 239.

[41] Keane to Manning, Rome, Feb. 28, 1887, cited by Leslie, *op. cit.*, p. 361.

[42] Keane to Manning, Rome, March 22, 1887, cited by Leslie, *op. cit.*, pp. 362–363.

> to Cardinal Monaco the volume of Proceedings of the Conventions of Knights of Labor last year, and the constitutions stating that the former gave the comment on the latter, — and that these, though the *latest* documents, are not *final,* as the constitution thus amended must be submitted to the local assemblies for adoption. They will be apt to see that this mass of English print is an elephant on their hands and they will be very slow to touch the matter again. Cardinal Monaco intimated as much.[43]

The efforts of Keane and his associates were ultimately rewarded with success and within a few years they felt completely vindicated in their labor views when Leo XIII published his encyclical *Rerum novarum* in May, 1891.

Before turning to the University work, for which Keane had been sent to Rome, it is necessary to consider here one other problem thrust upon the American prelates during their stay in the Eternal City. Edward McGlynn, a priest of the Archdiocese of New York, had for some years publicly espoused the questionable theories on land tenure proposed by Henry George in his book *Progress and Poverty*. McGlynn had also participated in meetings of the Anti-Poverty League which George had established for putting his theories into practice, and he had endorsed the no-rent policy of the Irish Land League. In doing so he incurred the displeasure of the Archbishop of New York, Michael Augustine Corrigan, who resorted to ecclesiastical censure when McGlynn refused to obey the command to discontinue these activities. Fearing that souls would be lost if public agitation over the case continued, Rome summoned McGlynn in the hope the differences between him and the archbishop could thus be settled. But this summons fell upon deaf ears.[44]

Such was the state of the case when Keane and Ireland appeared on the Roman scene. Soon McGlynn's case threatened to complicate the important Knights of Labor issue which was then the principal concern of Gibbons, Ireland, and Keane. In revealing his anxiety over

[43] AAB, 82-Q-1, Keane to Gibbons, Rome, May 14, 1887. Raffaele Cardinal Monaco was Prefect of the Congregation of the Holy Office. While Keane was in Rome on University business in 1894, the Pope discussed with him the tendency toward Socialism and the need of condemning dangerous societies in the United States. Keane said that he strongly protested against condemnations of labor organizations in America "as unnecessary, and as sure to prove pernicious" (ACUA, Bouquillon Papers, Keane to Bouquillon, Pegli, August 3, 1894).

[44] Stephen Bell, *Rebel, Priest and Prophet* (New York, 1937), pp. 41–47. This popular work on McGlynn, giving the broad outline of his career and the significant dates, is pro-McGlynn. There is no definitive biography of the priest.

this to Manning, the Bishop of Richmond referred to McGlynn as a "disobedient and cranky priest,"[45] and indicated in other ways that he was not in sympathy with his ideas. Naturally Keane was anxious, too, that the potential danger to the American Church should be averted. So at the request of Cardinal Simeoni,[46] Prefect of the Congregation of the Propaganda, he and Ireland sent a cablegram to McGlynn in which they said: "Have seen Cardinal, his feelings toward you are truly fatherly. We assure you all will be well. Answer."[47] Cardinal Gibbons and Keane then wrote letters to Father Richard L. Burtsell, the New York canon lawyer who was defending McGlynn's interests. Keane told Burtsell: "It is the most earnest wish of all the friends of the poor Doctor that you would exert your friendly offices to the utmost to induce him to come to Rome." He assured Burtsell that McGlynn would receive an impartial hearing and he urged that the voice of Rome be heeded in order "to still a tempest of controversy that will go far beyond his own individual case and involve peril to multitudes of souls and to the peace of the Church."[48] Burtsell's reply set forth the reasons for McGlynn's refusal to go to Rome,[49] but Keane tried again in more urgent language. "Let him," he said, "do his duty as a docile child of the Church by coming to the Father who has called him, without parley or hesitation, in full confidence that nothing but justice and charity awaits him and let him at once send a letter, long expected, respectfully giving the reasons for his delay."[50] To this Burtsell once more replied with reasons why the suspended priest would not proceed to Rome.[51] During the time Keane was corresponding with Burtsell a long article appeared in the New York *Morning Journal* which purported to quote Corrigan's secretary as saying that the documents reproduced in the *Journal* showing the loyalty of the clergy to the Archbishop of New York were "for use at Rome against the efforts of Cardinal Gibbons and Bishop Keane." When he learned this, the Bishop of Richmond addressed himself directly to Archbishop Corrigan. Keane stated that ordinarily he did not believe newspaper stories, but since the charge was publicly

[45] Keane to Manning, Rome, Feb. 10, 1887, cited by Leslie, *op. cit.*, p. 360.

[46] ACUA, "Chronicles," p. 17.

[47] ADR, Ireland and Keane to McGlynn (n.d.), copy of a cablegram.

[48] AANY, Burtsell Letterbook, Keane to Burtsell, Rome, Feb. 18, 1887, copy. The present writer is indebted to Father Henry Browne for obtaining this source.

[49] *Ibid.*, Burtsell to Keane, New York, Mar. 11, 1887, copy.

[50] *Ibid.*, Keane to Burtsell, Rome, Mar. 24, 1887, copy.

[51] *Ibid.*, Burtsell to Keane, New York, Apr. 22, 1887, copy.

made and attributed to Corrigan's secretary, he hoped the archbishop would recognize what he called "my right and a duty I owe to my reputation with the Holy See and with my brother-Bishops, to ask that your Grace will either send me a clear disavowal of the imputation, or, should it really have emanated from you, give its proofs."[52] Corrigan did not answer the letter for reasons that he communicated to Bishop Francis S. Chatard.

> On reflection, it seemed more advisable not to answer Bp. Keane, especially as the newspapers had already sufficiently accounted for the annoying rumor in *The Morning Journal.* The papers supposed to be favorable to Rev. Dr. McGlynn have repeatedly alluded to the friendly efforts in his behalf by American Prelates in Rome, and lately Dr. McGlynn himself has directly mentioned both Rt. Rev. Dr. Keane, and Rt. Rev. Dr. Ireland as giving him counsel and advice.[53]

This episode proved to be a serious bone of contention between the two prelates from that date. A year and a half later Bishop Keane explained to Monsignor O'Connell:

> Just before his jubilee, Abp. Corrigan wrote in reference to that letter of mine from Rome, which he had hitherto ignored. I responded most affectionately giving explanations for peace' [*sic*] sake. A correspondence has ensued showing a bitter spirit in him. His last clearly shows that my first reply to him was at once sent to la signora,[54] and that she has vigorously canvassed all available parties, from Card. Simeoni down, to prove that I was regarded as a meddler in the affairs of the Abp. of N. Y. This will doubtless raise embarrassments and hindrances in my way in Rome. Personally, I do not care, — but I regret the obstacles thus thrown in the way of what I firmly believe to be the work of God and His Church.[55]

[52] AANY, Keane to Corrigan, May 1, 1887. Keane told Gibbons that he had written to Corrigan "a very friendly but very frank letter on the subject, which I trust he will accept in the spirit in which it was written, and help to a fraternal good understanding all around" (BCA, 82-Q-1, Keane to Gibbons, Rome, May 14, 1887).

[53] AUND, Chatard Papers, Microfilm, Corrigan to Chatard, New York, June 1, 1887.

[54] "La signora" was Ella B. Edes, an American who had been received into the Church in 1852. She had resided in Rome for some time and seemed to have the confidence of some of the Roman and American Hierarchy. In the 1870's she was the Roman correspondent for the *Freeman's Journal.*

[55] ADR, Keane to O'Connell, Baltimore, Nov. 2, [1888]. The correspondence on the subject that passed between Keane and Corrigan included the following letters in the AANY: Corrigan to Keane, New York, Sept. 11, 24, Oct. 14, 31, copies; Keane to Corrigan, Chicago, Sept. 16, Oct. 1, Baltimore, Oct. 16, Nov. 1, 1888. In the last letter, Keane suggested to Corrigan that he might ask Ireland about the

Apparently Corrigan had misunderstood Keane's motives in entering the case. Certainly it was not because of personal regard for the unruly priest or because of a desire to interfere in the affairs of Corrigan's diocese. He was prompted solely by the urgency for peace and for the good of religion. Hence, when Rome sent an ultimatum to McGlynn in May, 1887,[56] requesting that he come to Rome within forty days or be excommunicated, Keane told Gibbons: "We have expressed our endorsement to the measure, provided the question is limited to the disciplinary case, and not permitted to drag us into a doctrinal and political discussion."[57]

Intimately connected with the McGlynn case and with the difficulties experienced by the American prelates in their efforts to prevent a condemnation of the Knights of Labor in the United States was the attempt on the part of the Archbishop of New York to have the writings of Henry George placed on the *Index of Prohibited Books*.[58] Corrigan's stand against McGlynn would have been fortified if he had accomplished this aim and those who sought condemnation of the Knights would have been given additional evidence for their position since McGlynn, George, and the Knights gave each other mutual support.[59] Here Keane clearly opposed Corrigan as was evident from his letter to Cardinal Manning of February 10, 1887,[60] and from his own later statement of his position:

> This condemnation Cardinal Gibbons and the rest of us opposed, not at all through any sympathy with the teachings of Henry George or of Dr. McGlynn, but because of the conviction that the conditions of economic science were not ripe for such a pronouncement from the Holy See; — because a condemnation would give a totally artificial importance to the theory in the U. S.; — and because the practical good sense of the American people could very well be trusted to deal wisely with the theory in the practical shape in which it came from them. This view of the matter finally prevailed, not increasing, of

---

manner in which they were authorized to bring about peace with McGlynn. He said that he did not intend to enter into a discussion of the affair and that this letter would end the matter as far as he was concerned.

[56] Bell, *op. cit.*, pp. 121–122. Also cf. Frederick J. Zwierlein, *The Life and Letters of Bishop McQuaid* (Rochester, 1925–1927), III, 1–83.

[57] AAB, 82-Q-1, Keane to Gibbons, Rome, May 14, 1887.

[58] Will, *op. cit.*, I, 362.

[59] Browne, *op. cit.*, p. 285.

[60] *Supra*, p. 73.

course, the friendliness of certain parties toward the University and those connected with it.[61]

With all these problems to distract Keane and his colleagues, it is a wonder that they accomplished the original purpose of their visit at all since the University question, too, was compelled to travel a thorny path in Rome. Shortly after their arrival Keane and Ireland had presented the letter of the University's trustees to Cardinal Simeoni while Ireland handed the other one to the Pope in the private audience accorded him as Bishop of St. Paul. He at that time requested a joint audience for himself and Keane to discuss the University business.[62] While they were waiting for this audience, it became all too evident that those who were opposed to the establishment of a university had lodged strong protests at the Vatican. As Keane later described it: "I was assiduous . . . in visiting Cardinals and other dignitaries of influence. From my conversations with them I gathered the difficulties which occurred to them, and printed a series of 'annuncio versiones' [*sic*] in reply, which I gave to those whom the business concerned."[63]

After they had waited about six weeks for an audience with the Holy Father the two bishops were informed that Archbishop Domenico Jacobini, Secretary of the Propaganda, had arranged with the Pope, as Keane stated, "that the matter of the University should be quietly laid aside until Cardinal Gibbons should come to receive the red hat, when it would be laid on the table indefinitely." This seemingly casual manner of disposing of the business that had brought them to Rome aroused the ire of Ireland and Keane. A show of indignation finally brought them an immediate audience with Leo XIII in which they learned the Holy Father's mind was not fully made up and that he wished them to remain in Rome until the arrival of Gibbons, in

[61] ACUA, "Chronicles," pp. 17–18. Keane, along with Gibbons, Ireland, and others, was against the attempts of others in that group to have Henry George's works condemned (AAB, 84-I-12, O'Connell to Gibbons, Rome, Apr. 17, 1888). The Congregation of the Holy Office condemned the false theories of Henry George by decree of February 6, 1889, but the decision was to be kept secret. Cf. Corrigan to McQuaid, Atlantic City, Apr. 24, 1889, in Frederick J. Zwierlein, *Letters of Archbishop Corrigan to Bishop McQuaid and Allied Documents* (Rochester, 1946), pp. 125–126.

[62] ACUA, "Chronicles," p. 11.

[63] *Ibid.*, pp. 12–13. This must be a reference to the document entitled, *Animadversiones quaedam de Universitate in America fundanda,* which bears the date of December 6, 1886, and the signatures of Keane and Ireland at the end of eight printed pages (AAB, 82-G-6, Document).

order, as he expressed it, "that his approval of the University might have greater solemnity."[64] When doubts were cast upon the sincerity of those who signed the petition to the Holy See for a university, Keane and Ireland sent off a circular to the signatories of the letters to Leo and Simeoni, requesting them to write individually affirming the validity and sincerity of their action.[65]

Following the joint audience with the Holy Father, Keane said that Leo XIII spoke "warmly, even enthusiastically of the University" on a number of occasions in public addresses, but that Propaganda continued to take a different view of the matter and to show an unfriendly spirit. When Gibbons arrived in Rome in February, 1887, Simeoni informed him of a lengthy protest against the University that had been submitted by the Archbishop of New York. Keane reported the reactions of himself and the cardinal to this news as follows:

> Cardinal Gibbons was so disheartened by this opposition that he proposed to me that we should abandon the undertaking and leave the responsibility of the failure where it belonged. To this I agreed very willingly, only too glad to escape from such contention. But when Bp. Ireland, who then was absent for a few days, returned to Rome, he protested bitterly against, as he expressed it, so cowardly a surrender to so unworthy an opposition, and insisted that we must at least win the approval asked for by the Board, and then give up the project if we thought it best to do so. His advice prevailed, Cardinal Gibbons answered the various objections to the entire satisfaction of the Holy Father, and the final decision was made.[66]

The papal approval finally came on Easter Sunday, April 10, 1887, in which Leo XIII gave his blessing to the establishment of the University in the form and under the conditions submitted by the American prelates.[67] In an audience that followed[68] Keane tried to persuade the Holy Father to entrust the new project to someone who had a greater inclination for university work. The Pope told him: "No — this is your work, you have been chosen for it by those whom the Bps. of America have entrusted with the work; regard their choice

[64] ACUA, "Chronicles," pp. 13–14.

[65] Ellis, *The Formative Years,* pp. 213–214.

[66] ACUA, "Chronicles," p. 19.

[67] *Ibid.*

[68] ACUA, "Report of Ireland and Keane to Trustees of the University on Their Mission to Rome," p. 4. This is an eleven-page typewritten report signed by Ireland and Keane and dated September 7, 1887.

as the will of God, take up the task bravely, do what you can; and even though you sh'd but make a beginning, you will have conferred a great benefit on the Church and on your country." Pope Leo then advised the Bishop of Richmond to retain his diocese until there was assurance that the University project would meet with success; as soon as it was evident that it would prove a reality, the Holy See would entertain his petition for resignation from Richmond.[69] Before leaving Rome Keane was asked by Leo XIII to assist him at the celebration of Mass. He spoke of this privilege later in a lecture in which he revealed the deep impression made on him by watching as the Pope offered the Holy Sacrifice. He said:

> During the celebration of the Mass his face was lighted up with a heavenly smile, and while receiving communion his whole countenance seemed as if it were transfigured. After the Mass was offered, he fell upon his aged knees and remained motionless for half an hour in conversation with his God.[70]

On May 15, when the negotiations on the University had been completed, Keane left the Eternal City[71] to visit some of the more famous universities on the continent and in England for the purpose of becoming acquainted with what he termed "the distinctive features which constitute a real University." In this way he added to the store of knowledge that he had gathered on university organization from Désiré Mercier of the University of Louvain, who was visiting in Rome at the same time as himself, and from Francesco Satolli, a professor of theology in the College of the Propaganda, both of whom had been recommended to him by the Holy Father.[72]

Keane had been away from the United States for seven months when he returned in June, 1887. When the Board of Trustees met on September 7, he was formally appointed the first rector of the Catholic University of America.[73] Naturally his chief concern after the appointment was the promotion of the enterprise so that its success would be assured. With that in mind in November, 1887, he began a series of articles on the European Catholic universities in the *Catholic World*. He also signed a circular, together with Bishops

[69] ACUA, "Chronicles," pp. 20–21.
[70] ACUA, scrapbook, Lecture on Leo XIII delivered in Washington on December 18, 1887.
[71] AANY, O'Connell to Corrigan, Rome, May 16, 1887.
[72] ACUA, "Chronicles," pp. 20–21.
[73] ACUA, MMBT, Baltimore, Sept. 7, 1887, p. 19.

Ireland and Spalding, which was sent to all the priests of the United States soliciting their financial support of the University.[74] But it was up to Keane to plan almost singlehandedly the erection of the building that was to house the University as well as to prepare the statutes which would be submitted for the perusal and approval of the University board and ultimately of the Holy See.[75]

After spending Christmas in Richmond, Keane began his travels again with the purpose of collecting for the institution. Gibbons, as chairman of the Board of Trustees, had paved the way for the tour by sending a circular to the bishops asking them to invite to their dioceses the University trustees engaged in collecting and urging that they help to secure the support of the wealthier Catholics in their jurisdictions.[76] In the company of Ireland, Bishop Keane spent two weeks in Baltimore where they enjoyed some success. Then he proceeded to Philadelphia, Boston, Chicago, Louisville, and other places in the East and Middle West, sometimes aided by Ireland or Spalding, at other times alone, speaking at meetings and in churches and interviewing persons of wealth.[77]

Evidence of the advancement of the University cause was furnished on May 24, 1888, when the cornerstone of Caldwell Hall, the University's first building, was laid. On that day President Grover Cleveland and several members of his cabinet joined the large crowd of prelates, priests, and laity to make an otherwise gloomy and rainy day a bright occasion in the annals of the University.[78] At the meeting of the Board of Trustees that followed the laying of the cornerstone the rector announced that six chairs had been endowed but that this was only a small part of the funds that were needed. For that reason he continued to ride the uncomfortable trains during most of the summer in search of generous hearts who would open to him their

[74] Ellis, *The Formative Years,* pp. 265–266. Keane wrote several articles for the *Catholic World:* "Leo XIII and the Catholic University of America," XLVI (Nov., 1887), 145–153; "The Roman Universities," XLVI (Dec., 1887), 313–321; "The Catholic University of Louvain," XLVI (Jan., 1888), 525–534; "The University of Strassburg," XLVI (Feb., 1888), 643–652; "The Catholic Universities of France," XLVII (June, 1888), 289–297; "A Chat about the Catholic University," XLVIII (Nov., 1888), 216–226.

[75] ACUA, "Chronicles," p. 23. Washington, D. C., was adopted as the permanent site of the University at a meeting of the Board of Trustees on September 7, 1887. Cf. Ellis, *The Formative Years,* pp. 241–242.

[76] Ellis, *The Formative Years,* pp. 258–259.

[77] *Ibid.,* pp. 269–275.

[78] ACUA, "Chronicles," p. 24.

treasures.[79] Meanwhile he awaited the action of Rome upon his request that he be relieved of his duties as Bishop of Richmond, since the success of the project seemed to be assured and it had reached a stage where it required all of his time.[80]

As we have seen John Keane's appointment to the University committee in 1885 had gradually led to almost complete responsibility for the University project by 1888. During that time he was also accountable for the administration of the Diocese of Richmond, nor did he neglect this charge despite the other obligations that forced him to absent himself from his see for long periods. During this time perhaps his most important accomplishment in the Diocese of Richmond was the convening of the second diocesan synod in the fall of 1886. He stated that he had prepared the outline himself after examining the decrees of the Third Plenary Council of Baltimore and the synods of other dioceses.[81] This he forwarded to his priests with the request that they examine it and then meet in Richmond on August 18 to discuss it. Thirty priests were present for the deliberations that continued for three days, during which public services were conducted on two nights. At the close of the synod Keane recorded in his diary: "The most beautiful harmony reigned throughout the deliberations of the Clergy, who examined all the decrees, first in committee, and then in general assembly. They asked for exceedingly few changes, which I very willingly made." He added that the decrees affecting the Germans had been drawn up after the synodal discussions by Father Willibald Baumgartner, Benedictine pastor of St. Mary's Church in Richmond, while those regarding the Negroes had been composed by Father Slattery, pastor of St. Joseph's Church. Of special importance to the priests of the diocese was the organization at this time of the Mutual Aid Society which would contribute to the support of priests whom ill health kept from performing regular pastoral duties. Keane allowed the pastors to take up a collection for the Society on Christmas day of that year, but for that year only.[82]

When the bishop returned to his diocese in the summer of 1887, he confessed that he had "a rather heavy heart" when the people manifested their joy at a reception that was attended by state dignitaries

[79] Ellis, *The Formative Years,* pp. 297–306.

[80] ADR, Bishops' Diary, p. 152.

[81] *Ibid.,* p. 144.

[82] *Ibid.,* pp. 144–145. For the officials of the synod and the names of the clergy who attended, cf. Magri, *op. cit.,* pp. 120–123.

including Governor Fitzhugh Lee.[83] The thoughts which produced this heavinesss of heart were recorded by him later. He stated:

> Though my diocese was one of the least important in the country, as to number of priests and people, yet I was one of the happiest Bishops in the world, owing to the perfect sympathy among us all and the absence of scandals, debts, etc. My work too, especially among the Protestants and negroes [*sic*] of the State of Virginia, was very congenial to my wishes; and I would have asked no better fortune than to spend all my life as I was.[84]

Meanwhile he took up the more pressing diocesan duties that had accumulated in his absence. Before the year ended the bishop had visited once more the chief missions and stations to confirm and to observe the state of religion. When the visitation was over he reported: "Religion is in a healthy condition everywhere, allowance being made for the great disadvantages of the poor little missions which can have the visit of a priest so seldom."[85] During this time he also purchased property for a church in the west end of Richmond and laid the cornerstone of the church that was later to be dedicated to the Sacred Heart. In Lynchburg, he bought land that was to be used for a school for the colored children, and at St. Joseph's Church for the colored in Richmond, he found it necessary to build another small school to provide for the industrial and normal students. To assist this apostolate among the colored people, the bishop had the money allotted to the diocese by the committee on Negro and Indian Missions and a portion of the money sent by the Propagation of the Faith.[86]

During the year 1888 Bishop Keane was almost entirely engaged in fulfilling his obligations as rector of the Catholic University of America. In Lent, however, he returned to Richmond for his usual course of sermons in the cathedral and for the annual meeting of the clergy.[87] After requesting release from his diocese in June, Keane anxiously awaited Rome's reply. Finally, on August 28 he was informed by Cardinal Gibbons that favorable action had been taken on

[83] ADR, Bishops' Diary, p. 148.

[84] ACUA, "Chronicles," pp. 21–22.

[85] ADR, Bishops' Diary, p. 151.

[86] *Ibid.*, pp. 149–151. When Keane was on a collecting tour for the University in the spring of 1886 he also made appeals in the churches on Sundays on behalf of his work among the colored people if the bishops permitted it (Archives of the Diocese of Albany, Keane to Francis McNierny, New York, Jan. 26, [1886]).

[87] ADR, Bishops' Diary, p. 152.

his petition. In acknowledging receipt of the news Keane told the cardinal: "While I cannot but feel the separation from the dear old Diocese, where I was truly the happiest bishop in America, I rejoice that the suspense is over, and that the Diocese can now soon have a bishop who can stay home and attend to it." He added that he had appointed Father Augustine Van de Vyver administrator of the diocese.[88] Within a few weeks Bishop Keane received the papal brief dated August 14, 1888, signed by Miecislaus Cardinal Ledochowski, which transferred him to the titular See of Jassus,[89] along with a cordial letter from Cardinal Simeoni, who told him that he could now give all his time and care to the University.[90]

On October 14 the former Bishop of Richmond preached a farewell sermon in the cathedral to those whom he had come to know and love during his ten years as their shepherd, and two days later the clergy assembled in the see city to extend their best wishes to their former ordinary.[91] Keane departed with the knowledge and satisfaction that he had gained the affection of most of those in whose behalf he had labored for a decade.

Prior to Rome's acceptance of Keane's resignation steps had been taken to fill the anticipated vacancy. At a meeting of the consultors and irremovable rectors of the diocese the choice fell on Daniel J. Riordan, a priest of the Archdiocese of Chicago and a brother of the Archbishop of San Francisco, Francis Janssens, Bishop of Natchez and former vicar-general of Richmond, and Augustine Van de Vyver in that order.[92] The bishops of the Province of Baltimore chose candidates for the see at a meeting on July 1, following the consecration of Leo Haid, O.S.B., as Vicar Apostolic of North Carolina. They nominated Van de Vyver, Denis J. O'Connell, and James M. Cleary of Wisconsin, who was later president of the Catholic Total Abstinence Union.[93] When Keane's resignation was accepted the *terna* was submitted and both Keane and Gibbons gave their support to O'Connell,[94]

[88] AAB, 84-Y-2, Keane to Gibbons, Notre Dame, Aug. 29, 1888.

[89] ACUA, Keane Papers, Ledochowski to Keane, Rome, Aug. 14, 1888 [Latin brief]. Jassus is a titular see of Caria in Asia Minor.

[90] ACUA, Keane Papers, Simeoni to Keane, Rome, Aug. 29, 1888 [Latin].

[91] ADR, Bishops' Diary, p. 152.

[92] AAB, Gibbons' Diary, July 1, 1888, p. 225.

[93] *Ibid.*

[94] Gibbons gave O'Connell strong support in a letter to Simeoni (AAB, 85-G-6, Baltimore, Oct. 19, 1888 [Latin], copy). Keane urged Gibbons to support O'Connell (AAB, 84-R-3, Richmond, July 3, 1888), and gave him support when he was in Rome (AAB, 85-G-2, O'Connell to Gibbons, Grottaferrata, Oct. 17, 1888).

which understandably pleased him very much.[95] Leo XIII and Simeoni indicated to Keane who was in Rome seeking professors for the University that they wanted O'Connell to remain at his Roman post,[96] so the bishops submitted another *terna* containing the names of Van de Vyver, George W. Devine, a priest of the Archdiocese of Baltimore, and Ignatius F. Horstmann, a priest of the Archdiocese of Philadelphia.[97] Gibbons spoke strongly in favor of Horstmann when he sent this list to the Holy See.[98] Keane, however, felt differently about Horstmann and he told the cardinal:

> I had a long talk with Mgr. Jacobini about the Richmond list. After reflection and prayer I felt compelled in conscience to differ from your Eminence's judgment in regard to Horstmann. . . . In all these respects, I think Devine will do far better, and so I spoke in his favor to the Propaganda. He is not a strong man, but seems the best available. Now I leave all to providence.[99]

To O'Connell Keane wrote: "Poor old Richmond I wonder how its fate is working out. The Card. will no doubt be cut at my having refused to endorse his support of Horstmann,—but, please God, I shall ever try to say and do what I think is right, coûte que coûte."[100] "Poor old Richmond" was vacant nearly a year before Rome finally appointed Augustine Van de Vyver, who had appeared first on both of the bishops' lists, although he was championed by neither Gibbons or Keane. Then the two former Bishops of Richmond participated in the consecration ceremony in St. Peter's Cathedral in Richmond on October 20, 1889, and the diocese had its sixth bishop at last.[101]

95 AAB, 84-V-2, O'Connell to Gibbons, Grottaferrata, Aug. 9, 1888; AAB, 84-V-6, O'Connell to Gibbons, Rome, Aug. 14, 1888.

96 AAB, 85-L-9, Keane to Gibbons, Rome, Dec. 18, 1888.

97 AAB, Gibbons' Diary, Feb. 27, 1889, p. 232.

98 AAB, 85-S-11, Gibbons to Simeoni, Baltimore, Mar. 8, 1889 (Latin), copy.

99 AAB, 85-V-7, Keane to Gibbons, Fulda, Apr. 5, 1889.

100 ADR, Keane to O'Connell, Liverpool, Apr. 27, [1889].

101 Magri, *op. cit.*, p. 128. O'Connell was among those who witnessed the consecration (Reily, *op. cit.*, II, 297).

CHAPTER V

First Rector of the Catholic University of America

DURING the eleven months that intervened between Keane's formal appointment as Rector of the Catholic University and his release from the See of Richmond, the University work had progressed to the point where the building that was to house the institution was in the process of erection, the corner-stone having been laid on May 24, 1888. A fairly promising beginning had been made toward the endowment of the chairs of Theology in response to the appeals of Keane and the collecting committee to wealthy Catholics; and a vice-rector in the person of Father Philip J. Garrigan, pastor of St. Bernard's Church in Fitchburg, Massachusetts, had been chosen to relieve the bishop of some of the burden that attended the administration of University business. Keane was at last free to give his full attention to the countless tasks that the head of an embryonic institution would inevitably encounter.

When the news of his release from Richmond reached him in August, 1888, Bishop Keane was at the University of Notre Dame preparing the statutes of the new institution. He had completed the fundamental governing laws of the University after having made a careful study of those at Louvain, Laval, and Lille. He planned to complete the special constitutions that must govern the School of Sacred Theology, after which he intended to submit the results of his labors to Archbishop Ireland and Bishop Spalding before sending them to Cardinal Gibbons for his approval.[1] During the first week of

[1] AAB, 84-Y-2, Keane to Gibbons, Notre Dame, Aug. 29, 1888. For a thorough treatment of this portion of the University's history, cf. Ellis, *The Formative Years,* p. 309 ff.

September, the rector told Gibbons: "Have finished the statutes, have sent an article to the Independent in reply to a couple of vile articles from a 'Catholic Layman' that were sent to me (they sounded very like McGlynn) — and am about beginning an article for the Cath. World. Enough to keep me out of mischief."[2] As a further precaution against idleness he had visited Archbishop Patrick A. Feehan of Chicago to arrange for himself and Spalding to collect in that archdiocese during the last weeks of September.[3] After completing their work in Chicago, the two bishops entrained for St. Paul where Keane preached on September 27, at the conferring of the pallium on Archbishop Ireland. In his long and flowery sermon, the rector traced the history of Catholicity in the Northwest beginning with the arrival of Mathias Loras in 1839 as first bishop of the Diocese of Dubuque. He attributed the rapid settlement of the one-time wilderness to the oppression of European peoples by rulers who, in their selfishness and greed for power, even sought mastery over divine things. The New World became the haven for downtrodden humanity because "the fathers of our country proclaimed to all the world that it is the land where humanity shall forever be free to pursue the end and enjoy the rights bestowed on man by his Creator." The preacher continued, "the New World proclaims as its first principle that man is dependent upon God alone, and has all his rights from God, that fellowmen must respect them, and the law protect them, but that the Creator's bounty is alone their origin, and His omnipotence their guarantee." The bishop further pointed out that it was "no wonder that the Church of God feels so entirely at home in such a country. She, too, had known what it is to be fettered and hindered and treated shamefully in the Old World, both by open enemies and by false-hearted self-seeking believers."

In his discourse Keane chose to praise Ireland especially for his labors in the cause of temperance. "The great army of those who are bravely striving in this noble cause," he stated, "look here to St. Paul for encouragement and counsel, while thousands of grateful hearts, lifted up from enslavement or from wretchedness, this day invoke blessings on your Archbishop as their deliverer and benefactor." As to Ireland's part in the founding of the Catholic University of America, the bishop exaggerated when he proclaimed:

[2] AAB, 85-A-5, Keane to Gibbons, Notre Dame, Sept. 6, 1888.
[3] *Ibid.*

> To him is the present assured success of the great undertaking to be attributed, and when the future historians shall be chronicling the incalculable good wrought by our Catholic University. . . . the voice of honest truth will declare that of this, as of most else that is good and noble of the period we live in, the credit is largely due to the Bishop of St. Paul.[4]

The invitation to speak at such an important event in the life of the Archbishop of St. Paul was a proclamation to all of the close friendship which existed between these two prelates — a friendship which was destined to endure until their deaths in 1918. Keane and Ireland probably first became acquainted while they were laboring for the cause of total abstinence. In the Third Plenary Council their sympathetic views on temperance, secret societies, and other subjects under debate likely forged a stronger bond between them. As we have seen,[5] while they were in Rome in the winter of 1886–1887, they worked together for what they considered the best interests of the Catholic Church in the United States, a mutual labor that caused them to unite more firmly as the opposition became more bitter. In their writings, public utterances, and private correspondence Ireland and Keane repeatedly indicated similar views on the Church's destiny in the United States. They foretold glorious days for American democracy while prophesying the downfall of decadent monarchy. The two bishops believed that the welfare of the Church in this country would be served best by keeping out Old World conservatism. They were convinced that if the Catholic Church humanly speaking expected to enjoy a prosperous future she must recognize the trends of the age and show a more sympathetic understanding in her relations with the people of the democracies. They were convinced that the Catholic Church would prosper in the United States as never before if she were allowed all the freedom that was consistent with essential dogmas untrammeled by annoying unessentials. So frequently and so persistently did Keane and Ireland treat these points that the name of one was often written and spoken with the name of the other, and those who opposed their ideas branded them and their sympathizers with the name "Americanizers," a term in which their opponents

[4] *Northwestern Chronicle* (St. Paul), Sept. 28, 1888. Keane had brought the pallium from New York and presented it to Ireland at Notre Dame "with a speech from His Eminence" (ADR, Ireland to O'Connell, St. Paul, Aug. 18, 1888). Also cf. Arthur J. Hope, C.S.C., *Notre Dame — One Hundred Years* (Notre Dame, 1943), p. 239.

[5] *Supra,* pp. 68–80.

included the notion of a dangerous philosophical liberalism.[6] The two prelates differed, however, in their attitude toward those who opposed their views. Calm and reasonable by nature, Keane was seldom, if ever, uncharitable to his opponents either in private correspondence or in public utterances. Ireland, on the other hand, seemed to enjoy a battle and his opponent was an enemy to be destroyed.

In inviting Keane to St. Paul in September, 1888, Archbishop Ireland also afforded the University rector an opportunity to win greater sympathy for the institution he represented. At several places in the

[6] For a list of eighty condemned propositions indicative of the "liberal" spirit of the nineteenth century, cf. the translation of the Syllabus of 1864 in Raymond Corrigan, *The Church and the Nineteenth Century* (Milwaukee, 1938), pp. 289–295. This Syllabus of Errors of Pius IX must be consulted to understand what was meant at that time by censorable liberalism. In summary form liberalism is defined as "a many-sided system or doctrine advocating the emancipation of man from the supernatural, moral, and divine-positive order. Essentially negative, it must be defined by reference to the thing from which the Liberal would be free. It may be political, economic, intellectual, moral, religious, or all of them combined. Integral Liberalism asserts the absolute freedom of the individual in thought, worship, conscience, speech, writing, and action, thus denying all authority derived from God. An all-pervading virus, impossible to isolate. In English-speaking lands a moribund and vague attitude of mind, but still virulent among Latin anticlericals" (*ibid.*, p. 306). The American churchmen to whom the term "liberal" was applied, were not liberals in this sense. Why were they called liberals then? An American contemporary furnished this acceptable answer: ". . . we have a country where those modern liberties [liberty of thought, of press, of worship and of teaching condemned by the Church as heresies in themselves, because they are utterly at variance with philosophy and revelation] are cherished; with us Church and State are separated (and both flourish). The question is — what attitude will the Church take to a state built up on such foundations and animated by that spirit!

"The Liberal and the Conservative appear, and they answer.

"The Liberal looks to present and future. He sees that the world cherishes what it calls its liberties and its supremacy of state over Church. He says to himself — seeing things as they are, 'the Church is well off separated; the constitution is all right; it lets us alone. We will flourish — Hurrah for the flag — God bless America — Let us be patriotic — We have a glorious country — Keep Church and State apart.'

"Thus you find the liberal — so to speak, in touch with the time.

"The Conservative however, looks back at the past and into books. He thinks of how much the world is out of plumb. He shudders at the recklessness of modern states — mourns over the heresies which develop daily; he can't live in a country which cherishes what he despises — he has nothing good to say of it. Patriotism doesn't exist outside of the dictionary; he can't pray for the flag which doesn't carry above its stars and stripes, the Papal colors. But the liberal is at one disadvantage, Progressive, he is constantly lecturing, talking, writing. He has new ideas, he is full of zeal — he preaches his ideas. The Conservative has nothing new to say — he is merely stationary, if he talks or writes he does two things — no more, no less.

"He constantly repeats principles absolutely true and denied by no one Catholic; secondly, he insinuates that the Liberal denies those principles" (ACUA, Kerby Papers, William Kerby to Edward Kerby, Louvain, Apr. 11, 1897).

Middle West he spoke to the clergy and laity of the importance of the University to the future of the American Church and of the need for the generous support of wealthy Catholics.[7] Then the bishop returned East to bid farewell to the priests and people of the Diocese of Richmond[8] before he accepted the hospitality of the pastor of St. Patrick's Church in Washington while the University building was under construction.[9]

Soon after he had taken up temporary residence at St. Patrick's, Bishop Keane prepared the letters which were to be presented to the Holy Father and to the Prefect of the Congregation of the Propaganda petitioning the approval of the University's statutes. He submitted these documents for the approval and signature of the Board of Trustees at their meeting in Baltimore on November 13, requesting at the same time that he be authorized to go to Europe to present the statutes for approval, to solicit all the necessary privileges and faculties for the University, and to meet personally those who were to be invited to fill the professorial chairs in the new institution. When these requests were all ratified by the members of the board,[10] the rector was prepared to set out on his mission.

Before sailing from New York on the *Gascoigne* on November 17, Keane preached one of the sermons in St. Patrick's Cathedral at the triduum in honor of Blessed (now Saint) John Baptist de la Salle. He indulged in a bit of exaggeration on the occasion by speaking of Archbishop Corrigan as "one of the foremost organizers and directors of the Catholic University,"[11] probably in the hope of easing their strained relations and at the same time conveying the impression that Corrigan was supporting the rector and the project he represented. He doubtless remembered the difficulties encountered on his previous visit to Rome on University business, difficulties that arose from the opposition of Archbishop Corrigan, and he now made a bid for peace in the hope that no obstacles would be placed in his way during his present trip. While he was in New York, the rector also gave an interview to the press on the purpose of his visit to Europe and on the progress so far made toward the establishment of the University. As in most of the interviews that he gave during these years, Bishop

[7] ADR, Ireland to O'Connell, St. Paul, Aug. 18, 1888.
[8] ADR, Bishops' Diary, p. 152.
[9] Smith, *op. cit.*, p. 64.
[10] ACUA, MMBT, Baltimore, Nov. 13, 1888, pp. 22–25.
[11] Ellis, *The Formative Years,* pp. 326–327.

Keane painted a very optimistic picture of the future of the institution and of its place and potential influence on American Catholic life.[12]

Upon his arrival in Europe, Keane stopped first at the Sulpician seminary at Issy to complete the arrangements, initiated by Cardinal Gibbons, for the Sulpicians to assume charge of the community life of the University's students.[13] Then he hastened to Rome to confer with some of the members of the American hierarchy who were to leave there soon, and to present at the Holy See the letters from the Board of Trustees. The Holy Father granted him an audience on December 17 and, as Keane expressed it, "he received quite eagerly and gladly all information in regard to the progress of the work, and heard with interest a general statement concerning the statutes to be submitted to him."[14] The statutes had been entrusted to Father James A. Corcoran of St. Charles Borromeo Seminary in Overbrook, Pennsylvania, for translation into Latin. He was slow in performing the task, and when they finally arrived, the rector was obliged to have that portion of the statutes that he himself had translated into Latin retranslated because, as he said, "I could not permit my plain Latin to stand in contrast to his slendid Latinity."[15] When the documents were printed the Holy Father appointed a special commission of six cardinals, under the presidency of Camillo Cardinal Mazzella, to examine them. The rector reported later that he had several conferences with the cardinals of the commission during which he answered the questions that were put to him and explained the reasons for a number of points that had been included in the statutes.[16] However, Bishop Bernard J. McQuaid, who was on the scene in Rome, obtained information which indicated that Keane's mission was not easily accomplished. In a letter to the Archbishop of New York, McQuaid said:

> All evidently is not plain sailing. There has been much consternation since the commission held its first meeting. Abbot Smith says, *sub sigillo,* of course, that the statutes will not pass unless the Pope over-

[12] *Ibid.*, pp. 325–326.

[13] AAB, 85-A-5, Keane to Gibbons, Notre Dame, Sept. 6, 1888. For a complete treatment of this trip to Europe, cf. Ellis, *The Formative Years,* p. 331 ff., and Patrick Henry Ahern, *The Catholic University of America, 1887–1896 — the Rectorship of John J. Keane* (Washington, 1948), p. 9 ff.

[14] ACUA, "Chronicles," p. 30.

[15] *Ibid.*

[16] *Ibid.*, p. 32. Keane had the documents printed in a small brochure which he sent from Rome to all the bishops of the United States (ACUA, Garrigan Papers, Keane to Garrigan, Rome, Mar. 14, 1889).

rides the decision of this commission. Bp. Keane has been busy visiting Cardinals, one after another and writing to Baltimore, etc.[17]

The Bishop of Rochester may have been indulging in a certain amount of wishful thinking, too, since he had originally opposed the establishment of a University on the grounds that diocesan seminaries should be erected first[18] and then later because he was opposed to the choice of Washington as a site for the institution.[19] Although McQuaid remained unalterably opposed to the University, he indicated some change of attitude toward its rector when he wrote that Keane was "wonderfully good-natured" about the teasing to which McQuaid subjected him.[20] Notwithstanding the opposition in Rome which Keane may have encountered, he accomplished that portion of his European mission when the secretary of the Congregation of the Propaganda signed the final approval of the statutes on March 7, the feast of St. Thomas Aquinas, and when, on the same day, the Sovereign Pontiff issued a brief in which all the rector's requests were granted.[21]

During the time that the statutes were under consideration in Rome, Keane was questioned about a lecture that he had delivered a year before on the subject of "The Providential Mission of Leo XIII." This lecture had been given in Washington on December 18, 1887, and it was published in English in pamphlet form in 1888. Monsignor O'Connell had a French translation of the pamphlet brought out in Rome which he judiciously distributed to some of the cardinals. However, a carefully annotated copy of the English pamphlet had been sent to Rome by someone. When Keane arrived Archbishop Domenico Jacobini, secretary of the Propaganda, told him that the Pope desired

[17] AANY, McQuaid to Corrigan, Rome, Feb. 16, 1889. In a previous letter to Corrigan, McQuaid had said: "What a craze the poor man has for knowing grand dignitaries!" (AANY, McQuaid to Corrigan, Rome, Dec. 8, 1888.)

[18] Ellis, *The Formative Years,* pp. 81–82.

[19] *Ibid.,* pp. 142–143.

[20] AANY, McQuaid to Corrigan, Rome, Jan. 22, 1889. Keane may have wished to relieve Gibbons of concern over McQuaid's opposition to the University when he stated: "I hope that weeks of familiar contact with Bp. McQ will remove somewhat of his animosities. He is evidently growing more tolerant of the University and its Rector" (AAB, 85-P-9, Keane to Gibbons, Rome, Jan. 22, 1889). But a month later McQuaid told Corrigan: "I have kept quiet, but never fail to insinuate that the U. will ultimately fail, and for sound reasons" (AANY, McQuaid to Corrigan, Rome, Feb. 16, 1889). After his work had been accomplished in Rome, Keane told Ireland: "Bp. McQuaid was a constant torture the whole time I was in Rome. He is *malignant* towards the University and all connected with it" (AASP, Louvain, Apr. 11, 1889).

[21] ACUA, "Chronicles," p. 32.

that he see Thomas Cardinal Zigliara, Prefect of the Holy Office, concerning it. The cardinal told Keane in their first meeting that, so far as he could remember, it was supposed that the lecture in some way favored the theories of Henry George and Dr. Edward McGlynn, but that he could not find the passages claimed to be objectionable in the French and English copies that the rector showed him. Regarding the episode Keane later stated that they considered the pamphlet page by page in four or five subsequent conferences during which Zigliara "dwelt on the exaggerated interpretation that might be put by European revolutionists on phrases which, he frankly acknowledged, were quite correct from our American standpoint." The cardinal also thought that Keane "had gone too far in citing the Holy Father as demanding, as a matter of *justice,* such measure of compensation for labor as w'd enable the laboring classes to live with human decency."[22] Actually there was nothing in the lecture that could be construed even remotely as an endorsement of George's theories. Keane had prepared the lecture for an American audience, therefore, he felt justified in making such statements as the following:

> This is the era of democracy, the day of absolute government is over and never again will a nation's laws be made by one man, or set of men, other than the agents of the people, for whose welfare alone laws should be made. . . .
>
> . . . He [Leo XIII] has laid down the law, the only law that laborers should have a just recompense for their work and has warned them to keep themselves within the circle of the law. He has said that Governments must protect them in their rights. Some may imagine that he is drifting away from the landmarks of his predecessors — what a mistake! He has simply laid down the only laws of the Democracy of the age. His unbounded love for America arises from the fact that he sees here the furtherest advance in the legitimate sphere of Democracy. He sees here a Republic which is at the same time a rebuke to the despotisms of the past and a protest to the Red Republicanism of France. He sees here the Church and State occupying the best positions which under existing circumstances could be expected. He loves America and his children here. He has shown that he has no fears of the Democracy of the age. . . .[23]

After the conferences with Zigliara, Keane said that the cardinal "acknowledged that there was nothing in the lecture that could be

[22] *Ibid.,* pp. 36–37.

[23] ACUA, Lecture on "The Providential Mission of Leo XIII," delivered in Washington, D. C., on December 18, 1887. Typed copy.

condemned, or need be changed; but added that if I issued another edition of it, it would be well to add a short preface to guard against the misinterpretation of Europeans." The rector told the Pope about the difficulty over his lecture in one of his audiences, and Leo XIII was quoted as having said:

> Oh yes, I knew it was all right; I told them that I knew you and your devotedness to the teaching of the Church and of the Holy See; but some of them thought there were things that could be misunderstood, and so I asked, to please them, that you should have these conferences with Card. Zigliara; and he has told me of it, and how delighted he is with you; and all is right.[24]

Keane was informed by O'Connell that the annotated copy of the suspected lecture had been sent from New York and that it had been placed in the hands of Cardinal Mazzella by Ella B. Edes, who was employed by Archbishop Corrigan and his friends to act as agent for some of their Roman business.[25] Gibbons must have made inquiries to ascertain if possible the identity of the person who had lodged the complaint against the lecture, for Archbishop Patrick J. Ryan of Philadelphia told Corrigan: "I wrote to Cardinal Gibbons in relation to the report about Bp. Keane's lecture. . . . I assured him most positively that you had nothing whatever to do with the complaints made of the obnoxious passages in the lecture."[26]

The University's rector must have been embarrassed by this first incident in which he was required to explain the meaning attached to his statements. Similar episodes were to be repeated in the following years and the cumulative effect of these rumors and suspicions about his orthodoxy caused a shadow to fall over his good name in the minds of some of the more conservative curial officials. Although the rector could point out to the satisfaction of the Roman authorities that there was nothing reprehensible in his statements, he nonetheless became the subject of unfavorable comments, similar to the one McQuaid relayed to Corrigan on this occasion. He said: "The Abbot [Bernard Smith, O.S.B.] told me that the Cardinals are quite disturbed by some of Keane's utterances, and they begin to fear that a mistake has been made in naming him as Rector."[27] Thus if it were the intention of an unfriendly critic to cast suspicion upon Keane's

[24] ACUA, "Chronicles," p. 38.
[25] *Ibid.*
[26] AANY, Ryan to Corrigan, Philadelphia, Sept. 21, 1889.
[27] AANY, McQuaid to Corrigan, Rome, Dec. 8, 1888.

reputation, some progress had been made to that end. In this instance and on subsequent occasions when his orthodoxy was questioned, however, Keane probably exposed himself to criticism by some imprudent statement. He insisted on great principles and ideas without too much anxiety about their precise expression and definition, and he did not set so high a value upon the minutiae of dogmatic and moral theology as many of his fellow ecclesiastics. For that reason he detested heresy-hunting; and yet his impulses were so strong that when anything seemed to conflict with any of his central religious convictions or practical ideals, he was likely to denounce it roundly and in unmeasured language, even though it lay within the boundaries of faith and morals. In the opinion of one writer, Keane and others who were identified as liberals gave the impression that they were mere youths, if not by a lack of force and of intelligence, certainly by an absence of criticism and doubt, by their exuberant enthusiasm and ingenuous sincerity. When they had exposed themselves to accusations of lack of orthodoxy, well-trained theologians and experienced masters of style among their antagonists were always ready to take advantage of their imprudence.[28] As we shall yet see, some of the difficulties which Keane experienced in promoting noble causes may be attributed to this apparent shortcoming.

During his Roman visit the bishop delivered a series of sermons in the Church of San Silvestro in Capite which attracted many of the English-speaking Catholics of the Eternal City who later, in appreciation of the preacher and his institution, presented the University with a bust of St. Thomas Aquinas.[29] On this visit the rector was also alert to the sentiments of the Vatican as to what would be considered a fitting protest on the part of the American hierarchy for the manner in which the Holy Father was then being treated by the Italian government. He advised Cardinal Gibbons to express the sentiments of the American Church on the subject of a demonstration of protest in the United States when writing the Holy See, and he added: "It might be well then to have some sort of public utterance in vindication of the Holy Father's *independence* and freedom of action without mentioning the *temporal power* at all. I am assured here that such declarations would be acceptable and useful."[30]

[28] Soderini, *op. cit.*

[29] New York *Herald,* Jan. 6, 1889. Cf. Ahern, *op. cit.,* p. 89.

[30] AAB, 85-L-9, Keane to Gibbons, Rome, Dec. 18, 1888. A few days later Keane said to Ireland: "You will all have to make *some* sort of a big fuss for the Pope's *religious independence* (nothing said of temporal power), or the Holy Father will be

The rector was still in Rome when he received the news of the death of Isaac T. Hecker, the founder of the Paulists. Keane's admiration for Hecker and his work dated from his first years in the priesthood when he became so strongly attached to the Paulists that he had sought permission to join them. Although his superiors did not permit him to take that step, Keane continued in the closest friendly relations with Hecker, reflecting his sympathy of views on such questions as temperance, the manner of converting American Protestants, and the providential mission of democratic America. Hence, even though he was deeply preoccupied with the business that had brought him to Rome, when he heard of Father Hecker's death he wrote a "warm article" in which he spoke of him as "a 'vessel of election' for the good of his generation." After tracing the steps that led to Hecker's conversion and ordination, Keane maintained that "never did a soul that had found grace and truth crave more ardently to share these blessings with all his kind, and never did a laborer in the harvest-field strive more earnestly for that end than he during the forty years of his priesthood." These labors among Protestants were crowned with success, said Keane, because Hecker understood the non-Catholic as a result of his own experience and, too, because "he never disparaged any particle of truth and goodness, wheresoever he might find it, but welcomed and utilized it." Keane likewise indicated some of his own convictions in attributing these views to Hecker:

> The fondest dream of Father Hecker's soul was a new and abundant outpouring of the Holy Spirit of grace and truth in our age and our country, for the sanctification of the new epoch in the history of the Church and of the world, which all can see unfolding. . . .
>
> His hope for America, his trust in her future, his confidence in her providential mission among the nations and peoples of the earth, were to him axiomatic convictions and springs of joyous energy. When he considered the providence of God leading up, through all history and through all the vicissitudes of the nations, to this wonderful new departure of human society, and pointing out its pathway and its work his whole being seemed to thrill with an enthusiasm that was electrical in its effect upon his hearers. . . .
>
> Some there were, doubtless, who thought him a visionary, dreamer, a dangerous theorizer. There are always whelps to bark at every great man's heels. There are always petty minds to look with pity, or with

far from content. After a few months, when the political field is quiet, it seems to me that could be done safely, and maybe with some good result" (AASP, Rome, Dec. 22, 1888).

suspicion, upon what transcends the measure of their small conservatism. . . .[31]

Throughout the article Keane gave abundant evidence to warrant the conclusion that he was sympathetic to all of Hecker's ideas even though some, as he said, would brand the founder of the Paulists as a "dangerous theorizer."

One of the objectives of Keane's visit to Europe in 1888 was the selection of a suitable staff of professors for the University. Hence, while in Rome he made inquiries about men whom competent authorities in Europe had recommended to him. Immediately after he had given an elaborate banquet at the American College in Rome to a select group of guests which included cardinals and news correspondents in celebration of the approval of the University's statutes,[32] the bishop set out on a tour of educational institutions to interview those who had been recommended to him or who had manifested an inclination to work in the United States. The search for professors took him to Pisa, Fiesole, Florence, Venice, Vienna, Munich, Fulda, Bonne, Cologne, Münster, Louvain, Liége, and Paris. Although at this time he selected some of the men who later formed the first staff of the Catholic University of America, they for the most part were not the ones upon whom his first choice would have fallen. He sought the most famous scholars in Europe but, unfortunately, they had no taste for an uncertain venture.[33] As he was going about in search of teachers, the rector added to his store of knowledge about university organization and administration and purchased some books and art treasures for the new institution.[34]

Having done what he could in Europe, Bishop Keane returned to the United States on May 5, 1889.[35] To the newspaper reporters who

[31] John J. Keane, "Father Hecker," *Catholic World,* XLIX (Apr., 1889), 1–9.

[32] Ellis, *The Formative Years,* pp. 347–348. Keane spoke in Latin and in French in reply to the speeches (Boston *Pilot,* Mar. 20, 1889). Extended and complimentary accounts of the banquet were carried in *Le Moniteur de Rome,* Mar. 20–21, 1889; *Osservatore Romano,* Mar. 20, 1889; *La Voce della Verità,* Mar. 20, 1889; Glascow *Herald,* Mar. 20, 1889; London *Tablet,* Mar. 30, 1889; Quebec *Morning Chronicle,* Apr. 20, 1889, and in many American papers.

[33] Ahern, *op. cit.,* pp. 10–25. The Rector wanted to offer a chair in the University to Alberto Lepidi, O.P., master of the Sacred Palace in Rome, who later gave the *imprimatur* to a book in which Keane was attacked, but, as he said to Ireland, "Riordon & Satolli both assailed the idea" (AASP, Rome, Dec. 22, 1888).

[34] ACUA, Garrigan Papers, Keane to Garrigan, Fulda, Apr. 5, 1889; ACUA, Keane Papers, Francis Jacquier to Keane, Paris, Apr. 24, 1889 (French); *ibid.,* Caen, Oct. 14, 1889 (French).

[35] Ahern, *op. cit.,* p. 25.

interviewed him at the dock in New York he gave once more a highly optimistic account of the future of the University and paid glowing tributes to the talents of the men selected for the faculty. Keane also seized the occasion for rebuking the critics who had construed the employment of European professors as evidence of an un-American sentiment on the part of the rector. The bishop protested his own patriotism and assured the American public that the Holy Father "fully appreciated that the American constitution contains the highest form of government for our country."[36] Three weeks later the *Church News* reported: "In Rome the Bishop was told that he was too loud in his admiration for America, to which he replied: 'Please God, I will never be less loud.' "[37] It was a view which the *Catholic Mirror* a few days later quoted Keane as having phrased in a slightly different way when he said: "During the past few years my duty has compelled me to cross the ocean four times, and I have never visited the old countries abroad that I haven't come back thanking God that I am an American."[38] Such expressions of Keane's patriotism found their way into the newspapers of Europe as well, and the strong statements which lauded American institutions and played down European systems helped to earn for him, in certain circles, the title of "Americanizer," a title in which he gloried, although to some minds it branded him as an enemy of the best interests of the Catholic Church.

While Keane was in Europe the University building program had been left in the capable hands of Philip Garrigan, the vice-rector. During that time the rector wrote to him frequently to make definite suggestions for changes in the building plans and to encourage his colleague to find a solution to such problems as supplying the institution with electric lights, gas, water, and heat.[39] The rector likewise looked ahead to the inauguration of the University in the fall of 1889 and here, too, he threw the burden of the remote preparation for the opening upon the shoulders of Garrigan.[40] The successful accomplishment of his mission in Europe and the progress made in constructing the buildings in Washington assured there would be no delay in the

[36] Ellis, *The Formative Years,* pp. 358–360. The *Commercial Advertiser* (New York), on May 6, 1889, had headlines reading, "A Foreign Faculty. No Americanism in the Catholic University."

[37] *Church News* (Washington), May 26, 1889.

[38] *Catholic Mirror* (Baltimore), June 1, 1889.

[39] ACUA, Garrigan Papers, Keane to Garrigan, Rome, Dec. 21, 1888; Jan. 22, 1889; Mar. 14, 1889.

[40] ACUA, Garrigan Papers, Keane to Garrigan, Rome, Mar. 14, 1889.

plans for beginning classes that fall. Hence, immediately after his return to the United States Keane began to visit seminaries of the East to speak of the advantages to be derived from the advanced theological courses that would be offered at the University to those who had completed their seminary training. After visiting the seminaries of Troy, Niagara, South Orange, New Jersey, Mount Saint Mary's in Emmitsburg, and Baltimore,[41] he returned to Washington to inspect the progress being made on Caldwell Hall,[42] and then continued his seminary visitations and his collecting tour in Philadelphia, Pittsburgh, Cincinnati,[43] Detroit, Notre Dame, Chicago, and Milwaukee. In all these places he described his reception as "most cordial," although the purpose of his mission was not strikingly fulfilled at any of his stops.[44]

While he was touring the country the rector wrote a short article on "The Clergy and the Catholic University" which was mainly an appeal for priest students and for the financial support of the clergy and of those whom the clerics could influence. He played on their pride as American priests and citizens by telling them:

> The clergy of the United States are an object of well deserved admiration to the universal Church. Their work during the century now closing stands almost without a parallel in ecclesiastical history, and they are rewarded not only with the grateful devotedness of their own people, but also with honor and praise from all the nations of the world.
>
> But the work accomplished forms only the foundations for the nobler work yet to come. The Church in America has only been preparing for the great part that she is to take in shaping the world's future. One need not be much of a diplomatist to recognize that America is giving tone and direction to the march of humanity; and one need not be a profound theologian and philosopher to see that on the influence of the Catholic Church in our country must it mainly depend that the direction given be wise and salutary.[45]

[41] ACUA, Garrigan Papers, Keane to Garrigan, Troy, New York, May 12, 1889.

[42] The rector was given a banquet at Welcker's Hotel in Washington on May 21, and on the evening of May 30 he was tendered a reception at Carroll Institute (Ellis, *The Formative Years,* pp. 361–362).

[43] *Catholic Mirror,* June 1, 1889.

[44] ACUA, Garrigan Papers, Keane to Garrigan, Cincinnati, June 6, 1889. Cf. also Keane to Garrigan, Notre Dame, June 13, 1889, and from Milwaukee, June 15, 1889.

[45] John J. Keane, "The Clergy and the Catholic University," *American Ecclesiastical Review,* I (July, 1889), 241–242. Thomas J. Shahan, a priest of the Diocese of Hartford, voiced this opinion about the clergy of the United States: "The noblest clergy on earth, all in all, is the clergy of the United States, and if only

He was so convinced of the importance of the University to the future of the Church in the United States that his statements at times may have been too sanguine, yet it must be remembered that essentially Keane was an optimistic man.

The inauguration of the Catholic University of America was planned for November 13, 1889, so as to take advantage of the large gathering expected in Baltimore during the preceding days for the celebration commemorating the centennial of the establishment of the hierarchy of the United States. Invitations were sent in advance to the hierarchy and to the leaders in various walks of life throughout the world and the rector engaged capable speakers for the occasion.[46] Keane kept the public informed of the progress that was made in erecting the building and of the work that was to occupy the professors and students when the University opened its doors.[47] Finally it was announced that Pope Leo XIII had chosen Archbishop Francesco Satolli as his representative for these celebrations.[48] This solution was a happy one so far as Keane was concerned, since he had come to know Satolli well when he was in Rome.[49] In a letter which conveyed the news to the rector, Edward A. Pace, a young priest of the Diocese of St. Augustine, who was in Europe preparing for the University faculty,[50] showed his mature judgment by making some observations about the Pope's rep-

---

we can fill up the deficiencies, we shall have the noblest the world ever saw, for, since the days of apostolic freedom, the world has never seen a time when the clergy and the people stood to each other as they do to-day in America. Hence our successes. Once let a certain policy, whose advancing foot is even now visible, obtain, and the apostolic and democratic simplicity of our first century will soon be a memory. This recalls to my mind that the present ablegate, Mgr. Satolli, once asked me if a Nuncio could not be appointed at Washington. Perhaps that unfortunate idea will crop up again, and a perpetual source of distrust, and a back-door government of the Church proposed as an ornament and utility to us who have made religion respectable, servatis servandis, in this age" (ACUA, Keane Papers, Shahan to Keane, Berlin, Oct. 10, 1889).

[46] Ellis, *The Formative Years,* pp. 375–385.

[47] ACUA, clippings.

[48] Ellis, *The Formative Years,* pp. 368–369. Francesco Satolli (1839–1910) was called to Rome by Leo XIII in 1880. He was appointed professor of dogmatic theology in the Propaganda and (1882) in the Roman Seminary, was rector of the Greek College (1884), president of the Academia dei Nobili Ecclesiastici (1886), and Archbishop of Lepanto (1888). Cf. Edward A. Pace, "Francesco Satolli," *Catholic Encyclopedia,* XIII, 486.

[49] Ahern, *op. cit.,* p. 8.

[50] Edward A. Pace had graduated in Rome with exceptional honors and he had been recommended to Keane for the University faculty by Leo XIII. The rector obtained his services from the Bishop of St. Augustine and sent him to Europe to pursue his studies further before he joined the faculty in 1891. Cf. Ahern, *op. cit.,* pp. 5–8, 50.

resentative, which in the light of later events proved remarkably accurate. He likewise suggested some interesting procedures that Keane followed with profit. Pace wrote:

> If we *must* have some one from Rome, he is about the best man they could send. From my knowledge of him, I think he is more sincere than the generality of Italians, and is rather an enthusiast for higher studies than a diplomat. No doubt you have had plenty of opportunities to measure him, and will know best how to fix him on the side of the University. Evidently this present mission is only a stepping-stone to something higher; and certainly Cardinal Satolli, either in the Propaganda or on the Congregation of Studies, will wield a mighty influence for, or against, the Catholic University. In any case, I think, considering his intimacy with the Pope, that his visit may have important consequences, not only for our new Institute, but for the whole American Church. He is very anxious, I am told, to meet me in Paris, not yet knowing that I have quit that city. I regret very much losing this opportunity, as I might have told him some plain truths. But of course you will arrange things for the best, so as to render superfluous what I have now to say.
>
> Satolli is a metaphysician, and he knows it: as a result, he is easily advised by others in practical matters. Again, this is the first visit he has ever made to a foreign country, and he will be open to all sorts of impressions. So long as he remains near the Cardinal or yourself or any of the right-minded Bishops, there is nothing to fear. But if he travels around, he may possibly pick up notions, for which an antidote should be provided. He knows American *students,* better than he does American Bishops; and he listens readily to what students say. Now the greater part of his former disciples are in New York, and his favorite, Dr. Hanna, is in the worst quarter of N.Y. I believe Hanna is right himself; but there's no telling what ideas he might *under instruction,* put into Satolli's head. Then, naturally, New York must be visited; perhaps a reception by the "Alumni Association" etc., etc. Possibly nothing may be done or said *directly* against the University — it would be poor policy to do so; but you know how a sneer, or a shrug of indifference opens up little cracks of mistrust through which suspicion creeps. The mere absence of enthusiasm in such a city as New York is a danger which should be guarded against. By keeping the right sort of men at Satolli's side, you can make sure that the favorable impression produced upon him at the opening ceremonies is not altered.
>
> If there is question of sending an American Priest round as his companion, it may be further suggested that one of his former students be selected for the position. In that case, the most trustworthy men

are those at Overbrook. Both Fisher and Kennedy know him well, and both are good men. I heartily trust that the dangers to which I have alluded, are rather imaginary than probable. It is only after due consideration of the circumstances, and after consulting Dr. Shahan, that I venture to make these suggestions, hoping that what is here respectfully submitted may save Mgr. Satolli and yourself from possible annoyance. . . .[51]

This sage advice helped to keep the University and its rector from "annoyance" on the occasion of this first visit of Satolli to the United States.

From November 10 to 12 the university rector was lost among the throng of prelates in Baltimore for the centennial. But on November 13 his eclipse had passed and he became one of the central figures in the ceremonies that accompanied the inauguration of the Catholic University of America.[52] As rector of the University, John J. Keane enjoyed at that time a popularity and prestige known to few bishops in the United States but, at the same time, the position carried commensurate burdens that few American prelates would have been willing or qualified to shoulder.

The story of Keane's life from 1889 to 1896 is largely the story of the development of the University.[53] He became so closely identified with the institution during those seven years that people began to call it "Bishop Keane's University."[54] It was not a misnomer in the sense that the first rector gave of himself and his talents unselfishly and unstintingly to bring to fruition the high ideals that he envisioned for the institution. During the first years of the University's life he was careful to seek the expert advice of the faculty he had chosen to join with him in the work. He encouraged these men to employ their

[51] ACUA, Keane Papers, Pace to Keane, Leipzig, Oct. 4, 1889. The Dr. Shahan referred to by Pace was Thomas J. Shahan, a priest of the Diocese of Hartford, who was in Europe preparing for a chair in the University.

[52] Ellis, *The Formative Years,* pp. 383–390. On this occasion Keane received an honorary doctorate in divinity from Laval University which had been brought to Washington by Monsignor Benjamin Paquet, the rector (New York *Freeman's Journal and Catholic Register,* Nov. 16, 1889). One of the guests at the inauguration complained to his diary: "The dignitaries had dinner. All under superiors of orders and rectors of Colleges had a wretched lunch. Dr. McSweeny and I returned to Baltimore after the disgraceful lunch: 200 priests and 100 laymen served by five waiters to coffee, and celery salad and bones of turkey" (AANY, Burtsell's Diary, Nov. 13, 1889).

[53] Ahern, *op. cit., passim.*

[54] *Seventh Annual Report of the Rector of the Catholic University of America, March, 1896* (Washington, 1896), p. 13.

aptitudes for the greatest advantage of the priest students and to evolve the best means for preparing them to satisfy the expectations of their bishops. The students' manifest interest in the work elicited frequent words of praise from Keane, while his great patience in the numerous discussions of his colleagues about academic and administrative problems won for him their respect.

In his relations with the members of the Board of Trustees, Keane was always evident as the promoter and the leader. It was he who made the recommendations which were calculated to advance the best interests of the University. Time after time he was forced to remind the trustees that the University was not his work alone, but his only in so far as he represented the choice of the board as the director of their institution. It must have been a difficult task to face the trustees year after year and to beg for financial and moral support as well as to plead for students to fill the classrooms. It was not that the members of the board were unsympathetic to the rector, but rather that they were so preoccupied with the responsibilities of their own dioceses that they had little time to give to the business of a university.

Finances, students, and academic progress were the chief concerns of Bishop Keane during his tenure of office. Each year he recommended that a general collection be taken up throughout the country for the benefit of the University and each year it was just as regularly voted down by the trustees. Hence, it fell to him to raise funds to keep the institution on a sound financial basis. Because there was an annual deficit in the current running expenses he borrowed from his experience in the financially embarrassed Diocese of Richmond to begin three organizations, called the Divinity Fund Association,[55] the University Fund Association, and the Chapel Fund Association, which helped to solve the problem. It was largely owing to Keane's efforts that at the end of his administration over $640,000 was invested from endowments for twelve chairs and thirteen scholarships and that the University was free from all debt.

In an effort to increase the enrollment at the University, Keane usually visited the seminaries of the country late in the spring to make the clerical students conscious of the need in the United States for a more thoroughly and broadly trained clergy. He wrote the letters

[55] To obtain priest members for the Association Keane found that personal autograph letters were more effective. He claimed: "I find a firm and general conviction that circulars are of no use, — priests especially will not heed them" (ACUA, Garrigan Papers, Keane to Garrigan, Boston, Oct. 25, [1890]).

which Cardinal Gibbons, as the chancellor of the University, sent to the bishops of the country each year urging them to give some of their subjects the advantages of graduate training. During Keane's administration there were never more than thirty-eight students residing in Caldwell Hall and during one year there were only twenty-six.[56] It was strong evidence of the failure of the hierarchy to use their institution for higher studies, and it was sufficient reason for the rector to be concerned about the future of the University. When it was decided to admit lay students in the fall of 1895, he was obliged to speak in many of the colleges of the nation to enkindle interest and to recruit the pioneer students. But response was disheartening, for only fifty-four reported to the various classes.

It was Keane's aim from the outset to found a complete university with all the faculties. He began with the Faculty of Theology which he was obliged to staff with foreign professors until American priests could be equipped by graduate training in European universities to replace them. He planned to add the Faculties of Philosophy and of Social Science shortly after the University had been inaugurated, but six years elapsed before the goal was fulfilled. The delay was due partly to the difficulty experienced in obtaining funds as a result of the Panic of 1893, and partly to a fear that there would not be sufficient lay students for the various courses to justify the monetary outlay. It was the rector's optimism, plus a large donation from Father James McMahon of New York, that finally won out when the business-minded trustees cautioned delay in enlarging the institution. Even then he added only two new schools during his administration.

As the Rector of the Catholic University of America and in his own right as a genial personality, Keane was shown many courtesies by university men. Charles W. Eliot, president of Harvard, invited him to deliver the famous Dudleian Lecture at that institution on October 23, 1890,[57] and three years later Eliot conferred the honorary doctorate of laws upon him.[58] At another time when one of the pro-

[56] For an interesting study of the inner life of the University and short sketches on some students enrolled in the academic year 1893–1894, cf. Henry J. Browne, "Pioneer Days at the Catholic University of America," *Catholic Educational Review,* XLVIII (Jan., Feb., 1950), 29–38, 96–103.

[57] ACUA, Keane Papers, Eliot to Keane, Cambridge, June 17, 1890; New York *Sun,* Oct. 24, 1890. For excerpts from a lecture which the rector delivered at Harvard on February 10, 1892, on "The Principles Taught by History," cf. *American Catholic Historical Researches,* XII (July, 1895), 197.

[58] Ahern, *op. cit.,* p. 67. On the occasion Eliot spoke of Keane as "virum eruditissimum, oratorem suave loquentem" (Kimball C. Elkins, assistant in the Harvard University Archives, to the author, Cambridge, Oct. 28, 1953).

fessors at Princeton heard that the Washington rector was scheduled to visit in the New England states he wrote:

> Mr. Marquand joins me in an earnest request for this visit. In staying with us you would see the working of a sort of Protestant monastery, for we two keep house together, surrounded by several thousand books, photographs, slides and the other implements of our work. We would give you a right cordial welcome, and all Princeton would do the same. . . . Our house is open to you at any time.[59]

Professional courtesy was again shown to Keane by secular educators when preparations were being made for the third annual convention of the College Association of the Middle States and Maryland to be held at Cornell University in November, 1891. Andrew D. White, president of Cornell, wrote the bishop a warm personal letter and invited him to be his guest. He told Keane that he was expecting "our common friend, President Gilman," to be with him at the same time,[60] and a short time later the president of Johns Hopkins University expressed his desire to travel to the convention in Keane's company.[61]

The rector's popularity was evidenced by the numerous requests he received to grace pulpits and platforms throughout the United States. Because of his clear, logical, and inspiring presentation of many subjects, the bishop always drew large crowds and attracted attention that was favorable to himself, but more important in his mind, to the institution he directed.

Keane and his professors co-operated to make the new institution a part of Washington's educational life by giving lectures which were open to the public. Since the rector was not a stranger to the people

59 ACUA, Keane Papers, Arthur L. Frothingham Jr. to Keane, Princeton, Jan. 7, 1890.

60 ACUA, Keane Papers, White to Keane, Ithaca, New York, Oct. 20, 1891. Keane read a paper on "The Idea and Scope of the Faculty of Philosophy" at the second annual convention of the College Association of the Middle Atlantic States and Maryland held on November 28 and 29, 1890, in Murray Hall, Princeton (ACUA, copy of *Proceedings*).

61 ACUA, Keane Papers, Gilman to Keane, Baltimore, Nov. 15, 1891. The rector's ability and personality also won the respect of men on the national scene. G. Brown Goode, assistant secretary of the Smithsonian Institution, wrote: "I know that you have been interested in the project for a Pan-Republic Congress, and have been consulted in regard to the address to the peoples of the world. . . . Would you be willing to look it [the address] over in its present form, and make freely any criticisms or suggestions which may occur to you?" (ACUA, Keane Papers, Goode to Keane, Washington, Nov. 4, 1891.)

of Washington, his lectures on various topics[62] were considered of special interest by the local journals.[63] On two occasions he preached in the chamber of the United States Senate. His funeral oration over the remains of Senator John Strode Barbour of Virginia was the first such eulogy in the history of the United States delivered by a Catholic bishop in that chamber. Members of the Congress, Supreme Court, cabinet, and diplomatic corps were present for the bishop's sermon which was "delivered in a clear, sonorous voice with all the grace and emotion of a pulpit orator." In it he explained that although the late senator was not a Catholic he had "expressed his desire and intention of becoming a Catholic" before his sudden death in Washington.[64] A faint note of censure could be detected in a contemporary's account of the event in which he stated: "The Church has been more liberal to the great men like Sherman, Barbour, Barrett and Florence, than to her own less fortunate members." The commentator continued by saying that if poorer men had led such lives they would have been held up as a terrible example and warning.[65] When the Roman authorities heard about Keane's sermon, Miecislaus Cardinal Ledochowski, prefect of the Propaganda, asked an explanation of Cardinal Gibbons concerning the circumstances under which the rector had taken part in the services.[66] In his reply, Gibbons indicated that Barbour was a catechumen who had died suddenly before a priest could be called and that Keane had taken particular care to elucidate the Church's discipline on catechumens and that both the sermon and the prayers

[62] The rector lectured on the following subjects during his time at the University: Jan. 29, Feb. 12, Feb. 19, 1890—"Herbert Spencer's 'First Principles'"; Oct. 8, 1890—"Statement and Nature of the Problem of Christian Education"; Oct. 15, 1890—"Difficulties of the Problem, and its Solution"; Mar. 4, 1891—"Edward Arnold's 'Light of the World'"; Nov. 19, 1891—"Leo XIII and the Social Problems of the Day"; Nov. 17, 1892—"The 'Rights of Man' in the Old World"; Nov. 24, 1892—"The Rights of Man in the New World"; Nov. 9, 1893—"Father Mathew's Apostolate in the Future" (First Annual Father Mathew Lecture); Nov. 8, 1894—"The Two World-Philosophies"; Jan., 1895—"The Philosophy of Literature." This list was compiled from the circulars announcing the lectures. Only the lecture delivered on November 24, 1892, was found during a thorough search of the ACUA, where the circulars are preserved.

[63] Washington *Star,* Feb. 7, 13, 20, 1890; Washington *Post,* Mar. 5, 1891. J. E. Rankin, president of Howard University, told Keane that he had attended the lecture on October 15, 1890, and he commented: "There was much in it that delighted me" (ACUA, Keane Papers, Rankin to Keane, Washington, Nov. 4, 1890).

[64] Smith, *op. cit.,* pp. 64–65. Also cf. Reily, *op. cit.,* II, 590 and Ahern, *op. cit.,* pp. 65–66.

[65] Reily, *op. cit.,* II, 590.

[66] AAB, 89-Y-9, Ledochowski to Gibbons, Rome, June 27, 1892 [French].

said by Father Cornelius Gillespie, S.J., had been previously approved by him.[67] On January 12, 1893, the bishop made his second appearance in the Senate chamber when he preached at the funeral service for the late Senator John E. Kenna of West Virginia, who was described by a Catholic chronicler as "a self-made man, Irishman and Catholic, honest, able, popular."[68]

Keane also spoke frequently outside the city of Washington. The president of the University of Notre Dame wrote in 1890: "Our faculty and students, having heard you last year, are — as men of taste might be expected to be — extremely anxious to enjoy the same pleasure again."[69] He accepted the invitation and delivered a lecture on "Christian Patriotism" in which he told his audience that "toleration is the watchword of American citizens — Catholic and non-Catholic. Catholics believe in the motto, 'Union in essentials, tolerance in non-essentials, charity to all.' Catholics are not opposed to state schools, but to unchristian state schools."[70] The Indianapolis *Journal* gave its approval to the University's rector by stating:

> That the Right Reverend John Keane, . . . is a man of remarkably clear prevision and exquisite tact is amply evidenced by his lecture on "Christian Patriotism." . . . With its large German following in Wisconsin, Illinois and a few other states displaying a stubborn inclination to drag it into politics, these be troublous times for the Catholic Church in America, and it needs just such men as Bishop Keane to pilot it through what promises to be a dangerous crisis.[71]

At approximately the same time an article entitled "Loyalty to Rome and Country" appeared from Keane's pen, containing the ideas embodied in his lecture, which Bernard O'Reilly, author of the life of *John McHale, Archbishop of Tuam,* thought to be so valuable that "it ought to be printed separately and circulated widely in town and country all over the United States, and by every channel of publicity we can avail ourselves of."[72]

[67] AAB, 90-A-8, Gibbons to Ledochowski, Baltimore, July 10, 1892 (French in Ireland's hand). It was also stated that shortly before his death Barbour attended a public banquet on Friday and refused to eat meat. In America such an act was a real confession of faith.

[68] Reily, *op. cit.,* II, 401–404; III, Part II, p. 29. Cf. *Catholic Mirror,* Jan. 21, 1894; Washington *Post,* Jan. 12, 13, 14, 21, 1894; James Thomas Curtis, "John Edward Kenna, A Sketch of a Brief Political Career" (unpublished master's thesis, Dept. of History, Catholic University of America, 1948).

[69] ACUA, Keane Papers, J. E. Walsh to Keane, Notre Dame, Feb. 22, 1890.

[70] New York *Herald,* June 1, 1890.

[71] Indianapolis *Journal,* June 7, 1890.

[72] ACUA, Keane Papers, O'Reilly to Keane, New Jersey, July 30, 1890.

Following a lecture which Keane had given before a large audience in Buffalo early in 1891 he received indications of the effect of his public statements upon some of his brother bishops. Cardinal Gibbons wrote: "Allow me to congratulate you on the splendid address you made in Buffalo, and its excellent effect on the large audience."[73] Richard Gilmour, Bishop of Cleveland, told him:

> If we all were as kindly frank and boldly outspoken as you we would be better off. With you I feel that we are much in the background. As well because we do not shoulder up to each other, as because we do not take our place among our fellow citizens. Thank God you and some few others are helping manfully to remedy the latter.[74]

John Ireland said: "Let me congratulate you on what I read as coming from yourself, whether in Washington or elsewhere. You are growing daily into a great Catholic thinker. The best service done of late years to the Church in America was the pulling you out from the obscure corner in Richmond."[75]

According to contemporary accounts Keane must have been an interesting and powerful orator. A professor of elocution and oratory at the University of Michigan told the bishop: "I have had occasion several times since your excellent address here[76] to commend your style of oratory to my classes as being the most finished and most direct of any we have had since I came."[77] Another educator was reported to have said that "he could sit at the feet of such a man as Bp. Keane and learn as he had heard him lecture at Harvard."[78] After

[73] ACUA, Keane Papers, Gibbons to Keane, Baltimore, Feb. 28, 1891.

[74] ACUA, Keane Papers, Gilmour to Keane, Cleveland, Jan. 10, 1891.

[75] ACUA, Keane Papers, Ireland to Keane, St. Paul, Mar. 30, 1891. A few years later a gentleman expressed the opinion: "If there were a dozen men like Bishop Keane to travel over the country to call out the people, thousands could be brought into the Church" (AUND, Brownson Papers, William Richards to Henry F. Brownson, Washington, Dec. 13, 1893).

[76] The rector lectured at the University of Michigan in May, 1891 (ACUA, Garrigan Papers, Keane to Garrigan, Detroit, May 11, 1891).

[77] ACUA, Keane Papers, T. C. Trueblood to Keane, Ann Arbor, June 10, 1891. After the bishop had addressed a large gathering of students of Brown University on "Philosophic Thought at the End of the Century," the Providence *Journal* reported: "The address was the best heard in Sayles' Hall for a long time" (*Church News,* Nov. 9, 1895).

[78] AAB, 92-K-5, Sylvester Malone to Gibbons, Brooklyn, Aug. 31, 1893. The chairman of the Kent Club, made up of students from Yale's law school, told Gibbons: "Five years at Yale have proved to me the need of such a revelation as was Archbishop [*sic*] Keane's lecture two years ago" (BCA, Unclassified, M[atthew] A. Reynolds to Gibbons, New Haven, Nov. 15, 1893). Bishop Keane had lectured before this club on "The Church and the Social Problems of the Day" on February

the rector had lectured on "Pope Leo XIII and Social Problems" before the Brooklyn Institute of Arts and Sciences in March, 1892, a reporter stated:

> As might be expected in one of such a nature his voice is clear and powerful, and his utterances incisive and intensely affirmative. His gestures, like his voice, reveal the same force of mind. To see him illustrating the word "relationship" by revolving the hands around one another, or the phrase, "the throbbing multitude" by wavelike movements, is to realize the expressiveness of mute language. . . . Those who have heard him speak say that when he is free of emotion he will put his fingers together as if thought were within them, twist them around several times simultaneously with the moulding of his idea, and then throw the palms wide open. When he does so everybody present realizes with the utmost certainty the import of his language. . . .
>
> The bishop is almost Delsartian in the philosophic sense of the word. He is calm, resolute, and vigorous. His aggressions reveal keen discernment and are marked by a princely nobility of purpose. His outbursts, when vehement, have the dynamic force of the cataract, but without splash or spray. He annihilates the victim of his reproach, whether physical or mental, without any shock to his own equanimity. Some orators swing and distort the body in many ways and wriggle the arms with every word. Bishop Keane deals his blows but apparently experiences no rebound. This is owing to his consummate self-control. In a word he is an orator, and one which any nation, clime or age, may be well proud to claim.[79]

In reporting one of the rector's lectures on another occasion, a writer in the Worcester *Spy* said:

> Bishop Keane is an orator to whom it is a pleasure to listen. His presence is dignified and gracious, his voice, clear, musical and penetrating, his enunciation distinct, his manner animated and engaging. The style of his address was controversial, but quite free from discourtesy, harsh judgment or invective. His rhetoric was admirable and his reasoning ingenious and forceful.[80]

Bishop Keane was also lauded for his outstanding ability when he

---

26, 1892 (ACUA, Keane Papers, William A. McQuaid to Keane, New Haven, Nov. 11, 1891 — on letter in Keane's hand, "Lecture delivered February 26, 1892").

[79] *Catholic Review,* Mar. 12, 1892. The bishop delivered an address before this group again in 1893 on "The Great Lessons Taught by History" (New York *World,* Feb. 3, 1893).

[80] Worcester *Spy,* Jan. 24, 1890.

lectured in the French language. In the *Revue Catholique de Bordeaux* a feature writer ventured this opinion:

> Very rarely have I had the opportunity of hearing such magnificent speech. It is not that you meet therein sonorous, emphatic passages with which many so-called orators bore their listeners. The eloquence of Monsignor Keane is essentially *real*. The deep impression it makes comes from the *things* said with simplicity, all the more perfect since those things are most important in themselves. . . . And what a surprising command of our language! Were it not for the accent which is strongly American, sentence structure is such, the appropriateness of diction is so excellent that one would think he were listening to the loftiest national eloquence. And beneath that distinguished demeanor marked with cold reserve, we feel the beat of a generous heart and the radiation of our Faith in all its splendor.[81]

On the other hand, a seminarian who heard the rector talk during this period of his career observed: "He's not a speaker, as Ryan, nor an essayist like Spalding, and I don't think he has the intellectual ability of either, but he's practical, outspoken, unpretending, and is the best man in my humble opinion they could have at the head of the University."[82] A more competent judge, John Cavanaugh, C.S.C., however, after speaking of Bishop John B. Fitzpatrick of Boston as a noted convert-maker and attributing his success in that work "to a remarkable group of intellectual gifts, a mind of much earnestness and seriousness and a gift of massive speech," claimed that "among the bishops of the modern period only one can be compared to him in these respects. That one is Archbishop John Keane. . . . His inspirational power was exceptional, and has been equalled only, so far as I have observed, by that of Archbishops Ireland and John Lancaster Spalding."[83] Again, Walter Elliott, C.S.P., an intimate friend of the bishop during most of his active career, observed:

> And what a treat it was to talk and listen in his company! He knew

[81] *Revue Catholique de Bordeaux,* Oct. 10, 1894, cited by *Catholic University Bulletin,* I (Jan., 1895), 90–91. A Paul Bourget made some flattering remarks about Keane in the *Figaro* (Paris) and the New York *Herald* (cited by *Church News,* Nov. 3, 1894).

[82] ACUA, Hyvernat Papers, James R. Mahoney to James Driscoll, Rome, Feb. 28, 1889. In "Pen-Pictures of the American Hierarchy," Merwin-Marie Snell observed that Keane was "more learned, probably, than either Archbishop Ireland, or his official superior, Cardinal Gibbons" (New York *Independent,* Apr. 27, 1893).

[83] John Cavanaugh, C.S.C., "Catholic Orators and Rhetoricians," *Catholic Builders of the Nation* (Boston, 1923), IV, 353.

> everything about religion, and he was gifted to impart it, as men are rarely gifted.
>
> The Archbishop's very extensive learning was wonderfully accurate, was maturely pondered, and was dispensed with fascinating kindliness. Yet he was anything but a conversational glutton — never interrupting, never unwilling to be himself interrupted. And what he uttered in his beautiful flowing style might well be printed without the least intrusion of the editor. He was always vivacious but never excited; not even in his most energetic public discourse did he ever lose that air of self-mastery which distinguishes the higher grade of eloquence.[84]

It was this remarkable power to express himself with unusual clarity and forcefulness, as well as his unlimited energy, boundless enthusiasm, transparent faith, and optimistic outlook on life, which brought Bishop Keane great popularity and respect among all classes of people. At the same time the institution which he represented greatly profited from his selfless use of his personal assets; in fact, it was principally owing to his personal popularity and resourcefulness that the venture gained sympathy and support during the first years. Moreover, in him the Catholic Church had an effective voice to carry its ageless message in words that penetrated the hearts of many in a materialistic and confused generation.

After the University's work was under way, Keane continued to use his oratorical abilities to promote the temperance movement. He preached at the opening of the twentieth national convention of the Catholic Total Abstinence Union of America in St. Paul's Cathedral in Pittsburgh on August 6, 1890,[85] and again, in August, 1891, he delivered the sermon at the opening of the national convention of the union in St. Patrick's Church in Washington.[86] On the second occasion he told his audience:

> . . . There has risen up in the land an evil that brings the blush of shame even upon the face of mother church itself, and there has also risen up a powerful army who are asking what they can do to down the demon of sin and misery and wretchedness. It is a noble thing this fighting valiantly for the love of humanity with this one sin

[84] Walter Elliott, C.S.P., "Personal Reminiscences of Archbishop Keane," *Catholic World*, CVII (Aug., 1918), 643.

[85] Ahern, *op. cit.*, p. 62.

[86] *Proceedings of the Twenty-First Annual Convention of the Catholic Total Abstinence Union of America, Washington, August 5–6, 1891*, in bound volumes entitled *Miscellanea de temperantia* (Mullen Library, The Catholic University of America), IV, 32–41.

> that is the parent of thousands and tens of thousands of other sins. Love is not true love that knows not how to be indignant; not the indignation born of anger or of hatred, but born of love of God.[87]

When the delegates to this convention met for their business session in the Academy of Music in Washington, the apparent endorsement of prohibition called forth a long debate, which only ended when Keane received permission from the chairman to speak. He said:

> I arise to address you as a friend of peace. No cause like this can get along without legislative help. We cannot ignore politics in one sense of the word. The commandments of God and the law of man must work together. The Church and State must work together; not after the old idea of amalgamation, but by the mingling of views upon those things affecting and operating upon human society. These resolutions bring in the important questions of labor and trade unions and the liquor traffic. We must meet them, but you must remember that you are handling dynamite. Your endorsement of labor unions must be carefully worded so as not to indorse modern socialism and ideas which no good Catholic can indorse.[88]

After an editorial had appeared in the *Catholic Total Abstinence News* urging that the friends of temperance support a paper for the dissemination of good literature which would be beneficial to the cause, the rector told the editor:

> If you know, dear sir, that there is any man endowed with the necessary ability and energy to practically inaugurate the work and push it on, I beg that no endeavors will be spared to secure his services and to see that he is supplied with the necessary means for putting the work into proper shape. Should it, as I trust, be thus undertaken, you can count on me as a friend and helper in every way in my power.[89]

As a partial fulfillment of his promise he wrote an eight-page article entitled "The Church is Against the Saloon," which appeared in *Temperance Truth*.[90] Because of his popularity among temperance workers, he was called upon to speak at a mass meeting of the convention of the Catholic Total Abstinence Union at Carnegie Hall, New York, after the scheduled speakers, especially the politicians Theodore Roosevelt

[87] *Evening Star* (Washington), Aug. 5, 1891.

[88] Washington *Post*, Aug. 7, 1891.

[89] Keane to the editor of the *Catholic Total Abstinence News*, Washington, June 4, 1892, cited in *Miscellanea de temperantia*, V, 12.

[90] John J. Keane, "The Church is Against the Saloon," *Temperance Truth*, Feb., 1893.

and Thomas C. O'Sullivan, had made it a lively affair.[91] In the same year, 1895, he was invited by the citizens of Buffalo, "irrespective of nationality or religious or political preferences,"[92] to address a mass meeting in the Music Hall there in an endeavor to check the spread of intemperance and to arouse public opinion so that the Sunday liquor law would be enforced. Sharing the platform with Theodore Roosevelt on this occasion, he spoke on "The Relation of Civil Legislation to Sunday Observance," which was a logical presentation of the purpose of civil legislation on this question.[93]

Besides exerting his influence in the temperance field, the bishop was an active participant in many ecclesiastical celebrations. He delivered the sermon at the dedication by Cardinal Gibbons of St. Joseph's Church in Washington on January 18, 1891. When the rector spoke at the laying of the cornerstone of the Church of the Holy Name in the same city that fall, he was quoted as having said:

> We will not come here to abuse Episcopalians, Presbyterians, or Methodists, but will worship God according to our faith, minding our own business and expecting our neighbors to do the same. The Church is one of universal charity, and instead of abusing the neighbors that do not agree with us in matters of faith we can but say, Brothers, though you do not serve God in our way, serve Him the best you know how in your own way.[94]

In Baltimore in that year, Keane delivered the sermon at the dedication of Calvert Hall and the unveiling of the Calvert Statue. The bishop told his listeners: "No narrowness or bigotry will ever be taught here. This school would be unworthy to receive the name of Calvert Hall if any bitterness should rule here. Here shall be taught the motto of the Fathers: 'In essentials, unity; in what is doubtful,

[91] Bland, *op. cit.*, pp. 197–202. After the meeting Roosevelt told Ireland that he and the mayor of New York had asked Keane to speak (AASP, New York, Aug. 19, 1895). In a letter to his sister on December 17, 1893, Theodore Roosevelt wrote: "Another evening we dined with the Storers, to meet divers Mick ecclesiastics; among others Bishop Keane whom I like." *The Letters of Theodore Roosevelt,* ed. Elting E. Morison (Cambridge, 1951), I, 343.

[92] Washington *Post,* Aug. 7, 1895.

[93] The lecture was later printed under the title *The Catholic Church and the American Sunday* (Buffalo, 1895). The Buffalo *Catholic Union and Times* reported on September 19, 1895, that "ministers of all denominations rubbed elbows with Catholic priests, and all were moved with the spirit of the great occasion." It added: "Bishop Keane displayed a magnificent voice and fine elocution in the delivery of his address, which was frequently interrupted by applause."

[94] Baltimore *Sun,* Oct. 19, 1891.

liberty, and in all things, charity.' "[95] Shortly after he had attended the centennial celebration of St. Mary's Seminary where he had been ordained twenty-five years before,[96] the University's rector delivered the sermon in the Baltimore cathedral when Placide L. Chapelle, pastor of St. Matthew's Church in Washington and a fellow student at St. Mary's Seminary, was consecrated by Gibbons as Coadjutor Archbishop of Santa Fe.[97] In the same city Keane preached at St. Vincent de Paul Church on the second day of the golden jubilee celebration of the foundation of the parish,[98] and again in Baltimore in 1893, when the cornerstone of St. John's Male School was laid.[99]

Keane did not confine his attendance at ecclesiastical functions to Washington and the surrounding area. When the Archdiocese of New Orleans celebrated its centennial in 1893, he spoke in French at the banquet in the Royal Hotel, and Francis Janssens, Archbishop of New Orleans, who had been vicar-general of the Diocese of Richmond during Keane's regime, noted in his diary that the bishop "spoke splendidly."[100] This appearance in New Orleans in a French address served as an introduction to the priests of that archdiocese who at a later date would desire him for their archbishop. The rector also became better known to the Catholics on the Pacific coast through his talks on the University and its work,[101] and San Francisco citizens especially benefited from his visit to the Far West, when in 1894 he gave a week's mission at St. Mary's Cathedral which received flattering publicity and was attended by large crowds.[102] Some of the people of the Middle

[95] Reily, *op. cit.*, II, 212. Keane had received some of his early training at Calvert Hall, cf. *supra*, p. 7.

[96] Reily, *op. cit.*, II, 150. John J. Kain, Bishop of Wheeling and classmate of Keane, who preached the sermon on the occasion, was one of the few to felicitate the rector on the occasion of the quiet celebration of his twenty-fifth anniversary as a priest (ACUA, Keane Papers, Kain to Keane, Wheeling, June 30, 1891). Garrigan also had sent silver jubilee greetings to Keane, who was resting in Far Rockaway, New York. In reply the bishop wrote: "The good priest here knows nothing of it, so the peace is without a ripple.

"The dear Master knows how much He must condone in the past — and He knows how completely my poor future is in the hands of His Providence — with no will of mine in regard to it. But may He, in His loving mercy, leave me where and what I am now, till He is pleased to grant His servant more quiet and peace" (ACUA, Garrigan Papers, Keane to Garrigan, Far Rockaway, New York, July 2, 1891).

[97] AAB, Gibbons' Diary, Nov. 1, 1891.

[98] Reily, *op. cit.*, II, 228–229. Cf. *supra*, p. 6, for a sketch on the parish and Keane's connection with it.

[99] Reily, *op. cit.*, III, Part I, 26–27.

[100] AANO, Diary of the Archdiocese of New Orleans, 1888–1896, Apr. 25, 1894.

[101] ADR, Keane to O'Connell, Washington, Jan. 5, 1894.

[102] San Francisco *Chronicle*, Feb. 12, 13, 15, 19, 1894. A former student said that

West learned to know Keane better at the time of the great jubliee celebration of Archbishop Peter Richard Kenrick in the fall of the year 1891. On this occasion all the visiting prelates were tendered a reception by the members of the St. Louis Exchange, and Keane addressed the group along with Gibbons, Ireland, and Ryan.[103]

While the archbishops were gathered in St. Louis, they held their annual meeting and agreed, among other things, to have a Catholic Congress in Chicago in 1893 in connection with the World's Columbian Exposition. It was decided that the subject matter to be treated by the congress should be mainly the social question, as suggested by Leo XIII's encyclical *Rerum novarum,* which had been issued the previous May, and there would be added the question of Catholic education and the present condition of the Holy Father *vis-à-vis* the Italian government. Keane was named by Gibbons as one of a committee of nine to supervise all the details.[104] The historian of the World's Columbian Exposition maintained that "the most imposing of all the denominational Congresses was that held by the Catholic Church."[105] Keane helped to make it imposing by reading a paper on "Catholic Higher Education," in which he developed the reasoning behind the conclusion that moral and religious training were abso-

---

the Far West ordinarily heard very little about the University except through the eastern papers (ACUA, Bouquillon Papers, Peter C. Yorke to Bouquillon, San Francisco, Apr. 29, 1892).

[103] Reily, *op. cit.,* II, 231. In 1896 Keane again preached in St. Louis when his friend, John J. Kain, received the pallium from the hands of Gibbons in the old St. Louis Cathedral (*ibid.,* IV, 517). The bishop also gave the sermon on the occasion of the golden jubilee celebration of Fathers Sylvester Malone and P. P. Dennis, S.S. (*Church News,* Oct. 20, 1894; New York *Sun,* Oct. 15, 1894). For the text of the sermon delivered at Malone's golden jubilee, cf. Sylvester L. Malone (ed.), *Memorial of the Golden Jubilee of the Rev. Sylvester Malone* (Brooklyn, 1895), pp. 89–98. He was also asked to preach on the second day of Archbishop John Joseph Williams' golden jubilee celebration (*Church News,* May 11, 1895).

[104] AAB, 89-D-5/1, Minutes of Meeting of Second Annual Conference of Archbishops, St. Louis, Nov. 29, 1891. AUND, Onahan Papers, Keane to William J. Onahan, Washington, June 6, 1892, gives the list of the laymen Keane had selected to prepare papers for the congress. Keane had written an exceptionally penetrating article on the encyclical *Rerum novarum* shortly after it had been published. Cf. John J. Keane, "The Encyclical 'Rerum novarum,'" *American Catholic Quarterly Review,* XVI (July, 1891), 595–611. In another article Keane attempted to demonstrate that "the efforts of social reformers can never succeed in their laudable purpose without the co-operation of religion and the church." Cf. John J. Keane, "The Catholic Church and Economics," *Quarterly Journal of Economics,* VI (Oct., 1891), 25–46.

[105] Rossiter Johnson (ed.), *A History of the World's Columbian Exposition held in Chicago in 1893* (New York, 1897–1898), IV, 331.

lutely necessary if an educational system was to be considered complete.[106] He also participated in the International Congress of Education of the World's Columbian Exposition and addressed the third session of the general assembly, which had as its theme "The Relation of Our Colleges and Universities to the Advancement of Civilization."[107] Furthermore, the bishop was assigned by Cardinal Gibbons and the archbishops the leading role in arranging for the Catholic participation in the World's Parliament of Religions, held from September 11 to September 28, 1893, as a department of the World's Congress Auxiliary of the Columbian Exposition at Chicago.[108]

There were times between 1889 and 1896 when alarming reports about Keane's health caused deep concern among those who regarded him as the chief hope for the University's success. When he sustained slight injuries in a railroad accident in 1890, which required a short period of hospitalization, some European papers reported him dead. The incident drew forth a number of comments indicating the high regard in which he was held throughout the world. Denis J. O'Connell, rector of the American College in Rome, told Keane: "I was truly touched by the devotion of Cardinal Manning. He was not able to give me the news of his fright without being moved with the deepest emotion." He added: "Had anything serious happened, what a change it would make in our American Church and for me."[109] When Maurice F. Burke, Bishop of Cheyenne, heard the news in Rome he wrote: "Bishop Keane will be an immense loss to the Church in America and an irreparable loss to the Catholic University,"[110] and a number of American bishops expressed their relief when they learned that his injuries were not serious.[111]

During the summer of 1890, Bishop Keane once more experienced impairment of his eyesight. So after he had visited his native Bally-

[106] *The World's Columbian Catholic Congresses and Educational Exhibit* (Chicago, 1893), pp. 95–99.

[107] *Report of the Commissioner of Education—1892–93,* I, 425. This report said that the third session was held on Friday, July 28. The historian of the World's Columbian Exposition said that Keane addressed the group on Monday, July 24 (Johnson, *op. cit.,* IV, 193). The historian also claimed that there were nine sessions over a period of two weeks, while the commissioner of education reported sessions from July 25 to 28.

[108] AAB, 90-Q-3, Minutes of the Third Annual Conference of the Archbishops of the United States, New York, Nov. 16–19, 1892, pp. 22–23. Cf. *infra,* pp. 144–148, for Keane's role in the Parliament of Religions.

[109] ACUA, Keane Papers, O'Connell to Keane, Paris, July 7, 1890.

[110] Diary of Maurice F. Burke, Bishop of St. Joseph, in possession of his niece, Miss Nellie A. Burke of Denver. Entry written at Rome, June 21, 1890.

[111] AAB, 88-B-3, Ryan to Gibbons, Philadelphia, June 21, 1890.

shannon and searched for an additional professor for the University in Ireland, England, and Belgium, he went to Lourdes to implore the intercession of our Lady, as he expressed it, "that my eyes may be made fit for my work." He told Garrigan just before he left for Lourdes: "The threatening condition of my left eye still continues. May God's holy will be done in the matter."[112] After he had made a novena at the world-famous shrine of the Virgin, he related to the vice-rector: "Thus far, it has pleased her and our Lord to leave my eyes as they were when I left America. Blessed be her will and God's will whatever it may be." He also informed his colleague that his general health was excellent.[113] His eyesight did not greatly improve, and it was a subject of general concern as long as he held his post in Washington. In letters from friends in Europe he was asked about his eyes and given the assurance of additional prayers.[114] Alarming reports in the American papers, very probably the result of an announcement that the bishop was to visit Lourdes again,[115] caused Thomas Bonacum, Bishop of Lincoln, to say in 1894: "I have read with a mournful interest the report in the newspapers that your eyesight is failing you."[116] However, despite the concern, his sight was never damaged to the extent that he was incapacitated for his duties as rector, nor did it keep him from continuous and fatiguing activity.

An attack of grippe in the spring of 1892 caused Keane to seek treatment in a hospital in Norfolk.[117] He recovered sufficiently to complete the year's work at the University and then, when it closed for the summer, he enjoyed another trip to Europe. He landed at Queenstown, whence he proceeded to Dublin, then going on to England where he made stops at Manchester, Birmingham, Oxford, and London.[118]

[112] ACUA, Garrigan Papers, Keane to Garrigan, "HMS Britannic," Aug. 7, [1890]; Keane to Garrigan, Louvain, Aug. 22, 1890.

[113] ACUA, Garrigan Papers, Keane to Garrigan, Lourdes, Sept. 7, 1890. Very probably it was on this visit to Lourdes that the bishop gave the sermon in the Basilica to which Mrs. Francis H. Throop of Brooklyn attributed her husband's conversion. The bishop also had the pleasure of baptizing the gentleman (*Church News*, Sept. 29, 1894).

[114] ACUA, Keane Papers, O'Connell to Keane, Grottaferrata, Sept. 7, 1890; Shahan to Keane, Berlin, Jan. 25, 1891; Shahan to Keane, Paris, May 8, 1891.

[115] ACUA, Garrigan Papers, Keane to Garrigan, Pegli, Aug. 2, 1894.

[116] ACUA, Keane Papers, Bonacum to Keane, Lincoln, Oct. 19, 1894.

[117] Ahern, *op. cit.*, p. 65. Charles Warren Stoddard reported that Keane was very sick but out of danger (AUND, Hudson Papers, Stoddard to Hudson, Washington, Jan. 12, 1892). Over two weeks later the same correspondent indicated that the bishop was, as he said, "very much pulled down," but he was up and about (AUND, Hudson Papers, Stoddard to Hudson, Washington, Jan. 27, 1892).

[118] ACUA, Garrigan Papers, Keane to Garrigan, Queenstown, July 7, [1892].

The rector told Garrigan after leaving England: "The weather was shockingly wintry during my entire stay in Ireland and England, and has greatly aggravated the grippe bronchial troubles still clinging to me."[119] He had consulted a physician in London who advised him to take a rest in Switzerland rather than in Arcachon, France, as he had planned.[120] The bishop followed the doctor's counsel and proceeded through Paris to Geneva where he spent nearly a month with his friend, R. J. Hemmick, the American consul,[121] and where Monsignor O'Connell joined him for a visit.[122] His summer of rest must have accomplished its purpose, since Stoddard, one of the professors, wrote in his diary when Keane returned to the University: "He welcomes us in his old breezy way. It is pleasant enough to have him back — so well and strong and full of life."[123]

These were years during which the bishop needed more than good health and full strength. The task assigned to him would have tested and strained the mind and body of the most talented and vigorous of men. Fortunately, he was further blessed with an unshakable optimism based upon an almost childlike trust in the Providence of God. Hence, he could say, when he was finding it impossible to obtain funds as a result of his labors, "there is *very little* harvest to gather here, but I am not disappointed."[124] On another occasion he had written, "I again had to postpone action, and be content with 'spreading the light' and make acquaintances useful for the future."[125] Keane's trust in Providence, so evident in many of his letters, in his annual reports on the University, and in his speeches, appeared to a man of the world like Maurice Francis Egan as "most beautiful and edifying."[126]

Indeed, all the gifts of mind and body, of spirituality and personality which he possessed were utilized by Keane during the nine years that he was rector of the Catholic University of America. He shouldered all the burdens of his office and carried them cheerfully and well until the day in 1896 when Pope Leo XIII ordered him to relinquish them.

[119] *Ibid.*, Paris, July 24, 1892.

[120] ADR, Keane to O'Connell, London, July 20, 1892.

[121] AAB, 90-C-6, Garrigan to Gibbons, Washington, Aug. 19, 1892.

[122] *Ibid.*

[123] ACUA, Charles Warren Stoddard's Diaries, Volume I, Sept. 27, 1892. In 1894 Keane suffered what he called "an acute attack of hay-fever" which was relieved after a brief stay at Atlantic City (NYAA, Keane to Corrigan, Atlantic City, May 26, 1894). During the summer months the rector either went to Europe or relaxed for a few weeks at Cape May, New Jersey, or Far Rockaway, New York.

[124] ACUA, Garrigan Papers, Keane to Garrigan, May 21, 1891.

[125] *Ibid.*, Detroit, May 11, 1891.

[126] Maurice Francis Egan, *Recollections of a Happy Life* (New York, 1924), p. 186.

CHAPTER VI

Dismissal From the University

POPE LEO XIII's decision to remove Bishop Keane from the office of Rector of the Catholic University of America in the fall of 1896 was undoubtedly dictated by weighty considerations. Although the deciding factors which prompted the action were not made known, it is possible to marshal considerable evidence which certainly had bearing on the decision. To do so, however, it is necessary to reconstruct partially the intricate mosaic which portrays the less constructive side of ecclesiastical affairs in the United States between 1887 and 1896. Moreover, it is also necessary to consider at some length and as far as the available evidence will permit, the rector's part in all the events which may have led his ecclesiastical superiors to look upon him with a jaundiced eye. Hence, seemingly isolated and insignificant matters must enter in along with matters of moment in order to furnish a true and complete setting for Rome's action against Bishop Keane.

During the years under consideration the hierarchy of the United States frequently appeared to be divided into two factions: the one, with John Ireland, Archbishop of St. Paul, as its recognized leader, was variously labeled by the religious and secular press as the liberal, progressive, forward, or Americanizing party; the other, with Michael A. Corrigan, Archbishop of New York, in the forefront, was sometimes referred to as the ultramontane or conservative party, or as the intransigents.[1] Keane was linked with the first party, along with

[1] Archbishop Domenico Jacobini, secretary of the Congregation of the Propaganda, told Monsignor Eugene Boeglin, the Roman Associated Press agent for Catholic news, that ". . . there were eight archbishops in the United States all liberals with Ireland at their head, and that there were three very obedient to the Holy See as we call them, intransigenti." O'Connell remarked when he reported Boeglin's version of the

Cardinal Gibbons — to a lesser degree, Denis J. O'Connell, rector of the North American College in Rome, the majority of the professors at the University, some of the Paulists, and a number of influential bishops and priests in the United States and in Europe, both secular and religious. The second party numbered among its supporters Bernard J. McQuaid, Bishop of Rochester, a number of American and European Jesuits, most of the German priests and bishops, with a mixture of prelates and priests of all nationalities. These two factions were formed as a result of differences of opinion over the issues of the day, and both were sincerely convinced that their point of view was the right one and, hence, to be maintained no matter what the cost. Their respective views on controversial subjects were thoroughly aired in the secular and religious press, much to the detriment of religion. Both sides besieged Rome from time to time with damaging accusations and counteraccusations about their opponents' motives and sometimes their orthodoxy, trusting that the See of Peter would vindicate their position.[2] As the story unfolds, it becomes evident that Keane played an important part in the drama and that the Roman authorities did not entirely approve of the role in which he was cast.

As previously mentioned, Keane's popularity as a public speaker prompted Charles W. Eliot, president of Harvard University, to invite him to deliver the Dudleian lecture at that institution on October 23, 1890.[3] Ordinarily, such an invitation would have been considered an honor, since it was given in recognition of outstanding merit. Undoubtedly, Eliot considered it as such, even though Judge Paul Dudley had originally donated the fund for the lecture in 1750 to expose the

---

conversation with the Roman official to Ireland: "If the narrow policy of the 'three intransigenti' Abps. is to govern America in the future, I can see nothing before it in the long run but the lot that befell the Church here" (AASP, Rome, Dec. 31, 1890). The word "intransigents" describes the party more accurately than the other terms. The members of the group were uncompromising and inflexible in upholding the letter of the laws of the Church and the opinions of theologians writing for a different period, while the forward party attempted to make the adjustments that in their opinion were demanded by reason of the novel conditions in the United States. In Soderini's opinion Corrigan was, as he put it, "somewhat secluded in his virtues as well as in his defects. His great virtue was his zealous custody of the integrity of his faith. His defect was the singular lack of charity he showed in condemning everything that appeared to be opposed to his ideas" (*op. cit.*).

[2] O'Connell wrote during the Cahensly controversy: "Rampolla said: 'Unfortunately there are two parties in the U. S. and the Holy See cannot favor either of them, it must stand between'" (AAB, 88-H-2, O'Connell to Gibbons, Rome, Jan. 19, 1891). On a few matters the prelates forming the factions joined ranks, e.g., in opposing the establishment of a nunciature in the United States.

[3] ACUA, Keane Papers, Eliot to Keane, Cambridge, June 17, 1890.

"damnable heresies" of the Catholic Church.[4] The rector accepted the invitation and chose as his subject "The Obviousness of Christianity," a topic which he developed in entire conformity with Catholic tradition. However, the next day the New York *Sun* reported:

> The Bishop appeared in his sacerdotal robes and spoke from the pulpit [in Appleton Chapel] which Phillips Brooks, Andrew P. Peabody, and other Protestant leaders have adorned. He gave out the hymn, "Nearer my God, to Thee," at the beginning of the service, and "Rock of Ages" at the conclusion, and dismissed the congregation with the regular apostolic benediction. The discourse was a powerful and eloquent portrayal of the groping of humanity after the light which was in Jesus, and an incisive demonstration of the truth that all existing error is due to deviation from the principles of Christianity.[5]

The bishop was pleased with the manner in which his discourse had been received, for he told Philip J. Garrigan: "The impression produced by my work at Harvard . . . seems to be very satisfactory."[6] Obviously, he considered the circumstances under which the lecture was delivered to be in keeping with his position as a bishop of the Catholic Church. When the president and faculty of Cornell University requested him to do them a similar favor, he informed Garrigan: "I declined the invitation to Cornell Univ'y. It was only to *preach,*— and I cannot get into jobs of that kind,— totally different from the Harvard lecture."[7] But the *Univers* of Paris took a somewhat different view:

> Monsignor Keane, Rector of the Catholic University, was called upon to give a speech, October twenty-third, in the chapel of the Protestant University of Harvard, near Boston. Such strange scenes can be seen only in America, sometimes in England.
>
> . . . The stranger who would have found himself that evening in that chapel full of Protestant ministers, among whom were some Catholics, would have been surprised, perhaps even a bit scandalized, at seeing Monsignor Keane, dressed in his episcopal garments, mount the pulpit and speak to an audience of heretics.
>
> Monsignor Keane was equal to the task of the hour, and without attenuating in any way the truths of Catholic dogma, without disguising his inalterable fidelity to the Roman Church and to his Chief, knew how to win his audience with his eloquence and his abundance of

[4] Boston *Herald,* May 11, 1891. Cf. Ahern, *op. cit.,* p. 62.
[5] New York *Sun,* Oct. 24, 1890.
[6] ACUA, Garrigan Papers, Keane to Garrigan, Worcester, Oct. 27, [1890].
[7] ACUA, Garrigan Papers, Keane to Garrigan, Kansas City, Nov. 21, [1890].

> arguments in favor of Christianity and of the divine mission of Jesus Christ. He received the congratulations of the reverend ministers, who will, no doubt, continue to accept but the Gospel of free interpretation, and refuse submission to the Pope and the Church.[8]

Evidently, the writer in the Paris newspaper was a bit shocked at the performance and very probably it had an unhappy effect on some of the more conservative French ecclesiastics who read it, especially since Keane was the representative of that institution which was supposed to train the future leaders of the Church in the United States. If his contemporaries were watching for liberal tendencies on the part of the rector — and there are usually close observers of such matters in every age — they certainly could point to the Dudleian lecture as evidence. It was an isolated incident without immediate repercussions, but it was significant in the light of subsequent happenings.

In 1891 there occurred a matter of greater importance and of more far-reaching consequences. At that time Keane became involved once more in the attempt to check the movement usually called Cahenslyism, which has been described as the "demand for a greater degree of ecclesiastical autonomy by foreign language groups within the United States."[9] It took its name from Peter Paul Cahensly (1838–1923), who served as general secretary for many years of the St. Raphael Society for the care of German immigrants. It will be remembered that while Keane was in Rome in the winter of 1886–1887, he, with John Ireland, had signed a telling memorial which labeled as false certain accusations brought against the English-speaking bishops in the United States, and as pernicious certain demands which had been presented to the Congregation of the Propaganda in a document presented by Peter M. Abbelen, Vicar-General of the Archdiocese of Milwaukee, as the representative of the German-speaking element in the American Church. Ireland and Keane's memorial, along with another document containing the individual answers of a great number of American bishops to Abbelen's pamphlet, influenced the Roman authorities to set aside most of the demands which the Germans had made.[10] Naturally, this created a certain coolness toward the rector

[8] *Univers* (Paris), Nov. 29, 1890.

[9] John J. Meng, "Cahenslyism: The First Stage, 1883–1891," *Catholic Historical Review,* XXXI (Jan., 1946), 390. Cf. also, Meng, "Cahenslyism: The Second Chapter, 1891–1910," XXXII, *Catholic Historical Review* (Oct., 1946), 302–340, and Barry, *The Catholic Church and German Americans.*

[10] For the documents submitted to the Holy See, cf. *Relatio de quaestione Germanica in Statibus Foederatis a Rev. P. M. Abbelen, Sac. Milw. conscripta, a Rmo.*

on the part of many Germans, while the more fanatic among them were at no point to conceal their hostility toward him.[11]

When the German question was revived in 1891 by the presentation of two memorials to Rome containing grossly exaggerated estimates of the number of German immigrants lost to the faith in the United States,[12] the majority of the American bishops united to expose the inaccuracies and to influence Rome to reject the demands. Since the memorials had been submitted by Cahensly, who was also a Catholic member of the German Diet, it was looked upon as "a plot to prevent 'Americanization' of the Church and to Germanize the United States." Those who supported Cahensly, however, "considered it nothing more than a pious philanthropic movement to better the material condition and to improve the spiritual welfare of German immigrants to the United States."[13] Hence, Cahensly and his followers considered those

---

et Illmo. M. Heiss, Archiep. Milwauk., approbata, et Sacrae Congr. de Propaganda Fide mense Novembri 1886, submissa. Sequuntur objectiones plurimarum Romarum Praesulum eidem S. Congr. propositae, e lingua Gallica in Anglicam translatae (n.p., n.d.).

[11] In answer to a letter from Keane asking that a promised subscription for the University be honored, A. C. Hesing, president of the Illinois Staats Zeitung Company, said that he had made the promise at a meeting in Chicago when "it was explicitly stated that the institution to be erected in Washington was intended to be — not a school for nursing and fostering certain narrow puritanical ideas apt to inculcate on [*sic*] the school for riding a hobby horse of those of our bishops and prelates who can only see safety and salvation for our Church in this country by thoroughly 'americanizing' as soon as possible everything that is called Catholic — but an institution of learning on the broadest basis after the model of German or European Universities, one of the purposes being to elevate the standard of education of our clergy by establishing chairs of German literature, for the German and other languages. . . .

"However the assurance then given and my expectations, I am sorry to say, have not been realized. For one reason or another Bishop Spalding, who always had my highest esteem and fullest confidence has withdrawn from the management of the University and control of the institution is now altogether in the hands of prelates who have made themselves conspicuous by their bitter opposition to everything that has a German name, going in their aversion against the Germans, their language, customs, and habits, even so far, as to denounce, traduce, accuse and malign the German Catholics, priests, and bishops of this country before the Propaganda and the Apostolic See at Rome" (ACUA, Keane Papers, Hesing to Keane, Chicago, May 21, 1890).

[12] For the Lucerne Memorials, cf. Peter Paul Cahensly, *Der St. Raphaelsverein zum Schultze Katholischer deutscher Auswanderer* (Freiburg im Breisgau, 1900), pp. 34–39, 42–44.

[13] Meng, "Cahenslyism: The Second Chapter, 1891–1910," *op. cit.*, p. 315. John Foley, Bishop of Detroit, gave interesting views on Cahenslyism in a letter to O'Connell. After labeling Cahensly as a "scoundrel" whose "infamous lies" did much harm to religion in this country, he said: "The Germans seem to strive after conquest. They brag that they have captured Milwaukee. Cleveland is now their

who opposed them as working against the best interests of the Catholic Church. This view was expressed by Cahensly in a letter to Corrigan:

> I am led to believe that the question at stake is: whether in the United States of N. America the principles of our holy Roman Catholic Church (as represented by Cahenslyism) will gain the victory or whether the Liberalism — as defended by Msgr. Ireland and colleagues — will conquer?[14]

The Cahenslyites, with Monsignor Joseph Schroeder as their leader in the United States,[15] therefore, took the position that there was a dangerous liberalism abroad in the American Church which could be traced to Ireland and his friends. That Keane was one of Ireland's close associates was well known, especially since the Germans had suffered one of their most decisive defeats as a result of the concerted action of the two prelates some years before. Furthermore, in 1892 Bishop Keane once more gave an unmistakable indication of his stand by censoring two of his German professors, Monsignor Joseph Schroeder and Father Joseph Pohle, for publicly aligning themselves with the German faction. Both of the professors had attended the general meeting of German Catholics at Mainz in August of that year and Schroe-

---

objective point and later they declare they will have Cincinnati and St. Louis. They want the earth. It is a noted fact, brought out by this agitation that the loss to the Church is greater in the dioceses under German Bishops than in any other. Where there are Germans, no other nationality has a showing, unless it adopts the German language. There is every danger of political capital being made of the excitement. The cry America for Americans will be heard before long and it will be reechoed by American Catholics. . . . Rome however should speak and destroy Cahensly and the miserable faction of this country, who would destroy the advancement of the Church to gratify their national feelings and their *personal ambitions*.

". . . Poles at times are troublesome. In fact every Polish priest believes he is going to be a Bishop, through the intervention of Cahensly" (ADR, O'Connell Papers, Foley to O'Connell, Detroit, July 5, 1891).

[14] AANY, Cahensly to Corrigan, Limburg am Lahn, Oct. 31, 1892. O'Connell observed that the occasion presented by the Lucerne Memorials could be utilized to work, as he put it, "the complete overthrow of the new attitude the Prop[agan]da wished to assume towards America. You were all represented as a dangerous set of liberals — yourself [Ireland] the worst, that must at any cost, but prudently be put down. The Germans were the only reliable Catholics in America, the only ones in favor of schools, etc., and they were to be patronized. Besides the Irish Bps. in America had the influence of no government to be gained; the American government would always remain indifferent. But the Germans had the patronage of a strong government about them, and the value to us here of the influence of the German government is incalculable" (AASP, O'Connell to Ireland, Rome, June 11, 1891).

[15] Barry, *op. cit.,* pp. 193–194. Archbishop Corrigan gave encouragement to the professor in his campaign against what appeared to him to be liberal tendencies in the United States.

der had given an address there before the general assembly of the St. Raphael Society in which he lauded the work of their general secretary, Cahensly, and made some imprudent remarks which were utilized by the liberals to frustrate the objective of the speech.[16] A month later Schroeder was present at the sixth annual *Katholikentag,* held in Newark, New Jersey, and he defended Cahensly and spoke on the subject of liberalism and nationalism.[17] On Schroeder's activities, Keane reported:

> Dr. Schroeder having, during vacation, gloried in Cahenslyism, when I did what I considered my duty expressing to him my disapproval of his having publicly advocated a policy condemned by the Holy See and the body of our Bishops, he received my words with contempt.[18]

Thus, the controversy over Cahenslyism placed the rector at odds with two of his professors who had the ear and the sympathy of those who controlled the German-language press in the United States, and this circumstance increased the conviction among some that Keane was a dangerous liberal unqualified to direct an institution which was meant to train priests for leadership.

The antipathy of some of the American Catholics of German origin toward the rector was also based upon his extreme views on temperance. By his constant identification with the total abstinence forces in the United States, he opened himself to criticism from those members of the Catholic Church who had a tradition of temperate use of alcoholic beverages. Hence, when it was announced that the Catholic Total Abstinence Union of America would provide the funds for a chair at the University, A. C. Hesing, president of the Illinois Staats Zeitung Company, took offense and adduced that act as one of his reasons for not honoring his subscription to the University, and he indicated that his paper, the Illinois *Staats Zeitung,* would be employed to defend the interests of German Catholics against the machinations of the liberals.[19] Certainly, Keane's conception of the best means to promote the temporal and spiritual welfare of Catholics was at variance with his conservative German correspondent.

The temper of a number of the German-language papers of that

[16] AANY, Cahensly to Corrigan, Limburg an der Lahn, Sept. 6, 1892. For a portion of Shroeder's speech, cf. Barry, *op. cit.,* pp. 208–210.

[17] Barry, *op. cit.,* p. 211; *Katholisches Volksblatt* (New York), Sept. 29, 1892, cited by George Zurcher, "Foreign Ideas in the Catholic Church in America," *Roycroft Quarterly* (Nov., 1896), p. 37.

[18] ACUA, "Chronicles," p. 56.

[19] ACUA, Keane Papers, Hesing to Keane, Chicago, May 21, 1890.

day, relative to the temperance question, was fairly well indicated by a statement in the Baltimore *Katholische Volkszeitung:* "The Irish may need total abstinence; they know best. The Germans, as a rule, do not need it."[20] As a consequence, advocates of total abstinence, like Keane, were actively opposed by many German-Americans, who looked upon such extreme views on the use of liquor as contrary to Catholic teaching and their own generally accepted practice. Schroeder was numbered among those who expressed opinions in opposition to those fostered by Keane and his fellow temperance workers.[21] This fact, along with the professor's stand on the German question and on the school controversy, constituted ample justification in the rector's mind for devising means which would bring about the return of Monsignor Schroeder to Germany. Hence, it is possible that Kean's views on temperance blinded him somewhat to the good in some of those who opposed him on very logical ground, although it must be said that usually their opposition was based upon a number of motives arising from partisan loyalty on controversial matters.

While the so-called liberals were fighting Cahenslyism in the 1890's, another and more acrimonious controversy raged over what was called the school question. In this issue the lines between the liberal and conservative viewpoints were more clearly marked, and Keane was definitely identified with those who were on the side of a liberal approach to the problem.

Prior to the controversy the rector had expressed his views many times on the importance of religious instruction in schools and on the great need for parochial schools, since the existing public school system left no room for this essential element in education. On the day of his consecration in 1878 as Bishop of Richmond he had told his people that the products of public schools in the United States would be as unfit to be good citizens as to be good Christians for lack of proper religious molding and principles.[22] And during the years he administered the Richmond see, Keane made heroic efforts to provide suitable parochial schools for both the colored and the white young people under his care. Moreover, he employed his pen in the widely read secular magazine, *North American Review,* to demonstrate that the system of public education as it was then conducted was not adequate

[20] *Katholische Volkszeitung* (Baltimore), Mar. 26, 1892, cited by Zurcher, *op. cit.,* p. 15.

[21] Zurcher, *op. cit.,* pp. 15–16.

[22] For the text of the sermon, cf. p. 37.

since it could not build up a thoroughly Christian generation. As for public aid to parochial schools, he "would rather continue forever to bear the unfairness and hardship of the present system, than purchase state aid at the cost of any danger to the thoroughly Christian character and perfect religious freedom of our schools."[23]

When Bishop Keane was appointed rector of the Catholic University of America, he looked upon his position as an invaluable opportunity to help perfect the Catholic school system in the United States. Secular educators often considered him to be the representative speaker for Catholic education in this country. Hence, the president of the National Education Association invited him to address the delegates to the association's convention in Nashville on July 16, 1889. When Keane received the invitation he told Garrigan:

> I am more than willing to say a good word for Christian education at his convention, provided that it can be done with propriety — and with hope for good results. This would evidently not be the case if any discourse were to be simply part of "symposium" or discussion because feelings on the other side would be apt to hinder fair play and to stir up strife, — and, of course, if the plan be anything of that sort I can take no part in it. But if I am invited simply to make an address in the interest of good understanding and peace, I will be happy to do so, and then to answer any questions that may be asked in a good and fair spirit.[24]

But, the next day Keane told Garrigan to accept the invitation for him without mentioning the reservations.[25] So he went to Nashville and read a paper which Cardinal Gibbons had prepared on "Should Americans Educate Their Children in Denominational Schools?"[26] as well as delivering one of his own on the same subject. He pointed out that each individual has an eternal destiny for which he must

[23] For the bishop's labors in Richmond, cf. Chap. III. John J. Keane, "What is the Catholic School Policy?" *North American Review,* CXL (June, 1885), 528–535.

[24] ACUA, Garrigan Papers, Keane to Garrigan, Rome, Feb. 12, 1889.

[25] *Ibid.,* Feb. 13, 1889.

[26] Keane was probably referring to an early draft of this paper when he told Gibbons that he had consulted William Byrne, vicar-general of the Archdiocese of Boston, and Archbishop John J. Williams of that see concerning the conclusion of his paper on the school question. The archbishop, he said, "agrees that the most prudent course would be to withdraw your paper at once, before it is made public, and to omit the portion referring to the public funds." Gibbons had evidently referred to the division of the school fund to help Catholic schools, for Williams was quoted as saying that "the question of the division of the school fund is one that they could not dare to open in New England" (AAB, 86-E-2, Keane to Gibbons, Boston, July 5, 1889).

prepare. During the child's early years, the parents are entrusted by almighty God with the obligation of directing the individual to his ultimate end. As the child grows, it belongs to the parent to choose those social institutions which are best suited to aid in accomplishing the primary purpose of life. Since the individual has an eternal destiny, he can be prepared for it only by being placed under Christian influence. Because the school plays a predominant role in shaping the mind of the child, the Catholic Church demands that her children be sent to schools where the instruction will aid, rather than hinder, the individual in his lifework. Keane pointed out that if there was any incompatibility between secular instruction and Christian teaching, the secular instruction would have to be sacrificed. In anticipation of the familiar objections that a Catholic cannot be a good American, the rector demonstrated "that the best Christian is sure to be the best American, and that the school which aims at sending forth his child a model Christian, in equal degree tends to send forth a model American." The bishop concluded his paper by refuting a number of fallacious arguments against Christian education.[27]

Keane was followed on the program by Edwin D. Mead, an educator from Boston, who read a paper entitled, "Has the Parochial School Proper Place in America?" in which he repeated many of the oft-refuted objections to the Catholic Church's teaching concerning the education of her children.[28] His lengthy paper was so offensive and misrepresentative of the Church's position, that Keane asked for and received permission from the president of the association to make a response. The reply was in good taste. Calmly the rector refuted Mead's more offensive statements, and, with less serenity, he concluded his rejoinder by stating:

> The American people will open their eyes, and no longer be hoodwinked nor duped by "clap-trap" of which we have heard so much this morning; "clap-trap" which would make men believe that by crying for an existing system they were doing all that was necessary for the public good.[29]

Certainly, no one could claim that he did not defend the parochial school system on this occasion. He told Father Pace, after the con-

[27] *National Education Association. Journal of Proceedings and Addresses. Session of the Year 1889, held at Nashville, Tennessee* (Topeka, 1889), pp. 114–123.

[28] *Ibid.*, pp. 123–147.

[29] *Ibid.*, pp. 147–152. Mead had used the word "claptrap" in criticizing some of Cardinal Manning's educational writings.

vention: "I went to Nashville, to defend, all alone, the Catholic position, before our national educators. The impression produced seemed to be deep and very favorable."[30]

The bishop also utilized the public press to clarify the Church's teaching on education, which had been so grossly misrepresented during the convention, and to point out the need for Christian teaching in the schools. He told a reporter from the New York *Herald*, when asked about the Nashville meeting:

> Never before had I so clearly appreciated the immense power, the all important influence, placed by the country in the hands of those to whom the education of our youth is entrusted. Never had I so keenly felt how essential it is to our country's welfare that the exercise of so tremendous a power should be guided by true and wise principles.
>
> I rejoice to pay the tribute of my admiration to the intelligence, the earnestness, the honesty of purpose, manifested throughout by that assemblage of educators. Every Christian heart must have been charmed by the applause which greeted every appeal for more Christianity in the schools. But it was unutterably sad to notice how vague were the ideas advanced as to the nature of the Christian teaching that could be imparted in the public schools, and as to the methods by which it could be introduced into them. Nay, I must say, in all kindness and charity, that the views and plans most ably advocated on this point fell lamentably short of any reasonable understanding of dogmatic Christianity. I am far from supposing that this argued either ignorance or unbelief. Hence I must conclude that the embarrassment lies in the difficulty of combining definite Christian teaching with the plan on which the public school system is at present shaped.
>
> If the present plan were final and irremediable, then indeed might the fate of Christianity in the schools be considered hopeless. But this is far from being the case. The system of public schools in our country is less than half a century old; and during that brief period it has been modified repeatedly. Therefore, it can still be acknowledged that the prevailing tendency in modifications hitherto has been toward the more and more complete exclusion of religion from the schools. But neither is this tendency irreversible. When the American people come to appreciate that more Christianity is needed in the schools they will not hesitate to modify any plan, to reverse any tendency, and to provide wisely for the public good.
>
> Now, to minds that reflect calmly and deeply, nothing can be more evident than the need of making the system of popular education more Christian, if our country is to be a Christian country, if our civilization

[30] ACUA, Pace Papers, Keane to Pace, Washington, Aug. 7, 1889.

is to be a Christian civilization . . . but thoughtful people are everywhere recognizing that there is not Christianity enough in our public schools; that the tendency to the secularization of education — that is to the exclusion of religion from the schools — logically tends to the exclusion of religion from the public and private lives of our people; that is a mistake that must be corrected, both for love of religion and for love of country. . . .

Others, less logical, or less courageous and generous, or perhaps in the hope of yet reversing the present tendency and infusing more Christianity into the present system, cling to it, and doubtless with the natural wish to make the most of what one is committed to, laud it as the best and the only admissible system. In the same breath, however, they give utterance to their anxiety about the gradual decay of clear and positive Christian belief and Christian principles among our people, and about the need of remedying this by making our educational system more Christian. Thanks be to God for this wide-spreading anxiety. It gives hope of turning into safer paths.[31]

After this admirable statement appeared in the papers, which no dyed-in-the-wool secular educator would endorse, the public press began to give more complete coverage to Keane's statements on education. When the bishop spoke on "The American Child and the Public School" before a large audience in Mechanics Hall in Worcester, Massachusetts, on January 23, 1890, the Worcester *Spy* reported that he had indicated the necessity of bringing Christianity to the schools.[32] The Springfield *Republican* criticized the discourse and, in doing so, indicated the prejudiced spirit that has always attended any discussion of the school question. It reported:

Bishop Keane proclaims his Americanism, and the Americanism of his church, and yet he cannot see how un-American this is, for if there be an American principle, it is the entire separation of Church and State, and here he is proposing that the public moneys be used to maintain schools for the teaching of religions according to the Roman Catholic, the Presbyterian, the Methodist, the Lutheran, — or whatever other church or sect shall establish them.

Then, after citing the Church's practice of refusing the sacraments to those who did not send their children to parochial schools as an example of compulsion, it added:

This is compulsion; and it is a sample of what must be expected to

[31] New York *Herald,* Aug. 29, 1889.
[32] Worcester *Spy,* Jan. 24, 1890.

occur when the church gets its grip thoroughly fastened on this great business. It has the additional evil quality that it is not the discipline of the state, in which citizens have a voice, and which they make for themselves, but it is the discipline of a hierarchy which professes to speak with divine authority, and against which the layman has no effectual protest.[33]

Bishop Keane gave practically the same lecture in Baltimore a few weeks later which the New York *Observer* reported and criticized in this case under the heading "The Public School Issue."

> This issue could not be more clearly defined than it is in a recent lecture in Baltimore by Dr. Keane. . . . He begins by assuming that Christianity must be taught in some way in the schools, for though the Church and the home are powerful religious influences, the school is of paramount importance, and cannot be left absolutely secular or irreligious. He then says that there are two policies by which religion may be incorporated with a school system that includes a vast variety of opinion and belief. The first is a compromise policy, which minimizes the Christianity taught until it is acceptable to those who have the least Christian faith. But this does not accomplish the end sought in teaching religion, and it soon becomes a source of strife and bitterness. As in many other compromises, the effort to please everybody results in pleasing nobody. The second policy, which is that advocated by the Roman Catholic Church under the present necessity, is to teach Christianity clearly and fully in all the schools by the regular denominational teachers of religion, the state retaining full control of the secular part of education.[34]

Although the *Observer* took exception to the policies which Keane had advocated, it was mild in comparison to the censures of some Protestant organs, which posed before the American people as the chief guardians of American institutions. The *Christian Union,* a denominational paper published in New York, printed an article that was typical of those to be found in non-Catholic journals relative to the school question. Since the Catholic Church was essentially un-American, "its members owing allegiance and obedience to a foreign potentate," the editor maintained, her opinions on the education of

[33] Springfield *Republican,* Jan. 26, 1890. The Milwaukee *Sentinel* clipped the item and published it on January 29, 1890.

[34] New York *Observer,* Mar. 6, 1890. Ireland advocated the same policies in his speech before the delegates to the NEA convention in St. Paul in July, 1890. Cf. John Ireland, *The Church and Modern Society* (Chicago, 1897), I, 197–214.

American citizens were not entitled to the same weight as those of any other large Christian body.[35]

Before July, 1890, therefore, Bishop Keane had changed his opinion about public aid to denominational schools and was advocating a national school policy which would relieve the Catholic Church of some of the financial burden which she had assumed due to the absolute necessity of providing her children with a religious training which could not be obtained under the existing public school system. Since he appeared to be the chief spokesman on education for the Catholic Church in America, his utterances received wide publicity, and, as we have seen, in some quarters they were sharply criticized. Some Catholic leaders, too, at this point were privately critical of the rector's proposed solution of the thorny problem, principally because the invoking of public aid for denominational schools implied direction which could and in all probability would be inimical to the objectives of such institutions. Others, however, believed that by adopting such a plan it would be possible to realize the objectives of parochial schools without the financial burdens which in some cases were unbearable.

In July, 1890, another powerful ecclesiastical figure took up the public school issue. John Ireland addressed the convention of the National Education Association in St. Paul on "The Relation of the State School to the Parish School." The policies that Keane had been advocating for a year were espoused by the Archbishop of St. Paul in language that lent itself to misinterpretation on the part of both Protestants and Catholics. Again there was an unfriendly reaction on the Protestant side. In reporting on the address, the *Evangelist* noted:

> . . . His gentlemanly tactics were very similar to those of Bishop Keene [*sic*] . . . , at the educational meeting at Nashville. When by general patriotic platitudes and universal good-will, he had won the sympathy and even the applause of his audience, he veered over to the "true Catholic" standpoint, when his large audience suddenly became

[35] *Christian Union* (New York), July 10, 1890. A Presbyterian minister at Adalbert College in Cleveland told Keane that he was "entirely out of sympathy with that apprehension so widely prevalent and so frequently expressed, that the Catholic Church is hostile to American civil institutions, and would, if she could, secure their overthrow in order to erect a temporal throne for the Pope upon the ruins of the American Republic." He added that he wished, as he expressed it, to "get at the best Catholic thought on the relation of the Catholic Church to our civil institutions. My object is to use what influence I may have, in a private way, to promote true views on this subject" (ACUA, Keane Papers, E. P. Cleaveland to Keane, Cleveland, Ohio, Nov. 17, 1890).

> still. But the expression of the faces showed very plainly that it was by no means the "silence that gives consent."[36]

Later Denis O'Connell remarked to Keane on the Ireland speech: "A number of persons tried to create trouble [in Catholic quarters] for Abp. Ireland on account of his address on the school question."[37] Actually, the interested parties succeeded in creating plenty of trouble for Ireland at the Holy See, for a year after the lecture had been delivered, it was still being considered with a view to censoring its contents.[38] Naturally, Keane maintained a lively interest in the fortunes of Ireland in Rome because any censorship of Ireland's ideas on the schools would be considered as a reflection on him, too, since he had advocated the same policies in clearer and less ambiguous language. Although in the sequel, Ireland's views were not condemned, the Roman authorities were doubtless more watchful for symptoms of liberal tendencies.

Archbishop Ireland was not content to allow his proposals for an acceptable national policy toward parochial schools to remain in the realm of speculation. He put them into practice in the schools of Faribault and Stillwater, Minnesota. Actually, Ireland's arrangement should have occasioned no alarm on the part of his fellow Catholics for the same practice of having the state pay the nuns for teaching secular subjects in the Catholic school, which was rented by the state for a nominal sum, had obtained in a number of other dioceses, among

[36] *Evangelist* (New York), July, 1890.

[37] ACUA, Keane Papers, O'Connell to Keane, Grottaferata, Sept. 7, 1890. The general outline of the school controversy and the events that led up to it have been taken from Daniel F. Reilly, O.P., *The School Controversy (1891–1893)* (Washington, 1943). This is very incomplete, especially because the Corrigan Papers in the AANY were not consulted, but the best over-all treatment of the subject to date. The Heuser Papers in the archives of the American Catholic Historical Society reveal the names of those who were active in the conservative camp during the school controversy. For copies of letters in this collection the author is indebted to Father Colman Barry, O.S.B.

[38] ACUA, Keane Papers, O'Connell to Keane, Rome, Mar. 30, 1891. O'Connell said: "The Pope has taken Dr. Chapelle's case from the Propda. and will treat it with Card. Gibbons. The same way the question of Abp. Ireland's discourse is to be settled." That the whispering in Rome about Ireland and Keane was gross and dangerous is evident from this statement, even though it may have been made in jest: "I told Denis the other day, that to my mind Mgr. Ireland was the stuff of which heretics were made, and that we would undoubtedly, hear from him, later, in that sense. . . . To him, comes next in order — the Rector of the University. God save the mark!" (Archives of the Abbey of St. Paul Outside the Walls, Rome, Abbot Bernard Smith Papers, Edes to Smith, Rome, Sept. 22, 1890, microfilm copy at St. John's University, Collegeville, Minnesota.)

them the Archdiocese of New York, over a period of years. However, the fact of Ireland's implementing his plan, plus the publication of a pamphlet in the fall of 1891, entitled *Education: To Whom Does It Belong?* by Thomas Bouquillon, professor of moral theology in the Catholic University of America, construed by the conservatives as an apology for Ireland's scheme, precipitated a crucial battle between the two ecclesiastical parties over the school question. The conservatives, believing that Ireland, supported by a theologian from the University, was committing the Church to a dangerous and unorthodox policy, used every available means to expose the plot and to acquaint the public with what they considered to be the true teaching of the Church. Meanwhile, Ireland could not speak in his own defense for reasons which he communicated to Gibbons.

> I have found myself in a triangular predicament on this whole Faribault matter. I am between two enemies — one Catholic and one Protestant. If I placate one, I arouse the other. The concessions to our school and its continued identity as a Catholic school are so important that I dare not fully state them lest I might bring down the wrath of anti-Catholic bigots. I am condemned to be silent. It is fair to add that the Faribault priest bungled things somewhat and in his desire to avert Protestant bigotry, used some expressions which Catholics may well criticize.[39]

Both secular and religious journals were filled with reports on the internecine war, and Rome was flooded with material from both parties.

Although Keane was not an active participant in the controversy, there could have been no doubt in the minds of the conservatives as to where his sympathy lay, since he had been proposing similar policies on a national scale. Furthermore, when Bouquillon's pamphlet was attacked, the rector defended his professor by stating:

> The pamphlet is nothing more than a quotation from the ecclesiastical authorities, theological and philosophical, in all ages. The only new thing about the matter is that people should so far forget this fact as to misrepresent the writer's views. It has always been understood that there are two forms of human society, the civil and the religious, and it has also been understood that these two forms of society should coöperate for the welfare of mankind. This is the true doctrine of union of Church and State, which does not mean that the Church should do the State's work nor that the State should do the Church's work,

[39] Archives of the Archdiocese of Cincinnati, letters, June 30 to Dec. 31, 1891, Ireland to Gibbons, quoted in Gibbons to Elder, Oakland, Maryland, Oct. 23, 1891.

> nor that either should interfere with the other in its legitimate sphere, but that each in its own sphere should coöperate with the other. As an example, the Church teaches us the commandments of the decalogue, and the State coöperates with the Church in bringing about an observance of the commandments. Nobody considers it an interference on the part of the State to have laws in regard to stealing, in regard to adultery, in regard to perjury, which are entirely in harmony with the laws of the Church of God. Education is considered to be one of the essentials of human welfare; and sound philosophy teaches us, as sound theologians have always understood, that here also civil and religious authority should coöperate for the teaching of men in all relationships toward this world and toward the world to come. The Church and State, therefore, should be united in education just as in everything else. This, Dr. Bouquillon shows, has been the teaching of the leading authorities of the Church in all ages. Therefore there is nothing new in his position. The only novelty is a short-sighted people with their false philosophy or their exaggerated ideas of either State or Church authority wish to keep education exclusively in the hands of either one or the other, whereas both ought to coöperate for its protection.[40]

After Ireland had been called to Rome to defend the practical application of his school policy — and incidentally to defend Bouquillon's writings — his partial victory, which also meant a victory for the university professor, was a cause for relief and elation to Keane, sentiments which he expressed in a communication to Ireland:

> How can I sufficiently congratulate you on the *glorious* news given us by yesterday's papers! It is a triumph which marks an epoch. It opens up a future of harmonious relations between America and the Church, and crushes the hindrances which would fain have barred the portals. Now let us have a pronouncement from the Pope, clear and unmistakable in meaning, which, while reasserting Catholic principles, as of course it is sure to do, and thus closing the mouths of those who

[40] *Globe Democrat* (New York), Nov. 29, 1891. On December 15 the *Church Progress* pointed to some inconsistencies between this statement and Keane's words in the *North American Review* in 1885 (cf. n. 23). The rector's letter explaining his views was printed in the same journal on January 8, 1893.

After Archbishop Corrigan had given the Paulists a veiled warning about maintaining an acceptable position in the school controversy, Elliott and Hewit suppressed articles that they had written in favor of Bouquillon and the Paulist superior general asked Keane to withdraw his offer of a lengthy article on the subject (AASP, Elliott to Ireland, Montreal, Mar. 25, 1892). It is very likely that the bishop used this article for a lecture which was published under the title *Catholic Education in America* (Washington, 1892) which was freely quoted in a review in the *Catholic World,* LV (Apr., 1892), 767–769.

are ready to assert that the Church is being committed to a false policy, will above all give the country clearly to understand that we recognize and admit civil rights and are ready to cooperate fairly in education as in all else that concerns the public welfare.[41]

The controversy did not end, however, when Rome indicated that Ireland's school plan could be tolerated. The Archbishop of St. Paul and his colleagues interpreted the Holy See's pronouncement as a complete vindication of their position, while the conservatives maintained that Rome merely tolerated it because of the alleged circumstances peculiar to the area in which the policy was in effect.

So the controversy continued. Keane, all the while, maintained his identity with the progressives and evidently from the way in which they watched his movements, he was considered to be the mentor of the group by some of the opposition. While he was in Europe in the summer of 1892, Bishop Zardetti of St. Cloud told Corrigan: "F. Brandi writes me 'that Bp. Keane went to Switzerland and will be met by Msgr. O'Connell.' See, they follow him." The Bishop of St. Cloud also remarked that Keane and O'Connell were working against the Archbishop of New York.[42] Meanwhile the rector feared that he would be needed in Rome to help Ireland's cause and, as he said, "that will mean hard work instead of rest. Blessed be the will of God."[43] Before Keane could make the journey, however, O'Connell informed him that his presence in Rome would not be necessary. Later the Rector of the American College joined the bishop in Switzerland.[44] Here they paid a joint visit to Cardinal Ledochowski, prefect of the Congregation of the Propaganda, who was spending his vacation at Lucerne,[45] a visit in which the Americans probably hoped to win that powerful ecclesiastic to their side and to counteract the representations of their opponents.

[41] ADR, Keane to Ireland, Washington, Apr. 29, 1892.

[42] AANY, Otto Zardetti to Corrigan, Bad Jordan, Aug. 4, 1892. Ten days later Zardetti wrote: "Just received news that Bp. *Keane* of the University and *Msgr. O'Connell* arrived in Lucerne and *paid visits* to C. *Ledocowski* [*sic*]. It would be good to print it in the papers" (AANY, Zardetti to Corrigan, Jorambad [?] Aug. 14, 1892). Miecislaus Cardinal Ledochowski was prefect of the Congregation of the Propaganda which handled American Church affairs. He was appointed to succeed Cardinal Simeoni on February 3, 1892.

[43] ACUA, Garrigan Papers, Keane to Garrigan, Paris, July 24, 1892. Ireland had urged Keane to go to Rome to see and talk with the Pope and some of the cardinals so it would be clear to them that Ireland had friends and supporters (AASP, Ireland to Keane, on shipboard, July 3, 1892).

[44] AAB, 90-C-6, Garrigan to Gibbons, Washington, Aug. 19, 1892.

[45] AANY, Zardetti to Corrigan, Jorambad, Aug. 14, 1892.

Since the controversy over the school question was not settled when the Holy See refused to condemn Ireland's school arrangements in his own diocese, the Holy Father decided to send a personal representative to the United States in an attempt to bring peace to the American Church. For this delicate assignment, the Pope chose Archbishop Francesco Satolli, the same prelate who had represented him at the celebration marking the centennial of the American hierarchy and at the opening of the University in November, 1889. It was significant that Satolli was accompanied by Denis J. O'Connell, who was identified with the so-called liberals, and that after they arrived in the United States in October, 1892, they proceeded to St. Paul, the stronghold of John Ireland, where they remained until the archbishops met in New York in November.

When the metropolitans opened their meeting at the residence of the Archbishop of New York on November 16, Satolli presented fourteen propositions which had been drawn up with a view to settling the whole school question. Immediately, the conservatives believed, with justification considering the circumstances, that the proposals had been dictated by the liberals who had won the Pope's representative to their side, and a few weeks later Zardetti told Corrigan: "Permit me to say that I think it is a mistake that after refusing signatures the Archbps. again negotiated with S[atolli]. They should have solemnly appealed to the H. Father. Its a prearranged conspiracy; I[reland], Gib[bons], Keane, Sat[olli], O'Connell."[46] Thus the unseemly bickering continued unabated. The conservatives showed in various ways that they were displeased with the personal representative of the Pope, who by the end of 1892 had taken up residence at the University in Washington where the liberal group's interests were represented by Keane — another significant coincidence that was not overlooked by their opponents.

Once more the Holy See received letters which indicated that the issue was not closed, and the public press, especially in New York,

[46] AANY, Zardetti to Corrigan, St. Cloud, Dec. 2, 1892. Zardetti was not wrong in concluding that there was complete accord between the liberals and the Pope's representative. Cf. AASP, O'Connell to Ireland, Rome, Aug. 3; Sept. 13 and 16, 1892. Two days after the meeting in New York, Satolli warmly recommended that Ireland be designated for the cardinalate (AUND, Soderini's notes, Satolli to Rampolla, Nov. 18, 1892). Satolli was told that the Pope did not deem it necessary at the moment to grant any pontifical distinction to Bouquillon (Rampolla to Satolli, June 14, 1893, cited by Soderini, *op. cit.*). Mariano Cardinal Rampolla del Tindaro was Papal secretary of State at this time.

heaped abuse upon Satolli, the ally of the liberals. As if in answer to Satolli's critics, the Pope appointed the Archbishop of Lepanto as the first apostolic delegate to the United States on January 24, 1893, and on the following May 31, he sent a long letter to the hierarchy of the United States which put an end to the controversy over the schools although it did little to obliterate the differences between the main contenders in the battle.[47]

Reflecting upon his own part in the school troubles, Keane later wrote:

> While trying to be friendly to all, my convictions were entirely on the side of Dr. B[ouquillon] and Mgr. Satolli, — and my feelings totally against the unfairness, the interested policies, the sophistry, by which they were assailed. As a matter of course, therefore, I came to be regarded with hostility by the other side, — and although my private utterances have ever been openly and strongly in favor of Catholic schools, they did not hesitate to represent me as their enemy! A glance at my lecture, "Christian Education in America," ought to be refutation enough of the calumny.[48]

As we have seen, it was true that Bishop Keane had been a champion of the parochial school, but his sympathies with Ireland made it more or less inevitable that he should suffer from the misrepresentations which arose during the heated controversy.

The school controversy served to intensify the distrust that the rector entertained for the Jesuits, since that order was most active in the battle. The bishop had discussed what he termed, "the too evident unfriendliness of the Jesuits toward the University," when he visited the Superior General in Fiesole in 1889.[49] In the quarrel over the parochial schools, he considered the Jesuit contenders as being there because of "interested policies" rather than because of certain conviction that the controversial matter was a danger to the welfare of the American Church. It is likely he was somewhat prejudiced in his estimate of the motives of the Jesuits, but it would have been difficult for him to overlook such evidences of unfriendliness as the articles

[47] On June 25 Keane told Rampolla how delighted he was with the letter and proceeded with a eulogy on the learning and the virtues of Satolli, refuting the objections against his proposals. He said that those who were now attacking the delegate were the same people who had earlier attacked the University (AUND, Soderini's notes).

[48] ACUA, "Chronicles," p. 55.

[49] *Ibid.*, p. 40.

that appeared in the Jesuit Roman journal, the *Civiltà Cattolica,*[50] and Ireland's report from Rome to the effect that the "worst enemy of the University is Card. Mazzella. He has ever a sneer for it."[51] A sneer for the University from the Jesuit cardinal was, indeed, a sneer for its rector. Hence, it must have been consoling to Keane to be told by Bouquillon, whose writings the Jesuits had attacked during the school controversy, that during his visit to the Eternal City he had an audience of the Pope, as well as visits to Cardinal Rampolla, Secretary of State and a classmate of the professor, and the two Cardinals Vannutelli, and that all these powerful figures, as he expressed it, "are entirely with the University and against the Jesuits."[52]

The controversy over the parochial schools also served to increase the antipathy between Keane and the Germans, especially the two professors who were teaching in the University at the time. During the early stages of the agitation over the question known as Cahenslyism, Schroeder had indicated to Gibbons that he was willing to remain at the University, although he had been offered a chair in the theological faculty at the University of Bonn. He told the cardinal: "I wrote to our beloved Rector, Msgr. Keane, about it, stating emphatically that I desired no other honor but that of my present position at Washington, and that honor itself makes it a duty for me not to abandon it."[53] The spirit of discord, however, resulting from the agi-

[50] Ireland wrote just before he received a decision on the school issue: "The field seems now clear of difficulties — except the Civilta, which to my mind is positively devilish. The next number will be out in a few [*sic*] and we shall see whether it has changed its tone. The Jesuits evidently make of the fight a question of life or death. Their intent is obvious. The last article finishes with an eulogy of the great Georgetown University — enumerating the many faculties, its hundreds of students in each faculty. The impression was that this is the only university in America" (ASMS, Ireland to Magnien, Rome, Mar. 17, 1892). Cf. *Civiltà Cattolica,* Vols. I, II, III [Series 15], for a number of references to American ecclesiastical affairs.

[51] ACUA, Keane Papers, Ireland to Keane, Rome, Apr. 26, 1892.

[52] AAB, 91-T-4, Keane to Gibbons, Washington, Aug. 25, 1893.

[53] AAB, 88-Y-5, Schroeder to Gibbons, Allentown, Pennsylvania, Sept. 24, 1891 (French). In an article written in 1891 Schroeder spoke of meeting Ludwig Windthorst at an annual congress of German Catholics at Coblenz in August, 1890. He said that the minister of state "spoke to us enthusiastically . . . of our beloved University" (Joseph Schroeder, "Windthorst," *American Catholic Quarterly Review,* XVI [July, 1891], 515–528). In 1892 Corrigan was apparently considering Schroeder for the faculty of St. Joseph's Seminary, for the rector of that institution said to his superior: "At the same time there was some difference of opinion about Dr. Schroeder. Father Puissant is afraid that he might not find everything so pleasant as at the University, and that there might not be that harmony which has reigned here for some time. . . . It was remarked also that his small class at the University was due to the fact that he is very theoretical, and spends weeks at times in going

tation over the problems of the day, created an entirely different attitude by the fall of 1892. At that time Cahensly, who maintained a lively interest in American ecclesiastical affairs, and incidentally in his two countrymen at the University, informed Corrigan:

> I know also from very good authority, that Msgr. Ireland, during his stay in Rome, passed unfair remarks about Msgr. Dr. Schroeder and Dr. Pohle, . . . saying, that they must quit their chairs. He now will surely, use all his endeavors with his friend Msgr. Keane, in order to get these men removed as soon as possible. Have the Most Rev. Membres [*sic*] of the University-board then no influence in the appointment of Professors? In the interest of the Catholic Church of America would I be sorry, were these learned men to get lost to the University.[54]

Cahensly's informant may or may not have been right about Ireland, but certainly his suspicions about the rector's role in accomplishing their removal from the University were valid. Furthermore, Cahensly was hopeful of a sympathetic correspondent in Corrigan since he, too, was opposed to some of the policies of Ireland and Keane.

When Schroeder and Pohle began to feel the pressure which was designed to bring about their resignation from the University faculty, the sympathetic ear of the Archbishop of New York opened to them. Schroeder wrote a number of letters which conveyed his "sentiments of profound affection" in which he wished, as he said, "to renew the expression of my veneration and respect which painful circumstances have only increased" for Corrigan after the latter's apparent defeat in the school controversy.[55] He also told his episcopal friend that he shared his views on the agitated question and he added, "I contented myself with making my opinions less secret than ever in surroundings where praise was reserved for others." Schroeder then remarked:

> Meanwhile the day which will decide my fate and that of Dr. Pohle draws near. I have many reasons to believe that my silence in the controversies of the day was not enough for Mgr. Keane or his friends and that they are still determined to have their victim. I can assure

---

into side issues and objections, which could not be considered at all in our Seminary course.

"The general opinion is however that he is undoubtedly a great man and that although the Professors might feel more at home with one of our own, yet they will welcome him if he should come" (AANY, William Livingston to Corrigan, New York, Apr. 8, 1892).

[54] AANY, Cahensly to Corrigan, Limburg, Oct. 31, 1892.

[55] AANY, Schroeder to Corrigan, Reading, Pennsylvania, Apr. 4, 1893 (French); *ibid.*, Schroeder to Corrigan, Staten Island, June 23, 1893 (French and Latin).

> you, Monsignor, that since October I have spent the most painful part of my life. Nevertheless, those gentlemen of the University are badly mistaken if they think that I am going to resign without being forced to do so. If they want to go to the extreme in this business of taking sides and forming parties, they will have to do it openly. They will not succeed in making me the scapegoat of the precarious situation of the University which, all during the past semester, has continually made itself the instrument, the active and avowed instrument, in public as well as inside, of the veritable conspiracy which is being plotted among the Catholics and against some Catholic prelates.[56]

Schroeder's suspicions about the designs against him were well founded, for Keane told O'Connell: "Schroeder holds on, and there is no way to oust him as yet, but he sees that he has to be quiet."[57] Meanwhile, Satolli, who was then accepting the advice of the liberals, had evidently concurred with their views on the German professor which prompted Schroeder to tell the delegate:

> 1° I candidly confess that if I am bound to follow the norms prescribed or wanted by the Most Reverend Ireland and Keane, I submit the privilege of teaching into your hands; 2° I ask you to tell me why you have punished me by ostracism for a whole year; 3° I will remain, although an excellent opportunity is now open to me (in Germany), and I will remain to show my gratitude to the eminent bishops who have protected me by their patronage.[58]

The professor later told Corrigan that Satolli "answered nothing to the first and third points, no more than to many others I submitted to him; as for the second, the only answer he gave me was: that I wasn't *Thomistic* enough."[59]

In the fall of 1893, Schroeder reported a change of attitude toward the two German professors on the part of the delegate. "I am happy to tell you," he wrote to Corrigan, "that His Excellency, Monsignor Satolli, received us most graciously; he even condescended to read, upon my asking him, my last year's lithographed lessons, and to express his complete satisfaction." Schroeder also spoke of their failure in an attempt to elect a dean for the faculty who would be suitable to them, but he added "we will quietly keep on doing what we

[56] AANY, Schroeder to Corrigan, Reading, Pennsylvania, Apr. 4, 1893 (French). The "precarious situation" mentioned by Schroeder probably is a reference to the lack of students.

[57] ADR, Keane to O'Connell, Atlantic City, Oct. 10, 1893.

[58] Schroeder's summary version of his letter to the delegate, in NYAA, Schroeder to Corrigan, Staten Island, June 23, 1893 (French and Latin).

[59] *Ibid.*

can. Our intention is not to disturb the peace, if that is left to us and if no more effort is made to pose as judges of persons and things which are beyond the province of professors of a University which should be that of the whole Episcopate."[60]

Pohle, however, yielded to the pressure on him to leave and accepted the chair of dogma at the University of Münster in Westphalia. In his letter of resignation the professor informed the Board of Directors that he was prompted to make the decision because of the partisan stand of some of the members of the University on the controversies which had disrupted the former amity among the professors of the institution. He said that he held the same views as Schroeder on the issues in question, and he justified his German colleague for taking an active part in them because, said Pohle, he did so "only after the University had already taken a decided position in the opposite direction." He further revealed Schroeder's unenviable position at the University by stating:

> But what has touched me most profoundly is the fact which I have observed during the last two years, that Mgr. Schroeder, who as a man and as a professor is, to say the least, equal to any of his colleagues, has become in consequence of his fearless attitude, at times the subject of treatment which is contrary not only to the courtesy due to such a distinguished man, but also to the most elementary principles of Christian charity. I myself have witnessed attacks whose evident purpose was to render his position at the University unbearable.[61]

Bishop Keane later said that the contents of this letter had to be "honestly denounced as downright misrepresentation of the spirit and conduct of the great body of Professors."[62] Nevertheless, it must have contained some truth, if Bishop Ignatius F. Horstmann of Cleveland was to be believed, for he said at the time:

> I feel that if he [Schroeder] considered that he can retire with honor, he will not remain at the University. The atmosphere is too chilly for him. There are two professors who have not spoken to him for two years in spite of his having humbled himself to make them do so.[63]

[60] AANY, Schroeder to Corrigan, Washington, Oct. 8, 1893 (French).

[61] AAB, 93-D-9, Pohle's "Letter of Resignation to the Board of Directors of the Catholic University of America, sent to his Grace the Archbishop of Philadelphia, Chairman of the Committee for the appointment of professors," Mar., 1894.

[62] ACUA, "Chronicles," p. 57.

[63] AANY, Ignatius F. Horstmann to Corrigan, Cleveland, Mar. 9, 1894.

Schroeder, of course, was loath to lose his friend and ally Pohle,[64] but Keane was elated. He was even more anxious, however, that Schroeder should leave, as he told O'Connell: "Would that Schroeder would do the same. He stands his ground, and the Board won't take action. But it won't last long so."[65] Nonetheless, it did last long for Keane, for he was still teaching at the University when the rector was dismissed, and to Schroeder were attributed some of the harmful accusations to powerful ecclesiastics which brought about the deposition.

Any judgment of Keane for his attempts to force the resignation of the two German professors must be made in the light of facts. It was a period in which there were unusual problems which divided men's loyalties, and he had the obligation of preserving harmony in his faculty. Then, too, it must have been common knowledge that the two had turned for support to Archbishop Corrigan who continued to oppose the University. Furthermore, the two German professors openly sided with their fellow nationals, many of whom carried on a campaign to discredit the University and its rector.[66] Under the conditions, Keane acted for the best interests of the University as he interpreted them.

Although the differences between the bishop and the Germans were a factor in bringing about his dismissal, the rector's active participation in the World's Parliament of Religions, held from September 11 to September 28, 1893, as a department of the World's Congress Auxiliary of the Columbian Exposition at Chicago, was a matter of greater moment, for it was construed as a sign of his liberal leanings by many of the more conservative churchmen in the United States and in Europe.

Owing to what he termed the "urgent solicitation of Abp. Ireland,"[67] the rector had presented a letter for the consideration of the archbishops at their annual meeting in New York in the fall of 1892, in which he explained the provisions that were being made for the par-

[64] AANY, Schroeder to Corrigan, Washington, Dec. 20, 1893.

[65] ADR, Keane to O'Connell, Washington, Jan. 5, 1894. Shahan, a professor at the University, voiced similar sentiments to O'Connell: "You know of course that Pohle is leaving us. . . . He was a good professor, would it were the other German [Schroeder]" (ADR, Shahan to O'Connell, Washington, Dec. 13, 1893).

[66] AAB, 93-J-7, Keane to Gibbons, Pegli, July 31, 1894. Keane reported that he discussed the opposition of Corrigan and the Germans to the University with the Pope.

[67] ADR, Keane to O'Connell, Washington, Oct. 10, 1893.

liament, and, after stating the pros and cons of the idea, he said: "It is not in our power to hinder the Parliament from taking place. It is already certain that all the other great forms of religion will be ably represented. *Can the Catholic Church afford not to be there?*"[68] The sequel to Keane's proposal was recorded by the secretary of the meeting when he wrote:

> After a thorough discussion of Bishop Keane's letter it was resolved that His Eminence should request him in the name of the Board to make suitable arrangements with those in charge of the so-called Parliament of Religions for having twenty Catholic speakers to be selected by the Rt. Rev. Bishop to expound Catholic doctrine at their meetings.[69]

Thus was the rector saddled with the responsibility of assuring the Catholic Church of full and suitable representation at the Chicago sessions. To that end in the months ahead he corresponded with prominent Catholics both at home and abroad and with the directors of the Parliament of Religions to whom he said on one occasion:

> It is only by a friendly and brotherly comparison of convictions that reasonable men can ever come to an agreement about the all-important truths which are the foundation of religion, and that an end can be put to the religious divisions and antagonisms which are a grief to our Father in Heaven. Such an assemblage of intelligent and conscientious men, presenting their religious convictions without minimizing, without acrimony, without controversy, with love and truth and humanity, will be an honorable event in the history of religion and cannot fail to accomplish much good.[70]

For the opening session, Keane was on the speakers' platform in company with Cardinal Gibbons and other prominent members of the hierarchy.[71] On the eighth day of the proceedings he delivered a paper on "The Incarnation Idea in History and in Jesus Christ,"[72] and on the seventeenth day he read a second paper on "The Ultimate Religion."[73] The historian of the World's Columbian Exposition ex-

[68] AAB, 90-P-6, Keane to the Most Reverend, The Board of Archbishops of the United States, Washington, Nov. 12, 1892.

[69] AAB, 90-Q-3, Minutes of the Third Annual Conference of the Archbishops of the United States, New York, Nov. 16–19, 1892, pp. 22–23.

[70] Barrows, *op. cit.*, I, 16–17. Keane was spoken of as the "able and liberal-minded" rector of the Catholic University of America in the same source.

[71] *Ibid.*, I, 64–66.

[72] *Ibid.*, I, 123.

[73] *Ibid.*, I, 151.

pressed the opinion that the latter paper summed up the results of the gathering, which in his mind were these:

> This comparison of all religions has shown conclusively that the only worthy idea of God is that of monotheism; that the belief in a divine revelation was a necessary step to religious unity; and that all human endeavors to tell of the means provided by Almighty God for unifying mankind with himself led logically and historically to Jesus Christ. As long as God is God and man is man, Jesus Christ is the center of religion forever; and because He is the ultimate center, His one original church must also and equally be ultimate.[74]

Besides presiding at a number of the sessions,[75] the bishop read papers at other sessions which had been written by Cardinal Gibbons, Professor Thomas Dwight of Harvard, and Father Charles F. Connelly of Boston.[76] The historian of the World's Columbian Exposition said:

> The [Catholic] delegation was exceedingly strong, and all the Catholic speakers kept strictly within the prescribed limits of the Parliament, stating their own views with frankness and ability, and refraining from criticism of others. Bishop Keane had put the different topics into the hands of specialists, all of whom were excellent speakers.[77]

At the close of the congress Keane was again on the platform with John Moore, Bishop of St. Augustine, and he ended the session with a prayer of benediction which was said to have been delivered "in great earnestness."[78] The historian of the parliament related that during the sessions "the popular and tolerant Bishop Keane . . . was received with the most cordial enthusiasm."[79] He further stated:

> Those who saw the Greek Archbishop, Dionysius Latas, greeting the Catholic Bishop Keane, with the apostolic kiss on the cheek and words of brotherly love, those who heard Bishop Keane relate how Archbishop Ireland and himself, finding that they were unable to enter

[74] Johnson, *op. cit.,* IV, 335. A short history of the parliament may be found in this volume on pp. 221–337.

[75] Barrows, *op. cit.,* I, 120.

[76] *Ibid.,* I, 116, 125, 136. Other papers were contributed by Augustine F. Hewitt, C.S.P., Walter Elliott, C.S.P., Monsignor Robert Seton, Professor Martin J. Wade of the Law Department of the State University of Iowa, Brother Azarias, F.S.C., D. J. Kennedy, O.S.B., Reverend James F. Cleary, Professor Thomas J. Semmes of the Law Department of Louisiana State University, the Reverends Thomas O'Gorman and John Gmeiner. Cf. *ibid.,* I, 112–146.

[77] Johnson, *op. cit.,* IV, 230.

[78] Barrows, *op. cit.,* I, 186.

[79] *Ibid.,* I, 182.

> the Hall of Columbus on account of the throng, went to the hall of Washington and presided over the Jewish Conference; . . . and the scores of thousands who beheld day after day the representatives of the great historic religions joining in the Lord's Prayer, felt profoundly that a new era of religious fraternity had dawned.[80]

But regardless of the show of brotherly affection, some Catholics were deeply shocked that Catholic bishops should appear at such a mixed gathering. The *Western Watchman* of St. Louis was loud in its denunciation of all the Catholics who participated in the parliament. Concerning the University rector it stated:

> Rt. Rev. John J. Keane thinks he sees much good to come out of the World's Parliament of Religions. We regret that we cannot see with the distinguished rector of the new University. We would like to be able to perceive with his optimistic eyes, but we cannot but feel that the Catholic participators were made the victims of unfortunate circumstances. They were indiscriminately *levelled* with publicans and heathens in that heterogeneous gathering making up a discordant babel of creeds.[81]

Keane was aware from the outset that he would be subjected to criticism as a result of his activity in Chicago, for he told O'Connell:

> I think he [Satolli] looks askance at our part in the Parliament of Religions, as do, no doubt, all the ultra conservatives. I got into it, first at the urgent solicitation of Abp. Ireland, — then at the request of the Abps. at their meeting in N. Y. — and I am confident that the result is an enormous advantage to the Church. But I take it for granted that I shall be denounced for it. So be it.[82]

Probably with a view to forestalling an inquiry on the matter, Gibbons wrote a long letter to Cardinal Rampolla to explain why

[80] *Ibid.,* II, 1559–1560.

[81] *Western Watchman,* Oct. 28, 1893. Herman J. Heuser, the editor of the *American Ecclesiastical Review,* who opposed the liberals during the school controversy, was convinced that the Holy Father had not been deceived, as he said, "about the aims of men here who under the pretense of national love propagate a ruinous Liberalism in religious matters," and he believed that the participation by these men in the Parliament of Religions would expose them further (AUND, Hudson Papers, Heuser to Daniel Hudson, Overbrook, Pennsylvania, Aug. 23, 1893).

[82] ADR, Keane to O'Connell, Washington, Oct. 10, 1893. Herman Heuser said: "Perhaps the Congress of Religions (with which I cannot feel any sympathy) may help to prove the worthlessness of the hope that concessions in Catholic teaching convert men to the true faith which, if it is animated by an unlimited charity, is nevertheless uncompromising and exacting in the maintenance of its traditional doctrine" (AUND, Hudson Papers, Heuser to Hudson, Overbrook, Pa., Aug. 23, 1893).

Catholics participated in the Parliament of Religions and to what extent they took part. The Baltimore cardinal told the papal Secretary of State that Keane had been assigned the difficult and delicate task of organizing the role the Catholics were to play. He stated that the rector had suggested the subjects of discussion to the directors of the enterprise and that they had endorsed all his suggestions. The bishop also obtained, said Gibbons, competent men to discuss the subjects, including several archbishops, professors of the University, presidents of seminaries, members of religious orders, distinguished Catholic laymen, and some famous foreign ecclesiastics.[83]

For the time being there was no repercussion in Rome, but the matter was not forgotten. In April, 1894, Keane remarked to O'Connell: "Mr. Haywood says that a dignitary of the Vatican wants a published report of the speeches of the Parliament of Religions. More complaints, I suppose!"[84] While the Roman authorities were giving their attention to the matter, it was kept before the public as an example of ecclesiastical liberalism in the United States by, among others, the Reverend Henry M. Tappert, of Mother of God Church in Covington, Kentucky, the delegate of the German American Catholic organizations to the general convention of German Catholics at Cologne, in a speech which he delivered before the assembled delegates on August 26, 1894.[85] At practically the same time, Bishop Keane was explaining the history and significance of the parliament before the delegates to the International Scientific Congress of Catholics at Brussels. "To love God," he said, "it is not necessary to hate our brother, only because he does not love God as we do. . . . To be faithful to our faith, it is not necessary to be in a state of war with those whose faith is different from ours." His words received a sympathetic echo in such Catholic papers as the *Journal de Bruxelles,* the *Voce della Verità,* and the *Bulletin Critique.*[86] Rome's final decision

[83] AAB, 92-P-5, Gibbons to Rampolla, Baltimore, Oct. 28, 1893 (French), copy. Keane received four letters from Monsignor Charles J. de Harlez concerning de Harlez's paper for the parliament (ACUA, Keane Papers, Louvain, Aug. 19, Sept. 12, 1892; June 16 and July 4, 1893 [French]).

[84] ADR, Keane to O'Connell, Washington, Apr. 13, 1894.

[85] ACUA, typed copy from the *Proceedings of the Seventh German-American Katholickentag, held in Louisville, Kentucky, September 24–27, 1894,* pp. 57–59. Tappert's discourse is quoted. In an interview which appeared in the *Journal de Bruxelles* on September 9, 1894, Keane took exception to and answered some points made by Tappert.

[86] *Catholic University Bulletin,* I (Jan., 1895), 90. The congress was held from September 3 to 7, 1894.

on such gatherings as the Chicago Parliament may have been influenced by Bishop McQuaid's explanation to Cardinal Ledochowski as to why he had assailed John Ireland by name from the pulpit of his cathedral in November, 1894. At the same time McQuaid unburdened himself of all his grievances against the liberals and the University, and among other things he told the cardinal prefect:

> Of late years, a spirit of liberalism is springing up in our body under such leaders as Mgr. Ireland and Mgr. Keane, that, if not checked in time, will bring disaster on the church. Many a time Catholic laymen have remarked that the Catholic Church they once knew seems to be passing away, so greatly shocked are they at what they see passing around them.[87]

At any rate, on September 18, 1895, in a letter to Satolli the Holy Father condemned further participation by Catholics in gatherings similar to the one held at Chicago.[88] By inference, therefore, it could be concluded that the course of action of those who had taken part in the Chicago parliament in 1893 had not met with the approval of the Holy See. Since Keane had planned and directed the Catholic participation another opportunity was thus afforded to deepen suspicions in Rome about his liberal tendencies.

But there were other considerations which had a bearing on the dismissal of Bishop Keane from the University; among them were the opposition to Archbishop Satolli and, what may be properly called, the campaign to discredit the University. Both of these situations stemmed from and formed part of the series of tensions between the conservatives and liberals. The University, of course, met with opposition from the very beginning, but the part played by Keane and some of his professors, especially Bouquillon and O'Gorman, in the controversies of the period increased the number of its adversaries and gave its original opponents additional motives for seeking to discredit it in the eyes of Rome. All this, as we shall see, naturally reflected on the principal administrator of the institution.

Satolli, on the other hand, was sent by Pope Leo XIII to restore peace to American ecclesiastical circles, but in the end he succeeded only in making an already bad situation worse. When he arrived in the United States in the fall of 1892, accompanied by Denis J.

[87] McQuaid to Ledochowski, 1895, original draft in the possession of Frederick J. Zwierlein, printed in his *The Life and Letters of Bishop McQuaid* (Rochester, 1927), III, 223–224.

[88] *Leonis XIII Acta,* XV, 323 ff., cited by Zwierlein, *op. cit.,* III, 238.

O'Connell and soon went to St. Paul where he spent a month with John Ireland, these circumstances were taken as signs by the conservatives that Satolli's sympathies were with the liberal group. Hence, when he presented his propositions on the school controversy some weeks later they were promptly rejected on the ground that they contained the liberals' views, very likely dictated by Ireland. Thus, almost from the very day that he set foot on American soil, Satolli met with opposition, and it would be difficult to determine whether or not he fully realized the real reason for it. Just as he was being subjected to the first wave of adverse criticism over his school propositions, Keane and the University entered the picture. Satolli took up residence at the University after the meeting of the archbishops in New York in November, 1892, a move which was likewise interpreted by the conservatives as evidence of his partisan leanings which would now be strengthened by contact with Keane and some of his faculty. Suspicions were seemingly corroborated in December of that year when the Roman archbishop rendered a decision in the case of Dr. Edward McGlynn which for some years had been a source of scandal and a matter of grave concern to Archbishop Corrigan. McGlynn's difficulties began in the 1880's when he became a follower of Henry George who advocated a single tax on land. Because he publicly advocated what seemed to Corrigan to be a questionable doctrine on the ownership of land and disobeyed his injunctions, he was ordered by his superior to cease such activity. When he failed to comply with the instruction, he was disciplined by Corrigan and excommunicated by Rome. He appealed his case to Roman authorities and they, in turn, instructed Satolli to weigh its merits. At the request of Satolli, therefore, a committee of four professors of the University reviewed a written statement of his teachings prepared by McGlynn and reported that he was not guilty of error, and rendered a verdict in favor of McGlynn. The rebellious priest was then restored to good standing by Satolli, an act which caused serious damage to Corrigan's prestige.[89] The New York prelate, therefore, felt he had solid reasons for opposing Satolli and additional reasons for resisting the University. One of his friends told him at the time:

> The newspapers, inspired by those inimical to Your Grace, have represented you as the leader of the opposition to the Delegate. The University has assumed, as it were, the office of defending the Delegate

[89] Bell, *op. cit.*

> and of teaching the hierarchy its duty to the Holy See. In assuming this office, it casts a slur on the Episcopate, who are bound by closer ties to the Holy See than any University and are not wanting in loyalty and devotion to the See of Peter.[90]

As the story unfolded it became evident that Corrigan was one of the delegate's chief opponents and that Keane was one of his stanch defenders.

Through the ensuing months Satolli continued to be identified with the liberals and, as Ireland said: "He is 'confirmed in truth and grace' — far more advanced in all our ideas than we are ourselves. He hates New York, and regrets that he ever put foot inside of Madison Av. house."[91] In an effort to silence his American critics, the delegate made a complaint to Leo XIII, and one of the Jesuits in Rome related to an American confrere:

> Mgr. Satolli, inspired no doubt by Archbishop Ireland and Co., has written to the Holy Father, complaining of the opposition made by our Fathers in the U. S. to the Apostolic Delegation and to himself. This has displeased the Pope very much who in consequence had had a letter written to the Very Rev. Fr. General asking him to put a stop to it.
>
> Of course, I know that the charge is not true and that its only foundation is in the false assumption that opposition to Archbishop Ireland is opposition to Mgr. Satolli.
>
> To remedy this false impression I was ordered by the Holy Father to write an article on the Delegation established by Him in the U.S.[92]

Chagrin over this complaint against the order may have prompted the statement in the New York *Herald* by one who was termed a "prominent Jesuit" in Rome:

> It is not exact to say that we [Jesuits] are making war on the University of Washington, but it must not be forgotten that for a century past the Jesuits had a flourishing university.
>
> When there was a question of establishing a Catholic University the Jesuits pointed out that it would be better to locate the projected university in some other city, as there was already such an institution in Washington.[93]

[90] AANY, McDonnell to Corrigan, Brooklyn, Feb. 10, 1893.

[91] AAB, 91-M-4, Ireland to Gibbons, St. Paul, June 13, 1893.

[92] Archives of Woodstock College, II, A8–b4, Brandi to René I. Holaind, S.J., Naples, July 26, 1893.

[93] New York *Herald,* Oct. 13, 1893. After this item had appeared, Ireland said to O'Connell: "Have you seen the late dispatch to the N. Y. Herald — an interview with a prominent Jesuit, saying that Satolli is, of course, accepted, but that no peace

Bishop Keane did not fail to answer the point in an interview with a representative from the *Herald,* and when the reporter wrote up his story, he named Salvatore M. Brandi, S.J., one of the editors of the *Civiltà Cattolica* who had written against the University during the school controversy, as the prominent Jesuit who had made the statement. The sequel was relayed to Monsignor O'Connell by Keane when he wrote:

> Fr. Brandi tried a trick on me lately. I rec'd a letter a few days ago from Card. Rampolla, saying that the Holy Father had learned that I had accused Fr. Brandi of being the author of an attack on the Univ. in the N. Y. Herald — that Fr. B. denied it, and that the Holy Father w'd be pleased if I would correct it. I answered by a statement showing that the charge ag'st Fr. B. was made by the Herald, an issue of veracity in which I could not interfere, and showing that as Fr. B. must have clearly understood this, his charge ag'st me was dishonest. The Cardinal forwards my letter with one of his own. I trust all will pass thro' your hands. Then comes a letter from Fr. B. to me, saying that he "repudiates and condemns" the attack on the Univ., and complaining that the *Herald* should have attributed it to him. I have answered, expressing my satisfaction at receiving his repudiation and condemnation suggesting that he make it public, and expressing my amazement that, knowing the charge to have come from the *Herald,* he should have accused me of it to the Pope. They too seem on the defensive, but their "art is long."[94]

Among the letters mentioned by Keane for the Papal Secretary of State, the one from Cardinal Gibbons had stated: "I cannot forbear showing you the deep sorrow that I feel at the continuation of attacks against the University in spite of the well-known intentions of His Holiness."[95] When the letters of protest were presented at the Vatican, Denis O'Connell reported after an audience with Leo XIII: "The Pope will support the University. We agreed that Father Brandi was provoking too many complaints."[96] Keane meanwhile had told Ireland that Brandi was the source for the *Herald* story, whereupon the Archbishop of St. Paul minced no words in a letter to O'Connell. "Brandi is a devil," he said. "He now writes to Keane that he never

---

can be made with Ireland or the Catholic University. I presume this is their program. Bp. Keane answered their attack on the University. He fears with reason that the war will continue" (ADR, Ireland to O'Connell, New York, Oct. 23, 1893).

[94] ADR, Keane to O'Connell, Washington, Nov. 16, 1893.

[95] AAB, 92-R-2, Gibbons to Rampolla, Baltimore, Nov. 14, 1893 [French], copy.

[96] ACUA, Keane Papers, O'Connell to Keane, Rome, Dec. 4, 1893.

spoke against the University, but the *Herald* told Keane that Brandi was its informant."[97] However, from the letter that was sent to Keane by the Washington bureau of the New York *Herald,* the only source available for information on the subject, the identification of Brandi as the "prominent Jesuit" was not evident.[98] At any rate, the accusation lodged against Keane by Brandi evidently was not warranted, for the Jesuit showed that he was concerned over the matter. In a letter to a confrere in the United States he expressed surprise at seeing in the *Catholic Mirror,* "written under the eyes of His Eminence," a statement to the effect that he had not denied the interview. Since the American Jesuit had written to him that the cardinal knew about Keane's letter to himself and to Rampolla, Gibbons should have known that he had made a disavowal to Keane.[99] In an attempt to close the issue Brandi cabled Keane to publish a denial of the *Herald* story in his name. But Keane told O'Connell: "I answered that as I had nothing to do with the mention of his name, I declined to have anything to do with his discussion of it."[100] It was an unfortunate and complicated incident which increased the animosity between the parties involved, but it was a logical outcome of the controversial spirit. Brandi had considerable influence in Rome and in Europe generally, which he employed to help destroy the so-called dangerous liberalism which he and his conservative friends attributed to Keane and other American bishops. It would be unjust to conclude that Keane's critics were intellectually dishonest, but it is not unlikely that personal antagonism colored their estimate of him when speaking to those in authority.

The continuing dissension between the so-called conservatives and liberals, which found the University identified with one side, evidently caused the misgivings of Roman authorities about the work of the institution, for in the fall of 1893, the Pope requested Satolli to submit a report on its condition. This prompted Keane to tell O'Connell: "I am very glad of it. We have nothing to fear in the facts of the case, and Satolli says it will redound to the good of the Univ'y."[101] A month

[97] ADR, Ireland to O'Connell, St. Paul, Nov. 24, 1893.

[98] Ahern, *op. cit.,* p. 146.

[99] Archives of Woodstock College, II A7B, Brandi to Aloysius Sabetti, S.J., Rome, Jan. 1, 1894 (Italian).

[100] ADR, Keane to O'Connell, Washington, Jan. 5, 1894.

[101] ADR, Keane to O'Connell, Atlantic City, Oct. 10, 1893. As an aftermath of the school controversy, the University was in disfavor with some of the bishops on the Board of Trustees, who voiced their complaints at their annual meeting in the spring of 1893. Keane answered the charges against the institution and they agreed

later the rector informed his friend in Rome: "Mgr. S. leaves us today for his own residence. He has shown his appreciation of the kindness we have in every way tried to show him for over a year, and the Delegation too. I feel sure that we have in him a true friend."[102] Surely, Keane had little to fear when the investigation of the University was in the hands of Satolli. Besides, there had been renewed assurances late that summer when O'Connell informed Gibbons that the Pope and Rampolla, as he put it, "will both undertake now the support of the University, and they are resolute."[103]

On the occasion of his annual report to the trustees in the spring of 1894, Keane said:

> If the University is to become what the Holy Father and the people of America expect it to be, energetic efforts need to be made both in

---

that he could not prevent the professors from talking and writing. He also rebuffed the accusation that the institution was instilling insubordination against episcopal authority and he told the trustees that they should see to it that the aspersions were denied (ACUA, Card with notes on "Sessio. Extra., April 14, 1893." Keane's report to the faculty on the meeting of the trustees). As an evidence of this episcopal displeasure Ryan had told Gibbons in February: "The clatter of Ireland and his rabble — Conway, Phelan, Cronin, Lambert, Malone, Ducey, O'Gorman — have added insult to injury and moreover tended fearfully to undermine all authority" (AAB, 91-F-7/1, Ryan to Gibbons, Alton, Pennsylvania, Feb. 24, 1893). Another indication of their low estate at the time was revealed when O'Connell told the Chancellor of the University: "Never did I dream that such foulness could ever come out of the American Church as the past two years have brought forth. The Episcopate has fallen greatly in the opinion of the Romans" (AAB, 91-G-10, O'Connell to Gibbons, Rome, Mar. 14, 1893).

[102] ADR, Keane to O'Connell, Washington, Nov. 16, 1893. In Gibbons' attempt to heal the breach between Satolli and Corrigan he had Keane write a letter for him (AAB, 91-S-3, Gibbons to Satolli, Baltimore, Aug. 9, 1893. Latin copy in Keane's hand). Later the rector told Gibbons: "Mgr. Satolli seems convinced that Abp. Corrigan has done all that could reasonably be asked of him towards giving his allegiance and establishing peace. He earnestly hopes that your Eminence may in like manner be able to bring about peace between Abps. Ireland and Corrigan when they are together in Chicago; and he suggests that it be on the basis of simply letting the past drop, since there w'd be little hope of success in explanations and vindications of things said and done hitherto" (AAB, 91-T-4, Keane to Gibbons, Washington, Aug. 25, 1893).

[103] AAB, 91-R-5, O'Connell to Gibbons, Rome, Aug. 4, 1893. Keane told Gibbons: "I have a splendid letter from Dr. Bouquillon. The Pope and Rampolla, and the Vannutellis also, are heartily with the University and against the Jesuits. The Pope promises a strong letter to that effect" (AAB, 91-T-4, Keane to Gibbons, Washington, Aug. 25, 1893). Bouquillon gave a long account of his audience with the Pope and other officials. They discussed the University and Satolli and the delegation. Bouquillon, of course, presented the views of the liberals (ACUA, Bouquillon Papers, Bouquillon to Monseigneur [Keane], Rome, n.d., [1893]).

order to encourage, solidify, and perfect the Faculty already in existence, and in order to render practicable and successful the Faculty which we have promised to shortly open for the laity.

This is rendered the more manifest and imperative by the efforts that are being made to discredit and injure the University. That such efforts were being made there has for some time been good reason to believe; as to their source and their motives only surmises could be formed. They recently culminated in the presentation to the Holy See of such charges and insinuations that the Holy Father judged it best to ask of his Apostolic Delegate an investigation and report, in order, as I am assured on the highest authority, to put an end to these calumnies. The Apostolic Delegate accordingly, after a careful inquiry, made a detailed report of the past work and present condition of the University, and has received from the Holy Father an assurance of his entire satisfaction. Is it not greatly to be desired that the guardians and friends were as vigilant and active as its enemies?[104]

After the meeting the rector remarked to O'Connell, "they did not, as I rather hoped, ask further about it, and thus give me an opportunity to give explanations which I w'd have been glad to present. They were evidently anxious not to probe and stir up depths."[105]

The trustees, however, were more anxious to probe than Keane suspected. The committee on studies and discipline, composed of Placide L. Chapelle, Ignatius F. Horstmann, and Thomas S. Lee, agreed that the small enrollment in the University was due to the lack of interest on the part of the hierarchy and of the clergy of the country. They recommended that an investigation be made to determine whether the reason for this defect arose from dissatisfaction with the University, and, if so, on what grounds.[106] Horstmann reported to Corrigan that when the committee report was made known, Keane, as he said, "immediately demanded whether that was intended as a reflection on him and the faculty." Chapelle had assured the rector that there was no such intention but that since a fact confronted them it was necessary to find out the causes of that fact.[107] Bishop Keane could not help realizing that the University was not prospering since at the time the number of matriculated students had decreased

[104] *Fifth Annual Report of the Rector of the Catholic University of America, March, 1894* (Washington, 1894), pp. 4–5.

[105] ADR, Keane to O'Connell, Washington, Apr. 13, 1894.

[106] ACUA, MMBT, Washington, Apr. 4, 1894, pp. 45–46.

[107] AANY, Horstmann to Corrigan, Cleveland, Apr. 21, 1894.

to twenty-six.[108] Evidently the depression from which the country was suffering at the time was not the sole cause for the situation, and Horstmann was probably right in telling Corrigan:

> I told them [the trustees] plainly that your [Corrigan's] cordial and generous support and that of your diocese was absolutely necessary, that it was more important than everybody else; that it was from the large cities of the East that the University would have for some time to look for its support and its students.[109]

While Keane might well have considered this statement as a complaint against him personally, since it was well known that he and Corrigan were at odds, yet, the rector's conscience was probably clear in the matter, for Corrigan had not been sympathetic to the project even before Keane's appointment as rector.[110]

[108] Ahern, *op. cit.*, p. 54. In a letter to Heuser on January 23, 1893, René I. Holaind, a Jesuit participant in the school controversy, made strong remarks against the liberal influence of the University: "If the University goes on giving the young priests who are *not posted at all* on philosophy a jumbling of lectures as diversified as the robe of Benjamin (I am told by respectable witnesses that one of the lectures defended evolution, not only for the body but for the soul), of course this will be counteracted by such men as Dr. Pohle, and if these young men were thoroughly grounded on the scientific basis of biology and psychology, very little harm would be done; but to present to them a panorama of incoherent systems before they are capable of finding their way, is to a practical teacher a lamentable piece of absurdity. . . . I am much afraid that unless a different impulse is given to the University, it will do more harm than good. First class seminaries is [*sic*] what we need most, we have several but all are not up to the mark. . . . In the meantime keep B. lively but smiling, and kill mercilessly any plan which would surrender our boys in the future of the Catholic Church in this country to a pack of evolutionists and free-masons" (cited by Barry, *op. cit.*, p. 191). Holaind's informants probably attended one or all of the four public lectures delivered at the University in January, 1892, by Robert Wilson Shufeldt, M.D., who by his own admission later was "not even an acceptor of the fundamental requirements of the Christian faith." The first two lectures were published in the *Catholic Mirror,* which deleted parts considered objectionable, and in the *Church News,* which prefaced each portion of the second lecture as it appeared with the statement: "The University assumes no responsibility for opinions advanced by lecturers in the public courses." According to the lecturer, the students disapproved of a few points in the second lecture and of many statements in the last two lectures. In fact, in one instance the interference of the rector was required to maintain order. The lectures were printed in full in the *American Field* in 1894 and reprinted from that journal in one volume under the title *Lectures on Biology Delivered before the Catholic University of America.* He spoke of the evolution of man in general in five places (pp. 8, 22, 43, 48, 56) and in a number of places in the last two lectures he inferred that the soul of man has evolved. It seems strange that such disturbances followed the lectures, since it must have been evident from the outset that the lecturer would put forth the views common to nineteenth-century materialists.

[109] AANY, Horstmann to Corrigan, Cleveland, Apr. 21, 1894.

[110] Ellis, *The Formative Years,* pp. 185–186.

In view of the precarious condition of the University brought about by the lack of interest and support from a great number of the hierarchy and by the unrelenting attacks which were designed to discredit it,[111] the rector was urged by a number of the University faculty to go to Rome in the summer of 1894 to gain support there. He told O'Connell:

> Our Faculty has been very anxious, as also Mgr. Satolli, that the Cardinal should go to Rome at the earliest possible day, in order to dispel these clouds of whisper and suspicion which so assiduously are gathered around the Holy Father, in regard to Mgr. Satolli, in regard to the University, in regard to the general tendency of so-called "liberalism" among us. . . .
>
> The faculty urged very strongly that I, as rector, ought to go to Rome along with the Cardinal. They think the University ought to show itself boldly and speak out strongly, — that we greatly need another clear and strong word from the Holy Father, in view of recent attacks on the University, and because of our opening the next Faculty, for the laity, in October '95, which calls for endless activity and generosity for the raising of funds and securing of students and for general encouragement and cooperation.[112]

The advice of the faculty was probably seconded by O'Connell, without whose approval few moves were made in Rome by the prelates of the progressive persuasion. Remote preparation, which might help to smooth the rector's course in the Eternal City, had been made by an unexpected discovery on the part of Archbishop Ireland. In April the Archbishop of St. Paul was successful in persuading Michael Walsh, the editor of the *Catholic Herald* of New York and up until that time Corrigan's friend, to bring him "*all* Corrigan's letters, and to relate *all* Corrigan's conversations," which, as Ireland expressed it, "plainly connect the latter [Corrigan] with the diabolical war waged against the delegation." A full statement from Walsh and copies of Corrigan's letters, said Ireland, were mailed to Cardinal Rampolla, and he added to Monsignor O'Connell: "We are most signally vindi-

[111] Some of the bishops were strongly for the University and anxious about the opposition. The Bishop of Mobile told O'Connell in the summer of 1894 that Bishop Thomas S. Byrne of Nashville had spoken in favor of the University on the day of his consecration. He added: "I hope the Holy Father will continue to uphold it. The failure of the University would be a calamity to the Church in the U. S. And yet there is grave danger that personal, sectional and national prejudices may render the great work a failure. I wish all were of the mind of Bp. Byrne, but he is in a small diocese and cannot do much" (ADR, O'Sullivan to O'Connell, Mobile, Aug. 18, 1894).

[112] ADR, Keane to O'Connell, Washington, Apr. 13, 1894.

cated. Deo Gratias."[113] Ireland's action in regard to the Corrigan documents afforded a more proximate preparation for the visit of Keane when O'Connell and O'Gorman decided to make good use of Ireland's discovery.[114] The full implications of the affair were revealed to Cardinal Gibbons by Keane after he had left Rome:

> My visit to Rome happened at a most critical moment, and was most opportune. Soon after his return from the East, Mgr. O'C. talked with the Pope and Cardinal Rampolla about the manifest policy of the Propaganda to disparage Mgr. Satolli's office. At their request he handed in a written memorial on the subject. The Pope looked into the matter, and became terribly indignant. They say Mgr. Ciaska, Secr. of Prop., fainted in the antechamber after his scolding. The Pope was determined to put the delegation beyond cavil and opposition, and a change of tone soon manifested itself all through Rome. Satolli's enemies were the Pope's enemies,—and he knew there were some in America, and seemed ready to take any measures to chastise them. O'C gave, of course, full information about the opposition of N.Y., and his trickery. Then Burtsell's statements fitted in, and were made welcome. Then O'Gorman arrived, introduced by Ireland. Rampolla had a long talk with him, pumped him thoroughly, and arranged that he should see the Pope, who for over an hour eagerly probed the condition, as to the delegation, as to the University, as to the condition of things in general.

[113] ADR, Ireland to O'Connell, New York, April 29, [1894]. Prior to this discovery Ireland had informed his friend in Rome: "Mgr. Satolli is himself quite discouraged and says that he will not stay here longer than spring. He feels that Propaganda is against him, that prelates here are plotting against him, that the Cardinal is playing a double role, that he has but *one* on whom he can absolutely count" (ADR, Ireland to O'Connell, St. Paul, February 16, 1894). Keane told the same correspondent: "Mgr. Satolli is in splendid health and good spirits, but eager to go home. When he must go, God grant that his successor may be as good a man" (ADR, Keane to O'Connell, Washington, April 13, 1894).

[114] In O'Gorman's audience with the Holy Father the chief matter considered "was the opposition to Mgr. Satolli on the part of the American Bishops and of Propaganda —and the best means to fortify the Delegate's position. . . . You may rest assured that I was without mercy for Corrigan. The pope wonders very much at the 'position indécise' of Card. Gibbons. Gibbons has certainly done himself injury in the mind and esteem of the pope by his seeming friendship with N. York" (ACUA, Bouquillon Papers, O'Gorman to "My dear friend" [Bouquillon], Rome, July 18, [1894]). In another letter O'Gorman told his friend that he had prepared and indoctrinated Keane so well that he had followed absolutely all the lines that O'Gorman had traced for him: University, Corrigan, Satolli (*ibid.*, July 23, [1894] [French]). Keane remarked to Bouquillon: "In two long audiences with the Holy Father I had abundant opportunity to give him *all* useful information as to the University, the Delegation, and the general condition in our country. The ground had been admirably prepared by Dr. O'Gorman" (ACUA, Bouquillon Papers, Keane to Bouquillon, Pegli, Aug. 3, 1894).

Thus all was well prepared for me. I saw Rampolla the day after my arrival, had a long talk with him in which we went over *all* the ground, as to things and as to persons. He begged me to speak to the Pope with equal fulness and clearness, — and in broad diplomatic hints gave me clearly to understand that the Pope was preparing to speak and act strongly.

Two days after I had an audience with the Pope, and for an hour and a half we were as hard at it as we could be. He was most cordial and affectionate, (and, by the way, in marvellously good health, as bright and strong as 5 yrs ago). After kind words about your Eminence whose respects I presented to him, as also to Rampolla, we got at the University. First I explained our success and presented an album of photographic views. Then we came to our difficulties, and discussed fully the opposition 1° of the Germans, 2° of the Jesuits, 3° of N. Y., 4° of all opposed to Mgr. Satolli and his policy, with which they identify the University. The last point launched us into the discussion of the delegation and Mgr. S. Here is where the Pope is most determined, because the delegation is simply an element in his "policy", which is, the breaking down of the influence of the Triple Alliance, — which means monarchism, militarism, and the oppression of the Papacy, — by enhancing the influence of democratic France and democratic America — an influence which presages a democratic Italy, or Federated Italy, with the Pope in a position suitable to him. On this policy he is inflexibly bent, and the welcome given to the representative of the Pope in America was a most hopeful sign of the rallying of all democracy around the Pope. In this there may be an exaggeration, but there is also a great truth, — the Church and the Democracies are fast drawing nearer. Hence opposition to Satolli and the delegation was the worst hostility to the Pope, and he is ready to discipline the opposition and to enhance the authority of the delegation. This is going to be the central feature and motive of what he will say and do, — and he told me plainly that he was going to speak and act. He did not give me details, and of course I did not venture to ask for them. But it seems most likely that he will make the delegation the *final and obligatory* court of appeal from the Metropolitan courts of the country, and enhance Mgr. S's dignity as much as possible.[115]

From the tone of the rector's letter, one would conclude that he had been successful in identifying for Leo XIII all those who were opposed to the University and to Satolli and that he could anticipate definite action by the Holy Father which would silence the critics of the institution he directed and of the delegate whom he so stanchly

[115] AAB, 93-J-7, Keane to Gibbons, Pegli, Aug. 3, 1894.

supported. On the same day that he wrote to Cardinal Gibbons the bishop informed his vice-rector that the Pope and Rampolla had assured him they were not at all impressed by whispers and insinuations against the University, that the report asked from Satolli was only for the vindication of the institution, and "that in the Encyclical for the U. S., which he is preparing, he will speak strongly in its favor."[116] Shortly after he left the Eternal City to rest from the labors of his eventful days there, Keane showed his renewed optimism when he told O'Connell: "I leave Rome with a more contented and hopeful mind than ever before. A wonderful transformation is being operated there. It will have resistance and temporary reversals, but it is sure to go on and to greatly modify the whole external administration of the Church. Blessed are you in being the chief instrument of Providence in bringing it about."[117]

In this case as in others Keane's optimism led him to entertain hopes for the future which, as it turned out, were quite unwarranted. The opposition of the University's adversaries was based upon so many and such complicated motives that the healing element of time was needed before peace could be regained. It must be remembered,

[116] ACUA, Garrigan Papers, Keane to Garrigan, Pegli, Aug. 3, 1894. He also informed the vice-rector that, besides the two long audiences with the Pope and three lengthy interviews with Cardinal Rampolla, he had talks with several other cardinals. Keane had discussed another matter with the Holy Father: "In my second audience with the Pope, we dwelt at considerable length on a point of great importance — the tendency toward socialism and the need of condemning dangerous societies. As far as this concerned our labor organizations in America, or even the Odd Fellows, etc., I strongly protested against condemnations, as unnecessary, and as sure to prove pernicious, as they have so manifestly done in Italy, etc. I quoted Card. Gibbons as earnestly deprecating any condemnations. — The Pope seemed impressed, but not convinced; so I went next day and had a very serious talk with Rampolla about it. He promised that he would speak strongly to the Pope and try to withhold all action till the Cardinal should come next fall. — O'Gorman and O'Connell thought this a serious indication of how the mind of the Pope has been influenced by recent protests that he was encouraging socialism. They thought it might be useful for you to come and discuss this matter thoroughly with Rampolla, the Vannutellis, etc." (ACUA, Bouquillon Papers, Keane to Bouquillon, Pegli, Aug. 3, 1894). O'Gorman then informed Bouquillon it would be well to come to Rome because, as he said, "you will be able to achieve by your influence the work that I have only begun. Keane is gone, not even having done as much as I. I see a disposition among the authorities to give you much more confidence than to him" (ACUA, Bouquillon Papers, O'Gorman to Bouquillon, Rome, Aug. 4, [1894] [French]). Gibbons wrote anent the question of publishing the decree on the secret societies in 1895; "The New Decree was issued against the Societies before I reached Rome. It was industriously circulated that I was to plead strongly for the societies, and hence I was forestalled" (ACUA, Keane Papers, Gibbons to Keane, Wörishofen, July 12, 1895).

[117] ADR, Keane to O'Connell, Pegli, Aug. 3, 1894.

too, that Keane's opponents had ears in the Vatican to hear about and to report on his activities and representations. Because of the leaks in official circles in those years, it is probable that Schroeder knew that Keane had told the Pope that he wanted to get rid of him.[118] It is likely, too, that the Jesuits' vigilance resulted in their being appraised of the situation and that Corrigan's friends in the Vatican informed him of the representations made against him. Indeed, some of the Jesuits were interested in the reason for the rector's Roman visit, for Brandi told an American friend that Keane said he was in Rome to offer explanations to the Holy Father concerning certain matters which had been censored by the bishops in their letters of reply to the Holy See on the state of the University.[119]

The encyclical which Leo XIII had promised during Keane's visit was finished on January 6, 1895, and dispatched to the United States. In his long letter to Gibbons after leaving Rome, the rector had accurately foretold the contents of *Longinqua oceani.* The apostolic delegation was the central theme; it was to be accepted by all parties because the delegate was the personal representative of the Sovereign Pontiff. He was the symbol of unity and his presence in America should be conducive to unity. Regarding the University, the Holy Father first recalled the "prosperity and glory" of the Belgian nation, which was ascribed in part to the influence of the University of Louvain, and then he added: "Equally abundant will be the benefits proceeding from the Washington University if the professors and students (as we doubt not they will) be mindful of Our injunctions, and, party spirit and strife being removed, conciliate the good opinion of the people and clergy."[120]

Despite the Pope's clearly expressed desires, however, "party spirit and strife" were not removed. A few months after the encyclical had been published the Sulpician president of Divinity College at the

118 ACUA, Bouquillon Papers, O'Gorman to Bouquillon, Rome, July 23, [1894] (French).

119 Archives of Woodstock College, II, A7b-8, Brandi to Sabetti, Naples, July 26, 1894 (Italian).

120 "Encyclical Letter," *Catholic University Bulletin,* I (Apr., 1895), 236. The Latin text and an English translation of the encyclical may also be found in *American Catholic Quarterly Review,* XX (Apr., 1895), 346–368. The Pope told O'Connell: "O'Gorman helped me a great deal: He gave me many notes but now I must go over them myself and make them my own. I shall give them another coloring, but the substance will be there" (BCA, 93-K-7, O'Connell to Gibbons, Grottaferrata, Sept. 9, 1894). Some weeks before O'Gorman told Bouquillon: "I am writing the whole Encyclical, the Holy Father will take what he wants of the text" (ACUA, Bouquillon Papers, O'Gorman to Bouquillon, Rome, Aug. 24 [1894] [French]).

University told a friend that there was much adverse criticism of the University in Baltimore.[121] Three months later the same correspondent was informed:

> Dissentions [*sic*] between Professors are far from healing. Last Sunday they had a very stormy meeting, 2 left the room, one was threatened with polite intervention and with expulsion, Dean followed 2 through the hallways, angry discussions, students hearing all, a P. one insulted in the room being qualified as the meanest fellow ever known leaves the meeting, students know who used the language and against whom used. Enough of it, such a state of things is sickening.
>
> Fr. Orban is well, greatly enjoys the comedy, as one of the Professors told me: what is worse is: so petty are the causes of such dissentions; Fr. Hogan would immensely enjoy all this.[122]

These unedifying disorders had arisen from the injured attitude assumed by Schroeder, George Périès, professor of Canon Law, and Henri Hyvernat, professor of Sacred Scripture, when the first issue of the *Catholic University Bulletin* appeared without articles from their pens. Keane later explained that a general invitation had been extended to the professors for contributions and, therefore, their complaint that they had been "boycotted" was repudiated by the *Bulletin* committee, which declared that the new publication was open to all. He stated further:

> But it did not satisfy Drs. S. and P. Dr. Hyvernat yielded and contributed. The others demanded public apology! and, this being very properly refused, as no offence had been given, or intended, they maintained their injured attitude. It was sent forth to the press, and the German papers of the country were full of "the boycott," and of denunciations of the Bulletin, of the University and its officials.[123]

Thus another internal misunderstanding had become a matter for public discussion, and a further occasion had been afforded for those who disliked the University to continue their opposition to it.

During the summer of 1895, Gibbons wrote to Keane from Rome to assure him that the University had been the subject of praise during his audiences of the Holy Father and the Secretary of State.

[121] ASMS, Francis Louis Dumont to Charles B. Rex, Washington, Mar. 20, 1895. Fr. Dumont feared that the two Sulpicians at the University might be unjustly blamed for spreading reports which gave rise to the criticism.

[122] ASMS, Dumont to Rex, Washington, June 6, 1895.

[123] ACUA, "Chronicles," pp. 58–59. The first issue of the *Catholic University Bulletin* appeared in January, 1895.

The Cardinal also told the rector that the Pope had given him a letter, which he had requested in view of the opening of the faculties for the laity that fall, in which Leo XIII, as Gibbons said, "refers to the Colleges as feeders of the University, speaks of it as an institution specially dear to him, and closes by a paternal allusion and blessing to the Rector, Professors, benefactors, and students."[124] This good news, however, was more than offset by the startling announcement that Denis O'Connell had resigned his position as Rector of the American College. It is certain that his resignation had been demanded,[125] but the real reason behind the deposition remains obscure.[126] Two years before Ireland had warned O'Connell of danger. He had then said:

> I am afraid that the war may now turn on you. I hear mutterings. Newey [*sic*] when in St. Paul dropped some words. Rooker has picked up others. Now, all will be right; the Cardinal says he will stick by you. Inordicus [*sic*] and I are sure he will. But take an advice: give up this trip to the Holy Land. . . . Keep some of your friends at a little greater distance.
>
> I am certain that our foes track us at every step, spy us. All this makes life a burden; but, then, for the time being, we must be careful.[127]

Ireland may have been right in foretelling this as part of the war against himself and his associates. At any rate, he was certainly right in his belief that Gibbons would remain loyal to his friend, for when the blow fell the cardinal appointed O'Connell vicar of his titular church, Santa Maria in Trastavere, where he remained in partial exile for the next eight years.[128] O'Connell's dismissal was a severe reversal for Keane, too, both as a member of the group to which O'Connell belonged and as Rector of the University, because he had always found in the gifted priest a friend capable of accomplishing a great deal for University interests through his close relations with many of the key men in the Roman Curia.

Since the internal strife among the faculty at the University had not been resolved when the scholastic year opened in 1896, Keane decided to dismiss George Périès who was considered the chief cause of the turmoil. The professor of Canon Law was informed that his con-

124 ACUA, Keane Papers, Gibbons to Keane, Rome, June 29, 1895.
125 Hogan, *op. cit.*, pp. 145–146.
126 *Ibid.*
127 ADR, Ireland to O'Connell, New York, Oct. 23, 1893.
128 Hogan, *op. cit.*, p. 146.

tract would not be renewed at the end of the year when it expired according to the terms agreed upon in 1893. At first Périès agreed to resign and, like others who had been dissatisfied with the administration, he turned to Corrigan to have him honor a promise of an official position in the Archdiocese of New York.[129] Then he changed his mind about resigning and appealed to the Board of Trustees to continue his services on the ground that his contract was not limited to three years. The board rejected his request after the rector stated that he had a limited contract and, as the report contended, that "Périès was incompetent to teach Canon Law for this country; that his students were dissatisfied with him; that his language concerning him as Rector had been most contemptuous, and that he had spoken publicly in Washington against the Rector and the University."[130] Moreover, some of the professors had stated, among other things, that if Périès remained they would be exposed to the danger of what they termed "intrigues and calumnies both among the students and the city."[131] When he failed with the trustees Périès carried his case to the apostolic delegate who, in turn, submitted the matter to the rector for reply. Bouquillon prepared the answer which was described as being "so clear and crushing that the Delegate declared that Dr. Périès had no case." Since there was no other avenue open to him, the professor reluctantly submitted his resignation.[132]

From what has been said thus far, it is evident that Satolli was considered to be the friend and protector of those who were identified as members of the progressive wing of the hierarchy,[133] and they, in

[129] AANY, Périès to Corrigan, St. Mande, Feb. 14, 1896.

[130] ACUA, MMBT, Washington, Apr. 18, 1896, p. 158.

[131] AAB, 94-Y-1, the confidential report of Bouquillon, Grannan, and Shahan to Cardinal Gibbons [1896]. George V. Leahy, a student at the University during these years, remarked in his "University Recollections" that Périès' apparent lack of interest in his work was observed by some and that all perceived that "the professor in question apparently preferred the social life; visiting frequently at the French Ambassador's downtown, none of our business to be sure, but significant" (cited by Browne, "Pioneer Days at the Catholic University," *op. cit.*, p. 31).

[132] ACUA, "Chronicles," p. 60. For a full treatment of the Périès case, cf. Ahern, *op. cit.*, pp. 153–156.

[133] J. Havens Richards, S.J., says that on March 7, 1893, Satolli spoke to him "of the Liberalism which he declared to be prevalent among some of the American clergy. He undoubtedly referred to Archbishop Ireland, Bishop Keane, and others associated with them, of Bishop Keane in particular he spoke strongly, saying that in the latter's recent address before the Unitarians there was nothing which any non-Catholic might not have said. This language surprised me exceedingly," Richards continues, "as it was still generally supposed that Satolli himself was allied to that faction" (E. J. Burrus, S.J. (ed.), Notes on the early relations of the Catholic Uni-

turn, were loyal to him when some of his policies met with criticism. The more conservative prelates, quite naturally, were at pains to win the delegate to their point of view on all of the burning issues then in dispute among the American bishops. As early as 1893, Archbishop Ryan of Philadelphia was of the opinion that Satolli could be won over to the wisdom of the conservative position, and he revealed his thoughts on the subject to Corrigan when he wrote:

> We have two of his favorite pupils, professors at Overbrook and from their account of him I formed the opinion that when thoroughly convinced of what is right, he is unyielding and impartial. One of these professors stated, that on his first visit to this country he spoke of you in the most laudatory terms as learned and pious, etc., but the change came in the interim, whatever caused it. I firmly believe that he will get right as he is really a pious interior man and open to conviction, after he has overcome those short spells of nervous passion which, it seems, he cannot control. Strange as it may seem to you now, he has more in common with yourself than one would think, and if you knew each other better you would become close friends.[134]

Such an acrimonious campaign was waged by those with opposite views on the problems peculiar to the American ecclesiastical scene that the Archbishop of Lepanto must at times have felt insecure on occasions when he favored the liberal group. It would be impossible

---

versity of America, Washington, D. C., with the members of the Society of Jesus of the Maryland-New York Province, prepared by Joseph Havens Richards, S.J., rector of Georgetown University, Washington, D. C., from August 15, 1888 to July 3, 1898," *Woodstock Letters,* LXXXIII [1954], 90).

[134] AANY, Ryan to Corrigan, Philadelphia, July 23, 1893. When Corrigan celebrated the anniversary of his consecration on August 15, 1893, he delivered a sermon in the presence of the delegate which Cardinal Rampolla termed the Archbishop of New York's profession of faith (AASP, O'Connell to Ireland, Rome, Sept. 12, 1893). According to O'Connell the following disastrous changes from the liberals' point of view resulted: "I open this to tell you the new combination, i.e., that the Holy Father is delighted with the adhesion of Corrigan, that in the future it will be Satolli, Corrigan and Co., with peace and harmony. Ireland and Gibbons being put aside, that henceforth in America all will move on in solid column, the Pope at the head. That Ireland's plan has failed, etc., in a word. That party to take now Satolli on their shoulders and march with him as their banner. That there was no real reason for disagreement. That they always wanted Satolli but not Ireland. So the program for Edes, Vetter, Geullaime, Baumgarten — all the German press. So too the last blow of the Civilta" (AASP, O'Connell to Ireland, n.p., Oct. 8, 1893). Satolli was informed by Rampolla on June 14, 1893, that the Pope was concerned about the consequences of the apparent dissension existing between the delegate and the Archbishop of New York. The Cardinal pointed out that the latter had "many connections, not only in the United States, but also in Rome, and eventually his followers could cause difficulties to the mission of the delegate" (cited by Soderini, *op. cit.*).

to reveal the thoughts that found a place in his mind, just as it would be presumptuous to attempt positively to identify the voices that found his ear to whisper the words that gave rise to uncertainty and suspicion. But one thing is certain, namely, that he did give these matters thought and that he did listen to utterances that were unfriendly to Keane and his friends.

The delaying tactics employed by the forward party, especially Gibbons and Ireland, to prevent the condemnation of the Knights of Pythias, the Odd Fellows, the Sons of Temperance, and similar societies, and their reluctance to promulgate the decree when the three societies mentioned by name were condemned by the Church, may have been the deciding factor in changing the delegate's attitude toward them. Over a period of several years the suspected lodges were discussed in the annual meetings of the archbishops, and in each instance the representatives of the forward group reasoned that the societies under consideration were not similar to the Freemasons, a secret society condemned by the Church, while the members of the conservative party argued that they were secret societies worthy of condemnation. Since the archbishops failed to reach unanimous agreement on the matter, they were required by a decree of the Third Plenary Council of Baltimore to submit it to Rome for a decision.[135] In 1894, while the Roman officials were studying the subject, Keane discussed the afore-mentioned societies in an audience with the Pope and "strongly protested against condemnation, as unnecessary, and as sure to prove pernicious." Since the Holy Father did not seem "convinced," as he said, he mentioned the matter to Cardinal Rampolla, who promised that "he would speak strongly to the Pope and try to withhold all action" until Cardinal Gibbons came.[136] However, on August 20, 1894, less than a month after Keane had "strongly protested against condemnation," the decree condemning the three disputed societies was forwarded to Archbishop Satolli in Washington. Owing to the campaign then being waged against the Catholic Church by the American Protective Association, the conservative archbishops joined the forward group when they met on October 10, 1894, in the resolution to withhold publication of the decree. Two months later the apostolic

[135] For an excellent treatment of this phase of the problem, cf. Ellis, *The Life of James Cardinal Gibbons,* pp. 454–475. For a detailed treatment of the problem down to 1895, cf. Fergus Macdonald, C.P., *The Catholic Church and the Secret Societies in the United States* (New York, 1946). Also cf. Moynihan, *op. cit.,* pp. 214–218.

[136] ACUA, Bouquillon Papers, Keane to Bouquillon, Pegli, Aug. 3, 1894. Also cf. n. 116.

delegate informed Gibbons that it was the wish of the Holy Father that the decree be promulgated. This information distressed the cardinal, and it made Ireland indignant. Both refused to publish the decree and both submitted arguments against publication to the Roman officials. Up to this point Satolli seems to have left the impression on those who were against the condemnation that he was in sympathy with their views. This refusal to carry out a papal command probably startled the delegate and caused him to wonder whether his sympathy had been misplaced. On January 5, 1895, he reported to Rampolla that for the first time he had to face an attitude on the part of Gibbons which he could interpret in no other way but as "insubordination."[137] Six weeks later he could report that Gibbons as well as the other bishops had finally promulgated the decree,[138] but the memory of the events of the past weeks may have resulted in a decision to give his support to the group that had promptly obeyed the Pope's command.

The laying of the cornerstone of the new St. John the Baptist school at Pottsville, Pennsylvania, on April 21, 1895, was the first public occasion, so far as the present writer could determine, on which Satolli gave some indication that he could no longer be identified with the liberals. The delegate was accompanied to this German parish by August J. Schulte of St. Charles Seminary, Overbrook, Pennsylvania, former Vice-Rector of the American College in Rome, and by Monsignor Schroeder, who preached at the pontifical Mass in the morning and at the cornerstone laying in the afternoon. At a banquet that evening, the pastor, Frederic W. Longinus, said of Schroeder:

> His name is dear to all the German Catholics in America. In him we salute an ornament to the Catholic University in Washington. Him we honor not only as our friend, but also as our guide, and we look upon him with just pride, because we see his devotedness to the Holy See, and always see him in the front ranks to defend the rights of our holy Church.[139]

[137] Satolli to Rampolla, Jan. 5, 1895, in AUND, Soderini's notes.

[138] Satolli to Rampolla, Feb. 18, 1895, in AUND, Soderini notes.

[139] *Church News,* Apr. 27, 1895. Schroeder was among the University professors who claimed that they had been excluded from the first issue of the *Catholic University Bulletin* which appeared in January, 1895. Some of the German papers cried out against this apparent discrimination (cf. *supra,* p. 162). William Warren Stoddard, another University professor, appraised the situation in this way for his friend, Daniel Hudson: "The German element will never be reconciled or the one German left in the Faculty [Schroeder] — who does not recognize his fellow profs except at the table, where he cannot avoid it — he will do all he can do to kill the 'Bulletin'" (AUND, Hudson Papers, Stoddard to Hudson, Washington, Feb. 11, 1895).

The pastor did not need to add: "Hear ye him." Satolli then delivered an address in Latin,[140] which Schroeder translated into German and English, in which the delegate expressed the "warmest gratitude and sincere appreciation" for the manner in which he had been received by the community. He claimed that he found three things which characterized the work of the German Catholics in the United States, in illustration of which he referred to three expressions from Sacred Scripture. In developing the points the representative of the Pope put his stamp of approval on all the German activities, some of which had been, as he expressed it, the "subject of false charges and accusations." He commended them for supporting and furthering "genuinely Catholic movements," and, above all, he claimed that the past and present history of the United States testified clearly that "the German Catholics also as good citizens of this great republic stand second to none."[141]

That the Pottsville speech was "hailed with delight by the German

[140] *Catholic Mirror,* Apr. 27, 1895. The Washington *Post* of October 28, 1896, reported that Satolli addressed the assembly in Italian and that Schroeder translated it first into German and then into English. According to Alexis Orban, S.S., Satolli had been notified by this time that he was soon to be given a position in Rome (AANO, Orban to Chapelle, Washington, May 8, 1895).

[141] *Katholische Volkszeitung* (Baltimore), May 4, 1895. For the Italian version of the speech, cf. *Civiltà Cattolica,* III [Series 16] (July, 1895), 244–245. For an English translation of the speech, cf. Barry, *The Catholic Church and German Americans,* Appendix viii. This speech became the subject of some newspaper comment when Keane was removed from the University. It was then reported that Frederick Z. Rooker, who had been appointed secretary to the apostolic delegate late in 1894, when Papi, the delegate's former secretary, announced his intention of entering the Jesuit novitiate at Woodstock, Maryland (*Church News,* Dec. 22, 1894), would also be removed from his office because Satolli took offense at his having "suppressed the famous Pottsville speech." According to the Washington *Post* (Oct. 28, 1896), the "suppression" amounted to this: John R. Slattery, S.S.J., who had published the delegate's addresses in this country prior to the speech in question, decided to publish a second edition of Satolli's discourses. When this edition appeared, the Pottsville speech was missing. Cf. Francis Satolli, *Loyalty to Church and State,* ed. J. R. Slattery (2nd ed., Baltimore, 1895). Suspicion was thrown on Rooker as the one responsible for keeping the discourse from being printed. Rooker averred that he had nothing to do with it. Satolli said that he had sent the speech to Slattery, and the latter claimed that he had not received it. Cf. *Civiltà Cattolica,* VI [Series 16] (May, 1896), 752–753, for its comment on the suppression of the discourse. Sebastian Martinelli, Satolli's successor as apostolic delegate, temporarily suspended the controversy, according to the New York *World* (Nov. 2, 1896), by telling "both of the principals of this discussion, Mgr. Schroeder and Dr. Rooker, that such controversies are necessarily hurtful to the Church, and as they have both written Cardinal Satolli, it would be wiser to await his reply before making any further public utterances." The question as to whether or not the speech was deliberately or inadvertently omitted from the published addresses of the delegate still remains unanswered, but in view of Slattery's sympathy with the liberals it is not unlikely that he was not guilty of an oversight.

and certain other Catholic papers"[142] was quite understandable, for certain pointed questions could now be asked. For example, who was responsible for publishing "false" charges and accusations against the Germans? The liberals? Who supported and furthered movements that were not "genuinely" Catholic? The liberals? Who accused the Germans of being second-class citizens? The liberals? Some of those who heard or read the speech had no difficulty in answering the questions that naturally found a place in their minds by the statement: "The liberals are guilty of all these things." Undoubtedly, Satolli's contemporaries interpreted his words on this occasion as a statement of his future policy toward the German Catholics in the United States, although there is nothing in the correspondence of the progressive prelates to indicate that they were alarmed by what could be construed as an indictment of them.

Three months after the delegate's discourse had been delivered in Pennsylvania, he sought instructions from the Holy See concerning the participation of Catholics in meetings similar to the Chicago Parliament of Religions in which Catholics and Protestants discussed religious matters. He suggested that Catholics be advised to hold their own congresses, admitting Protestants as auditors, and he asked that the decision include some laudatory comments about the work of the Paulists so it could not be construed as a victory for the "Germans" over the "Irish."[143] Not long after that the Holy Father issued instructions in the sense of Satolli's request,[144] and it then became publicly known that the officials in Rome frowned on gatherings such as the Parliament of Religions in Chicago, which had been supported by the liberals.

Less than a year after the Pottsville manifesto, Satolli pontificated at the opening of the Forty Hours' Devotion at St. Mary's Church for the Germans in Washington. This, too, became an occasion for impressing the delegate with the importance of maintaining national parishes so the German Catholics could preserve their language and some of their national customs. In the course of the dinner following the ceremonies, the pastor, George Glaab, claimed that the length of time it would take before the complete amalgamation of all the races in this country was left to the "inscrutable disposition of Divine Providence," but he was certain, as he put it, "that the transition of it, if it

[142] Washington *Post,* Oct. 28, 1896.
[143] Satolli to Rampolla, Aug. 2, 1895, cited by Soderini, *op. cit.*
[144] *Leonis VIII Acta,* XV, 323 ff, cited by Zwierlein, *op. cit.,* III, 238.

must come, must be permitted to take its natural course. Any other method of effecting a change of a sudden and violent character," he said, "would unquestionably be productive of most disastrous consequences."[145] On this question Satolli was reported to have made the following observation:

> If left to the operation of natural causes, the question of amalgamation of the various races coming to this country would solve itself without disturbance or difficulty, and that the interference by violence in either one direction or the other could only be productive of bad results and retard the solution of the question itself.[146]

Surely, if these were his sentiments, they were not identical with those of his friends, Keane and Ireland, to whom it was paramount that the Americanization of Catholics of various nationalities should advance as quickly as possible in order to deprive unscrupulous critics of the opportunity of accusing American Catholics of a lack of sympathy for American institutions.

While Satolli was giving the Germans good reason to believe that he was in sympathy with their ideas — perhaps, one could also include those regarding the University and its rector — Keane was made aware of the fact that the delegate entertained doubts about his scholarship and that he was listening to adverse criticism of him. The delegate and the rector were among those invited to New Orleans to participate in the ceremonies attending the opening of the first Catholic Winter School on February 20, 1896. At the evening session on the first day, Keane gave the substance of Satolli's Latin discourse, and then he delivered his own lecture.[147] According to Alexis Orban, S.S., the assist-

[145] *Church News,* Feb. 1, 1896. Schroeder preached the sermon on this occasion. Glaab, who received his licentiate in theology at the University in June, 1896, spoke in the name of the theological students on the day the degrees were conferred. Cf. "Graduating Exercises, 1895–96," *Catholic University Bulletin,* II (July, 1896), 447–449.

[146] *Church News,* Feb. 1, 1896.

[147] Keane delivered three lectures on "Modern Philosophical Thought" during the Catholic Winter School. In the New Orleans letter which appeared in the *Church News* on March 7, 1896, it was stated that "the announcement of the first lecture of a series by Bishop Keane . . . was the cause of a large audience assembling in Tulane Hall . . . despite the inclement weather." In his summary of the rector's lecture on "The Philosophy of History," the correspondent quoted the bishop as having said that "civilization has been kept back by narrowness, too much Caesarism and militarism, sectarianism and religious hate — all these things still exist." Then, looking to the future, Keane proclaimed: "In the better times the dominant force must be Americanism. It is America that has taught the world that if they love God not to hate one another. Once the dominant force was wealth and might; in the future it

ant spiritual director of the ecclesiastical students and librarian at the University, who was acting as secretary to the delegate at the time, Keane's discourse was "an exposition of the philosophy of the ancients touching on God, the human soul, and the future life. He took one after another the great philosophers of Greece and Rome and made them say things which often they had not said at all." Satolli was not able to prevent, what Orban called, "a show of impatience and resentment"; also "he chose to leave the platform quietly under the pretext of the advanced hour." Orban further observed that the priests "clearly evidenced their disappointment," but, because Keane "had facility in speaking, the good people did not notice the basic inaccuracies, taking it all in and finding no fault."[148] William Macon Coleman, a feature writer for the Washington *Post,* asserted that afterward Satolli, "with more than ordinary rudeness, twitted Bishop Keane with putting sentiments into the mouth of Plato which that philosopher never uttered." Since the apostolic delegate did not comprehend English well enough to have understood the philosophical terms which Keane had used, Coleman pointed out that he must have had the aid of someone to indulge in such criticism, and he said that Orban had been accused of "coming to Satolli's aid in this vulgar impeachment of Bishop Keane's scholarship."[149] Unfortunately, the present writer could not find a copy of the lecture for an objective analysis of it. However, these facts seem to be clear. Satolli left at 10:15 p.m. during Keane's lecture, which lasted for another hour. Orban, who was acting as Satolli's secretary, believed that the rector was guilty of dishonestly attributing statements to the ancient philosophers. If Satolli could not understand English well enough to follow the discourse, it is likely that Orban furnished the impressions which were the basis for the displeasure the delegate is supposed to have shown to Keane.

---

must be right. The American of the future will be the kind of man we make him, and the future must be guided by the hand of God."

A later issue of the *Church News* (Mar. 14, 1896) claimed that Keane was the "highest single drawing card at the door."

148 Archives and Library of the International Benedictine Collegio di Sant' Anselmo, Manuscript journal in French (pp. 130) among Satolli's books bequeathed to the College after his death in 1910. The present writer has established that Alexis Orban, S.S., wrote the journal, which contains his impressions on the Church in the United States, after he had accompanied the delegate on a trip which lasted from February 12 to March 13, 1896. The writer is indebted to Father Colman Barry, O.S.B., for a copy of the journal and a translation of it. Orban made numerous uncomplimentary remarks about Irish bishops and priests, and it is evident that he agreed with those who considered Keane an ultra liberal.

149 Washington *Post,* June 5, 1899.

Within two months of this incident, the rector was warned by Ireland that Satolli had received serious charges against him, and the Archbishop of St. Paul advised the bishop to answer some of them. It was with that in mind that Keane communicated with his erstwhile friend whose elevation to the cardinalate had been announced only a few months before.

> I am extremely sorry that the impression should have been produced upon the mind of your Eminence that I have at various times spoken or acted in a way that was imprudent, unfair to others, or in any way prejudicial to the interests of the University. I am well aware of my innumerable deficiencies, and have not the least doubt that often, while aiming to serve the interests of the University or of religion, I may have in some way exceeded and gone beyond the bounds of prudence. On any such occasion, or whenever I in any way fail in duty, I am most grateful for a word of fraternal monition, and I would have been most thankful if your Eminence had kindly called my attention to such things at the time. And if now, or in the future, anything of the kind concerning me should be known to your Eminence, I shall consider it an act of friendship and charity that it should be made known to me plainly and at once.
>
> There is one of the charges made against me which Archbishop Ireland considers it my duty to explain immediately. He tells me that your Eminence was informed that on a certain occasion when visiting Doctor Peries' class of Canon Law, I spoke to the students in a manner that was derogatory of the importance either of Canon Law in general, or of what was then being taught in class. I declare unhesitatingly and absolutely that this is not true. Whenever I have visited the classes of the University, I have done so with the sole and single aim of encouraging the students, and of enhancing the importance of the course. I am absolutely certain that the words which I spoke in the class of Doctor Peries were meant solely and entirely for this purpose. I can hardly have been so stupid as, while meaning this, to have said the very opposite.[150]

It would be impossible to determine the source of the delegate's information and the value of the allegations, but in view of Périès' violent opposition to the attempts to terminate his contract at this time, it is not unreasonable to suspect that he might have been the

[150] ACUA, Keane Papers, Keane to Satolli, Washington, Apr. 22, 1896, copy. After Keane's dismissal from the University, the New York *World* announced on October 20, 1896, that when Satolli had been asked his opinion of Bishop Keane "a few months ago," he had replied that "the rector of the Catholic University never opened his mouth without contradicting the theological and philosophical teachings of the Church."

source of a damaging statement against Keane. Moreover, the prominent role he played as the author of some scathing and fallacious articles against the American Catholic liberals in the *Vérité,* a Paris newspaper, under the name "Saint-Clément,"[151] a short time later, would prompt one likewise to believe that the allegations made to Satolli were false. Furthermore, Keane must have suspected Orban of playing an unfriendly role for he insisted that the Superior General of the Sulpicians recall his subject from the University at the end of that school year.[152] The fact that the delegate listened to such accusations and reported them to Ireland was significant, for it indicated a preoccupation with and, perhaps, a certain scrutiny of the activities of Bishop Keane and his friends. Keane's letter, on the other hand, revealed a humble submission to authority and an utter lack of self-righteousness which is so often the mark of the proud man. There is no evidence to indicate whether or not Satolli expressed his satisfaction with the rector's explanations, and it would, therefore, be gratuitous to surmise that their friendly relations remained unimpaired by these episodes, although there were no striking signs to the contrary.

Unfortunately, Satolli's reconciliation with those who had opposed him during his first years in the United States was not the subject of comment in the correspondence of the progressive bishops. They may have looked upon his actions as those of an astute politician who sought peaceful relations with all parties, with no implication that he thought any less of those who had supported him from the day he arrived on American shores. Bishop Keane, in particular, certainly did not convey the impression that he feared for his career at the hands of the Holy Father's representative. To him the future looked especially bright, for at the end of the seventh scholastic year (1896), the University faculty's relations seemed to approach the ideal of unity that had been so strongly urged by the Holy Father in his encyclical over a year before. The Périès case had been settled for all practical purposes, and Keane's daily prayer that the professor might be kept in Paris since, as the rector said, "his mercurial temperament would keep us in constant uncertainty all next year,"[153] was answered favorably.[154] Moreover, the Superior General of the Sulpicians had agreed

[151] Hogan, *op. cit.,* p. 160.

[152] AAB, 94-P-5, Garrigan to Gibbons, Washington, Aug. 1, 1896. The Superior General of the Sulpicians had visited the University the previous May (*Church News,* May 23, 1896).

[153] AAB, 94-M-13, Keane to Gibbons, Washington, May 23, 1896.

[154] ACUA, *Letter of Resignation to the Board of Directors of the Catholic Uni-*

to recall Alexis Orban.[155] As for Schroeder, Keane later stated that "after a conversation with Abp. Ireland, [Schroeder] expressed his good will for peace, and promised to write for the Bulletin and work for the establishment of a Chair of German, which I had public [*sic*] recommended and strongly urged." The rector added: "He was met more than half way by myself and all. And so harmony and union seemed to have prevailed at last."[156] With a light heart, therefore, Keane left the United States to spend the summer resting at St. Gildas de Rhuys in Brittany and in the Channel Islands.[157]

Although Bishop Keane felt that he could now look forward to a period of peace within the University, there were indications that those outside the institution were not of a mind to abandon their campaign against it. When two of the professors, Thomas O'Gorman and Edward A. Pace, were engaged by the chairman of the committee on study and lectures for the Columbian Catholic Summer School for the summer of 1896, the president of the school, Sebastian G. Messmer, Bishop of Green Bay and former professor at the University, made an unsuccessful attempt to have them cancel their engagement on the ground, as he expressed it, that "the Catholic University and its Professors and Rector are not looked upon with favor by many of our Catholics."[158] As John Zahm, C.S.C., chairman of the committee, pointed out to Pace, Messmer was a conservative prelate and his objections consisted of doubts about the soundness of their philosophy and their tendency toward a dangerous liberalism. Zahm, in urging the University men to come, observed that the University's interests were at stake and that he trusted that they would not see them sacrificed to satisfy

---

versity of America sent to his Grace the Archbishop of Philadelphia, chairman of the Committee for the appointment of Professors, St. Mande, September 8, 1896. This printed letter bears George Périès' signature.

[155] AAB, 94-P-5, Garrigan to Gibbons, Washington, Aug. 1, 1896.

[156] ACUA, "Chronicles," p. 61. Gibbons had requested Schroeder to write for the *Bulletin* (AAB, 94-L-10, Apr. 23, 1896, copy), and Schroeder had answered: "I shall cheerfully comply with your request as well as that of the Apostolic Delegate" (AAB, 94-L-13, Apr. 26, 1896). The professor had delivered a Latin oration on the work of St. Patrick on March 17 (*Church News,* Mar. 21, 1896).

[157] ACUA, "Chronicles," p. 61. St. Gildas de Rhuys was a secluded spot on the Breton coast, fifteen miles from railroad and telegraph. A small hotel attached to a convent was the favorite resort for the old aristocrats of France, according to Bishop Keane in an article which appeared in the New York *Freeman's Journal,* Oct. 10, 1896.

[158] ACUA, Pace Papers, Messmer to Pace, Green Bay, Jan. 20, 1896. For a more complete treatment of this topic, cf. Ahern, *op. cit.,* pp. 157–159. Thomas O'Gorman was consecrated Bishop of Sioux Falls on April 19, 1896.

Messmer and Father Michael Hughes, S.J., whom he characterized as "two self-constituted inquisitors."[159]

Opposition to the University and its rector continued; nor was it confined to private correspondence, as Keane indicated to George Zurcher, a priest of the Diocese of Buffalo:

> Permit me to ask of you a great favor. You have doubtless noticed the persistency with which many of the German Catholic papers have kept up an attack of insults and misrepresentations against the institution. Every approval of the Holy Father here only serves to intensify their malignity. You have yourself suffered enough from similar attacks to be able to appreciate the animus of them. We have thus far let these insults and calumnies pass unnoticed, but now it seems plainly our duty to ask the attention of the board of directors to the matter. . . . Could you, dear friend, from such of these papers as you are acquainted with, make a small collection of such pieces, with name of paper and date, and send them to me?[160]

This unrelenting agitation to discredit the University and the bishop reflected the determination of a certain group among the conservative churchmen to stamp out all that was obnoxious to them. Under such conditions it was to be expected that Satolli should receive charges against Keane and, since his recent activities indicated a change of sympathy, it was not surprising that he forwarded these unfavorable views of the rector to Rome.[161] The delegate told Ireland that the

159 ACUA, Pace Papers, Zahm to Pace, Notre Dame, Jan. 27, 1896. Herman J. Heuser, the editor of the *American Ecclesiastical Review* and the friend and adviser of many conservatives, also had misgivings about the soundness of Pace's philosophy. To Daniel Hudson he had said two years before: "Fr. Zahm writes me from Paris; he is surely very busy, and if I could suggest any work for him, it would be to see how much soundness there is in the psychological speculations at the W.[ashington] University, of which Dr. Pace has given us a recent example in the 'Quarterly.' I hear the paper is much praised — and by sensible and erudite men; and yet cannot help feeling that there is much of the quality which makes his former teacher at Leipzig one of the most powerful agents for spreading materialistic doctrines in Germany. However, I may be wrong. Videbimus" (AUND, Hudson Papers, Heuser to Hudson, Overbrook, Aug. 23, 1894).

160 Cited by the Buffalo *Express,* Oct. 6, 1896, from what seems a private letter.

161 In 1897 Keane told Ireland: "Satolli lately expressed his apprehension that if I went back to America this summer, I would say to the newspapers 'that it was he who had done it, refering [*sic*] of course to the University episode. The poor man seems to have forgotten that he not only said to you and Archbishop Riordan that he had done it, but that he declared it aloud in Major Keiley's parlor, and gloried in having done it. However, I of course have not the slightest intention of saying anything against him or about him" (AASP, Keane to Ireland, Rome, June 4, 1897). In reporting a conversation with Cardinal Rampolla to a friend, Mrs. Bellamy Storer quoted the cardinal as having said that Keane was dismissed from the University be-

bishop had been accused of making unorthodox utterances and of teaching views that were contrary to faith and morals. It had been said that he was furthering personal ambition in his administration of the University and that the students there doubted the solidity of his doctrine. Finally, it had been claimed that he was guilty of liberalism in an odious sense.[162]

Were these serious accusations founded on reality or were they the product of prejudice and imagination? To help in arriving at the truth in the matter, Camillus P. Maes, Bishop of Covington, wrote a lengthy communication in which the charges against Keane were refuted point by point. He reminded the bishop of their own previous differences of opinion on certain questions, especially the school controversy, the Parliament of Religions, and, on a few occasions, the nomination of professors. But these instances Maes cited for the purpose of giving more weight to what he expressed as his "condemnation of the plots against your Excellency; and to protest against the insincere criticism and the unjust accusations of which you have been made the object." The Bishop of Covington stated that he had heard Keane preach, give clerical conferences, and had frequently spoken with him in private

---

cause of a struggle among the professors. When she heard this she told the cardinal that when Satolli was asked the reason for Keane's dismissal, he had replied: "It is because 3,000,000 Germans asked for it." Rampolla claimed that he never knew that (AASP, Maria Longworth Storer to Monseigneur [?] Barcelona, Oct. 18, 1900 [French]).

[162] ADC, Maes to Keane, Covington, Nov. 27, 1896 (French), copy. A postscript in English at the end of the letter read: "Archbishop Ireland publicly stated in our University meeting that His Eminence Cardinal Satolli had said to him that these accusations were the reasons of your removal." To a Jesuit in Washington the delegate is reported to have said that Keane had "no philosophy, no theology and no (I think it was) administrative ability" (Burrus, *op. cit.*, p. 95).

The present writer drew up the list of charges against Keane from Maes' letter written in answer to them and from the rector's own letter to Garrigan in which he said: "I wish a document from yourself and the Professors of Divinity, and such of the clerical Professors of Philosophy as could with propriety sign, as for example, Dr. Pace, to this effect:

"That they had sufficient opportunity to know of the character of my teaching to my students, and that they are convinced that I never taught them anything heterodox, contrary to the Syllabus, prejudicial to their priestly spirit or the good of religion — but the contrary.

"And if they could add the same in regard to my public utterances, I would be very glad" (ACUA, Garrigan Papers, Keane to Garrigan, San José, Nov. 19, 1896). It seems to have been Soderini's private opinion that Keane was retired from the University only because of a lack of firmness of character and for not having a degree. The lack of formal training on the graduate level made it difficult for him to supervise the examinations (AUND, Soderini's notes).

conversation and that never had he heard him give expression to unorthodox opinions. He then continued:

> Always, in public and in the intimacy of private conversation, I have admired your devotion to the Catholic Church, your affection and respect for Leo XIII, and your adhesion to the Church's doctrines. Finally, I am convinced that never have you knowingly said anything contrary to the Syllabus, the encyclicals and the doctrines of the Holy Apostolic See. To speak frankly, I believe that you are incapable of doing it in view of my knowledge of your honesty and candor.
>
> As rector of the Catholic University in Washington you have worked with selflessness at all times, and always in its interests. It is due to your labors that the University today enjoys a position of influence without rival in the country; its material prosperity, miraculously accomplished, and its scholastic reputation are your work. Never have I heard a student of the University question the solidity of your doctrine; all admire the sanctity of your life and the salutary effects of your example. In your zeal for the advance of the Church and for the success of the University you have been neglectful, or rather unmindful, of your personal interests.

To this strong defense the bishop added that he believed the only reasons why Keane had gained the name of being a "liberal" were his position in the school controversy in support of Satolli and his oratorical efforts to bring about the conversion of heretics.[163]

From a careful study of Keane's utterances, his correspondence, and the general conditions of the time, the historian is inclined to agree with Maes' judgment. True, there were a few quotations from his speeches in the press which could easily have been misconstrued when taken out of context, or were open to question by those whose training and temperament was of an ultraconservative character.[164]

[163] ADC, Maes to Keane, Covington, Nov. 27, 1896 (French), copy.

[164] After Leo XIII in 1895 had forbidden further participation in gatherings such as the Chicago Parliament of Religions, the *Western Watchman* (Oct. 24, 1895) of St. Louis proudly stated: "When Bishop Keane went over the country a few years ago advocating Protestant teaching in the public schools where the people submitted to it, and Catholic teaching where the people desired it, we pronounced the scheme silly and almost heretical. The Holy Father has just knocked in the head the neo-pelagianism that teaches that Protestantism is better than no religion." A month later the same paper again revealed its pique at Keane when it said: "Some time ago we wrote a petulant note upon a speech delivered by the President of the Catholic University at Buffalo, on the subject of Sunday observance [lecture given in September, 1895] which many of our friends thought too severe. . . . We were deeply provoked at the Bishop for his persistency in maintaining a wrong position, and one against which we had expostulated in vain. . . . Bishop Keane has repeated his offense in Rhode Island. . . .

However, it must be remembered that the rector was never called upon by the Holy See to answer any of the charges lodged against him. As for Satolli, one may conclude that, having been won over by conservatives, he sincerely believed that he was acting for the best interests of the Church in the United States in general and for the welfare of the University in particular.

In Rome the curial officials doubtless took many things into consideration. They were aware of the opposition to the University on the part of a few from the very moment of its conception. They knew that the institution and its rector were identified with the so-called liberal bishops in the United States because, as we have seen, numerous representations reached them from time to time. Finally, they received serious accusations against the rector from the papal representative himself. Apparently in Rome's mind the situation was too grave to be dismissed as a harmless struggle between contending parties. A solution was demanded. Thus after weighing the facts of the case as they were presented, the Roman authorities reached a decision. When Keane returned from his summer in Europe, which he ended by an eight-day retreat in the Maison St. Louis, the Jesuit scholasticate on the Island of Jersey,[165] he was refreshed and ready to renew his work for the University. But on September 28 Cardinal Gibbons telegraphed for him to come to Baltimore and there he handed to him a letter from Pope Leo XIII dismissing him from his office as Rector of the Catholic University of America.[166] The future that had seemed so bright in June was now dark, indeed.

"The Bishop wants all public, educational, reformatory and charitable institutions placed under church control and management; and openly declares that he would rather see our public schools, hospitals and prisons in the hands of Episcopalians or Methodists or Baptists or Presbyterians, than have them purely secular or unchurched as they are. Against this all the Catholics of the country protest" (*Western Watchman,* Nov. 21, 1895).

Pelagianism designates a heresy of the fifth century, which denied original sin as well as Christian grace. The statements attributed to Keane, even out of context, contain none of the elements of this heresy.

[165] *Church News,* Oct. 17, 1896.

[166] ACUA, "Chronicles," p. 62. When John A. Zahm, C.S.C., was told that some were saying that he could have saved Keane from the humiliation, he labeled the idea as "preposterous" and added: "It was settled nearly a year ago that he should be guillotined" (AUND, Zahm Papers, Zahm to Albert Zahm, Rome, Nov. 11, 1896).

Chapter VII

The Aftermath

Pope Leo XIII's letter of September 15, 1896, removing Bishop Keane from the rectorship of the Catholic University of America, was couched in affectionate terms. The Pontiff pointed out that it was customary to limit the term of those who presided over Catholic universities and since Keane had held his office for several years, during which he had displayed "laudable zeal and diligence," the Pope now invoked that custom as the sole reason for terminating his tenure as rector. The Holy Father then assured Keane of honorable positions for the future in these words:

> Being solicitous for your future welfare we leave it to your own free choice either to remain in your own country, or, if you prefer it, to come to Rome. If you choose the former, we will destine for you some archiepiscopal see, by vote of the Bishops of the United States. If you prefer the latter we shall welcome you most lovingly, and will place you among the Consultors of the Congregation of Studies and the Congregation of the Propaganda, in both of which you could do much for the interest of religion in the United States. In this case we would also assign you a suitable revenue for your honorable maintenance.[1]

When the rector received the letter from the hand of Cardinal Gibbons on September 28 at St. Mary's Seminary in Baltimore, he read it carefully and repaired to the chapel where he spent "fully an hour before the Blessed Sacrament." Then he returned to the presence of the cardinal and his Sulpician friends and stated: "This is God's will, and who am I to question it?" Father John B. Hogan, S.S., who re-

[1] Pope Leo XIII to Keane, Rome, Sept. 15, 1896, quoted in "Right Rev. John Joseph Keane, D.D.," *Catholic University Bulletin,* II (Oct., 1896), 583.

vealed to a friend the admirable resignation of Bishop Keane on this occasion, added: "That is the man."[2] Indeed, it was typical of him for he had always displayed an almost childlike trust in the Providence of God. To one of those who expressed sympathy when the news of his demotion became known, he answered: "Thanks be to God, it costs me no effort to say hurrah for the will of God! I have only a sense of immense relief,"[3] and to another, "From the first I have found in my removal only the greatest relief, for which I am profoundly grateful to our Divine Master. And I welcome the act of the Pope without the slightest desire to ask why it has been taken, or how it was brought about."[4] The chancellor of the University told the Cardinal Secretary of State that Keane received the Holy Father's letter "with the greatest calm and, without a moment's hesitation." He received the decision, said Gibbons, "not only with the respect due to the will of the Pope, but also, I am able to say, with a sensible joy, seeing in it the manifestation of the will of God in his regard."[5]

However, in the bishop's reply to the letter of dismissal, in which he assured Leo XIII that his administrative act was unhesitatingly accepted "as a manifestation of the providence of God," there was a note in the last paragraph which might have revealed a certain petulance when he said: "Thanking your Holiness for the freedom of choice granted me, I choose to remain in my own country, and, moreover, without any official position whatsoever, in tranquility and peace."[6] The Hartford *Times* on October 5, 1896, pointed out in an editorial that Keane's reply contained a tone of displeasure. Moreover, Bishop John M. Farley, a member of the University's Board of Trustees, remarked to Archbishop Corrigan: "I am somewhat afraid that the tone of the Bp's reply will get him into trouble. I don't like it, I must say."[7] It would be impossible to surmise the motives which prompted Keane to express himself in this manner if he honestly regarded his dismissal as providential. In such case, he might be expected to have humbly stated a preference for one of the honorable positions offered to him. Since he did not do that, one may conclude that although he

[2] AUND, Hudson Papers, Katherine E. Conway to Hudson, Boston, Oct. 23, 1896. Miss Conway was on the editorial staff of the Boston *Pilot*.

[3] AJF, Keane to Slattery, San Jose, Oct. 19, [1896].

[4] AANO, Keane to Chapelle, San Jose, Oct. 26, 1896.

[5] AAB, 94-T-7, Gibbons to Rampolla, Baltimore, Nov. 24, 1896 (French), copy.

[6] Keane to Pope Leo XIII, Washington, Sept. 29, 1896, printed in *Catholic University Bulletin,* II (Oct., 1896), 584.

[7] AANY, Farley to Corrigan, New York, Oct. 5, 1896.

may have accepted his removal as the manifestation of God's will, at the same time he resented the misrepresentation of himself personally and its acceptance by Roman authorities without giving him an opportunity to defend himself. However this may be, it is certainly true that the events following his dismissal would have taken a different turn had he immediately stated a preference for an archiepiscopal see in the United States.

Keane and Gibbons had not intended to publish the correspondence between Rome and the rector because it was especially humiliating that the matter could not be satisfactorily explained before the public. Besides, the action of Rome seemed to imply a lack of confidence in the cardinal, who as chancellor of the University normally should have been consulted on the matter. Had their plan been allowed to materialize, Keane's retirement would have been simply announced on October 4, at the opening exercises of the scholastic year. But, as frequently occurred during the controversies of those years, the story leaked out to the newspapers, and since they knew that a change had been demanded by Rome, Keane could do no more than attempt to explain away the seemingly unfriendly action of the Holy Father by making a statement to the representatives of the press. It was in that spirit that he said:

> I welcome my release from the office of Rector of the University with profound gratitude, both to Divine Providence and to the Pope. While I always regarded its duties as a labor of love, they had grown to be far beyond my strength and abilities, and the deliverance from the burden is a response to my prayers. . . . Of course no one needs to be assured that the action of the Holy Father is prompted not only by personal kindness toward myself, but also by earnest solicitude for the best interests of the University.[8]

Therefore, when Keane addressed those gathered in the chapel of Caldwell Hall for the opening exercises of the new year, he could say: "I had a secret to tell you this morning. It is a secret no longer."[9] Then, after speaking in a vein similar to the published interview, he concluded his remarks on this note: "I ask no reasons why. I request you, my friends and students, to do likewise. Do not question why the Holy Father has done this. It is sufficient that he has done it, therefore it is wisely and well done."[10] If a reporter for the *Irish World* gave an

[8] *Catholic University Bulletin,* II (Oct., 1896), 584.
[9] *Catholic Standard and Times* (Philadelphia), Oct. 10, 1896.
[10] *Irish World* (New York), Oct. 10, 1896.

accurate account of the reactions of the assembly, emotions were at a high pitch. "Many of the students and visitors sobbed audibly," it was said. Moreover, the reporter related that when Cardinal Gibbons began to speak "his voice trembled and broke, and he made no effort to hide the tears that rushed to his eyes." According to the same writer, the cardinal stated in a half sobbing tone:

> "I am a hard man to move, but to-day I am moved with the most profound sorrow I have ever felt in a long life full of sorrow."
>
> "I trust," he concluded, "that the Catholic University is destined to have a long line of distinguished and able rectors, but I know that none will be more courtly, more able, more thoroughly a man of God than the one we lose to-day."[11]

Such public manifestation of the esteem of the chancellor must have been comforting to the sorrow-laden heart of the deposed rector. Furthermore, the resolutions formulated and formally presented to him by both the faculty and the students on the same day were surely calculated to raise his spirits. The professors expressed regret over his departure and assured him of their "unalterable affection, of their prayers, and of their determination to work unitedly and perseveringly for the great object to which he has consecrated so large a portion of his life."[12] The students conveyed their appreciation for Keane's labors on their behalf, and they informed him that "his manner of departure was worthy of those heroes and saints, whose example, his words and work have taught them to follow."[13] After the formalities Keane tarried only long enough to take lunch with his former confreres before departing for California in search of "tranquility and peace."

[11] *Ibid.* According to the report in the October 10, 1896, issue of the *Catholic Standard and Times* Gibbons said: "I always admired him and respected him before, but his conduct on this occasion edified me most highly and made me love him more than ever.

"You may have many rectors whose names will be brilliant in the annals of the University, but never will you have one more notable for zeal, devotion and, above all, for absolute disinterestedness and self-denial than John Joseph Keane." The reporter concluded: "Gibbons spoke with more feeling than he had displayed for years." The *Freeman's Journal* for October 10, 1896, also reported that the cardinal displayed deep emotion. For an edited account of Gibbons' address, cf. *Catholic University Bulletin,* II (Oct., 1896), 585.

[12] *Catholic University Bulletin,* II (Oct., 1896), 586–587.

[13] ACUA, "Resolutions." These were signed by twenty-nine students. On October 24, 1896, a similar sentiment was voiced in the *Catholic Columbian* (Columbus, Ohio): "Bp. Keane is more useful teaching in the eminently Christian manner in which he has taken his removal from the rectorship of the Catholic University than he was ever at the head of that institution. He has taught a great lesson of humility and respect for authority."

Quite naturally, the announcement of Bishop Keane's dismissal from the University occasioned some interesting comments in the correspondence of those who had been conspicuous in their opposition to him while he was rector of the institution. Bernard J. McQuaid, Rochester's uncompromising critic of the so-called liberals and of the University, stated his views in a letter to his equally inflexible metropolitan, Archbishop Corrigan. The Bishop of Rochester wrote:

> The news from Rome is astounding. The failure of the University is known in Rome at last, and the blame is thrown on Keane. Much of it is due to him, but other causes are there. These causes are irremediable now. The failure implicated the Holy Father, who was made to father the undertaking from the beginning.
>
> What collapses on every side! Gibbons, Ireland, and Keane! ! ! They were cock of the walk for a while and dictated to the country and thought to run our dioceses for us. They may change their policy and repent. They can never repair the harm done in the past.[14]

Ignatius F. Horstmann, Bishop of Cleveland and a member of the Board of Trustees, who was identified with the conservatives, informed Joseph Schroeder that the removal of Keane had come as a thunderclap to everyone. He then commented: "You know I will be blamed for the action that has been taken. You are blamed as the major cause — the Germans and Jesuits come in for their share also, as for myself it is impossible to think of any name." The bishop concluded by telling

[14] AANY, McQuaid to Corrigan, Rochester, Oct. 3, 1896, cited by Zwierlein, *op. cit.*, III, 241. Later Corrigan wrote to Keane to express his condolence and the bishop answered: "I welcome the release as a great blessing, but am none the less thankful for your kind sympathy" (AANY, Keane to Corrigan, San Jose, Oct. 23, 1896).

Some of the correspondence at this time indicates that the bishops of the Province of New York were fearful that Keane would be appointed to the See of Buffalo that had been vacant since the death of Stephen V. Ryan on April 16, 1896. With evident pleasure the Bishop of Newark informed Corrigan that Satolli positively declared that the former rector would not be appointed to Buffalo (AANY, Wigger to Corrigan, South Orange, New Jersey, Oct. 9, 1896). Later, McQuaid said to the same correspondent: "It seems that nothing kept Keane out of Buffalo but his own folly in publishing, as he did, the Pope's letter asking for his resignation. Divine Providence often intervenes to upset man's plans. The first news kept me awake two nights in succession. An unusual occurrence" (AANY, McQuaid to Corrigan, Rochester, Jan. 20, 1897). George Zurcher, pastor of St. Joseph's Church in Buffalo and one of Keane's supporters, on the other hand, thought that the former rector "as Bishop of Buffalo could do even more good than in the University," and that such an appointment "would satisfy American sentiment" (AAB, Unclassified, Zurcher to Gibbons, Buffalo, New York, Oct. 13, 1896). The New York *Staatszeitung* (Nov. 7, 1896) informed its readers that Buffalo was to be made an archdiocese with Rochester and Syracuse as suffragan sees, and that Keane was to be its first archbishop.

the professor that he would soon stop at the University and talk matters over since it was, as he expressed it, "a critical period not only for the University, but also for the Church in this country."[15] On the other hand, Father Herman J. Heuser, editor of the *American Ecclesiastical Review,* who had disagreed with Keane's stand on all the controversial issues of the day, expressed to Daniel Hudson, C.S.C., his edification and pleasure with the laudatory article on the deposed bishop which the latter had published in his religious journal, the *Ave Maria.* In explanation of his partial change of attitude toward the former rector, Heuser told his friend:

> I have a dread of being connected with party people and so long as the faction at the University lasted never went near it; but when, some time ago, I learnt how Bp. Keane had offered the hand to those who opposed his policy, I realized that a man may have strong convictions which sometimes stamp him as hostile to what seems true, and yet be noble-hearted and self-sacrificing. Hence, I rejoice to see him praised, although I do not think that in his zeal for the introduction of progressive methods he took sufficient account of the ancient conservative wisdom on the one hand, or of the material with which he had to deal, on the other. Hence I believe in the advantage of a change, although it will be difficult for any man (not excepting your friend Bp. Spalding who is, I suppose, the most probable candidate) to do more for the material prosperity of the University than the late rector.[16]

Even some of Keane's critics, therefore, could not honestly find words to condemn him completely after he had been toppled from his exalted position. As for his friends and admirers, they strongly rallied to his support in the hour of trial. On the evening of October 8, a public mass meeting was held in Washington, in the hall of Carroll

[15] Archives of the Diocese of Cleveland, Horstmann to Schroeder, Cleveland, October 10, 1896, copy. Two German-language papers, the *Staatszeitung* (Chicago) and *America* (St. Louis), announced on October 13, 1896, that Horstmann would be the next rector of the University.

[16] AUND, Hudson Papers, Heuser to Hudson, Overbrook, Oct. 18, 1896. Heuser's statement, "Bp. Keane had offered the hand to those who opposed his policy," may have been a reference to McQuaid, for the Bishop of Rochester had written to Corrigan: "Father [John Joseph] Fedigan [O.S.A.] was here ten or twelve days ago. I did not meet him being out of town at the time. A priest told me that his object in coming to Rochester was to bring about a *rapprochement* between Keane and myself. This is best obtained by each keeping far from the other. I imagine, however, that he had in view a different purpose. It seems to me that he wished to bespeak my good will in favor of Martinelli. This was unnecessary, as Martinelli, or any other Delegate is sure to have my best wishes and my help" (AANY, McQuaid to Corrigan, Rochester, Oct. 3, 1896, cited by Zwierlein, *op. cit.,* III, 241).

Institute, for the single purpose of sending after Keane an expression of regret at his departure from their midst. This demonstration, attended by the presidents of all the universities in Washington, by representatives of the various branches of the national and city governments, by generals of the army, by men prominent in society and business, by Catholic clergy of the city, and by "a crowd which filled the hall and galleries and overflowed into the corridors and reception rooms," was an extraordinary revelation of the esteem felt for the deposed rector in the nation's capital by citizens in all walks of life and of all religious faiths.[17] When a similar meeting did not materialize in Baltimore, perhaps because of the disapproval of Cardinal Gibbons, William L. Starr, the prominent pastor of Corpus Christi Church in that city, expressed his disappointment to the cardinal, and he added: "I cannot refrain from the impulse to convey to your Eminence the assurance of my burning indignation at the manner of his removal and of the indignity thereby put upon your Eminence."[18]

Among the many heart-warming expressions of admiration for Keane personally and of regret at his departure from the University, he must have especially cherished a letter he received from Gibbons which was written at the request of and in the name of the Board of Trustees. It breathed sincere affection for him in every line, while it praised and thanked him for his untiring labors and apostolic disinterestedness in the founding and developing of the institution over a period of nine years.[19] Furthermore, the University's trustees showed their continued confidence in him by retaining him as a member of the board.[20]

For the most part, the secular and religious press, too, was most generous in estimating the qualities of the bishop and of the work that he had accomplished. However, after the Holy Father's letter and Keane's answer had been published on October 4, the secular dailies and a few of the religious journals began to speculate on the causes for

[17] Washington *Post,* Oct. 9, 1896. The *Philadelphia Public Ledger,* under a Washington date line, stated: "No prelate or priest who has ever served in the national capital was so widely esteemed among all classes and conditions in this community" (Oct. 12, 1896).

[18] AAB, 94-R-9, Starr to Gibbons, Baltimore, Oct. 9, 1896.

[19] ACUA, Gibbons to Keane, Baltimore, Oct. 31, 1896. This letter and Keane's reply were published in the New York *Democrat,* Nov. 22, 1896. The members of the Board of Trustees voted in their meeting of October 21 and 22 to send a letter to the Holy Father in which their high esteem for Keane would be mentioned among other things. Since they could not agree on a communication that would be suitable to each member, it seems that none was dispatched. Cf. Ahern, *op. cit.,* pp. 177–178.

[20] ACUA, MMBT, Oct. 21–22, 1896, p. 61.

the rector's removal, evidently refusing to accept the Pope's statement that the act was based upon a long-standing custom in ecclesiastical administration. Keane may have been inadvertently responsible for causing the Holy Father's motives to be questioned by the secular press owing to his admonition that none should question why the Holy Father had acted as he had. "It is sufficient that he has done it," said the bishop, "therefore it is wisely and well done." But in view of the controversies between the liberal and conservative bishops that had been thoroughly aired in the newspapers during the preceding years, it was natural for the sensation-loving journals to look behind the scenes in this case for causes that did not appear on the surface. Many writers, not without foundation, viewed the dismissal as a continuation of the battle between the two groups that divided the American episcopate with the conservatives now enjoying the upper hand. Some attributed their apparent success in ousting Keane to alleged representations made in Rome against him by Satolli and Schroeder, who were labeled as reactionists. Others claimed that the Jesuits were the responsible parties, and they pointed an accusing finger at the German Jesuit, Andreas Cardinal Steinhüber, whom Schroeder supposedly visited while he was in Rome that summer. As a result, the press heaped abuse upon the so-called German party in the United States. In all of this the liberals were especially alarmed by the frequent expression of the view that they were completely disgraced in Rome — an opinion that was supported by a number of cablegrams that were supposed to have originated from high sources at the Vatican.[21]

Some Protestant papers also gave considerable space to the issue. They tended to look upon the Pope's act as a "high-handed interference in American affairs" and "an arbitrary act," and thus it was uti-

[21] Ahern, *op. cit.*, pp. 167–180. These pages give excerpts from a number of papers. Concerning the cablegrams, McQuaid wrote on November 13, 1896: "The long telegram from Rome, in yesterday's *New York Journal* reads to me like the truth. It explains much. They are determined to break up liberalism in the University as its center and thus in the U. S.

"The forbearance of Rome deceived the poor fellows. But, at their age, they ought to have known better. They are not talking now of knocking your mitre or mine off our heads. They had things their own way for a long while" (AANY, McQuaid to Corrigan, Rochester, Nov. 13, 1896, cited by Zwierlein, *op. cit.*, III, 242).

On the same subject Ireland had stated: "We have come upon terrible times: those telegrams have alarmed the American people to a very high degree. We must stop such things one way or another. I have written a strong letter to Card. Rampolla — and I have written two letters to Satolli demanding from him a denial or a confirmation of those stories" (ACUA, Bouquillon Papers, Ireland to Magnien, St. Paul, Nov. 19, 1896).

lized as an occasion for further abuse of the Papacy and was pointed to as another example of the Catholic Church's un-American quality. Simultaneously, these non-Catholic journalists seemed to vie with one another in compliments for Keane personally.[22]

A few Catholic writers, notably Father David S. Phelan, editor of the *Western Watchman,* and William Henry Thorne, a convert who was then editing a magazine called the *Globe,* and who had previously printed unflattering opinions about the bishop, gave the public the benefit of their "positive knowledge" as to the reasons for his deposition. Phelan stated "positively that Bishop Keane was removed from the rectorship of the Catholic University, in Washington, D. C., for persistently maintaining a wrong position in regard to public schools and other public institutions." This certain knowledge, he said, was based on the sentiments which Satolli had expressed to him a few weeks previously in Baltimore on the occasion of the delegate's investiture with the red biretta of the cardinalate.[23] Thorne, on the other hand, in a typical unrestrained article entitled "Fool Newspaper Correspondents," maintained that the removal was not caused by the reasons broadcast by the press, but rather, he said, it was brought about "because of a contention between non-Catholic posing, American Brummagemism and quasi-Protestantism in the name of Catholicism on the one side and true Catholicism, without regard to language, race or national prejudice, on the other."[24] In general, however, the Catholic press refrained from the wild speculation so prominent in their secular counterparts, and they confined their remarks to inoffensive and ineffective denials of the unfounded rumors then being widely circulated.[25]

[22] Ahern, *op. cit.,* pp. 173–174.

[23] *Western Watchman,* Oct. 9, 1896, cited in the Washington *Times,* Oct. 10, 1896.

[24] Wm. Henry Thorne, "Fool Newspaper Correspondents," *Globe,* VI (Dec., 1896), 400. In another place in the same issue Thorne stated: "[Keane] has never accomplished anything to justify his perpetual posing as a public man of special interest to the 'American public,' and if at this juncture he could only banish this idea utterly from his mind and life, and accept such position of trust and honor as the Holy Father may choose for him, and be done forever with all concern what 'the American' or any other 'public' may think of him, thousands of Catholics will give him greater reverence and honor in his silent and faithful modesty than they have ever been able to bestow upon him or upon the amateur university which he has boomed out of all just and true proportion. . . . His friends write me that 'his enemies (I among them) have made a saint out of him.' I am delighted to hear that. There was good material to work upon, and lots of room for improvement" (Wm. Henry Thorne, "Globe Notes," *Globe,* VI [Dec., 1896], 442–443).

[25] Ahern, *op. cit.,* pp. 169–171. An editorial writer on the staff of the Boston *Pilot,* commenting on the fact that the *Catholic Citizen* of Milwaukee had said that Bishop Keane was resigned to the change because he had to be, asked a private corre-

The German language papers, too, at first limited themselves to unadorned reports on the fact, and published the letters of the Holy Father and the rector.[26] However, as the members of the fourth estate began to speculate on the reasons for the deposition, the German editors joined in by ascribing it to his co-operation with John Ireland in building up a liberal spirit in the American Church.[27] The bishop's position in support of Ireland on the school question was most frequently cited as the cause for his downfall,[28] and some German newsmen hopefully viewed the event as the death knell to Ireland's ideas both here and in Rome as well as the vindication of the German language.[29] The New York *Staatszeitung* scoffed at the charges that had appeared in the New York *World* and the New York *Journal* to the effect that the harmful representations responsible for Rome's actions against the rector were traceable to the Germans. Rather, this journal maintained, the Holy See had feared the chauvinism of the liberals, and it had sent Satolli to curb them. In spite of this, it said further, Gibbons, Ireland, and Keane, who were termed the "liberal triumvirate," pursued their dream of converting the whole United States and establishing a national church. Keane, especially, according to the *Staatszeitung,* was so given to making concession to attain this end that he even praised Protestantism. The Holy See, therefore, fully aware of such absurd notions, merely removed the rector to put an end to them.[30]

Bishop Keane's deposition also received wide notice in the newspapers in England and on the continent. Nearly a month after the first announcement, the *Catholic Times* of London informed its readers that "the strong feeling against what is called 'the German Party' excited amongst the Catholics in the United States by the removal of Bishop Keane . . . has by no means subsided."[31] In France such journals as the *Peuple Français* and the *Bien Public* merely printed

---

spondent: "Is all idea of the possibility of heroic virtue going out of the minds of these people who claim especially to represent Catholic opinion?" (AUND, Hudson Papers, Katherine E. Conway to Hudson, Boston, Oct. 23, 1896.)

[26] *Herold* (Milwaukee), Oct. 5, 1896; *Herold des Glaubens* (St. Louis), Oct. 7, 1896; *Germania* (Akron, Ohio) and New York *Staatszeitung,* Oct. 8, 1896.

[27] Denver *Journal,* Oct. 10, 1896.

[28] *America* (St. Louis), Oct. 8, 1896; Denver *Journal,* Oct. 10, 1896; *Herold des Glaubens* (St. Louis) and New York *Staatszeitung,* Oct. 14, 1896.

[29] *America,* Oct. 8, 1896; *Herold des Glaubens,* Oct. 14, 1896.

[30] New York *Staatszeitung,* Oct. 14, 1896.

[31] *Catholic Times* (London), Oct. 30, 1896.

the letters that had appeared in the American papers, but other news organs demonstrated a hostility to the former rector that could only be attributed to a personal antipathy. The evil genius of this poisonous print was none other than George Périès. Frustrated in his efforts to retain a position at the Catholic University of America after his contract had expired, he had vowed revenge against those who refused to profit by his services.[32] In a letter signed "Saint-Clément," which appeared first in the *Vérité* of Paris and which was copied by the *Espérance du Peuple* of Nantes, Périès claimed that Keane and Ireland, whom Félix Klein and Victor Charbonnel were holding up for the admiration of the French, were neo-Christians. Keane was famous, he said, for his invention of the Parliament of Religions of Chicago and for his attempts to promote the universal congress of religions at Paris, which was to be its complement. The untruthful Frenchman concluded that the bishop was removed because the Holy See was putting an end to what he termed "such dangerous tendencies of the liberal party and their chiefs." For some unknown reason the former professor thought it important in this connection to point out that Keane's "hostility to France was no longer a secret" by quoting an article on "The Decline of France" which the rector had published in the Washington *Post* after his return from St. Gildas de Rhuys.[33] Concerning the meeting of distinguished Washingtonians on October 8 to honor the bishop, Périès said: "He and his friends succeeded in provoking a meeting of protestation in Carroll Institute in Washington, to which heretics of all denominations and unbelievers, and a mixture of ignorant Catholics, common people and loafers, came to acclaim him."[34] In this manner did the former professor give conclusive evidence of his perverseness.

The *Croix,* another influential French paper, reprinted the New

[32] Périès had threatened the trustees by stating: "I do not want any scandal, but I must warn you that if something is made against me, the country at large and the Roman competent congregations will know what has been the spirit of this house, and I will do that, not in view of a mean revenge, but for the interests of the Church" (cited by Hogan, *op. cit.,* pp. 165–166).

[33] Washington *Post,* Sept. 30, 1896. Among other things, Keane said: "France is termed a republic, but has a republican form of government that is really more autocratic than when monarchical. It is a strong centralization, and Paris is the center around which all France revolves.

"It is hard for the French Legitimist or Imperialist to give up his opinions and conform to the republic, but it is slowly being done."

[34] *Espérance du Peuple* (Nantes), Oct. 22, 1896. In its issue of November 9 this paper quoted the *Western Watchman's* statement that Keane's removal was the deathblow to liberalism.

York *Journal's* sensational story from its Roman correspondent in which it was stated that, upon his return to the Vatican, Satolli had submitted a report on the religious question in the United States. In this report, as the *Journal* expressed it, "the Cardinal accuses Keane of having, in many discourses, enunciated opinions which border on heresy and says that in accord with Ireland, he has tried to acclimate his neo-Catholicism on American soil."[35] Equally unflattering opinions concerning the former rector appeared in the *Courrier de Bruxelles*. According to this journal, the reason adduced by the Holy Father for terminating Keane's rectorship was not the real one; rather, it was because he was too liberal. This paper maintained that "the liberal Catholicism, crushed by Pius IX, is reborn in America under the cover of democratic Christianity. Keane leaned to that side, along with Ireland and Gibbons." As evidence of the bishop's liberal leanings, it cited his part in the congress of religions in Chicago, and a supposed lack of sympathy for the monastic orders.[36]

Such universal newspaper agitation caused Gibbons to fear lest the partly healed wounds of former controversies be reopened and religion would thereby suffer. Further, he was faced with impudent stories that gave the party alignment of the University's Board of Trustees and that predicted an "open fight between Gibbons and the German party."[37] For this reason, during the second week of October, the cardinal authorized the publication of a statement in which the public was assured that far from there being any disagreement or antagonism or want of harmony among the members of the Board of Directors of the University, there was, as it was said, "a full and perfect unanimity of sentiment and purpose in all that regards the direction and government of the institution."[38] Yet, despite this effort to pour oil on the troubled waters, the storm continued unabated. Therefore, when the Board of Trustees held a special meeting on October 21 and 22 to select Keane's successor, a second attempt was made to put an end to the public discussion of a purely ecclesiastical matter. The trustees tried to give the impression that peace reigned in Church circles

[35] New York *Journal,* Nov. 12, 1896, cited by the *Croix,* Nov. 20, 1896.

[36] *Courrier de Bruxelles,* Oct. 25, 1896.

[37] *Globe Democrat,* cited by *America* (St. Louis), Oct. 13, 1896. The Washington correspondent of the *Globe Democrat* claimed that the Germans were in the majority and they would choose Spalding as Keane's successor. The German language paper sensibly maintained that "no bishop is likely to resign to take that position, at least for a few years."

[38] New York *Freeman's Journal,* Oct. 17, 1896; *Rochester Union and Advertiser,* Oct. 12, 1896, cited by Zwierlein, *op. cit.,* III, 241–242.

by stating that there were "absolutely no factions nor sectional differences among the members." It was said: "To speak of the triumph of this or that party as conservatism or liberalism, Nationalism or Americanism, is to misrepresent the whole situation. All the members of the Board are equally American in spirit."[39] Once more the newspapers paid no attention to the honest efforts of the Church authorities to remove a matter of internal ecclesiastical business from public discussion. Yet, the storm they brewed served a useful purpose, for it brought fully and forcibly to the authorities in Rome the undeniable fact that Bishop Keane had won many stanch friends during his career as rector of the Catholic University of America. Moreover, the Holy See could expect storm signals to be raised again unless the greatly esteemed prelate was justly treated according to the newspaper editors' standards. Furthermore, the support which the liberal cause received from the press must certainly have been pointed out at the Vatican, and it may have influenced Leo's future policy toward the Americanists.[40]

Meanwhile, Keane had placed the whole American continent between himself and the University. On his way to California he had stopped at Chicago to confer with Archbishop Riordan of San Francisco and Archbishop Ireland of St. Paul, who were visiting in that city. After the

[39] New York *Tribune,* Oct. 23, 1896. The editor of the *Shepherd of the Valley* applied the board's statement to Keane in these words: "If the retirement of Bishop Keane, by invitation of the Pope, simultaneously with the advent of Mgr. Martinelli, new Papal Delegate, as advised by Mgr. Satolli, former Papal Delegate, means anything, it means that the 'tendencies of Bishop Keane' are no longer to tend. If it means otherwise, the proper thing to have been done would be the re-election of Bishop Keane, as proposed by Archbishop Ireland the moment Bishop Keane's deposition was announced, in spite of the decision of the Pope that he must go and some one else take his place.

"One of the tendencies of Bishop Keane has been, wittingly or unwittingly, to impose upon the Protestant public the absurd notion that there is, in the Catholic Hierarchy and citizenship of this country, a distinction of Americanism and Non-Americanism, of Liberalism and Ultramontanism. And the last act of the Board of Directors of the Catholic University yesterday, before adjournment was to pass and promulgate a resolution of repudiation of the nonsense" (*Shepherd of the Valley,* Oct. 23, 1896, cited by Zwierlein, *op. cit.,* III, 242).

[40] After he had been in Rome a short time, in answer to the summons of the Holy Father, Keane indicated that the newspaper agitation was utilized to good advantage by telling Ireland: "But *events* in America and in France spoke so loud, and were so well made use of by our friends in Paris and by O'Connell here, that the transformation is complete" (AASP, Keane to Ireland, Rome, Dec. 21, 1896). A biased writer later claimed: "Keane and Ireland are responsible for the hub-bub after Keane's dismissal" (Wm. Henry Thorne, "Catholic Liberalism and Nationality," *Globe,* VII [June, 1897], 187).

meeting the bishop reported to Gibbons that both, as he said, felt "very gloomy" over the situation.[41] Upon his arrival in San Francisco on October 10, he was met by Father Peter C. Yorke, a former student at the University,[42] and the San Francisco *Monitor* of which Yorke was then editor welcomed him in these words: "He will receive a kindly welcome from Catholic Californians. He is not to us 'a tramp and a beggar,' but our homes are his home and the best we have is not too good for him. The friends he made three years ago have not forgotten him."[43] A few days later he went to San Jose to take up residence in a sanatorium conducted by the Sisters of Charity, which had been founded by Judge Myles P. O'Connor, the bishop's friend and a benefactor of the University.[44]

Although a great distance separated Keane from the scene of his former labors, the University remained uppermost in his thoughts. On the day after he arrived in California, he wrote a long letter to the University's vice-rector, Philip J. Garrigan, to inform him that Archbishop Riordan, as he put it, "was hopeless in the extreme, both as to the Univ'y, and as to the general condition now facing the Church in the U. S." According to the former rector both the Archbishop of San Francisco and Father Yorke considered George T. Montgomery, Bishop of Monterey-Los Angeles, whom Keane had proposed to them as a possible candidate for the rectorship, as "utterly unfit" for the post. Hence, the bishop concluded:

> I can only pray that God may grant to the Directors lights invisible now to me. The two things to be seen to are, first, that one sh'd be appointed who is not a partisan but will be a loyal friend of the Univ'y; secondly, that the collection be granted. Even if the Rectorship remained vacant a long time, you could hold the institution together and give it a chance to assume solid shape, if only the means were put in your hands by the collection. Insist on this as the essential thing.[45]

Garrigan did not answer this letter immediately, very likely because his time was fully taken up with the administration of the institution as acting rector. Over two weeks later Keane wrote again and he asked especially that he be given news of what he called the "true

[41] AAB, 94-R-6, Keane to Gibbons, Chicago, Oct. 7, 1896.
[42] ACUA, Garrigan Papers, Keane to Garrigan, San Francisco, Oct. 11, 1896.
[43] *Monitor* (San Francisco), Oct. 10, 1896.
[44] AANO, Keane to Chapelle, San Jose, Oct. 19, [1896].
[45] ACUA, Garrigan Papers, Keane to Garrigan, San Francisco, Oct. 11, 1896.

inwardness" of the Board of Trustees' meeting. In this remarkable letter he also revealed the state of his mental and physical health and of his deep piety. He said:

> Doubtless you have had an anxious and weary time of it. And what a storm the press did raise for a while! It was well indeed that I was far beyond their reach, and could look down on the tumult from my hilltop of solitude and peace. Though I cannot lose sight of the fact that I am *in exile;* yet no place of exile was ever sweeter, and no exile was ever more peacefully content than I. The interior calmness which upheld me under the strain of those last days at the Univ'y has continued always. No reaction, no break of the nerves, health and strength all right.
>
> How has it been with you, dear friend? Your health was not good when I was leaving; and the strain has naturally been heavy on mind and body. But in your case, as in mine, God's Providence makes no mistake, and His grace must be sufficient for you. As His docile and faithful servant, *stand your ground firmly and bravely* until *His* voice calls you from it, if it ever does. Don't take your course in your own hands. We have no right to do that.[46]

Some days before, the bishop had told another friend: "Providence gives me a lovely home and kindest care. I have lots of health and peace, and lots of good work mapped out. I only pray that I may be left in quiet to enjoy it all."[47]

Although Keane's friends must have understood why he desired peace and quiet after so many years of unrelenting warfare, yet it was impracticable in view of the fact that he, as well as the ideas and the party for which he stood, were dangerously near to complete disgrace. All the evidence pointed to the fact that the conservatives, in the hope of dealing the deathblow to those whom they styled liberals, were pursuing the advantage they had gained by Keane's removal to give the American people the impression that all those who had been frequently described as progressives were in disfavor in Rome and that it was only a matter of time before the rest of them would be deposed

[46] ACUA, Garrigan Papers, Keane to Garrigan, San Jose, Nov. 1, 1896.

[47] AJF, Slattery Papers, Keane to Slattery, San Jose, Oct. 19, [1896]. The New York *World* (Nov. 2, 1896) reported that Keane had written the following to a friend in Washington: "I am living in a beautiful, quiet spot, away from all the rush and cruel jars of life, and can just now think of nothing that will tempt me to leave my retirement for the disappointment and incompleteness which makes up a public office. I have earned my rest, and I hope it will continue for long." This does not read like a letter composed by Bishop Keane.

by their ecclesiastical superiors.[48] Commenting on this state of affairs, Ireland had said to Alphonse Magnien, S.S.:

> Recent occurrences show us the necessity of being frank and courageous. Satolli is determined to sustain his action toward Bp. Keane, by arraigning others — Card. Gibbons included, and if we lie down as cowards we shall be ruined. Boeglin and others write to me that we do not know Rome; that Rome respects only those whom she fears.[49]

Owing to alarming rumors of this kind, Keane was finally convinced early in November that he could not honorably remain longer in what he termed his "sweet retirement." After his plans for the immediate future had been formulated, he revealed them to Garrigan in these words:

> Abp. Riordan has convinced me that it is my duty, for the good of religion, to sacrifice my sweet retirement in which I am so content,— go to Rome, accept the position there offered me by the Holy Father, (and which Card. Satolli said to Abp. Riordan w'd remain always open to me), and *then,* demand an investigation of the charges of heterodoxy made ag'st me by Card. Satolli, and, thro' me, against so many others.
>
> Of course I must have *documents* for the fight. These I am asking of the friends of truth and justice under whose eyes I have acted and spoken. I would not dare to ask them were I not certain that I have never knowingly taught anything heterodox, and, please God, never shall. . . .
>
> I feel that this is the most important step of my life, and I ask the prayers of you all in regard to it.
>
> There can be no objection to its getting out that I have been persuaded to go to Rome and accept the Holy Father's offer there, as likely to be more useful to religion than my remaining in retirement. But of course there must be not a whisper of my expecting to "make a fight."[50]

[48] On November 12, 1896, the New York *Journal* published a cablegram that was supposed to have originated in Rome in which it was said that Ireland, who was called an "apostle of heresy," would be summoned to Rome. It also stated that Satolli had counseled the Holy Father to depose some of the professors at the University because they were dangerous disciples of Keane.

The New York *Tribune* (Nov. 14, 1896) included Gibbons among those held in disfavor and liable to removal from his position.

[49] ACUA, Bouquillon Papers, Ireland to Magnien, St. Paul, Nov. 19, 1896. Monsignor Eugène Boeglin, a friend of the forward group, had employed his pen on their behalf as the Roman Associated Press agent for Catholic news.

[50] ACUA, Garrigan Papers, Keane to Garrigan, San Jose, Oct. 19, [1896]. The bishop had requested similar documents from Maes and Chapelle. Cf. ADC, Maes to Keane, Covington, Nov. 27, 1896 (French), copy; AANO, Keane to Chapelle, San Jose, Nov. 18, [1896].

When John Ireland communicated the news about Keane's decision to Abbé Magnien, one of Gibbons' most intimate friends, he spoke in his familiar warlike tones:

> Bp. Keane has recovered himself: and he is willing to be the soldier rather than the hermit. He has realized that he is disgraced, that he must fight for his honor, and for the cause which he represented. He goes to Rome, nominally as "conciliarius," really in order to fight Satolli and Satolli's allies. I have written to Rampolla that I will go to Rome soon after McKinley's inauguration. I shall wait until I can go with all the prestige of my American influence. This influence is, thank God, immense just now.
>
> Satolli has killed himself out. Stand by Bp. Keane and myself—and ask Card. Gibbons to stand by us, and "loquemur victorias."[51]

Gibbons, too, expressed joy over the bishop's intention to answer the summons of Rome in a letter to Rampolla, in which he also told the papal Secretary of State: "I have well-founded confidence that by his piety and his zeal, he will usefully serve in Rome the general interests of the Church and in particular the interest of the Church in the United States."[52] Some of the newspapers also seemed to reflect the rejoicing among Keane's friends. One went to the extreme of announcing that his intimates in San Jose thought that he would be made a cardinal.[53] Others, taking up this new theme, opined that although it was hardly possible that he would be made a cardinal immediately, yet, as they expressed it, "there is but little doubt of his elevation to that exalted position within a reasonable time."[54]

After he had decided to "fight for his honor," Keane lost little time in preparing for his return to the East. Upon his arrival in Washington, in the last week of November, he conferred with Garrigan on the future of the University and, as a result, he urged Gibbons to ask Rome to delay the promulgation of Father Thomas J. Conaty's selection for the rectorship so as to give him an opportunity to seek the appointment of Camillus P. Maes, Bishop of Covington, for that post. The deposed rector sought this favor of the cardinal because Garrigan and others thought, as he said, "that not to have a Bishop for Rector will hopelessly lower the Univ'y to the level of a mere college or seminary,

[51] ACUA, Bouquillon Papers, Ireland to Magnien, St. Paul, Nov. 19, 1896.
[52] AAB, 94-T-11, Gibbons to Rampolla, Baltimore, Nov. 30, 1896 (French), copy.
[53] LCLD, clipping with dateline, San Jose, California, Nov. 24.
[54] LCLD, clippings.

deprive it of all its prestige, and ensure its utter failure."[55] Keane made the same representation to Rome and the Holy See authorized the cardinal to suppress Conaty's appointment, if he deemed it advisable. Since it was left to Gibbons' discretion, he chose to publish the selection when the official papers were in hand, principally because he feared that the newspapers would, as he expressed it, indulge in "all kinds of surmises, suspicions and perhaps insinuations" if it became known that a choice had been made and the announcement withheld.[56]

One of John Keane's principal objectives upon returning to the eastern seaboard, however, was to counteract the impression that he and his friends were held in disfavor by their ecclesiastical superiors. Therefore, he told reporters that he had received a second call to Rome to "take up the honors and duties" which awaited him there. "The reports," he remarked, "which were prevalent that the Pope desired to degrade me when he relieved me of my duties at the University are entirely without foundation. The kind expressions used in the letter which was printed were repeated and even more strongly in the second communication."[57] The New York *World* quoted the bishop as having said: "I should have preferred to remain always at rest and in retirement, but again the Holy Father in his wisdom saw fit to

[55] AAB, 94-Y-2, Keane to Gibbons, Washington [written between November 30, the day on which he arrived in Washington, and December 3, the date of his departure, 1896]. Charles Warren Stoddard, the occupant of the chair of English literature at the University, who by his own admission was an unstable person, made a series of interesting comments on conditions at the institution during this period of trial: "I am disgusted with the institution I am associated with and have been for some long years" (AUND, Hudson Papers, Stoddard to Hudson, Washington, Oct. 10, 1896); "This university scandal is killing me, it is killing the institution. Yesterday I got out of bed to go out to lecture, came home to get into bed again for it always makes me ill to spend any time in that atmosphere" (*ibid.*, Nov. 12, 1896); "Yes, the Varsity [University] is crippled forever. They have killed the goose that laid the golden egg and now 'twill live hand to mouth to the end of its days" (*ibid.*, Nov. 22, 1896); "The Varsity is wearing me out, it is telling on my nerves and I have lost all interest in life. I have to go this afternoon to a special faculty meeting when the priests will fight like cats and dogs and I shall come home in a state bordering on hysteria" (*ibid.*, Dec. 17, 1896).

[56] Hogan, *op. cit.*, p. 25. As early as October 22 it had been announced in the New York *World* that Conaty was first on the list for the rectorship submitted to Rome by the trustees.

[57] Washington *Post*, Nov. 30, 1896. In a note to Ireland written shortly after his arrival in Rome on October 31, Satolli revealed that he intended to speak to Leo XIII about Keane and that he would suggest that the Sovereign Pontiff again express to the bishop in a paternal manner his desire that he come to Rome where he would be honored with the title of archbishop and of assistant at the pontifical throne. Such a letter from the Holy Father, the cardinal added, would amount to a command (AASP, Rome, Nov. 5, 1896 [Italian]).

call me to a much higher post of honor and responsibility in the Church." The *World* then reported that Keane's friends were certain that the former rector would be appointed to the Congregations of the Propaganda and of Studies.[58]

Fortunately, the deposed rector could honestly appear before the American people and assert that his future and the outlook for the liberals was not as dark as some newspapers had painted it, for, along with a letter dated November 23, 1896, to Gibbons from Leo XIII announcing Conaty's appointment to the rectorship, Rampolla had sent a note in which he had said at the end:

> As regards Rt. Rev. Bishop Keane, that all animadversions and calumnies should cease, let it be known that the confidence and esteem of the Holy Father for him has been in no sense lessened, and he desires him to remain in Rome, where he will associate him as a canon to one of the patriarchal basilicas and give him place among the bishops who attend at the pontifical throne.[59]

Furthermore, the bishop had received advice which gave him positive assurance that he would not be called upon to defend his orthodoxy against the charges allegedly made by Satolli, since it would not be questioned.[60]

After he had spent several days with his friends in Washington, Bishop Keane was ready to continue on his way. On December 3 he was escorted to the station by a large and distinguished group, including many of the clergy of the city. The students of St. John's College also were present and, according to a Washington paper, "they cheered the bishop with a college yell as he went aboard the train."[61] Two Washington pastors, John Gloyd of St. Patrick's and James F. Mackin of St. Paul's, who were to be Keane's companions on his trip to Rome, as well as other clergymen from the University and the city and men prominent in government and business boarded the train to accompany him as far as New York. On the way to New York, they stopped at Baltimore and Philadelphia where others joined the delegation that was to see him off on his ocean voyage.[62]

On the day after they had arrived in New York, the publication of

[58] New York *World,* Dec. 1, 1896.

[59] Reily, *op. cit.,* IV, 731–732.

[60] AANO, Keane to Chapelle, Chicago, Nov. 26, [1896]. The bishop told Chapelle: "Never mind that document which I asked of you. Later and satisfactory information shows that there will be no need of it." Cf. *supra,* p. 194 *n.*

[61] Washington *Post,* Dec. 3, 1896.

[62] LCLD, clippings.

a telegram from Cardinal Rampolla to Sebastian Martinelli, in which the papal Secretary of State emphatically denied that the Holy See was contemplating the deposition of any American prelate or the removal of some professors from the University,[63] gave Keane an opportunity to speak out against those in Archbishop Corrigan's see city who, he was convinced, constituted a bureau for the spread of false rumors. To a representative of the press he stated:

> I very much regret that there has been a bureau of mischief at work in this country and in Europe, founded for the manufacture and dissemination of pernicious rumors of all sorts against Christians and distinguished Catholic prelates in this country. I am delighted to see the crushing blow inflicted upon them by the telegram from Cardinal Rampolla to the Apostolic Delegate. I hope the telegram will convince the American public that they ought never again to pay heed to the fabrications of the mischief bureau.[64]

The bishop also let it be known that he expected to find it convenient to return each year to attend the October meetings of the University's Board of Trustees and, as he said, "keep myself informed of the spirit of the Church in America."[65]

During his short stay in New York, the former rector called upon New York's metropolitan, who, as Keane later revealed, "spoke quite

[63] AAB, 94-U-2, Martinelli to Gibbons, Washington, Dec. 3, 1896.

[64] Rochester *Union and Advertiser,* Dec. 5, 1896, cited by Zwierlein, *op. cit.,* III, 245. The most disturbing rumor spread by the so-called mischief bureau involved Gibbons, Ireland, and three University professors, Thomas Bouquillon, Thomas J. Shahan, and Edward A. Pace. Newspapers reported that the two prelates had been called to Rome and that they would be removed from their sees. As to the professors, they were to be dismissed from the University. Sebastian Martinelli, the Apostolic Delegate, wrote to his superiors in Rome about the matter and on December 3 he received a cablegram from Cardinal Rampolla which authorized him to label the rumors as lies. Cf. Hogan, *op. cit.,* pp. 10–11.

Ireland gave evidence of concern over the matter in a letter to Gibbons on December 2 (cf. n. 49 for his previous statements on the subject). "Many Americans are beginning to believe that there is some truth in all those reports of papal disfavor," he said. "Something must be done to stop this dreadful and diabolical conspiracy."

"Of course," he continued, "Bp. Keane's presence in Rome will be a wonderful help. Our enemies did not know what they were doing when they had him removed from Washington. Was not Satolli's letter sweet? I frightened him in my last interview in Brooklyn. Nothing but stern courage on our part will avert disaster from us. We are timid children, and we are treated as children. Our enemies are not timid.

"The University is dead: nothing can revive it. The Jesuits have triumphed there for good" (AAB, 94-U-1, Ireland to Gibbons, St. Paul, Dec. 2, 1896).

[65] LCLD, clippings.

plainly about the statement that I had made to the press concerning the New York breeders of mischief and slander." Corrigan declared, according to the bishop, "that forty-nine out of fifty priests in the New York diocese and the public generally would infer from my language concerning the 'bureau of mischief' that I meant him," and the archbishop, as Keane remarked, "urged me to say to newspaper men before I sailed the next day that my published remarks were not intended to apply to him." To this request Keane claimed that he simply replied: "All I could say to the public was that my remarks referred to the same persons denounced in Cardinal Rampolla's telegram."[66] Thus, the breach between the two eminent ecclesiastics remained unhealed.

On December 5, Bishop Keane's loyal admirers gathered about him on the pier as the French liner, *La Bretagne,* prepared to sail. According to one witness, when the call "All aboard!" was heard, "he started to go up the gang plank, then stopped and turned again, a noble enthusiastic figure, and called in a loud voice for 'three cheers for the United States!' which were given with a will."[67] On the day after the former rector left the American shore, a cleverly composed piece, labeling Keane as a heretic, appeared in the New York *Tribune.* Its author undertook to give the public the real truth behind the claim that the bishop had been summoned to the Eternal City for the purpose of assuming, as his friends said, "a very important office in connection with the Propaganda Fide, the Roman institution that controls the affairs of the Catholic Church in America." First of all he pointed out that the Congregation of the Propaganda, which was supposed to exercise an all-powerful influence over the Catholic population in the United States, actually exerted very little control over the American Church, principally because the cardinal prefect of that congregation, realizing that Americans resented foreign influence, left the control and direction of the Church in the United States to its own hierarchy and to the apostolic delegate. Then, after showing to his satisfaction that the Propaganda's main function, so far as the American Church was concerned, was to keep a watch over doctrinal matters, the writer came to the real purpose of his news story. He wrote:

> Just what position the friends of Bishop Keane expect him to occupy at the Propaganda it is difficult to understand. For Cardinal Ledochowski is hardly the man to consult, with regard to the doctrinal affairs of

[66] New York *Journal,* Feb. 12, 1897.
[67] Elliott, *Catholic World,* CVII (Aug., 1918), 643–644.

the Church in the United States, a prelate who has been removed by the Pope from his responsible office of rector of the University at Washington for having identified himself with teachings that entailed displeasure to even so liberal and broad-minded a Pontiff as Leo XIII, the most enlightened and progressive priest that has ever occupied the chair of Peter. Bishop Keane's summons to Rome, while nominally to assume the purely titular and honorary office of Conculter [*sic*] to the Propaganda — they are numerous, and have no voice in the Congregation — is far more likely to have been issued for the purpose of enabling him to receive new inspiration at the fountain-head of Catholicism with regard to its dogmas. Whenever a prelate shows by his teachings or by his attitude that he has, so to speak, lost touch with Rome, that he has forgotten his early training and permitted new and unacceptable ideas to predominate over the true dogmas of the Church, he is usually called to the Eternal City and subjected to a sort of moral discipline. Nor is he permitted to depart until he has become once more thoroughly imbued with the true spirit of Catholicism, as understood at the Vatican and at the Propaganda.

The author of this attack either must have been convinced that Keane was guilty of teaching heretical doctrines or he was inspired by a deep personal animosity. In any case it would appear from the following that the writer was proud of the Archdiocese of New York:

Thanks to the relative freedom and latitude accorded to the American episcopacy, there is no branch of the Catholic Church in all the world that shows such marvelous growth and vitality and rapidity of development. Although the youngest of all the offspring of the Mother Church at Rome, the Catholic Church in America is already the most prosperous, its wealth being entirely built up by the voluntary contributions of its adherents, and at Rome to-day the archdiocese of New York is renowned as the wealthiest and, in point of its philanthropic and educational institutions, the most important of the entire Catholic world.[68]

[68] New York *Tribune,* Dec. 6, 1896. Thomas Gambon, a priest of the Diocese of Louisville, who was in Rome at this time, reported to Corrigan: "Rampolla has written another letter for Keane and he is expected here in a few days. He will be made Canon of St. John Lateran where he can say his office piously according to the Roman Ritual, and will have an opportunity to study sound Catholic Philosophy if he feels so inclined.

"Cardinal Satolli's suggestions I think will be carried out to the letter regarding American Church affairs and popular lecturers are not as much appreciated here as they may appear to be in America and the one who attends to his work quietly is the one who meets with and has gained golden opinions with the Powers that be" (AANY, Gambon to Corrigan, Rome, Dec. 10, 1896).

One would surmise, therefore, that those whom Keane had referred to as the "New York breeders of mischief and slander" were not frightened off from utilizing for their own ends the advantage gained over the liberals by the bishop's deposition.

On the day that this article appeared, Bishop Spalding, whose disposition certainly was not improved by the fact that he was suffering at the moment from an attack of rheumatism, revealed his thoughts on American Church affairs to his friend Father Hudson:

> The impression in Rome is that the Pope, in slapping Bp. Keane in the face, has given a death blow to the University. With Bp. Keane himself I have lost patience. If the Pope had him down on all four kicking him, each time he lifted his foot, the enthusiastic bishop would shout; — See how the Holy Father honors me. A more disgusting state of things than our ecclesiastical situation is hardly conceivable. The only important question, it seems, is whether Abp. Ireland is falling or rising in favor with Rome. If we could only hear nothing more of him, it matters little whether he fall or rise. I am sick of it all and only wish that I were away from it all.[69]

On the other hand, John R. Slattery, Keane's loyal friend since the days of their co-operation on behalf of the colored in the Diocese of Richmond, communicated his ideas to the bishop in words that bear complete reproduction:

> For the nonce, let Laertes now address Polonius, but in his father's words. Nine years of blowing hot and blowing cold are signs enough of the atmosphere into which this transatlantic trip will introduce you. The mystic is now walking down the valley of silence of which the poet-priest, Father Ryan sang; but the man of affairs has set his candle upon the mountain, yea, the mountain of God.
>
> This seems the first element in your present position. You are a representative man. You stand not alone. The bulk of the Archbishops and very many of the Bishops will turn to you; the Catholic University is your "Alter ego," devoted friends here in the hierarchy and out of it look towards and up to you, who have grappled them to your soul with hoops of steel.
>
> On the other hand, the Ethiopian cannot change his skin, nine years have proven that.
>
> Sings Longfellow,
>
> "Tell me of the voices four that fill the world,
> The voice of the sun in heaven's dome

[69] AUND, Hudson Papers, Spalding to Hudson, Peoria, Dec. 6, 1896.

> The voice of the angel of the rain
> The voice of the soul going home
> The voice of the murmuring of Rome."

The Sphinx of Diplomacy is gazing upon you, double eyed as it were from the Vatican and the Propaganda,

> "Give thy thoughts no tongue
> Give every man thine ear, but few thy voice
> Take each man's censure, but reserve thy judgment"

Such are some of Polonius' words.

The Lord Chamberlain of Hamlet never knew a newspaper: if he did, he would have said, give thy thoughts no press interview.

No man can safely rest upon his strong points, save in defence.

It is better to recognize one's defects and an enemy's strongpoints, than vice versa.

No one will challenge your character, your singleness of purpose, your love of prayer, your noble high-mindedness; but those surrounding you will edge on your impulsiveness; will catch the chance word let drop unawares; will flatter your past successes; will repeat the garbled news of a letter or a press dispatch, in order to carry a point. "Timeo Danaos et dona ferentes."

No doubt the sense of loneliness will be among your greatest crosses. There are some characters who rise above such oppression and ride every occasion to victory. Such seems to be Archbishop Ireland. Your present status is like the Rectorship at Washington, papal. A word made and another word may unmake it. Not so your nearest and dearest hierarchical friends in the United States. They are within Canonical confines. If driven to the wall, you cannot count upon them because of the Superior you are dealing with. Rex lex ipsa. Not only is this true, but more, you are now a novice, learning one of the most ungrateful tasks it falls to the lot of man to master. The web and maze of a policy, which has outlived all that the best minds of Europe have conjured up.

You need not expect any changes. The glory and prestige of the Roman Curia is the uppermost aim. Souls and knowledge, jure Divino apparently, must yield to it. Surely you will need to consult. . . .

While Mgr. O'Connell is in Rome, you have a true friend. But Italy may be too small for the both of you. If so, better to write to Baltimore or to St. Paul than to act alone. Festina lente, says St. Francis de Sales. Indeed the congregations of Rome are no mean examples of waiting. They never seem to be in a hurry. "Go thou and do likewise."

Pardon this long letter. Be certain that my unworthy prayers shall

> follow it. In the long run, you will gain a glorious victory; for after all "Universae viae Domini misericordia et veritas."[70]

The letter of Father Slattery clearly revealed his affection and esteem for the bishop, even if its strictures on the latter's opponents were severe. Such a message was naturally welcomed by the bishop who told the Josephite Superior that every line of his letter came from the heart of a true friend. "As such," he said, "never hesitate, I beg of you, to offer me such counsel as you see to be opportune." At the same time Keane indicated that others had proffered similar advice to him. He wrote:

> Your exhortation to prudence was in perfect accord with similar counsel given by others who understood the nature of the atmosphere that I was about to be committed to. Knowing well how foreign it is to my nature to deal with insincerity, pray that God may grant me the virtue of prudence, which, as a distinguished prelate here said to me, is often considered in Rome a substitute for all other virtues! Or rather ask for me, in the spirit of your good old mother — God rest her — the Gift of Counsel.[71]

While his friends were volunteering suggestions which, they hoped, were calculated to ensure a happy future for him, Keane and his companions arrived in Paris where they spent a few days before they went on to Rome.[72] Upon reaching the Eternal City on December 18, the bishop began to tread the thorny road that would lead him into an uncertain future. As his foot touched that path he said to Garrigan: "It costs my heart a severe wrench to settle down here and as it were, give up my country. But it seems to be clearly the will of Providence and for the best."[73]

[70] AJF, Slattery Papers, Slattery to Keane, Baltimore, Dec. 8, 1896, copy. "Song of the Mystic" by Father Abram J. Ryan, herein referred to, may be found in his *Poems: Patriotic, Religious, Miscellaneous* (10th ed.; Baltimore, 1884), pp. 1–3.

[71] AJF, Slattery Papers, Keane to Slattery, Rome, Dec. 29, 1896.

[72] AANO, Orban to Chapelle, Issy, Dec. 18, 1896, (French). Orban said that "Keane left Paris yesterday." He also spoke of their visit to Captier. Keane wrote to Garrigan that he had made satisfactory arrangements with the Superior General of the Sulpicians in regard to some University business (ACUA, Garrigan Papers, Keane to Garrigan, Rome, Jan. 22, 1897). Cf. Ahern, *op. cit.*, pp. 115–120, for an account of the business discussed. The bishop had told Félix Klein that he would stay with Madame Roux while he was in Paris and that he would pay his respects to Captier. He also hoped to see his correspondent (APF, Klein Papers, Keane to Klein, San Francisco, Nov. 22, 1896).

[73] ACUA, Garrigan Papers, Keane to Garrigan, Rome, Jan. 4, 1897. Soon after Keane had arrived in Rome, Satolli told Ireland: "I have tried very gracefully to see that he has decent hospitality amongst the fathers who have charge of the

On the very evening of his first day in Rome, Bishop Keane had a long talk with Cardinal Rampolla who, as he said, "was evidently rejoiced to see me in Rome, and was profuse in assurances that all was well."[74] During his meeting with the papal Secretary of State Keane applied for an audience with the Holy Father, who must have been anxious to see him since he named the following Sunday, December 20, at noon, as the hour for the audience.[75] In a letter to John Ireland on the day after the audience Keane reported:

> As I telegraphed this morn'g, all goes well. A few weeks ago, things here were quite as bad as we feared. But *events* in America and in France spoke so loud, and were so well made use of by our friends in Paris and by O'Connell here, that the transformation is complete. The Pope sees that he was duped into an action whose bearing he did not suspect. You may imagine this did not please him. Now he is eager to repair the mischief, and so all has turned in favor of the good cause which we represent.

During the audience with Leo XIII, which lasted an hour, the bishop stated that "the whole situation [was] discussed, the tergiversation of Satolli, and that imputed to himself, fully talked out."[76] Concerning this audience the former rector informed Garrigan:

> The Holy Father was most loving in his welcome, said it was God who had counseled me to come, and was both emphatic and cordial in declaring that there was absolutely no charges ag'st me, or the Univ'y, or the Professors, or Abp. Ireland. He repudiated with indignation the imputation of his having at all changed or modified his ideas and his policy. He gave abundant assurances that my future position sh'd be honorable, useful, and satisfactory.[77]

---

church of San Silvestro. . . . The Holy Father has deigned to make me archpriest of St. John Lateran and perhaps he will make Mgr. Keane canon of the same church" (AASP, Satolli to Ireland, Rome, Dec. 20, 1896 [Italian]).

[74] ACUA, Garrigan Papers, Keane to Garrigan, Rome, Jan. 4, 1897.

[75] AAB, 94-W-2, John Gloyd to Gibbons, Rome, Dec. 29, 1896.

[76] AASP, Keane to Ireland, Rome, Dec. 21, [addition on Dec. 23], 1896. On December 23, Keane said that he had not visited Satolli, nor the other cardinals, "lest it sh'd be said I was intriguing," but he was going to call on the former delegate and others the next day.

[77] ACUA, Garrigan Papers, Keane to Garrigan, Rome, Jan. 4, 1897. The bishop also assured William J. Kerby, who was preparing himself for a chair at the University by completing his studies at the University at Louvain, that the Holy Father held absolutely nothing against the University or its professors (ACUA, Kerby Papers, Keane to Kerby, Rome, Jan. 4, 1897). Kerby was welcomed to the University's staff in the fall of 1897. Cf. Hogan, *op. cit.*, p. 35.

To his clerical correspondents Keane also revealed that he had found in Rome devoted and powerful friends and advisers in Denis O'Connell, John A. Zahm, C.S.C., David Fleming, whom he described as the "celebrated English Franciscan," Bishop Carl Mourey, the representative of the French Church in the Curia, and the two Cardinals Vannutelli. "So the phalanx is a good strong one," he optimistically told Ireland, "and I think it is bound to do work that will tell. The enemy's hand is not seen, but we are not off our guard a moment."[78]

Truly, a strong phalanx was needed, for the former rector learned within a few days after his first satisfactory conversation with the Holy Father of what he called "a temperizing policy on foot," which he attributed to resistance to his being appointed consultor of the Propaganda. Because of this, as he remarked to Ireland, "O'C. advised that we sh'd not proclaim peace and draw off our forces until promises have been kept. And as yet it is all promises."[79] As evidence of the temporizing policy Keane cited what he termed "the higgling of the Pope," over the question of salary. The Sovereign Pontiff had asked: "Could not a pension be imposed on the income of the Univ'y! or on the salary of its Rector! or on the Amer. College in Rome! ! !" All of these suggestions the bishop showed to be impossible and he added: "I would rather live on charity than be a burden on these institutions, that the Amer. people would not be pleased with it." When he reported this conversation to the papal Secretary of State he also told him: "While I must receive a salary, lest some sh'd conclude that I was not a real official of the curia, still I did not care what might be its amount, as I was assured enough would be sent from America to supply my wants." In relating all of this to the Archbishop of St. Paul, he concluded by saying: " 'Tis a risk, I know, but O'C advised it, to facilitate their action, and it was the decent American thing to do."[80]

Over a week after he had paved the way for action, the bishop had to confess that he was still waiting for a definite word from the Vatican as to his future position. Among other things he told Archbishop Ireland:

> We are still standing to our guns; for it seems certain that the hostile influences are at work to hinder my appointment as Consultor

[78] AASP, Keane to Ireland, Rome, Dec. 21, [addition on Dec. 23], 1896. Bishop Carl Mourey was an official in the Roman Rota. Father David Fleming, O.F.M., was a consultor in the Congregation of the Inquisition. Cf. *La Gerarchia Cattolica* (Rome, 1897), pp. 675, 708.

[79] AASP, Keane to Ireland, Rome, Dec. 21 [addition on Dec. 23], 1896.

[80] *Ibid.*

> of the Propaganda. To give empty honors, *and shelve me,* would be natural policy; and O'C, Mourey, and Father David warn me strongly against it. Ledochowski don't [*sic*] want me in the Propaganda for he is *absolutely* with the Germans. The Jesuits don't want it; we believe Satolli doesn't want it. But without it my position here would be migratory and *a farce.*

It was because of circumstances such as these, he told the archbishop, that he had been prompted to send cablegrams to him and to Cardinal Gibbons requesting that they immediately write to Rampolla to urge him to use his influence to secure Keane's appointment to the consultorships which had been explicitly promised by the Holy Father in the letter announcing the bishop's dismissal from the University. Keane insisted that great good could be accomplished in time if he was successful in obtaining the appointments. If he failed to receive an assignment in the Propaganda it was Keane's conclusion that he might better have remained in California than be relegated to what he called the "Congregazione dei Sepolti Vivi [Congregation of the buried alive]."[81]

Ten days later the bishop again summarized the situation for Ireland by telling him that Rampolla had sent for him on January 9 and had told him that the Holy Father had appointed him a titular archbishop, assistant at the pontifical throne, and a canon of St. John Lateran. Keane said that he had thanked both the cardinal and Pope, but he had explained to the Secretary of State that all these honors would mean little without the consultorship. This, he told Rampolla, had been promised by the Holy Father and was expected by the bishops and people, and not to grant it would subject him to ridicule and be a source of disappointment to many. Besides, he had made it clear to the cardinal that he was in Rome not for honors but for work, and he must insist on getting the position which meant work. Keane maintained that he had been advised to follow such a line of argument by all his friends in Rome and it seemed to be successful, for Father David had assured him, as he said, "that my stand had *settled* the

[81] AASP, Keane to Ireland, Rome, Jan. 1, 1897. Cardinal Gibbons wrote to Rampolla relative to the consultorships, as Keane had requested, but the letter arrived after Rome had decided to honor the promise. In his letter the Archbishop of Baltimore had remarked: "It is important not to revive the public sentiment which has calmed. A long delay would make them angry and respect for pontifical authority would suffer" (AAB, 95-B-19, Gibbons to Rampolla, Baltimore, Jan. 15, 1897 [French], copy).

question and I w'd surely receive the Consultorship."[82] On January 15, the bishop announced to Gibbons that he had received the honors mentioned in his letter to Ireland as well as the appointment as a consultor of the Propaganda. "All is now certain," he wrote, "but still I make no move, and publish nothing, till the documents are in my hands." Keane gave the chief credit for their success in securing the consultorship to O'Connell's advice and to the latter's influence with the Vannutellis, especially Vincenzo, who, he explained, had spoken plainly and strongly to the Pope about it, and Leo XIII had agreed with him and had asked Cardinal Vannutelli to go personally to Ledochowski, Prefect of the Propaganda, and order the appointment to be made out immediately.[83] On January 18, Archbishop Keane wrote that he had now been appointed to all the offices mentioned in his previous letter but that he valued only the consultorships,[84] especially that of the Propaganda because it meant, as he said, "*practical* utility, work for the Ch. in the U.S., while the others are simply tinsel honors."[85]

With his position in Rome thus assured, Keane and his faithful friends had ample reason to rejoice. Yet, the newly created titular Archbishop of Damascus was faced with two pressing difficulties, namely, an adequate income to defray his expenses and a suitable permanent residence, the latter being conditioned by the former. It was no secret that he had little if any money when he left the Catholic University of America. When, for example, Gibbons had expressed the sorrow of the Board of Trustees at his departure from the University he had remarked to Keane: "We know you leave the university as poor as when you began it."[86] J. Havens Richards, S.J., the presi-

[82] AASP, Keane to Ireland, Rome, Jan. 11, 1897.

[83] AAB, 95-B-9, Keane to Gibbons, Rome, Jan. 15, 1897. In this letter Keane said: "Strong effort was made by all the hostile influences, especially American, to hinder my being admitted to the Propaganda; and even Rampolla, while talking fair, was at least passively holding the appointment back."

After Keane had received the coveted appointments, O'Connell told Ireland: "There was a determination never to let him into the Prop. But I overcame it through V[incenzo] V[annutelli]" (AASP, O'Connell to Ireland, Rome, Jan. 28, 1897).

[84] AAB, 95-C-4, Keane to Gibbons, Rome, Jan. 18, 1897.

[85] AAB, 95-B-9, Keane to Gibbons, Rome, Jan. 15, 1897.

[86] ACUA, Keane Papers, Gibbons to Keane, Baltimore, Oct. 31, 1896. After his deposition from the University Keane had asked Gibbons to help someone, as he said, "among the charity pensioners whom I now must cease to provide for" (AAB, 94-R-6, Keane to Gibbons, Chicago, Oct. 7, 1896).

When Gibbons wrote to Rampolla after Keane's dismissal from the University, he told the cardinal that the former rector did not have any money to provide the

dent of Georgetown, in his discourse on the occasion of the demonstration for Keane in Carroll Institute shortly after his deposition, had likewise stated: "His salary was spent on others much more than himself. The only luxury which he allowed himself was his books; and countless poor will render an account, on the last day, of the disposition of the scanty sums that came into his own hands."[87] Another who knew the archbishop intimately, namely, Walter Elliott, C.S.P., had said of him: "While Rector of the Catholic University, it was his custom every month when he received his salary to go about Washington incognito and distribute the money among the needy whom he knew."[88] The evidence of Keane's great charity was, therefore, known to many. After his position in Rome was made clear it was not surprising that Keane should reveal his financial status to his intimate friends. To Gibbons he wrote: "My total Roman salary will not be over $850, the canonry bringing only $60 a month, I am told, and the Consultorship $80 a year! I have to enter on my new career, with all its difficulties and financial responsibilities, trusting to the Providence of God and the kindness of my friends in America, and must pray: 'non confundar in aeternum.' "[89] And a few days later he asked the cardinal to send the $500 which his Eminence had offered because, as he put it: "The expenses entailed by the fees for these honors will be something enormous — the am't I do not know as

---

necessities of life because of his extensive charities (AAB, 94-T-7, Gibbons to Rampolla, Baltimore, Nov. 24, 1896 [French], copy).

In a long article in the Washington *Post,* June 5, 1899, William Macon Coleman expressed the opinion that Keane should not have gone to Rome, and he compared the material comforts there of Satolli and Keane. "Satolli," he said, "was now in the Eternal City, with ample means to provide himself with a palace from generous offerings bestowed on him as apostolic delegate to the United States." Then Coleman said that when the former rector was leaving for Rome in the fall of 1896 Archbishop Riordan of San Francisco supplied him with $1,000, with the remark, "if you need me, let me know, and I will follow you by an early steamer."

[87] *Church News,* Oct. 17, 1896.

[88] Elliott, *Catholic World,* CVII (Aug., 1918), 644. While he was rector, Keane enclosed a list of the people he aided each month in a letter to Garrigan, and he told the vice-rector to provide for them while he was in Europe for the summer (ACUA, Garrigan Papers, Keane to Garrigan, New York, July 5, 1894).

In 1893 Bishop Keane appealed to Father Hudson to collect funds for Mrs. Anna H. Dorsey, who was experiencing poverty in her old age because the revenue from her books would, as the rector said, "hardly keep her in salt." The Bishop said that he would take the blame if she complained (AUND, Hudson Papers, Keane to Hudson, Washington, Apr. 18, 1893; *ibid.,* New Orleans, Apr. 28, 1893; *ibid.,* Chicago, May 4, 1893; *ibid.,* Washington, May 19 and May 20, 1893).

[89] AAB, 95-B-9, Keane to Gibbons, Rome, Jan. 15, 1897.

yet."[90] Two weeks later he revealed his circumstances and state of mind in more detail to Archbishop Ireland when he said:

> We have all calculated the cost of my living here, if in an apartment, — and all agree that, for myself and Secretary, it w'd be about $4000 a year! As I have next to nothing, and only hopes and promises (vague) and probabilities ahead, all have concluded that I dare *not* launch into that now. I go next Wednesday to two rooms in the Canadian College, via Quattro Fontane, where I can be very comfortable at very moderate cost, and will stay there till America makes some *certain* and *permanent* arrangements, enabling me to take quarters suitable to my quasi-representative character. Judge O'Connor insists that a fund of $100,000, or at least $80,000, must be raised, the income to support me and any one succeeding me, and, if the office lapse, the whole to go to the Univ'y. He offers to give *one tenth* of the am't, if the other nine tenths be raised. He has no confidence in promises to give an *annual* am't. O'C. can tell how soon people get tired and drop off, and then some one is left in the lurch. As I have no desire to find myself worse in the lurch than I have been, I shall stay quietly with the Canadian Sulpicians till my friends make it possible to do better.[91]

Keane's decision to live modestly at the Canadian College proved a wise one for there was no evidence of any effort to raise the fund suggested by O'Connor. Furthermore, there were no signs that Gibbons was successful in making provision for the archbishop, as William Henry Elder had understood him to have stated that he would do at the meeting of the Board of Trustees in October, 1896.[92] During the two and a half years that Archbishop Keane was in Rome, therefore, he lived in two rooms on the first floor of the Canadian College where, as he told Ireland, "my hosts will in no way hamper

[90] AAB, 95-C-4, Keane to Gibbons, Rome, Jan. 18, 1897.

[91] AASP, Keane to Ireland, Rome, Jan. 31, 1897.

[92] AAB, 94-Y-3, Elder to Gibbons, Cincinnati, Nov. 20, 1896. O'Connell suggested that a new chair be founded at the University in Keane's honor and to bear his name, the interest to go to him during his life, and then to the University. "The University feels mean in having done nothing for Keane," the monsignor said, "and it is believed that this move will draw to the University all the sympathy of Keane's friends and strengthen the institution even financially. Abp. Keane could also accept it honorably, and the aching uncertainty of his present way of living would be at an end" (AASP, O'Connell to Ireland, Fribourg, Aug. 26, 1897). Chapelle was chosen to introduce the motion at the subsequent meeting of the Board of Trustees, but he found Gibbons, Ireland, and even Keane, vehement in their opposition to the idea. Gibbons was reported to have gone so far as to say that he would resign from his position as chancellor if Chapelle insisted on carrying out the plan (ADR, Chapelle to O'Connell, New York, Oct. 23, 1897).

my ideas or action, nor I identify myself with theirs."[93] His friends were generous during his Roman residence; nonetheless, Keane was keenly conscious of the fact that he was an object of charity, for as he remarked to Thomas M. A. Burke, Bishop of Albany, in thanking him for a contribution toward his support, "may you never need one like it."[94]

Amid his anxieties over his future status in Rome, Keane did not lose interest in the institution that had claimed much of his energy during the previous nine years. Shortly after he had arrived in the Eternal City he had shown this clearly when he told Garrigan:

> Please impress strongly on the Professors that there is no fear of an attack on them; — that they must have confidence in us here, and leave all things peacefully in our hands; that they must simply redouble their energy at their work, make it tell, and so save the reputation of the Univ'y; — that they must *work together* to make the Bulletin a greater and greater success; that their work is *right there* and they must be in it with all their hearts.
>
> My cordial greetings to Dr. Conaty. I hope he rec'd my telegram from Paris. May his Rectorate be a splendid success. Rally round him and stick to him, all of you, and *you* especially.[95]

[93] AASP, Keane to Ireland, Rome, Jan. 31, 1897. In reporting to Gibbons, John Gloyd said, anent Keane's taking up residence at the Canadian College: "This step was strenuously opposed by his advisors for some time, . . . Of course you understand this is only a temporary arrangement" (BCA, 95-E-6, Gloyd to Gibbons, Rome, Jan. 28, 1897).

[94] Archives of the Diocese of Albany, Keane to Burke, Rome, June 7, 1899. This letter, as well as others, indicate that John J. Kain, Archbishop of St. Louis, forwarded to Keane any gifts toward his support which were made by the American hierarchy. Cf. AANO, Kain to Chapelle, St. Louis, Mar. 27, and June 12, 1899; Keane to Chapelle, France, July 29, 1899. The Paulist Fathers, Deshon, Doyle, and Elliott, also contributed various sums (APF, Keane to Elliott, Rome, May 5, 1899).

Despite his dependence on others for funds, Keane sent Conaty $500 for, as he expressed it, "this year's subscription to the funds of the University" (ACUA, Conaty Papers, Keane to Conaty, Rome, Nov. 11, 1898).

[95] ACUA, Garrigan Papers, Keane to Garrigan, Rome, Jan. 4, 1897. A few months later, the former rector had this to say to the same correspondent: "I hope that in this critical period of the life of the University, yourself and all its old soldiers will stand firmly by the colors and by the new captain and not give the evil one the satisfaction of bringing harm to an institution which ought to prove such a blessing to the Church of God in America" (ACUA, Garrigan Papers, Keane to Garrigan, Rome, Mar. 19, 1897).

In a letter to the alumni of the Catholic University of America on the occasion of their second annual meeting on May 12, 1897, he spoke of the University as one of his "sacred interests" and he urged them to hold its advancement as one of their chief objects in life (Keane to the Alumni, Rome, Apr. 28, 1897, cited by the *Catholic University Chronicle,* I [May–June, 1897] 74). The *Chronicle* formed a part

In view of an expression of this kind, those whom he had left behind could have had no misgivings about the constancy of his devotion to the work which he had inaugurated. In turn, the former rector was the subject of praise that would prompt the most humble of men to pride, when Thomas J. Conaty was installed as the second rector of the Catholic University of America on January 19, 1897. Cardinal Gibbons, after speaking of the Holy Father as the first and chief founder of the University, said of Keane: "He is justly entitled to be called its second founder." It was largely owing to Keane's efforts, Gibbons pointed out, that the institution knew material prosperity and academic excellence.[96] The new rector, too, devoted a part of his inaugural address to an expression of admiration for the one whom he had succeeded in office. Concerning him Conaty said:

> My illustrious predecessor, the beloved, scholarly Bishop Keane, has given to the world marked evidences of marvellous enthusiasm and unstinted disinterestedness, by means of which he has been enabled to place this University upon a plane of usefulness which is the wonder and admiration of all lovers of education. I realize the difficulty of succeeding to such earnestness and devotion, for it is not given to many men to imitate so noble a model. The country honored him with its confidence and support. The Church is proud of his magnificent labors, and the Supreme Pontiff has rewarded him with high marks of esteem, affection, and distinction. The University owes him a debt of gratitude which can only be met by the best possible results in its efforts for the attainment of the high ideal which he set before it.[97]

The newspapers picked up these complimentary allusions to the former rector and one reporter gave further proof of the hold which Keane had on the affectionate regard of so many when he stated:

> No man will question the fact that it will be difficult to fill the place made vacant by the retirement of Bishop Keane. No man could have done more than he for the young University. Eloquent, industrious, zealous, with a most attractive personality, Bishop Keane did the work of a dozen men, and in the short space of nine years accomplished what generally requires a quarter or a half century to achieve. His retirement from the Catholic University has created profound regret, and he will ever enjoy the respect, confidence, and love of American Catholics.[98]

---

of the *Catholic University Bulletin* except in 1897, when one volume consisting of twelve numbers, issued two at a time, was published.

[96] "Inauguration of the Very Rev. Dr. Conaty," *Catholic University Chronicle,* I (January–February, 1897), 5.

[97] *Ibid.,* p. 14.

[98] LCLD, clippings.

Moreover, in Rome, Keane's work for the University was not ignored, for in the letter by which Augusto Guidi, titular Archbishop of Nicaea and auditor of the Holy Father, announced to the College of Cardinals and to Keane himself his promotion to the titular Archbishopric of Damascus, he enumerated among the bishop's qualifications for the advancement the following:

> Under his guidance the new University was not only erected, but through his care became one of the most flourishing universities of the world. He was not only its first rector, but he is also to be considered as the principal founder of that great athenaeum. He is a man of great doctrine, of great prudence, and, in a special way, a man fitted to accomplish the greatest good for our Catholic faith, and in every way worthy of being promoted to the said archiepiscopal Church of Damascus.[99]

Although the letter contained obvious exaggerations which were probably designed to be a balm to the wounded feelings of Archbishop Keane, it may have comforted a little the saddened heart of the man who was now embarking on a new field of labor.

[99] *Catholic University Chronicle,* I (May–June, 1897), 71–72. The apostolic brief in which Keane was promoted to the titular Archbishopric of Damascus was sent on January 9, 1897.

CHAPTER VIII

Roman Interval

ARCHBISHOP KEANE began his Roman career early in 1897 loaded with honors, but, as he remarked more than once to his American friends, he was interested only in "*work* for the Church in America."[1] His appointment as a consultor to the Congregations of the Propaganda and of Studies seemed to offer the opportunity he desired. However, when he called upon Cardinal Mazzella, Prefect of the Congregation of Studies, he was informed, according to O'Connell: "There is practically no Congregation, the Consultors were not consulted, the Prefect did all."[2] The Secretary of the Congregation of the Propaganda, on the other hand, put the archbishop to work immediately by giving him, as Keane expressed it, "a pile of documents on an American case."[3] Three months after the archbishop had been given his first case Brandi reported to Archbishop Corrigan that up to that time Keane had not been consulted by any congregation.[4] He was, nonetheless, an active consultor, although it must have been obvious to his friends as well as to those who had been opposed to him that his influence in that capacity would be very limited.

Moreover, as a canon of the Basilica of St. John Lateran, the archbishop was placed in a very trying position. In that role he was

[1] ACUA, Garrigan Papers, Keane to Garrigan, Rome, Jan. 22, 1897.

[2] AASP, O'Connell to Ireland, Rome, July 24, [1897].

[3] ACUA Garrigan Papers, Keane to Garrigan, Rome, Jan. 22, 1897. Some days later Keane told Ireland: "Ciascha welcomed me very kindly and gave me a case at once to work up. He has told me that my ponenza was entirely satisfactory, and that the case was settled in congresso according to my recommendation. You will be amused when I *tell* you some day what the case was" (AASP, Keane to Ireland, Rome, Jan. 31, 1897). Also cf. AAB, 95-E-6, Gloyd to Gibbons, Rome, Jan. 28, 1897.

[4] AANY, Brandi to Corrigan, Rome, May 1, 1897.

under the jurisdiction of Francesco Cardinal Satolli who had been in great measure responsible for the difficulties which Keane had experienced. In writing to Garrigan, shortly after he had been assured of an honorable place in Rome, the former rector optimistically averred: "Yesterday I had my first meeting with Card. Satolli — I was as off-hand and friendly as if nothing had happened. He responded, and no allusion was made to by-gones. The fight is over; the Pope has made all the atonement he can; and I have only to be agreeable, and useful."[5] Nevertheless, the strife between them was continued for the next two and one-half years, during which time Satolli maintained an uncompromising attitude toward Keane that was difficult of explanation except on the basis of a deep personal antipathy.[6]

While the archbishop was in some respects hampered in his desire to work for the welfare of the Church in the United States, he did have many opportunities to engage in labors which brought him favorable public notice. Less than three months after he had taken up residence in the Eternal City, he told Garrigan that he had done more preaching and lecturing than ever before in the same length of time. He trusted that Providence was directing him in this regard and that it was for the best interests of his Roman mission. And to this he added the comment: "It certainly has made me quite a noted Roman institution already."[7] On March 10 he spoke for more than an hour in Palestrina Hall on the subject of "Christian Civilization," and the papers reported that this lecture was attended "by the most distinguished audience that could be furnished by the English-speaking colony of Rome."[8] Each year between 1897 and 1899, by invitation of the Very Reverend William Whitmee, rector of the Church of San Silvestro in Capite, who was also the Superior General of the Pious Society of Missions, Keane preached a series of sermons in English

[5] ACUA, Garrigan Papers, Keane to Garrigan, Rome, Jan. 22, 1897.

[6] Cf. *infra,* pp. 239, 307. According to reliable reports, Satolli ordered Keane from one of the principal altars to a side altar in St. John Lateran on one occasion when it had been announced that the archbishop would pontificate and preach (William Macon Coleman in the Washington *Post,* June 5, 1899).

[7] ACUA, Garrigan Papers, Keane to Garrigan, Rome, Mar. 19, 1897. He added: "Our Lord is pleased to give me, moreover, an amount of contentedness in my new position which quite astonishes myself.

"So, I go on, peacefully doing each day's work, and leaving the future absolutely in God's hands."

[8] LCLD, clippings. O'Connell stated that Satolli had been invited to preside on this occasion but, as the monsignor put it, "Satolli curtly refused, giving no reason" (AASP, O'Connell to Ireland, Rome, Mar. 6, 1897).

on Sunday afternoons and Thursday evenings during Advent and Lent, which were attended by people of all classes and of all faiths.[9] That these discourses bore fruit was testified to by the Roman correspondent of the Baltimore *Sun,* who reported that among the archbishop's converts were to be found the Countess Andreozzi of Rome and a Miss Baxter of Maine.[10] O'Connell, in commenting on the tangible effects of Keane's preaching in Rome, remarked to Archbishop Ireland: "I don't think Mgr. Keane can with any safety take up his residence outside of the Canadian College. All the noble ladies of Rome are rushing after him with their doubts and sorrows, and were he living alone, in spite of his saintly life calumniators in Rome would not leave him a shred of reputation."[11] Leo XIII was also aware of the good results of the archbishop's work for during a special audience he advised Keane never to refuse an invitation to preach, and he dwelt at length on the great good which such work would produce among the English-speaking people in Rome.[12] That the archbishop had spoken to the Sovereign Pontiff about the time and energy that was consumed in such an important function of the ministry seems evident from an account of another audience in which it was reported that the Pope offered to grant an indult to Keane relieving him of some of his duties as canon of the Basilica of St. John Lateran.[13]

Besides the series of sermons which the archbishop gave each year in San Silvestro in Capite, he was called upon, among other things, to deliver one of the two English sermons given during the octave of the Feast of the Epiphany in the Church of San Andrea della Valle[14]

[9] *Church News,* Dec. 4, 18, 1897; Jan. 1, 22, Apr. 9, May 7, Dec. 31, 1898; Apr. 29, July 15, 1899. In January, 1898, Keane sent Garrigan a nine-page letter which included the sermon outlines for his discourses delivered during Advent of 1897, and those to be given during the Lent of 1898. He had taken the Incarnation for his theme on both occasions (ACUA, Garrigan Papers, Rome, Jan. 3, 1898).

[10] Baltimore *Sun,* cited by *Church News,* July 15, 1899.

[11] AASP, O'Connell to Ireland, Rome, July 21, 1897. For his sister, Agnes, Father William Kerby summed up the results of Keane's sermons and lectures in these words: "The Church is always crowded—his sermons for charity net from 500 to 1400 francs—extraordinary when you remark that heretofore 100 francs attracted by famous men was considered splendid. Rich ladies even give bracelets, jewelry, etc. to the collections" (ACUA, Kerby Papers, Kerby to Mrs. R. J. McHugh, Louvain, June 13, 1897).

[12] *Church News,* Jan. 1, 1898. A similar statement appeared in William J. D. Croke's column in the *Catholic Standard and Times,* cited by *Church News,* December 31, 1898.

[13] LCLD, clippings.

[14] *Ibid.*

and to lecture for a charitable purpose in the *aula maxima* of the palace of the Cancelleria, the use of which was specially granted by the Holy Father.[15]

But what was, perhaps, Archbishop Keane's most impressive discourse during this period of his career was the one delivered on May 15, 1897, in the Church of Sant' Agata, in Rome, in memory of the fiftieth anniversary of the death of Daniel O'Connell. According to one report, the archbishop preached on this notable occasion at the invitation of Michael Cardinal Logue, Primate of all Ireland.[16] The choice proved a happy one for Herbert Cardinal Vaughan, Archbishop of Westminster, pronounced the discourse of Archbishop Keane to be one that merited to rank with the masterpieces of Ventura, Lacordaire, and Dupanloup.[17] Certainly, the superb style in which the archbishop portrayed the Irish patriot's formative years as well as his relentless labors for the spiritual and political liberation of the people of Ireland would appeal to every lover of finished composition. But it was his masterful manipulation of the delicate subject of England's relations to Ireland, revealing his all-embracing charity, even as he rapidly reviewed the historical record that must have prompted Englishmen and Irishmen alike to agree with Vaughan's conclusion that the discourse had produced great good.[18]

In their reports on Keane's public appearances in Rome the foreign correspondents frequently pointed out that whenever the archbishop was scheduled to appear, the church or auditorium in which he was to speak was filled, and that fact in itself, as one writer said, was an event of rare occurrence.[19] The orator was also spoken of as "unquestionably one of the most effective preachers and one of the most zealous and industrious workers that America has sent to Rome."[20] Another enthusiastic account maintained that Keane's public address was beyond all praise, and the most striking element in the composition of his sermons was that they were quite scriptural.[21] The in-

[15] *Church News,* Mar. 19, 1898. The lecture was entitled: "The Boy is Father to the Man."

[16] J. J. Sisk (ed.), *Ancient and Modern Masterpieces of the Leading Lights of the Catholic Church* (New York, 1906), II, 592.

[17] *Ibid.,* II, 593. A Mr. Nerincx heard this sermon and reported to Father Kerby that the power of Keane's eloquence was so great that the Italian audience wept over the great emancipator just as Ireland must have wept when he died (ACUA, Kerby Papers, Kerby to Mrs. R. J. McHugh, Louvain, June 13, 1897).

[18] Sisk, *op. cit.,* II, 594–616. [19] LCLD, clippings. [20] LCLD, clipping, May 7, 1898.

[21] William J. D. Croke in the *Catholic Standard and Times,* cited by *Church News,* Dec. 31, 1898.

terest which the press manifested in Archbishop Keane — some of which was inspired by his friends — kept the people in the United States from forgetting the prelate during his exile in Rome. Furthermore, his yearly visits home afforded him opportunity to accept the invitation of journalists to express himself on many matters, to appear before select as well as large audiences in Washington and elsewhere, and to maintain personal contact with ecclesiastical activity in the United States and in his beloved University.

Each year as he returned and made St. Patrick's Church in Washington his headquarters, the archbishop devoted himself to the work of the ministry among the people of the national capital. He spoke at the annual meetings of the Washington Tabernacle Society;[22] he delivered lectures for such charitable institutions as the Home of the Good Samaritan;[23] he preached frequently in the Churches of St. Patrick, St. Paul, and St. Augustine in the city;[24] and he gave instructions to those who sought them.[25] In turn, he received testimony of the esteem in which he was held in the city, for a newly-erected dormitory at the University was named Keane Hall in 1897,[26] and, in the following year, Washington's second council of the Knights of Columbus was designated as Keane Council.[27]

On the occasion of Keane's visit to the United States in August, 1897,[28] his friends contrived to give his return the appearance of a

[22] *Church News,* Oct. 23, 1897; Oct. 15, 22, 1898.

[23] *Church News,* Oct. 15, 1898. William F. Downey, founder of the League of the Good Samaritan in Washington, had established the home in 1894.

[24] *Church News,* Oct. 23, 1897. The reporter claimed that the congregation that assembled in St. Paul's Church on the occasion was the largest since the edifice was dedicated. *Ibid.,* Sept. 17, Oct. 1, 15, 22, 1898.

[25] ADR, Fannie Whelan to O'Connell, Washington, Oct. 1, [1897]. This correspondent said of Keane: "His hands full of work — he gives himself no rest. He has at least a half dozen converts under instruction and last week received into the church young Lt. Field a navy officer — son of Mrs. Field whom you knew in Richmond."

[26] Hogan, *op. cit.,* p. 30. This building is today known as Albert Hall.

[27] *Church News,* June 18, 1898. The council was instituted on June 5, with eighty-six members. Philip J. Garrigan, Thomas Shahan, and Edmund T. Shanahan from the University's faculty entered at this time.

Outside the city of Washington the archbishop graced the pulpit at the Baltimore cathedral (Reily, *op. cit.,* IV, 942) and he delivered the opening sermon of the scholastic year at Notre Dame on September 18, 1898. Cf. John J. Keane, *The Man; The Christian; The Worker* (University of Notre Dame Lecture Series, I [Notre Dame, 1898]).

[28] Reily, *op. cit.,* IV, 918. He arrived in New York on August 12 on the steamer *Trave.* Some months before his visit, Keane had told Ireland: "Satolli lately expressed his apprehension that, if I went back to America this summer, I would say to the

triumph. When the superior of St. Mary's Seminary in Baltimore revealed to O'Connell that a banquet would be held in the archbishop's honor, he said in anticipation: "It will be a grand affair owing to the quality of many of the guests, not even the refractaires of the French 'La Vérité' will be able to deny that the elite was there and that Abp. Keane occupies a prominent place in the esteem and respect of his fellow countrymen." Abbé Magnien then added: "But, inter nos, please to watch his tongue: I always fear that he will commit himself to some extraordinary and very suspicious statement."[29]

The superior of St. Mary's was correct in his prediction and, to some extent, justified in his fears, for Keane was to give a significant address. The guest list for the celebration contained the names of men holding the highest offices in the Church in the United States and five members of the President's cabinet.[30] After the sumptuous feast in the Shoreham Hotel on October 13, the Archbishop was eulogized by the Honorable Webster Davis, Assistant Secretary of the Interior, in response to the toast, "The American Citizen," and by Cardinal Gibbons in reply to the toast, "The Holy Father." In the first address of the evening, the Honorable James G. Berret, ex-mayor of Washington, paid homage to Keane as "The Model Christian and the typical patriot." Then the honored guest delivered a strong patriotic discourse which contained both an answer and a challenge to those who had been critical of him in recent years. He first told how he had come to appreciate Washington's providential significance as the capital of the country. Having taken up residence in the nation's capital in 1866, when it clasped North and South with outstretched arms, he "came to love the Union, to love the whole country, and sectionalism became an impossibility." Next, he stated that he had been influenced by the peculiar relation of the city to the politics of the country. Independent of state control and political strife, she symbolized to him the union of all parties for the general weal. Therefore, just as sectionalism had

---

newspapers 'that it was he who had done it,' referring of course to the University episode. . . . However I of course have not the slightest intention of saying anything against him or about him" (AASP, Rome, June 4, 1897).

[29] ADR, Magnien to O'Connell, Baltimore, Sept. 27, 1897.

[30] Cardinal Gibbons, the apostolic delegate, five cabinet members, and 150 distinguished Americans were there, according to a cablegram sent to Rampolla by the committee in charge of the banquet (*Church News*, Oct. 16, 1897). One chronicler recorded that the President's cabinet was represented by the Secretary of the Treasury, the Attorney General, the Secretary of the Navy, the Postmaster General, and the Secretary of the Interior (Reily, *op. cit.*, V, 334–335).

become an impossibility for him, so did partisanship. By this, he said, he did not mean to criticize parties, party men, and politics. But he was grateful that identification with the national capital had lifted him to what he considered "a higher level than the party arena," and had left him not only the friend of what was true and right in each of the parties, but also "a counsellor of that unselfish patriotism which makes the interaction of the different parties co-operate for the promotion of public-mindedness, and for the symmetrical, harmonious, justly balanced and safe advance of our country in her march of onward progress." Subsequently he had come to appreciate the influence of the United States in the politics of the world and in the social advance of mankind. The republic had received wisdom from the old world, only to return it fresh and new for the welfare of older peoples. "And thus," said he, "I came to recognize that our country, in being, as Leo XIII called her, 'the land of hope, the land of the future,' was destined by providence to be such not only for her own welfare, but for the welfare of all the upward struggling races of mankind." Hence, he came to hold America dear more and more "with the heart not only of a patriot but of a priest." He was absolutely convinced that America's influence in the world was meant to ennoble and uplift it. "In so important and so every way desirable a work," he continued, "it was manifest to me that the old Church of Christ, the mother of Christian civilization, ought to have a prudent and even a principal part." As he grew in age and in influence he thought it was his duty to impress this conviction on everyone. On this note the speaker became more eloquent as he told his audience:

> The more fully I came to appreciate both the spirit of the Church and the genius of America, the more profoundly did I become convinced of the essential harmony between them and of their heavenly-imposed duty to co-operate with each other for the welfare of America and of the world. If there has been anything specially characteristic in my career, it is to this conviction that it is due, and I am deeply grateful to providence that so it has been.
>
> For the realization of so vast and noble a purpose, I have been not only anxious to do conscientiously my own humble part, but ready to give just recognition to whatever any believer in Christ, or even any believer in God, might be striving to do towards the same end. Carping critics have asserted that in this I minimized Catholic truth, and dragged it down to the level of man-made and imperfect Christian systems, or even of heathen unbelief. In so saying they have totally and, I cannot but fear, wilfully misrepresented me. I have always been

glad, and even proud, to utter the fulness of the truth to any assemblage of human beings who care for the truth; for I hold with St. Paul that to believers and unbelievers, to Gentiles and to Jews, the Church of Christ is still a debtor. But I have never forgotten that the power of the truth consists in its presentation in all its symmetry and beauty and fulness; I have never sacrificed one tittle or iota of it; and they who assert that I have assert what is false. May God forgive them; I have no controversy with them.

In conclusion he spoke of his work in Rome, where he said he was useful and happy, and, according to his conviction that "Providence makes no mistakes," he would continue to work for the Church, for humanity and for America.[31] Shortly after the celebration, the archbishop writing of it to O'Connell said: "I had a splendid opportunity to speak a clear strong word at the banquet tendered me last Wednesday night. All whose opinion I care much for are glad I spoke it. The Cardinal was afraid, but could not help noticing that the points which he dreaded were the most vehemently applauded."[32]

Keane had another chance to speak "a clear strong word" when he addressed those assembled at the Catholic University of America on October 20, to participate in the investiture of Thomas J. Conaty as a domestic prelate. In his discourse on this occasion the archbishop pointed to three qualities which in his mind made Conaty particularly desirable for the position of rector of the institution, namely: he was a typical American priest, a representative American worker for the modern elevation of American youth, and a representative American educator. Then, alluding to the whispers and rumors about the University which had called forth various endorsements of the institution by Leo XIII, he remarked: "A year ago the Holy Father said to me: 'All these things these people have been telling me are lies, manufactured by men who hate, not only the University, but me; by refractaires who hate my policy. I will show them by my treatment of you what I think of them and the University.'" In conclusion, he maintained that the honor bestowed upon his successor was another answer to those who had been so tireless in their efforts to destroy the institution that crowned the American Catholic educational system.[33]

[31] *Church News,* Oct. 16, 1897. One journal reported that the Washington papers, *Post, Times* and *Star,* gave full coverage to the banquet and it added: "Memories such as these may well prove a solace to a beloved prelate without a rival in the esteem of the American people" (LCLD, clippings).

[32] ADR, Keane to O'Connell, Washington, Oct. 15, 1897.

[33] "The Investiture of the Right Reverend Rector," *Catholic University Chronicle,*

The vigorous language employed by Archbishop Keane in public addresses during his visit to the United States in 1897 was doubtless prompted in part by the continuation of the struggle between the two parties in the American Church. To offset the results of adverse newspaper reports attending his dismissal from the University, his liberal friends had utilized every available means to foster the impression that their so-called influence in Rome had not been in the least bit diminished. It was with this in view that wide publicity had been given to the honors bestowed on the archbishop by the Holy Father. As soon as his position was assured, Keane, for personal as well as for party reasons, had begun to clear his record before the American people and, at the same time, to point out those who were responsible for the sensational stories calculated to embarrass his friends. On February 12, the New York *Journal* printed on the front page a report from its Roman correspondent, James Creelman, under the headline "Keane in Favor with the Pope." In the interview Keane stated that the Pope was greatly shocked and grieved by the mischief-makers who were so busy in the American press, and Leo XIII was quoted as having said: "I protest against this malice and falsehood. The idea that anyone would try to put me in the position of disapproving the splendid service of Cardinal Satolli or of publicly disgracing you never occurred to me." The former rector maintained that the Holy Father was indignant and astonished when he learned that the meaning of his act in bringing about a change in the rectorship at the University had been misrepresented and that he would answer Keane's enemies by giving substantial evidence of the love and esteem in which he was held by the Vicar of Christ. Creelman then quoted Keane as having asserted:

> It is a remarkable thing that when the so-called liberals are dominant in America no one is attacked by them, but when the so-called conservatives appear to have gained a victory the mischief-bureau in New York suddenly starts into activity, and the whole press of the country teems with scandal, falsehood and venemous abuse.
>
> Archbishop Ireland, one of the purest and noblest prelates in America, who is loved and admired by the Pope for his zeal, ability and piety, has been outrageously villified, and because I taught in Washington

---

I (July–Oct., 1897), 87–88. Accounts of Keane's address may also be found in *Church News,* October 23, 1897, and in Reily, *op. cit.,* IV, 951. Reily gives October 19 as the date of the investiture. A misprint in Father Hogan's volume on the University makes the ceremony take place on October 30 (*op. cit.,* p. 104).

> University that the truth of God's word was not inconsistent with facts revealed by science I was denounced as a heretic, who had been rebuked by removal from office.
>
> All these stories, originating in New York, are pure inventions of malignant minds. I would be sorry to hold Archbishop Corrigan responsible for all that has been said or written by those who appear to be his friends, and I cannot be brought to believe that he would consent to or authorize all of this mischievous work.[34]

When Thomas F. Gambon read this account, he hastened to tell Corrigan that there was "a loud mouthed Canon by the Tiber," and he added: "From the tone of the Canon's utterances one can easily fancy that Keane now feels that he is in tight traces but this roar across the waters will make the Archpriest of St. John's [Satolli] keep his eye on some of his Canons and he is the man that will do so."[35] Brandi, too, took notice of American newspaper stories by informing the Archbishop of New York that although certain papers in the United States were full of news concerning American prelates in Rome, the Catholic papers in the Eternal City had ignored them entirely, to which he added, "E 'tutto fumo senz' *arrosto* [all smoke and nothing cooking]. The smoke is easily recognized in Rome, but not in the U.S., at least by all." Brandi then observed that to believe that these American prelates or anybody else of the same stamp could exercise in Rome, under the prevailing circumstances, any influence over the Holy Father or the congregations was an illusion and a grievous error.[36]

Some weeks after Creelman's piece had appeared in the *Journal,* the New York *World* printed a staff correspondent's story with a Washington date line under the headline "Corrigan vs. Keane." The *World's* representative claimed that Keane was threatened with an ecclesiastical examination by the Congregation of the Holy Office which he described as "the most solemn and rigorous of the Roman Church." He gave as the immediate cause the archbishop's utterances in the published interview in which he had expressed surprise and indignation because Archbishop Corrigan, as he expressed it, "had continued to lend the dignity and authority of his high position to the attacks made on him and his associates, Cardinal Gibbons and Archbishop Ireland."

[34] New York *Journal,* Feb. 12, 1897.

[35] NYAA, Gambon to Corrigan, Louisville, Feb. 20, 1897. He stated further that he would write to Satolli, since, as he expressed it, "it is well to let him know how the world wags on this side of the pond."

[36] AANY, Brandi to Corrigan, Rome, Mar. 1, 1897.

The correspondent further attributed to Keane a statement to the effect that the stories originating in New York concerning his deposition and the future policy of the Vatican toward the so-called liberals of the Catholic Church in the United States were directly traceable to the Metropolitan of New York. The journalist maintained that it was no secret that the Archbishop of New York had forwarded a mass of material to Lucido Mark Cardinal Parocchi, the vicar-general of Rome, with the request that Keane be subjected to examination and disciplinary action. Parocchi was a warm friend of Corrigan and an open champion of the conservative party in the American Church, the article stated, and it was contended that through the cardinal's influence and that of Cardinal Ledochowski Keane had received only minor offices at the Vatican. The writer also professed to see a foreshadowing of the conservatives' protest to Rome about Keane in an article, signed Romanus, which had appeared the week before in the St. Louis *Review,* a journal which he described as a Catholic periodical of German inspiration. According to the *World,* it was known that Schroeder was the author of the *Review's* article which was especially critical of Keane's farewell address at the University and of his declaration: "In Rome, as elsewhere, I will fight for my American idea against man and devil," and in which Keane and his friends were accused of having inspired the dispatches to the newspapers after his dismissal from the University, and therefore Keane was the head of what was termed the "Ecclesiastical Bureau."[37]

Thus was the contention between the two groups in the American hierarchy kept before the people by outside interests. But the real purpose behind the party strife was not evident to the general public. New issues now divided the American bishops, and Keane, as one of the leading members of the liberal group, became deeply involved in furthering the interests of his party. It was later known that the archbishop's thinly veiled attack on Corrigan was part of a plan to prevent his elevation to the cardinalate and to promote the candidacy of Archbishop Ireland for that honor. If the Holy See selected the Archbishop of New York without choosing Ireland at the same time for the high office, it would be a sorry blow to the prestige of the friends of Ireland. But, on the other hand, if their candidate was

[37] New York *Evening World,* Mar. 23, 1897. According to another source (cf. *infra,* p. 227) the writer was correct when he stated that Cardinal Parocchi was "a warm friend of Corrigan." Although Schroeder denied that he had written the article, signed Romanus, he did say that he had written a similar article in German (cf. *infra,* p. 237).

singled out for the position their ideas would appear to be vindicated before the world, and the ugly shadow cast over them by Keane's dismissal from the University would be largely dispelled. O'Connell was sure that two New York millionaires then in Rome, whom he described as "ardent Corriganites," were, as he phrased it, "no doubt at work." He also claimed that a "very eminent person" believed that Satolli was actively engaged in promoting the New York metropolitan's candidacy for the red hat. This unnamed ecclesiastic, O'Connell reported, had expressed the opinion that the Pope set more store on "one word from a diplomat than on all the letters from Bps." Since Keane was on intimate terms with Bellamy Storer, the United States minister to Belgium, the monsignor suggested that Storer, or some other man high up in the government, be employed to counteract the work that he surmised was being carried on by the friends of Archbishop Corrigan.[38] In writing to Gibbons on the same subject, Keane remarked: "There is so much talk now of the red hat for N. Y., called by the knowing ones the *'capello d'oro'* [hat of gold] — that the risking of a little *oro* on the right side becomes indispensable." The risk that was suggested to the cardinal would take the form of assistance to the niece of the Cardinals Vannutelli and her doctor husband who were experiencing difficulty in establishing a professional practice in Baltimore. Keane observed that the gratitude to Gibbons would in this case come not from the doctor but from the cardinals which he thought a most desirable consummation. The archbishop then concluded: "All seems to go well; but we are passing thro' a critical period between now and the next consistory."[39]

[38] AASP, O'Connell to Ireland, Rome, Mar. 6, 1897. In a letter to Ireland on March 24, Keane identified the wealthy friends of the Archbishop of New York as Norton Otis, Eugene Kelly, and Bourke Cockran (AASP). After Corrigan died his brother told Arthur Preuss that the archbishop had been offered the red hat many years before but he did not wish to accept it "as it might give rise to jealousy on the part of others — on account of his youth, etc., and because New York had already once had this honor, and that he would ask that the Cardinalate be conferred either on Abp. Williams, or on Msgr. Gibbons on account of his being Primate" (Archives of the Central Verein, St. Louis, Arthur Preuss Letters' Collection, Box 1900–14, Central Bureau Library Vault, Joseph F. Corrigan to Preuss, New York, June 29, 1902, copy through the kindness of Father Coleman Barry, O.S.B.).

[39] AAB, 95-K-12, Keane to Gibbons, Rome, Mar. 18, 1897. The archbishop did more than his share to help the unfortunate immigrants. One of O'Connell's correspondents told him: "If the Cardinals Vannutelli have rendered him [Keane] service in Rome he is returning it a hundred fold by his brotherly care of these two exiles." She said that Keane had them as his guest at a hotel, gave her a hundred dollars to use for them, and was giving of his time to introduce the doctor to the physicians of the city (ADR, Fannie Whelan to O'Connell, Washington, Oct. 1, [1897]).

Archbishop Keane also kept Ireland informed on the Roman sentiment in regard to the liberals and the behind-the-scenes maneuvering for the red hat. In his first audience with the Holy Father, Keane maintained that he had "entered an earnest and most solemn protest against the idea that there existed among us any disaffection to the Holy See." That the Pontiff had heard such accusations was evident from the archbishop's account of his reply. He told Archbishop Ireland:

> He received the assurance most kindly and added that he had always said to those who spoke to him, that he was sure there could be no danger of schism in the United States, that he had alleged the example of a Mexican bishop who had left the Church and had been powerless to draw others after him. Whence he agreed that if ever a similar thing should happen in the United States there would be no following there either.
>
> This, as you'll see, shows clearly to what extent misrepresentation had gone. Under the circumstances, it is marvellous that the Holy Father has done as well as he has.[40]

The charges against the so-called liberals had, indeed, been serious and, if they were believed by the Pope, they constituted a threat to the hopes of the Archbishop of St. Paul. In a later summary of events to Ireland, Keane reported that Leo XIII was alleged to have expressed a doubt concerning the loyalty of the American progressive bishops toward him. Keane consulted Serafino Cardinal Vannutelli and Monsignor Raffaele Merry del Val on this matter to determine whether or not the Pope had made such a statement and they both emphatically stated that it could not be true. Nonetheless, Keane declared that he would mention the subject to the Pope, and in the meantime, as he told his friend, "we simply *cannot, and must not,* be disheartened or pessimistic. As long as Providence puts before us things to be said and to be done, we simply must keep on saying and doing."[41]

Concerning the red hat there were other things to be considered. Norton Otis, Eugene Kelly, and Bourke Cockran, citizens of New York with considerable wealth and political influence, had been in Rome in quick succession and at the time Bishop Henry Gabriels of Ogdensburg, one of Corrigan's suffragans, was also there. Keane believed that it was their object, and especially that of Cockran, to prove that the center of American Catholic political influence was in

[40] AASP, Keane to Ireland, Rome, May 9, 1897.
[41] *Ibid.,* Mar. 24, 1897.

New York. He felt prompted to remark: "We are doing our best to head off mischief; but this fighting in the dark is wretched work."[42] Later the archbishop stated that when he had mentioned to Rampolla the various emissaries from New York who had been in Rome, the cardinal, with what he described as "a very meaning look," had replied: "Rest assured that these tricks are fully understood in the Vatican."[43]

To keep Ireland's name before the Holy See in a favorable light, Keane made it known that he was having the St. Paul prelate's volume of sermons and addresses, entitled *The Church and Modern Society,* prepared for presentation to the Pope by having it bound over in papal style, for, as he remarked, "I dare not have an offering from *you* especially in the slightest degree out of form. This will give me an occasion for a little plain talk."[44] Less than a month later he was given an opportunity to present the book to Leo XIII, and on the same day he wrote to Ireland:

> I told him of the various social topics which it treated, and told him it was virtually a commentary on the various encyclicals issued by His Holiness on the social questions of the day. I took care to present him all these points in writing, giving him in French the titles of the various discourses contained in the volume.

Keane then assured Ireland that there was little danger that Corrigan would be selected in the May consistory and as to the future, he contented himself with his favorite formula, "Providence will make no mistake."[45]

The consistory of May, 1897, which the liberals seemed to view with a degree of apprehension, did not announce any new cardinals for the United States. Nevertheless, neither party relaxed its vigil.

[42] *Ibid.* While thus advancing this particular cause of the Archbishop of St. Paul, Keane was likewise helping him to obtain his candidate for the Diocese of St. Cloud which had been vacant since the death of Martin Marty, O.S.B., on September 19, 1896. He sent Propaganda, what he called, "a strong doc.," and he talked to Ciascha, Secretary of the Propaganda, as well as to Rampolla and Serafino Cardinal Vannutelli. Sarafino promised to stand by them and to get his brother to do likewise. At Rampolla's suggestion, Keane submitted to him a strong letter about it for the Pope.

[43] *Ibid.,* Apr. 10, 1897.

[44] *Ibid.,* Mar. 24, 1897.

[45] *Ibid.,* Apr. 10, 1897. According to a newspaper report, at the same time that he presented Ireland's volume Keane also presented *The Ambassador of Christ* by Cardinal Gibbons (LCLD, clipping). Concerning Gibbons' volume, the archbishop said: "Satolli is talking shamefully about Card. Gibbons book; says he has not a chapter about the Pope!! etc. If he attacks him in the press, we must make it hot for him" (AASP, Keane to Ireland, Rome, Mar. 24, 1897).

Joseph Bonnet, chaplain of De La Salle Institute in New York City, stated to Corrigan shortly after his arrival in Rome in January, 1898:

> Last night, I called on Cardinal Parocchi, whom I had not seen in ten years, and did not fail to convey to him the greetings of Your Grace, which were extremely well received. It would be unpleasant to your humility to hear in what terms His Eminence spoke of Your Grace, of your episcopal virtues, of your attachment to Catholic traditions, of the soundness of your views on the policy of the Church.

He then recounted a conversation in which he had said to the substitute Secretary of State: "It would be extremely sorrowful that the annual vacation trips of Archbishop Keane to America become an occasion for disturbing the peace of the Church, as has been the case last year."[46] The very next day he again wrote to inform Corrigan that Vincenzo Cardinal Vannutelli had expressed himself concerning the Archbishop of New York in the same way Cardinal Parocchi had done.[47] Since the cardinal himself had opened the subject he was emboldened, he said, to speak freely and he continued:

> I explained again what circumstances and utterances had attended the last trip of Archbishop Keane, and how necessary it was that such a thing should not be repeated. I remarked also that it was apparent from that very fact that Archbishop Keane had not remained inactive

[46] AANY, Joseph Bonnet to Corrigan, Rome, Jan. 24, 1898. Besides the speeches at the banquet and at Conaty's investiture (cf. *supra,* pp. 218 ff), which received wide publicity, Keane was obliged to answer the charge that he had slighted Archbishop Corrigan by not calling on him when he disembarked at New York (LCLD, clippings). This promoted O'Connell to say: "The noise made unnecessarily on Abp. Keane's return proves that Corrigan will never give the Church peace" (AASP, O'Connell to Ireland, Freiburg im Breisgau, Sept. 5, 1897). Some of the journals, such as the New York *Independent,* carelessly spoke of Keane's having "the right to speak as the representative of the Holy See." This called forth a blistering answer from William H. Thorne who said: "In a word, while an excellent gentleman, and doubtless a faithful Catholic, Keane is, in his posing public attitudes and speeches, a wind-blown, blustering humbug, and the first thing for the entire Catholic Church in America or elsewhere to do is to have done forever with the kind of humbuggery that Keane and his master, Ireland, represent in this poor world" ("Globe Notes," *Globe,* VII [Dec., 1897], 494). In another issue of his magazine "About the Hierarchy," *Globe,* VII (Sept., 1897), 266–275, Thorne maintained that McGolrick, Spalding, Horstmann, McQuaid, Becker of Savannah, and others were "in every way superior to Keane but who hears about them."

[47] It is interesting to note in this connection a comment made by O'Connell to Ireland: "I am delighted with your letter of Jan. 18th. Card. Vincenzo [Vannutelli] was here just now and I read portions of it to him which made him really enthusiastic. Again he said with much confusion that so many affairs had hindered him from writing and he asked me to write you again his sentiments of admiration and thanks. They are both [Serafino and Vincenzo] grand men and perfectly devoted" (AASP, O'Connell to Ireland, Rome, [Jan., 1897]).

> in Rome and had found propitious hearing. As the Cardinal asked a question about some favor of Archbishop Ireland with President MacKinley, I had to tell him the cause why the Republican platform had been so openly advocated at St. Paul, and how it was that public opinion did not hold Archbishop Ireland in higher esteem for it. His Eminence had the notion that the differences existing in America came from the nationalities. I told him that Your Grace was in no way more favorable than Archbishop Ireland to undue preservation, for instance, of German privileges, and that it was the Catholic spirit that made all the difference, the vast majority of American bishops being in favor of imparting that spirit to their country in the greatest possible measure, while a few seemed anxious to bring into catholicity such spirit as was spread in their country, even amongst Protestants and infidels.

Corrigan's correspondent also spoke to Father Esbach, rector of the French College, about what he termed the manner assumed by Archbishop Keane the previous September in Washington which "could not possibly be construed otherwise than as an indication of a change in the view of His Holiness." Bonnet felt certain that the Pope put exceptional trust in Esbach.[48]

However, the advocate for the Archbishop of New York was unsuccessful in his attempt to persuade the Roman officials to prevent vacation trips to the United States, just as he proved incapable of successfully promoting the New York prelate's cause. Some weeks later O'Connell told Ireland there would be no cardinals in the coming consistory and none before June, to which he added, "have nothing definite about N. Y.'s chances."[49] At the same time Keane informed Ireland that their friends, Bellamy Storer, American Minister to Belgium, and his wife, had obtained a private audience during which they had spoken with great plainness about American Catholic conditions, needs, and dangers on which they had been thoroughly coached. The Storers had also presented Cardinal Rampolla with a written statement on the same matters which the Secretary of State promised to communicate to the Holy Father. Alluding to Corrigan's recent episcopal silver jubilee Keane said that some of the remarks of Leo XIII had indicated that the jubilee influences had been at work and had impressed him, and Keane hoped that the visit of the Storers would provide an antidote.[50]

[48] AANY, Bonnet to Corrigan, Rome, Jan. 25, 1898.
[49] AASP, O'Connell to Ireland, Rome, Mar. 9, 1898.
[50] AASP, Keane to Ireland, Rome, Mar. 8, 1898.

During the last week of March the efforts which Ireland's friends had put forth to impress the Holy See with his American influence seemed to be rewarded. Because of the lamentable conditions in Cuba, the government of the United States was threatening to interfere actively in the island. Such an intervention would naturally result in warfare with Spain. When it appeared inevitable that the United States would engage in a test of arms with Spain over Cuba, Leo XIII determined to use his good offices to promote a peaceful settlement of the problem. Since the Holy See did not have an accredited minister to the United States Government, someone who was in favor with the administration at Washington was sought and found in Archbishop Ireland.[51] While Keane was preaching in the Church of San Silvestro in Capite on the afternoon of Passion Sunday, March 27, a messenger, bearing a letter from Cardinal Rampolla, hurried to the church and handed it to him as he descended from the pulpit. The cardinal asked the archbishop to get in touch with the Archbishop of St. Paul and to urge him to use his influence with the American President to maintain peace.[52] Archbishop Keane and O'Connell recognized the great honor of the mission entrusted to Ireland, but, as O'Connell later said, they also saw its delicacy.[53] Nonetheless, Keane immediately telegraphed to Archbishop Ireland and sent him the cardinal's letter

[51] In replying on December 15, 1897, to a letter from the nuncio to Germany in which it had been suggested that the Pope intervene in the Cuban question, Rampolla said that it was impossible under the circumstances. The Holy Father's only hope, said the prelate, was the Archbishop of St. Paul, who was on intimate terms with President McKinley, and he intended to look into the possibilities in that direction on the occasion of Ireland's next visit to Rome (Rampolla to Francesco Nava, Dec. 15, 1897, cited by Soderini, *op. cit.*). The Holy Father probably knew that Ireland intended to be in Rome the next year after Easter (ADR, Ireland to O'Connell, St. Paul, Aug. 9, 1897). On March 8, 1898, Keane told the Archbishop of St. Paul that "the Holy Father said repeatedly and strongly that he wished you would come to Rome, as did also Cardinal Rampolla. Whatever be their motives for so much wishing it, it is quite evident you ought to come as soon as possible" (AASP).

[52] AASP, Rampolla to Keane, Rome, Mar. 27, 1898 (Italian); Baltimore *Sun,* Apr. 23, 1898. During the early part of 1897, O'Connell had urged Ireland to use his influence with the administration to bring about the appointment of someone favorable to the Vatican as the United States ambassador to Italy. Failure to do so would be disastrous he said (AASP, O'Connell to Ireland, Rome, Jan. 7 and 28, 1897). When William F. Draper received the appointment and arrived in Rome, his wife gave Ireland credit for securing the favor. This prompted O'Connell to remark: "The impression at the Vatican was surprising. They are glad to have a favorable man here, and still embarrassed at the great power of those *Americani*" (AASP, O'Connell to Ireland, Rome, July 21, 1897). Draper turned out to be anything but friendly to the Vatican. Cf. John T. Farrell, "Archbishop Ireland and Manifest Destiny," *Catholic Historical Review,* XXXIII (Oct., 1947), 285–287.

[53] AASP, O'Connell to Ireland, Rome, Apr. 24, 1898.

enclosed in one of his own urging that the commission be accepted.[54] To the papal Secretary of State Keane wrote on the same day that in a long conversation with William McKinley in October, the President had assured Ireland and himself that he earnestly desired to keep peace. Keane believed that the Roman officials seeking the same objective should concentrate upon having the argument concerning the origin of the explosion which caused the *Maine* to sink suspended and made subject to arbitration. It was his opinion that this could be achieved and that it would satisfy those who were clamoring for war, especially if it was combined with an armistice of six months. The archbishop emphasized the fact that the President was under strong pressure from the public whose indignation against Spain could be attributed, in part at least, to the conviction that the explosion had been caused by external force. He hoped that the influence of Ireland, or those whose influence he could win, would be able to keep the President firm in his decision to maintain peace. If Spain would not change her attitude on the cause of the explosion, however, he believed that it would be difficult to avert war. On the other hand, if the Spanish government admitted that the explosion was caused as the Americans were claiming, but that it was the act of villainous individuals rather than the government, which had no knowledge of the attempt, the President would be in a position to resist those who were urging armed intervention.[55] The Holy See immediately communicated the contents of this letter to the Spanish government and to the apostolic delegate in Washington.[56] On March 29 Keane sent another cablegram to Ireland urging him to go to Washington at once and to employ strong action there so that the government would accept arbitration on the explosion and abstain from intervention in Cuba.[57] The Archbishop of St. Paul hurried to Washington where he labored with all his customary energy, but his failure became public on April 19, when Congress passed a joint resolution which declared Cuba to be independent and directed the President to use the military and naval forces to maintain its independence.[58] Yet, Ireland's lack

[54] AASP, Keane to Ireland, Rome, Mar. 27, 1898.

[55] Keane to Rampolla, Mar. 27, 1898, cited by Soderini, *op. cit.* The Spanish Minister of State said that Spain was ready to accept an arbitration of the *Maine* incident (Gullon to Merry del Val, Mar. 31, 1898, cited by Soderini, *op. cit.*).

[56] Soderini, *op. cit.*

[57] AASP.

[58] For an account of Ireland's efforts to preserve peace, cf. Moynihan, *op. cit.*, pp. 162–168.

of success did not discourage his American friends in Rome. O'Connell looked upon the mission as the most important sanction ever given to Ireland and his views before the whole world, and he pointed out to the Archbishop of St. Paul, who was bitter over his defeat, that his influence over the people of the United States must be maintained to prevent any other man from being called upon to represent the Church at the end of the struggle.[59] Archbishop Keane also wrote to Ireland in an endeavor to counteract the depression which the latter had revealed in a letter about his Washington mission. Keane stated:

> No indeed, Providence will not permit you to remain shut up *at home*. Nor would it have been better in any way if you had so done instead of going to Washington on that mission. That mission not only put the Pope and the Church as well as you in their true light before the world. While it is true that failure is unpardonable here, as in other diplomatic centres, still, you are *the man* of the situation, the one to be looked to for future aid, if only you set right their view of having positively promised peace almost on the very eve of war.[60]

It became part of Keane's unpleasant task to dispel the impression that Ireland had been overly optimistic in his reports to the Holy See concerning the progress of his Washington negotiations. For this purpose the Archbishop of St. Paul sent him all the documents pertaining to his brief excursion into diplomacy,[61] and the archbishop put them to work immediately. He later informed Ireland concerning these documents:

> Their chief value here is to open the eyes of Cardinal Serafino [Vannutelli]. He declares himself *simply astounded, dazed*. He didn't understand it so at all, — sees that the notion of your having been "a child", piping *peace* all the time, was a monstrous misrepresentation. He is still studying them and will find opportunity to use them for justice sake.[62]

59 AASP, O'Connell to Ireland, Rome, Apr. 24, 1898. He also said: "The philosophic view over here of the situation is Pan Anglosaxon against the world. Eichthol says there is simply consternation in Europe at the spread of American influence. Soon, they say, America will ask a voice even in European affairs. Now you can shape the future and do it. There is a mission for John Ireland."

60 AASP, Keane to Ireland, Rome, May 24, [1898].

61 ADR, Ireland to Keane, St. Paul, May 28, [1898]. The documents are in AASP.

62 AASP, Keane to Ireland, Rome, June 19, 1898. At approximately the same time Monsignor O'Connell had stated to Ireland: "I have gone over your diplomatic correspondence three times, and reading it now, even in the light of accomplished events I am struck with admiration for the perfect manner in which the whole series was intoned, and the deep honesty and insight that mark it throughout. I study it in

Mrs. Storer, wife of the United States Minister to Belgium, told the Archbishop of St. Paul that Keane was anxious to have the Nuncio in Brussels write a favorable account to the Vatican of Ireland's work in Washington, and he suggested that Mr. and Mrs. Storer should give him the necessary information. They hesitated about doing that, she said, because any overture made by them would be suspect. However, she did work out a plan by which a favorable view of Ireland's mission reached the papal Nuncio to Belgium and he, in turn, according to Mrs. Storer, had sent it at once to the Vatican.[63]

While the archbishop was striving to bolster Ireland's cause, he was constrained to live in a generally unfriendly atmosphere because of the widespread sympathy in Rome, as in other European capitals, for Spain in her war with the United States. Concerning his own attitude and conduct during the war, he told Gibbons:

> While I am not aggressive, they find me unflinching in standing up for my country. Weighing on the one side the old worn out "vested rights" that are being broken up, and, on the other, the interests of civilization which our cause represents, I could not, even as an impartial judge, hesitate as to which way my sympathy should go. I thank God ever more and more for being an American.[64]

To Ireland he also revealed his determined judgment concerning the rightness of the conduct of the American government despite the charge of unjust aggression:

> Your acknowledgement concerning the "wrong" of the war is painful in the extreme. It is hard to be enthusiastically loyal to one's country if you believe she is *wrong*. I view it in the light of the "higher law." I say humanity demanded that Spain sh'd simply get up and leave, as she had to do in all those other colonies of hers, and that I am proud of our country for doing a service to humanity and Providence.[65]

---

order to expound it to some eminent friends" (AASP, O'Connell to Ireland, Rome, June 16, [1898]). If O'Connell's information, gained two years after the event, was correct, Ireland's work for peace was sabotaged to some extent by some of the very men he was serving. "I have learned on undoubted authority," he said, "that regularly for one month before the Spanish War, Rampolla, Merry del Val, père et fils, Père Martin, general of the Jesuits and Camilla Pecci, as representing land in Cuba and a traveler from that island, held regular meetings at the Vatican, and out of those meetings came the telegrams to the Paris N. Y. Herald" (AASP, O'Connell to Ireland, Rome, Feb. 28, 1900).

[63] AASP, Mrs. Storer to Ireland, Brussells, June 15, 1898.

[64] BCA, 96-H-1, Keane to Gibbons, Rome, May 15, 1898.

[65] AASP, Keane to Ireland, Rome, May 24, [1898].

His "impartial" judgment concerning the justice of the American cause, however, was based upon the premise that the United States was fighting for the welfare of humanity and not for the extension of her possessions. As he expressed it to Ireland:

> But how ominous what you say that: "finally, Cuba should have come to us"! Were Congress and the Pres. insincere in declaring we did not want her and would not take her? Will they break the word they have pledged to the world? *This* is the danger looming up ahead, and it behooves men of influence to guard against it, and to insist that we *must* keep our word, — and we *must not* go into the *colony business,* no matter how great the scramble of other nations in that line. But I greatly fear our country is changing her base completely, and is drifting into the militarism of the old world. Do work against it. We must *win,* and then disarm, or keep up only the *essentials* of armament.

Since Archbishop Keane was convinced of the justice of American intervention in Cuban affairs, and since he was by nature outspoken in voicing his convictions, it was inevitable that he should be subjected to some unpleasant situations in the hostile surroundings in which he found himself. In June of 1898 he informed Ireland: "Feeling is more and more intense for Spain, and we are *the enemy.* I simply have to stand up to it, as our sailors and soldiers do. Yet I shall be glad to leave here next Saturday."[66] After spending the early part of the summer of 1898 at Houlgate and at Brussels with the Storers, Keane visited friends in the United States,[67] and then returned to his work in Rome. The red hat for Ireland was not forgotten by him or by the rest of the friends who continued to champion their candidate against the supporters of Corrigan until the latter's death in 1902.

Although keeping the red hat from Archbishop Corrigan was regarded as extremely important to the liberals, it was not their only concern. What was called the German question continued to occupy them and at this time (1897) it centered chiefly in Joseph Schroeder, professor of dogmatic theology at the University in Washington.

[66] AASP, Keane to Ireland, Rome, June 19, 1898. According to one observer, the mother of Monsignor Merry del Val, who was the wife of the Spanish ambassador to Vienna, was guilty of treating Keane and O'Connell "shamefully" at this time (ADR, W. E. Mantini to O'Connell, New York, May 19, 1901).

[67] AASP, Keane to Ireland, Rome, June 19, 1898. He planned to leave Rome on June 25, remain at Houlgate until July 20, visit the Storers in Belgium for a week or more, and then sail from Liverpool in the first week of August. He made his headquarters at St. Patrick's in Washington until after the meeting of the University's Board of Trustees.

Shortly after Keane had come to Rome, the friends of Ireland there formed a combination and decided on a program which they fully expected to demoralize those who were classed as the opponents of the Archbishop of St. Paul and to multiply greatly the number of his friends.[68] In the opinion of Monsignor O'Connell it was time to clear the air of false notions about their aims and to publish their real program before the world. There was not, as he said, "a war of race on race, but of idea on idea, of progress on stagnation." In this vein O'Connell continued:

> The little clique of Germans that attacked you in America do not represent the Germans. Germany is a most progressive country and the reactionaries are in a minority. Schroeder is more hated in Germany than in America. Germany would never say "Schroeder is my leader." You have more sympathizers in Germany than Schroeder has. It was a trick of that clique in America to make it be believed that you made war on the German race. Even among the Jesuits you have sympathizing friends.[69]

A few days later Keane endorsed the monsignor's approach to their problem and he proceeded to furnish John Ireland with additional material for meditation on the subject of the Germans when he said:

> We have no *German question*. We only hold to *true ideas* ag'st the clique of Germans who have attacked them, thro' revenge for having been defeated in their ultra Germanism. That clique do not represent the German people in Europe or America. Multitudes of Germans are in no way committed to their ultra narrowness, but are, on the contrary, at least as far advanced as we in many lines of ideas. But even these are banded ag'st us, because of their mistaken notion that we are hostile to the Germans as such, which we of course are not. They must be undeceived. The lines ought to be drawn between those who hold to true ideas and those who oppose them, — by no means between nationalities as such, a mediaeval [*sic*] and cursed notion. I feel confident that you will sympathize with all this and respond to it actively. I will do all that I can here to remove the mistaken notion; and surely you will do your very best for the same end.[70]

[68] AASP, O'Connell to Ireland, Rome, Jan. 7, 1897. The little coterie of friends in Rome held their meetings in O'Connell's "fine set of rooms" which he also described as the "Committee Room of the Lodge" (*ibid.* [late in Jan., 1897]). At another time, speaking of the necessity of keeping Keane in Rome because he was a "necessary point for rallying and a centre of force," the monsignor stated: "I have things far more widely organized now than ever I had at the College" (*ibid.*, July 21, 1897).

[69] *Ibid.*, Jan. 7, 1897.

[70] AASP, Keane to Ireland, Rome, Jan. 11, 1897.

Toward the end of January Monsignor O'Connell again urged Ireland on and gave him additional ammunition for the fight for support of the liberal cause from many angles. The progressive group in Rome had determined that they should attempt to make the world understand that they were not really a party, but rather that they were the true representatives of the old Church; whereas their opponents constituted a party which they had decided to designate as the "Refractaires." O'Connell admitted that he did not much care for the sound of the word but it had what he called "a deep meaning and a power of demarcation," since it was the word recently used by the Pope in speaking of all those persons in France who opposed his policy. If Ireland applied the term to reactionaries and obscurantists the world over, the monsignor was positive that the Sovereign Pontiff would understand it well, and if he used it in the French original, it would be an international term, and he ventured the prediction that soon it would be anglicized like Cahenslyism.[71] On the heels of O'Connell's letter there followed one from Keane urging the Archbishop of St. Paul to speak along the lines which their friend had indicated and he optimistically stated that their plan of dividing the German ranks had already produced some good fruit.[72]

During the last week in March, the Archbishop of St. Paul found an opportunity to utilize the ideas forwarded by his Roman friends when he delivered a sermon in St. Patrick's Church in Washington. Employing his favorite theme about the Church's capacity for embracing and turning to account all that was good in every age, he pointed to the noble ambitions and the great progress which characterized the age in which they lived, and he singled out Leo XIII as the protector and the guardian of every grand work which the spirit of the age had produced. It was their clear duty, therefore, to follow the lead of Leo. However, he claimed that some Catholics refused to emulate the enlightened Pontiff because they believed that there was nothing but evil in their age. Concerning them he said:

> Refractaires, rebels against Leo, are found outside of France. They are found where we should least expect to find them in America. There are unfortunately divisions among Catholics in America, not indeed, in strict matters of faith and morals, but in tendencies and movements, and in adaptations of action to modern circumstances and surroundings. There should be for us but one tendency, one move-

[71] AASP, O'Connell to Ireland, Rome, Jan. 28, 1897.
[72] AASP, Keane to Ireland, Rome, Jan. 31, 1897.

ment, one mode of adaptations — those indicated by Leo. Separation from Leo, opposition to his direction, however much it clothes itself in America, as it does in France, with the specious titles of conservatism and traditional Catholicity, a religious fear of novelties is nothing but rebellion. Those in America who resist the direction given by Leo are rebels and refractaires, however much they dare push themselves forward as the only true and trustworthy Catholics. It is thought sometimes that Catholics in America are divided sometimes on lines of race and language. It is not so. The loyal Catholics and the refractaires are confined to no one language. I speak now for myself, but in what I say, I know, I speak for all the loyal Catholics of America. There is for me no race, no language, no color. I rise above all such accidentals. In seeking out my brethren, I wish to find those who work for God and for truth, those who work with Leo. When I move away from Catholics, I move away from the refractaires and from none other. I would scorn to draw distinctions among Catholics because of race or language. I am — I must be — as Catholic as is God's Church. I differ from men, I war with men on account of ideas, not on account of race. And so it is with Leo. And so it is with all loyal Catholics. It is well that this be understood and proclaimed aloud, far and wide. Efforts are being made to identify certain refractaires with certain races of Catholics. To do so is an injustice. Again, I say Leo is our leader. Under Leo's banner we shall fight. Under his banner we shall win — win for God, for the Church and for humanity.[73]

Archbishop Keane hastened to inform Ireland that the sermon had done great good in the right direction. He said that Rampolla had read it in the *Petit Moniteur,* and that at the cardinal's suggestion they were having the text printed in the *Univers,* and then they would spread it in Belgium and Germany.[74] On the occasion of congratulating Ireland a month later on a discourse delivered in Cleveland before the Chamber of Commerce, Keane asserted: "We shall keep on looking for other strong utterances, emphasizing and rubbing in the Thesis of your Washington sermon."[75]

[73] *Freeman's Journal,* Apr. 7, 1897. The sermon was delivered on March 26.

[74] AASP, Keane to Ireland, Rome, May 9, 1897. On the same day the archbishop told Gibbons about the impression Ireland's speech had made on Rampolla and he added: "He must speak again and again on this theme during the next six months before his arrival in Rome, so as to completely remove the mistaken impression that we are engaged in a war of races, and to make clear that it is only a war of ideas — a war between those who advocate *and* disseminate the ideas of Leo XIII, and those, on the other hand, who are refractaires against those ideas, as in France" (AAB, 95-P-3).

[75] AASP, Keane to Ireland, Rome, June 4, 1897. The subject of Ireland's Cleveland

O'Connell, too, was extremely pleased with Ireland's sermon.[76] It was his opinion that the Washington sermon had rendered all explanation about opposition to the Germans superfluous and the active element in Germany was now with Ireland. However, he advised him to proceed cautiously regarding Father Franz Xavier Kraus, professor at the University of Freiburg in Baden and an influential liberal political journalist, with whom Ireland had reached some kind of an understanding. According to O'Connell the priest was the antithesis of the Pope's policy in Europe, but he could serve their cause, for his letters in the press about Schroeder had made a tremendous impression in Germany; in fact, the one verdict in Germany was that they destroyed the University professor.[77]

Although Keane and his associates were apparently meeting with some success in their campaign to inform Europeans about their true ideas and thus win friends, they were faced with the continuing embarrassment of Schroeder's presence in the University at Washington. The professor was accused in the public press of having written an article in which charges of heresy were lodged against some members of the hierarchy, whom the reader could readily identify as the liberal wing among the bishops.[78] Schroeder disclaimed any responsibility for that particular piece, according to the editor of the *Globe*, but he did admit that he had written such an article in German, and he stated that he would not retract a single sentence of it.[79] Whether the University professor was the author of the article could not be determined, but the papers reported that Ireland was resentful of the attack and that he had invoked the aid of the apostolic delegate.[80] At the same time the Washington *Post* printed a long story about

---

discourse was "Conscience: The Mainstay of Democracy." Cf. his *The Church and Modern Society* (Chicago, 1897), II, 85–100.

[76] AASP, O'Connell to Ireland, Rome, July 21, 1897.

[77] *Ibid.*, July 24, [1897]. Kraus' letters were published in *Beilage zur Allgemeinen Zeitung*.

[78] New York *Evening World*, Mar. 23, 1897.

[79] AASP, clippings, Preuss' *Review*, Apr., 1897. O'Connell stated that "in the press and out of it, publicly and privately in Europe and America, [Schroeder] showed what heretics his fellow professors were, and how Ireland and his party were a generation of viperous liberals. He even publicly boasted that he had put Mgr. Keane out" (La Contessa Sabina di Tarravicino di Revel Papers on microfilm in AUND, O'Connell to Sabina, Rome, Dec. 1, 1897).

[80] *Ibid.* Cf. William H. Thorne, "Catholic Liberalism and Nationality," *Globe* VII (June, 1897), 180–192. Thorne expressed the view that Keane and Ireland were very near to heresy.

Schroeder in which it was stated that he was seeking a position elsewhere because he had been defeated in his attempt to gain control of the University and principally owing to the fact that he was emphatically *persona non grata* with the rest of the faculty and the trustees.[81]

The real effort to bring about Schroeder's removal from his position at the University did not begin, however, until the summer of 1897, when O'Connell broached the subject to Ireland after he had met some of the University's professors. He said:

> Schroeder must go. All the professors are determined upon it, and demoralization will follow in the University if the Board of Directors decide to continue the division and the humiliation of the Corps. They will bring severe charges against [him] and naturally they count on you among others, to see the thing goes through. In Germany all are surprised that he is harboured so long and enquire in wonder why he is not sent away. Nearly all the members of the Board will be written to.[82]

To be sure, Ireland needed no urging to take part in the fight against Schroeder which Ireland himself christened the "War of 1897." Neither did he find it hard to rally forces from among those bishops who had been charged with heresy by the professor. In September he let O'Connell know that he and Archbishop Riordan of San Francisco were strongly against Schroeder, and that Riordan would lead the campaign. "All America is laughing at us," he complained, "deriding us for being kept in awe by a Dutch beerguzzler."[83] When the Board of Trustees met, therefore, the forces arrayed against Schroeder were powerful. Keane, who had returned to the United States and was on

[81] Washington *Post,* May 24, 1897.

[82] AASP, O'Connell to Ireland, Freiburg im Breisgau, August 26, 1897. A month later O'Connell said to the same correspondent: "Be sure you put Schroeder out. See Spalding, Foley, Maes, and Riordan. You will have a sufficient bill of charges to work on, of a pure University kind" (*ibid.,* Munich, September 14, 1897). The monsignor, seeking the weight of Chapelle in their campaign against the professor, stated: "The Germans especially are our staunch friends and they want to follow us. They have absolutely no sympathy whatever with Mgr. Schroeder and his narrow American faction. On the contrary everywhere men ask in surprise why Schroeder is kept in Washington. They regard him as a kind of fanatic, and hitherto could never remain more than three years in any one position. Wherever the Washington professors went they were twitted about Schroeder and jeered a little bit as being all intimidated by a poorly educated man who remains there only for the sake of his salary" (AANO, O'Connell to "My dear Friend" [Chapelle], Freiburg im Breisgau, August 27, 1897).

[83] ADR, Ireland to O'Connell, St. Paul, Sept. 13, 1897. Cf. Hogan, *op. cit.,* pp. 153–157, 188–190, for further particulars on the Schroeder case.

hand for the meeting, engaged actively in the heated debate, and according to his later report to Ireland from Rome, it seems that he was entrusted with the task of bringing the case to a happy conclusion for their party. At any rate, he wrote at that time:

> Our victory seems to be complete. Rampolla assured me yesterday even'g that he had written to the Delegate to say to the Cardinal that all must be settled according to the desire of the Bps. — that the thing was ended, and that now they only asked silence. You may rest assured that the victory was not won without some tough fighting. They have my long memoir and 15 corroborative documents in their archives, and lots of strong talking besides. The Delegate must have sent a statement agreeing with mine; and so they simply had to surrender, though it must have been a painful step back for the Pope, and the enemy had evidently prepared for a long and bitter war. They say Steinhuber is outraged. Satolli, now more despotic and fierce than ever, and bitter in his hostility to me, must see that he simply cannot play the despot. But his sway over the H. F. grows every day greater! And he fumes ag'st the opposition of the American Bps. . . .
>
> Now you must see that the Cardinal will not attempt any conciliatory measures as to Schroeder, but simply stand to the situation as it is, that we have received his written promise of his resignation before the end of the scholastic year, and that we simply are waiting for it, and must have it.[84]

A week later Keane appeared to be nearing the end of the troublesome problem, when he told Walter Elliott of the Paulists that the question seemed to be settled satisfactorily. At the same time he prayed that God would grant them peace in truth, justice, and charity.[85]

The Roman opinion of the opposing camp in the Schroeder case was expressed by Brandi to Archbishop Corrigan when he wrote that it had produced a painful impression in high circles. He believed, nevertheless, that it had also done a great deal of good in Rome where Schroeder had powerful friends by showing, as he said, "the animus of certain of his declared opponents and the real state of

[84] AASP, Keane to Ireland, Rome, Nov. 17, 1897. In October Chapelle had written that the Schroeder case was nearly finished and that it was only the interference of Andreas Cardinal Steinhüber, a Roman official, which had prevented "absolute and final" action on the part of the Board (ADR, Chapelle to O'Connell, New York, Oct. 23, 1897). T. H. Malone, editor of the *Colorado Catholic,* probably expressed the views of many when he said that he believed it wise to condemn the action of such men as Schroeder, "who ignore the American episcopate and seek foreign influence to override the wishes of those who are immediately responsible for the Church's welfare in the United States" (AANO, Malone to Chapelle, Denver, Dec. 24, 1897).

[85] APF, Keane to Elliott, Rome, Nov. 24, 1897.

affairs in Washington."[86] Indeed, it was to be expected that any solution of the case would produce conflicting emotions. O'Connell was of the opinion, nevertheless, that as a result of the professor's dismissal things looked much better in Rome for the cause, although he confessed that there was no great love for certain individuals.[87] He likewise told the Abbé Klein: "I know they are terribly angry about the removal of Schroeder and I am watching to see how they will have revenge. Once it was said they would have Mgr. Keane removed from Rome, but that danger is now passed."[88] When the matter was completely settled to the satisfaction of Archbishop Keane and his friends and shortly before the professor submitted his resignation on December 29, 1897, Keane made the following observations to the University's vice-rector:

> Now the University has ended the chapter of its first and greatest difficulties. . . . Henceforth there ought to be nothing but unity, harmony, and concerted energy for the highest purposes in the work of the University. The Institution may still feel for some time the results of the storm through which it has passed, but it has weathered the storm, thank God, and now it need not be long till every vestige of it shall have disappeared. If every man do his full duty at his post, and this I'm certain they will do, the Providence which started the Institution will ensure its future success.[89]

A parting shot at the liberals was taken by Schroeder when he finally left the United States to assume a position at the Catholic Academy of Münster. It prompted Keane to exclaim, with more partisanship than objectivity: "It was an admirable specimen of the spirit and the movement in which he was ring leader and inspirer. What a service we did to the Church in getting rid of such a man!"[90]

[86] APF, Brandi to Corrigan, Rome, Nov. 21, 1897 (photostat).

[87] APF, O'Connell to Elliott, Rome, Dec. 3, 1897.

[88] APF, O'Connell to Klein, Rome, [1897].

[89] ACUA, Garrigan Papers, Keane to Garrigan, Rome, Dec. 16, 1897. A few weeks later Keane stated: "Once more thanks be to God for the happy solution of the Schroeder difficulty. The price you had to pay for the final riddance was cheap enough" (*ibid.*, Jan. 3, 1898).

[90] AASP, Keane to Ireland, Rome, Mar. 8, 1898. In the same letter the archbishop said that Kraus, who was visiting in Rome, had stated: "Schroeder's chances in Germany are not brilliant since the 'Spectator' letters have made the Government acquainted with his antecedents and his character." To which Keane added: "I wish him no harm but I wish no increase of his power for mischief."

O'Connell told the same correspondent that the German chancellor was withholding his confirmation of Schroeder's appointment due to the revelations in the "Spectator" letters, and that a friend of Ireland's in Berlin, a certain Mr. White, had written an

That Keane was rendering yeoman service in Rome for the progressive bishops became evident during the summer of 1897, when there seemed to be a possibility of his returning to the United States to take an archiepiscopal see. The death of Archbishop Francis Janssens of New Orleans on June 9 opened that see and there were a number of Keane's fellow bishops who thought that he could fill the post very well. Bishop Edward Fitzgerald of Little Rock, who was anxious about the choice of a new metropolitan, inquired of Cardinal Gibbons and Archbishop Ireland as to the availability of the former University rector for the position and his willingness to accept it. He, as well as other suffragans of the Province of New Orleans, believed that the choice of Keane would be an admirable one since he could speak French fluently and, too, because he was generally popular.[91] With his customary caution, Gibbons replied that the archbishop's transcendent abilities were known to the country, and he presumed that if he were nominated the Holy See might induce him to accept.[92] When the Bishops of the Province of New Orleans met on July 14, therefore, to express their preferences for Janssens' successor Keane was their first choice, with the Bishops of Covington and Natchez taking second and third place respectively.[93] Gibbons, O'Connell, and Maes all rejoiced in the fact that for reasons of prestige and personal vindication the archbishop's name had appeared first on the *terna*. As Maes said:

> His exaltation would be looked upon as a vindication of our self-sacrificing friend whose treatment by passing powers has aroused the best feeling of the whole Catholic world. During my recent trip through Europe, I have been able to gauge the Catholic opinion in many lands: all agree that the vindication of this good man by our Holy Father was called for and was not made too emphatic.[94]

To O'Connell the choice of the New Orleans prelates represented a delightful compliment to the archbishop and what he termed "a sweet

---

article, signed Mr. Evans, confirming all that had been written in the letters (AASP, O'Connell to Ireland, Rome, Mar. 9, 1898).

[91] AAB, 95-Q-2, Fitzgerald to Gibbons, New Orleans, June 17, 1897; AAB, 95-Q-5, Fitzgerald to Ireland, Little Rock, June 20, 1897.

[92] AAB, 95-Q-4, Gibbons to Fitzgerald, Baltimore, June 19, 1897, copy.

[93] AANY, Thomas Heslin to Corrigan, New Orleans, July 15, 1897. The Bishop of Natchez, Thomas Heslin, was secretary of the bishops' meeting, so it devolved upon him to send the *terna* to all the archbishops. Camillus P. Maes of Covington was second and Heslin was third on the list.

[94] AAB, 95-R-5, Maes to Gibbons, Covington, July 19, 1897.

lesson to Satolli."[95] But Keane cabled that he preferred for the time being to remain in Rome. In this decision the cardinal and his other friends wholeheartedly agreed. Gibbons believed that it would be a pity to remove Keane from Rome just then,[96] and he conveyed the same sentiment to the Prefect of the Propaganda.[97] It was an opinion which Bishop Maes thoroughly endorsed when he told the Cardinal of Baltimore:

> I have witnessed the work which Archbishop Keane is doing in Rome. There we have a man occupying the position, enjoying and asserting the influence over American interests, which had been denied for years to the entreaties of Your Eminence and of the whole American Hierarchy; he is doing an untold amount of good. Besides, the Archbishop himself asserts that he has never been so happy; he realizes that he is doing a good work; he is enthusiastic about his many and great opportunities in Rome to serve the Church of America. I therefore agree with Your Eminence, that it is better for the good of religion to allow Archbp. Keane to have his wish and have him remain in the Eternal City to watch and further the Catholic interests of the United States.[98]

O'Connell, too, thought that it would be ruinous to remove Keane,[99] and he grew emphatic when he told Ireland: "Don't allow Keane to go from here. He is a necessary point for rallying and a centre of force. . . . Keane says last winter was the happiest of his life."[100]

Since Keane and his friends were of one mind about his future, in so far as they were capable of directing it, it was not surprising that the archbishop was so emphatic in telling the American public, when he returned to the United States during the summer of 1897, that he had no desire to be appointed to the vacant see and that he did not believe that Rome would select him against his express wish.[101] Actually, if O'Connell's information was correct there was no danger that the archbishop would be removed from Rome, for the monsignor confided to Gibbons: "I hear again that the Pope would not approve the nomination of Mgr. Keane. Satolli's opposition is like a passion."[102]

[95] AASP, O'Connell to Ireland, Milan, Aug. 12, 1897.
[96] ADR, Gibbons to O'Connell, Baltimore, July 23, 1897.
[97] AAB, 95-S-3, Gibbons to Ledochowski, Baltimore, Aug. 10, 1897 (Latin), copy.
[98] AAB, 95-R-5, Maes to Gibbons, Covington, July 19, 1897.
[99] AAB, 95-R-2, O'Connell to Gibbons, Rome, July 18, 1897.
[100] AASP, O'Connell to Ireland, Rome, July 21, 1897.
[101] ACUA, clippings.
[102] AAB, 95-U-5, O'Connell to Gibbons, Genazzano, Oct. 21, 1897.

And, even after Keane had privately informed Placide L. Chapelle, Archbishop of Santa Fe, that it was on him that Propaganda had decided to place the burdens and honors of the See of New Orleans,[103] O'Connell stated that there had been fears about the confirmation of Chapelle for the office, owing, as he said, to the fact that some in Rome had put forward Keane's name with the idea of getting rid of him.[104] When the news of the confirmation of Chapelle's appointment was finally dispatched by Keane on November 30,[105] all danger that his enemies would immediately get revenge for his part in ousting Schroeder from the University and for his championing of the liberal cause was averted. Doubtless this was especially pleasing to O'Connell who mapped out many of the liberal campaigns in which Keane was given a stronghold to defend. By remaining in Rome a little longer, he was in a strategic spot to fight one of the major battles between the liberal and conservative factions. The "War of 1897" and the Corrigan-Ireland campaign were mere skirmishes when compared to the struggle that occupied the contenders from 1897 until 1899. The war was known as Americanism.

[103] AANO, Keane to Chapelle, Rome, Nov. 17, 1897.

[104] AANO, O'Connell to Chapelle, Rome, Nov. 30, 1897. O'Connell told Ireland: "We were afraid at the last moment that Abp. Keane would be sent there, because the Pope was hesitating and the enemies' papers said Keane would do less harm there" (AASP, O'Connell to Ireland, Rome, Dec. 2, 1897).

[105] AANO, Keane to Chapelle, Rome, Nov. 30, 1897, cablegram. A few weeks later Keane advised Chapelle that he had written to Gibbons, Ireland, Riordan, Kain, and Fitzgerald to insist, as he said, "upon the great importance of your suffragans' being in perfect accord with you. I sincerely trust that no clashing whatsoever will result from the fact of your not having been on their list. You will I'm sure be magnanimous and friendly with them, as I take every opportunity of insisting that they must be with you.

"Their advice will of course be invaluable to you, and I'm sure they will always find you ready to take it in the spirit of friendship and trust" (AANO, Keane to Chapelle, Rome, Dec. 17, 1897).

Chapter IX

Americanism

THE controversy over what came to be called Americanism,[1] in which Archbishop Keane became so deeply involved in the last years of the century, was the flowering of the seeds of discord which had been planted on two continents some years before. In preceding chapters we have seen how the justifiable differences between zealous and talented American ecclesiastics degenerated into acrimonious controversies and personal intrigues.[2] Some of the

[1] Since the literature on Americanism is so voluminous, no attempt has been made here to include an exhaustive bibliography. The following, however, will supply the reader with many details of the controversy, as well as giving its background. These articles from the *Catholic Historical Review,* besides being scholarly and penetrating, give reference to many other works in the footnotes, John J. Meng, "A Century of American Catholicism as Seen Through French Eyes," XXVII (Apr., 1941), 39–68; Vincent F. Holden, "A Myth in 'L'Américanisme,'" XXXI (July, 1945), 154–170; Thomas T. McAvoy, "Americanism, Fact and Fiction," XXXI (July, 1945), 133–153. Abbé Félix Klein's *La route du petit morvandiau. Souvenirs.* Vol. IV. *Un hérésie fantôme, l'américanisme* (Paris, 1949) is especially interesting since it gives some of the true inwardness of the controversy. A translation of this work, in which the material has been rearranged with a Foreword by James M. Gillis, C.S.P., bears the title *Americanism: A Phantom Heresy* (Atchison, Kansas, 1951). The biographies of James Cardinal Gibbons by John Tracy Ellis and of Archbishop John Ireland by James H. Moynihan contain much hitherto unpublished material on the subject.

[2] Cardinal Gibbons may well have had in mind the controversies during those years when he wrote: "Animosities are engendered, also, by religious discussions; and the *odium theologicum,* though more rare than other causes of enmity, is proverbially intense and implacable. The contestants in the controversy confine themselves for awhile to the subjects under consideration. After hotly arguing the question for a time, they gradually glide into personalities, and impugn each other's motives. While both were probably within the line of orthodoxy, one took a conservative, the other a liberal view of the subject. The one leaned to the side of authority, the other contended for freedom. The conservative begins to call his liberal opponent a radical; the liberal stamps the conservative a reactionary. The conservative goes a step further, and throws out thinly veiled hints about his antagonist's heterodoxy — a method of

dissension centered about the most effective method of gaining recognition for the Roman Catholic citizen as a devoted and loyal supporter of the American democracy. A few prelates, notably Ireland, Gibbons, and Keane, were in favor of the rapid Americanization of the large foreign element in the Catholic Church in the United States. It was their frequently expressed desire that these recently arrived sons of the Church should become familiar with the language and the institutions of their new environment and take their place alongside their fellow citizens in a democratic society actively supporting the republican form of government. There were others in the American Church, however, who believed that too rapid Americanization was a danger to the preservation of the faith of the newcomers and for that reason they felt bound in conscience to resist the well-meant efforts of their colleagues. It so happened that the churchmen who were most conspicuous for their endeavor to Americanize the Catholic immigrants were also noted for their attempts to propagate the truths of the Catholic faith among their non-Catholic countrymen. However, the methods which they employed were sometimes regarded with suspicion by their more conservative brethren, and for that reason the Americanizers were accused of liberalistic tendencies which were not in keeping with the traditions of the true Church. Hence, Americanism became an ambiguous term, bearing a patriotic sense on the lips of those who employed it in the sense of loyalty to the Constitution, but smacking of dangerous liberalism when it was employed by the conservatives.

Despite the differences between its bishops over some important questions, the Catholic Church had prospered in the United States as it had seldom done in any other country. The progressive bishops claimed that the complete freedom of the Church from interference by the State was in a great measure responsible for the unprecedented success which she enjoyed; furthermore, the Catholic citizens in America supported the government and actively participated in the affairs of state without in any way compromising their loyalty to the See of

---

controversy which is aptly styled 'poisoning the wells.' The liberal retaliates by calling his opponent a fossil. The respective allies of the two combatants take up the dispute and fan the flame. The arena of this war of words is still more widened when the newspapers plunge into the debate and sometimes, without caring to ascertain the original basis of the discussion, decide the dispute with oracular dogmatism according to their individual prejudices. Once the subject of discussion has drifted away into the open sea of promiscuous controversy, it is as hard to lead it back to its first moorings as to gather up feathers scattered by the winds." *The Ambassador of Christ* (Baltimore, 1896), p. 111.

Peter. Since many Catholics in France, Germany, and Italy held themselves entirely aloof from the political arena, if they were not openly hostile to their governments, and since the Church had been suffering reverses in those countries at the hands of the element in power, it was natural for those who were sincerely seeking a solution to their dilemma to investigate the enviable position of the American Church to determine if an answer to their problem could be found there.

Just as the European liberals began to probe in earnest the relations of Church and State across the Atlantic, Bishop John J. Keane, who had frequently lauded the Church's position *vis-à-vis* the State in the United States, was removed from his position as rector of the Catholic University of America and those who had opposed him and his friends during the preceding years attempted to create the impression that the Americanizers were evidently held in disfavor in the highest ecclesiastical circles. In part to counteract this unfavorable attitude, Keane accepted Leo XIII's offer of an honorable position in Rome and thus he became, as it were, the recognized representative of Americanism in Europe.

As soon as Bishop Keane arrived in Rome in December, 1896, Denis O'Connell began a campaign, which was seconded by Keane, to remove the false impression that the Americanizers were motivated by prejudice against any race or against any religious community in the controversies that had occupied them prior to this time. If the enthusiastic letters of the Americanists in Rome are to be credited, their efforts met with considerable success. At least, many Europeans who had previously opposed the Americanists solely because they misunderstood their motives, now began to accept and to give active support to their principal conviction that it was imperative for the Church to recognize the spirit of the age and to espouse all that was noble and good in it.[3]

As one would expect, as Keane pointed out to both Gibbons and Ireland early in May, 1897, not all Europeans were won over to their point of view. He told his correspondents that Cardinals Satolli and Mazzella had recently opened a new and fierce war in the Vatican against Americanism but, as he informed Ireland, he supplied the Vatican with a full memoir on American conditions which he hoped would "antidote their poison." To Gibbons the bishop remarked: "How

[3] AASP, O'Connell to Ireland, Rome, Jan. 7, 1897; Keane to Ireland, Rome, Jan. 11, 1897; O'Connell to Ireland, Rome, Jan. 28, 1897; Keane to Ireland, Rome, Jan. 31, 1897; O'Connell to Ireland, Rome, Feb. 5, 1897.

I wish that your Eminence could come here every couple of years to let these people see that what Satolli and Mazzella attack as 'Americanism' is simon-pure Catholicity and disinterested devotedness to the Holy See."[4]

An item published in the *Civiltà Cattolica* during the same month probably afforded a clue to what the two cardinals were attacking as Americanism, at least it reflects the opinions of men who were very close friends of the prelates. After giving an analysis of the figures representing the membership in the various denominations in the United States and an especially searching treatment of the status of the Catholic Church in the United States, the unnamed author launched into a criticism of an element among the American Catholics whom he described as "zealots." He claimed that they wanted to replace the language of the Church with their own, to tolerate secret societies, and to send their children to state schools. They aimed, he said, to make Christianity an easy, broad religion by softening the dogmas that were offensive to unorthodox ears, such as the doctrine that outside the Church there is no salvation. He further stated that the so-called zealots condemned the union of Church and State as the greatest calamity and that they advocated complete separation of the two powers. Furthermore, he averred that they taught that the lay state was to be preferred to the religious state because the latter was not conformable to the times, besides, vows as taken by the members of religious orders were not necessary because a free clergy could work better among a free people. The author concluded his exposé of these American churchmen by saying that they believed that if all of their ideas were accepted, the United States would not only be Christian, it would be Catholic.[5]

While such a distorted and untrue picture of the aims of the prelates who were called Americanists was being painted in Italy, there arose

[4] AAB, 95-P-3, Keane to Gibbons, Rome, May 9, 1897; AASP, Keane to Ireland, Rome, May 9, 1897. Keane added in his letter to Ireland: "There are storms around us but things are moving well for the True and the Right. This is no time to trifle with pessimism. Everyone needs to be firm and alert at his post."

[5] *Civiltà Cattolica* (Series 16) (May, 1897), 509–510. O'Connell showed that he was especially incensed over this issue of the Jesuit's review. To Ireland he wrote: "All that I consulted agreed that a protest should be entered against the Civilta Cath. of May 15, but how? Best, if possible by the Archbishops in their approaching meeting. If that could not be carried then it would devolve upon Cardinal Gibbons. And if he would not do it, then let it alone and give the Civilta free rope to show the American Catholics what the Jesuits are" (AASP, O'Connell to Ireland, Rome, July 21, 1897). In the same letter O'Connell related: "Satolli told Chapelle there was none of the 'supernatural' in the Church of America."

in France a similar misrepresentation of their ideas. The remote causes of this lamentable state of affairs were the sincere efforts of one group of influential French Catholics to foster the policy of Leo XIII, known as the *Ralliement,* which favored greater Catholic co-operation with the republic, and also the attempts of another Catholic group in that country to spread an excessive spirit of freedom in religious matters. Both parties thought that support for their activities could be found in the United States where Catholic prelates extolled the harmony which existed between the Church and the State and where they engaged in progressive activities such as the Chicago Parliament of Religions.[6] The immediate cause of the Americanism controversy in Europe, however, was the publication of a French translation of Walter Elliott's *Life of Father Hecker,*[7] a work which the Catholic liberals in France seized upon as containing the best expression of the ideas which they were striving to promote among their fellow Catholics. Within a short time this French life of the founder of the American Paulists passed through seven editions. Its popularity must undoubtedly be attributed to a thirty-five page preface by Abbé Félix Klein, a young journalist and professor of the Catholic Institute of Paris, in which the force and originality of Hecker's ideas were stressed.[8] It was from this quite unreliable literary production and

[6] Cf. McAvoy, *op. cit.,* pp. 140–142.

[7] *Le Père Hecker, fondateur des "Paulists" Américaines 1819–1888,* par le Père Elliott de la même compagnie. Traduit et adapté de l'anglais avec authorisation de l'auteur. Introduction par Mgr. Ireland. Preface par l'Abbé Félix Klein (Paris, 1897). The original had appeared under the title *The Life of Father Hecker* (New York, 1891). In 1889 O'Connell said that "insinuations come from N. Y. against Fath. Hecker's orthodoxy and in the same place suspicions were cast on Bp. Keane" (AASP, O'Connell to Ireland, Grottaferrata, July 23, 1889). In view of that information the forward group should have foreseen the danger in promoting the book.

[8] Cf. Holden, *op. cit.,* and McAvoy, *op. cit.,* pp. 142–143. Concerning the translation Father William Barry stated: "This translation abridges and omits, and in some very serious points has fallen into error. It cannot be relied on as giving the sense of the original which must always be consulted." "An American Religious Crusade," *National Review,* XXXIII (Mar., 1899), 121 n. This was written by a friend of the Americanists after the French work had been subjected to scrutiny and attack. Keane at one time corresponded with Barry concerning a position at the University in Washington and the talented Englishman was strongly inclined to accept the work (ACUA, Barry to Keane, Dorchester, Aug. 16 and Oct. 15, 1890, and May 2, 1891). When the translation had first appeared, however, O'Connell said: "It is surprising how circumstances are combining in favor of the new idea. Hecker's Life gives a tremendous impulse. You can hardly imagine it. Klein wrote a masterly preface that is a tour de force of itself, and that has received a stupendous welcome. Klein is a noble fellow, body and soul in your idea and ready, he writes me, to sacrifice everything to the cause. I shall write Fr. Elliott asking permission to have his Father Hecker translated into Italian. Klein has already placed his preface at my

especially from the preface that the liberal French press in enthusiastic reviews garnered the doctrines which some came to regard as true Americanism and which were roundly criticized under that heading.

Misrepresentation of the aims and tenets of the Americanists was so widespread and persistent during the summer of 1897 that John A. Zahm, C.S.C., a supporter of the progressives who was president of the Anthropological Section of the Fourth International Catholic Scientific Congress scheduled to be held in Fribourg, Switzerland, in August, was prompted to give Monsignor O'Connell an opportunity to appear before the delegates to the congress and to deliver a paper in which Americanism would be rightly defined. On August 20, therefore, the monsignor presented to that group what might be called the American definition of Americanism in an address that was later published under the title, *A New Idea in the Life of Father Hecker.*[9] On the basis of O'Connell's exposition of the ticklish question it would be impossible to accuse either Father Hecker or the Americanizing ecclesiastics of being guilty of expounding the dangerous doctrines which were being paraded in Europe as Americanism. Furthermore, all those who were identified as Americanists or who were in sympathy with them had nothing but praise for the manner in which the monsignor presented their true ideas,[10] and one of them believed that Keane would have "put his two feet in it" if he had treated the subject."[11] Nevertheless, at the congress Charles F. Turinaz, whom Klein described as "the windy Bishop of Nancy, the bore of the Congress," charged that Hecker was a Protestant because he left Catholics to follow, like Protestants, the internal guidance of the Holy Spirit. This accusation Klein claimed to have refuted himself "amid the

---

disposal. *Father Hecker's Life is regarded as the supernatural philosophy of the whole movement — given out by a saint*" (author's italics) (AASP, O'Connell to Ireland, Milan, Aug. 12, 1897). Nearly four months later O'Connell admitted that he had never read the book. "It is too long," he said (La Contessa Sabina di Tarravicino di Revel Papers on microfilm in AUND, O'Connell to Sabina, Rome, Dec. 1, 1897).

[9] (Breisgau, 1897). It was published in French under the title, *L'Américanisme d'après le P. Hecker, ce qu'il est et ce qu'il n'est pas* (Paris, 1897).

[10] O'Connell informed Klein that his pamphlet had been enthusiastically received by Cardinal Gibbons, Abbé Magnien, Francis Aidan Gasquet, O.S.B., and Father William Barry. Father Elliott had written: "I applaud your mingled audacity and prudence" (APF, Klein Papers, O'Connell to Klein, Rome, Oct. 18, 1897). Keane had simply stated that it was just the "definition" that they needed (ADR, Keane to O'Donnell, Washington, Oct. 15, 1897). Chapelle called it a "masterly presentation" and swore that he subscribed to every word of it (AANO, Chapelle to O'Connell, New York, Oct. 23, 1897, copy).

[11] ADR, Magnien to O'Connell, Baltimore, September 27, 1897.

applause of the gathering," and at the meeting of the board after the session it was decided that Bishop Turinaz's remarks would be struck from the minutes and that no official record of the episode would be kept.[12]

Within a month after the Fribourg gathering O'Connell revealed some of the thoughts that had found a place in his mind as he prepared his definition of Americanism. To Ireland he wrote:

> So many accusations were laid to your charge on the score of "Americanism" that I thought I would avail myself of the opportunity presented by the Fribourg Congress to give the mis-used term a proper definition. . . .
>
> You will have the brochure in a few days and I hope you will be pleased with it and stand up for it. I identified it with the Declaration of Independence and the Constitution, and so understood, all censure of the term ought to end.[13]

Two days earlier he had told Klein:

> It was deemed best to send out my paper on Americanism and, in the public mind, transfer the combat from the theological to the political issue. Every American in America must endorse Fr. Hecker's Americanism, because it is defined as nothing else than devotion to America and to its Constitution. To put that on Index would be to condemn our government and that would create too great a controversy. In your Review you might show how Americanism in its political phase is nothing else than the policy the Pope recommends to France. In America, I don't see how the Fathers [Jesuits] could safely attack Hecker's politics and, in the public mind, the two questions will be merged into one.[14]

[12] APF, Klein to Elliott, Milan, Oct. 12, 1897. It would seem, however, that the record of the episode was kept. Cf. McAvoy, *op. cit.*, p. 143.

[13] AASP, O'Connell to Ireland, Freiburg im Breisgau, Sept. 5, 1897.

[14] APF, Klein Papers, O'Connell to Klein, Freiburg im Breisgau, Sept. 3, 1897. Besides O'Connell at the congress, there was John Zahm, Edward A. Pace, and Charles Grannan, Americanists all and the latter two professors at the Catholic University of America. O'Connell reported that on the last evening they had given a banquet to the leaders of the gathering and, as he expressed it, "prepared ground for future operations." He told Ireland: "You are right, our friends are in Germany, men of strength, courage and conviction and only longing to unite with us. They all believe we are the future and now Americanism as represented by you is the Catholic watchword of Europe" (AASP, O'Connell to Ireland, Freiburg im Breisgau, Aug. 26, 1897). O'Connell kept insisting that Ireland's field was outside France, where, as he said "no ten men stand together and you would fail" (AASP, O'Connell to Ireland, Freiburg im Breisgau, Sept. 5, 1897). A little later, he wrote: "The more I study these people the more I am convinced that your strength lies here [in Germany]. There are 24 millions of them Catholic, all educated, and their chiefs the best and most

While O'Connell was seeking to place the term "Americanism" beyond the reach of hostile critics in Europe, Keane was visiting in the United States where he boldly proclaimed his political Americanism on diverse occasions,[15] at one time stating: "America is to my mind the embodiment of ideas, conditions, and influences, which are the best that the world has yet beheld for the furtherance of human welfare."[16] Because Keane was to return to the continent after a brief vacation in the United States, O'Connell sought to impress Klein with the importance of seeing the archbishop when he arrived in Paris. "He is the greatest admirer living of Fr. Hecker," the monsignor claimed, "and he says everywhere that he owes all he has to Fr. Hecker. They were bosom friends."[17] After he had seen their friends in Paris, Keane informed John Ireland that they were in excellent spirits, principally because the Holy Father continued to support the *"rallies."* Hence, as he put it, "the good leaven is working irresistibly."[18]

The "good leaven" to the mind of Keane and his friends was the Americanism which was being spread through Europe by means of Hecker's life, O'Connell's Fribourg paper, and Klein's translation of some of Ireland's conferences, as well as the more recent discourses of the Archbishop of St. Paul which had been widely publicized by his friends on the continent.[19] Archbishop Keane was especially anxious

---

advancedly educated men in the Church" (AASP, O'Connell to Ireland, Munich, Sept. 14 1897).

[15] Cf. *supra,* pp. 218–220.

[16] LCLD, clippings, Washington *Post* (1897). In his old age Archbishop Keane underlined this statement.

[17] APF, Klein Papers, O'Connell to Klein, Rome, Oct. 18, 1897. Eleven days later the monsignor said: "You may regard Mgr. Keane as Fr. Hecker's spiritual child in everything" (*ibid.,* Genazzano, Oct. 29, 1897). To Walter Elliott, C.S.P., O'Connell wrote: "This success (of the French translation) brings great joy to the heart of Archbishop Keane who loves Fr. Hecker as his father in the spiritual life" (APF, O'Connell to Elliott Rome, Dec. 3, 1897).

[18] AASP, Keane to Ireland, Rome, Nov. 17, 1897. Nearly a month before O'Connell had said to Klein: "Still it is true that the Holy Father is growing stronger in his dislike of these new notions under the influence, I understand, of Cardinal Mazzella, S.J. The Holy Father is growing old, and they impose on him" (APF, Klein Papers, O'Connell to Klein, Genazzano, Oct. 22, 1897).

[19] Monsignor O'Connell joyfully related to Ireland: "The whole atmosphere of Europe is now redolent of Americanism. Your Conferences, Hecker's Life and my little brochure. It is now three months that the French press has been occupying itself with that little paper, and the subject assumes greater proportions the more they handle it. Americanism now means no longer provincialism but modern society. Modern law in contrast to Ancient Law. In France the movement only needs watching. In England some of the best writers have placed themselves at my service, and I hope to avail myself of their offer. Klein writes me that a new edition of your

that Hecker's life, which he had but recently presented to the Holy Father,[20] should reach a larger circle of readers. To that end he strongly urged Father Elliott to prepare a new biography, much shorter than the original English version, which could be translated into Italian. This shorter volume was to give, as the archbishop expressed it, "in quintessence the great majestic, powerful Father Hecker, as an ideal for the Catholic Clergy and the Catholic people of today." Furthermore, it would make Hecker, as he put it, "accessible to tens of thousands of people who need him and who cannot be reached by him otherwise." Four months later, however, the archbishop told the Paulist that he and O'Connell were convinced "that Europe has as big a dose of Heckerism and Americanism as it can stand."[21]

At the beginning of the year 1898, therefore, the spirits of the Americanists in Rome seemed to be very high, although they had lost one of their number when John A. Zahm, C.S.C., returned to Notre Dame. "The 'triplex funiculus' has lost one of its cords," Keane commented when announcing their friend's departure.[22] Gibbons was told by the archbishop that peace reigned in the Vatican and that a great deal of attention was being attracted to Americanism because of the French edition of Hecker's life and O'Connell's essay. Although what he called "a spirit of narrowness" was manifesting itself, yet he reported "the bulk of sentiment is on our side."[23] Keane also drew the notice of both Gibbons and Ireland to a current article in the *Civiltà Cattolica,* then eliciting newspaper comment in England and Rome, which hinted that a republic would be a better form of government for Italy than a monarchy. The archbishop claimed that it was known that this was the Pope's private conviction, but it was highly significant, in his opinion, that the first public utterance of it should appear in an article which, as he said, "could not have been published without the Pope's knowledge and approval." Such a pronouncement of Leo XIII's policy, Keane concluded, although it did not appear in an official statement, "ought naturally to prove favorable to Americanism."[24]

'L'Église et le Siècle' will soon appear in Flemish. There is more Americanism here than in the Church in America and when you arrive you will be everywhere regarded as a colossus. The question is really the conflict of two civilizations, as Archbishop Keane puts it" (AASP, O'Connell to Ireland, Rome, Dec. 2, 1897).

20 APF, Klein Papers, O'Connell to Klein, Rome, [Dec. 3, 1897].

21 APF, Keane to Elliott, Rome, Dec. 13, 1897; Apr. 18, 1898.

22 AASP, Keane to Ireland, Rome, Jan. 24, 1898.

23 AAB, 96-A-10, Keane to Gibbons, Rome, Jan. 24, 1898.

24 *Ibid.,* AASP, Keane to Ireland, Rome, Jan. 24, 1898.

That O'Connell shared Keane's optimistic view of the future of Americanism in Europe was evident in his correspondence with Abbé Klein. "All eyes are now turned towards France and are watching with profound interest the growth of the movement you have created," he wrote to his friend in Paris. "It is in France that the issue will be fought out, and the moments of greatest danger seem past."[25] Keane also sent encouraging words to the abbé who, in view of the disquieting criticism of Heckerism from the pulpit of the Church of St. Sulpice in Paris, was preparing a conference on Americanism which the archbishop expected to be crushing to their enemies.[26] Since his loyal ally in France had asked for some ideas which he could embody in his conference on true and false Americanism, Keane complied with a long letter which is especially interesting for, as Klein wrote a half century later, it showed "Americanism in its indisputable authenticity just at the moment when its adversaries began to attack it most violently and in the most depraved manner." Furthermore, in the opinion of the French priest, Archbishop Keane was then the person, as he put it, "most truly representative of the American Church: more reserved than Ireland, less reserved than Gibbons, in the manifestation of his thoughts; uniquely solicitous (and here I no longer contrast him with other archbishops) uniquely solicitous to interpret the truth and promote good, absolutely above all personal seeking."[27] This, then, is Archbishop Keane's conception of Americanism at that moment:

> In order to keep to our text, it seems to me that the showing of what Americanism is not, as well as of what it is, had better be drawn

[25] APF, Klein Papers, O'Connell to Klein, Rome, Jan. 13, 1898. In this note the monsignor refers to the Abbé Alphonse Magnien, S.S., president of St. Mary's Seminary in Baltimore, who was then visiting in Paris, as "the head and heart of the whole movement in America."

[26] APF, Klein Papers, Keane to Klein, Rome, Jan. 17, 1898. Cf. Holden, *op. cit.*, p. 158 n. Edouard Trogan, the Paris correspondent of the *Revue Générale* of Brussels, wrote in his letter of November 22, 1897, published in the January, 1898, issue, that Father R. P. Coubé, whom he described as one of the best Jesuit orators, had delivered a sermon in the Church of St. Sulpice in Paris which was out of place according to several very competent persons. Although the speaker mentioned no names, he struck at the Chicago Parliament of Religions, Ferdinand Brunetière, editor of the *Revue des Deux Mondes,* Hecker, and Maurice Blondel. When he had finished criticizing Blondel's theories, he ended: "The Church cries out to you: Pelagius and heresy!" Furthermore, Father A. J. Delattre, S.J., scourged Klein in a brochure entitled *Un congres d'intellectuels a Gand en fevrier, 1897.* Keane requested Klein to forward the facts concerning the attack on Hecker and Americanism and similar attacks that may follow (AUND, Klein Papers, Keane to Klein, Rome, Jan. 9, 1898).

[27] Klein, *La route du petit morvandiau: Souvenirs,* IV, 177.

from Monsignor O'Connell's Essay. In his concluding paragraph you find these three points: "It is no new form of heresy, of Liberalism, of Separatism."

No. I — not heresy. — Our enemies in America have accused us lately of being neo-pelagians. The charge is absurdly false and calumnious. There is no country in the world where the Supernatural and the channels of Grace are so insisted upon and are so appreciated by the people as in the United States. Our clergy work as hard as any priests in the world, and I think it will be readily admitted that our people flock to the Sacraments as frequently as any other people. The devotions to the Holy Eucharist and to the Sacred Heart are universal.

Again Monsignor O'Connell says expressly that Father Hecker recognized in the social principles of the United States a broad basis whereon to bring among men the work of the supernatural.

Our adversaries cannot cite a single utterance of any prelate of the United States to the contrary. We insist of course upon the natural virtues, and we are glad that these are very strong in the American character; but never for one moment do we forget that these are only the basis of the supernatural virtues. To assert it is a calumny.

No. II — not Liberalism.

Liberalism is rejection in various degrees of the authority of God, or of the Church, or of the Pope. I defy our enemies to show a single instance of this among the Bishops or people of the United States. There is no country in the world where the authority of the Church and of the Pope is as free and as lovingly honored as in the United States. It is the only country in the world to-day where the Pope can exercise his authority without limit, and where it is always bowed to most lovingly. Only in one instance did it seem as if a papal decision was not welcomed as heartily as it ought to be. This was in regard to the fourteen propositions on the question of Christian schools presented to the Bishops by the Apostolic Delegate, Monsignor Satolli.

The partial and temporary want of agreement then manifested did not at all arise from any tendency towards Liberalism on the part of the Bishops, but on the contrary was owing to their belief that these propositions were too liberal and could not represent the mind of the Pope. For it must be known that at that time Monsignor Satolli had not presented any credentials to show that he had been sent as Delegate to America by the Pope. As soon as the Pope made it clear that these propositions were his own, there was no more opposition either to them or to Monsignor Satolli.

In his Encyclical "Libertas" the Holy Father has defined the various degrees of Liberalism which the Church condemns, and the one degree of Liberalism which the Church approves. I defy any man to show a single instance in which the teaching or action of the Church in

America transcends the limits of the Liberalism there approved by the Holy Father.

No. III — not Separatism.

No American could be such a fool as to have any desire for a separate national Church. They see too plainly that the idea of national and Catholic are contradictory. Even were they free to choose they would infinitely rather be a portion of the Universal Church than be a Church to themselves. It would be atrocious calumny to assert the contrary.

Finally, Americanism does not mean a Propaganda, aiming at imposing American conditions on the rest of the world. We mind our own business and only assert and defend what concerns our own country. What fits our circumstances would of course not fit countries where the conditions are different. We are not foolish doctrinaires. We agree absolutely with the wisdom of Leo XIII in saying that our conditions are not to be regarded as a rule for the rest of the world.

I hope, dear friend, that these suggestions may be somewhat useful. The attacks of your adversaries will I'm sure supply you with any other notions to refute that you may desire.[28]

While the archbishop was jotting down these thoughts for his friend in Paris, he prepared an article on "America as Seen from Abroad" for the *Catholic World*. Evidently, he was concerned with the almost complete misunderstanding of American conditions on the part of Catholic Europeans which resulted in baseless criticism of American ecclesiastics who were at once thoroughly devoted to the Holy See and to their country. He pictured the American visiting on the continent as being puzzled because of the difficulty Europeans found in comprehending the spirit and institutions of the new world, and he sought to explain that, because of a difference in traditions and institutions, what seemed unorthodox to the mind molded by ancient custom and prejudice was actually in complete harmony with the teachings of the Church. He then expressed the opinion that intelligent interest in America and Americanism was increased by the publication in French of Hecker's life and by O'Connell's essay on "Americanism," but "as might be expected," he continued, "Father Hecker and 'Americanism' have had their assailants. The adherents of the old schools could, of course, not permit them to pass unchallenged." Letting his optimism influence his judgment, he concluded:

But the comparative mildness of the protests shows that the old bitter spirit of partisanship is passing away; and the disfavor with

[28] APF, Klein Papers, Keane to Klein, Rome, Jan. 18, 1898.

which the attacks have been generally regarded proves that the acceptance of providential development is becoming universal, that the synthesis between these developments and devoted Catholicity, as exemplified in Americanism, is more and more generally recognized to be both possible and desirable, and that Father Hecker is carrying on an apostolate to-day more wide-spread and more efficacious than during his lifetime.

So, God speeding the good work, there is reason to hope that, ere many years, America, as seen from abroad, will not inspire so much suspicion and dread, and that the American will find himself more at home among his fellow-Catholics in Europe.[29]

Although the archbishop viewed the future hopefully, he was well aware, as he said to Elliott, that Heckerism was at that moment passing through a crisis. But he believed that such an interest in Heckerism was not to be regretted, since the final result was sure to be good.[30]

[29] John J. Keane, "America as Seen from Abroad," *Catholic World,* LXVI (Mar., 1898), 721–730. The article was reprinted in *The Light of the Cross in the Twentieth Century* (New York, 1908), I, 289–300. The London *Tablet* (Apr. 2, 1898) printed extracts from the article which were prefaced by the statement: "The article explains the supposed Liberalism of American Catholics, and pleads for a right understanding of the loyal spirit of progress which is working in the Church in America. No one is better qualified than his Grace for the task which he has undertaken." From John R. Slattery, S.S.J., the archbishop received a congratulatory letter, thanking him especially for the omissions in the article. "There is no arguing with passion or prejudice," he said. "It must be lived down. Eventually Socialism may become the means of proving American orthodoxy." He concluded: "At last after long years of separation, Hecker and Keane are united. Both are invading Europe and knocking at the Vatican. Hecker in his Americanism: Keane, its embodiment." In his reply, Keane stated: "You are right in judging that the Church in the United States cannot expect to be understood by people over here, but must go quietly on her course, true to principle and duty, content to be misunderstood, trusting in Providence" (AJF, Slattery Papers, Slattery to Keane, Baltimore, Feb. 26, 1898, copy; Keane to Slattery, Rome, Mar. 16, 1898).

[30] APF, Keane to Elliott, Rome, Feb. 5, 1898. In this same epistle, the archbishop advised Elliott not to present the Paulist rule for the approval of Rome yet, because, among other things, he felt convinced that the proposed preamble to the rule would not receive approval. Nearly three months later, Keane wrote: "I am glad that you have come around to my views in regard to keeping Father Hecker's teachings for the home interpretation and spirit of the Rule rather than presenting the mere letter of it to men who surely would not accept it. I am glad that you also agree that no formal approval ought to be asked just yet. Meanwhile let all efforts at home be concentrated towards growing under the spirit of your founder. May the love of God, the love of Mother Church, the love of souls, the love of our Country, and the love of the interior guidance of the Holy Spirit, become the very life and soul of the Congregation." Since the Paulist had mentioned founding a religious order for women, Keane advised him to consider carefully the experience of Father Sorin, superior general of the Holy Cross Fathers, in that regard and he added that Rome would not look with favor upon any relationship between the two

Nevertheless, the Paulist author of Hecker's life gave voice to his apprehension about the attitude of the continental Jesuits toward the French translation, and he added:

> Men must have time to think to assimilate Heck. Here one, there another, will be led to understand that what we desire is only the normal condition of the spiritual regimen of the Church and the Gospel, to be unloaded of some of the extra and useless and encumbering pieces of our spiritual harness. Do I object to a Jesuit burying himself in 'Methods'? Not in the least. But why can't he let me try the fight without so many obediences, resulting as they too often do in really less actual obedience. . . . I am the man of my age — how often dear Lacordaire said those words — the man who did so much to show his age the road to Jesus Christ.[31]

Elliott's misgivings were amply justified within the next few months when the *Vérité Française* began to print a series of articles attacking the Americanists and Hecker in particular, basing its knowledge of his views on the French translation of his life. Keane identified the authors of the articles, who used the pen names "Martel" and "Saint-Clément," as Charles Maignen, a priest of the Congregation of the Brothers of St. Vincent de Paul who had gained some notoriety for his attacks on Count Albert de Mun and who, as Keane expressed it, "is noted as hot-brained and unscrupulous." The second writer was George Périès, who according to the archbishop, now was getting the revenge which he had threatened when he was removed from his position at the Catholic University of America. Because he was sure that one class in France and in Italy would strive to have the French translation of Hecker's life put on the Index — he was just as positive that they would not attack the English original — Keane strongly advised Elliott to obtain a letter from Cardinal Gibbons, containing an approval of Father Hecker and of the spirit and work of the Paulists, which could be inserted into the next French edition of their founder's life. "Such a letter will tell in France," the archbishop assured his correspondent,

---

organizations. "If Providence has raised up a woman capable of founding a community in the lines indicated by Fr. Hecker," he said, "they had better I think stand rigorously separate and independent" (APF, Keane to Elliott, Rome, Apr. 19, 1898).

31 APF, Klein Papers, Elliott to Klein, New York, Feb. 14, 1898. The distinguished Paulist was also uneasy because it had been announced to George M. Searle, C.S.P., by the Vatican directly, that he was to be appointed Director of the Vatican Observatory, but now the appointment seemed to be slow in coming, a fact which Elliott attributed to the enemies of Americanism.

"but will especially tell here in Rome."[32] Gibbons, of course, needed no urging to comply with such a request, for he could honestly commend the founder and the members of the American congregation. Besides, he was in complete sympathy with the ideas which the Americanists sought to present in a proper light to the people of the world.[33]

Shortly after the outbreak of the Spanish-American War, which served to intensify the anti-republican spirit in Europe generally and in France particularly, Félix Klein determined to utilize the cardinal's letter in praise of the Paulists to bolster the cause of Americanism and to counteract the effects of continued attacks on Heckerism. "The peaceful silence we observed for two months," he told Elliott, "only encouraged our opponents. I believe they are now in as bad a position as mere Spaniards." He had reliable information, he said, that Father Maignen was going to enlarge the articles attacking the Americanists which had appeared in the *Vérité* and publish them in a book and that the priest hoped to obtain an *imprimatur* from the Archbishop of Paris or a letter from the Bishop of Nancy. However, François Cardinal Richard of Paris was hesitating about granting his approval to the work because of conflicting advice from the Jesuits and the Sulpicians, the latter having told him that his approbation of the book would hurt the feelings of the Archbishop of Baltimore. Therefore, Klein believed

[32] APF, Keane to Elliott, Rome, Apr. 18, 1898. In a postscript the archbishop related: "A Jesuit Bolandist told me this afternoon that from conversations with Fr. Brandi he is certain that there is no danger of any attempt by the Index or Holy Office on Hecker and Americanism. There is too much dynamite in things just now, and they are going to let us alone. So without saying anything about it to the public, simply take it for granted that you are in no danger."

[33] APF, Gibbons to Elliott, Baltimore, Apr. 14, 1898. Alphonse Magnien, S.S., Gibbons' close friend and adviser, who was in Europe at this time, was interviewed by William J. D. Croke, a Roman correspondent for the *Catholic Standard and Times,* and reportedly stated that there was great interest in Paris among the members of the clergy and among Catholic laymen in the Church in America. He had found that some entertained strange notions on this subject but that they were ready to receive explanations and correct information. There was also, he said, "always a great sympathy when American ideas were properly explained and understood, and all seemed to feel that in Europe there were hindrances to progress from which we did not suffer, and that they would like to have the same free and untrammeled action of the Church as in America. They feel that freedom prospers the Church" (*Church News,* Apr. 30, 1898). Shortly after Magnien's death Gibbons said of him: "He was a loyal citizen of the United States, and had a great admiration for the civic and political institutions of the country. He took delight in expatiating on the happy relations existing here between Church and State, in contrast with the incessant conflict between the ecclesiastical and civil authorities in his own distracted native land." Cf. *Very Rev. A. L. Magnien, A Memorial* (Baltimore, 1903), p. 7. In this same volume Keane and Ireland testified to the fact that he held the same ideas as they did. Cf. pp. 84–87.

that his publication of Gibbons' letter in the *Univers* would have a salutary impression on the Cardinal of Paris who, as Klein put it, "dislikes conflicts between bishops and who, personally, told me he read with edification the life of Father Hecker."[34] Either Klein's plan was effective or some other consideration induced Richard to refuse Maignen an *imprimatur*. In any case, Maignen applied to Rome for permission to print his book, and with that maneuver the controversy took on an entirely different color, and the scene of the more important aspects of the conflict shifted from France to Italy.

As soon as it was known that Maignen had received a favorable hearing in Rome, O'Connell hastened to assure Klein that grave consequences would follow for those who had been responsible for such an unusual procedure which so completely revealed their hostility to Americanism.[35] The very next day, after having obtained a copy of the book[36] and after assuring himself of the libelous nature of its contents, the monsignor expressed the opinion that its publication should not be regretted, for it furnished them, as he put it, "with an arm we were long in need of. The *imprimatur* must be satisfactorily explained or our confidence in the Curia Romana is over."[37]

During the next few months Keane and O'Connell maintained that the granting of an *imprimatur* by the Roman officials, Alberto Lepidi, O.P., Master of the Sacred Palace, and Francesco Cassetta, Viceregent of the Cardinal Vicar of Rome, was surprising because it was contrary to the letter and the spirit of a recently published constitution of the Index, which required that the ordinary of the place where a book was printed should give the approval, and he presumed that Lepidi did not receive powers from his superiors to dispense from the provisions of

[34] APF, Klein to Elliott, Paris, May 5, 1898 (French). In the margin Klein added: "And thus, if a French bishop sides with Martel, he will have the odium of opposing Cardinal Gibbons. Otherwise, we would have seemed to create the conflict." Later in the conflict Corrigan stated to George Deshon, superior general of the Paulist Fathers, that the Archbishop of Paris had denied the *imprimatur* to Maignen's book, not because he disapproved of it but to avoid responsibility. The Cardinal had advised an application to Rome for it, and Lepidi acted under orders (APF, Deshon to Elliott, New York, Feb. 26, 1899).

[35] APF, Klein Papers, O'Connell to Klein, Rome, June 1, 1898.

[36] Charles Maignen, *Études sur l'americanisme, le père Hecker — est-il un saint?* (Paris, 1898). "The Americanists were accused of limiting the external submission to the Church, of advocating a false liberalism in their dealings with non-Catholics, of advocating a complete separation of Church and State, of opposition to the evangelical virtues and the older religious orders, and of advocating the practice of active virtues over the supernatural" (McAvoy, *op. cit.*, p. 144). The abbé based his charges on Klein's preface and the writings of Ireland, Keane, and Charbonnel.

[37] APF, Klein Papers, O'Connell to Klein, Rome, June 2, 1898.

the constitution. Furthermore, since Cardinal Richard had written to the Holy See to inform them of his action, the granting of the *imprimatur* for a book printed in Paris by Retaux was a direct slap to the Archbishop of Paris as well as an indication that the principals in this action knew that they were engaged in what O'Connell called "sneaky work." In the face of this unprecedented situation O'Connell's thoughts grew somewhat bitter. He told Ireland:

> Now come the considerations: for years (six) the Curia Romana has been playing a double part with us. While openly giving us smiles and fair words, it has covertly given every encouragement in its power to our enemies, and never lost an opportunity of hurting us. It cherished Schroeder in its bosom, never put any check upon the false correspondence of [Paul Maria] Baumgarten [a German priest residing in Rome]. This patronage of Peries and Company is nothing but the continuation of the same false system and now that the Curia has publicly shown its hand it is in order for us to ask it; where we stand and what are their intentions. They don't own the Church. For hundreds of years history shows that the Curia Romana has been in constant conflict with the Church and now let us know openly where we are and not await any more dark policy. If we are not Catholic let them frankly say so . . .
>
> All this corresponds with the rules given by Rampolla to the Roman press under his control, that your name should never appear in it. I know the Correspondent for American letters intimately. Time and again all letters or allusions to you were rejected or suppressed and finally they told him "We can print nothing about these men." But the Correspondent added "they print everything I give them about Corrigan."[38]

Keane's account of the events leading to the publication of the slanderous book was forwarded to Ireland without interpretations such as those which O'Connell had presented. He did report, however, that the volume was *"launched"* by the *Voce della Verità* in a review from the pen of a Jesuit, and that the same paper had announced two days later that it had been necessary to obtain another large assignment of the book from Paris, in which the table of contents was printed so as to attract more readers. Concerning the work itself, the archbishop said that it contained "only a vein of insinuation" against the

[38] AASP, O'Connell to Ireland, Rome, June 3, 1898. Baumgarten looked upon himself as a Roman agent for Catholics in Germany and he showed an interest in the cause of German Catholics in the United States. Cf. Barry, *The Catholic Church and German Americans*, p. 167.

Archbishop of Baltimore, but that Ireland was spoken of as the future head of the schismatical American Church, and that he himself had been pictured, as he stated it, "as a rationalist, throwing all dogma over to modern ideas, and author of the [unsigned] article of the English rationalist in the Contemporary Review, of whom I know nothing, and with whose ideas I have no sympathy." He referred to Rome's "blunder" in granting the *imprimatur* as a fortunate mistake for him and his friends because it enabled them to lodge strong protests, whereas otherwise they would have been inclined to allow the matter to pass unnoted. Keane said that after he had read the Maignen volume he had written out a protest for Rampolla and for the Holy Father, which he read to Serafino Cardinal Vannutelli, who expressed indignation over such a publication and who endorsed his deprecation.[39] The archbishop had concluded his letter of protest to Rampolla with the statement: "If, in the opinion of the Holy See, I am really the man Maignen is making his readers believe, I cannot see how the Holy See can tolerate my presence in Rome, or even in the church. If not, the official authorization given to such calumniation requires an equally official and public repudiation."[40] When he presented this document to the papal Secretary of State, the cardinal, as Keane expressed it, "professed himself astonished, sorry, indignant, and assured me that due action would be taken, at any rate, upon receiving the protests to the Holy Father which he *expects* from you and Cardinal Gibbons." Furthermore, Rampolla stated that neither he nor Leo XIII knew anything about the granting of the *imprimatur*.[41] This last bit of information, as well as the statement attributed to Rampolla that "energetic action would promptly be taken to do justice to those who had been greviously wronged," shortly appeared in some of the principal papers in England and on the continent.[42] Nevertheless, O'Connell,

[39] AASP, Keane to Ireland, Rome, June 4, 1898.

[40] Keane to Rampolla, June 2, 1897, cited by Soderini, *op. cit.* Keane also stated that several quotations from his speeches were falsified.

[41] AASP, Keane to Ireland, Rome, June 4, 1898. The next day Klein was informed about the highest Church officials' complete unfamiliarity with the *imprimatur,* but O'Connell added: "Not one Catholic paper in this city would venture to publish Cardinal Gibbon's letter to Father Elliott, and a mot d'ordre has gone out vs. Americanism and Heckerism" (APF, Klein Papers, O'Connell to Klein, Rome, June 5, 1898).

[42] *Catholic Times and Catholic Opinion,* June 17, 1898. This journal added: "Singularly enough, the work was highly lauded in a review edited by the Jesuit Fathers, and was recommended to all readers in all quarters of the earth." Besides giving the general report, a French paper (AASP, clippings, Vol. L, pp. 97–99) pointed out that Lepidi was a Dominican who disliked Americanism and who had joined forces with

who was familiar with procedures in Rome, remained dissatisfied with Rampolla's statements to Keane, and he told Klein: "It is hard to conceive how Cardinal Rampolla and the Pope would both be unacquainted with this fact if we suppose that Padre Lepidi had been informed, as he should have been, of the intention of the author to publish his book in Paris, and the fact that Cardinal Richard had already denied the imprimatur."[43]

Keane used a different approach, demonstrating in a letter to his friend in Paris an understanding of the French temperament. He offered Klein his congratulations upon the attacks which Maignen had made on him and he added: "The spirit of the poor man is so obviously evil, the opposite of the spirit of our Lord, that to be attacked by him is an honor for you." Concerning the charges against himself, Keane remarked: "His efforts to show that I myself am a dangerous rationalist, have naturally saddened me by their sophistic venom, but leave me without any indignation, rather with a heart full of pity." Klein was then asked to express to the Archbishop of Paris Keane's recognition of his friendliness in refusing to grant permission to have the book printed, and he concluded by voicing the hope that Cardinal Richard, as he said, "whose authority has been so sadly outraged in this affair, would make a strong protest to the Holy See," especially in view of the fact that Rampolla had professed ignorance of the event and had promised to make amends.[44]

Contrary to their expectations, instead of receiving a satisfactory explanation of the granting of the *imprimatur* for such a book by a Roman official, Keane was favored by a letter from Lepidi in which the Master of the Sacred Palace expressed regrets at the pain which the work had caused the archbishop. At the same time, however, he justified his grant of the *imprimatur* on the ground that it was his duty to safeguard faith and traditions, and he thought that the publication of Maignen's work would provoke a thorough discussion of Americanism to which were attached doctrines which lent themselves to false and dangerous interpretations.[45] The archbishop immediately

---

the Jesuits. O'Connell told Klein that Keane had given him permission to send the item to the *Tablet,* and that it would be well to publish it in the *Univers* (APF, Klein Papers, O'Connell to Klein, Rome, June 8, 1898).

[43] APF, Klein Papers, O'Connell to Klein, Rome, June 8, 1898.

[44] APF, Klein Papers, Keane to Klein, Rome, June 9, 1898 (French).

[45] Lepidi to Keane, June 12, 1898, cited by Soderini, *op. cit.* The original letter must have been in French for O'Connell quotes from it in that language (AASP, O'Connell to Ireland, Rome, June 16, 1898).

replied that the explanation was not satisfactory, for Rampolla had expressly said to him that it was unbelievable that an *imprimatur* was granted for such a book while Lepidi's letter justified the act. The book could only do harm, said Keane, and its approval constituted an odious attack on respectable bishops. He continued: "I declare that no bishop in the United States will feel obliged to make any declaration in answer to such a libelous and vile book."[46] On the same day Archbishop Keane informed Rampolla that Lepidi's reply was inadequate and that the bishops, priests, and faithful in the United States would naturally ask him if that official's statement expressed the opinion of the Holy See. He pointed out that it was common knowledge that the master general of the Dominicans was the first and most active supporter of Spain against the United States and expressed himself with bitter hostility against that country. Ten million Catholic Americans would not be happy, therefore, that the judges of their country and of Americanism were the Dominicans, and sixty million of their fellow citizens would think likewise and would ask him if the Dominicans really reflected the sentiments of the Holy See. "Americanism," the archbishop continued, "is merely the sentiments of Catholics in the United States toward their country, a feeling of satisfaction, of gratitude and of devotion to which Archbishop Carroll first gave expression. It is not a system, nor a doctrinal program, nor any kind of propaganda. . . . The definition of Americanism as given in the book of Maignen is an infamy, whereas the one given in the letter of Lepidi is a distorted and unjust one." Keane concluded by stating that the men attacked did not have to give any explanations of Americanism to Lepidi and certainly no one would offer them to Maignen, but they would gladly present them to the Holy Father or to Rampolla.[47] A few days later, in order to demonstrate the lengths to which the adversaries of Americanism were prepared to go, the archbishop sent Rampolla a copy of the *Croix* which stated that Lepidi had studied the matter very carefully and had consulted Vatican officials and that the whole matter had then been laid before the Pope before the *imprimatur* was given. Keane reminded the papal Secretary of State that this was not the explanation given to him and he asked that an official declaration be issued to clarify the matter.[48] At this

[46] Keane to Lepidi, June 13, 1898, cited by Soderini, *op. cit.*

[47] Keane to Rampolla, June 13, 1898, cited by Soderini, *op. cit.*

[48] Keane to Rampolla, June 18, 1898, cited by Soderini, *op. cit.* Cf. Klein, *La Route du petit morvandiau: Souvenirs,* IV, 250–251, for the text of the *Croix* and Klein's answer.

point O'Connell stated that Keane's influence on the subject was exhausted and that his efforts must now be strongly seconded from the United States. He rightly concluded: "I am afraid they are making Archbishop Keane's life bitter."[49]

John Keane and Denis O'Connell were not lacking the sympathy and the support of the Americanists in the United States, for the latter responded to Keane's requests for protests to Rome against the granting of the *imprimatur* for such a book. Gibbons wrote that he could perceive its venom after having only glanced at it and he stated: "I regard the attacks of Protestantism as mild compared with the unprincipled course of these so-called Catholics. Our mission is surely a hard one here. While trying to exhibit the Church in all her beauty, we are assailed by those who would exhibit her in an odious light. But truth will prevail."[50] Archbishop Ireland wrote a nine-page letter to Rampolla in which he showed that in the eyes of Europeans and Americans the granting of the *imprimatur* meant the almost official approval of the Vatican and as a result it was announced, as he said, in American newspapers: "Americanism condemned, Paulists are anathema, Gibbons, Keane, Ireland and their friends are under papal censure." According to Ireland, the lay journals were amazed, and they imagined that a new war was announced, a war between Rome and America. After devoting some space to protesting the devotion of the Paulists to the Church and to answering some of the charges lodged against him, Ireland pointed out that the Maignen book would do great harm. He showed that the word "Americanism" was sacred, a symbol of everything that Americans held dear, and now it was cursed with the *imprimatur* of Rome. As a consequence, he concluded:

> The Americans will say, our institutions are condemned in Rome. Rome is opposed to America. The bishops who work with all their might to show that the Catholic faith is compatible with the civil duties

[49] AASP, O'Connell to Ireland, Rome, June 16, 1898.

[50] ADR, Gibbons to O'Connell, Baltimore, June 16, 1898. It seems that the cardinal delayed some time before sending the protest, for his letter to Rampolla is dated August 27. The original, in Magnien's hand, praises the work of the Paulists and deprecates the use of the word "Americanism" in an odious sense against American prelates. The letter is chiefly devoted to a protest against Lepidi's granting the *imprimatur* because it seemed to indicate that the Holy See was in sympathy with the contents (BCA, 96-M-6, [French] and APF, in English). On the last day of July Gibbons had inquired of Elliott whether the Paulists had taken any steps to prevent placing the *Life* on the Index and whether they had instituted any action against Maignen's book (APF, John S. Foley to Elliott, Southhampton, New Jersey, July 31, 1898).

> of a citizen are put under censure: the Church and America cannot, therefore, live in harmony. America will soon decide the fate of 12 million Catholics in the old Spanish colonies. The time is badly chosen. We are accused of wishing to invade Rome and conquer with our ideas the government of the Church. What dreams of crazy brains! The bishops who are attacked have only one system — that of the Holy See; hence only one kind of ideas — that of the Holy See. They obey the least word that comes from Rome. In what case have we not followed the wish of the Pope?[51]

Among the American newspapers, the Baltimore *Sun* deplored the attacks on Americanism and claimed that the chief object of Maignen's malevolence was Archbishop Keane. This journal published the archbishop's denial of any connection with the article on liberal Catholicism which had appeared in the *London Contemporary Review* for December, 1897, signed "Romanus," which, according to Maignen, expressed Keane's ideas.[52] The New York *Sun,* on the other hand, merely commented that nothing had created such a sensation in Catholic circles in two continents in many years as the appearance of Maignen's book in which the "honesty of the Catholicity" of the Paulists, Gibbons, Keane, Ireland, and O'Connell was questioned.[53]

It was in Rome, however, that the chief work was being done. By the middle of June Keane believed that he had convinced his ecclesiastical superiors that it would be folly to pursue the war on Americanism.[54] When he left the Eternal City at the end of June for his annual vacation, in his customary optimism he felt confident of the future. To Elliott he gave the information and assurance that although their enemies had arranged a program of aggression which included the determination to place Hecker's life on the Index of Prohibited Books, their guns had been spiked, and the Paulists were free from danger. He warned the Paulists, however, that they might be subjected to further attacks, and that eternal vigilance, as well as fearlessness and persistence, were needed.[55] Less than a week after Elliott had

[51] Ireland to Rampolla, July 11, 1898, cited by Soderini, *op. cit.*

[52] Baltimore *Sun,* June 20, 1898.

[53] New York *Sun,* July 11, 1898. On July 1, the *Catholic Times and Catholic Opinion* reported an article written by Klein in the *Correspondent* of June 25 defending Ireland and Keane against Maignen's attacks.

[54] AASP, Keane to Ireland, Rome, June 19, 1898.

[55] APF, Keane to Elliott, Paris, July 4, 1898. To Alfred Vicomte de Meaux Keane wrote: "The outburst of hostility against what is termed 'Americanism,' is quite phenomenal. It is made up of misunderstandings and calumnies, it is persistent, unrelenting in its campaign of violence and injustice; it can hardly fail to do much

received such heartening news, O'Connell warned all interested parties that all negotiations had failed and that there seemed to be danger ahead. In a long letter to Keane he revealed the reasons for this alarming statement of conditions. After the archbishop had left Rome, the monsignor had discussed with Lepidi the meaning of Americanism, and he had offered to publish a new edition of the life of Hecker which would be satisfactory to the Master of the Sacred Palace. Lepidi was pleased with O'Connell's conciliatory spirit, and he seemed to favor the idea of the new edition as a means of promoting peace, but he said that he would require a few days to reflect and "to consult upstairs." When O'Connell saw him a few days later, he was told that the Pope had reserved the matter to himself, that replies would be written to Gibbons and Ireland, and that a new edition of Maignen would be prepared. O'Connell then said to him: "You will have war, I foresee it. Nothing could be more fair than my offer and hearing is given to secret whispers and none of the honest men implicated is interrogated." In subsequent conversations, the Dominican said that further information which was very damaging to the Americanists had been received from a reliable person in high position in America, whom O'Connell identified as Sebastian Messmer, Bishop of Green Bay. According to this informant, Lepidi stated, "there was Americanism all over America. Hecker founded a Congregation for the diffusion of his ideas. That Congregation started a Review to help them do the work and Keane is one of the contributors. Between the Paulists and the Chiefs in France there is regular communication. The movement is all one and its object is to make a new phase of religion." The monsignor claimed that he had evidence to show that a committee was studying the life of Hecker "in *English*" and from that he inferred that the committee included Mazzella, Brandi, and Satolli, men who knew English. Moreover, it was his decided impression, as he said, "that widespread and numerous forces have labored, with a spirit of madness, to prove that Monsignor Keane is infected with what they call 'Heckerism.'" In conclusion he informed Keane that they were preparing an English translation of Maignen in Rome.[56]

---

harm, for it is listened to, but, 'magna est veritas, et praevalebit'" (Archives du Château d'Ecotay, Keane to Vicomte de Meaux, Calvados, July 15, 1898, copy through the kindness of Father McAvoy).

[56] AASP, O'Connell to Keane, Rome, July 12, 1898. In a postscript O'Connell added: "Messmer had audience with the Pope June 27. The Benedictine priest that accompanied him begged not to hurry or curtail the conversation 'as his Lordship had matters of great importance to treat with the Pope.' He gave the information and

Keane rushed O'Connell's letter to Archbishop Ireland with one of his own in which he pleaded his helplessness in the face of conditions in Rome. He would hasten back there to fight, he said, but he knew it would be useless for he would be kept from seeing the Holy Father, and he had learned from recent experience that it would be of little value to put papers in Rampolla's hands. Therefore, he told Ireland:

> You are the only man who now can speak so as to be heard and heeded. How I wish that you would just run to Rome, talk and act as you alone can, crush the vipers and avert the danger! Soon, very soon, it may be all too late. Once they get the Pope to act and sign, the harm is done irretrievably. . . . For the moment, the all-important thing is to avert the critical and awful danger; and I cannot see any other way to do it.[57]

O'Connell, too, was at his wit's end. Doubts cast on Rampolla's veracity concerning the conditions surrounding the granting of the *imprimatur,* the unsuccessful negotiations with Lepidi, the ammunition against the Americanists which came from certain bishops in the United States, the books and the articles published in Europe against them, and the fear of the Catholic press to publish anything on the American side of the question — all contributed to the monsignor's distress of mind. "It is impossible to say what may come out," he told Ireland. "Now I feel for the first time what fury rages in Theological controversies, especially when pent-up rage for ten years is let loose on it." Then, after disagreeing with Keane as to the advisability of Ireland's hastening to Rome because, as he pessimistically stated, "you might arrive late, and besides their mind is made up," he concluded: "I am

---

increased the existing bitterness." To Ireland O'Connell wrote: "He [Messmer] also said in Suisse that he left the University on account of his dislike for liberalism, that his friend Schroeder likewise; that it was all nonsense to say that it was a racial fight; it was a fight for religion" (AASP, O'Connell to Ireland, Rome, July 20, 1898). Furthermore, Corrigan had written Lepidi a letter of approval and congratulations after the *imprimatur* had been granted (APF, Ireland to Deshon, Rome, February 24, 1899). Then too, the Bishop of Grand Rapids had said to Corrigan in April, 1898: "I hope that God will spare you long to continue as a bulwark against the spirit of false liberalism which threatens us in the United States. Popularity bought at the sacrifice of principle is a sham. Your example as the head of the largest diocese in the U. S. exerts a great influence over the whole country. I wish the Holy Father would give you a seat in the senate of the Church to increase your influence and reward your labors" (AANY, Henry J. Richter to Corrigan, Grand Rapids, Michigan, Apr. 27, 1898).

[57] AASP, Keane to Ireland, France, July 16, [1898].

tired and exhausted. Can't you do something?"[58] O'Connell must have sent a telegram to Keane at this time to apprise him of the fact that Rome was distinguishing between American and European Americanism, and that the latter only was worthy of condemnation, for, in relaying the information, the archbishop grasped it as evidence which should give them hope. But, as he told Ireland, even though they must keep out of the public arena, there was a greater and greater need of, what he termed, "strong action" in the Vatican, and he was convinced that Ireland could do the most effective work there. In fact, as he said, "in the present emergency, you alone have entree and power."[59]

Despite the conviction that he could do nothing more for the cause in Rome, because, as he told Rampolla, "past experiences do not permit me to have any hope of remedial action," Keane wrote to the papal Secretary of State once more on July 25 to invite his attention to a bibliography of anti-Americanist publications in the *Voce della Verità* to show the extremes to which the opponents of the Americanists had gone. "Finally," he said, "one has gone as far as to accuse us of wanting to give the heretics a new Church, one deprived of all the characteristics of true religion, and such calumnious assertion is published under the approval of the Vatican! It appears as if there was a desire to provoke some desperate step," he continued. "It will be a futile one, but it must be feared that this systematic campaign of falsehood and of hatred will bring no good to the Church."[60]

By this time Archbishop Ireland had been sufficiently bestirred to write Rampolla, as he put it, "two terrible letters," and he assured Father Elliott that since they must conduct a vigorous campaign he was "a veteran, ever ready for re-enlistment."[61] Shortly thereafter he

[58] AASP, O'Connell to Ireland, Rome, July 20, 1898. Concerning the granting of the *imprimatur* O'Connell said to Keane: "On certain authority I hear the Pope compelled him to give the *imprimatur* in the first instance" (AASP, Rome, July 12, 1898). On the same subject Brandi stated: "As to the story which Archbishop Keane is now repeating in the U. S., it may be that Cardinal Rampolla using a diplomatic language told his Grace, that he [Rampolla] and the Holy Father knew nothing of the *Imprimatur* given by Fr. Lepidi to Abbé Maignen's book; but it is a fact that the Holy Father knew everything about it, and that the *Imprimatur* was given with the *express* consent of His Holiness. On this point there is no doubt whatever" (APF, Brandi to Corrigan, Rome, Sept. 3, 1898 [photostat]).

[59] AASP, Keane to Ireland, France, July 20, 1898.

[60] Keane to Rampolla, July 25, 1898, cited by Soderini, *op. cit.*

[61] APF, Ireland to Elliott, St. Paul, July 30, 1898. He also stated: "The Pope is sick and weak and Brandi and Company think their opportunity has come." O'Connell reported that Ireland had sent Rampolla nine pages of "fiery protest" (APF, Klein Papers, O'Connell to Klein, Freiburg im Breisgau, Aug. 21, 1898).

received a communication from Cardinal Rampolla in which he was urged to be calm and patient and to ignore the controversy. The papal Secretary of State assured him that Leo XIII would pass judgment on the question in due time.[62]

While Rampolla was advising Ireland to retain his composure, the adversaries of the Americanists continued the work which had given rise to the controversy. The English translation of Maignen's work appeared with the new *imprimatur* given in Rome[63] and with a commendatory letter to its author from Francesco Cardinal Satolli, dated August 4, 1898, in which Satolli stated, among other things: "Your reverence may rest assured of having done a work exceedingly useful and commendable. Whoever may be touched by its pages, instead of being offended, should rather acknowledge that unconsciously he has erred, and duly regretting it, profit by the information received."[64] In his reply to the papal Secretary of State, therefore, Ireland spoke of the Satolli letter and other recent manifestations of the unfriendliness of some Europeans to Americanism, but he gave assurances that he would acquiesce in the wishes of Rampolla to remain calm.[65] Nonetheless, by this time the Archbishop of St. Paul had determined to go to Rome.[66]

Lest Ireland should become complacent after reading reports that the Americanists were winning the fight, O'Connell kept prodding him with information which would sting him into action. He pointed out that the publication of Maignen's book in English with the *imprimatur* of Rome, in the face of all the protests from American prelates, was an audacious step by which their enemies desired to discredit all the leading Catholics in the United States. "It is the crisis," the monsignor stated, "and there [in America] the decisive battle of the war must

[62] Rampolla to Ireland, Aug. 6, 1898, cited by Soderini, *op. cit.* 287.

[63] Charles Maignen, *Studies in Americanism — Father Hecker, Is He a Saint?* (Rome, 1898). Keane was attacked on pp. 322 ff. and 222–245.

[64] Washington *Post,* June 5, 1899. Also cf., William H. Thorne, "Fact and Fiction in Recent Prose," *Globe,* IX (Sept., 1899), 260. The English translation contained commendatory letters from the Cardinal Archbishop of Rennes, and the Bishops of Annecy and Mende (Maignen, *Studies in Americanism,* pp. vii–x). Benziger Brothers were requested by Maignen to take the American agency for the English edition, but they honored Father Elliott's plea that they refuse the overture. In reporting this, Thorne remarked: "Of course Keane or the Paulists made this money making crew of saintly publishers believe that the Pope was against the book, that Ireland was with the Paulists, that Ireland, in fact, was just next to the Almighty if not His tutor" (William H. Thorne, "The Benziger Boycott," *Globe,* IX [June, 1899], 227–231).

[65] Ireland to Rampolla, cited by Soderini, *op. cit.*

[66] AASP, O'Connell to Ireland, Freiburg im Breisgau, Aug. 28, 1898.

be fought—the Waterloo." He further claimed that he had heard that Hecker's Life had been put on the Index, and that Roman officials were merely waiting for an opportune time for publishing the sentence. In view of these facts he urged the Archbishop of St. Paul to rally his forces for "one supreme decisive effort," namely, to bring about a united protest from the archbishops of the United States against the granting of an *imprimatur* to Maignen's book.[67]

It would be gratuitous to assume that Ireland was in any way responsible for the long memorial signed by George Deshon, superior of the Paulists, deprecating the attacks on American prelates and the Paulists, which Archbishop Corrigan read at the annual meeting of the archbishops of the United States in October, 1898.[68] Moreover, the attitude which the Archbishop of New York would assume on the subject had been foreshadowed in the fact that he had been told shortly before the meeting by Bishop Bernard J. McQuaid of Rochester, his constant episcopal adviser: "We have nothing to do about the Paulists. They are your diocesans, and, if they are teaching heresies, it is your business to reprove them. If they are not, there is nothing to be done.

[67] AASP, O'Connell to Ireland, Freiburg im Breisgau, Sept. 27, 1898. At this time John A. Zahm, C.S.C., who had left Rome only a short time before and who was now the provincial of the Congregation of the Holy Cross, received notice from Rome that his book *Evolution and Dogma* had been placed on the Index of Prohibited Books. Keane advised him that he must "stoop to conquer" (AUND, Zahm Papers, Keane to Zahm, Washington, Sept. 28, 1898; ADR, Keane to O'Connell, Washington, Oct. 7, 1898). Serafino Cardinal Vannutelli asked the Pope to prevent the publication of the sentence and the Holy Father granted the request (AAB, 96-S-8, Keane to Gibbons, Rome, Nov. 9, 1898). However, Zahm was worried about continual reports in the papers that the book would be condemned. Besides, as he told Ireland, "Corrigan announced publicly to his seminarians some days ago, after some literary exercise, in which 'Evolution and Dogma' had been quoted and commended, that the work would soon be condemned." So, he urged the Archbishop of St. Paul to work to have the decree suppressed forever for the sake of the cause (ADR, Zahm to Ireland, Notre Dame, Mar. 31, 1899). In this they failed also. The *Church News* (July 9, 1899) published Zahm's letter to Alfonso Maria Golea (Notre Dame, May 16, 1899), one of the translators of the book, in which he informed his friend that the Holy See was adverse to further distribution of the volume and, therefore, he should use his influence to have it withdrawn from sale. Golea's public announcement asking his true friends neither to read nor to give further publicity to the work was also published. O'Connell considered the condemnation of Zahm's book as another example of some ecclesiastics in Rome, as he put it, "working like demoniacs against the Americans" (AUND, Zahm Papers, O'Connell to Zahm, Rome, Apr. 12, 1899). Also cf. Thomas F. O'Connor, "John A. Zahm, C.S.C.: Scientist and Americanist," *The Americas,* VII (Apr., 1951), 440–455. On September 1, 1898, Father George Zurcher's pamphlet, *Monks and Their Decline* (1898), was placed on the Index. This priest of the Diocese of Buffalo was a temperance fanatic and a supporter of the Americanists. Cf. McAvoy, *op. cit.,* p. 152 n; Bland, *op. cit.,* pp. 211–212.

[68] Cf. Holden, *op. cit.,* pp. 165–168, for the complete text of the memorial.

They should not be made scapegoats to cover up Ireland, Keane, and Company."[69] Likewise Corrigan's attitude was known from the statement he made to Elliott during the controversy when he said: "The main trouble with your *Life of Father Hecker* at Rome is due to your connection with Archbishop Ireland and Bishop Keane, who are in great disfavor there. If you will repudiate them all will go well."[70] Besides, it will be remembered that the Archbishop of New York congratulated Lepidi for giving the *imprimatur* to Maignen's book. Hence, it was not at all surprising to find Keane communicating the following impression of Gibbons' report on the meeting: "Archbishop Corrigan presented with much trepidation and depreciation a protest from the Paulists. He argued that they had better keep out of the controversy, so did Feehan, so did Ryan, so did Katzer, *so did Williams*. And so it was dropped, just as he anticipated. No strong voice there for truth and justice."[71]

Not even Ireland's voice was heard; he was not there. After the meeting he wrote to Elliott in a manner which must have disgusted the Paulist who was being so sorely tried because of conditions that could be partly traced to Ireland:

> I regretted very much that I was not to be there — as I was anxious to break a lance against all comers in defense of Heckerism.
>
> You, no doubt, have heard how your cause was treated at the meeting. The Archbishop of New York timidly and as acting under protest, offered a paper from the Paulists — and added at once his own opinion, which was that the hierarchy of America should lie low in this war. No voice bellowed out in the name of justice — and all was over.
>
> It is as well: I like to fight — and to conquer with few allies. You owe nothing, or but little, when the victory is won.
>
> We are going to win — The last letter I have from Cardinal Rampolla, written on the field itself — in the Vatican, is most encouraging. Besides I shall soon invade Africa and either Lepidi or Ireland will go into winter quarters.[72]

Elliott, however, entertained the most charitable interpretation of the results of the meeting. He believed, as he said, that "*all* are against Maignen," and that they did not take any action because Gibbons had received some reassuring counsel from Rome. He then added:

[69] McQuaid to Corrigan, Aug. 30, 1898, cited by Zwierlein, *op. cit.*, III, 246.
[70] Cited by Holden, *op. cit.*, p. 168.
[71] AASP, Keane to Ireland, Washington, Oct. 18, 1898.
[72] APF, Ireland to Elliott, St. Paul, Nov. 6, 1898.

"America is mute with the exception of the Review, edited by Preuss. We are glad that the Jesuits of America have been silent. The American Jesuits are very strong. They are fine men, full of peace and good will. Their leading men are among our warmest friends."[73]

Whether or not Gibbons received information from Rome early enough to render united episcopal action in the United States unnecessary and unwise or whether the cardinal did not press the issue because he feared lack of unanimity is not clear. It is certain, however, that during October the Archbishop of Baltimore was apprised of the fact that the Pope had reserved the entire problem to himself, for when Archbishop Keane returned to his post in Rome during the first week of November, he immediately visited Rampolla who, as Keane informed Gibbons, "renewed the assurances of his letter to you — that the Holy Father, having now taken the whole matter into his own hands, would be sure to act in a way not hurtful to us, — that his sentiments of affection and confidence were in no way altered, etc." The Archbishop claimed that he had been told by Serafino Vannutelli that during an audience the Holy Father had said to him: "They (without saying *who*) have been urging me to be severe with the Americans: but I am convinced that gentle measures will do more good." Keane further averred that this fortunate change in the Roman climate had been brought about by the protests which had rained upon Leo XIII, especially by the one which had emanated from the Archbishop of Baltimore.[74] As a result, the archbishop continued, the matter had been withdrawn from those who were rejoicing in having it all their

[73] APF, Klein Papers, Elliott to Klein, New York, Oct. 20, 1898. After the meeting, O'Connell asserted that no effort was made to have a collective protest of the archbishops because there were, as he put it, "fears about unanimity" (APF, Klein Papers, O'Connell to Klein, Rome, Oct. 31, 1898). On the same day O'Connell said to Zahm: "At present you can't get anybody in Rome to open his mouth about Americanism. Something most ominous. Everything is absolute uncertainty, only the Jesuits see their way" (AUND, Zahm Papers, O'Connell to Zahm, Rome, Oct. 31, 1898).

[74] On this subject O'Connell had said: "You may know by this time that during vacation everything was prepared for the condemnation of Hecker and the decree was placed before the Holy Father on his table for his signature. Just at that time however a letter came from Cardinal Gibbons that 'shook him.' When they pressed him to sign he replied 'No, I can do no more against those Americanists. Moreover I reserve now the entire affair to myself and I permit no more examination of books or anything else. I will arrange all myself with an encyclical" (APF, O'Connell to Elliott, Paris, Dec. 10, 1898). After a conversation with Corrigan, Deshon related that the archbishop had said that a commission of ten cardinals had examined the English edition carefully and, as he put it, "what a fist they made of it." Deshon concluded, "I console myself much with the reflection that neither we nor Fr. Hecker have been responsible for this thing" (APF, Deshon to Elliott, New York, Feb. 26, 1891).

own way, and the Pope had appointed a special commission to study the question and report to him directly. He added: "this is considered in Rome as a defeat of the extremists who have been hounding us." Furthermore, Keane had learned from Cardinal Serafino, who had been told by the Pope, that the encyclical which was being prepared on the question would treat of Church and State, individualism, and the vows. "As to each," he said, "only the familiar warning not to represent the contingently useful as the *ideal.*" So he concluded with seeming satisfaction that they could hope that there would be no danger ahead.[75]

Meanwhile, Archbishop Ireland stated that he believed the veracity of an Associated Press cablegram which made public the fact that the Sovereign Pontiff had ordered silence on American questions. "I do not see what else the Pope could have done," he stated, "if letters from Cardinal Gibbons and myself have weight any longer."[76] A few days later, he related to the same correspondent Monsignor Boeglin's assurance that "the present tempest has blown over," and his counsel of moderation on the part of all the friends of Americanism. Furthermore, Boeglin had insisted that Ireland should hurry to Europe so as to enforce the discipline. For that reason the Archbishop of St. Paul was working hard to be in Rome around Christmas time if possible.[77]

While Ireland was making final preparations to invade Europe, Klein was being informed that victory was near, but, as O'Connell put it, "our enemies are wild and are watching some act of imprudence of ours to destroy it."[78] A few weeks later the abbé received assurances from his Roman correspondent that neither Hecker's life nor the

[75] AAB, 96-S-8, Keane to Gibbons, Rome, Nov. 9, 1898. During the month of October O'Connell had been cautioned by Zahm, whom Keane had so advised, "to keep quiet and not to fight Lepidi" (APF, Klein Papers, O'Connell to Klein, Rome, Oct. 15, 1898), and on the last day of the month the monsignor informed Klein that Gibbons had received notice that the Pontiff would send a letter on Hecker (APF, Klein Papers, O'Connell to Klein, Rome, Oct. 31, 1898). Concerning Keane, O'Connell said at this time: "He is opening his eyes to facts about him and says he sees he is 'to count for nothing in Rome' and that 'they want to stop his preaching.' But I think he will keep out of trouble" (AUND, Zahm Papers, O'Connell to Zahm, Rome, Nov. 10, 1898).

[76] ACUA, Bouquillon Papers, Ireland to Magnien, St. Paul, Nov. 6, 1898.

[77] ACUA, Bouquillon Papers, Ireland to Magnien, St. Paul, Nov. 8, 1898.

[78] APF, Klein Papers, O'Connell to Klein, Rome, Nov. 8, 1898. According to O'Connell, Serafino Cardinal Vannutelli "had one day informed Rampolla that he had just come from the Pope and that His Holiness has said he intended publishing a letter favorable to the Americans and tranquillizing to them. Whereupon Rampolla drew himself up and looking at Vannutelli with surprise said, 'But Eminence, have you read Maignen's book?' When Vannutelli replied negatively, Rampolla said 'you must read it, for it is most important'" (AASP, O'Connell to Ireland, Rome, Feb. 28, 1900).

preface would be condemned, much less examined, and that the encyclical under preparation, which he presumed to outline, would not represent all that they would wish but it would certainly fall short of what their enemies desired and expected. He concluded:

> Defeat has added a bitterness to anger, and all are recognizing that everything indicates that eventually and inevitably, things will move that way [towards Americanism]. We are trying to have a look at that papal letter and a suggestion, if need be, before it appears.[79] A cruel thrust made at Mgr. Keane, we have been able to defeat and turn it with most favorable circumstances, upon its authors.[80]

During the time that the Americanists were speculating on the contents of the expected papal letter, they utilized every opportunity to acquaint the Holy See with the consequences of ill-considered action. Rampolla was given a note which Ferdinand Brunetière had sent to Keane in which the influential editor of the *Revue des Deux Mondes* had said: "Any measure of severity taken in Rome now against Hecker

[79] O'Connell had written the following to Magnien at this time: "I desired Abp. Keane to see the encyclical before its publication and I got a friend to suggest it to the Pope. He said: 'I wished to do something acceptable for these Americans, but when I had the letter almost finished I asked myself what the Spaniards would say if I were to publish favorable things about their conquerors in this moment. No, then now, I will not publish it at all.' My friend suggested: 'Publish something nice without any reference to politics.' 'No, now I rather not publish anything at all' " (Archives du Château d'Ecotay, Magnien to Vicomte de Meaux, Baltimore, Jan. 3, 1899 [French with quotation from O'Connell's letter in English]). O'Connell had given the same information to Klein. Cf. Klein, *Americanism: A Phantom Heresy,* p. 205.

[80] APF, Klein Papers, O'Connell to Klein, Rome, Dec. 1, 1898. Shortly before this, Father David Fleming, O.F.M., whom the Americanists in Rome had looked upon as their friend and supporter up to this time, wrote to Abbé Klein: "I have read your preface carefully. I think that you should suppress it entirely if you wish to avoid disastrous misunderstanding. In spite of my good will, I cannot conscientiously approve it. I believe that you will endanger the whole situation in your dear country. The alliance, or rather the basis, that you are looking for is not to be found in Heckerism. I am afraid that the result will be the same as the attempt made long ago by Lamennais to transplant into France the ideas and the methods which the great O'Connell had adopted so successfully in Ireland. In the present case, on the contrary, Heckerism has not been a success in the United States. A little clique has taken hold of his name. Mgr. O'Connell, ex-rector of the American College, like many another, trifles with it. Mgr. Ireland has hardly any authority even in America . . . Mgr. Keane does not shine as a theologian, and the Paulists themselves have given up the ideas of Fr. Hecker. Therefore, I see nothing but disaster if you pursue the exact ideas you receive by following the will-of-the-wisp of Heckerism. You will end up like Schell in Germany and others elsewhere. The Holy See may keep silent for a time but not forever" (APF, Klein Papers, Fleming to Klein, Rome, Nov. 16, 1898 [French]). Fr. Fleming, who was at one time on the side of the liberals, changed his views and became as O'Connell put it, "a most hurtful enemy" (AUND, Zahm Papers, O'Connell to Zahm, Rome, Apr. 12, 1899).

or Americanism will be considered in France as an evidence of the consolidarity of Catholicism and Jesuitism." And the papal Secretary of State was told by Wilfrid Ward in the name of the Duke of Norfolk, the English Catholic leader: "severe measures against Hecker or Americanism would hurt Catholicity in England."[81] Then, in the last week of January,[82] the chief of the United States Americanists stormed into the Eternal City to do battle with all their opponents. First of all, according to Archbishop Keane, Ireland saw Cardinal Rampolla and was informed that the encyclical had not been sent out yet, but between that interview and Ireland's audience with the Holy Father three or four days later, it was dispatched to Gibbons.[83] As soon as the American progressives found out that the letter had been mailed they strove to prevent its publication. For that purpose Gibbons cabled Rampolla on February 7, but the Secretary of State answered two days later that publication could not be long delayed as some copies had been sent to American bishops and, moreover, the dissensions in France had to be ended. Furthermore, he was sure that Gibbons would be satisfied with it.[84]

For the same end Keane and Ireland labored in Rome, but in vain. The Archbishop of St. Paul explained their defeat by saying: "The

[81] APF, O'Connell to Elliott, Paris, Dec. 10, 1898.

[82] ACUA, Garrigan Papers, Keane to Garrigan, Rome, Feb. 2, 1899. A few days after Ireland arrived in Rome he wrote to Countess Sabina di Tarravicino di Revel in Milan, asking her to translate a volume of Satolli's discourses published in America under the title *Loyalty to Church and State*. He stated that "Satolli was when in America the most Americanist of all of us," so he wished to "show to Rome what he once was." Besides, he believed that the translation of those discourses "will be a most valuable aid in our Roman campaign for Americanism." Since Satolli, as he said, "will not like to see himself confronted in Italy by his own words spoken in America; he will likely be quite angry," she was to engage a printer "whom you can trust, or, at least one whom you would approach through a reliable intermediary," so Ireland's part in the work would not be known. When the translation was completed, Ireland urged her to publish it as soon as possible, he would stand all the expenses. "I believe," he said, "the translation will be a 'coup' for our arch-enemy." Cf. La Contessa Sabina di Tarravicino di Revel Papers on microfilm in AUND, Ireland to Sabina, Rome, Jan. 31, Feb. 6, and Mar. 12, 1899.

[83] ACUA, Bouquillon Papers, Keane to Magnien, Rome, Feb. 11, 1899. A copy of the encyclical was sent to Gibbons on January 31 and 100 copies were sent to the delegate (Rampolla to Gibbons, Jan. 31, 1899, cited by Soderini, *op. cit.*). Rampolla told Ireland that after the letter had been signed and printed, he had it softened in the beginning and in the end in deference to Ireland's words. Therefore, Ireland believed that a second printed edition was made (APF, Ireland to Deshon, Rome, Feb. 24, 1899). However, Ireland arrived in Rome on January 26 and the encyclical was dated January 22, 1899.

[84] Gibbons to Rampolla, Feb. 7, 1899, cablegram, and Rampolla to Gibbons, Feb. 9, 1899, cited by Soderini, *op. cit.*

forces against us were enormous — Jesuits, Dominicans and Redemptorists fought for very life, and again and again Archbishop Corrigan's letter to Lepidi was flung in my face."[85] Characteristically, Keane thought mostly of the effect of their defeat upon others when he mused:

> We have the consolation of knowing that we did our full duty. The blow will, I fear, be a sad one for the Paulists and for the memory of Hecker, and a blow to the Cardinal and Ireland who wrote in their behalf. We must simply make the best of it, and carry on our game of explaining away to the American people the administrative blunders of our superiors.[86]

During the time that the encyclical was under consideration and just prior to its publication, Archbishop Keane gave yet another example of the complete selflessness that drew him so close to the hearts of those who knew him intimately. His friends, knowing that his position in Rome was unenviable, offered to use whatever influence they possessed to bring about his appointment to the metropolitan see of Oregon City made vacant by the death of William H. Gross on November 14, 1898. In fact, Cardinal Gibbons wrote to the Prefect of the Congregation of the Propaganda on January 24, 1899, to state that the bishops of that western province had informed him that they would welcome Keane as their metropolitan and that he was simply adding his voice to theirs and including as well a list of the archbishop's qualifications which made him especially suitable for the office.[87] Of course, when Ireland arrived in Rome, the matter was considered, and Keane gave this report on the results of their discussion:

> After a brief informal discussion of pros and cons, I left it to Ireland and O'Connell to think and talk over for a day before we would come to a final decision. O'Connell was very positive that it was wiser not to cut the knot just now, but to wait and see whether circumstances would have so changed, by the time that I would have finished my proposed work for the University, that it would then be well for American interests that I should return to Rome. If not, why Providence would then show what to do. But the main contention was that we had better not relinquish our hold on Rome at present, but wait and see how things would develop. I could see that this was also

[85] APF, Ireland to Deshon, Rome, Feb. 24, 1899. The archbishop also claimed: "All that giant will could do was done by me to prevent the publication. It had been signed, sealed and printed before my arrival. And in what I did I can thank the strong co-operation of Cardinal Gibbons by cablegram."

[86] ACUA, Bouquillon Papers, Keane to Magnien, Rome, Feb. 11, 1899.

[87] AAB, 97-B-9, Gibbons to Ledochowski, Baltimore, Jan. 24, 1899 (French), copy.

> Ireland's conviction, even though personal kindness toward me made him ready to work to have me sent to Oregon if I so desired. Of course I put self out of the question and agreed with them. While I would rather be in the humblest parish in the U. S. than in Rome, still I would not desert a post of duty simply because it was disagreeable.

In further proof of his loyalty to the cause and of his personal friendship for John Ireland, he said: "I would not dare to leave Europe at present, nor as long as Ireland is in Europe; for I believe the attacks and the need of standing on the defensive will last as long as he is over here, and the united counsels and action of us three is indispensable."[88] When Alexander Christie's appointment to Oregon City was announced on February 12, 1899,[89] the matter was settled. The three would continue to work at Rome as one.

During the third week of February, the contents of the papal letter on Americanism, entitled *Testem benevolentiae,* were finally released to the public and to the fearful Americanists. The Sovereign Pontiff pleaded his affection for the people and the Church of the United States as the principal reason for pointing out erroneous opinions arising from the preface of the French translation of Hecker's life which should be avoided or corrected. If by Americanism one meant that the Church should adapt herself to the age and relax her laws as well as her traditions and minimize or completely forget certain points of doctrine, it was to be rejected. To be repudiated, too, were the corollaries of such a false doctrine; namely, that individual spiritual direction was not as necessary in these times because the Holy Ghost is now more lavish in His gifts; that the natural virtues are to be held in higher regard than the supernatural; that the virtues are to be divided into the active and the passive and that the former are to be practiced because they are more suitable to the age; that the vows taken by religious restrict the liberty of the individual and they are of little value for the welfare of society and for Christian perfection; and, finally, that established methods for bringing the truths of reli-

[88] ACUA, Bouquillon Papers, Keane to Magnien, Rome, Feb. 11, 1899. At the same time there were rumors that Keane had been appointed as apostolic delegate to the Philippines (*Church News,* Jan. 14, 1899; LCLD, clipping with Jan. 31, 1899 dateline). On February 4, 1899, shortly after Ireland entered the Eternal City, the first issue of the *True American Catholic* appeared in Rome. By its vicious articles against Ireland and Keane it proved that its only purpose was to discredit these ecclesiastics.

[89] Reily, *op. cit.,* V, 495. Satolli had stated that Keane would not be appointed to the Philippines or Oregon City (AANO, Orban to Chapelle, Issy, Feb. 7, 1899).

gion to those outside the fold should be rejected in favor of entirely new and untried ways. On the other hand, if by "Americanism" one understood the national traits which were exceedingly honorable, as well as the laws, customs, and conditions prevailing in the republic, Leo saw no reason for questioning the term in that sense.[90] Just before the encyclical appeared, Rampolla had told Ireland to do his best to spread the view, as he said, "that the words of the letter allow us to say that the things condemned were never said or written in America, not even by Hecker, but were set afloat in France — as 'Americanism' at the occasion of the Life, and especially of its translation, and of interpretation given in foreign languages."[91] So, it was on this note that the two American prelates in Rome penned their adhesion. Ireland's letter, in which he accepted the encyclical and swore against all the opinions condemned in it on the grounds that they were foreign to the United States and that it was an insult to his country to cover such extravagances with the name "Americanism," was published in the *Osservatore Romano* on February 25, 1899.[92] Archbishop Keane, writing at the same time, said:

As for myself, I declare that I accept and admit completely and

[90] For a translation of the letter, cf. *Catholic World,* LXIX (Apr., 1899), 133–141. The letter was, as Magnien said, "purposely exclusively given to the Baltimore Sun" (APF, Magnien to Ireland, Baltimore, Mar. 9, 1899). When the Boston *Review* reprinted the document from that source (Mar. 4, 1899) it stated: "We presume it authentic." For a summary of the letter, cf. Condé B. Pallen, *"Testem benevolentiae," Catholic Encyclopedia,* XIV, 537–538. For an excellent commentary on the apostolic letter, cf. Joseph Clifford Fenton, "The Teaching of the Testem Benevolentiae," *American Ecclesiastical Review,* CXXIX (Aug., 1953), 124–133.

[91] APF, Ireland to Deshon, Rome, Feb. 24, 1899.

[92] *Ibid.* Ireland summarized the contents of his letter for this correspondent and said: "Fanatics conjured up an 'Americanism,' and put such before the Pope. Lepidi and Mazzela [*sic*] wrote the body of the letter. I cannot pray that God forgive them." After Ireland's adhesion appeared, Zahm stated: "The effect of your Osservatore letter was simply immense. It completely nullified the well-laid plans of the enemy — made their work ridiculous. It was a veritable coup on your part and coming immediately after the Pope's letter was specially effective. Nothing could have been more timely or more telling in its results. It was the *mot d'ordre* for your friends in this country and all considered it as such. The enemy at once felt that the wind had been taken out of their sails and that you had pitted them against a man of straw. What can they do now? The Pope has spoken and he will not take up the question again. Americanism, thanks to your letter, remains untouched, and we can now go on more bravely than ever before. Nobody in this country is interested in the vagaries of Hecker and Heckerism will not be more than a nine-day wonder at most. To me the future is more promising than ever. The enemy has done its best to crush progress and has failed most signally. A German editor declared a short time ago that 'Ireland had already been condemned three times, but, the trouble is, he won't stay condemned!' " (ADR, Zahm to Ireland, Notre Dame, Mar. 31, 1899).

unreservedly everything that Your Holiness sets forth in this letter. I declare that I repudiate and condemn everything therein condemned by Your Holiness, and I declare to Your Holiness, calling God to witness, that I have never in my life taught or maintained any part of what is therein reproved by Your Holiness.[93]

On February 28, Klein also wrote a note of adhesion, and at the same time announced that the French edition of Hecker's life had been withdrawn from the market.[94]

The reaction to the document itself and the letters submitted to Rome concerning it took many forms in the United States. Gibbons was pleased with the tone of Ireland's reply, but anent the letter itself he said: "It is very discouraging to us that the American Church is not understood abroad, and that its enemies are listened to, and that they can lie with impunity. I do not think any of the questions discussed was a living question here. But I suppose the Holy Father had to act."[95] In his letter to the Holy See on the matter, therefore, the cardinal wrote that no American bishop, priest, or layman was guilty of advocating or holding the doctrines which the Holy Father had condemned.[96]

Frederick Z. Rooker, an ardent supporter of the Americanists and secretary of the apostolic delegate, made this analysis of the document:

It strikes at no objective reality. Being such, it is clear, as in all such cases, that it is a veiled attack on persons deliberately done for purposes of personal spite. It does show to what a complete extent the Vatican is under the influence which hates America and everything American. The allusions are all perfectly clear, and Mgr. Ireland and

[93] San Francisco *Argonaut*, Apr. 17, 1899. For a little different translation, cf. Zwierlein, *op. cit.*, III, 249. The present writer was unable to find a copy of Keane's letter to the Pope and the original letter has never been published by the Vatican. In the Boston *Journal* (Mar. 5, 1899) it was stated: "Not even the news that Archbishop Keane, the American representative at the Vatican, has sent a letter to the Pope wholly accepting the Pontiff's declarations on 'Americanism' need cause the least suspicion that the so-called American party in the Roman Catholic Church has surrendered its position. It merely accepts the Pope's views on the writings of Father Hecker and the evangelical methods of the Paulists, which views cannot be construed as antagonistic to the work done and approved by the liberal leaders of the Roman Church in this country."

[94] Klein, *Americanism: A Phantom Heresy,* p. 230. In a recent publication Klein asserted that he would not have withdrawn the book from the market if he had known the tone of the replies of Ireland and Keane. *La route du petit morvandiau.* Vol. V. *Sans Arret* (Paris, 1949), p. 10.

[95] ADR, Gibbons to O'Connell, Baltimore, Mar. 4, 1899.

[96] For Gibbons' letter to the Holy Father in French, cf. "Notes and Comments," *Catholic Historical Review,* XXX (Oct., 1944), 347–348.

Mgr. Keane are the ones directly and systematically and hypocritically attacked. . . . They did not dare to say what they really meant and make an open fight on Americanism in the only form in which it actually exists, so they picked out a measly little religious organization which has no backers and few numbers, and they poured out the vials of their wrath on those poor unprotected heads.[97]

The Abbé Magnien, who at one time was described by O'Connell as the head and heart of the movement in the United States, complained: "The tone of the letter is really fierce and contrary to custom, there is not even a soothing word for the Paulists. The Pope seems to have forgotten that only a few years ago, he praised their work and their methods."[98]

Bishop Thomas O'Gorman of Sioux Falls, a close friend of Keane and Ireland, made these interesting comments on the subject:

The Pope's letter has fallen flat. No interest. The doctrines treated appeal to nothing in Catholic or protestant mind or heart. The Catholic laity are puzzled to know when where by whom such outlandish doctrines have been taught, they conclude it must be something between priests and monks, something in which they have no stake. Intelligent men wonder at a document basing itself, not on any original source but on a translation and a misinterpretation; wonder too that the Pope did not know what is Americanism and stumbles between two "ifs" — if Americanism is such, anathema, but if it is such, hurrah! It is no use trying to get up a fight on this letter. The press, feeling the Catholic laity take no interest, is indifferent.[99]

Walter Elliott, the brave Paulist whose labor of love had produced unexpected thorns, remarked after the encyclical appeared:

Of course we were all immensely surprised at the contents of the letter. For those who really know our prelates, priests and people, know full well that they are sound and true in all the points touched on by Pope Leo, most of which we never had a discussion about, even privately.

You offer us your sympathy. But I feel sure that our dear friends in France have had a harder time than we.

But God is above all. We have only one purpose — to serve God and to do so in a way that will not meet the disapproval of the rulers of His Church. There are some influential persons and even classes

[97] ADR, Rooker to O'Connell, Washington, Feb. 24, 1899.
[98] ADR, Magnien to O'Connell, Baltimore, Mar. 9, 1899.
[99] ADR, O'Gorman to Ireland, Washington, Mar. 13, (1899).

as we now know, whom we cannot succeed in pleasing. As regards them, why we can still cultivate a friendly feeling, we can and must endeavor to offend them as little as possible, and meantime pray for them. I know not if I have passed a single day for many months without very earnestly praying for the Abbé Maignen, especially during the H. Sacrifice, also for the men who have worked hardest against us in Rome.

But what vast, almost resistless power these men have in the Church in our day. It seems as if God willed that progressive spirits shall be forced to work harder to be *allowed to work* than to overcome the difficulties of the work itself after beginning.[100]

Charles P. Grannan, professor of Scripture in the Catholic University of America and one of the Americanists who had accompanied O'Connell to the Freibourg congress, wrote on the matter in his usual breezy style:

The letter contains no doctrine but what is taught here in the Catechism class, or in the Sunday School. At the same time the letter is harsh, and written in evident anger and provocation. The man who wrote it is a partisan, and wrote in great exasperation and irritation of spirit. But it is weak. It is a "Brutum Fulmen," a "Fulmen sine ictu." I don't know but it will strengthen the so-called Liberal Party. It certainly has called forth a vast amount of sympathy for the Paulists.[101]

Such were the comments of those in sympathy with the Americanism which Keane and Ireland stood for, but their opponents in the United States viewed the encyclical as "admirable"[102] and "oppor-

[100] APF, Klein Papers, Elliott to Louis Marie Olivier Dufresne, Thomaston, Connecticut, Apr. 29, 1899. Keane said to Elliott at this time: "It always does me good to hear from you — a whiff of refreshing earnestness and honesty and zeal coming to one whose sojourn in an atmosphere not made up of those elements is a good deal of a soul crucifixion.

"I agree with the advice which you have determined to follow concerning the apologia of Fr. Hecker and the Paulists. *Theoretically* it ought to be made, so as to make the historical record right. But *practically* your advisers are correct. Divers influences here would be ready to distort and discolor it, as they do all that concerns us, and so it might do more harm than good, and at home I trust it is not needed, and that is the most important consideration. Go ahead bravely then in your noble work for God and souls, and let there be no more explanations or apologies or protestations" (APF, Keane to Elliott, Rome, May 5, 1899).

[101] ADR, Grannan to O'Connell, Washington, [Postmark, Mar. 11, 1899]. Another American stated: "Think of it; Cardinal Gibbons given an *Instruction* only suited to a two cent catechism for children. Great God — are we made of such material that we will longer stand this infamy?" (ADR, Joseph E. Hayden to O'Connell, Castellammare di Stabia, May 10, 1899). Mr. Hayden wrote on European subjects for the *Church News*. Cf. June 11, 1898.

[102] AANY, Winant M. Wigger, Bishop of Newark, to Corrigan, Hamilton, Bermuda, Mar. 14, 1899.

tune."[103] Archbishop Corrigan, in a letter to the Holy See drawn up by Father Philip Cardella, S.J., to which the signature of the bishops of the Province of New York were affixed, avowed that the germs of the errors were stifled in time by this pontifical action, while the Archbishop of Milwaukee and his suffragans told the Roman officials that the errors known and proscribed under the name of Americanism were common among the clergy and the people, and that those who denied the fact were modern Jansenists having recourse to the famous distinction of *jus et factum.*[104]

In the newspapers of both continents much space was devoted to the papal document but their commentary on the question for the most part was favorable to the Americanists.[105] The *Civiltà Cattolica*

[103] AANY, Frederick X. Katzer, Archbishop of Milwaukee, to Corrigan, Milwaukee, May 1, 1899.

[104] APF, Klein Papers, O'Gorman to Klein, Sioux Falls, Mar. 7, 1900 (French). This document would appear to be a summary of the reception of the encyclical in the United States for Klein's use in the newspapers. O'Gorman says that of the fourteen American archbishops, three kept silence, namely, Chicago, Dubuque, and Santa Fe; four acknowledged receipt of the letter, but made no allusion to the question of fact, neither admitting nor denying that the errors existed in their flocks, namely, Cincinnati, New Orleans, Portland, and Philadelphia, the last said one would have difficulty finding them. Then, as we will see, four denied the existence of the errors among them, and two recognized explicitly that the Church in the United States was tainted. The Bishop of Sioux Falls also claimed that two of Corrigan's suffragans, whose names were affixed to the letter that emanated from that province, were not familiar with the contents of the letter and had refused to sign without such knowledge. Zwierlein states that the explicit approval of the suffragans was given, and he reproduces the letter that was sent to Leo XIII. Cf. *Letters of Archbishop Corrigan to Bishop McQuaid and Allied Documents* (Rochester, 1946), pp. 199–201.

[105] Grannan reported: "The Public Press is a study. Many newspapers have noticed it. Some of them seriously refute the letter; others minimize the contents; but the majority treated it very gallantly, hit at the men who wrote it, or urged the Pope to write it, and even made fun of it, as the enclosed will show [Boston *Republican* and *Review,* New York *Commercial Advertiser* and *Churchmen* for March 4; Boston *Journal* for March 5; New York *Tribune,* March 6]. Even the Catholic papers, such as the *Providence Visitor,* the *Catholic Citizen,* the *Colorado Catholic,* the *Standard* and *Times* of staid old Philadelphia, come out and tell us that the letter contains nothing that concerns us. One of them says it would be better if Rome established bands of missionaries after the pattern of the Paulists and sent them throughout Italy to preach the Gospel and to convert them to the Catholic Religion. Another calls it a storm in a tea-pot. And most of the Catholic papers say that the thing is gotten up by Satolli, Mazzella, the Germans, the Jesuits, the Monarchists, the retrogrades in theology, and by the Anti-American, Pro-Spanish partisans of Europe. The Jesuits here are chafing under the imputation that they are anti-American. But if they do not wish to be blamed, why do they persist in doing what is blameworthy. 'If a man will persist on sitting down on a red-hot stove, he must carry the blister'" (ADR, Grannan to O'Connell, Washington, [Postmark, Mar. 11, 1899]). Gibbons said: "The Catholic and secular press is very friendly to the Paulists, and the animus of the

for March 18, 1899, however, rejoiced that Americanism had been condemned root and branch, and later it published the letters from New York and Milwaukee recognizing the existence of the errors in the United States, whereas the denials that the errors existed in their flocks from the Archbishops of Baltimore, San Francisco, St. Louis, and Boston were conspicuously absent from its pages.[106] The Jesuit journal's continuation of the war prompted Ireland to exclaim: "The Civiltà is venomous. I now believe all our efforts for 'a vindication' will be fruitless, and I am afraid to go on."[107] Nevertheless, he continued to fight so as to clear the Americanism of the American prelates from the taint attached to the word through its use in the encyclical.[108]

---

attack is transparent to them" (ADR, Gibbons to O'Connell, Baltimore, Mar. 15, 1899). The *Church Progress* of St. Louis claimed: "The letter on Heckerism was the excising of the vicious doctrine of Liberalism at the roots" (cited by *Weekly Register* [London], July 22, 1899). Cf. Félix Klein, *La route du petit morvandiau. Souvenirs.* Vol. IV. *Une hérésie fantome, l'Américanisme* (Paris, 1949), pp. 399–436. The abbé treats the effects of the letter in America, England, and France. The clippings, on which he based this portion of the book are to be found in APF, Klein Papers, where they were studied by the author. Bishop Maes of Covington said that one of the German papers gave a pointed history of Jansenism and, as he put it, "creates the impression that some ultras would not be sorry if they succeeded in driving the Paulists to retaliate and in goading them into rebellion, as some tried to do with Lacordaire!" (APF, Maes to Elliott, Covington, Apr. 12, 1899). Thorne continued to use his journal for tirades against the Paulists, Ireland, and Keane. Cf. William H. Thorne, "Globe Notes," *Globe,* IX (Mar., 1899), 96 ff.

[106] APF, Klein Papers, O'Gorman to Klein, Sioux Falls, Mar. 7, 1900 (French); Reily, *op. cit.,* V, 842. In another place Reily stated: "The course of the *Civiltà Cattolica* of Rome is also beyond comprehension; . . . an enemy of democracy — an enemy of America." Then after speaking of the evident lack of friendship for the United States on the part of the editor of the *Vérité* of Quebec, Jules P. Tardivel, Monsignor P. L. Péchenard, rector of the Catholic Institute of Paris, Cardinals Mazzella and Satolli, and Father David Fleming, he labels them as the "reactionary enemies of the republican institutions, enemies of the present, lovers and sighers for the past that is past by the will of God and the people. Despite all their efforts the Holy Father was not misled" (Reily, *op. cit.,* VI, 850). "Monachus" in *Rassegna Nazionale* (Mar. 16, 1899) printed matter favorable to the American Americanists.

[107] ADR, Ireland to O'Connell, Naples, Mar. 23, 1899. Also cf. APF, Klein Papers, Ireland to Klein, St. Paul, Sept. 15, 1899.

[108] On May 8, at the invitation of the Bishop of Orléans, France, John Ireland preached at a grand celebration commemorating Joan of Arc's deliverance of the city. Keane called the discourse admirable and, as he said, "it gives in its latter part the best exposition that could be desired of his [Hecker's] ideas and ours" (ADR, Keane to Ireland, Rome, May 14, 1899). For the text of the talk, cf. John Ireland, *The Church and Modern Society,* St. Paul, 1905), II, 29–66. Later Ireland experienced triumphs in Paris (Klein, *op. cit.,* IV, 438) and while he was there he gave a long interview on Americanism which was designed to remove the stigma from the term (New York *Herald,* Paris edition, June 23, 1899). At this time he obtained and published Périès' letter threatening revenge against those who desired to remove him

On October 12, during the annual meeting of the archbishops, he further sought to have the American bishops express their opinion as to whether or not the errors existed anywhere in their country as the bishops of the Province of Milwaukee had asserted. He failed to accomplish what he desired because, as he told O'Connell, "Baltimore cried 'peace — peace, death, even for the sake of peace' — and nothing was effected."[109]

At the end of the year 1899, O'Connell wrote from the Eternal City to say that things were quieter there on Americanism, but, as he expressed it, "the Jesuits are as furious as ever. They must prove they were right."[110] A little later he told his friend in St. Paul that they could all hope for peace during the next year because the authorities wished for that condition during the Holy Year.[111]

Indeed, relative peace reigned during the year 1900. But in view of Rampolla's statement that the words of the letter allowed the

---

from his position at the Catholic University of America, thus giving the impression that it was personal spite that prompted Périès to engage in the anti-American campaign. Cf. Hogan, *op. cit.*, pp. 165–166. The Archbishop of St. Paul also went to England where he received favorable publicity in the *Weekly Register* (London) on July 8, 1899, and in the *Catholic Times and Catholic Companion* (Liverpool) on July 14, 1899. Meanwhile, Rooker was seeking Storer's appointment to Spain because of the advantage that would result to the Americanists. Storer was to be instructed to tell the Pope that his position would require him to avoid all appearance of diplomatic complications, but that he would be glad to give all the assistance in his power. He could not, however, receive hints from anyone except Ireland and Keane (ADR, Rooker to O'Connell, Washington, Apr. 14, 1899).

[109] ADR, Ireland to O'Connell, New York, Oct. 21, 1899. The minutes of the meeting show that Archbishops Riordan of San Francisco and Kain of St. Louis joined Ireland in the fight, but they met the opposition of Archbishops Corrigan of New York and Ryan of Philadelphia, and Cardinal Gibbons cast the deciding vote putting an end to the matter (AAB, 97-R-5, Minutes of the Meeting of the Archbishops of the United States, Catholic University of America, Oct. 12, 1899). O'Connell must have feared that Ireland was getting tired of the fight and discouraged with the prospects for the future, for John A. Zahm assured the monsignor that after meeting Ireland and spending two days with him he could say that "I never saw him in such high feather, or more determined to fight until victory is ours . . . 'The Cause,' I think, is stronger than ever. Ireland agrees with me on this. And 'Americanismo,' too, is on firmer ground, and the followers are rapidly increasing in number. I am more hopeful of an early victory than ever" (ADR, "Parnasso" [Zahm] to O'Connell, Washington, Oct. 6, 1899).

[110] AASP, O'Connell to Ireland, Genazzano, Nov. 14, 1899.

[111] AASP, O'Connell to Ireland, Rome, Dec. 7, 1899. O'Connell gave evidence of being disheartened in a letter to Humphrey Moynihan, Ireland's secretary, who was thinking of writing on Americanism: "But when it came to the scratch, we made a very poor show, and much of our glory is vanished. But the work will yet be done by England, France in a way, and Germany. Those countries are more educated than ours" (AASP, O'Connell to Moynihan, Rome, Jan. 30, 1899).

Americanists to say "that the things condemned were never said or written in America, not even by Hecker," the main question as to whether or not the highest officials in Rome believed that the errors condemned in *Testem benevolentiae* were held and taught by American prelates remained unanswered. However, when Archbishop Keane received a letter from the Holy Father, dated August 18, 1900, along with his appointment to the See of Dubuque, he was made certain of the mind of the Holy See on that point. Leo XIII exhorted Keane in the new career now opening before him, to keep in mind the encyclical to Cardinal Gibbons on Americanism in which he showed, as he said, "for many reasons, which we mentioned there, the piety of the faithful was endangered." The Pope went on to say that these dangers must be combated by every means, especially by fostering Catholic schools. "Nor do we doubt," he continued, "that you will work hard to suppress the errors spreading there and to foster the union of souls with this seat of infallible truth." In passing on this information to the Archbishop of St. Paul, Keane remarked with understandable bitterness: "He simply reiterates the assertion made in the Encyclical—and this at the very time when he was virtually apologizing to you for it, and saying it was needed only in France; . . . It made me sick—and it was a painful blow to the Cardinal too. I have not told a living soul of it besides him."[112] But he did speak of it to someone else even before he had communicated with Ireland. And Rooker, whom Keane had so favored, interpreted another event, considered highly significant by some of the Americanists, in the light of this information. Rooker stated:

> When you get down to the bottom of facts, there is but one thing in the recent visit of Mgr. Ireland to Rome which has any particular significance, and that is the opportunity he was given to talk at the "circolo," and the speech he there made. Now, I have, of course, been glad to see that incident being made good use of and turned into a very high compliment to him. So far it has done and will do good in this country. But at the same time the real significance of the thing is

[112] AASP, Keane to Ireland, Dubuque, Oct. 29, 1900. It was only five months previously that Keane had said: "The Holy Father is beginning to recognize that there has been a mistake, and that the errors which he condemns have no existence among us" (Archives of the Diocese of Albany, Keane to Thomas M. Burke, Rome, June 7, 1899). On August 5, 1900, Ireland had said to Mrs. Storer: "The Pope told me to forget that letter on Americanism, which has no application except in a few dioceses in France!" (Ireland to Mrs. Storer, Rome, Aug. 5, 1900, in Maria Longworth Storer, *In Memoriam Bellamy Storer* [Boston, 1923], pp. 46–47).

> not understood here to be particularly favorable to him. It is taken to have been a pre-arranged profession of faith, which he was "invited" to make in the most solemn and public and universal possible manner. Color is given to this interpretation by the autograph letter which accompanied the Brief appointing Archbishop Keane to Dubuque. That letter re-iterated and rubbed in the whole letter on Americanism; reasserted the existence of dangerous tendencies among American Catholics; insinuated plainly that Archbishop Keane himself was tainted by those tendencies; and called on him to devote himself and his energies to rooting them out of himself and his people. This is a very strong expression of what was contained in the letter, and perhaps someone will tell you that I have exaggerated. But it seems perfectly plain to me that anyone who knows how to read a pontifical letter will see all this very clearly contained in that letter. Archbishop Keane himself admitted to me that he could see a complete re-iteration and even an ill-natured insistence of all that was in the letter on Americanism. Now, that letter was written at almost precisely the time when Archbishop Ireland was making his speech in the "circolo." It seems to me therefore that the incident of the "circolo" is to be interpreted in the spirit of that letter of Archbishop Keane and not as a high honor to Archbishop Ireland. Of course, the intention of Rome in both instances was the same so far as the individuals were concerned. You know as well as I do the little Italian couplet about spreading honey on the lip of the cup from which a child is to take medicine. Both the Archbishops were to get a dose, and the lip of the cup was sweetened in each case. It was a great honor to allow an Archbishop to "speek in meetin'." But it was clearly understood beforehand what he was to say, and strangely enough what he said happened to be a perfect rectification of the very points on which he had of late been suspected to be a little off. It was an unusual honor for the autograph letter to accompany a Brief, and the style of the letter was very affectionate and paternal; but the letter clearly stated, however, that American tendencies are dangerous and must be suppressed. So, I say, it seems to me that it is quite impossible to understand late events as meaning any real, substantial return to favor or power or influence, either on the part of Monsignor Ireland.[113]

In view of the Pope's letter accompanying Keane's appointment to Dubuque it would seem that Rooker's analysis was in good measure

[113] ADR, Rooker to O'Connell, Washington, Oct. 22, 1900. For further evidence to support the belief that the Holy Father understood that the errors condemned under the name of Americanism existed in the United States, cf. Holden, *op. cit.*, p. 162 n.

correct and that Archbishop Keane was still suspected of being tainted with a tendency to what was termed the errors of Americanism.

It would appear from the ever-busy Mrs. Storer's report of a conversation with Cardinal Rampolla, however, that the Roman officials did not want the American public to conclude from recent events that the progressive bishops were suspected of tendencies that were to be reprobated or to get the impression that the conservative ecclesiastics were considered by Rome to be the only orthodox representatives of the true church. Especially did they want to avoid the appearance of foreign influence on Rome in her guidance of the internal affairs of the Church in the United States. The appointment of Keane to Dubuque, Rampolla said, was their reply to the calumniators of the forward group and to those who claimed that Europeans, the Germans in particular, exercised an undue influence on the Holy See.[114] The appointment of a progressive prelate to the Archdiocese of Dubuque and the Pope's personal letter to him in which it was made clear that he was suspected of dangerous tendencies, therefore, appear to have been designed to prevent either of the contending parties in the United States from claiming a victory in the Americanism controversy.

As to the factual basis for the suspicion of Roman officials that Keane held and advocated the errors condemned by Leo XIII under the term "Americanism," none can be found. A theologian, writing about the men who have encouraged devotion to God the Holy Ghost in the United States, states:

> . . . it is worse than nonsense to hold that Bishop Keane, to quote but one example, could have encouraged anything like naturalism when we know that great prelate did all in his power to practice and to inculcate those very spiritual exercises which would render naturalism impossible. [The man who is aware of the part these men played in encouraging devotion to the Holy Ghost] knows that the tremendous accomplishments of these men were possible only because they were aware of the worth and the necessity of the Christian dispensation in the one Catholic Church.[115]

It must be noted, however, that a historian has claimed that "the doctrines of the condemned Americanism had their counterpart in tendencies among the Catholics of the day." These tendencies, however, were, as he pointed out, "entirely unrehearsed and unplanned and con-

114 AASP, Mrs. Storer to "Monseigneur" [?], Barcelona, Oct. 18, 1900 [French].

115 Fenton, "Devoton to the Holy Ghost and Its American Advocates," *op. cit.*, p. 501.

sisted mostly of unconnected incidents which can be grouped into tendencies from the perspective of history."[116] To say, then, that in the actions and utterances of Keane, as well as of the other members of the forward group, it was these tendencies which the Roman officials detected and warned against lest they be consciously cultivated, would presume uncommon vision on their part. Considering all the circumstances which provoked the Pope's letter, unquestionably it was the theological opinions formulated in Europe and called "Americanism," because their basis was the supposed teachings of Hecker and of Keane, Hecker's chief disciple in Europe, which called for the papal document. Hecker, Keane, and his friends had not formulated any new doctrines. The archbishop and his associates were merely of the opinion that the clergy in Europe would render greater service to the Church if they imitated the best characteristics of the American clergy — exemplified in Hecker — whom Keane considered to be in many respects the most excellent the world had known since the time of the Apostles and who in nearly all respects would be the greatest, once their intellectual defects were remedied through study in institutions such as the Catholic University of America. By pointing out to European audiences the laudable traits of the American clergy, which to their mind helped to explain the prosperous and happy condition of the Church in the United States, a criticism of their counterparts in Europe was implied. Naturally, many of the clergy in Europe resented the insinuation that they lacked energy in the pursuit of souls; that they were devoid of charity in their relationship with those outside the fold; that they showed little concern about the promotion of *practical* remedies for social evils; that they were losing the sympathy and love of their people because they had locked their doors to them; that their relationship with civil authorities was strained because they refused to recognize the changes in civil society; that these inevitable changes were taking the wrong course because they were not providing the necessary direction. Moreover, by picturing the brighter future of the Church in the democratic United States and by saying that the monarchies were dead, their past glory never to be revived, and that the United States would now assume the role of world leadership for which providence had destined her, they brought upon themselves the wrath of the monarchists among the clergy, and they were in the majority, who were familiar only with the European

[116] McAvoy, "Americanism, Fact and Fiction," *op. cit.*, pp. 149–150.

meaning of democracy, which to them represented much that was damnable in the spirit of the age. When Keane spoke on such matters, even some of his closest friends at times expressed concern, principally because his forthright nature — or, from another viewpoint, his lack of tact — led him to wound the sensibilities of clergymen who resented the attempts of the clergy of a young nation without Catholic traditions to tutor them. History bears out the conclusion that the priests in Europe could have listened to Keane with profit, and it demonstrates that his statements about the role to be played by the United States in world affairs and concerning the Church's prosperity under her flag were prophetic. The evidence also proves that the firmness of his adherence to the true faith and the constancy of his devotion to the Holy See cannot be questioned.

The uncensorable Americanism which Keane and his friends represented did not die. Bishop O'Gorman wrote from Rome in 1902: "On all sides it is proclaimed that Americanism, which was supposed to be our defeat, has been turned into a glorious victory. We are surely on top,"[117] and in 1903, when the papers announced that Leo XIII had appointed Denis O'Connell third rector of the Catholic University of America, the irrepressible Ireland fairly shouted: "O'Connell in Washington — Simply impossible. Well, here he is — Viva L'Americanismo! Viva sempre!"[118]

[117] AAB, 99-R-6, O'Gorman to Gibbons, Rome, May 17, 1902, cited by Hogan, *op. cit.*, p. 167.

[118] ADR, Ireland to O'Connell, St. Paul, Jan. 14, 1903, cited by Hogan, *op. cit.*, p. 172. Father Hogan has an interesting treatment of the events that led to O'Connell's appointment (pp. 167–172). On the same subject, cf. Barry, *The Catholic University of America, 1903–1909,* pp. 24–33.

Chapter X

Release From Exile

ARCHBISHOP KEANE'S exile in Rome ended in the fall of 1899, when he returned to the United States to collect funds for the Catholic University of America. After he had been dismissed from the rectorship of the University in 1896, he continued to use every opportunity to promote the welfare of the institution that had caused him so much toil and anguish of spirit.[1] By returning to the United States each year to attend the meetings of its Board of Trustees, of which he continued to be a member, he gave evidence of his unflagging interest in the institution, and at the same time he thus kept himself fully informed about its progress and its difficulties.

In the trustees' meeting in the fall of 1898, the members of the board were confronted with a report that foretold the inevitable doom

[1] We have seen the evidence of this in preceding chapters. Additional evidence of his interest in the University appeared when he wrote to Ireland on January 24, 1898: "Let me ask you to do a service to the Catholic University. When Father Zahm was leaving Rome he begged of me that a strong pressure be brought to bear by his Eminence, Cardinal Gibbons, yourself, and a few other Archbishops, upon the Father General of the Holy Cross and upon himself as Provincial to prevent the removal of the Holy Cross from connection with the Catholic University" (AASP). Keane wrote to Gibbons on the same subject on the same day (AAB, 96-A-10). A few months later he told Vice-Rector Garrigan: "Especially am I glad that Mgr. C. [onaty] gives so great satisfaction in his difficult position and is so loyally co-operated with by all in the University, now that the elements of discord are gone" (ACUA, Garrigan Papers, Keane to Garrigan, Rome, May 24, 1898). Archbishop Keane received a beautiful souvenir volume, containing thirty photographs of persons connected with the institution during his rectorship and seventeen views of the buildings, in which the following inscription in English and in Latin appeared: "To the Most Rev. John J. Keane, D.D., Archbishop of Damascus. From the professors of the Catholic University. In grateful memory of their association with him, in the foremost undertaking of the Church in America" (*Church News,* Nov. 6, 1897).

of the institution unless effective methods were initiated to raise sufficient funds to wipe out the recurring annual deficits. Since the University's governing board maintained the policy of seeking funds only from Catholics with considerable means and since Archbishop Keane had enjoyed some success in procuring donations from such sources during his administration while his successor had not made any conspicuous progress in financial matters, with Keane's consent and with Conaty's approval the board authorized the cardinal chancellor to request Pope Leo XIII in their name that the former rector be released from his duties in Rome so that he could devote at least a year to the important work of completing the endowment of the institution and of obtaining the necessary funds for its further development.[2] On November 1 of that year Gibbons carried out the wishes of the Board of Trustees by sending to Cardinal Rampolla a letter in which he outlined the financial condition of the University and requested that the Holy Father permit Keane to return to the United States for the purpose of collecting, since the members of the board thought that Keane, as he said, "with his talents, the esteem in which he is held, the affection and popularity he enjoys could successfully perform that difficult but important task."[3] In his reply Rampolla conveyed the sentiments of the Pontiff which, while not adverse to granting the board's request, indicated some delay before favorable action would be taken.[4] It is quite probable that the Pope's reluctance to release Keane at the time was owing to the fact that the controversy over Americanism was then in an acute stage both in Rome and in France. In any case, it was this controversy which posed a difficulty for the archbishop himself, inasmuch as he felt, as he informed Conaty, that he would be ill-advised to leave Rome as long as the storm raged.[5]

Meanwhile, Bishop Spalding, one of the founders of the University, who had grown pessimistic about its future during the period of its greatest trials, took a more hopeful view of its success when he learned that Keane had consented to become a beggar again on its behalf.[6]

[2] ACUA, MMBT, Oct. 11, 1898.

[3] ACUA, Gibbons to Cardinal Rampolla, Baltimore, Nov. 1, 1898 (French), copy. For a translation of the complete text from AAB, 96-S-1, cf. Hogan, *op. cit.*, pp. 39–40.

[4] AAB, 96-T-3, Rampolla to Gibbons, Rome, Nov. 16, 1898 (Italian).

[5] ACUA, Conaty Papers, Keane to Conaty, Rome, Feb. 1, 1899; ACUA Bouquillon Papers, Keane to Magnien, Rome, Feb. 11, 1899.

[6] AUND, Hudson Papers, Spalding to Hudson, Peoria, Oct. 28, 1898. One of the archbishop's Washington admirers ruminated concerning his agreement to collect for the University: "And what do you think of the heroism of his willingness to put his shoulder to the wheel at the University and finish collecting for the endowments he

Not to be completely outdone in generosity to the imperiled cause, the Bishop of Peoria accepted an invitation to give some lectures in Washington for the institution, and his efforts, according to Gibbons, created great interest and met with gratifying success. Furthermore, Spalding offered to accompany Keane and to help him in the task of collecting, as far as his episcopal duties would permit.[7] When Archbishop Keane heard about the manifestation of good will and generosity toward the University which Spalding had elicited, he expressed the hope that it would deepen and spread so that there would be no need of what he called his "proposed crusade." Nonetheless, as he put it, "it is a task which I shall willingly undertake, as requested by the Directors, but which I should still willingly relinquish if circumstances would fortunately render it unnecessary."[8]

Conditions made it absolutely necessary for the archbishop himself to shoulder the burden, however, and Gibbons and Spalding were both anxious that he begin the work as soon as possible, since the financial conditions of the country at that time looked very favorable.[9] The cardinal suggested that Keane ask the Holy Father to permit him to come at the close of Lent so as to begin at the very latest in the month of May. But when Rampolla informed Keane in March that he could begin collecting whenever the cardinal and the bishops thought that the time was opportune, the archbishop continued to plead to Gibbons that circumstances required his presence in Rome. Besides, he and Ireland agreed that there would be little use in beginning the work in May since it would have to be suspended in June because of the impracticability of engaging in such activity during the summer. Therefore, in Keane's judgment, it would be best to wait until the fall and then launch an intensive campaign during the Holy Year.[10] This opinion finally prevailed, and it was decided that Keane

---

had begun. Is there any other man in the whole world who would be willing to do it?" (ADR, Fannie W. Whelan to O'Connell, Washington, Nov. 13, 1898). The Archbishop of St. Paul also regained confidence in the future of the institution because of Keane's consent to work for it. Keane reported: "Ireland, who used to be so hopeless about the University, acknowledged that the prospects were never as bright as at present" (ADR, Keane to O'Connell, Baltimore, Nov. 3, 1899).

[7] AAB, 97-C-1, Gibbons to Keane, Baltimore, Jan. 26, 1899, copy.

[8] ACUA, Garrigan Papers, Keane to Garrigan, Rome, Feb. 2, 1899.

[9] AAB, 97-C-1, Gibbons to Keane, Baltimore, Jan. 26, 1899, copy; Spalding to Conaty, Peoria, Nov. 15 and Dec. 4, 1898, cited by Hogan, *op. cit.*, p. 41.

[10] ACUA, Garrigan Papers, Keane to Garrigan, Rome, Mar. 25, 1899.

should make his headquarters at the University when he returned in the fall.[11]

When it had been determined that the archbishop would engage in the work, the newspapers were so informed and at once began to shout his praises. The Roman correspondent for the *Freeman's Journal* mentioned that he would leave behind a host of friends in the Eternal City and that the throng of English-speaking people there would certainly miss him from the pulpit of San Silvestro.[12] The Baltimore *Sun's* correspondent wrote a factual note on the proposed utilization of what he called Keane's "admirable eloquence and his indefatigable energy" to complete the University's endowment.[13] The London *Tablet*, along with the information that the archbishop was to devote two years to this special work, denied the rumor that Conaty was to be moved to Columbus so that Keane could be reinstated as the University's rector.[14]

Since Rome's decision to release Keane from his duties in the Eternal City came early in the summer, he had ample time to rest and to plan for the work that would begin in the autumn. After winding up his affairs in Rome at the end of June,[15] he visited a few places in Italy before going to France to spend part of July and August with some friends.[16] During his stay with these American friends he learned from them that it would be possible to obtain relief for an annoying heart complaint at Bad Nauheim in Germany, and hurrying there he found, as he claimed, that he had more need of treatment than he

[11] ACUA, Garrigan Papers, Keane to Garrigan, Rome, Mar. 25, May 5, and June 9, 1899.

[12] *Freeman's Journal*, cited by *Church News*, Apr. 15, 1899.

[13] Baltimore *Sun*, cited by *Church News*, July 15, 1899.

[14] London *Tablet*, June 17, 1899. Hogan quotes the denial of the rumor from the Washington *Times* (May 29, 1899) which stated: "This report was unfounded, according to an official of the University. If Rome were to reinstate Archbishop Keane, this official said, it would be an acknowledgement that it had erred in displacing him so summarily, and Rome never acknowledges that it makes an error" (*op. cit.*, p. 42). The University's *Bulletin* could hardly have done otherwise than speak of him thus when announcing his return to work for the institution's welfare: "His vigorous enthusiasm, his high ideal of University life and work, his numerous devoted friends in every rank and calling, his winning manner and rare eloquence, — above all, his absolute unselfishness and spirit of self-sacrifice, make it sure that wherever he goes he will meet with no uncertain or hesitating response" ("Archbishop Keane," *Catholic University Bulletin*, V [July, 1899], 395).

[15] ACUA, Garrigan Papers, Keane to Garrigan, Rome, June 24, 1899. He says here that he is leaving Rome tomorrow.

[16] AANO, Keane to Chapelle, France, July 29, 1899.

had supposed. According to his own estimate the sixty-year-old prelate profited by remaining at the health resort during a portion of August and the greater part of September, for he told O'Connell later, "Roman malaria *of all sorts* has ceased to bother me, and I am well."[17] However, when the archbishop arrived in the United States just in time for the meeting of the University's trustees on October 11,[18] those who had not seen him for some time noted that his personality had undergone a change and that he seemed to lack his customary physical stamina. Charles P. Grannan remarked in one letter that "Broad John looks wish-washy,"[19] and in another he said: "He is not the same man he was three years ago. Every one notices the change. He must have been dreadfully hammered, cuffed, kicked about, mauled, and battered (metaphorically) to be so demure as he now is. He is a crushed man." The University professor then observed:

> Perhaps the free air of the country, and the kind attention of friends may restore him to his former spirits. But if his present psychic condition is the result, not of personal ill-treatment, but of an inside knowledge of the trend of events, then it is pessimism; and he, who was always so optimistic, can not survive pessimism. He has not enough character for that.[20]

[17] ADR, Keane to O'Connell, Baltimore, Nov. 3, 1899. Keane was suffering from a valvular lesion of the heart (ADR, Keane to O'Connell, Bad Nauheim, Aug. 14, 1902).

[18] He arrived in New York on October 8 (ACUA, Garrigan Papers, Keane to Garrigan [postmarked New York, Oct. 8, 1899]); ACUA, MMBT, Oct. 11, 1899.

[19] ADR, Grannan to "Dear Doctor" [O'Connell], Hartford, Conn., Oct., 1899. Ireland was referred to as "Big John" and Keane as "Broad John."

[20] ADR, Grannan to O'Connell, written shortly after Keane had begun collecting. In June, 1899, Keane said: "Rome has not been a pleasant place to live in, these months past" (Archives of the Diocese of Albany, Keane to Thomas M. Burke, Rome, June 7, 1899.) In December of the same year he revealed to Zahm that he had moved out of the Canadian College to the Procure. "There was Montreal spite in it," he stated, "rather tell about it sometime. But I am all the better off" (AUND, Zahm Papers, Keane to Zahm, Rome, Dec. 10, 1898). According to O'Connell, Satolli had suggested to the Sulpicians who presided over the Canadian Seminary that Keane should be asked to leave his rooms there. Captier, the superior general of the Sulpicians, was "bold enough," as he said, to invite the archbishop to the Procure of St. Sulpice (Klein to Abbé de Tourville, Dec. 20, 1898, cited by Klein, *Americanism: A Phantom Heresy,* pp. 204–205). In a "Letter from Rome" by an anonymous author, published in the *Vérité* of January 11, 1899, it was stated that Keane had been obliged to leave the Canadian seminary in Rome because he was exercising a "pernicious influence" on the students and that it was the friendship of Cardinal Vannutelli which had secured his admission to the Procure (cited by Klein, *Americanism: A Phantom Heresy,* p. 210). Reporting this treatment of Keane on November 13, 1899, the New York *Herald* stated: "These facts are confirmed by a Protestant convert to Catholicism, who is scandalized at the unchristian proceedings by which the Canadian priests sought to find favor with the Pope."

Another correspondent remarked after a first glimpse of the bishop: "I was *so shocked* by his appearance so grieved so indignant so stunned by all he had to tell me . . . I have never seen any one so changed, his vim is all gone, he fatigued so easily." Then, on a more hopeful note, she continued: "We thank God every month is doing him good. His reception at the Catholic University. The warm greeting of the Archbishop [Gibbons], his own assured position for at least two years — the unchanged devotion of his friends has done more for him than all the 'cure of Bad Nauheim.' "[21]

Despite this evidence of a physical and psychological deterioration, Keane managed to enter upon the familiar paths of former years with some of his old enthusiasm. During the meeting of the University's Board of Trustees, in which he received a hearty welcome from Cardinal Gibbons as their spokesman,[22] the archbishop read Rampolla's letter to him under date of June 22, 1899, in which were expressed the constant and deep interest of the Holy Father in the University and his earnest prayer for the success of Keane's mission.[23] After the meeting Keane prepared a letter which was sent out to all the bishops over Gibbons' signature, in which the hierarchy of the United States was reminded that each was pledged by the action of the Third Plenary Council of Baltimore to the full establishment and maintenance of the University. A quotation from Rampolla's letter to Keane was included and plainly indicated that Leo XIII desired that the pledge be kept. For these reasons the bishops were asked to welcome the archbishop and to lend him their co-operation.[24] It was then up to him to launch the drive for funds.

Furthermore, Cardinal Parocchi, acting on orders from the Vatican, prohibited any preaching by Keane in Rome during his last days there (AAB, 98-F-12, Kain to Gibbons, Lucerne, June 27, 1900).

At another time O'Connell remarked: "Abp. Keane has turned away in despair from all things earthly and spends the whole day in his lonely room with the Holy Ghost" (La Contessa Sabina Papers on microfilm in AUND, O'Connell to Sabina, Anzio, May 19 [1899]).

[21] ADR, Fannie Whelan to O'Connell, Washington, Dec. 10, 1899.

[22] ACUA, MMBT, Oct. 11, 1899; Riley, *op. cit.*, VI, 252.

[23] "University Chronicle," *Catholic University Bulletin,* V (Oct., 1899), 522; *Church News,* Oct. 14, 1899. ACUA, Gibbons to Monsignor, Washington, Nov. 4, 1899, in Keane's hand, quotes a portion of Rampolla's letter. A copy of this letter was sent to all the bishops. Cf. AANY, Gibbons to Monsignor, Washington, Nov. 20, 1899, and Hogan, *op. cit.*, p. 42, for the same extract from the Roman cardinal's letter. The archbishop received this letter in June before leaving Rome (ACUA, Garrigan Papers, Keane to Garrigan, Rome, June 24, 1899).

[24] ACUA, Gibbons to Monsignor, Washington, Nov. 4, 1899.

On Sunday, October 22, Archbishop Keane inaugurated the campaign in St. Patrick's Church in Washington where, as he put it, he had practically started the University.[25] Effective advance publicity had drawn a large number of Washingtonians to hear the prelate,[26] but the financial results were not immediately apparent. On the next Sunday he appeared in Gibbons' cathedral,[27] and he had the satisfaction of having the cardinal recommend his work on behalf of the University. After preaching in St. Paul's Church in Washington on November 5,[28] the archbishop moved on to Philadelphia where he delivered a discourse at the dedication of the Church of Our Lady of Mercy on November 19.[29] He then spent a few weeks in that city calling on people of means. Here his appeal gained a sympathetic reception.[30] The next scene of his labors was Boston, where he preached in the cathedral on Sunday, December 3.[31] Finding that prospects for funds were not very good in that archdiocese he asked Archbishop Williams to allow the use of his name for a University chair as the only hope for a successful campaign. Williams gave his consent, but at the same time he upset Keane's calculations by forbidding him to appeal to the clergy from whom their Archbishop himself was shortly to seek funds for the chapel of St. John's Seminary which had just been completed. Nonetheless, Archbishop Keane obtained subscriptions amounting to $20,000 in Boston, and he collected $6,000 toward the endowment of the Archbishop Williams Chair during the short time that he was there. Furthermore, Bishop Matthew Harkins of Providence, Rhode Island, and Bishop Thomas D. Beaven of Springfield, Massachusetts, in whose cathedrals he preached during these

[25] *Church News,* Oct. 28, 1899. On Sunday evening Keane visited the Good Samaritan Home in Washington where he spoke after he was welcomed by William F. Downey, its founder. Riley erred in stating that "Keane made the first public announcement of his mission" in the Baltimore cathedral on October 29 (*op. cit.,* VI, 255). Cf. "Archbishop Keane's Collecting Tour," *Catholic University Bulletin,* VI (Jan., 1900), 130. This gives a partial report on the work.

[26] *Church News,* Oct. 7 and 14, 1899.

[27] Riley, *op. cit.,* VI, 255. Keane's record of the money collected or promised and a partial list of the people he approached may be found in the ACUA in a small notebook with the title "Subscriptions and Contributions to the Catholic University of America. October, 1899 — June, 1900." Washington is not mentioned and there is very little entered under Baltimore.

[28] The *Church News* announced this sermon on October 28 and the same paper reported on it on November 11.

[29] Riley, *op. cit.,* VI, 263.

[30] ACUA, "Subscriptions and Contributions."

[31] *Church News,* Dec. 16, 1899.

days,[32] assured him of their full co-operation in securing the necessary amount for the chair bearing their metropolitan's name.[33] At the approach of the Christmas holidays the archbishop made his way back to Washington to rest before resuming his labors in the middle of January.

While he was relaxing in his rooms at the University, Keane indicated to O'Connell that in some respects the collection tour had been good for him. As he expressed it, "I meet nothing but friendliness so warm and so sincere that it makes my heart young again — and it had grown right old." As for the various items of news which the monsignor had sent from Rome, he claimed that they were of little interest and he stated:

> It is wonderful how Rome has got out of my spinal marrow, — out of it as completely as I am out of Rome. It interests me now not in the least for what is, but only for what I hope and pray is to be. More and more am I convinced that individual endeavors count for very little. — but that there is a great avalanche movement, irresistible, certain, which in some respects will be like the landslide of Amalfi, but will bring order out of chaos. And amid all my work, and I have plenty of it, I never lose sight of "respice finem."[34]

Such were the subjects of some of his holiday meditations.

Since he had no invitation to collect in any diocese immediately after the opening of the new year, Keane remained in Washington and fulfilled requests to open the Forty Hours' Adoration at the Church of the Sacred Heart on January 7, and to speak before the annual meeting of the Tabernacle Society on January 9.[35] At the same time he made final arrangements with the Archbishop of New York for a sermon in the cathedral of that important see on January 14, and he accepted Corrigan's gracious offer of hospitality while collecting in his archdiocese.[36] During his stay in New York Keane gave an interview to a reporter from the Brooklyn *Eagle* in which he outlined the

[32] *Ibid.*, Jan. 27, 1900.

[33] ACUA, Conaty Papers, Keane to Conaty, Philadelphia, Dec. 20, 1899.

[34] ADR, Keane to O'Connell, Washington, Dec. 25, 1899.

[35] *Church News*, Jan. 13, 1900. These activities were announced in the same journal on January 16.

[36] AANY, Gibbons to Corrigan, Baltimore, Nov. 23, 1899. The cardinal thanked Corrigan for inviting Keane to New York. AANY, Keane to Corrigan, Washington, Jan. 2 and 6, 1900, furnish the evidence for the final arrangements for the visit. Concerning the invitation to stop at Corrigan's residence, Keane remarked: "His invitation is cordial, and for the good of the cause I am glad it should be so, — but it will be awkward, very" (ADR, Keane to O'Connell, Washington, Dec. 25, 1899).

University's position in the struggle between Christianity and agnosticism and took occasion to stress the importance of endowing the institution. No collections were taken up for that purpose in the churches in which he spoke, he reported, since he only sought to awaken interest in the institution and so to invite offerings. "I am planting the seed," he said, "not yet gathering the harvest. But the assurances already given me made me feel confident that before the end of the two years which I am consecrating to this task, nearly one million of dollars will have been added to the endowment fund."[37] This note of optimism was certainly tailored for the public, for at approximately the same time he informed Monsignor Conaty that he expected very little in New York City, and he added: "One of my millionaires ill in bed for weeks, another worried by attacks on his syndicates."[38] After preaching at St. Stephen's Church in New York on the third Sunday in January, the archbishop began to visit the principal cities in the state of New York. He hurried through Buffalo, in which he had found "a collapse from an absurdly inflated boom," to Syracuse where, as he said to Garrigan, "things are slow, slow, slow." On February 8, he returned to Buffalo to speak at a banquet of the Knights of Columbus, and the next day he entrained for Albany for three speaking engagements on Sunday, February 11. After spending three days there visiting many people whom he described as not ready to act, he returned to the archbishop's house in New York, his headquarters while mapping the strategy to be used on the rich in that area. As soon as he had delivered a sermon at St. Agnes' Church on February 18, he quit the New York area for Washington, and more calls upon wealthy Catholics.[39]

Some months before this, the archbishop had promised a lecture for the benefit of the Washington Tabernacle Society on February 23. Although the members of that organization were interested in a handsome financial return from the lecture, they had deliberately set out to make of it an occasion for honoring their benefactor.[40] The results

[37] Brooklyn *Eagle,* Jan. 20, 1900.

[38] ACUA, Conaty Papers, Keane to Conaty, New York, Jan. 17, 1900.

[39] ACUA, Garrigan Papers, Keane to Garrigan, Syracuse, Feb. 2 and 7, 1900; ACUA, "Subscriptions and Contributions." Keane requested a few days hospitality from Corrigan (AANY, Keane to Corrigan, Albany, Feb. 14, 1900).

[40] They had asked him to talk on Rome but, as one member said, he had no heart for it. She also related: "I am trying to work it out to have him introduced by Governor Roosevelt. It will be a big card for us, for we could then be sure to secure the attendance of the President and I am determined to make of the occasion an ovation to the Bishop as well as fill the purse of the Society" (ADR, Fannie Whelan to O'Connell, Washington, Dec. 10, 1899).

of their labors must have been gratifying to them, for the audience at the Lafayette Square Opera House on that memorable afternoon was considered by one writer as "the most distinguished audience assembled at the capital of the nation since James G. Blaine pronounced the eulogy upon President Garfield in the hall of the house of representatives."[41] The reporter could have added that it was most unusual for a relatively unknown organization to succeed in assembling an audience which included the President of the United States and many men prominent in the national government to hear a lecture by a Catholic prelate. Archbishop Keane had an enviable reputation as a speaker, however, and his discourse on George Washington, under the title "The Star of Destiny," was a fitting celebration of the birthday of the father of our country. The archbishop portrayed the character of Washington by comparing him with other historical figures, and he concluded that our national hero was the typical embodiment of the American genius. Washington was truly the instrument of the Providence which shapes our ends, Keane told his audience, and his greatness resulted from the Christian ideal which fired his soul. By stating the conviction that owing to Washington's Christian ideals he would, if he stood before them at that moment, denounce agnosticism in education as the greatest danger to the country, the archbishop launched forth on a subject that had distressed him throughout his life and which must have caused discomfort to some in his audience. True to his duty as a patriot and as a Catholic prelate, nonetheless, he warned his listeners that Americans of the future must have the Christian ideal impressed upon their minds more and more strongly in order that the safety of the nation might be assured.[42]

With the applause of official Washington still ringing in his ears,

[41] *Church News,* Mar. 3, 1900. The lecture was announced in Washington's Catholic paper on February 10 and 17. On February 10, Emma Luke Perley stated in her column: "The names on the list of patronesses show how well the Archbishop stands with the best people. The name of the Austrian ambassadress is significant." On February 17 the same journal printed the information that Miss Fannie Whelan had invited the members of the Keane Council of the Knights of Columbus to sit in the gallery during the lecture at a reduced fee.

[42] *Church News,* Mar. 3, 1900. The complete text of the lecture is given. Miss Whelan received credit for the success of the benefit lecture which brought $1,100 for the Tabernacle Society. A portion of the lecture was reprinted in the *American Catholic Historical Researches,* XVII (Oct., 1900), 166. In the *Review* Preuss quoted from the *North Western Review* of St. Boniface (Apr. 4) in which Keane's statement about Washington as a Christian was challenged by the statement that the father of his country was a godless man who refused to hear the word of God or to receive any clerical ministrations at the time of his death. Cf. *Review,* VII (Apr. 19, 1900), 37.

Archbishop Keane set out for the West to resume the work of collecting for the University. Naturally, prior announcement of his intended visit appeared in many of the journals, but bitter comment such as that of the *Herold des Glaubens* of St. Louis, was not anticipated. They wrote:

> We wicked Germans; we "refractaires"; "antiquated theologians"; "nest of Cahenslyites"; come in all at once for honors. The deposed rector of the University in Washington, the discoverer of the "aristocracy of Learning," is coming to St. Louis with bag and bell to collect for that institution, German contributors will be welcomed. In this way we rascally Germans are again assumed as dear children into the council of the cultivated.[43]

Fortunately, such feelings were not general among the Germans in that gateway to the West. The co-operation of Archbishop Kain and the priests enabled Keane to succeed in his attempt to endow a chair which would bear the name of the late Archbishop Peter Richard Kenrick of St. Louis. After a visit to Kansas he reported that he had hopes of obtaining about $20,000. He had greater success in Chicago where he received $50,000 from Michael Cudahy and a few small subscriptions after calling on many people. From Chicago the archbishop went to Milwaukee where he preached two sermons and visited several people without immediate results. At the end of May he made a stop at Detroit, preaching in the Cathedral of Saints Peter and Paul and in the Jesuit church with the same patrons. Again, he obtained very little, but he could see the hope of greater success in this area during the fall and winter. As he told Garrigan: "I have done an enormous amount of preaching, lecturing, talking; let us hope the seed will not be wasted."[44] When he arrived in Washington during the last week in May he was almost empty-handed; yet he had well earned the words of praise that Conaty spoke during the commencement exercises. The rector said:

> The University has been encouraged in its financial efforts during

[43] AASP, clippings, the *Western Watchman's* version of the *Herold des Glaubens'* story. Father Phelan referred to the German-language paper as "The official organ of the Vicar General of this diocese." Keane left for St. Louis on March 15 (ADR, Fannie W. Whelan to O'Connell, Washington, Apr. 30, 1900).

[44] ACUA, Garrigan Papers, Keane to Garrigan, Detroit, May 21, 1900. This letter contains a picture of his fortunes during the western tour. The eccesiastical authorities in St. Paul had asked him to postpone his visit there until Ireland returned in the fall. ACUA, "Subscriptions and Contributions" has nothing entered under Kansas City and Milwaukee.

the year by the magnanimous action of Archbishop Keane, its first Rector. With singlemindedness and devotedness which have never been surpassed, or, I may say, equalled, he has accepted the burden of laboring for the completion of the endowment fund, the foundation of which he so successfully laid several years before.[45]

On March 4, 1900, while the archbishop was collecting in the western part of the United States, Archbishop John Hennessy of Dubuque died. Immediately the newspapers began to suggest Keane for the position.[46] In fact, so many journals were guilty of naming Keane as Hennessy's successor that the San Francisco *Monitor,* Archbishop Riordan's official organ, felt justified in stating on March 24: "Nothing, we imagine, could be more distasteful to the Archbishop himself, than this constant and gratuitous 'booming' at the hands of the officious scribblers." This merely led Preuss, who could not resist an opportunity to strike at Keane, to remark: "From the way the *Western Watchman* has participated in 'booming' Mgr. Keane for the see of Dubuque, it would seem that the association of his name with such important vacancies is not as distasteful to the archbishop of Damascus as the Monitor 'imagines.' "[47] The *Northwestern Catholic* of Sioux City, recognizing that there would be opposition to such an appointment, told its readers: "It is an open secret that his selection would be fiercely opposed; and this opposition is being moulded and organized. Whether it will outweigh the weighty influence in his favor remains to be seen."[48]

As the papers continued to mention Keane's name most frequently as the likely successor to Hennessy, the consultors and irremovable rectors of the Archdiocese of Dubuque met to present and consider the names of men who represented their choice for the vacant see. When their votes were counted John Patrick Carroll, president of St. Joseph's College in Dubuque, was in first place, Keane was their

[45] "Commencement Exercises," *Catholic University Bulletin,* VI (July, 1900), 454. Also cf. *Freeman's Journal,* June 16, 1900. Keane was in Washington by May 26 (ADR, Keane to Kain, Washington, May 26, 1900). The archbishop reported on the results of his tour at the October 11, 1900, meeting of the board. It was supposed to be encouraging. Cf. "Meeting of the Board of Trustees," *Catholic University Bulletin,* VI (Oct., 1900), 551.

[46] On March 10, 1900, Riley wrote that it was the general opinion that Keane would succeed Hennessy (*op. cit.,* VI, 344). The archbishop had attended Hennessy's funeral, cf. *Annals of Iowa,* IV (1899–1900), 399.

[47] *Review,* VII (Apr. 5, 1900), 24. By this time Father Phelan had changed his attitude toward Archbishop Keane and had become friendly (AASP, O'Connell to Ireland, Rome, May 25, 1900).

[48] *Northwestern Catholic* (Sioux City, Iowa), Mar. 29, 1900.

second choice, and Edward John McLaughlin, pastor of St. Mary's Church in Clinton, Iowa, was in third position. Shortly after this list had been drawn up, the bishops of the province assembled to prepare their *terna* and they placed Keane, Bishop O'Gorman of Sioux Falls, and Bishop Lawrence Scanlan of Salt Lake City on it in that order.[49] That Keane's name was found on both lists was a cause for unrestrained elation among the archbishop's closest friends who felt that they could now use whatever influence they possessed to assure his selection. For Cardinal Gibbons it proved a splendid opportunity to prove further his esteem and love for the man whose trials he had made his own. In a letter to Cardinal Ledochowski, Prefect of the Congregation of the Propaganda, Gibbons invited his attention to the fact that Keane's name was the only one on both lists and that he was the first choice of the bishops. Moreover, he was already an archbishop, and while it had happened once that a simple priest was made a coadjutor archbishop with the right of succession, never had anyone but a bishop been made a reigning archbishop immediately. Furthermore, Gibbons continued, when the Holy Father removed Archbishop Keane from the University he had said that if he preferred to remain in the United States he would receive an archiepiscopal see, selected by vote of the bishops of the United States. Pursuing this point, the cardinal added: "Now the very best opportunity is offered for fulfilling this council of the Holy Father, and at the same

[49] AANY, Henry Cosgrove to Corrigan, Davenport, Mar. 28, 1900; AAB, 98-C-4, Cosgrove to Gibbons, Davenport, Mar. 28, 1900. Cosgrove was Bishop of Davenport from 1884 to 1906 and was the senior suffragan of the Archdiocese of Dubuque at this time. According to the late Monsignor Peter D. O'Malley, pastor of St. Anthony's Church in Dubuque, Cardinal Gibbons told Monsignor Roger Ryan, the administrator of the archdiocese, that if Keane's name was put on the *terna,* the archbishops would assure his appointment (written statement in the author's file).

This may have been the reason for the following letter that was signed by a number of priests: "We, the priests of the Archdiocese of Dubuque, having only the glory of God and the interests of the Church in view, would humbly submit our judgment as to the person to our mind most fitting to occupy the vacant See. We are not all the clergy of the Archdiocese, but we are a great majority of them, and those who are not with us are, we fear, influenced from without. We think, if left to their own feelings and convictions, the clergy of Dubuque, with the Rt. Rev. administrator at their head, would record their unanimous judgment that the bishop most fitting to fill the See made vacant by the death of the illustrious Archbishop Hennessy, is Most Rev. John Joseph Keane, DD., Ex. Rector Catholic University, Titular Archbishop of Damascus.

"He would be acceptable to priests and people because they respect his virtues and constructive qualities, that would perpetuate the prestige of this great metropolitan See." A printed copy of this letter may be found in Monsignor O'Malley's files. The present writer could not determine to whom it was dispatched.

time put an end to that state of things, which, on account of many and evident causes, brings injury both to the prelate himself and to Americans and to the Church."[50] At the same time, to help insure the accomplishment of his desire, the Cardinal of Baltimore wrote to Cardinal Rampolla to urge him to use his influence with the Pontiff to have Keane appointed to Dubuque. He reminded the cardinal that the Pope had promised the deposed rector an archbishopric in the United States and that Dubuque was a suitable see for his dignity. In his inimitable way Gibbons stated that he was certain that Rampolla could recall the public clamor in the United States which had followed upon Keane's removal from the University, and he was happy to report that it had greatly calmed. He pointedly added that Keane's present position was regarded as humiliating by very many people in the United States.[51] Such forceful expressions from the only prince of the Church in the United States were certainly unusual and bespoke the cardinal's strong feeling. Besides, his views were sure to receive careful consideration from the authorities in Rome.

Among Keane's closest friends John Ireland was the first to urge O'Connell to enlist the support of powerful Roman ecclesiastics for Keane's nomination. Along with his comments on the *terna* from Dubuque, he remarked concerning the archbishop: "Nearly all the archbishops, of course, will opine for him. The Germans of the whole country are up in arms, and will work against him. Please speak to both the Vannutellis. The opportunity has come to do him some justice."[52] Archbishop Riordan of San Francisco had thoughts on the subject which were similar to those expressed by the Archbishop of St. Paul. He told O'Connell: "His appointment would be most acceptable to all the educated Catholics in America, who still feel bitterly the removal from the University. He has the ability, the zeal and piety needed for such a place as Dubuque, and his appointment would be a great blessing to the entire Province." He urged the monsignor to have Spalding, who was then in Europe, contact some of the cardinals and even the Pope himself on the matter.[53] A short time later

[50] AAB, 98-D-6, Gibbons to Ledochowski, Baltimore, Apr. 15, 1900 (Latin), copy. Gibbons said that he did not know anything about Carroll and McLaughlin, but he spoke a good word for O'Gorman and Scanlan.

[51] AAB, 98-U-6, Gibbons to Rampolla, Baltimore, Apr. 15, 1900 (French), copy.

[52] ADR, Ireland to O'Connell, St. Paul, Apr. 4, 1900. He described Carroll as a young man nine years ordained and McLaughlin as a broken-down man.

[53] ADR, Riordan to O'Connell, Paris, Apr. 18, 1900. Spalding said that he would send a letter to Serafino Cardinal Vannutelli or anyone else if O'Connell thought it would help Keane (ADR, Spalding to O'Connell, Paris, May 3, 1900).

the Archbishop of San Francisco remarked to O'Connell: "I thought of writing to Satolli a frank letter on this subject. If the Archbishop is not sent to Dubuque it will be because Satolli opposes him. What do you advise? I will do nothing until I receive an answer from you."[54]

By the third week in May, all of the archbishops in the United States — even Corrigan, O'Connell reported with some amazement — had written on behalf of Keane. Such extraordinary unity of sentiment was breaking down the conviction in Rome of the strength of the American opposition to the archbishop.[55] Since Gibbons had already heard from Rampolla that the Holy Father seconded the cardinal's desire to put Keane in Dubuque,[56] he was not surprised when O'Connell cabled on May 21 that Keane would undoubtedly be nominated.[57] But the news was so important to the superior of the Josephites, to whom it had been confided, that he could not contain his joy. "Liberty Hall" [the American College in Rome], he said, "never sent forth a more joyous message than yesterday's: that Damascus will be swallowed up in Dubuque." He continued: "We know how glad J. J. K. will be to find himself once more anchored and beyond the call of the chapter of San Giovanni in Laterano."[58]

But Archbishop Keane, knowing that he would be opposed by some of the cardinals in the Propaganda,[59] did not put full trust in

[54] ADR, Riordan to O'Connell, Paris, Apr. 29, 1900. Since Camillo Cardinal Mazzella had died in March, 1900, his opposition to Keane would not be felt. An American correspondent in Rome said in a private letter that Mazzella, as he put it, "had been in great measure Pope during late years" (Howard Family Papers, Columbus, Ohio, W. J. Croke to Francis W. Howard, Rome, Apr. 14, 1900).

[55] AASP, O'Connell to Ireland, Rome, May 25, 1900. This was also reported in the *Western Watchman,* May 21, 1900. The anti-clerical *Tribuna* gave the alarm that Corrigan was in Rome for the principal object of preventing Keane's nomination to Dubuque (*Freeman's Journal,* June 16, 1900). Shortly after the archbishop of New York died, his brother said that the archbishop "had told me that the question of appointment or not had been virtually referred by Rome to him — and that if he approved, the appointment would be made. The deciding reason was that Rome wished it, and that the Monsignor was giving trouble there — and that it probably would be better to have him in Dubuque" (Archives of the Central Verein, St. Louis, Arthur Preuss Letters' Collection, Box 1900–14, Central Bureau Vault, Joseph F. Corrigan to Preuss, New York, June 29, 1902).

[56] AAB, 98-D-12, Rampolla to Gibbons, Rome, Apr. 30, 1900 (Italian).

[57] AAB, Cablegram, Marathon [O'Connell] to Gibbons, Rome, May 21, 1900 (Latin).

[58] ADR, Slattery to O'Connell, Baltimore, May 22, 1900.

[59] Shortly after sending the cablegram, O'Connell had written: "They would have to choose between Keane and O'Gorman and then face the certainty of meeting Keane again for Chicago. Still there are in the Prop. many cardinals opposed to Keane." In view of the unity among the archbishops, however, the monsignor felt that the opposition would dissolve (AASP, O'Connell to Ireland, Rome, May 25, 1900).

O'Connell's message. He calmly pursued the work of collecting according to plan, and he begged Archbishop Kain of St. Louis, his classmate, who was then visiting in the Eternal City, to ascertain, if he could, when they were likely to act on the appointment.[60] Since no appointment had been made by the time Keane concluded his collecting schedule, he consulted the apostolic delegate, Archbishop Martinelli, to determine whether it would be advisable to leave the United States for Europe in view of the possibility of his selection as Hennessy's successor. The delegate assured him that there would be no objection on his part so long as Keane avoided newspaper correspondents who might assign unworthy motives to such a trip at that time.[61] So, before sailing at the end of June the archbishop instructed Garrigan to use the title "Reverend" on all correspondence to him since he was to travel *incognito*.[62] On July 21, Keane arrived at Bad Nauheim and registered at the Hotel Schuchardt where he took treatments for his heart condition and awaited further news from Rome.[63]

Meanwhile, the journalists continued to stimulate the public interest in the topic of Hennessy's successor by publishing sensational stories that were generally the result of little more than a fertile imagination. Preuss, for one, accused the *Western Watchman* of trying to incite the German clergy of the Archdiocese of Dubuque to petition Rome against the appointment of Keane.[64] Although this charge against Father Phelan may have had little foundation, so many statements had appeared in the press about the opposition of the German priests to the archbishop, that Father F. J. Brune of Alton, Iowa, wrote this note to the Sioux City *Times* on April 5:

> The German priests generally are busy attending to their duties; they have no time left to devote to making of bishops and episcopal sees. They will reverently accept whomsoever the proper authority will send us. It is a pity and a scandal to see the serious matter of selecting a successor to the late Archbishop Hennessy treated as if any political office were to be filled. The Catholic politicians in Dubuque and Fort Dodge and Sioux City would do well to let the proper authority

[60] ADR, Keane to Kain, Washington, May 25, 1900.

[61] ADR, Keane to O'Connell, Bad Nauheim, Germany, July 22, 1900.

[62] ACUA, Garrigan Papers, Keane to Garrigan, Gloucester, Mass., June 26, 1900. On June 28 the *Northwestern Catholic* said that he had quietly stolen out of the United States bound for Rome.

[63] ADR, Keane to O'Connell, Bad Nauheim, Germany, July 22, 1900.

[64] *Review,* VII (Apr. 19, 1900), 36.

> attend to such important matters; or, at least, if they are anxious to place their nonsense before the public they ought to refrain from spreading falsehoods about the German clergy.[65]

Despite such strictures, lively newspapermen like Preuss would not keep any interesting copy from the public. On April 26, he said that he understood that the German clergy favored Father Carroll, but that they had not taken any steps, as he expressed it, "to counteract the movement that has been started within the diocese and outside, privately and in the public press, for Monsignor Keane." To show how the alleged movement was conducted, he reproduced a circular which had been sent to a considerable number of the Dubuque clergy by Father T. F. Gunn of Cedar Rapids, Iowa, under the date of April 10, 1900, in which the priest had stated:

> Though there seems to be little doubt as to the appointment of the Most Rev. Dr. Keane to our great Arch-Diocese, nevertheless there is some apparent opposition.
>
> With all due honor and respect for any names offered in preference, we must admit, the vast experience of the Most Rev. Doctor in matters of religion and education places him in the ranks of the "few." Considered in this light, it has been thought proper and just to select him as successor to our grand and highly esteemed deceased.
>
> An unanimous appeal would secure for us this "Light" of christian education, this grand talented ecclesiastic, who would ably erect thrones for our already honored brothers and with a master mind and hand continue the noble work awaiting the incoming Prelate.
>
> Being the eldest orphan of this widowed Arch-Diocese, I have been charged with the pleasant duty of circulating a petition in his behalf and trust you will kindly assist in the good work by signing the inclosed and returning it as quickly as possible.[66]

But in the final analysis, Gunn's effort had no more influence on the selection of Hennessy's successor than Father Brune's statement had in quieting the accusations against the Germans.

When no definite news of Keane's appointment to Dubuque was forthcoming, the *Northwestern Catholic* indulged in some fantastic speculation by printing that Alexander J. McGavick, Auxiliary Bishop

[65] Sioux City *Times* quoted in the *Northwestern Chronicle,* Apr. 12, 1900.

[66] *Review,* VII (Apr. 26, 1900), 44. A printed copy of the circular was forwarded to the author by the late Monsignor O'Malley of Dubuque, to whom the author is grateful.

of Chicago, would resign soon to make way for the appointment of Keane to that see as coadjutor with the right of succession and that Bishop O'Gorman of Sioux Falls would be transferred to Dubuque.[67] Another Catholic journal, basing its information on the opinion of the editor of a paper in Rome, said: "Those who like to be in advance of the events of the day may with some degree of assurance proclaim it to be settled that the ex-Rector will not rule the See of Dubuque."[68] At approximately this same time the *Catholic Universe, Freeman's Journal, Catholic Standard and Times,* and *Catholic Tribune* claimed that their Roman correspondents announced positively that Keane would be approved for the vacancy.[69]

During this period of general uncertainty, the archbishop's friends believed that his appointment would soon be officially announced. Late in June Archbishop Kain of St. Louis spread the good news that Ledochowski had assured him, as he said, "whilst Mgr. Keane was not a *persona grata* to Cardinal Satolli, yet seeing that all wanted Mgr. Keane in Dubuque, he would not oppose the appointment." He further reported that Cardinal Rampolla was strongly of the opinion that the archbishop would be the successor of Hennessy and that Cardinal Parocchi "was loud in his eulogies of Mgr. Keane's learning and eloquence and piety and expressed his confidence that, if he would accept, he would certainly go to Dubuque." Most important of all was the fact that in Kain's audience with the Pope, the Holy Father had said that he had confirmed the appointment of Archbishop Keane to the Iowa See.[70] Thinking that the matter was definitely settled, one of O'Connell's less reserved lay correspondents remarked: ". . . and now Bishop Keane is free; all glory to God and no thanks to them. Is it not strange that they continue to say the Lord's prayer; for surely with the 'coming of His Kingdom' there will be an end to

[67] *Northwestern Catholic,* May 24, 1900.

[68] *Intermountain Catholic,* June 16, 1900.

[69] *Catholic Universe* (Cleveland), June 29, 1900; *Freeman's Journal,* July 7, 1900. The latter said that Corrigan's name was first on the petition for Keane's appointment to Dubuque. Gerald P. Coghlan reported on the Philadelphia Catholic paper (ADR, Coghlan to O'Connell, Philadelphia, July 14, 1900). *Catholic Tribune,* (Dubuque), July 20, 1900. Late in July an Associated Press dispatch from Rome announced that Keane certainly would be appointed (*Review,* VII [July 26, 1900] 151). On August 9 and 30, 1900, the *Catholic Tribune* had to admit that no official news of the appointment had been received in Dubuque.

[70] AAB, 98-F-12, Kain to Gibbons, Lucerne, June 27, 1900. O'Connell had told Gibbons on June 15 that the appointment was certain (ADR, Gibbons to O'Connell, Woodstock, Maryland, June 27, 1900).

theirs. You see I can't help being critical—but this is all right as long as I remain just."[71] Among those who had received almost positive assurance from O'Connell that Keane would be honored was Father James Nugent, editor of the Liverpool Catholic *Times,* who was incited to say: "I am rejoiced to hear that Archbishop Keane goes to Dubuque. There is a field where he can show his power and sterling worth. It is a vast diocese with vast resources and great opportunities."[72]

Although Archbishop Keane had also received similar encouraging dispatches from Monsignor O'Connell, he told his friend in Rome that he could not consider the matter settled until the Pope had given his approval and that in the meantime the monsignor was to send on any information that he could gather.[73] During the last week in July the archbishop's faithful Roman correspondent sent word that the appointment had been made. In acknowledging the good tidings, the harassed prelate poured out the sentiments that he had hidden in his heart for several years. He wrote:

> Impersonal as I have endeavored to be in this whole matter, still I must and do say Deo Gratias from the depths of my heart for this solution of my life problem. And I do most gratefully and affectionately thank all the dear good friends who have shown in the matter a practical sympathy far beyond my deserts. To Cardinal Serafino Vannutelli especially I am profoundly grateful, and I beg of you to say this to him for me, being convinced that the expression of my gratitude through you, dear friend, will be better than through letter.
>
> The action of the Holy Father in sending, virtually, his instructions to the meeting of the Propaganda in my favor, seems to me very unusual and significant. It is a very nice and welcome settling of the score which, after all, really stood between us.[74]

Despite this absolute assurance that the appointment had been made, fully a month later the archbishop told Garrigan that although he was quite sure that his selection had been confirmed, he had not received official notification.[75] Finally, as he sipped his coffee at the German spa on the morning of his sixty-first birthday, September 12, 1900, a

[71] ADR, Joseph E. Hayden to O'Connell, Castellammare di Stabia, July 19, 1900.

[72] ADR, Nugent to O'Connell, Liverpool, July 28, 1900. Earlier in the month Nugent had said: "I hope you can secure Dubuque for Archbishop Keane. It would be such a blessing for that part of the country to have such a man" (ADR, Nugent to O'Connell, Liverpool, July 6, 1900).

[73] ADR, Keane to O'Connell, Bad Nauheim, July 22, 1900.

[74] ADR, Keane to O'Connell, Bad Nauheim, July 27, 1900.

[75] ACUA, Garrigan Papers, Keane to Garrigan, Bad Nauheim, Aug. 26, 1900.

cablegram from the apostolic delegate at Washington settled all doubts.[76] Indeed, it was a happy solution to his "life problem," and some of his friends looked upon it as his complete vindication by Rome.[77]

The archbishop did not tarry at Bad Nauheim after the delegate's cablegram had reached him. That very day he left for the Palace Hotel on the Champs Elysées in Paris where the banquet table was spread. Among those present for the celebration were Ireland, who was still in Europe savoring the acclaim following his discourse at the unveiling of the statue of Lafayette on July 4; Monsignor Boeglin, who had supported the Americanists in European journals with his pen during their worst days and who still championed their cause in the New York *Sun* over the pen name "Innominato"; Father Phelan of the *Western Watchman,* a former critic of the archbishop but now a partial convert to his ideas; Bellamy Storer, who was then the official representative of the United States at the Spanish court, and his wife; and Father M. Guyot, editor of the *Gaulois*.[78] After the last toast had received an adequate response, Keane left by train for Hamburg to be ready to sail on September 14.[79] Eight days later he

[76] AAD, "Record of the Administration of John J. Keane, Archbishop of Dubuque," p. 1. This is a diocesan diary of 152 pages in Keane's hand for the years 1900 to 1911, hereafter referred to as AAD, Dubuque Diary.

[77] Father Phelan, whom Preuss described as "loudmouthed," claimed that the appointment was a vindication of the American party. Cf. *Review,* VII (Nov. 15, 1900), 267. Rampolla stated that the appointment of Keane to Dubuque was an answer to those who averred that the Americans were condemned by the encyclical on Americanism (AASP, Mrs. Storer to Monseigneur [?], Barcelona, Oct. 18, 1900, [French]). In an article in the New York *Sun* (May 5, 1901), over the pen name "Innominato," Monsignor Boeglin said: "Mgr. Keane has endured cruel humiliation for the sake of this movement [Americanism] and this idea. Against him as well as against Mgr. Ireland bitter campaigns were waged. More than the Archbishop of St. Paul he has suffered for the policy which Leo XIII is making general in the main government of the Church.

"What the Church and Rome celebrate . . . in Keane's promotion is the consecration of the methods of work which we call 'Americanism'; the life full of faith, the apostolate of Mgr. Keane; the Christian movement of which Mgr. Ireland is the most illustrious representative."

[78] *Review,* VII (Oct. 11, 1900), 229. Without any apparent emotion, O'Connell stated in a letter to Ireland in 1915: "At the dinner table of St. Sulpice, Rome they told me in a clear voice that Boeglin was dead: "il est mort misérablement à Vienne abondonné de tous" (AASP, O'Connell to Ireland, Richmond, Virginia, Sept. 8, 1915). Besides the important talk in France, Ireland had delivered a discourse before the cardinals in Rome at the invitation of Leo XIII. Cf. *supra,* p. 285.

[79] ACUA, Garrigan Papers, Keane to Garrigan, Gloucester, Massachusetts, June 26, 1900. He had booked passage for September 13 he said. According to a statement after the fact he claimed that he sailed on September 14 (AAD, Dubuque Diary, p. 1).

arrived in New York and on the same day[80] received from the hand of the apostolic delegate in Washington the papal brief dated July 24, 1900, and a personal letter from Leo XIII.[81]

As soon as the official documents were in hand, the archbishop opened a correspondence with Monsignor Roger Ryan, the administrator of the archdiocese during the interregnum, to set the time for his installation. When Keane was assured that everything was in readiness for the ceremony, he informed the administrator that he would arrive at 4:20 p.m. on September 27,[82] and he expressed the wish that there would be no public display when he arrived. Despite the explicit manifestation of his desires, he and his companions, Garrigan and Kerby of the University, were greeted by a large delegation from Dubuque at Apple River, a little town fifteen miles from Galena, Illinois. Then, as the train rounded the curve leading to the depot in Dubuque the archbishop saw thousands of people of every class, creed, and nationality, waiting to welcome him by their cheers as he left the train and made his way to the cathedral rectory in a carriage. At the same time the great bells of the cathedral rang out the joyful news that the new shepherd of the Archdiocese of Dubuque had arrived.[83]

Within an hour after he had stepped on Iowa soil, the archbishop was vested and with the clergy proceeded to the Cathedral for the ceremony prescribed in the *Pontificale Romanum* for the installation of a bishop. When this short rite was completed, John Carroll, whose name had appeared first on the priests' list for the vacant see, read and gave a short explanation of the papal document transferring the Archbishop of Damascus to the See of Dubuque. His place in the pulpit was then taken by Monsignor Ryan, who welcomed the archbishop in the name of the clergy and the laity of the archdiocese. Then, the one whom all had come to see and to hear raised his voice to express his gratitude for the warm reception accorded him and to

[80] On that day the archbishop asked for an appointment with President McKinley, saying that it was very important, and he mentioned that he had just left Europe where he had a momentous discussion with Ireland (Library of Congress, Manuscript Division, McKinley Papers, Keane to the Secretary of the President, Washington, Sept. 22, 1900).

[81] AAD, Dubuque Diary, p. 1.

[82] John J. Toomey and M. C. Sullivan (eds.), *Souvenir of the Installation and the Investiture with Pallium of Most Rev. John J. Keane, D. D., as Archbishop of Dubuque* (Dubuque, 1901), p. 5; AAD; Dubuque Diary, p. 2.

[83] Toomey and Sullivan, *op. cit.*, p. 57. As early as September 8, the *New Century and Church News* had reported that all the leading citizens without regard to religious affiliation had expressed the desire to make the reception a notable event.

give his inaugural sermon. After paying tribute to Leo XIII and to his predecessors in the See of Dubuque, Keane praised Monsignor Ryan, whom he continued in the office of vicar-general, and expressed his high regard for the priests, religious, and laity, whom he looked upon as his greatest comfort and most effective aids in carrying out the work which he outlined. Their personal sanctification through co-operation with the graces merited by the Redeemer and the uplifting of the age and the country through their spiritual activity were the goals to be achieved. They were bound, as well, to make good Christians of the coming generation, an object that could only be accomplished by perfecting the system of Catholic education in the archdiocese. "We must press on in the resolve to build up in this archdiocese a perfect system of Christian education," he said, "bringing within the reach of every Catholic child such training as will fit him both to fill an honorable place in this world and to secure his eternal salvation in the next."[84]

Five days after the installation ceremony, nearly 250 out of the 273 priests under Keane's jurisdiction assembled at the Hotel Julien in Dubuque for a dinner in the archbishop's honor.[85] On this occasion, according to the Catholic paper in Dubuque, he created quite a sensation when he was reported to have said:

> He had been called a Liberal, a heretic, and that he was imbued with Americanism. But he defied those who had thus characterized him to show that there was any foundation for their assertions and declared that there was not a single act of his life nor word that he had ever spoken that justified any one in making such charges against him.

At the same time the archbishop made some sharp references to Arthur Preuss whose *Review* had given ample evidence that its editor's sympathies were not with Keane.[86]

[84] Toomey and Sullivan, *op. cit.*, pp. 8–18. The discourse may be found on pp. 10–18. He had the sermon printed, and he asked the pastors to read it in their churches (AAD, Dubuque Diary, p. 3). According to an intimate friend, the archbishop frequently said during these years "that his few years' sojourn in the Eternal City had given him a deeper insight into the Church's universality, and had at the same time intensified his love of America as God's gift to Holy Church, in our times, for the conversion of the world to the true Faith of Christ." Cf. Elliott, "Personal Reminiscences of Archbishop Keane," *op. cit.*, p. 644.

[85] AAD, Dubuque Diary, pp. 3–4.

[86] *Catholic Tribune*, Oct. 4, 1900. Concerning Preuss this journal reported that he said that "he had nothing for the 'poor creature' but pity, and that 'some one ought to take him in hand and teach him his catechism.'" Preuss then reminded his readers and Keane that it was the *Western Watchman* of the same city, not the *Review*,

During these first days in Dubuque Keane made a favorable impression on his new subjects, according to the reports that reached his friends.[87] He, in turn, claimed that the reception which the priests and laity had accorded him "was all that heart could wish."[88] Hence, the future looked unusually bright for him as he entered his new field of work full of peace and charity.

Before Archbishop Keane could be truly considered the shepherd of the flock in the Archdiocese of Dubuque, however, it was necessary that he be invested with the pallium. When this highest badge of the metropolitan's office arrived in Dubuque late in January, 1901,[89] the date for conferring it was set for April 17. For over two months preceding that day, the clergy and laity of the archdiocese were engaged in preparations for the occasion which they had fully resolved to make memorable in the history of Dubuque. Since the archbishop had most emphatically expressed himself as being opposed to any celebration apart from the ceremony prescribed by the *Pontifical,* and since he frowned on any token for him personally, their energies were admirably exhausted in seeking perfection in all that concerned the ecclesiastical function and in the preparations for the fitting reception of distinguished guests.[90]

The dawn of April 17 foretold a balmy spring day. By ten o'clock the unreserved portions of St. Raphael's Cathedral were filled with

---

which had referred to Keane as a semipelagian heretic at the time of his deposition (*Review,* VII [Oct. 11, 1900], 229).

[87] AUND, Hudson Papers, Spalding to Hudson, Peoria, Oct. 8, 1900; ADR, Ireland to O'Connell, St. Paul, Oct. 27, 1900.

[88] AASP, Keane to Ireland, Dubuque, Oct. 29, 1900. Nugent told O'Connell: "The first dinner given to Archbishop Keane after his arrival was given by Mr. Connolly. I was staying with them at the time" (ADR, Nugent to O'Connell, Nice, Mar. 18, 1901).

[89] *Catholic Tribune,* Jan. 31, 1901.

[90] R. Ryan and John J. Toomey to Dear Rev. Father, Dubuque, Feb. 8, 1901, quoted in Toomey and Sullivan, *op. cit.,* pp. 28–29, asked the priests of the archdiocese to subscribe the amount which had been determined at a meeting of a representative group of the clergy so all expenses could be defrayed. Among other things they said: "In the past on similar occasions we have shown ourselves as not disposed to do things by halves. On this occasion to not only maintain but to surpass our former reputation is a sacred duty we owe to ourselves as priests, to the fair name of our great and historic diocese, and in an especial manner do we owe it as our first expression, feeble and inadequate though it be, of our loyalty and reverence to the person and sacred office of that peerless character among the grand galaxy of the American hierarchy whom the Holy Ghost has sent to be not only our chief pastor, but our father and friend." The accounts of the celebration indicate that they met with success in all that they undertook. Cf. Toomey and Sullivan, *op. cit.,* pp. 28–31.

people who had been waiting since the early hours of the morning to be sure of a place, and the large number who had been disappointed in their attempt to enter the church lined the path over which the procession would go from the rectory to the cathedral. Promptly at ten o'clock the clergy, numbering about 400, marched to their places in the pews in the middle aisle of the richly decorated church. They were followed by twenty-one bishops and four archbishops who took their places in the sanctuary. After them came the principals of the Mass with Archbishop Kain of St. Louis, the celebrant, followed by Archbishop Keane and his deacons.[91] In the place of honor was James Cardinal Gibbons flanked by his chaplains. Never in the history of Dubuque had so many prelates graced an occasion, nor had the cathedral ever contained so many laymen from abroad and from many states in the Union.[92] All followed the first portion of the pontifical Mass, and then they focused their attention upon the pulpit as John Ireland, the "Apostle of the New Era," began a lengthy discourse on his favorite theme "The Church in America, Its Yesterday and Its Tomorrow." A critical auditor accurately summarized its contents when he called it "a repetition of the old subject. The Church—the Age—America, upon which was tacked a few rounding out [*sic*] on Christian Education, Catholic Colleges and Schools."[93] Besides, as an introduction, the Archbishop of St. Paul gave a short summary of the mother see of the Northwest, and, in conclusion, he directed these words to Keane:

> Friend of my priestly and episcopal years, my fellow-soldier and my leader in all causes that we believed to be serviceable to church and to country, I shall not this morning speak for myself; it is needless, is it not, that I do so? You know me too well.
>
> But I will speak in the name of the church of America and of America, and say how exceedingly one and the other rejoice today that you are seated in the full panoply of archiepiscopal dignity and authority upon Dubuque's Cathedral chair. The church of America and America are sure that from Dubuque will go forth in sweetness and power a mighty influence for good in the aid of religion and of

[91] Keane had chosen for his deacons the Sulpicians, Alphonse L. Magnien, president of St. Mary's Seminary in Baltimore, and Charles B. Schrantz, president of St. Charles College, Ellicott City, Maryland. When Magnien died in December, 1902, Keane was prevented from attending his funeral because he was recovering from an attack of bronchitis, but he wrote a warm personal note to the Baltimore *Sun* (*Very Rev. A. L. Magnien, A Memorial* [Baltimore, 1903], pp. 86–87).

[92] LCLD, Clippings.

[93] ADR, Bro. Joe [J. R. Slattery, S.S.J.] to O'Connell, Chicago, Apr. 18, 1901.

> patriotism. You are not an untried public servant. Your deeds of valor upon many fields of labor, your high endowments of mind and of heart, your exalted personal and priestly virtues, the esteem of love which you have never failed to win wherever you set foot in America or in Europe, the encomiums awarded you by the chief pontiff of the church — all this is remembered today, and is taken as an augury of the trophies of victory which the future reserves for you! Yes, the church and country rejoice and congratulate you.[94]

After the Mass, Gibbons seated himself before the altar and, after receiving in the name of the Sovereign Pontiff the promise of fidelity to the Holy See and to its teachings from Archbishop Keane, placed the pallium on his shoulders. Returning to his throne, the cardinal announced that Leo XIII had revealed his affection for the archbishop by sending a cablegram conveying the pontifical blessing to him and to his priests and people on that day.[95]

When all of the ceremonies had been completed, Father John P. Carroll addressed the archbishop on behalf of the priests of the archdiocese.[96] Replying to this address, Keane expressed his gratitude, and thanked Leo XIII, "who today," as he said, "has crowned his many acts of paternal benevolence toward me by placing on my shoulders the pallium of Dubuque." To Gibbons the archbishop manifested his deep gratitude for investing him with the sacred symbol of his office and concerning the cardinal he stated:

> For nearly forty years I have honored and loved him as a friend, and rejoiced at each new upward step in his marvelous career. Well have I

[94] Toomey and Sullivan, *op. cit.*, p. 60. For the complete text of the sermon, cf. pp. 44–61. Ireland's sermon at Dubuque was answered by Archbishop Ryan of Philadelphia on the occasion of the conferring of the cardinal's biretta on the apostolic delegate. The Archbishop of St. Paul, who was present for the discourse, said of it: "Yesterday was made famous by the horrid sermon of Archbishop Ryan — attacking the age, the government of the United States, France (in presence of its ambassador) — defending *a outrance* the religious orders, etc. You will read it. But what is printed does not give all his words, especially those of his attack on our government for its supposed rulings in Indian education. I gave out at once an interview to the Press, stating the exact position of the government. I owed this to the government, which had made at my request the needed changes in its rules" (ADR, Ireland to O'Connell, Baltimore, May 9, 1901). Another auditor made this comment: "At Martinelli's 'Red Hat' Ryan answered St. Paul's Dubuque sermon, hitting straight from the shoulder. Alas! Alas!" (ADR, Bro. Joseph [J. R. Slattery, S.S.J.] to O'Connell, New York, May 19, 1901.)

[95] Two months before the ceremony Ireland had asked O'Connell to obtain a pontifical blessing for the occasion through the Vannutellis (ADR, Ireland to O'Connell, St. Paul, Feb. 23, 1901).

[96] Toomey and Sullivan, *op. cit.*, pp. 62–66.

experienced his friendship, sincere, unselfish, generous, as true in the darkest days of life as in the brightest; above the wealth of worlds I prize it; and for this latest proof of it he has thanks too deep for words.

The archbishop's next words were addressed to his beloved friend from St. Paul, whose discourse made him, as one observer put it, "The Sun and Keane a pale Moon,"[97] and to his lifelong friend and comrade, Archbishop Kain, who had invoked the blessing of heaven on the day. Then to his suffragans he said, pointing to the pallium: "It looks soft and light; but we know well how weighty is the burden of care and toil which it implies. Yet we shall not fear it, nor stagger under it, because we shall carry it together as friends and brothers in the Lord, strong in our love for one another and in our devotedness to the Divine Master to whom our lives belong." Turning next to the prelates and priests who had come from a distance, he addressed sentiments of gratitude. Finally, to the priests of Dubuque he directed the major portion of his speech. After assuring Father Carroll, as he said, that "your words of esteem and affection will spur me to redoubled endeavor to be all that you have pictured; and if I still fail to reach the level of your overkind estimate, it will be through lack of power, not through want of will," the archbishop told his priests that they would work together "in spirit and in truth," for the ends designed by Providence.[98]

Shortly after two o'clock, all the priests and prelates moved from the cathedral to the Hotel Julien for the elaborate banquet which the clergy of the archdiocese had so carefully planned. After the last course had been served, Archbishop Keane, acting as master of ceremonies, pronounced some eulogistic words on the Holy Father and proposed the toast "All Hail to the Great Leo XIII, Pastor of the Universal Church." In his response Cardinal Gibbons recalled the occasions on which he had been privileged to see the Pontiff, and he spoke of the greatness of this successor to St. Peter. He singled out for special consideration the encyclical on the *Christian Constitution of States,* in which Leo XIII had reasserted that the Catholic Church was at home under every system of government. With this as an introduction to his theme, the cardinal stated:

[97] ADR, Brother Joseph [J. R. Slattery, S.S.J.] to O'Connell, Chicago, Apr. 18, 1901. He also said: "One ray illumined all with Ireland as the 'lumen originis' save Spaldings' eclipse in part. Was it defiance to the Consistory of April 15? Or was it the first note in the campaign for the Consistory of June . . . ?"

[98] Toomey and Sullivan, *op. cit.,* pp. 67–70.

> Certain people believe that Catholicity and republicanism cannot go together, but the Holy Father says the church can and will exist under all forms of government. While the church is hampered where despotism casts its dark shadow, it blooms like a rose under the light of liberty. In no country is her expansion or development more pronounced than in the United States. Where is the nation in which the church has not some grievance? And I don't believe there is any country on earth where it is smaller than here. We enjoy here liberty without license and authority without despotism.

After this expression of patriotism so characteristic of Gibbons, he said of Keane:

> I confess that the elevation of Archbishop Keane has lengthened my life for many years. It has cheered my heart, has brought sunshine to me, and to me has been the happiest incident of my life in the last ten or fifteen years, and I propose the health of the Archbishop of Dubuque, in his most cherished beverage.

After the cardinal had replaced his glass of water and after the merriment caused by the gesture had subsided, Keane introduced the next toast by stating, "After love for the church our next sentiment should be love for our country." In his reply to the proposal that they drink to the sentiment "God Bless Our Country, the Home of Civil and Religious Freedom," John Lancaster Spalding, the popular Bishop of Peoria, maintained that patriotism could not be founded on warfare or gold, and he spoke of liberty, civil and religious, as the chief basis of that civic virtue. Since liberty could not endure unless it was based upon intelligence and education, the bishop said that he agreed with the Archbishop of St. Paul — with whom he admitted disagreement on other things — that we ought to find wherein we can reach accord with our fellow men on the matter of education and, as he expressed it, "stand side by side battling to put down evil and all foes of God and Man."

The responses to the toasts "Welcome to Our Cardinal, to Our Archbishops and Bishops and to All Our Honored Guests" by Archbishop William Henry Elder of Cincinnati and "Success to the Catholic University of America, the Glorious Crown of our Catholic Educational System" by Bishop John S. Foley of Detroit were not marked by any significant remarks, except for Foley's humorous comparison between Keane and his patron saint who was thrown into a caldron of boiling oil and came out unharmed. The kettle into which the archbishop had been immersed was filled with misrepresentations and calumny but, as Foley put it, "the Lord rescued and vindicated the rector of the University by placing the pallium upon his shoulders."[99]

Bishop O'Gorman's response to the toast "The Church of the Great Northwest," was replete with implications as well as direct statements which were not calculated to please all those who wore clerical garb. He pointed out that in the Northwest there was to be found one quarter of the Catholic population of the United States — two and a half million souls, almost one quarter of the hierarchy, and more than one quarter of the priesthood. Giving further facts, he said that outside of Chicago, Milwaukee, and St. Paul, the Catholic population was in the rural areas and that the clergy caring for these people were affiliated with a diocese for the most part. With this background the Bishop of Sioux Falls launched into his main theme by stating:

> You will find less religious communities because of the few centers of population. The proportion of the regulars to the diocesan in the United States is 1 to 3 and in the northwest 1 to 6, and if you leave out the large cities it is much smaller. Therefore the first result is that the real diocesan life of the clergy, which is the ideal apostolic character, is to be found in the diocese of Dubuque. The second result is that the western priest is self-reliant and a sturdy man. He lives alone in his rural parish, and the breezes, and sometimes blizzards, blow about him and brace him up physically and spiritually. I take off my hat and give my hand to the sturdy priest of the northwest.[100]

It was on this slightly discordant note that the festivities came to an end.

After his intimate friends had departed for their own fields of labor, Keane continued to utilize those gifts which enabled him to make loyal friends among all classes and to win people to the only cause in which his whole life proved him to be truly and irrevocably interested, namely, the salvation of souls. Thus, "letting civil and ecclesiastical politics alone, and doing the work of an American Bishop," as he had advised Ireland to do,[101] Keane's life became full of usefulness and peace as he took up his new task in Dubuque.

[99] For an account of the banquet, cf. Toomey and Sullivan, *op. cit.*, pp. 71–80. The rector of the University was in Dubuque the day before the celebration, but he had to leave before the ceremony to attend the funeral of Monsignor James McMahon of New York, one of the institution's chief benefactors.

[100] *Ibid.*, p. 80.

[101] ADR, Keane to O'Connell, Dubuque, Dec. 24, 1901.

CHAPTER XI

Active Years in Dubuque

WHEN he assumed the administration of the metropolitan See of Dubuque, which then embraced the northern half of the state of Iowa, Archbishop Keane brought to his assignment twenty-two years of experience as bishop. The broad knowledge that he had gained during the years that he held responsible positions in the Church enabled him to grasp the crosier with a sure grip; while his naturally zealous soul impelled him to meet this new challenge without hesitation. Upon his arrival at his new post, he immediately dispatched the routine matter of the appointment of diocesan officials by the simple expedient of continuing them all in their offices, with the exception of the chancellor-secretary, whom he appointed as rector of St. Raphael's Cathedral.[1] Before accepting the archdiocesan properties from the executors of the former archbishop, however, he first obtained the best legal advice about incorporation, and only when he was satisfied that the method of holding the property in fee simple, which had obtained in Dubuque for some time, was the most practical under the circumstances, did he have the transfer effected and recorded in every county of the archdiocese. At the same time he had his will prepared to ensure the transmission of all ecclesiastical property to his own successor.[2]

Like most bishops entering a new see, Keane deemed it advisable

[1] AAD, Dubuque Diary, p. 4. On October 2 he also held the first meeting of the six archdiocesan consultors. The archbishop told them that he would call them together monthly and ask their advice on all important diocesan business (*ibid.*, p. 6). Ecclesiastical officials in Dubuque told the present writer that the Diocesan Diary is the only document from Keane's administration in the archives. It is presumed that he destroyed the rest of his personal and official papers.

[2] *Ibid.*, pp. 6–7.

to spend some time in observing conditions before he would launch any projects for the spiritual and material welfare of his people. For that reason, he merely told his clergy, at their first meeting within a week after his arrival in Dubuque, that he expected to administer the sacrament of confirmation in every parish and mission of the archdiocese, and that, in the visitation which would be made at the same time, he would expect to find all the parish records and all the articles utilized in the liturgy in proper order.[3] The period of careful observation began immediately. Within the first month he had inspected all the schools and religious houses of his see city and had attended receptions in his honor tendered by several local Catholic associations. Then, on November 3, he embarked on a schedule that called for the administration of confirmation and the visitation in one parish a day on weekdays and in two parishes on Sundays. He found during the first tour, which took him to the country missions in the neighborhood of Dubuque, that the sacrament had not been conferred in most of the parishes from seven to thirteen years or even longer, but he noted with pleasure that in nearly all of the parishes the organization, equipment, and management were excellent.[4]

While Keane was carrying out his resolve to visit approximately 250 parishes scattered over an area of 32,602 square miles,[5] he was constrained also to direct his attention to many other things which pertained to their welfare. Even before he had been appointed to Dubuque, the suffragans had petitioned the Holy See to form a new diocese out of the western portion of the metropolitan see with Sioux City as its center. In the brief appointing him to Dubuque, therefore, the contemplated division was explicitly mentioned. Keane readily admitted to his priests that he was in favor of multiplying centers of episcopal jurisdiction. In this particular case, however, he had heard that the division had not really been sought by the majority of the

[3] *Ibid.*, pp. 3–5. Keane informed the priests that he wanted them to come to him in their troubles and trials and that he would be a brother to them. He insisted that he did not believe in ruling by force; rather, he was convinced that gentleness and devotion to a common cause would bring the best results in religion (*Catholic Tribune*, Oct. 4, 1900).

[4] AAD, Dubuque Diary, pp. 10–11.

[5] *Catholic Directory, Almanac and Clergy List . . . 1901* (Milwaukee, 1901), pp. 60–70. It took Keane over two years to complete the visitation of the entire archdiocese (AAD, J. J. Keane to the Clergy and Laity of the Archdiocese of Dubuque, Dubuque, Easter Monday, 1903, inserted in the Dubuque Diary, between pages 38–39). He completed the second visitation in May, 1906 (*ibid.*, p. 67) and he was in the midst of a third tour when his health began to fail in 1908. James J. Keane, Bishop of Cheyenne, confirmed for him in 1909 (*ibid.*, p. 119).

clergy and people, but had been urged by some "businessmen," backed by a very small number of priests. If these allegations were true, he averred that those who were opposed to the division had a duty to state their reasons frankly. The matter was agitated with such warmth pro and con by the clergy, and even in the newspapers, that the archbishop was anxious to have the subject definitely settled.[6]

On December 4, 1900, the suffragan Bishops of Davenport, Omaha, Lincoln, and Cheyenne met with Archbishop Keane to consider the contrary petitions sent in by the clergy within the limits of the proposed see. After discussion, the bishops voted four to one in favor of the new diocese and signed a letter containing the results of the voting and the reasons therefore to the Propaganda. The officials of the Roman congregation, in turn, referred the case to the apostolic delegate in Washington with the request that he obtain further facts on which to base his recommendation. Keane supplied the delegate with all the pertinent documents, a fact which moved Archbishop Sebastiano Martinelli to make a decision favorable to the proposal. On May 30, 1901, Archbishop Keane was informed that the new see would be erected, and he was asked to forward to Rome the names of suitable candidates for the post which could be proposed only by the bishops of the province. The archbishop and his suffragans met immediately and selected Thomas M. Lenihan, Bishop of Cheyenne, James M. Cleary, pastor of St. Charles Church in Minneapolis, and Philip J. Garrigan, vice-rector of the Catholic University of America, in that order.[7] After the death on December 15 of Bishop Lenihan, who, as Keane was informed, "would surely have been appointed to Sioux City," Garrigan was finally chosen as the first bishop of the new see.[8] It certainly was a source of great happiness for Keane to preach on the occasion of Garrigan's consecration in Springfield, Mas-

[6] AAD, Dubuque Diary, p. 5. On October 25, 1900, the *Catholic Tribune* reported that the priests had petitioned for a new diocese. Cf. *Western Watchman,* April 8, 1900, and *Review,* VII (April 19, 1900), 36.

[7] AAD, Dubuque Diary, pp. 12–13, 25. After Keane and the suffragans had met the *Catholic Tribune* (Dec. 6, 1900) reported that the question of the new see had been referred to Rome and that the archbishop had refused to give an interview on the subject. The same journal (Dec. 13, 1900) claimed that there were many conjectures about the case in the secular press.

[8] AAD, Dubuque Diary, p. 28. Bishop Lenihan died at Marshalltown, Iowa. Keane preached the funeral sermon (Reily, *op. cit.,* VII, 1311). On February 18, 1902, the bishops of the province submitted the following names for the vacant suffragan see: James J. Keane, pastor of the Church of the Immaculate Conception, Minneapolis, J. A. Connolly, pastor of St. Theresa's Church, St. Louis, and M. F. Cassidy, pastor of St. Patrick's Church, O'Neil, Nebraska (AAD, Dubuque Diary, p. 30).

sachusetts, on May 25, 1902, and to assist at the installation on June 18, for the events marked the recognition of the merits of a friend whom he had long held in high esteem and brought to the province a man who had, as John Keane had said of him some years earlier, "a record of self-sacrificing devotedness to duty."[9] Furthermore, the advent of this companion of former years in the University at Washington relieved him of the care of about 50,000 Catholics scattered over twenty-four counties, including a territory of 14,518 square miles in the northwestern part of Iowa.[10] But the release from burdens in that area only served to focus his attention on many other problems elsewhere.

From his earliest days in Dubuque, as one might expect from a man who had for years displayed such energy in the field of Catholic education, the archbishop was conscious of a serious obligation to perfect the parochial school system in the archdiocese as well as to foster native vocations. In the first meeting with his clergy in October, 1900, Keane urged the priests to take an active interest in St. Joseph's College in Dubuque which served as the preparatory seminary, and he exhorted them likewise to increase the number of Catholic schools. Archbishop Hennessy had left a rich inheritance of 125 parochial schools, sixteen academies for girls, and one college for young men. Thus it was Keene's concern to add to their number and to make all these institutions more effective in accomplishing the goal sought in establishing them.[11]

While Archbishop Keane urged the priests and people to build an elementary school wherever thirty or forty pupils could be gathered together, even offering to pay the teachers' salary if the parish found it impossible to do so,[12] he gave much of his personal attention to

[9] AAD, Dubuque Diary, p. 34; ACUA, Garrigan Papers, Keane to Garrigan, Rome, Dec. 16, 1897.

[10] Philip J. Garrigan, "Diocese of Sioux City," *Catholic Encyclopedia,* IV, 16. Late in 1902 Keane and his suffragans petitioned Rome to create a new province comprising Nebraska and Wyoming with the metropolitan see at Omaha. At the same time they requested a division of the Diocese of Davenport with a new see at Des Moines. The Holy See refused both petitions (AAD, Dubuque Diary, pp. 34–38). Keane was quoted as favoring the erection of the new province (*Catholic Tribune,* Dec. 25, 1900) and as intending to urge it while at Rome in 1903 (*Catholic Tribune,* July 9, 1903). During his visit *ad limina* in 1905 he asked again for the new province but once more it was not granted (AAD, Dubuque Diary, p. 56). Keane declared that Hennessy had promised the Bishop of Omaha to get this through.

[11] AAD, Dubuque Diary, pp. 6–7. Keane tried to establish uniformity of textbooks in the parochial schools. Cf. the *Catholic Directory . . . 1901,* p. 70, for statistics on the schools.

[12] LCLD, clipping, dateline, June 18, 1901.

the development of St. Joseph's College. In this he was prompted no doubt by his earnest desire to increase the number of native vocations which would be fostered and nurtured under the eye of the ordinary. His determination to provide a native clergy was strengthened as the years went on because of the difficulties he experienced in finding suitable priests to care for some of the national groups, who often proved troublesome when a priest speaking their own language fluently could not be found.[13] At any rate, the archbishop decreed that all young men who aspired to the priesthood in the Archdiocese of Dubuque must take their classical and philosophical studies at St. Joseph's College. At the same time, the plan calling for the construction of a major seminary was abandoned,[14] and the money collected for that purpose, as well as the funds provided for such an institution in the will of Archbishop Hennessy, were legally transferred to the college to be used for the expansion of its facilities. By the end of 1902, in addition to the acquisition of small parcels of land adjoining the campus, a large wing had been added to the building that housed the college; and before the termination of Keane's chancellorship a large structure containing a chapel and an auditorium had been completed and paid for.[15]

The material prosperity of St. Joseph's College was a real consolation to Archbishop Keane, and he experienced further joy as the number of its students increased, the standard of its work reached a higher excellence, and the products of its training took their places as zealous workers in the vineyard entrusted to his cultivation. In-

[13] AAD, Dubuque Diary, has a number of entries which indicate that his difficulties with some parishes were due to the lack of priests who could speak the native language of the parishioners. The Germans at Williams, Iowa, instituted a civil suit to recover $2,400 which had been given to rebuild the church there, alleging that the sum had been given on condition of having a German-speaking priest (*ibid.*, pp. 20–21). In 1902 the *Catholic Tribune* stated that Keane won the case (Apr. 17, 1902). The Catholics of Williams must have appealed, for the same journal reported on January 8, 1903, that the bishop was defeated in the suit. Keane, in turn, appealed the verdict but he ended up by paying the claim in 1905 (AAD, Dubuque Diary, p. 57).

[14] AAD, Dubuque Diary, pp. 7–8, 13–14. A month before he had told the clergy that he endorsed his predecessor's plan for a seminary (*Catholic Tribune,* Oct. 4, 1900).

[15] M. M. Hoffmann, *The Story of Loras College, 1839–1939* (Dubuque, 1939), pp. 166–173. On July 15, 1902, the *Telegraph-Herald* said that Keane had purchased two parcels of land during the previous year. In 1904 the archbishop made a strong public appeal for funds for the development of the college in a letter to the clergy and the laity. Cf. Sister Mary Innocentia Sanner, P.B.V.M., "Archbishop John Joseph Keane as a Devotional Writer and Speaker" (unpublished bachelor of arts thesis, Columbia College, Dubuque, Iowa, Apr., 1937), p. 32.

deed, he contributed his share to ensure such happy results. He regularly gave lectures to the student body; he was often found in the classrooms; and he frequently was present at the meetings of groups engaged in special studies.[16] Furthermore, by his open confidence in Father John P. Carroll, the president of the college until 1904, and by the appointment of a capable successor to that office in the person of Father Daniel M. Gorman,[17] Keane was partially responsible for promoting the institution's healthy intellectual atmosphere which won the trust of the people of Iowa and which ultimately caused its name to attract young men from many states.

While Archbishop Keane was taking an active part in the development of the institution that is now known as Loras College, he did not fail to give encouragement to the sisters who were instructing nearly 3000 young women in the higher branches of learning.[18] A Dubuque secular paper said of the prelate after he had been in their midst for a year: "His interest in educational matters has given all the Catholic educational institutions a new inspiration and impetus. Extensions and additions have been built and are being planned and those in charge are filled with a new ambition."[19] In fact, he made frequent visits to all of the academies for young women, and he never failed to speak of the blessings of a Christian education for women and to assure them that he would always work to have them as well instructed as men.[20] In fulfillment of this pledge he added twelve academies for young women during his eleven-year tenure of the see.[21]

Keane was not so successful, however, in rousing the Catholics of Iowa to a realization of the benefits that young men could derive from a Christian high school training. It was true that the boys were needed on the large farms so they could be tilled with profit, and it

16 The *College Spokesman*, a student publication, made numerous references to the archbishop's visits and to his lectures. Sanner summarizes a few of the discourses delivered at the college (*op. cit.*, p. 35).

17 Hoffmann, *op. cit.*, pp. 160, 168–169. When Carroll was consecrated on December 21, 1904, as Bishop of Helena, Keane claimed that he had no one of equal ability to put in his place (AAD, Dubuque Diary, pp. 50–51).

18 *Catholic Directory . . . 1901*, p. 70.

19 *Sunday Herald* (Dubuque), Sept. 22, 1901, Supplement.

20 *Daily Herald* (Dubuque), Feb. 11 and Mar. 26, 1901; June 17, 1902; Jan 30 and Sept. 4, 1905; *Catholic Tribune*, Mar. 28, 1901; Sept. 11, 1902, June 23, 1904; Sept. 3, 1908.

21 Cf. *Catholic Directory* for 1901, 1903, and 1911. In 1901 there were sixteen academies (p. 70). Three were in the Sioux City territory when it was cut off from Dubuque (1903, p. 542). When Keane resigned in 1911, there were twenty-five academies (p. 90).

was likewise evident that it would have meant financial suicide to attempt the construction and the staffing of high schools in the rural areas. Nevertheless, despite the obvious difficulties, Dubuque and Dyersville were provided with secondary schools for boys under the direction of the Brothers of Mary of the St. Louis Province.[22] Thus, there was created a small nucleus of young men who were more suitably prepared to portray and to promote the Christian ideal.

While the archbishop was trying to make provision for the education of the young in his flock, he did not allow the priests to succumb to the notion that their intellectual training was complete. In 1903 he introduced the practice of an annual examination of the junior clergy which entailed for them a detailed review of portions of the sacred sciences. During the same year, with some apprehension which proved to be unfounded, he revived the custom of holding semiannually in every deanery regular theological conferences at which serious papers were read and discussed.[23] Furthermore, because the Third Plenary Council of Baltimore had recommended the holding of diocesan synods in 1884, and because his experience as Bishop of Richmond had shown their value, he called the second, third, and fourth diocesan synods in 1902, 1905, and 1908, respectively, to ensure among the clergy a clear understanding of the archdiocesan regulations which were based on the Baltimore decrees.[24] Besides, Keane promoted organizations, such as the Priests' Eucharistic League, which was designed to increase the spirit of devotion. Moreover, by personally

[22] The brothers had established a high school in Dubuque by 1907 and one in Dyersville in 1910. Cf. the *Catholic Directory* for the respective years.

[23] AAD, Dubuque Diary, p. 39. The *Catholic Tribune* (May 14, 1903) merely mentioned the first annual conferences of priests.

[24] At a meeting of the consultors on May 29, 1901, Keane appointed a commission, consisting of the consultors and five others, to study the material for the synod (AAD, Dubuque Diary, pp. 24–25). For the statutes of the second synod, held on April 29, 1902, cf. *Synodis diocesana Dubuquensis secunda, die 29ª mensis Aprilis, A.D. 1902, in ecclesia metropolitana Sancti Raphaelis Archangeli Dubuquensi habita* (n.p., n.d.). Besides the fifty pages devoted to the statutes, this volume contains fifty-seven pages of appendixes, giving the archdiocesan faculties and other information useful to the priests. The *Catholic Tribune* (May 1, 1902) reported that during the synod the archbishop exhorted the clergy to work diligently against intemperance, to keep preaching proper observance of the Sabbath, and to continue inveighing against secret societies and mixed marriages. He also asked that the children be trained to sing parts of the Mass. The salary of pastors was set at $1,000 for country and city pastors after some discussion about making the salary for country pastors lower. Priests were urged to form parish libraries.

The third synod was held on April 4, 1905, and the fourth on May 31, 1908 (AAD, Dubuque Diary, pp. 54–55, 101). The statutes of the third synod take up only three printed pages. Cf. *Tertiae synodi Dubuquensis, die 4ª Aprilis, A.D. 1905 habitae.*

conducting the annual clergy retreat during his first two years in Dubuque, Keane furnished them with an admirable example of the results of a lifetime of study and deep devotion.[25]

Just as the archbishop's experience had equipped him for the struggle to increase the educational opportunities in the archdiocese, so his earlier training had prepared him for another important endeavor for the welfare of his people. In the early nineteen hundreds, Dubuque was known as "a wide open town," owing principally to the number of unregulated saloons within its limits which were open even on Sundays. As compared to the rest of Republican Iowa, Democratic Dubuque as regards the liquor traffic was a law unto itself and for that reason it was often called "the State of Dubuque." Because the Democratic politicians were lax and the saloonkeepers were entrenched, patent abuses could have been eradicated only by drastic and sensational action. Early in his Dubuque career Keane saw the need of some action for he had noted that a Catholic total abstinence society was sorely needed, and he confided to his diary that this would be seen to without delay.[26] True to his word the campaign was launched immediately. In his inaugural sermon in the see city he scored impurity and intemperance "as pests which disgrace and destroy the individual life, and sap the foundations of social existence," and in an introductory address before the Catholics of Fort Dodge, he denounced evils that follow in the train of excessive drink with, what a daily journal called, "all the ardor of a third party prohibitionist."[27] Besides, the papers reported that in his first meeting with the city officials of Dubuque he definitely left the impression that he would not stand idly by in the battle for the abolition of what was called, "officially protected dens of vice." Those who were unfamiliar with Keane's past record may have entertained doubts about his determination to carry on an effective campaign against drink and its attendant evils, but their incredulity was dispelled prior to the Lent of 1901 when, in nearly all of the churches, they heard sermons stressing the importance of abstinence from intoxicants and when

[25] AAD, Dubuque Diary, p. 22; *Catholic Tribune,* Aug. 15, 1901; Sept. 4, 1902.

[26] AAD, Dubuque Diary, p. 10. There is no history of the city for the period after 1900. The present writer obtained information on conditions in Dubuque during the period under discussion through the kindness of Monsignor Isidore Semper, who consulted people who have a memory of those days. According to a story relayed by the monsignor, the archbishop's residence was pointed out to a stranger in the city, who inquired of a Dubuquer on a Sunday evening where he might procure a drink, as the "only place in Dubuque where you can't get a drink."

[27] *Daily Herald,* Oct. 2, 1900; Jan. 16, 1901.

they were given cards containing the pledge to abstain from liquor during Lent, to avoid saloons, and to pray for the suppression of intemperance.[28] Moreover, in the sermons which the archbishop preached in the cathedral every Sunday afternoon during the Lent of that year, great stress was placed on the obligation of Catholics to give up the liquor business and to stay away from saloons. His last sermon in this Lenten series became the occasion of a great deal of discussion when he declared that he had heard that the city government was under the control of those who were engaged in the sale of liquor. The mayor countered by stating that the Dubuque government was "a pure and unadulterated people's Government,"[29] and on that note the matter was allowed to rest for a time.

Meanwhile, Keane was successful in establishing, in a number of the parishes in Dubuque, two Catholic temperance societies, the Happy Home League for the men and the St. Veronica League for the women.[30] So satisfied was he with the temperance campaign after his first year of effort that he optimistically assured one of his friends: "The reign of whiskey and of vice that had settled down like a pall is being thrown off."[31]

Although the archbishop utilized almost every appearance before an audience during the year 1901 to inveigh against the evils that surrounded the saloons, he merely suggested at that time that legal action should be taken to make certain that the laws regulating good morals were obeyed. During the second week in January, 1902, however, Keane began a vigorous campaign to clean up his see city.[32] Among other things, he and the pastors of the Catholic churches in Dubuque petitioned the city council for an ordinance which would close the saloons entirely on Sundays, election days, and legal holidays, and at reasonable hours on weekdays, and would prohibit the presence in

[28] *Catholic Tribune,* Jan. 3, 1901; Feb. 21, 1901. By "dens of vice" Keane probably meant the unregulated saloons and their unsavory clients as well as houses of prostitution which in some cases were located in the same buildings.

[29] *Daily Herald,* Apr. 1, 1901; *Catholic Tribune,* Apr. 4 and 11, 1901. During Lent he discovered that a saloon was to be found in what was called the "Bishop's Block" in Dubuque. He ordered it removed immediately and it was closed without contest (AAD, Dubuque Diary, p. 21). He preached in the cathedral on Sunday afternoons during Lent and Advent.

[30] *Catholic Tribune,* Oct. 24, Nov. 14, Dec. 12 and 26, 1901. The Happy Home League had for a badge a medal with a portrait of Keane (*ibid.,* Jan. 30, 1902). The Cathedral society was known as the St. Raphael's Abstinence League.

[31] ADR, Keane to O'Connell, Dubuque, Dec. 24, 1901.

[32] *Catholic Tribune,* Apr. 18, May 30, June 6, and Nov. 14, 1901; Jan. 16, 1902.

them of women either as employees or as customers.[33] This effort to control by city ordinance the places dispensing liquor was endorsed by Dubuque's Protestant ministers.[34] But despite their influence on public opinion and the tremendous pressure exerted by the archbishop in his Sunday afternoon sermons during the lenten season, a special committee of the city council killed the proposed ordinance on the grounds that it conflicted with the Mulct Law which gave the control of liquor to the state government. This action drew sarcastic criticism from Keane, and he suggested that the citizens of Dubuque attend the caucuses of the various parties to see that the proper men were selected to name the candidates for the city offices.[35]

Before attempting anything further along the lines of the proposed ordinance, Keane must have decided that he needed the backing of a strong diocesan temperance organization. Such an organization was required, too, if Dubuque was to be successful as host to the national temperance meeting that was scheduled to meet there in the fall. At any rate, in a pastoral letter of April 29, 1902, Keane stated:

> On account of the great sins and shameful scandals that arise from the excessive use of drink, priests are exhorted to have in their parishes temperance societies by which the young will be reared and by which the vice will be overcome. Catholics engaged in the saloon business are expected to find other occupations or at least under penalty of denial of the sacraments to observe the Sabbath.[36]

During the month after the episcopal letter had been received, there was intense activity in the parishes in the cause of temperance so that everything would be ready for the formation of a state union of the

[33] *Ibid.,* Mar. 6, 1902; *Telegraph-Herald,* Mar. 1, 1902 (the *Daily Herald* was merged with the *Telegraph* on October 27, 1901). In his diary Keane stated that the petition was submitted on February 15. He continued by stating that the opposition was chiefly furnished by the Malting Company, which, as he put it, "has long controlled the politics of the city, in the interest of the saloon." The archbishop, contrary to the reports in the papers, claimed that the council yielded a little and ordered the saloons to stay closed until two o'clock on Sunday afternoon (AAD, Dubuque Diary, pp. 31–32).

[34] *Telegraph-Herald,* Mar. 2, 1902. The Dubuque *Times* stated that Keane had refused an offer made by the City Ministers' Association to co-operate in the temperance work. The archbishop replied through his secretary that the proposition had not been conveyed to him. Had the offer reached him, said the secretary, "he would not be guilty of the discourtesy of failing to return an answer" (*Telegraph-Herald,* Apr. 4, 1902).

[35] *Telegraph-Herald,* Feb. 10, 15, 24; Mar. 10, 12, 17, 19, 29, 1902.

[36] *Ibid.,* Apr. 29, 1902.

Happy Home League.[37] On May 30, the date set for the convention in Dubuque of all the parish temperance societies, it was reported that the Grand Opera House was filled to capacity with the delegates from thirty-six societies representing a membership of nearly 3000 who listened to inspiring speeches given by the archbishop, a Paulist from New York, and Father John Toomey, rector of the cathedral and Keane's chief aid in this work. The climax of the convention was reached when the Archdiocesan Total Abstinence Union was formed with Father Toomey as its first president.[38]

Soon after the archdiocesan union was established, Keane sought to whip up more enthusiasm for the movement by making the meetings of the Happy Home League memorable occasions and by holding public meetings in the Grand Opera House which were usually attended by citizens of all denominations.[39] By August 6, the date for the opening of the three-day national convention of the Catholic Total Abstinence Union of America, a large number of the inhabitants of the "Key City" were prepared to tender a fitting welcome to the temperance delegates from every part of the nation. The convention was opened with a pontifical Mass in St. Raphael's Cathedral where Archbishop Keane formally welcomed all those whose sentiments on the question were akin to his own. So many able speakers addressed the delegates during the three days that the *Catholic Tribune* was prompted to remark: "Temperance eloquence and lots of it was on tap during the convention."[40] Of course, the archbishop contributed his share of the eloquence. At the same time, as one who had worked for the cause for thirty-two years and had but recently revived the issue in Dubuque where it had been dead since the time of Bishop Loras, he was the object of some of the most laudatory oratory.[41]

[37] On April 24, 1902, the *Catholic Tribune* announced the purpose of a scheduled temperance convention.

[38] *Telegraph-Herald,* May 31, 1902. Six years later the same paper claimed that at this meeting there were delegates representing twenty-six societies with a membership of 1625 (*ibid.,* June 7, 1908). These figures are probably more accurate in view of the fact that twenty-nine societies of the archdiocese joined the national union a few months later (AAD, Dubuque Diary, p. 35). It was reported that nearly 3000 members of the St. Veronica League were affiliated with the national union at the same time (*Telegraph-Herald,* Sept. 22, 1902).

[39] *Catholic Tribune,* June 5 and 26, 1902.

[40] *Ibid.,* Aug. 14, 1902. The *Telegraph-Herald* gave an account of the proceedings on August 6, 7, and 8. For an account of the convention, cf. Bland, *op. cit.,* pp. 229–230.

[41] *Catholic Tribune,* Aug. 15 and 14, 1902. Keane was not completely satisfied with the showing made by his archdiocese during the convention, for he wrote in his

Shortly after the delegates to the national temperance convention had completed their work in Dubuque, the local papers began to give a great deal of publicity to the city council's practice of countenancing vice by forcing the keepers and inmates of immoral houses to pay a monthly fine. Such evidence of flagrant violations of the civil and moral laws gave Keane an opening for the renewal of his campaign to rid his see city of all vice. He began by characterizing the heads of municipalities that failed to fight gambling, impurity, and intemperance as "dirty dogs," and he declared that they should be thrown in jail where they might "stink" in their rottenness without endangering the morals of those entrusted to their care.[42] When Chris H. Berg, mayor of the city, was informed that the Catholic authorities of Dubuque were determined to have all the houses of ill fame in the city closed within a month, and that they would attempt to secure his indictment by the grand jury if he failed to aid them in the effort, he replied:

> You may say for me that I don't care a continental for the threats of these so-called reformers to secure my indictment by the next grand jury for countenancing houses of ill repute in the city. I have no fear of them, and furthermore, if they can produce evidence that I am in league with the immoral element and gamblers of Dubuque, let them furnish such information to the grand jury and I will graciously face the charges.[43]

Keane pressed the attack on the mayor during the second annual convention of the archdiocesan temperance union held at Dubuque in June, 1903. The *Telegraph-Herald* gave the following as the gist of the archbishop's remarks:

> Speaking of municipal corruption caused by the influence of liquor traffic the archbishop declared that because of his great love for Dubuque he would never give up the fight against intemperance until the mayor's office is filled by a man who will not bow down to the liquor traffic. . . . He appealed to the people to rise up and clean the stables, referring to the mayor's office as a stall that is rotten with filth. Moreover he declared that he would continue to fight intemper-

---

diary: "The Germans have, as a body, held coldly aloof from the Convention. They seem to consider free beer essential to civilization & human welfare, and are *intolerant* of the total abstinence movement" (AAD, Dubuque Diary, p. 35).

[42] *Telegraph-Herald,* Jan. 3, Feb. 9, Mar. 2 and 6, 1903; *Catholic Tribune,* Mar. 17, 1903.

[43] *Telegraph-Herald,* Mar. 12, 1903.

ance until the primary elections ceased to be controlled by the liquor power and until decent men will no longer be afraid to enter politics.[44]

Throughout the summer and into the autumn of that year the prelate carried on the fight to oust the mayor. He told a reporter of the Dubuque daily paper in September, "What the people of Dubuque need is a new mayor. We need a man who has courage, convictions and a desire to do right — a man who is not afraid to do his duty no matter what the people think or say." Keane also declared that he believed there was little use in trying to reform the administration since someone else was needed in the mayor's chair before changes in the city's moral atmosphere could be anticipated.[45] Finally, the mayor was called before the grand jury in connection with the investigation of houses of ill fame, and he testified under oath that he knew the houses accused but that no one had told him that they were bad houses. Reporting on the incident, a local paper added, "Comment is unnecessary."[46] While the grand jury continued to investigate the brothels, Mayor Berg announced that he was a candidate for renomination. At the same time, one of the Dubuque papers announced as a fact that the archbishop had consulted with some prominent citizens concerning a more suitable candidate for the office and that certain names had been proposed, but it was equally certain that the prelate would not take any part in the political struggle.[47] Although Keane was not publicly active in the combat, it seems evident that it was his powerful influence which was in good measure instrumental in bringing Henry A. Schunk to the mayor's seat.[48] For a time after the election of 1904 there was peace between the metropolitan and the city officials.

In the fall of 1906, Archbishop Keane again declared that he was dissatisfied with conditions in Dubuque, and he made a public appeal to the city officials to eliminate what he called "the agencies of public corruption," which included public dance halls and saloons. The mayor

[44] *Ibid.*, June 10, 1903.

[45] *Ibid.*, Sept. 25, 1903.

[46] *Ibid.*, Oct. 27, 1903.

[47] *Catholic Tribune*, Nov. 30, 1903; *ibid.*, Dec. 6, 1903.

[48] *Telegraph-Herald*, Feb. 14, 1904. The newspaper reports on Keane's temperance work in Iowa are numerous for the rest of his administration.

On November 7, 1903, the *Happy Home*, the official organ of the Catholic temperance societies of Iowa, first appeared. This monthly magazine received many contributions from the pen of the archbishop.

quickly announced that there was no law which could be invoked to close the dance halls but that he would give full co-operation as soon as some method of procedure could be determined upon. Shortly thereafter the press stated that the mayor had ordered the police to supervise the dance halls rigidly, and especially to see that minors were not allowed in them.[49] Still Keane was not completely satisfied. On Sunday evening, February 9, 1907, he revealed to a large temperance rally at St. Raphael's Cathedral that he felt keenly disappointed and humiliated because many Catholics in Dubuque had refused to stand by him in the crusade to better the moral atmosphere in their city. He especially rebuked the Catholic families in power, the professional men, and the men in politics, who, he said, were too cowardly to advocate and to work for what was right.[50] In a sermon given in the cathedral a few weeks later, he approved the efforts of the Reverend George L. Cady, a Congregational minister of the city, on behalf of the cause of sobriety and decency, and shortly thereafter he appeared with the minister on the same platform in the Grand Opera House on the occasion of a mass meeting to discuss ways of obtaining law and order in Dubuque.[51]

The mass meeting proved to be the beginning of an effective movement to accomplish some of the aims of the temperance advocates. Many of those present signed petition blanks asking for the enforcement of the Mulct Law, and the assembly adopted the archbishop's resolutions which called for the enforcement of the liquor law and for the formation of a Law and Order League to encourage and to cooperate with the public officials in carrying out the duties of their office. A committee was then assigned to handle applications for membership in the new league which would meet in St. Raphael's Auditorium. During the next few months Keane begged the citizens of Dubuque to support the movement for the enforcement of the Mulct Law, principally its provision for Sunday closing. Many of the saloonkeepers expressed a willingness to keep their places closed on Sundays,[52] but by that time Keane declared that he was tired of half measures. He insisted on the full enforcement of the Mulct Law. Evidently, the archbishop hoped to accomplish this aim through the Law

[49] *Telegraph-Herald,* Nov. 5, 6, 25, 1906; *Catholic Tribune,* Nov. 8, 1906. He also denounced political candidates who won votes by treating in the saloons.

[50] *Telegraph-Herald,* Feb. 11, 1907.

[51] *Ibid.,* Mar. 1, 1907; *Catholic Tribune,* Feb. 21, 1907.

[52] *Telegraph-Herald,* Mar. 1, 4, and 6 and Apr. 22, 1907.

and Order League which soon met to ratify plans of procedure and to raise funds so these plans could be carried out.[53]

During May and part of June, 1907, Mayor Schunk, as the head of a wholesale liquor firm, and many saloonkeepers were served with notices to appear in court to answer charges made by Archbishop Keane and Dr. Cady. Much to his chagrin, Keane was subpoenaed by the attorneys for the defendants who intended to have him tell under oath all that he knew of the saloons which he swore in his complaint were not conducted according to the law. Before he could appear, however, the judge postponed the cases on technical grounds. The attorneys for the saloonkeepers met with the members of the Law and Order League and their lawyer in an attempt to reach a settlement. When it was found that a compromise could be effected, they appeared in court, a priest representing the archbishop. After eight hours of deliberation, they heard the judge read a decree which called for the closing of saloons on Sundays, general election days, and Christmas; opening at 5:00 a.m. and closing at 11:00 p.m. on weekdays; no sale of liquor to men who had taken the drink cure, minors, and drunkards; no sale to any person whose wife, husband, parent, child, brother, sister, guardian, or ward over fourteen years of age, or employer, should by written notice forbid the same; no obscene pictures in the saloons; no gambling, music, or dancing; no women employees; no free lunches; no wine rooms as a part of the saloon.[54] The court decree was sent to the mayor, and he conveyed the contents to the police. On Sunday, June 16, 1907, the saloons of the city of Dubuque were closed for the first time in fifty years.[55]

Archbishop Keane, to whom the temperance workers gave the credit for bringing about the decree, publicly expressed his gratitude for this solution of a great evil. He said that the saloonkeepers themselves would be the ones who, after a few months, would be most thankful for the changes. Their families would be most grateful, too, he stated, because they could have a day to themselves without giving scandal to the world. In the same issue which carried the archbishop's sentiments, the *Telegraph-Herald* pointed out that some of the disciples of Bacchus followed well-worn paths to Kimbel's Island and other outlying saloons to obtain relief for their parched throats. Because beer had flowed faster than the Father of Waters at Kimbel's Island,

[53] *Ibid.,* Mar. 23, 1907; *Catholic Tribune,* Apr. 25, 1907.
[54] *Ibid.,* May 9, 1907; *Telegraph-Herald,* May 24 and 27, June 2, 6 and 11, 1907.
[55] *Telegraph-Herald,* June 16, 1907.

the temperance workers in Dubuque announced that they would take steps to change the course of one or the other. Lest there be a leak in Dubuque, moreover, the Law and Order League set aside a sum to be used in securing evidence on violators of the decree and for pushing prosecutions.[56]

In the same year that marked his successful campaign in Dubuque, the archbishop was honored by election to the highest office in the Catholic Total Abstinence Union of America. His many years of energetic and successful labor on behalf of the great cause, coupled with the widely publicized victory recently gained in his see city, prompted the delegates to the thirty-seventh annual convention of the union in Cleveland to vote unanimously for him although he was absent at the time.[57] The archbishop wrote in his diary that their selection of him was a very foolish move since he was not even able to attend the meetings of the executive council.[58] The next year, when indifferent health prevented him from attending the national convention in New Haven, he said in a letter to the delegates, "especially I shall pray that you may secure for President some Prelate, full not only of zeal for the cause, but also of the health and strength which I no longer possess."[59] As long as he had the energy to speak, however, he made temperance the theme of many of his sermons and lectures.[60]

While the Archbishop of Dubuque was striving to banish intemperance and some of its attendant evils from the city and the Archdiocese of Dubuque, he was at the same time warning Catholics about agencies which were spreading a spirit of irresponsibility in society. In the course of a talk given in Omaha in 1902, for example, he scored socialism as one of these agencies, and he claimed that the rapid development of trusts within recent years had much to do with the growth of socialism in the United States. He said:

[56] *Ibid.*, June 17, and July 12, 1907. In January, 1908, on the first anniversary of the establishment of the Holy Name Society in Dubuque, the archbishop praised the members for their help in curtailing abuses (*ibid.*, Jan. 20, 1908).

[57] *Proceedings of the Thirty-Seventh Annual Convention of the Catholic Total Abstinence Union of America, held in Cleveland, Ohio, August 7, 8, 9, 1907* (Cleveland, 1907), p. 70.

[58] AAD, Dubuque Diary, p. 90. The *Telegraph-Herald* (Nov. 20, 1907) erroneously stated that he had presided over a meeting of the executive council in November, 1907.

[59] *Proceedings of the Thirty-Eighth Annual Convention of the Catholic Total Abstinence Union of America, held in New Haven, Connecticut, August 11, 12, 13, 1908* (New Haven, 1908), pp. 10–12. On August 13, 1908, the *Catholic Tribune* said that he was presiding over the convention.

[60] Keane's name appeared each year on the advisory board of the Union, and in 1917, he was given the title of spiritual director of the National Union.

> Their enormous earnings have aroused the envy and cupidity at the same time that their success has been an object lesson in the importance of consolidation and combination of which the socialists have not been slow to take advantage. This is the age of combinations; we cannot hope, successfully, to check it, and should not wish to if we could. What we would strive to do is fasten the responsibility on power. It is there that the golden medium lies. There should be no irresponsible power. Combinations of capital, as well as combinations of labor, should be held strictly accountable, by government, for those things which they do that affects the public.[61]

When members of an electrical workers' union in Dubuque gave evidence of the spirit of lawlessness by destroying property and attacking defenseless pedestrians during a strike, the archbishop denounced the men who were leading the labor unions astray. He pleaded with the laboring classes to drive the socialists and anarchists from their midst and to fight instead for law and order. Lest some think him unfriendly to labor and to unions, Keane cited his successful struggle, along with Ireland and Gibbons, in 1886 and 1887 to keep the Knights of Labor from being condemned by the Holy See. He believed in labor unions because, as he put it, "in union there is strength and so long as the labor unions are rightly directed they will be the instruments of good, the world will applaud them." On the other hand, as he added, "as soon as reckless, unprincipled men get control of them they become dangerous and are open to suspicion."[62]

It is evident from many of John Keane's sermons and addresses that he blamed the socialists for the tendency toward anarchy manifested in some of the disorders created by labor unions throughout the country during the early years of the century. He observed how the leaders of that political faith were fomenting discontent by teaching the poor to hate the rich, by setting class against class. However, the prelate predicted the failure of socialism because it was founded on rationalism and because it ignored the Creator as the solver of man's social problems.[63] Where, then, would society find the solution to its

[61] *Telegraph-Herald,* Dec. 5, 1902. Keane had been invited to deliver two lectures before the Twentieth Century Club of Boston on the topic of the rights and duties of capital and labor (*ibid.,* Oct. 23, 1902). It is very likely that these talks were the basis of a number of his discourses at this time.

[62] *Ibid.,* June 22, 1903; *Catholic Tribune,* June 25, 1903. The results of the strike were reported in the *Tribune* on June 18, 1903. For Keane's role in the Knights of Labor episode, cf. Browne, *The Catholic Church and the Knights of Labor.*

[63] *Telegraph-Herald,* Sept. 28, 1903; *Catholic Tribune,* Oct. 11, 1903.

ills? This question he answered for the students of the State University of Iowa in a baccalaureate address in 1906, when he stated:

> Christian socialism can alone be the safety of the future, perfectly reconciling rights and liberties and energies and prosperity with the general welfare, and founding them both, not on the law of force (which always defeats itself at last), but on the law of love — love of God, love of Christ, love of humanity, love of the true, good, and beautiful, which is the Christian religion.[64]

Besides giving reasons for the condemnation of socialism, communism, and anarchy, Keane gave positive instructions to those who were most likely to succumb to the allurements of such false philosophies. At one time, he said:

> No man or set of men should be exempt from the law. Much of the trouble between labor and capital is due to irresponsible power. On the one hand we find a body of capitalists banded together. They make their own laws. they plan to do certain things, and they consider themselves exempt from the law. Likewise on the other hand we find a body of laboring men banded together, making their own laws, planning to follow a certain course of action and they also refuse to obey the law. It is wrong for men to act thus. No man or set of men should be exempt from the law; irresponsible power always causes trouble.[65]

At another time he outlined the ideal condition of things thus:

> A man's duty toward the public welfare is as sacred as it is to his family. In this world of industry the rule that must govern is that of justice and not only justice but good will. He who gets wages is bound to give honest labor for his wages, and he who gets work is bound to give honest wages for the work. He who gets work and doesn't give honest, square work is a thief, he is not merely indolent, he is a thief. Any labor union that aims at helping workmen to give less work than the wages demand, is a school of thievery. The industrial world must be dominated by justice, employers seeking the welfare of employees and employees seeking, in turn, the welfare of employers.[66]

Since Keane crusaded against all social evils, it is not surprising to find that he was a member of the National Committee on Child Labor and that he denounced the existence of child labor as a "menace to

[64] *Telegraph-Herald,* June 11, 1906.

[65] *Ibid.,* Nov. 23, 1903. This was the theme of a number of his addresses, cf. *ibid.,* Oct. 19, 1903; *Catholic Tribune,* Oct. 22, 1903, Sept. 10, 1908.

[66] *Telegraph-Herald,* Feb. 12, 1906.

civilization." In 1906 he congratulated the people of Iowa in that it had not been found necessary in that state to enact legislation to prevent the exploitation of children, but he expressed himself in favor of reasonable statutes which would label the use of child labor as a crime and he urged the Catholic people of the state to support this view.[67] When a bill to prohibit the employment of children under fourteen years of age was before Congress in 1907, Keane urged the state's two senators to use their influence to secure the passage of the law, and he appeared before the public in the hope of prompting them to follow the same course.[68]

While the archbishop displayed remarkable energy in the administration of the See of Dubuque, he was strong enough and cosmopolitan enough to show lively interest in many ecclesiastical affairs outside his immediate jurisdiction. From 1901 to 1908, he attended and took an active part in the annual meetings of the archbishops of the United States held at the Catholic University of America.[69] In the first meeting which he attended he was appointed secretary to the group, in which capacity he served until 1904. Moreover, in his first appearance at the metropolitans' annual conferences he was named, along with the Archbishops of St. Paul and Milwaukee, to a committee charged with making a study of catechisms to determine on one for universal adoption.[70] The next year this committee reported that there was no existing catechism which they could fully recommend, and if such a book for instructions was prepared, the board of archbishops had no authority to order its general use. Since such was the case, they could only postpone action, and Keane was given the duty of learning from the Holy See if a catechism for the Universal Church was in the course of preparation.[71]

In 1904 Keane, with the Archbishops of St. Paul, Milwaukee, and St. Louis, constituted a committee to obtain information from the highest officials of the Knights of the Maccabees, the Improved Order of Red Men, and the Modern Woodmen of America so that they might

[67] *Ibid.*, Jan. 8, 1906.

[68] *Ibid.*, Jan. 28, 1907. In 1908 the archbishop asked his clergy to solicit support for the child labor law (*ibid.*, Jan. 27, 1908).

[69] The minutes of the meetings of the archbishops show that Keane was not present after 1908.

[70] AAB, 99-F-8, Minutes of the Meeting of the Archbishops, Washington, Nov. 21 and 22, 1901; 101-E, Minutes of the Meeting of the Archbishops, Washington, Apr. 14, 1904.

[71] AAB, 100-D-4, Minutes of the Meeting of the Archbishops, Washington, Nov. 13, 1902.

determine whether these groups should be reported to the Holy See for condemnation as secret societies.[72] As secretary of the committee Keane reported the next year on the results of the deliberations of the four prelates during a meeting in Dubuque.[73] Confining his commentary to the Maccabees and Woodmen, the Archbishop stated that the officials of these organizations had shown an eagerness to please the committee members and that the societies were not so secret as to exclude investigation by Catholic authorities. For these reasons they believed, as he said, "that it would be unwise, undesirable and, from a standpoint of Catholic Theology, apparently unnecessary to condemn them."[74] After the committee had continued its investigation for two more years, a similar report was made concerning the Red Men. At the same time Archbishop Ireland suggested that the metropolitans request the Holy See to reconsider the condemnation of the Odd Fellows and the Knights of Pythias. Keane claimed that full rituals and pertinent documents had been freely supplied to the committee by the chief officers of these organizations and that they had found nothing in them worthy of condemnation. The archbishops decided to allow the committee to present the report on this delicate matter to the apostolic delegate, who would be urged to forward the views of the metropolitans on the subject to the Holy Father.[75]

Shortly after the archbishops' meeting in 1907, Keane made a statement to the press on the attitude of the Church toward secret organizations. First of all, he made it plain that the Church was not concerned with the business matters of such associations, nor did he question the high moral principles of many of the federated societies. Rather, it was for the following reasons that they were subjected to scrutiny:

> We feel that the Church should know what manner of organization her children belong to, and whether it embodies anything contrary to Catholic principles. This is the historic attitude of the Church toward secret societies. It is the religious question solely which concerns the Church. We want to know if there is danger to the faith of our people, if there is a tendency to indifferentism and carelessness in religious matters on their part. Membership in these societies often tends to

[72] AAB, 101-E, Meeting in 1904.

[73] AAB, 102-G, Ireland to Gibbons, St. Paul, Mar. 22, 1905.

[74] AAB, 102-K, Minutes of the Meeting of the Archbishops, Washington, May 4, 1905.

[75] AAB, 104-G, Minutes of the Meeting of the Archbishops, Washington, Apr. 10, 1907.

> weaken the loyalty of a Catholic to his Church. We gauge this by results and know that many become lukewarm by their membership in these societies. Lodge members may come to think that the lodge offers them sufficient religion if they live up to its rules. The Catholic Church cannot, therefore, on principle permit her people to join societies that refuse to permit those who have the guidance of her children's conscience, to judge whether the influence is to be good or bad.[76]

It was only in 1908 that the report of the committee on secret societies was sent to Rome, together with a request that the Holy See reopen the case of the condemned societies named.[77] A year later the Prefect of the Congregation of the Holy Office informed the American bishops that there was not enough information on the societies examined to justify condemnation, so it was up to individual bishops to permit their subjects to join the organizations so long as there was no danger to the faith of the person seeking membership.[78] Not until 1910, however, did Rome answer the request for a reconsideration of the two condemned societies by announcing that the ban on them could not be lifted unless there was a change in the rules and practices of those organizations. By this time, Keane was no longer active as a member of the committee entrusted with the task of inducing the leaders of the Odd Fellows and Knights of Pythias to make the necessary changes.[79]

During the 1907 meeting of the archbishops, Keane made a plea for greater generosity to the Peter's Pence collection. Besides pointing out that the Holy Father could no longer depend on such countries as France for large donations, he said: "Ridiculous statements have been made from time to time concerning the great wealth of the Vatican; the truth being that there was scarcely enough to meet the necessary expenses of the Holy See." In consequence of this argument the assembled prelates voted that a strong letter be sent to all the bishops of the country on the subject, and they commissioned the Archbishop of Dubuque and his colleague from St. Paul to prepare the document.[80]

Among Keane's interests outside of Dubuque, however, the Catho-

[76] *Telegraph-Herald,* Apr. 19, 1907.

[77] AAB, 104-Y, Minutes of the Meeting of the Archbishops, Washington, May 8, 1908.

[78] AAB, 105-L, Minutes of the Meeting of the Archbishops, Washington, Apr. 22, 1909.

[79] AAB, 106-E, Minutes of the Meeting of the Archbishops, Washington, Apr. 7, 1910.

[80] AAB, 104-G, Minutes of the Meeting of the Archbishops, Washington, Apr. 10, 1907.

lic University of America was the one which most frequently absorbed his attention. Since he had been taken from its service as a collector in 1900 to fill the Iowa See before he had realized the fruits of his mission, he tried to finish the work by mail and by visits to a few of those who had shown some inclination to open their purse for the cause.[81] Apparently, he soon found that this method was ineffective or that his time was too limited for such work, for he informed Monsignor O'Connell, the rector, that he could do it no longer.[82] This certainly did not mean a lack of interest in the welfare of the institution which had already cost him so much, for he told the vice-rector at about the same time in a letter which contained his donation of $1,000 for the current expenses of the institution, "whatever I can do for the interests of the University, I shall always consider it both my pleasure and my duty to do."[83] Since the university continued to be plagued by internal disorders and financial difficulties, Keane was given many opportunities to prove that his was no idle promise.

So many complaints had been lodged against Conaty's administration of the University by the fall of 1901 that the trustees of the institution appointed Keane, Bishop John Lancaster Spalding of Peoria, and Bishop Camillus P. Maes of Covington to investigate the financial and academic condition to determine its true standing so that practical suggestions could be made for its improvement.[84] When this committee was established one of the professors who was most responsible for spreading the impression that the rector was entirely incompetent, told his friend, Denis O'Connell, that he believed that the Bishops of Peoria and Covington would be able to dominate Keane during the investigation, even though the former rector was, as he put it, "wedded to his blunders."[85] After the episcopal committee had spent six days at the University in February, 1902, devoting six hours a day to their work, the same professor stated that Keane "took it all

[81] ACUA, Conaty Papers, Keane to Conaty, Barnum, Iowa, Jan. 12, 1901.

[82] ADR, Jeshurun to Dear Doktor [Grannan to O'Connell], [postmarked, Washington, Mar. 3, 1901]. On the subject of collecting for the University, Grannan said: "Broad John of IOA was in Washington and Philadelphia, to give some of his friends an opportunity to redeem their promises to shell out. I have not heard that he got so much as ten cents. . . . He told the administration that he had done his share, that he can do no more, that folks are tired of hearing him talk money, that now some one else must go out and collect, that we must help ourselves as best we can & cetera. 'Live or die, sink or swim, survive or perish, root hog or die.' Which is it?"

[83] ACUA, Garrigan Papers, Keane to Garrigan, Dubuque, Mar. 26, 1901.

[84] ACUA, MMBT, Washington, Nov. 20, 1901, p. 95.

[85] ADR, Jeshurun to Dear Doktor [Grannan to O'Connell], [postmarked, Washington, Nov. 24, 1901].

better than I would have expected. At the same time some of the comparisons were purposely made flattering to him."[86] Of course, a man like Professor Grannan would find it hard to believe that the archbishop could approach the problem in an objective manner and, despite the colored information presented by an interested professor, be a party in the formulation of important recommendations for the welfare of the institution which were presented to the trustees at their meeting on April 9.[87]

Although it was not apparent from the recommendations of the special investigating committee that Conaty was not doing his duty, enough evidence was unearthed to show that it was very likely that the institution would fare better under the direction of another head. Since Conaty's first term was to expire in January, 1903, Grannan began to maneuver for the appointment of O'Connell, with the latter's knowledge and approval. The two men spent the summer of 1902 together in Europe mapping their strategy. When they were assured that Cardinal Satolli, the Prefect of the Congregation of Studies and the person who for all practical purposes would appoint the next rector, was definitely in favor of O'Connell for the post, the monsignor's friends on the Board of Trustees were so informed. Gibbons, Ireland, and Keane were surprised at this change in the attitude of the former apostolic delegate toward their friend in Rome, but they were glad of it for his sake as well as for the sake of the University.[88] On hearing of it, Archbishop Keane wrote to O'Connell:

> I am convinced that if you threw all your energies cum amore into the development of the Univ'y, you could do more for that end than anyone else. And it needs it badly. The Univ'y is a case of arrested development; it is in the hands of a body of men whose *primary* concern is financial economy; — whereas that ought to be secondary, though important; & the primary aim ought to be the creation of a true University & the doing of true university work, & the offering of true university advantages, even tho' a lot of hustling had to be done for the funds. A *soul* is needed for the institution; and you have it in you to be that.[89]

[86] ADR, Jeshurun to Dear Doktor [Grannan to O'Connell], [postmarked, Washington, Feb. 11, 1902].

[87] Cf. Hogan, *op. cit.*, pp. 131–137, and Barry, *The Catholic University of America*, pp. 59–62, 77-78, for a complete treatment of this phase of the University's history.

[88] Hogan, *op. cit.*, pp. 167–170; Barry, *The Catholic University of America*, pp. 25–30.

[89] ADR, Keane to O'Connell, Dubuque, Sept. 26, 1902.

A short time later Ireland told O'Connell that "Keane was admirable" in the meeting of the trustees which witnessed the battle to put the monsignor in second place on the *terna* for the rectorship, it being understood that Satolli would see to it that O'Connell was appointed.[90] Everything developed according to plan. On January 12, 1903, the University's third rector was named.[91] Upon O'Connell's arrival in the United States, Keane could not refrain from revealing the joy he experienced in seeing him, as he said, "in a post that will fit you so well. May you have only peace and contentment in it, even amid all the problems that you will have to overcome. You will be more than ever a soldier of the Lord, and He will give you the victory all along the line."[92] A month later the archbishop extended a personal welcome to his Roman friend when the members of the Board of Trustees gathered in Washington for their semiannual meeting, the installation of the new rector, and the laying of the cornerstone of the Apostolic Mission House on the campus. On this occasion Keane was featured as the principal speaker.[93]

During O'Connell's first appearance before the trustees in April, 1903, Archbishop Keane supported the new rector's request that the members of the board petition the Holy See to order, for a period of ten years, an annual collection for the University in every diocese in the United States.[94] When the newly elected Pius X granted the petition in a message that gave evidence of his paternal interest in and support of the institution, Keane joined many of the bishops of the country in issuing a pastoral letter to his clergy and laity, containing the papal brief, in which he recalled that ten years of his life had been given to the labor of laying the foundations of the University, to which he added: "The seven years which have since elapsed have only deepened my conviction that the future of the University is inseparably bound up with the future of the Church in our country." He ended by ordering the collection to be taken up in every parish in the archdiocese to help, as he put it, "to solidify the foundation of the University forever."[95]

[90] ADR, Ireland to O'Connell, St. Paul, Nov. 28, 1902.

[91] Hogan, *op. cit.*, p. 170.

[92] ACUA, O'Connell Papers, Keane to O'Connell, Dubuque, Mar. 26, [1903].

[93] For a sketch of the Apostolic Mission House up to 1908, cf. Barry, *The Catholic University of America*, pp. 110–115. Cf. also Walter Elliott, "Catholic Missionary Union," *Catholic Encyclopedia*, III, 453–454.

[94] Barry, *The Catholic University of America*, p. 39.

[95] ACUA, O'Connell Papers, John J. Keane to the Clergy and the Laity of the Archdiocese of Dubuque, Dubuque, Nov. 3, 1903, printed.

In the year following the first collection for the University, Keane attended all of the meetings of the investigating committee and the special board meetings in which the precarious financial condition of the institution was gradually unfolded and revealed in all its dire aspects when involuntary bankruptcy proceedings were instituted against the University's treasurer.[96] The need for funds was greater than ever after that catastrophe. Keane joined the hierarchy of the United States in presenting an especially strong appeal to the people to be generous toward the University collection that fall; yet he realized only $3,400, just $400 more than the previous year.[97]

Although he could not furnish O'Connell with very much money to help maintain the institution, Keane was in a position to supply him with some helpful advice — at least it was meant to be beneficial. In a letter to the third rector in April, 1906, he pointed out these facts on handling the University's Trustees:

> I always considered myself the responsible executive; and in the meetings of the Board I never dealt with them as a Bishop with fellow Bishops, but as the Executive of the Univ'y dealing with its over-Senate.
>
> Such too seemed always to be Dr. Conaty's view. He really *bossed* our every meeting, and we were all glad that he did, for it was the only way to have deliberation & action strictly *ad rem*.
>
> Allow me to take the liberty of a loving old friend, and say that you have not seemed to take this view, — that you have not sufficiently bossed our meetings, — that in your actions on these occasions there has been too little of *initiative,* of *direction* of debate, of shaping our conclusions. Your answer, that you were "a simple priest" don't [*sic*] seem to me to meet the case at all. It is *not* as a "simple priest" that you were there, but as the *Executive of the Univ'y,* bound to be acquainted with every detail of its life & its needs, far beyond what any of us could be, and bound as such and as member of the Board, to be not only outspoken, but the leader in all debate & the most potent influence in all action. Your view, or your action, has been, as we used

[96] Barry, *The Catholic University of America,* pp. 79–100.

[97] *Telegraph-Herald,* Nov. 28 and 29, 1905. In 1906 the archbishop said that practically the same amount was given by the people for the Holy Father. "It is impossible to enthuse these hog & corn people of the West" (ACUA, O'Connell Papers, Keane to O'Connell, Dubuque, Dec. 7 [1906]). A letter in which Keane commended the cardinal for his showing in these collections could be taken as a sly dig. He said: "No other influence can possibly count in this matter like the personal influence of your Eminence. The misfortune of the present moment is a great blessing, in having set you so earnestly to work for the gathering of funds" (AAB, 101-R, Keane to Gibbons, Dubuque, Dec. 7, 1904).

to say in olden days, *"too subjective."* More *objectivity,* regardless of *personality,* is what will bring you up to the full level of your situation. That with patience, tact, considerateness, which circumstances so demand, cannot but win.[98]

Frank counsel of this kind would be graciously received by Denis O'Connell since his long years of intimate association with Keane certainly revealed that the archbishop had nothing but the highest motives when he gave advice to his friends. That O'Connell was his friend no one could doubt and further evidence of their fraternal bond was furnished nearly two years later when the monsignor invited Dubuque's prelate to be one of the assistant consecrators on the occasion of his elevation to the episcopacy.[99] Indeed, Keane was a true friend to O'Connell and to his successor at the University, just as he was a stanch supporter of the institution as long as he lived. Even when he was forced to remain in Dubuque by a gradual deterioration in his physical and mental powers, he spent his energy for it by praying that it would continue to develop and to know prosperity at last.[100]

During the time that John Keane was active as the Archbishop of Dubuque, nearly every year he spent the summer months in Europe in the hope of regaining some of the vitality which was being dissipated by his strenuous life and a valvular lesion of the heart. Before settling down for an extended rest at his favorite spot in Bad Nauheim, Germany, in 1901, however, he stopped in Ireland to preach on June 16 at the dedication of the new Cathedral of St. Eunan at Letterkenny in the Diocese of Raphoe, County Donegal, the see in which he had been born. The archbishop's reputation as a pulpit orator had occasioned the invitation in part, and he did not disappoint Bishop Patrick O'Donnell, who had also invited Michael Cardinal Logue,

[98] ACUA, O'Connell Papers, Keane to O'Connell, Dubuque, Apr. 2, 1906.

[99] ACUA, O'Connell Papers, Keane to O'Connell, Dubuque, Feb. 28, 1908. In this note Keane agreed to act in such a capacity. Later he was forced by failing health to ask to be excused. When he did so, he declared: "I shall make up for it by praying for you all the more earnestly" (ACUA, O'Connell Papers, Keane to O'Connell, Dubuque, Apr. 2, [1908]).

[100] AAB, 105-G, Keane to Gibbons, Dubuque, Nov. 11, 1908; AAD, Dubuque Diary, p. 148. That Keane was deeply devoted to the University is unmistakably revealed in these words: "Not a day since we parted but I have prayed as earnestly as I knew how for you and for the University. God grant that, through the 'fortiter in re & suaviter in modo,' you may yet have the institution where God wants it to be, the cornerstone of unity and peace, as well as the sanctuary of highest learning, for the whole Church in America" (ACUA, O'Connell Papers, Keane to O'Connell, Christmas Eve, n.d.).

Archbishop of Armagh, to preside at the ceremony and Bishop Francis J. MacCormack of Galway and Kilmacduagh to preach in Gaelic at the evening exercises. Among other things, Keane said that it made him sad of heart to be told about the gradual extinction of the Irish people, but he was sure that it was God who was scattering them to every part of the world to plant the faith in the cross of Christ. Wherever they went, he averred, they retained a love for the land of their birth so that the Irish would never die. He urged the people to muliply their industries and to get possession of the land of Ireland. "There are," he said, "thousands and tens of thousands of acres of grass that only stand in need of Irish arms to make them bloom, and bloom like a rose."[101]

Leaving Ireland, the archbishop tarried a little while in London where he visited Herbert Cardinal Vaughan, Archbishop of Westminster. While in England he gave an interview in which he expressed his trust in the fair play of England which eventually would see to it that Ireland had a Catholic university and that a parliament would be given not only to Ireland, but also to Scotland and Wales.[102] Upon unburdening himself of the expressions which marked him as a true Irishman, he went on to the continent where he suffered an illness which, as he told O'Connell, "shook me pretty badly." But he was completely recovered when he returned to his archdiocese in September in time to conduct the retreat for the clergy.[103]

While Archbishop Keane was at Bad Nauheim taking the rest ordered by his physicians[104] in the summer of 1903, his silver episcopal jubilee passed with barely a notice.[105] During this same period Pope Leo XIII's death was announced and his successor was chosen. Keane was certain that he would miss Leo whom he knew so intimately, but he said of the new Pope Pius X: "I feel as if he would prove to be a decent good Vicar of Christ."[106] When he went to Rome in 1905 for

[101] Reily, *op. cit.,* VI, 1022. During his stay in Letterkenny, the archbishop gave a fairly complete summary of his life on the occasion of a visit to one of the schools of the Presentation Brothers (*ibid.,* p. 1029; *Catholic Tribune,* Aug. 1, 1901).

[102] *Catholic Tribune,* June 20, 1901.

[103] ADR, Keane to O'Connell, Dubuque, Dec. 24, 1901. The archbishop had asked the monsignor to spend some time in Bad Nauheim with him. Taking the "liberty of an old friend," as he put it, he sent O'Connell $100 for expenses (ADR, Keane to O'Connell, Letterkenny, June 18, 1901; ADR, Keane to O'Connell, Bad Nauheim, July 10, [1901]).

[104] AAD, Dubuque Diary, p. 40.

[105] *Catholic Tribune,* Aug. 27, 1903.

[106] ACUA, O'Connell Papers, Keane to O'Connell, Bad Nauheim, Aug. 14, [1903].

his *ad limina* visit, he had his first opportunity to meet Leo's successor. After submitting to the secretary of the Congregation of Propaganda Fide his report on the Archdiocese of Dubuque, the archbishop saw Rafaelle Cardinal Merry del Val, the papal Secretary of State, whom he had known in various capacities during the previous years and to Merry del Val he made application for an audience. On June 16 he ascended the Scala Regia to the Pope's chamber, as he had done once as a priest to see Pius IX and many times as a bishop to visit Leo XIII. Pius X motioned him to a chair by his side after the exchange of the usual formal courtesies and they conversed in Italian for half an hour.[107] He described this meeting as interesting and pleasing in every respect, "but it lacked," as he said, "the element of old acquaintances and of many thoughts in common, which was the charm of my interviews with Leo." At the request of Cardinal Gibbons, the Archbishop of Dubuque probed the mind of the Pontiff during the audience to determine the extent to which His Holiness would go in insisting on the application of the principles for the reform of Church music which he had laid down in the *Motu Proprio* of November 22, 1903. Concerning this Keane later reported to the cardinal:

> You need have no fear whatever of any drastic measures or commands in regard to the exclusion of women from the choirs of a country situated like ours. Male choirs are indeed the principle and the rule; "but," said he with a very pleasant smile, "in the practical application, one must use a very large dose of salt, not merely a grain of salt." He has no thought of sweeping commands, and no expectation of sweeping results, but is naturally gratified by every compliance with the rule he has laid down.[108]

Pius X doubtless found it gratifying to learn from Keane that a Commission on Church Music had been established in Dubuque in compliance with the papal instruction,[109] and that the duties of the commission would be further outlined in a pastoral letter which he would write soon after he reached home.[110]

[107] Eugene J. Manning, "The Archbishop's Visit to Rome," *College Spokesman,* III (Nov., 1905), 13–20.

[108] AAB, unclassified, Keane to Gibbons, Rome, June 16, 1905.

[109] AAD, Dubuque Diary, p. 54. On Pentecost, 1904, Keane had established the commission. The four priests constituting the commission submitted conclusions based on the encyclical letter in April, 1905, which were published in a twenty-two page pamphlet entitled, *Ecclesiastical Music for the Archdiocese of Dubuque* (Dubuque, 1905).

[110] John J. Keane to the Clergy and Laity of the Archdiocese of Dubuque,

When he returned to the United States after being absent from May 13 until August 22, the papers announced that the archbishop had a message to deliver to President Theodore Roosevelt from the Pope.[111] Very probably it was nothing more than a request to convey good wishes to the President, since Keane had come to the conclusion after his conversation with the New Pontiff that, as he put it, *"the West* don't [*sic*] seem to count for so much, and the importance of winning the friendship of our President or our country, does not seem to be a dominant thought."[112]

During the years that he graced the See of Dubuque, Keane also absented himself for short periods of time to attend functions calling for his presence by reason of his position or owing to his former attachments. In May, 1902, he attended the celebration accompanying the consecration of St. Mary's Cathedral in Peoria which took place on the twenty-fifth anniversary of Bishop Spalding's elevation to the episcopacy.[113] In the same month he was present in St. Patrick's Cathedral in New York for the funeral of Archbishop Michael A. Corrigan, an event that marked the passing of one of the principal ecclesiastical figures of an important period in the history of the American Church.[114] In December of that year an attack of bronchitis prevented him from attending the obsequies of one of his dearest friends, Alphonse L. Magnien, S.S.,[115] whom he had seen a month before while in the East attending a meeting of the University's Board of Trustees.[116] However, Keane prepared the following tribute on

Dubuque, Pentecost Sunday, 1905 in AAD, Dubuque Diary, pp. 59–60. Archbishop Robert Seton, who is revealed in his diary as a somewhat eccentric ecclesiastic, wrote after he had spent an hour with Keane during this visit to Rome: "I had not seen him for some years & found him slightly deteriorated in appearance, but he remains still the same man *in nubibus;* seeing certain things (the University for example) & persons (Mgr. O'Connell, rector, for example) always *couleur de rose*. He is lacking in worldly wisdom" (New York Historical Society, Robert Seton's Diary, June 15, 1905, p. 166, procured for the present writer by the Reverend Henry J. Browne).

[111] *Catholic Tribune,* Sept. 7, 1905.

[112] AAB, unclassified, Keane to Gibbons, Rome, June 16, 1905.

[113] AAB, 99-K-3, Spalding to Gibbons, Washington, Feb. 6, 1902; statement by Monsignor Valentine Casey, personal interview, Dec. 28, 1948.

[114] ADR, Jeshurun to Dear Doc [Grannan to O'Connell], [postmarked Washington, May 30, 1902]. Cf. [Joseph F. Mooney], *Memorial of the Most Reverend Michael Augustine Corrigan, D.D. Third Archbishop of New York* (New York, 1902).

[115] Keane to Dyer, Dubuque, Dec. 21, 1902, telegram, quoted in *Very Rev. A. L. Magnien,* p. 86.

[116] ADR, Ireland to O'Connell, St. Paul, Nov. 28, 1902. The Archbishop of St. Paul, who had been in the East for the same purpose said: "Poor Magnien is dying — sure. I cried when I saw him: 'Many battles you & I have fought,' I said to him — and he smiled."

Magnien for the Baltimore *Sun:*

> The name of Father Magnien will be held in loving remembrance by the hundreds of American priests who made their ecclesiastical studies under his direction. It will be held in honor by the still greater number who have regarded him as a conspicuous type of the priestly character demanded by our age. He admirably combined the faith and piety and learning of the apostolic past with the energy, the adaptability, the intellectual receptiveness demanded by the circumstances of our new world. His life has taught us that this blending of the past, the present, and the future in man's intellect and character works well. His death has taught us to persevere in that course nobly and fearlessly unto the end, and then lay the result trustfully at the feet of the just Judge.[117]

On October 31, 1904, another cherished friend, William Henry Elder, Archbishop of Cincinnati, died, and it became Keane's sad duty to deliver the funeral oration in St. Peter's Cathedral, which had been the scene of the fine old prelate's labors for over twenty years.[118] It was in this same year that Archbishop Keane was afforded the only opportunities of his episcopal career to exercise his power to perpetuate the episcopacy. Some weeks before Elder's death, Keane had used this power for the first time in his twenty-six years as a bishop when he consecrated Mathias C. Lenihan, pastor of St. Mary's Church, Marshalltown, Iowa, as first bishop of Great Falls. Three months later he raised to the episcopal dignity James Davis, rector of Sacred Heart Cathedral, Davenport, Iowa, as coadjutor with the right of succession to Bishop Henry P. Cosgrove of Davenport, as well as John P. Carroll as John B. Brondel's successor to the See of Helena.[119]

In the fall of 1904, the archbishop's oratorical gifts were in demand on the occasion of the dedication of the new academy of Carroll Hall, when the 110th anniversary of the founding of St. Patrick's Church in Washington, D. C., was also commemorated. Martin I. J. Griffin thought Keane's talk on Christian education on this occasion "a great discourse," and he reported that President Roosevelt and Archbishop

[117] Baltimore *Sun,* quoted in *Very Reverend A. L. Magnien,* pp. 86–87.

[118] AAD, Dubuque Diary, p. 49. Elder had been in Cincinnati from 1880 to his death in 1904; and had been ordinary of the See from 1883.

[119] *Ibid.,* pp. 47, 50–51. Joseph B. Code errs by stating that James A. Duffy was consecrated by John J. Keane in 1913 and that Archbishop James J. Keane (who was still only a bishop) elevated John P. Carroll to the episcopacy in 1904. John Keane consecrated Carroll and James Keane consecrated Duffy. *Dictionary of the American Hierarchy* (New York, 1940), pp. 42, 88–89. The same mistake is made in Jesse M. Lonsway, *The Episcopal Lineage of the Hierarchy of the United States, 1790–1948* (New York, 1948), Plate A, No. 114, and Plate B, No. 75.

Ireland also lent color to the celebration by giving speeches at different hours during the same day.[120] It was in the course of the same year that the archbishop prepared for the Second Australian Catholic Congress a paper which appeared in pamphlet form under the title *Mary Immaculate and Democracy*.[121] The *Review* of St. Louis, whose editor had lost none of his earlier hostility to Dubuque's metropolitan, declared that it was "a novel aspect of that sacred subject, to be sure!"[122] Yet, the title in no way revealed the contents of the paper, and it was probably chosen to point up the fact that as soon as the United States had a Catholic hierarchy, they placed the nation under the patronage of Mary Immaculate. Most of the space was devoted to the development of his ideas on the role that the democracies were playing in the plan of Providence. The following were some of Keane's thoughts on the subject:

> It is in the youngest outgrowth of the great Christian civilization, in America and Australia, that the normal evolution of civil society, and the marvelous adaptation thereto of the Church's spirit and life, can be observed, and studied, too, with gladness, with hope, with confidence for the future. . . . In the nations of the Old World, the study is often more sad than consoling, showing, as it too frequently does, the endeavor of outworn or unfit civil forms to coerce or hinder the spiritual life of the Church. . . .
>
> Nothing is more plainly implied in the principles of Catholic philosophy and theology than the ultimate right of civil society to self-government. . . . Throughout nearly all Christendom the whole of the nineteenth century was spent in shaking off one after another of the trammels of civil childhood, in asserting and winning one after another of the rights of civil manhood. Even imperialism can no longer mean absolutism. Monarchy has become simply a form of constitutional government. Popular rights and free institutions have won the day against all resistance. Suffrage, growing more and more universal, rules the world. We are fully launched on the age of Democracy. . . .
>
> And it is under the inspiration and guidance of Christianity that civil society has grown to this. Christianity has been the inner soul,

[120] *American Catholic Historical Researches,* XXII [New Series I] (Jan., 1905), 64.

[121] Most Reverend John J. Keane, D.D., Archbishop of Dubuque, U.S.A., *Mary Immaculate and Democracy* (Melbourne, [1904]). Keane's discourses over a period of years were used by Maurice Francis Egan for a book of thoughts for each day. Since most of the pieces are separated from their context and since none of them was identified as to the time and place of delivery, the author did not think it advisable to use this work. Cf. Maurice Francis Egan (compiler), *Onward and Upward: A Year Book Compiled from the Discourses of Archbishop Keane* (Baltimore, 1902).

[122] *Review* of St. Louis, quoted in the *Catholic Tribune,* Nov. 10, 1904.

> through whose native power the intellect and the conscience and the will of human society have expanded into Christian manhood. But now the humanitarianism of the nineteenth century asserts that civil society, having reached its manhood, no longer needs the guidance of Christianity, but can dispense with this, as with the other appurtenances of bygone tutelage. And civil society has, on occasions, shown itself ready to act on the insidious advice. History records the results as a lesson of warning and wisdom.

Keane then spoke of France's failure in the attempt to establish a democracy without God. The American experiment, on the other hand, was launched with the invocation of God's blessing and for that reason, as he said, "it is today the chief home of peace and prosperity — as well as of liberty and equality — in the world." There was a tendency, however, to have, as he remarked, "the national intelligence alienated from Christian truth, and the national conscience alienated from Christian principles," the only remedy for which was the Christian education of youth. Furthermore, the greed of a few anti-Christian socialists constituted a threat to American institutions. But he concluded in his customary optimistic vein, "we cannot believe that the Providence of God will allow such a reversal of the natural Christian growth of civil society. Therefore, we feel assured that the men of the future will come back to Christianity, as the sole guarantee of peace and welfare both for individuals and for society."[123]

To return to the account of the archbishop's trips to various sections of the country, it should be noted that in May, 1906, he delivered a discourse on Father Edward Sorin at the University of Notre Dame when a statue of the venerable founder of the institution was unveiled.[124] And in the fall of that year, he went across the country to the scene of his first episcopal struggles to witness in Richmond the dedication of a new cathedral under the patronage of the Sacred Heart. There he met once more one of his earliest friends and a frequent benefactor, Thomas Fortune Ryan, who had donated generously toward the erection of Richmond's beautiful cathedral.[125] In June,

[123] Keane, *Mary Immaculate and Democracy, passim.* During 1904 an article from Keane's pen, entitled "Mission of St. Paul," appeared in the *Catholic World,* LXXVIII (Mar., 1904), 711–724. In 1907 he wrote a short, clear explanation of what is meant by the Hierarchy of the Catholic Church. "The Catholic Hierarchy," *Catholic World* LXXXIV (Jan., 1907), 453–461.

[124] Arthur J. Hope, C.S.C., *Notre Dame — One Hundred Years* (Notre Dame, 1943), p. 283.

[125] *Telegraph-Herald,* Nov. 27, 1906.

1907, Keane was in St. Paul for the laying of the cornerstone of Ireland's magnificent cathedral which was, as he said, "a superb demonstration." Approximately a year later he went East again to attend the centennial of the Archdiocese of New York, as well as to be present for Denis O'Connell's consecration in Baltimore on May 3 and for a meeting of the University's trustees.[126]

While the Archbishop of Dubuque was devoting himself to a wide variety of activities, he was comforted by the support of priests and religious who were faithful to their ordinary duties and zealous in fulfilling the special tasks which he assigned to them or which he encouraged them to undertake. When he had completed the second visitation of the archdiocese in May, 1906, he expressed great satisfaction with the improvements that had been made, and chiefly with the number of new churches and schools that had been built.[127] And in June, 1907, during his third visitation of parishes he stated: "Nearly everywhere I find regularity of pastoral service; good care of the young; especially as our schools are nearly everywhere; and neatness in all altar equipment."[128] The gradual increase in the number of clergy had enabled him to assign resident pastors to places which had formerly been missions, and to appoint priests to serve areas which had received little attention previously.[129] Furthermore, the mission band, made up of three priests whom he had sent for training to the Apostolic Mission House at the Catholic University of America, was instrumental in breaking down prejudice against the Church by spreading the real truths of the faith where erroneous views about it had previously held sway and by instructing Catholics so that they could answer intelligently some of their non-Catholic neighbors' inquiries.[130] Moreover, by inviting to the archdiocese the Sisters of the Third Order of St. Dominic of Sinsinawa, Wisconsin, an invitation that was accepted in

[126] AAD, Dubuque Diary, pp. 91, 103; *Catholic Tribune,* Apr. 30, 1908.

[127] AAD, Dubuque Diary, p. 67. He had said in a pastoral letter after his first visitation of the archdiocese: "Everywhere I have been comforted by the evidence of your zeal for the upbuilding of the Church and the honor of the Kingdom of Christ. Very often I have been greatly edified and profoundly touched by the sacrifices which both priests and people have made, either in the starting of new parishes or in the improvement of old ones" (AAD, Keane to the Clergy and Laity of the Archdiocese of Dubuque, Dubuque, Easter Monday, 1903, in AAD, Dubuque Diary, pp. 38–39).

[128] AAD, Dubuque Diary, p. 90.

[129] For an estimate of the parishes established and the churches built during John J. Keane's administration, cf. M. M. Hoffmann, *Centennial History of the Archdiocese of Dubuque* (Dubuque, 1938) and *The Catholic Directory* for the years 1901 to 1911.

[130] AAD, Dubuque Diary, p. 52.

1901, and the Sisters of the Congregation of Our Lady of Charity of the Good Shepherd of Angers, who came to Dubuque in 1903,[131] Keane made a distinct contribution to the educational and charitable work for which the Archdiocese of Dubuque has been justly praised by American Catholics everywhere.

It is understandable enough that Keane's obvious solicitude for the mental, moral, and material welfare of all the people within his jurisdiction, regardless of their religious affiliations, would win for him the respect and admiration of most of the clergy and laity of all faiths. But there was one aspect of his character of which they were positively enamored, namely, his all-embracing charity. From his very first days in Dubuque he was generous to nearly everyone who could make the slightest claim upon his purse. About six months after he had taken possession of the see, the papers announced that he had provided a home and an income for an elderly woman who had been the housekeeper in the cathedral rectory for years.[132] From time to time the journals became aware of his large donations for charitable purposes and they mentioned such things as his contributions for a new hospital in Cedar Rapids,[133] a new altar at St. Ambrose College in Davenport,[134] the monument fund of the veterans of the Spanish-American War,[135] the completion of the Cathedral of the Epiphany in Sioux City,[136] the chapel fund of St. Joseph's College, Dubuque,[137] the San Francisco Relief Fund,[138] and the struggling parishes in his archdiocese with a large debt for a new church or school.[139] There was no publicity, however, for the sums which he gave out privately to the indigent in Dubuque and elsewhere.[140]

[131] Hoffmann, *Centennial History,* pp. 631, 637.

[132] *Catholic Tribune,* Mar. 21, 1901.

[133] *Ibid.,* Apr. 11, 1901; *Telegraph-Herald,* Apr. 9, 1901.

[134] *Catholic Tribune,* Jan. 9, 1902.

[135] *Telegraph-Herald,* May 25, 1902.

[136] *Ibid.,* June 24, 1902; *Catholic Tribune,* July 3, 1902.

[137] *College Spokesman,* VII (Mar., 1910), 168.

[138] *Catholic Tribune,* May 3, 1906.

[139] *Ibid.,* Mar. 20, Oct. 23, 1902; Mar. 28, 1903; *Telegraph-Herald,* Oct. 28, 1901, May 25, 1903.

[140] When his health was very bad, in 1909, Keane wrote in the diary: "Absolutely my only solicitude in facing eternity, are my poor charity pensioners. To them I have instructed my secretary, Father Barry, to send in usual monthly installments any funds remaining to my credit. And I make bold to appeal to the charity of my successor, that he may send them, for awhile, not the entire amount I have been sending them monthly, but such proportion of it, as may seem reasonable to him" (AAD, Dubuque Diary, p. 119). When Archbishop Henry P. Rohlman was a young priest studying in Washington, at Keane's request he visited some of the pensioners

A few people were critical of Keane because of his charity, owing to their belief that he scattered diocesan funds about too freely, especially to clever priests who took advantage of the archbishop to obtain money which they should have raised through their own efforts.[141] It is true that he did display a certain lack of financial wisdom in dealing with the more worldly-wise, a fact that was in part reflected in the need for the archdiocese to borrow $10,000 at the end of 1906.[142] Yet, the urge within him to spread accumulated treasures where they could be most profitably used, his utter disregard for material goods, was just another sign of his detachment and deep spirituality. It was the spirituality behind the magnanimity which attracted the people to John Keane and won their affection.[143]

With each passing year the archbishop had a greater need for the loyalty and unselfish devotion of those who were closest to him in the work of promoting the interests of religion in northeastern Iowa. The cardiac trouble, which had been the chief reason for his need of a long vacation each summer, became progressively worse. In the fall of 1907 it was so aggravated that he was forced to miss the meetings of the University's trustees in Washington and of the officials of the Catholic Total Abstinence Union of America of which he was then president.[144] By the spring of 1908, however, he was sufficiently recovered from the attack to be able to preside at the fourth archdiocesan synod and, as has been mentioned, to attend the Archdiocese of New York's centennial celebration, the consecration of O'Connell, and the meetings of the archbishops of the United States.[145] Still, Keane was in such a weakened condition that the doctors advised him to seek

---

who had been the archbishop's converts years before (statement by the Most Reverend Henry P. Rohlman, Archbishop of Dubuque, personal interview, Dec. 28, 1948).

[141] This view was expressed by a number of people in Dubuque during personal interviews.

[142] AAD, Dubuque Diary, p. 79.

[143] Shortly after he had arrived in Dubuque the Catholic paper observed: "He is adverse to accumulating financial wealth for his own person. With all his accomplishments he has never attempted to build up a bank account" (*Catholic Tribune,* Apr. 18, 1901). Some may have construed this as a criticism of the former archbishop who left a large fortune, most of which had come to him from his family.

[144] AAD, Dubuque Diary, p. 99. During the summer of 1907 he had confided to his diary: "I have found that seven weeks is too long a strain of daily preaching, traveling, etc. It has told severely on my heart, and made me anxious for Bad Nauheim. Four weeks must be about the average, each Spring and Fall" (p. 91). He spent two and one half months in Europe that summer (*Telegraph-Herald,* Sept. 27, 1907).

[145] AAD, Dubuque Diary, pp. 101–103.

a rest completely undisturbed by the cares of his see. In the summer of 1908, therefore, he visited in Boston whence he went to Nantucket as the guest of Father T. J. McGee, his classmate, who was pastor of the Church of Our Lady of the Isle.[146] On August 9 he announced that he was feeling much better and that he would return to Dubuque in time to dedicate a convent on August 31.[147]

After a few months at home, Archbishop Keane found that he was far from having regained his health. In fact, his brain and nerves were in such a condition that partial unconsciousness was produced at times, and occasionally he lapsed into a coma.[148] During a short sermon on a Sunday in late November he told the people, "they are going to pack me off to the Mission Home of the Paulist Fathers, down in Tennessee," and while urging his flock to pray to our Lady, he added, "just at the present time I ask you to pray to her for me."[149]

Before he left Dubuque in the middle of December, he appointed Monsignor Roger Ryan to be administrator of the archdiocese during his absence. Keane remained in the South and the East until a Boston physician advised him that, all things considered, home was the best place for him. On the eve of St. Patrick's Day, therefore, Keane once again, but this time much more slowly, mounted the steps of the cathedral rectory on Bluff Street.[150]

When it became apparent that the Archbishop could not expect to regain his former vigor after some weeks of "rural repose" at the St. Paul Seminary during the summer of 1909, he decided to petition the Holy See for a coadjutor with the right of succession.[151] Before he had obtained the permission of the Sovereign Pontiff to do so, he called a meeting of the diocesan consultors and irremovable rectors and then

[146] *Catholic Tribune,* July 11 and 23, 1908.

[147] *Telegraph-Herald,* Aug. 15, 1908.

[148] AAD, Dubuque Diary, p. 113. The archbishop had intended to be in Chicago on November 15, 1908, for the solemn pontifical Mass which opened the first American Missionary Congress. Cf. Francis C. Kelley, The *First American Catholic Missionary Congress* (Chicago [1909], p. 426).

[149] *Catholic Tribune,* Nov. 19, 1908.

[150] AAD, Dubuque Diary, pp. 113–114. When he left Dubuque, the Catholic paper announced that the archbishop was going to southern Florida and Cuba (*Catholic Tribune,* Dec. 24, 1908). The *Telegraph-Herald* for January 2, 1909, quoted from a New Orleans paper which said that Keane was on his way to Cuba and Mexico and that he had declined to comment on any civil problems. In February the archbishop wrote to O'Connell from the Piney Woods Hotel in Thomasville, Georgia, to tell him that St. Patrick's in Washington would be his place of residence while in that city (ACUA, O'Connell Papers, Keane to O'Connell, Thomasville, Georgia, Feb. 12, [1909]).

[151] AAD, Dubuque Diary, p. 123.

of the bishops of the province to select the names to be submitted for the position.[152] As soon as he became aware of the improper procedure, he wrote to Pius X through Cardinal Merry del Val for authority to hold the prescribed meetings. In a short time he was informed that the petition should be made through the apostolic delegate in Washington. This he did, and on October 19 he was granted the authority to proceed in compliance with the canonical regulations.[153]

At the time that Keane was groping his way toward some solution of his problem, Cardinal Gibbons heard that the archbishop's condition had become alarming. In making inquiry of Archbishop Ireland to determine the facts, the Cardinal bared his love and esteem for his old friend in these touching words:

> I am profoundly grieved that a luminous mind is clouded, and that a Prelate hardly surpassed for eloquence, zeal and piety is no longer able to exercise his apostolic ministry. He was one of the most beautiful and disinterested souls that I have ever encountered. I hope that the unfavorable report I have heard of him is exaggerated.[154]

Unfortunately, the report was not exaggerated. In a hand that was no longer firm and sure, Keane scrawled in his diary that he was beginning the new year with "greatly weakened physical powers," and as he said, "waiting prayerfully, for an answer from Rome as to the Coadjutor, — and looking to our Divine Master for guidance and help, for He well knows that His Divine Will is the only object and rule of my desires."[155] Early in that year 1910, he was notified by the Consistorial Congregation that it would not be advisable to transfer to the coadjutorship any one of the bishops on the list which had been submitted. Realizing that he could no longer fulfill the duties of his position and that he could expect further deterioration rather than improvement in his health, Keane then wrote at once to urge the appointment of Bishop John P. Carroll of Helena as his successor. When this suggestion was declined by Rome, the bishops of the Province of Dubuque were called to prepare another list for the coadju-

[152] Statement by Archbishop Henry P. Rohlman, personal interview, Dec. 28, 1948. On August 2, the *Telegraph-Herald* stated that Keane had asked for a coadjutor. The *Catholic Tribune* announced on August 5 that the qualified clergy would meet to select the *terna* on August 18 and that the bishops of the province would convene later.

[153] AAD, Dubuque Diary, pp. 123–124. He wrote the Papal Secretary of State on August 23, and the authorized meeting of the bishops took place on November 4.

[154] AASP, Gibbons to Ireland, Baltimore, Sept. 13, 1909.

[155] AAD, Dubuque Diary, p. 133.

torship.[156] While waiting for an answer to this latest petition, his growing awareness of an increasing impairment of his memory and of his continual decrease in bodily strength prompted him to confide to his diary: "This makes me hope that Divine Providence will, ere long, solve the coadjutor or successor problem, by kindly calling me home."[157]

It was not until the end of October, after he had returned from several weeks spent at the St. Paul Seminary, that he learned that no action would be taken on a coadjutor and that a renewal of the petition would not be viewed with favor.[158] On January 10, 1911, John Ireland arrived in Dubuque to consult with him on the next step that should be taken. They decided that he should submit his resignation of the see. Thus on that very day the letter to the Holy Father was composed and mailed to Archbishop Diomede Falconio, the apostolic delegate. When Keane revealed this action to Gibbons on the following day, the broken archbishop humbly asked this "beloved Old Friend" if he would object to an archbishop taking up residence in his jurisdiction in the home of Monsignor James F. Mackin of St. Paul's Church in Washington, when it was time, as he added, "to step down and out."[159]

On the very day that the Archbishops of St. Paul and Dubuque were in consultation, Baltimore's cardinal had written to advise Keane to ask for an auxiliary, a request which Gibbons felt would be granted.[160] The information, arriving in Dubuque two days after the letter of resignation had been dispatched, was to Keane "as balm from heaven," and as he informed the cardinal, "welcome as an Angel's visit."[161] Immediately, he asked the delegate by telegraph to withhold his letter of resignation. Then, he pleaded with the Holy Father's representative, and especially with Gibbons, to use their influence so that the choice for auxiliary might be Father Michael Barry, who had been a faithful secretary and chancellor during most of Keane's administration in Dubuque.[162] A month later the archbishop received word

[156] *Ibid.*, p. 138. On April 28 the *Catholic Tribune* reported that the prelate's health was much improved and that he would administer the sacrament of confirmation in five Dubuque parishes during the month of May.

[157] AAD, Dubuque Diary, p. 139.

[158] *Ibid.*, p. 142.

[159] AAB, 107-A, Keane to Gibbons, Dubuque, Jan. 11, 1911.

[160] AAB, 107-A, Keane to Gibbons, Dubuque, Jan. 12, 1911; AAD, Dubuque Diary, p. 145.

[161] AAB, 107-A, Keane to Gibbons, Dubuque, Jan. 12, 1911. The Archbishop wrote two letters to Baltimore on the same day.

[162] *Ibid.*; AAB, 107-C, Falconio to Gibbons, Washington, Jan. 14, 1911.

from Falconio that the Holy See had declined to grant him an auxiliary, trusting that he could get along with the help of neighboring bishops. Upon the receipt of this disappointing news, he calmly noted, "of course, I have sent my respectful Amen."[163]

Less than a month after his revived hopes had been completely dashed, Archbishop Keane again asked the delegate in Washington to submit his resignation of the See of Dubuque and to urge it at Rome with all his power.[164] On April 25, Archbishop Falconio informed him that he had received a cablegram from Cardinal Merry del Val announcing the acceptance of Keane's resignation by Pius X. "His Holiness," the delegate stated, "greatly regrets that the state of your health has been such as to render this step necessary, and he trusts that the complete release from responsibility and the rest to which this action will lead will conduce greatly to your restoration."[165] On June 29, he received notification that his bulls as titular Archbishop of Ciana — the fifth episcopal title to be held by him — were ready, and it found Keane fervently praying: "May His Divine Providence direct and shape all my future; and may He soon take me to our Eternal Home."[166]

In view of the years of splendid service which Archbishop Keane had rendered to the Church of the United States, it is not easy to explain the attitude of the Roman officials in their treatment of him as an old and broken man. Many felt that he deserved to retain the security and the honor of an archiepiscopal see in his own country until his earthly sojourn was completed, even though it would have been necessary to appoint someone to help him shoulder the burdens. As it turned out he was practically forced to resign his see and to depend on the charity of his successor and of the faithful in Dubuque during his remaining seven years. Archbishop Keane himself, however, accepted the decision with the spirit of obedience and resignation to the will of superiors that had characterized all his life.

[163] AAD, Dubuque Diary, p. 147.

[164] *Ibid.*, p. 149.

[165] AAD, Falconio to Keane, Washington, Apr. 25, 1911. This letter was inserted in the Diary. It also advised the archbishop that he was to act as administrator of the archdiocese until his successor had been appointed. The resignation was officially accepted on April 3, 1911, and the *Catholic Tribune* printed the news on May 4, 1911.

[166] AAD, Dubuque Diary, p. 151. The bulls appointing him to the titular see were dated April 28, 1911.

CHAPTER XII

The End

LIKE many other bishops who in the best interests of religion have sacrificed the security that jurisdiction over a see afforded them, Archbishop Keane was faced in 1911 with the problem of making provision for whatever time remained to him. In a short while another prelate would come to rule the archdiocese, and it would be necessary to give over everything into his keeping. Still he had to reside somewhere. But among all the places open to him in Dubuque, which one could he enter without causing some alteration of the normal routine? Would he be sincerely and wholeheartedly received? How many years would he live to be a burden on others? Cardinal Gibbons had told him that he would be welcome to take up residence in the Archdiocese of Baltimore, but, after all, would that be wise? After some consideration, he decided that when his successor arrived he would, as he told the cardinal, "simply take up quarters in our Mercy Hospital, and there await the summons to our Home."[1] When he had finally determined to leave the cathedral rectory, however, he took a cab to the mother house of the Sisters of Charity at Mount Carmel with the intention of residing there indefinitely.[2] Nevertheless, in a short time he returned to the episcopal residence and remained until it was announced that Bishop James John Keane of Cheyenne had been elevated to the archiepiscopal dignity and transferred to the See of Dubuque. John Keane then moved to Mercy Hospital in the city, as he said, "to be out of the way."[3] Imme-

[1] AAB, 107-G, Keane to Gibbons, Dubuque, May 25, [1911]. *The Catholic Tribune* reported on April 27 that the archbishop was at Mercy Hospital in serious condition.

[2] *Catholic Tribune,* July 6, 1911. He left the cathedral on June 26.

[3] Statement by Monsignor Michael L. Kerper, pastor of Nativity Parish, Dubuque, Iowa, personal interview, Aug. 3, 1949. Monsignor Kerper was assigned to the

diately after James Keane had been installed as Dubuque's third archbishop on September 12, the seventy-third anniversary of John's birth, he went up to Mercy Hospital all alone to persuade the retired prelate to return to the cathedral rectory and to take his own rooms. This the archbishop did on October 2 insisting, however, that he take the quarters in the back of the house on the second floor rather than those which he had formerly occupied in the front of the house.[4] Within a year thereafter, the Archbishop of Dubuque moved to the new episcopal residence which he had obtained, and the old titular archbishop was once more master of the house that had sheltered him for eleven years while he had administered the see.[5] Here he lived and worked, suffered and prayed, for seven more trying years.

When James Keane received the pallium on January 22, 1912, it was the hands of the retired archbishop which put it in place while the words of the ritual were spoken by him "in a solemn, resonant voice that thrilled the vast congregation."[6] One evening at the dinner table those same hands had taken from his own breast the pectoral cross and had given it to his successor with the words: "You have assumed the burden, you may as well wear the cross."[7] On the occasion of the conferring of the pallium, however, it was the voice of Archbishop Ireland, which was more familiar to Dubuque's new shepherd, which gave suitable praise to the illustrious prelates who had graced the see. When he came to the name of John Keane, the preacher paused in thought before speaking of him in these words:

> How much my heart fain would say! How much his merits should bid me say! But only this: splendid the virtues of mind and of will,

---

cathedral as an assistant when he returned in 1908 from his studies in Rome. For a short time he read meditations in Italian to the archbishop. According to another source, as soon as Archbishop Ireland heard of James' appointment to Dubuque he rushed down from St. Paul and moved John to the hospital (Monsignor Isidore Semper to the author, Dubuque, Apr. 16, 1953). James Keane's appointment to Dubuque is treated by Sister Mary Rosinda O'Neill, B.V.M., "A Sketch of the Life of the Most Reverend James John Keane, Third Archbishop of Dubuque, 1856–1929" (unpublished master's thesis, Dept. of History, Catholic University of America, 1947).

[4] Statement by Monsignor Kerper. The *Catholic Tribune* (Oct. 12, 1911) spoke of James' invitation to share the dwelling and gave the date on which the archbishop returned to it.

[5] *Official Catholic Directory . . . 1912,* p. 86; statement by Monsignor Kerper.

[6] "Quiet Event," *College Spokesman,* IX (Mar., 1912), 161. At this time the new archbishop appointed his predecessor archdiocesan vicar-general. Cf. *Catholic Bulletin* (St. Paul), Feb. 3, 1912.

[7] Statement by Monsignor Kerper. The archbishop did not wear the pectoral cross after this event.

> brought by him to Dubuque; splendid the outpouring of those virtues while step was agile and hand was free to the uplift. The see of Dubuque lost naught of its splendor, while John Joseph Keane clasped its regal sceptre.[8]

Now his palsied hand had released its grasp on Dubuque's scepter, and life continued. He maintained the same precise daily routine that he had followed for many years, and he was faithful besides to set aside periods of repose in the morning and afternoon for the sake of his health. He rose each morning at six o'clock and said his Mass in the cathedral chapel an hour later, assisted by one of the curates who was present in case he should be seized by an attack which might result in total unconsciousness. After breakfast the mail was read and answered immediately, and then he took a siesta until ten or ten thirty. In the afternoon he invariably went for a walk up Bluff Street and around the park where he was met by those who found it profitable to appeal to his generosity. In fact, those who knew his habits made it a point to meet him on both sides of the park so he could gain twice as much merit by contributing a second time to the maintenance of their carefree existence. Since the archbishop's heart was bigger than his bank account, it was necessary to deprive him of the use of a checkbook and to give him a small amount in silver each day for this purpose. After the evening meal, which consisted of plain food of which he partook sparingly in keeping with his general habit at table, the priests frequently read to him and received ample correction if their enunciation was not clear and precise enough to satisfy his critical ear. As soon as James had made his nightly visit, John paced in the hall on the second floor and said the fifteen decades of the rosary. Punctually at nine o'clock he retired in a room that was tightly locked to keep out all air. The assistants who served at the cathedral during this period of his life, as well as at the time of his active days, found him as simple and as humble as a child. Frequently, he would seek one of them out to hear his confession. In his conversations with them he would make use of some peculiar expressions. He did not have many of them, but the few he had he used often. He was fond of repeating the phrase: "Hurrah for nothing! Everybody has it, nobody wants it. Hurrah for nothing!" Again, when someone told him of difficulties they were experiencing, he would say: "The best cure for all ills is three big cheers for the will of God." Then he would loudly fill the

[8] "Archbishop Ireland's Sermon," *College Spokesman,* IX (Mar., 1912), 119.

prescription, sometimes to the utter amazement of a listener who was not familiar with his ways. During any discussion on the subject of smoking, he would jokingly say: "I am a firm believer in the adage that those who smoke here are preparing to smoke hereafter."[9]

During the first three years of his retirement, the old archbishop could not appear before a public audience. The frequent attacks which rendered him semiconscious also distorted his face and made communication impossible. While he was saying Mass one morning in November, 1913, he was seized by an exceptionally severe spasm which lasted for fifteen minutes. When he reached the breakfast table after his normal period of thanksgiving that morning he asked the young priest who had assisted why it was that they were late for the morning meal. He had no recollection of the difficulty experienced, and apparently it had not caused him great pain, but from that time on his memory was partially restored. Shortly after this incident Archbishop Ireland, who visited John Keane often and was like a brother to him, stopped at the rectory and on hearing the archbishop give from memory the first verse of the Canticle of Moses in Greek, Hebrew, Latin, and Italian, threw out his arms and joyfully proclaimed: "Wa-a-a-l, you are the old Keane again."[10]

During the month in which he had gained greater control over his faculties, the archbishop appeared at a regular meeting of the Sacred Thirst Society at St. Joseph's College. After urging the young men to be temperate in public and private, he declared that his one great occupation during the rest of life would be persevering prayer for a united Christendom. This evidence of renewed life caused the college publication to report: "The welcome extended him by the students seemed to electrify him and bring back all the old-time spirit of eloquence. In appearance, voice, and power of thought, he was the same prelate that has thrilled audiences on both sides of the Atlantic."[11] Although it was certainly an exaggeration to claim that he had fully regained the powers that he had enjoyed during the days that marked his greatest contributions to the Church, the archbishop had, indeed, sufficiently recovered to say a public Mass and to preach a short devotional sermon nearly every Sunday at eight o'clock up to the time of his final illness.[12] Besides, he administered the sacrament of Con-

[9] Statement by Monsignor Valentine Casey, pastor of St. Raphael's Cathedral, Dubuque, Iowa, personal interview, Dec. 28, 1948; statement by Monsignor Kerper.

[10] Statement by Monsignor Casey.

[11] "Our Retired Archbishop," *College Spokesman,* XI (Nov., 1913), 37–38.

[12] Statement by Monsignor Casey; AAB, 112-D, Edward A. Pace to Gibbons,

firmation on a few occasions and offered the funeral Mass for some of the clergy.[13]

The labor to which he set himself most arduously after his partial recovery, however, was the composition of a book, entitled *Emmanuel,* which appeared in 1915.[14] From its contents it seems evident that he conceived it as a contribution to the efforts for the reunion of Christendom which his failing heart seemed to yearn for in union with that of Pius X. Since it was composed in years that witnessed the loss of clear perception, accurate memory, and lucid expression, it does not represent the John Keane who, as he was once described, "dropped the lower jaw and words flowed out as water from a fountain."[15] For that reason it might have been much better had he heeded the advice of the friends who urged him not to submit the manuscript for publication.[16] Nonetheless, the little volume reveals the results of what he himself called "the life-long prayerful reflection on the teachings of our Divine Lord, on the example of His life, on the spirit of His Sacred Heart, on the history and present condition of His Holy Church."[17] These reflections appear in scriptural form and in content they deliberately resemble the Apocalypse of the beloved apostle, another John.

On July 6, 1916, Archbishop Keane celebrated the fiftieth anniversary of his priestly ordination. During the pontifical Mass, which he himself celebrated, he heard read a letter from the apostolic delegate, Archbishop John Bonzano, in which he was congratulated because of his co-operation with the grace of God and his loyalty to the fulfillment of duties entrusted by Divine Providence. Moreover, there was an address on behalf of the priests of the archdiocese by Monsignor

---

Dubuque, July 19, 1915; "Scholachronicon," *College Spokesman,* XIII (Dec., 1915), 54; (Mar., 1916), 134–135.

[13] Statement by Monsignor Casey.

[14] John Joseph Keane, *Emmanuel* (Philadelphia, 1915).

[15] The statement of Bishop John P. Carroll, quoted in Sanner, *op. cit.,* p. 3.

[16] The writer was told that he had submitted the manuscript to some of his Sulpician friends and they had advised him to defer publication. The archbishop arrived at St. Charles College, Ellicott City, Maryland, on April 19, 1915, for an extended visit. Cf. *The Catalogue of St. Charles College, 1914–1915* (Baltimore, 1915), p. 46. On April 25 he gave the first of a series of weekly conferences to the student body (*ibid.,* p. 47). On May 31 a reception was given for the archbishop at the college (*ibid.*). Father John J. Tierney, S.S., who supplied the author with the above information, stated that John Keane had intended to retire at the college but for some unknown reason he had left during the summer, according to a story that has been handed down (Tierney to the author, Catonsville, Maryland, May 9, 1951).

[17] Keane, *op. cit.,* p. vii.

George Heer and one on behalf of the people by P. J. Nelson, a prominent attorney.[18] When Archbishop Ireland rose to deliver the principal address of the day, he was mindful of the archbishop's expressed wish that the discourse be brief and that its theme would not be "praise or eulogy, but simply a reminder of the favors granted to him during his long career by Almighty God, and of the responsibilities those favors had imposed upon him." Among the favors granted, the Archbishop of St. Paul pointed to time, the priesthood, the episcopate for thirty-eight years during which he had served in Richmond, Washington, Rome, and Dubuque, and the final gift of peace and opportunity for plenary preparation to meet God. Then with evident feeling he faced the venerable prelate and addressed to him these words:

> John J. Keane, you and I have been friends for many a year. No cloud ever passed across the horizons of our life to darken the light of our friendship, to lessen its freshness and strength. Together we have fought the battles of the Lord. Together we have walked in days of peace, together in days of war. We have stood side by side to fight the battles of the Church and of country. Fellow soldiers we are, and friends ever.[19]

To which he might have added Bishop Denis O'Connell's words to himself: "The sun's going down and evening is coming on, let us continue the journey together."[20]

For two more years these old friends could sit and reminisce about their role in shaping the destinies of the Church in the United States. But after that it was time for the sun to set for both of them, leaving, as they did, another beloved old friend, James Cardinal Gibbons, to mourn their departure and to long to be with them again in eternity. John Keane was confined to his bed in the cathedral rectory in June, 1918. At half past four o'clock on Saturday morning, June 22, he peacefully answered the Lord's summons as loving hands ministered to his needs.[21] On Monday evening his body was carried in solemn pro-

[18] "Our Grand Old Man," *College Spokesman,* XIII (July, 1916), 348–349. Cf. "Contemporary Items," *Acta et Dicta,* V (July, 1917), 120, for a list of the dignitaries present.

[19] "Fifty Golden Years," *College Spokesman,* XIII (July, 1916), 314. When he was in the pulpit on this day, John Keane rambled on and on until James sent the pastor of the cathedral to tell him to stop. This he gladly did and went on with the Mass (statement by Archbishop Rohlman).

[20] AASP, O'Connell to Ireland, Richmond, Sept. 8, 1915.

[21] "Archbishop Keane Obeys Summons," *Apostolate,* XIV (May and June, 1918), 3–5.

cession from the rectory to St. Raphael's Cathedral where it lay in state until Wednesday morning, when a solemn pontifical requiem Mass was celebrated by Archbishop James John Keane.[22] Denis O'Connell, then Bishop of Richmond where he had labored as a young priest under the deceased, preached the funeral oration. Because of his lifelong association with the late archbishop, he made no mistake when he observed: "He measured all things by the light of eternity, and acquired the habit, when a student, of considering everything in Christ. He acted as he thought Christ would have acted in similar circumstances and spoke as He would have spoken."[23] Finally, Keane's remains were taken to Mount Olivet Cemetery at Key West where the earth received them at the spot that had already embraced others of Dubuque's former prelates.[24]

Many citizens of the Key City attempted an expression of their esteem for the shepherd who had spent nearly eighteen years among them, but they ended for the most part with such inadequate phrases as "he was a man who labored tirelessly for the social uplift of humanity, and his every effort was made for the honor and glory of God,"[25] and, "a man of God, a citizen who inspired all citizens regardless of creed, a noble friend, has passed away, whose memory will always be revered."[26] Numerous references were made to his charity to all men, to his gentleness and sweetness. In the words of one secular journalist: "His love for a mere human, no matter what his station in life, was beyond understanding."[27] To him and to many others, this portion of the archbishop's will must have been the source of further confusion:

> I have always considered it my duty, as a priest of Jesus Christ to have no personal belongings whatsoever beyond the books, clothing and the like utilities, called for by my daily life; and I am happy to be able to declare that substantially such has always been my condition and such it is today. Any personal revenue that has been mine has been held and used solely to meet the appeals of charity, which have never failed to be equal to the total of my income. For that end alone have

[22] *Catholic Tribune,* June 27, 1918.

[23] Sanner, *op. cit.,* p. 57.

[24] *Catholic Tribune,* June 27, 1918.

[25] James Saul, Mayor of Dubuque, quoted in *ibid.*

[26] Reverend Henry F. Milligan, Pastor of the First Congregational Church, quoted in *ibid.*

[27] *Telegraph-Herald,* June 22, 1918. John Keane's gentleness won for him the title "Sugar Keane," while certain qualities in his successor resulted in the priests speaking of him as "Hickory Keane."

> I ever had, or have now, a bank account,— simply as a means for sending such contributions. Hence, if there happen, at the time of my death, to be any balance to my credit in our Second National Bank, it belongs to any charity claimants who may apply for it; or it may be used for the expenses of my funeral, which I wish to be as simple and inexpensive as possible.[28]

Thus, did the warmth of his charity linger after the hand extending it was cold in the grave.

The people who were privileged to know Archbishop John Keane during his whole life were immeasurably more capable of the difficult task of giving an analysis of his character and an evaluation of his career. Those who knew him most intimately agreed on one thing, that he was completely disinterested in the world's goods and honors. Gibbons said of him: "He was one of the most beautiful and disinterested souls that I have ever encountered,"[29] and Ireland expressed the same thought when he remarked: "He was a great and good churchman, ever untiring, ever disinterested."[30] Mrs. Maria Longworth Storer used these words:

> He had no pride. He was gifted with a wonderful talent of speech and with a profound inrooted faith— the faith of an apostle, which he was able to impart with the warmth of delightful, clear and poetical language. . . . One could not help being fond of Archbishop Keane. He was so good, so genuine, in a way, so childlike, although robust and straightforward in his convictions. And he was so strikingly unworldly. A little more worldliness would have carried him to the most enviable positions in the Church. But his character would have lost some of its charm if he had been worldly wise. And I dare say now he rejoices to have become a Saint in Heaven, and a little less prominent on earth.[31]

From the pen of one of his former confreres in the institution which he loved as a father loves a son came the most detailed and balanced tribute to the man who had served God and the Church so faithfully for nearly eighty years. It read:

> Few men have deserved more richly of the American Catholic Church than John Joseph Keane, whose death, though at a patriarchal age, is mourned sincerely in every Catholic household of our country. If there is a Catholic University of America, it is in great measure owing

[28] *Catholic Mirror* (Baltimore), Nov. 16, 1918.
[29] AASP, Gibbons to Ireland, Baltimore, Sept. 13, 1909.
[30] *Catholic Tribune,* June 27, 1918.
[31] AAB, 118-Q, Mrs. Storer to Gibbons, Saranac Lake, New York, Sept. 8, 1918.

to him. As Bishop Keane, the power of faith in a lofty ideal became synonymous with him and won recognition and admiration even from those without the fold. In a less sophisticated age he would have been accepted as a God-given popular leader, whatever the cause to which he might have adhered, so compelling among men is the power of faith in a noble cause, of total self-devotion to an ideal once accepted, of the sacrifice of self at all times and in any required degree. He did not originate, it is true, the idea of an American Catholic University, but from its inception threw himself, with characteristic ardor into all the plans, journeys and toils which the great work called for at once, given the breadth of the concept, its future hopes, the gravity of its needs, and the very vastness of our American life. It was a gospel that he was called to preach, the gospel of more education for our Catholic people, of a higher and better education, but under strictly Catholic auspices and without any compromises. This gospel, the cause of the Catholic University of America, he preached with success throughout our beloved land. And whereas, when he began, every fundamental help or instrument had to be fashioned, knowledge and grasp of the new educational ideal, enthusiasm, a temper of sacrifice, confidence and sympathy, patience and insight (the whole "morale" of a long and trying conflict), when he died he had won out in a degree and on a level which may have surpassed his hopes and dreams.

The happy site of the University, the original funds, the first chairs, the professorate, the buildings and equipment, the student body — all this is owing to one decade of an activity that was simply tireless, though with a superb faith in his work and sustained by a physical energy that acknowledged no right or duty of rest. His appeals, individual and collective, opened up the treasures of the Catholic heart, simply inexhaustible when rightly solicited. And what man ever spoke with a richer and sweeter diction, a more persuasive heart, a braver Catholic "vision," more candid trust in the simple truth, than Bishop Keane? Some called him an idealist, a dreamer of dreams; but, accepting their good faith, did not this man rouse the Catholic conscience in the matter of education as it was never roused before him? And has he not a fair share in the creation of that large Catholic generosity to which we owe the educational progress of the last generation? Did all those noble discourses, clean across the continent, vanish into thin air, or did they sink into the hearts of many thousands, who crowded to hear a perfect orator on issues that were no less fundamental for our American state than for our American Catholic Church?

His moral influence, we may rightly claim, is disseminated throughout our entire American life, since the apostolic spirit so vividly active in him never goes without a perenduring response.

> It is a rare thing in history that the pioneers of movements which uplift, or try to uplift, the settled convictions of their time or its institutions, escape the great law of suffering, in whatever form or degree it comes to them. Bishop Keane was no exception. He bore his great trials with more than ordinary meekness, and lived to know that he had been greatly misunderstood. His saintly life, his broad charity, his liberal view of enmity, disarmed eventually his opponents of good faith. He would not have been true to himself did he not sympathize with every great moral cause and offer it the aid of voice and pen. He lived out fully the ideals of the holy priesthood as he had learned them from men of God and had seen them exemplified in his own youth and early manhood. In turn he has left, East and West, an imperishable memory of goodness, zeal and charity which will long survive to enkindle the noblest ambitions in the hearts of those to whom his life will one day be a spur and an impulse.[32]

During the thirty-six years that have passed since the death of John Joseph Keane most of those who had been directly influenced by him lost the voice by which the memory of his apostolic life was kept vividly alive. He can never be forgotten by Americans, nonetheless, while the Catholic University of America stands as a monument to this greathearted selfless man who showed his generation how to love God, the Church, and America.

[32] "Necrology," *Catholic University Bulletin,* XXIV (Nov., 1918), 128–129.

Bibliography

MANUSCRIPT SOURCES

Archives and Library of the International Collegio di Sant' Anselmo, Via di Porta Lavernale 19, Roma. Manuscript journal in French written by Alexis Orban, S.S., giving some of his views on the Church in the United States after a tour of the United States with Francesco Cardinal Satolli in 1896. The present writer received a copy of this journal through the kindness of Father Colman Barry, O.S.B.

Archives of the Archdiocese of Baltimore, 408 North Charles Street, Baltimore 1, Maryland. Spalding, Bayley, and Gibbons Papers.

Archives of the Archdiocese of Dubuque, 1100 Bluff Street, Dubuque. A diary in Keane's hand entitled "Record of the Administration of John J. Keane, Archbishop of Dubuque, 1900–1911." Ecclesiastical officials in Dubuque say that no other records remain from Keane's administration. According to a tradition the prelate destroyed all of his correspondence.

Archives of the Archdiocese of New Orleans, 7845 Walmsley Avenue, New Orleans 18. Chapelle Papers.

Archives of the Archdiocese of New York, St. Joseph's Seminary, Yonkers 4. Corrigan and Farley Papers.

Archives of the Archdiocese of St. Paul, St. Paul Seminary, St. Paul 1. Ireland Papers.

Archives of the Catholic University of America, Catholic University of America, Washington 17. The Papers of Bouquillon, Conaty, Garrigan, Keane, Kerby, O'Connell, and Pace; miscellaneous correspondence. Some time after the present writer had completed his research these materials were gathered together and located in the Department of Archives and Manuscripts of the University which is housed in Room 33 of the Mullen Library. A copy on microfilm of the Manning Papers obtained in England by Father Ellis may be found there. The "Chronicles of the Catholic University of America from 1885" and the "Minutes of the Meetings of the Board of Trustees" are kept in the office of the University's rector.

Archives of the Diocese of Covington, 1140 Madison Avenue, Covington. Maes Papers.

Archives of the Diocese of Richmond, 807 Cathedral Place, Richmond 20. Keane and O'Connell Papers; Bishops' Diary.

Archives of the Josephite Fathers, 1130 North Calvert Street, Baltimore. Leeson and Slattery Papers.

Archives of the Paulist Fathers, 415 West 59th Street, New York City 19. The

Papers of Deshon, Doyle, Elliott, and Hecker of the Paulists; Klein Papers.

Archives of the University of Notre Dame, Notre Dame, Indiana. The Brownson, Edwards, Hudson, Klein, McMaster, Onahan, and Zahm Papers; a copy on microfilm of the Contessa Sabina di Tarravicino di Revel Papers and of the personal papers of Leo XIII and Rampolla copied by Eduardo Soderini.

PRINTED SOURCES

Acta et decreta concilii plenarii Baltimorensis tertii. Baltimore, 1884 [private edition].

Burrus, E. J., S.J., (ed.). "Notes on the early Relations of the Catholic University of America, Washington, D. C., with the members of the Society of Jesus of the Maryland-New York Province, prepared by Joseph Havens Richards, S.J., rector of Georgetown University, Washington, D. C., from August 15, 1888 to July 3, 1898," *Woodstock Letters*, LXXVIII (1954), 79–101.

The Catalogue of St. Charles' College, 1914–1915. Baltimore, 1915.

Concilii plenarii Baltimorensis II. Baltimore, 1894.

The Constitution and the Proceedings of the Catholic Total Abstinence Union of America, issued from the First Annual Convention held at Baltimore, Maryland, February 22nd and 23rd, 1872. Baltimore, 1872.

The Constitution and the Proceedings . . . , issued from the Fourth Annual Convention held at Chicago, Ill., October 7th and 8th, 1874. Philadelphia, 1874.

Fifth Annual Report of the Rector of the Catholic University of America, March, 1894. Washington, 1894.

Miscellanea de temperantia (A collection of temperance literature bound and preserved in the Mullen Library, Catholic University of America), Vol. VII, *Official Declaration of the Catholic Total Abstinence Union of America, 1917;* Vol. IV, *Proceedings of the Fourteenth Annual Convention of the Catholic Total Abstinence Union of America, Chicago, Ill., August 6th and 7th, 1884*, and *Proceedings of the Twenty-First . . . , Scranton, Pennsylvania, August 4th and 5th, 1891;* Vol. V, *Proceedings of the Tenth . . . , Washington, D. C., August 5th and 6th, 1891*.

National Educational Association. *Journal of Proceedings and Addresses. Session of the Year 1889, held at Nashville, Tennessee*. Topeka, 1889.

Proceedings of the Thirty-Eighth Annual Convention of the Catholic Total Abstinence Union of America, held in Cleveland, Ohio, August 7, 8, 9, 1907. Cleveland, 1907.

Report of the Commissioner of Education, 1892–93. Vol. I. Washington, 1893.

Seventh Annual Report of the Rector of the Catholic University of America, March, 1896. Washington, 1896.

Shea, John Gilmary. "Catholic Congresses," *Official Report of the Proceedings of the Catholic Congress, held at Baltimore, Md., November 11th and 12th, 1889*. Detroit, 1889.

Zwierlein, Frederick J., *Letters of Archbishop Corrigan to Bishop McQuaid and Allied Documents*. Rochester, 1946.

SECONDARY WORKS

Adams, William Forbes, *Ireland and Irish Emigration to the New World from 1815 to the Famine,* New Haven, 1932.

Ahern, Patrick Henry, *The Catholic University of America, 1887–1896. The Rectorship of John J. Keane,* Washington, 1948.

The Baltimore City Directory, Baltimore, 1858.

Barrows, John Henry (ed.), *The World's Parliament of Religions,* 2 vols., Chicago, 1893.

Barry, Colman J., O.S.B., *The Catholic Church and German Americans,* Milwaukee, 1953.

——— *The Catholic University of America, 1903–1909. The Rectorship of Denis J. O'Connell,* Washington, 1950.

Bland, Sister M. Joan, S.N.D., *Hibernian Crusade. The Story of the Catholic Total Abstinence Union of America,* Washington, 1951.

Browne, Henry J., *The Catholic Church and the Knights of Labor,* Washington, 1949.

Buckingham, James S., *America, Historical, Statistic, and Descriptive,* Vol. I, London, 1840.

——— *Canada, Nova Scotia, New Brunswick, and the Other British Provinces in North America,* London, 1843.

Cahensly, Peter Paul, *Der St. Raphaelsverein zum Schutze katholischer deutscher Auswanderer,* Freiburg im Breisgau, 1900.

The Catholic Directory, for the years between 1877 and 1912.

Catholic Red Book, Baltimore, 1908.

Cavanaugh, John, C.S.C., "Catholic Orators and Rhetoricians," *Catholic Builders of the Nation,* edited by Constantine E. McGuire, Vol. IV, Boston, 1923.

Code, Joseph B., *Dictionary of the American Hierarchy,* New York, 1940.

Corrigan, Raymond, *The Church and the Nineteenth Century,* Milwaukee, 1938.

Egan, Maurice Francis (compiler), *Onward and Upward: A Year Book Compiled from the Discourses of Archbishop Keane,* Baltimore, 1902.

——— *Recollections of a Happy Life,* New York, 1924.

Elliott, Walter, C.S.P., *The Life of Father Hecker,* New York, 1891.

——— *Le père Hecker. fondateur des "Paulists" américains, 1819–1888.* Traduit et adapté de l'Anglais avec authorisation de l'auteur. Introduction par Mgr. Ireland. Préface par l'Abbé Félix Klein. Paris, 1897.

Ellis, John Tracy, *The Formative Years of the Catholic University of America,* Washington, 1946.

——— *The Life of James Cardinal Gibbons,* 2 vols., Milwaukee, 1952.

Fosselman, David H., C.S.C., "The Parish in Urban Communities," *The Sociology of the Parish, An Introductory Symposium,* edited by C. J. Nuesse and Thomas J. Harte, C.Ss.R., Milwaukee, 1951.

Foster, John Campbell, *Letters on the Condition of the People of Ireland,* London, 1846.

Gabriel, Brother Angelus, F.S.C., *The Christian Brothers in the United States, 1848–1949,* New York, 1949.

La gerarchia cattolica, Rome, 1897.

Gibbons, James Cardinal, *The Ambassador of Christ,* Baltimore, 1896.
Guilday, Peter (ed.), *The National Pastorals of the American Hierarchy* (*1792–1919*), Washington, 1923.
Hall, Clayton Colman (ed.), *Baltimore, Its History and Its People,* Vol. I, New York, 1912.
Hansen, Marcus Lee, *The Atlantic Migration, 1607–1860,* Cambridge, 1940.
Herbermann, Charles G., *The Sulpicians in the United States,* New York, 1916.
Hoffmann, M. M., *Centennial History of the Archdiocese of Dubuque,* Dubuque, 1938.
——— *The Story of Loras College, 1839–1939,* Dubuque, 1939.
Hogan, Peter E., S.S.J., *The Catholic University of America, 1896–1903. The Rectorship of Thomas J. Conaty,* Washington, 1949.
Hope, Arthur J., C.S.C., *Notre Dame — One Hundred Years,* Notre Dame, 1943.
Johnson, Rossiter (ed.), *A History of the World's Columbian Exposition held in Chicago in 1893,* Vol. IV, New York, 1897–1898.
Keane, John Joseph, *Emmanuel,* Philadelphia, 1915.
Kelley, Francis C., *The First American Catholic Missionary Congress,* Chicago, 1909.
Klein, Félix, *Americanism: A Phantom Heresy.* Translated by the Paulist Fathers with an introduction by Archbishop John Ireland (reproduced from Walter Elliott's *Life of Father Hecker*) and a foreword by James M. Gillis, C.S.P., Atchison, Kansas, 1951.
——— *La route du petit morvandiau. Souvenirs.* Vol. IV. *Un hérésie fantôme, l'américanisme.* Paris, 1949.
——— *La route de petit morvandiau. Souvenirs.* Vol. V. *Sans arrêt.* Paris, 1949.
Leslie, Shane, *Henry Edward Manning, His Life and Labours,* London, 1921.
Levinge, R.G.A., *Echoes from the Backwoods,* London, 1846.
The Light of the Cross in the Twentieth Century, Vol. I, New York, 1908.
McCarthy, Justin, *A History of Our Own Times,* Vol. I, New York, 1880.
Macdonald, Fergus, O.P., *The Catholic Church and the Secret Societies in the United States,* New York, 1946.
Mackay, Alex, *The Western World; or Travels in the United States in 1846–47,* Vol. I, 4th ed., London, 1850.
[Magri, F. Joseph], *The Catholic Church in the City and Diocese of Richmond,* Richmond, 1906.
Maignen, Charles, *Études sur l'américanism, le père Hecker — est-il un saint?* Paris, 1898.
——— *Studies in Americanism — Father Hecker, Is He a Saint?,* Rome, 1898.
Malone, Sylvester L. (ed.), *Memorial of the Golden Jubilee of the Rev. Sylvester Malone,* Brooklyn, 1895.
Marmion, Anthony, *The Ancient and Modern History of the Maritime Ports of Ireland,* 3rd ed., London, 1858.
Matchetts Baltimore Directory for 1847 and *for 1851,* Baltimore, 1847 and 1851.
The Memorial Volume: A History of the Third Plenary Council of Baltimore, November 9–December 7, 1884, Baltimore, 1885.

[Mooney, Joseph F.], *Memorial of the Most Reverend Michael Augustine Corrigan, D.D. Third Archbishop of New York,* New York, 1902.

Moynihan, James H., *The Life of Archbishop John Ireland,* New York, 1953.

O'Reilly, Bernard, *John McHale, Archbishop of Tuam,* Vol. I, New York, 1890.

R. L. Polk & Co's. Baltimore City Directory for 1887, Baltimore, 1887.

Reilly, Daniel F., O.P., *The School Controversy (1891–1893),* Washington, 1943.

Reily, John T., *Collections in the Life and Times of Cardinal Gibbons* [Titles vary], 10 vols. McSherrytown, Pennsylvania, 1890–1903 [imprint varies].

Russell, William Howard, *My Diary North and South,* New York, 1863.

Ryan, Abram J., *Poems: Patriotic, Religious, Miscellaneous,* 10th ed., Baltimore, 1884.

Satolli, Francis, *Loyalty to Church and State,* edited by J. R. Slattery, 2nd ed., Baltimore, 1895.

Schmeckebier, Lawrence F., *History of the Know Nothing Party in Maryland,* Baltimore, 1899.

Shea, John Gilmary, *Our Faith, Its Defenders,* New York, 1894.

Sisk, J. J. (ed.), *Ancient and Modern Masterpieces of the Leading Lights of the Catholic Church,* Vol. II, New York, 1906.

[Smith, Milton E.], *History of St. Patrick's Church, Washington, D. C.,* Washington, 1933.

Storer, Maria Longworth, *In Memoriam Bellamy Storer,* Boston, 1923 (privately printed).

Tindall, William, *Standard History of the City of Washington,* Knoxville, 1914.

Toomey, John J., and M. C. Sullivan (eds.), *Souvenir of the Installation and the Investiture with Pallium of Most Rev. John J. Keane, D.D., as Archbishop of Dubuque,* Dubuque, 1901.

Trollope, Anthony, *North America,* Vol. I, London, 1862.

[Viger, George Ernest, S.S.], *Golden Jubilee of St. Charles' College, Near Ellicott City, Maryland, 1848–1898,* Baltimore, 1898.

——— *1791–1891 Memorial Volume of the Centenary of St. Mary's Seminary of St. Sulpice, Baltimore, Md.,* Baltimore, 1891.

Walter, Joseph M. (ed.), *A Memorial Tribute to Rev. J. A. Walter, Late Pastor of St. Patrick's Church, Washington, D. C.,* Washington, 1895.

Very Rev. A. L. Magnien. A Memorial, Baltimore, 1903.

Ward, Leo Richard, C.S.C. (ed.), *The American Apostolate. American Catholics in the Twentieth Century,* Westminster, Maryland, 1952.

Will, Allen Sinclair, *Life of Cardinal Gibbons,* 2 vols., New York, 1922.

Wood's Baltimore Directory for the years 1856, 1860, 1864, 1867, 1872, 1873, published in Baltimore on the same dates.

The World's Columbian Catholic Congresses and Educational Exhibit, Chicago, 1893.

Zardetti, Otto, *Devotion to the Holy Ghost, I, Special Devotion to the Holy Ghost. A Manual for the Use of Seminarians, Priests, Religious and the Christian People,* Milwaukee, 1888.

Zwierlein, Frederick J., *The Life and Letters of Bishop McQuaid,* 3 vols., Rochester, 1925–1927.

BROCHURES AND PAMPHLETS

Animadversiones quaedam de universitate in America fundanda, Rome, 1886 [privately printed].

Bouquillon, Thomas, *Education: To Whom Does it Belong?*, Baltimore, 1891.

——— *Education: To Whom Does it Belong? A Rejoinder to Civiltà Cattolica*, Baltimore, 1892.

——— *Education: To Whom Does it Belong? A Rejoinder to Critics*, Baltimore, 1892.

Centenary Manual of St. Vincent de Paul, Baltimore, 1841–1941, n.p., n.d.

Centennial Souvenir of St. Thomas the Apostle Catholic Church, Wilmington, North Carolina, 1947.

A Complete List of the Students Entered at Saint Charles' College, Ellicott City, Maryland, from the Opening October 31, 1848 until the Golden Jubilee, June 15, 1898, n.p., n.d.

Ecclesiastical Music for the Archdiocese of Dubuque, Dubuque, 1905.

Keane, John J., *A Sodality Manual for the Use of the Servants of the Holy Ghost*, Baltimore, 1880.

——— *The Catholic Church and the American Sunday*, Buffalo, 1895.

——— *Catholic Education in America*, Washington, 1892.

——— *The Man; The Christian; The Worker*, "University of Notre Dame Lecture Series," I; Notre Dame, 1898.

——— *Mary Immaculate and Democracy*, Melbourne [1904].

O'Connell, Denis J., *A New Idea in the Life of Father Hecker*, Breisgau, 1897.

——— *L'américanisme d'apres le p. Hecker, ce qu'il est et ce qu'il n'est pas*, Paris, 1897.

La question Allemande dans l'église des États-Unis, Rome, 1887.

Relatio de questione Germanica in Statibus Foederatis a Rev. P. M. Abbelen, Sac. Milw. conscripta, a Rmo. et. Illmo. M. Heiss, Archiep. Milwauk., approbata, et Sacrae Congr. de Propaganda Fide mense Novembri 1886, submissa. Sequuntur objectiones plurimorum Rvmorum Praesulum eidem S. Congr. propositae, e lingua Gallica in Anglicam translatae, n.p., n.d.

Rommel, H., *Thomas Bouquillon, notice bio-biographique*, Bruges, 1903.

St. Mary's Seminary, Baltimore, List of Superiors, Professors and Students Ordained, 1791–1916, New York, 1917.

ARTICLES

"Archbishop Keane Obeys Summons," *Apostolate*, XIV (May and June, 1918), 3–5.

Barry, William, "An American Religious Crusade," *National Review*, XXXIII (Mar., 1899), 115–128.

Bouquillon, Thomas, "The Catholic Controversy About Education. A Reply," *Educational Review*, III (Apr., 1892), 365–373.

Browne, Henry J., "Pioneer Days at the Catholic University," *Catholic Educational Review*, XLVIII (Jan., Feb.), 29–38, 96–103.

Cassidy, Francis P., "Catholic Education in the Third Plenary Council of Baltimore. II," *Catholic Historical Review*, XXXIV (Jan., 1949), 414–436.

Catholic University Bulletin:
"Archbishop Keane," V (July, 1899), 395–396.
"Archbishop Keane's Collecting Tour," VI (Jan., 1900), 130–131.
"Commencement Exercises," VI (July, 1900), 452–457.
"Encyclical Letter," I (Apr., 1895), 231, 247.
"Graduating Exercises," II (July, 1896), 447–449.
"Meeting of the Board of Trustees," VI (Oct., 1900), 550–551.
"Necrology," XXIV (Nov., 1918), 128–129.
"Rev. Denis J. Stafford, D.D.," XIV (Feb., 1908), 209.
"Right Rev. John Joseph Keane, D.D.," II (Oct., 1896), 583–592.
"University Chronicle," V (Oct., 1899), 521–525.

Catholic University Chronicle. The "Chronicle" formed a part of the *Catholic University Bulletin,* except in the year 1897, when one volume consisting of twelve numbers, issued two at a time, was published.

College Spokesman:
"Archbishop Ireland's Sermon," IX (Mar., 1912), 105–119.
"Fifty Golden Years," XIII (July, 1916), 309–315.
Manning, Cyrus J. "The Archbishop's Visit to Rome," III (Nov., 1905), 13–20.
"Our Grand Old Man," XIII (July, 1916), 348–349.
"Our Retired Archbishop," XI (Nov., 1913), 37–38.
"Quiet Event," IX (Mar., 1912), 161.
"Scholachronicon," XIII (Dec., 1915), 54; (Mar., 1916), 134–135.
"Contemporary Items," *Acta et Dicta,* V (July, 1917), 120–127.

Elliott, Walter, C.S.P., "Catholic Missionary Union," *Catholic Encyclopedia,* III, 453–454.

——— "Missionary Society of St. Paul the Apostle," *Catholic Encyclopedia,* X, 368–369.

——— "Personal Reminiscences of Archbishop Keane," *Catholic World,* CVII (Aug., 1918), 641–646.

"The Encyclical," *American Catholic Quarterly Review,* XX (Apr., 1895), 346–368.

Farrell, John T., "John Ireland and Manifest Destiny," *Catholic Historical Review,* XXXIII (Oct., 1947), 269–301.

Fenton, Joseph Clifford, "The Teaching of the Testem Benevolentiae," *American Ecclesiastical Review,* CXXIX (Aug., 1953), 124–133.

——— "Devotion to the Holy Ghost and Its American Advocates," *American Ecclesiastical Review,* CXXI (Dec., 1949), 486–501.

Garrigan, Philip J., "Diocese of Sioux Falls," *Catholic Encyclopedia,* XIV, 16.

Green, James J., "The Organization of the Catholic Total Abstinence Union of America, 1866–1884," *Records of the American Catholic Historical Society of Philadelphia,* LXI (June, 1950), 71–97.

Guilday, Peter, "John Gilmary Shea," *Historical Records and Studies,* XVII (July, 1926), 5–171.

Holden, Vincent F., C.S.P., "A Myth in 'l'américanisme,'" *Catholic Historical Review,* XXXI (July, 1945), 154–170.

Keane, John J., "America as Seen from Abroad," *Catholic World,* LXVI (Mar., 1898), 721–730.

——— "The Catholic Hierarchy," *Catholic World,* LXXXIV (Jan., 1907), 453–461.

——— "The Catholic Church and Economics," *Quarterly Journal of Economics,* VI (Oct., 1891), 25–46.

——— "The Catholic Universities of France," *Catholic World,* XLVII (June, 1888), 289–297.

——— "The Catholic University of Louvain," *Catholic World,* XLVI (Jan., 1888), 525–534.

——— "The Clergy and the Catholic University," *American Ecclesiastical Review,* I (July, 1889), 241–245.

——— "The Encyclical 'Rerum Novarum,'" *American Catholic Quarterly Review,* XVI (July, 1891), 595–611.

——— "A Chat About the Catholic University," *Catholic World,* XLVIII (Nov., 1888), 216–226.

——— "The University of Strassburg," *Catholic World,* XLVI (Feb., 1888), 643–652.

——— "What Is the Catholic School Policy?" *North American Review,* CXL (June, 1885), 528–535.

Kelly, Blanche M., "Tabernacle Societies," *Catholic Encyclopedia,* XIV, 426.

Kerby, William J., "John Joseph Keane," *Dictionary of American Biography,* X, 267–268.

——— "Thomas Bouquillon," *Catholic Encyclopedia,* II, 716.

Lerner, Max, "Thomas Fortune Ryan," *Dictionary of American Biography,* XVI, 265–268.

McAvoy, Thomas T., C.S.C., "Americanism, Fact and Fiction," *Catholic Historical Review,* XXXI (July, 1945), 133–153.

——— "Liberalism, Americanism, Modernism," *Records of the American Catholic Historical Society of Philadelphia,* LXII (Dec., 1952), 225–231.

Meng, John J., "Cahenslyism: The First Stage, 1883–1891," *Catholic Historical Review,* XXXI (Jan., 1946), 389–413.

——— "Cahenslyism: The Second Chapter, 1891–1910," *Catholic Historical Review,* XXXII (Oct., 1946), 302–340.

——— "A Century of American Catholicism as Seen Through French Eyes," *Catholic Historical Review,* XXVII (Apr., 1941), 39–68.

"Notable Deaths," *Annals of Iowa,* IV (1899–1900), 398–402.

O'Connor, Thomas F., "John A. Zahm, C.S.C.: Scientist and Americanist," *Americas,* VII (Apr., 1951), 435–462.

Ott, Michael, "Saint Joseph's Society for Foreign Missions," and "Saint Joseph's Society for Colored Missions," *Catholic Encyclopedia,* VIII, 521–522.

Pace, Edward A., "Francesco Satolli," *Catholic Encyclopedia,* XIII, 486.

Pallen, Condé B., "Testem Benevolentiae," *Catholic Encyclopedia,* XIV, 537–538.

R[eilly], W. S[tephen], S.S., "St. Charles' Alumnus Writes Reminiscences," *Voice,* X (Feb., 1933), 8–9.

Russ, William A., Jr., "Disfranchisement in Maryland, 1861–67," *Maryland Historical Magazine,* XXVIII (Dec., 1933), 309–328.

Schroeder, Joseph, "Windthorst," *American Catholic Quarterly Review,* XVI (July, 1891), 515–528.

Stockbridge, Henry, Sr., "Baltimore in 1846," *Maryland Historical Magazine,* VI (Mar., 1911), 20–34.

Sullivan, W. L., "Catholic Young Men's National Union," *Catholic Encyclopedia,* X, 712.

Thorne, William Henry, "About the Hierarchy," *Globe,* VII (Sept., 1897).

——— "The Benziger Boycott," *Globe,* IX (June, 1899), 227–231.

——— "Catholic Liberalism and Nationality," *Globe,* VII (June, 1897).

——— "Fact and Fiction in Recent Prose," *Globe,* IX (Sept., 1899), 260.

——— "Fool Newspaper Correspondents," *Globe,* VI (Dec., 1896), 395–401.

——— "Globe Notes," *Globe,* VI (Dec., 1896), 435–448; VII (Dec., 1897), 480–500; IX (Mar., 1899), 96–108.

Zurcher, George, "Foreign Ideas in the Catholic Church in America," *Roycroft Quarterly,* I (Nov., 1896), 1–55.

UNPUBLISHED MATERIAL

Carlin, Sister Mary Angela, O.S.U., "The Attitude of the Republican Party Toward Religious Schools, 1875–1880," unpublished master's thesis, Catholic University of America, 1953.

Curtis, James Thomas, "John Edward Kenna, A Sketch of a Brief Political Career," unpublished master's thesis, Catholic University of America, 1948.

McKeon, Sister Francis Joseph, S.N.D., "The Formation of the Catholic Total Abstinence Union of America," unpublished master's thesis, Catholic University of America, 1946.

O'Neill, Sister Mary Rosinda, B.V.M., "A Sketch of the Life of the Most Reverend James John Keane, Third Archbishop of Dubuque, 1856–1929," unpublished master's thesis, Catholic University of America, 1947.

Sanner, Sister Mary Innocentia, P.B.V.M., "Archbishop John Joseph Keane as a Devotional Writer and Speaker," unpublished bachelor's thesis, Columbia [Loras] College, Dubuque, Iowa, 1937.

Soderini, Eduardo, "Leone XIII e gli Stati Uniti di America," unpublished MS. in the Vatican Library. There is a complete copy of this work on microfilm in AUND and a typescript of part of the MS. in APF.

NEWSPAPERS

The writer used the newspaper files at the Mullen Library of the Catholic University of America, the Library of Congress, and the Public Library and the Loras College Library in Dubuque, as well as clippings filed in the Mullen Library, the Loras College Library, AANY, AASP, APF, and AUND.

Akron *Germania,* Oct. 8, 1896.

Baltimore:

Catholic Mirror, July 14, 1865; June 30, 1866; 1872–1874; 1878; June 1, 1889; Jan. 21, 1894; Apr. 27, 1895; Nov. 16, 1918.

Katholische Volks-Zeitung, July 4, 1863; Aug. 31, 1878; May 4, 1895.

Sun, Apr. 2, 1883; Oct. 19, 1891; Apr. 23, 1898.

Boston:
Herald, May 11, 1891.
Journal, Mar. 5, 1899.
Pilot, Mar. 20, 1899.
Review, Mar. 4, 1899.
Brooklyn *Eagle,* Jan. 20, 1900.
Courrier de Bruxelles, Oct. 25, 1896.
Journal de Bruxelles, Sept. 9, 1896.
Buffalo *Express,* Oct. 6, 1896.
Chicago *Staatszeitung,* Oct. 13, 1896.
Columbus *Catholic Columbian,* Oct. 24, 1896.
Denver *Journal,* Oct. 10, 1896.
Dubuque:
Catholic Tribune, 1900–1911.
Daily Herald and *Sunday Herald,* 1900–1901.
Telegraph, 1900–1901.
Telegraph-Herald, 1901–1911
Glascow *Herald,* Mar. 20, 1889.
Indianapolis *Journal,* June 5, 1890.
Liverpool *Catholic Times and Catholic Opinion,* June 17, 1898; July 1, 1898; July 14, 1899.
London:
Catholic Times, Oct. 30, 1896.
Tablet, Mar. 11, 1899; Mar. 30, 1899; June 17, 1899.
Weekly Register, July 8, 1899; July 22, 1899.
Milwaukee:
Herold, Oct. 5, 1896.
Sentinel, Jan. 29, 1890.
Nantes *Espérance du peuple,* Oct. 22, 1896; Nov. 9, 1896.
New Orleans *Morning Star and Catholic Messenger,* June 8, 1879.
New York:
Catholic Review, Mar. 12, 1892.
Christian Union, July 10, 1890.
Commercial Advertiser, May 6, 1889.
Democrat, Nov. 22, 1896.
Evangelist, July 10, 1890.
Evening World, Mar. 23, 1897.
Freeman's Journal and Catholic Register, Nov. 16, 1889; Dec. 24 and 31, 1893; Jan. 7, 1893; Oct. 10 and 17, 1896; Jan. 16, 1900.
Herald, May 29, 1879; June 6, 1889; Aug. 29, 1889; June 1, 1890; Oct. 13, 1893; (Paris edition) June 23, 1899.
Irish World, Oct. 10, 1896.
Journal, Nov. 12, 1896; Feb. 12, 1897.
Observer, Mar. 6, 1890.
Sun, Oct. 24, 1890; Oct. 15, 1894; Dec. 20, 1895; July 11, 1898; May 5, 1901.
Tribune, Nov. 14, 1896; Dec. 6, 1896.
Straatszeitung, Oct. 8 and 14, 1896; Nov. 7, 1896.

World, Feb. 3, 1893; Oct. 20, 1896; Nov. 2, 1896.
Paris:
Croix, Nov. 20, 1896.
Univers, Nov. 29, 1890.
Philadelphia:
Catholic Standard, Oct. 27, 1877.
Catholic Standard and Times, Oct. 10, 1896.
Public Ledger, Oct. 12, 1896.
Quebec *Morning Chronicle,* Apr. 20, 1889.
Richmond *Daily Dispatch,* Dec. 19 and 21, 1880; Oct. 18, 1881.
Rome:
Civiltà Cattolica, [Series 15] Vols. I, II, and III; [Series 16] Vols. VI and X.
Moniteur de Rome, Mar. 20 and 21, 1889.
Osservatore Romano, Mar. 20, 1889; Mar. 6, 1899.
Voce della Verità, Mar. 20, 1889.
St. Louis:
America, Oct. 8 and 13, 1896.
Herold des Glaubens, Oct. 7 and 14, 1896.
Review, 1899–1901.
Western Watchman, Oct. 24, 1895; Apr. 8, 1900; Nov. 21, 1895.
St. Paul *Northwestern Chronicle,* Sept. 28, 1888; Aug. 25, 1893; Sept. 1, 1893.
San Francisco:
Argonaut, Apr. 17, 1899.
Chronicle, Feb. 12, 13, 15, 19, 1894.
Monitor, Oct. 10, 1896.
Sioux City *Northwestern Catholic,* Mar. 29, 1900; Apr. 12, 1900; June 16 and 28, 1900.
Springfield *Republican,* Jan. 26, 1890.
Washington:
Church News (in 1900 became *New Century and Church News*), May 26, 1889; 1894–1900.
Evening Star, Aug. 26, 1878; Aug. 5, 1891.
Post, Mar. 30, 1878; Mar. 18, 1879; Mar. 5, 1891; Aug. 7, 1891; Jan. 12, 13, 14 and 21, 1894; Oct. 9 and 28, 1896; Dec. 3, 1896; May 24, 1897; June 5, 1899.
Star, Feb. 7, 13, and 20, 1890.
Worcester *Spy,* Jan. 24, 1890.

Index